Everything You
Ever Wanted to Know About

# Mormonism

# Everything You
# Ever Wanted to Know About
# Mormonism

## JOHN ANKERBERG
### & JOHN WELDON

**HARVEST HOUSE PUBLISHERS**
Eugene, Oregon 97402

This text constitutes an expanded revision of chapter 50 of Dr. Weldon's unpublished 8,000 page "Encyclopedia of American Cults and Religions." Interested publishers only, corporate or individual, should contact the author directly at P.O. Box 8977, Chattanooga, TN 37411.

Chapter 3 was excerpted from the authors' text *Cult Watch* (Harvest House, 1991), Part 1, Question 3.

**EVERYTHING YOU EVER WANTED TO KNOW ABOUT MORMONISM: THE TRUTH ABOUT THE MORMON CHURCH**

Copyright © 1992 by John Ankerberg and John Weldon
Published by Harvest House Publishers
Eugene, Oregon 97402

Library of Congress Cataloging-in-Publication Data

Ankerberg, John, 1945–
    Everything you ever wanted to know about Mormonism / John Ankerberg, John Weldon.
    ISBN 0-89081-908-4
    1. Church of Jesus Christ of Latter-Day Saints—Controversial literature.    2. Mormon Church—Controversial Literature.    I. Weldon, John    II. Title.
    BX8645.A68    1992
    289.3—dc20                                      91-38068
                                                                           CIP

**Printed in the United States of America.**

*The authors would like to dedicate this book to the staff and personnel of the John Ankerberg Show for their sacrifice, commitment to integrity, and heartfelt service to the Christian community. In addition, the authors express their special gratitude to the following word processors and editors: Louise Ebner, Terry Grazier, Rebecca Carol Harris, Ruth and Esther Wilson. Finally, we would like to thank Jerald and Sandra Tanner for their assistance in helping us secure large numbers of primary source documents.*

# Foreword

This year approximately 45,000 young Latter-day Saint (LDS) missionaries will be sent around the world to recruit 400,000 new members for the Mormon church. They will be viewed by many people as part of accepted Christian missionary agencies and various Christian denominations.

Mormonism views all other churches, ministers, and church members as being in a state of apostasy with no assurance of eternal life, a wrong understanding of God, and in dire need of Mormon baptism and secret temple rituals. How is the average Christian to evaluate such claims? John Ankerberg and John Weldon have performed a great service to the Christian community by spelling out the differences between LDS beliefs based on Joseph Smith's revelations and standard Christian concepts based on the Bible.

Jesus warned that in the last days there would arise false prophets promoting a false Christ (Matthew 24:24). As Christians familiarize themselves with the material in this book, they will be better equipped to recognize heresy and to relate the biblical message of salvation through Christ and His grace to their Mormon friends and neighbors.

*Sandra Tanner*

# Contents

## Section 1
### *Mormon Power and Origins*

## Section 2
### *Mormon Belief and Practice*

## Section 3
### *Mormon Religion and Christianity*

## Section 4
## *Mormon Theology and Its Doctrine of God*

## Section 5
## *Mormon Salvation and the Quest for Godhood*

## Section 6
### *Mormon Religion and the Occult*

## Section 7
### *Mormon Revelation and New Scripture*

# Section 8
## *Mormon Religion and Its Fruits*

# The Importance
# of the Subject
# of Mormonism

◆

The need for this book derives from the particular claims made by the Mormon church. These claims have caused widespread confusion concerning the nature of Mormonism.

Mormonism claims it represents true Christianity. Mormonism contends it believes in the biblical God. Mormonism teaches it trusts in the true Jesus Christ and that He alone is the atoning savior who died for the sins of the world. Mormonism emphasizes it depends on salvation by grace. Mormonism asserts it places full confidence in the Bible as the authoritative Word of God. Mormonism holds it accepts the biblical teaching concerning heaven and hell. But none of these claims are true, as we will document.

This means that by whatever process Mormonism has arrived at such beliefs, the church as a whole has misled the public concerning its true teachings. Therefore, our book, *Everything You Ever Wanted to Know About Mormonism: The Truth About the Mormon Church*—is written to help set the record straight.

The current prophet and president of the Mormon church, Ezra Taft Benson, has stated the following:

> The Church and kingdom of God has no fear of the truth. . . .
> Let us never fear truth, but only its misuse. On the contrary, let
> us love truth above all else, for God Himself is truth.[1]

But to love truth "above all else" can be difficult when it brings unexpected or painful conclusions. When the price of truth is high, it is easy to conclude that its cost is beyond our means.

But truth cannot be ignored: if neglected too long, it has a nasty habit of coming back to haunt us. But Benson is correct—truth should not be feared, whatever its consequences. This is why we have subtitled our book *The Truth About the Mormon Church*. More than anything else, both Christians and Mormons—and the general public—need to hear the truth.

## Why Are the Authors Qualified to Write this Book?

John Ankerberg has two graduate degrees in Christian History and the History of Christian Thought and is therefore qualified to evaluate historic Christian belief and doctrine in light of Mormon claims to represent authentic Christianity. In addition, he has researched and hosted three separate television programs with Mormon leaders, former Mormons and Christians on the subject: Is Mormonism Christian?

John Weldon holds two masters degrees in biblical studies and is a graduate of law school, where he majored in the subject of evaluating evidence for the true claims of Christianity. He has minored in both theology and philosophy and has a Ph.D. in comparative religion, including a second doctorate specializing in cultic theology. He has studied Mormonism for many years.

## Why Is Mormonism Important?

The Mormon church is a multibillion dollar institution with eight to nine million members worldwide.[2] The church's size and its some forty-five thousand missionaries explain why a prominent non-Mormon scholar could recently forecast that in two generations the Mormon religion will be a world faith with approximately sixty million adherents.[3] This tallies with the estimate of church authorities that in forty to fifty years Mormonism will have seventy to one hundred million members.[4] Further, sociologist Rodney Stark conservatively estimates that Mormonism will have over two hundred million followers within a hundred years, given present growth rates. This means that "Mormonism has the potential to become the first world religion to emerge since the birth of Islam in the seventh century."[5]

Perhaps sensing a large market by which to secure such expansion (especially in mainline and more liberal denominations), Mormonism has recently targeted the Christian church for evangelism. In January 1989 seminars were instituted to teach church leaders how to befriend Christian clergymen. The basic theme of the seminars is: "Win a Minister and Influence a Thousand." The goal is to convert Christian pastors in order to reach their flock with the message of Mormonism. (See preface appendix.)

Significantly, one reason cited for this program is that Mormons claim they have been "misunderstood" by Christians and are thus seeking to "set the record straight." By convincing Christians that Mormonism truly is Christian—that it believes in Jesus Christ and His atoning death on the cross—they would like to eventually win millions of converts to the Mormon faith.

But such a program illustrates two key problems facing Mormonism.

The first is the Mormon claim to be Christian. Many biblical and Christian terms are used by Mormons, but they are given entirely different meanings. In this book, we will prove that Mormonism is not Christian.

The second problem is that many Mormons are uninformed concerning their own history and doctrinal teachings. Darl Andersen, a leader in the Mormon evangelization of the Christian church, illustrates this quandary. In his *Soft Answers to Hard Questions*, he describes his feelings after attending a so-called "anti-Mormon" lecture by Christians:

> Much of the doctrine they explained as being Mormon, I had never heard in a Mormon church during 50 years of active participation. . . . It was a bit amusing to me when they commented that Mormons may deny believing many of their statements. But then, they said, Mormons really don't know what their own church leaders teach.[6]

Or, perhaps Mr. Andersen is himself uninformed. Perhaps he has never heard of this material in "50 years of active participation" because church leaders have kept it from him. Or, perhaps Mr. Andersen is unwilling to speak frankly about his church's true beliefs. That Mormons could be uninformed about church teaching is not surprising. Members of all religious faiths are frequently ignorant in matters of doctrine and historical theology. For example, our research into over one hundred religions has revealed that for a variety of reasons, the *average* member was ignorant of 1) the details surrounding the origin of their religion, 2) their historical theology: how their religious teachings had evolved and changed over the years, and 3) their current doctrinal beliefs. Now, if members of all these religions are often uninformed on such issues, why should it surprise anyone that Mormons may also be uninformed? Even official Mormon literature concedes that Mormons can be ignorant of Mormon doctrine. For example, one student manual confesses, "The gospel of Jesus Christ teaches that man is an eternal being made in the image and likeness of God. . . . These truths are generally well understood by Latter-day Saints. Less well understood, however, is the fact that God is an exalted man who once lived on an earth and underwent experiences of mortality [and that] . . . his marriage partner is our mother in heaven. We are their spirit children."[7]

But if in addition to this, church leadership has lied to Mormons and concealed the truth, then responses like Mr. Andersen's are not unexpected. However, it is the discovery of what Mormonism truly believes—and the realization that church leaders have been untruthful with them—that is responsible for tens of thousands of Mormons becoming disenchanted with their church.

Perhaps it is significant that leading Mormon researchers such as

Jerald and Sandra Tanner "are very encouraged by recent developments." They note that thousands of Mormons are no longer willing to uncritically accept the pronouncements of the church. Further, they express their personal conviction "that we will see tens of thousands of them" turning to true Christian faith.[8]

What is Mormonism and what does it really believe? What is the truth about Mormonism? These questions can only be answered by examining the authoritative sources of Mormonism itself, sources that Mormonism claims accurately reflect its teachings. These sources include its scriptures, such as the *Book of Mormon* and *Doctrine and Covenants*, as well as the writings of its "presidents and prophets," which are also considered to be scripture. In addition, there is a great deal of other literature which the church considers authoritative. By examining all this material, it is possible to arrive at an accurate understanding of what Mormonism really teaches and believes.

If modern Mormons claim that they do not believe these teachings, then 1) they are ignorant concerning what Mormonism is, or 2) they are being less than frank.

In this book, we have attempted to fairly and accurately describe the teachings and beliefs of the Mormon religion. If any individual Mormon truly does *not* accept these teachings, then he or she should ask themselves, "Why am I a Mormon?"

In essence, Mormonism is important because of its increasing influence in the world, its attempt to influence the Christian church, and most importantly because of its influence upon people who become Mormons.

## Special Note

It should be stressed that any claims by Mormon leaders and writers concerning official Mormon history, early doctrine, apologetics, etc., are generally not to be trusted.

The Mormon church has engaged in a protracted whitewashing of its early history and doctrines. As a result, most Mormons are unaware that previous "divinely inspired" teachings may contradict official Mormon doctrine. While it is regrettable that devout Mormons are unable to trust their leaders, this is not a unique phenomenon in the history of religious cults and sects.

It does underscore the dilemma faced by the average Mormon. Does he or she accept the claim that early prophets *were* prophets and hence authoritative? If so, they must charge modern Mormonism with apostasy, for it denies many of its own prophets' early teachings.

Or, on the other hand, since many of their doctrines are rejected by modern church leadership as false, do they disregard the early Mormon presidents and prophets?

If so, then the authority of the entire Mormon church collapses, for it is based entirely upon the divine inspiration of such men. An examination of the teachings of the presidents and prophets of his own church will force the average Mormon to conclude that the leaders of Mormonism as a whole are frequently guilty of either apostasy or deception.

The response of the average Mormon is to ignore the historical data which forces such a conclusion, appealing instead to either spurious arguments or subjective or psychic religious experiences as "proof" of the legitimacy of one's faith. Thus, contemporary Mormons may speak of "relative," "dispensational," or "developmental" truth—that is a developmental understanding of divine truth on the part of the church. Unfortunately, when examined, such arguments provide little assistance and neither explain nor justify the kind of problems one encounters in a historical study of Mormon religion. Even modern Mormon teachings are not consistent, with one Mormon leader or scholar contradicting another.

In conclusion, the reader should recognize that talking with Mormons may represent a doctrinally diverse exercise even among members of the Utah church. In addition, historically there have been over one hundred different sects within Mormonism. These range from the five-hundred member "Church of Christ with the Elijah message" in Independence, Missouri, to the Reorganized Church of Jesus Christ of Latter-day Saints (RLDS) in Independence, Missouri, with a membership of two-hundred thousand plus, to the seven to eight million member Church of Jesus Christ of Latter-day Saints in Salt Lake City. Almost all Mormon groups do agree in accepting the *Book of Mormon* as scripture and Joseph Smith as a true prophet.*

Nevertheless, the fact that many Mormon sects accept new revelations as scripture has caused numerous contradictions of belief and practice. This has led nearly every Mormon sect to claim it is the best or only true church. Dr. Gordon Melton's four-point classification of Mormonism gives one an idea of the diversity:

1. Utah Mormons (for example, the Church of Jesus Christ of Latter-day Saints, the Aaronic Order, Zion's Order of the Sons of Levi, LDS Scripture Researchers);

2. Missouri Mormons (for example, the Reorganized Church, the Church of Christ, Temple Lot and Fettingite);

---

* The five-hundred member "Elijah Message" Church offers its own newer revelations—e.g., *The Word of the Lord* (describing ninety-eight additional revelations) plus a prophet to replace Smith; one Mormon sect even rejected Joseph Smith as an apostate—the Church of Christ founded by Mrs. Pauline Hancock. For information relating to splinter groups, see Kate Carter's *Denominations That Base Their Belief on the Teachings of Joseph Smith the Mormon Prophet*, printed by the Mormons (Daughters of the Utah Pioneers Press). See also Steve Shield's, *Divergent Paths of the Restoration*. In addition, both Gordon Melton's *Encyclopedia of American Religions*, 2:1-21 and Gordon Fraser's *Sects of the Latter-day Saints* discuss the Reorganized Church and some of Mormonism's many polygamist groups.

3. Polygamist sects (for example, the Church of the First Born, the Church of the Lamb of God, the Perfected Church of Jesus Christ Immaculate Latter-day Saints);

4. Variant sects (for example, Church of Jesus Christ—Strangite, Bickertonite or Culterite).[9]

The Utah church is by far the largest and most influential of Mormon bodies, and this is the version of the Mormon religion which is evaluated in this book.

We wish to express our indebtedness to Jerald and Sandra Tanner's printing of early Mormon documents and their research in general for its contribution to understanding the Mormon religion.

## ♦ ♦ *Appendix* ♦ ♦

*How Mormons May Attempt to Reach Christian Ministers.*

The "Love Thy Minister Neighbor Workshop Outline" by Darl Andersen contains thirty-nine suggestions for reaching Christian ministers. We cite examples below. Under the category of "Common Ground" (p. 6) it suggests that the following questions be asked of Christian ministers:

5. We really want to be your friends. What can we do to be better neighbors?

6. What can LDS do to support your Christian influence in our community?

7. Without communication we may offend you. We don't want to do that. How can we open channels of communication to reduce offenses?

8. What can we do to make it easier for you to love us so you can be a better Christian?

9. How can our relationship be an example that we truly love our neighbors so that "all men may know we are His disciples?"

11. What joint responsibilities do we have to the community?

13. How can we lift up the example and teachings of Jesus as a solution to many of our community needs and problems?

Under the category of "Suggestions" (p. 7) it encourages the following actions:

> Make a map of the Stake area. Circle and number each church location. List the church name, address, phone number, and minister's name.

Call as many as needed, preferably couples, under the PCD organization, to be a kind of "Home Teachers" to the ministers. People such as Patriarchs, Temple workers, Ex-stake Presidents, Ex-Bishops, Ex-R.S. Presidents can be effective.

Below we supply a verbatim list of recommendations:

## Possible Things to Do

1. Visit each minister at his church.
2. Attend special events at his church.
3. Invite him to lunch.
4. Attend clergy council as an observer or friend.
5. Send congratulations or recognitions whenever appropriate.
6. Offer a special shrub or tree for their new buildings.
7. Invite them to "clergy only" open house at new LDS churches.
8. Offer your service in response to their needs such as fires, emergencies, etc.
9. Send flowers for special events such as Easter and Christmas.
10. Support anti-pornography efforts.
11. Community needs—drug abuse, youth and alcohol, law enforcement.
12. Support Anti-Defamation League with the Jews.
13. School needs—Bibles in libraries, drugs on campus, student discipline, etc.
14. Tours to view church welfare programs.
15. Open house for temple.
16. Joint Thanksgiving Services.
17. Inter-denominational choir performances.
18. Family of the year events.

Although Mormons attempt to use such means to convert Christian pastors, such encounters may also effectively be used to help Mormon leaders understand the truth about Mormonism.

# General Information
# on Mormonism

———————— ◆ ————————

*Name:* The Church of Jesus Christ of Latter-day Saints (Mormon)

*Purpose:* To evangelize the world with the message of Jesus Christ as interpreted by Joseph Smith and the Mormon church; to baptize the dead for their salvation, and for individual members to strive to attain godhood on the basis of personal righteousness and merit.

*Founder:* Joseph Smith

*Source of Authority:* Supernatural revelations received by Joseph Smith, Brigham Young and other prophets and presidents

*Revealed Teachings:* Yes

*Claim:* To be the only true church of Jesus Christ on earth

*Occult Dynamics:* Historically and at present necromantic and spiritistic revelations and other contacts; development of psychic powers interpreted as gifts of the Holy Spirit.

*Size:* Eight to nine million worldwide; five million in the U.S.

*Key Literature:* Scripture: The Bible, the *Book of Mormon, Doctrine and Covenants, The Pearl of Great Price;* while the revelations of Mormon prophets and presidents are also considered scripture, these are only occasionally added to the canon.

*Other Authoritative Literature: Journal of Discourses* (26 volumes of writings by leading early Mormon presidents and prophets and other authorities); Joseph Smith's *History of the Church* (7 volumes); Bruce McConkie's *Mormon Doctrine* and *Doctrinal New Testament Commentary* (3 volumes); Joseph Fielding Smith's *Doctrines of Salvation* (3 volumes); *Answers to Gospel Questions* (4 volumes); *Teachings of the Prophet Joseph Smith;* and *Gospel Doctrine;* James Talmage's *Articles of Faith* and *Jesus the Christ;* LeGrand Richards' *A Marvelous Work and a Wonder; Ensign* (periodical) conference addresses, etc.

*Attitude Toward Christianity:* Hostile

# Mormon Theology
# at a Glance

———————————————  ◆  ———————————————

*God:* An exalted physical man; "Elohim" of the Old Testament; a deity "created" (technically, "fashioned") by sexual union of his divine mother and father. As an infinite number of gods and earths exist, God the Father of Jesus Christ is creator and ruler of this earth only. He is (in early Mormonism) Adam who fell in the Garden of Eden, then located, accorded to Mormonism, in what is now Independence, Missouri.

*Jesus:* "Jehovah" of the Old Testament; the first begotten spirit child of Elohim ("God the Father"), who "created" (or fashioned) him by physical, sexual union with Mary, one of his wives.

*Trinity:* Mormonism rejects the Christian Trinity for a belief in *henotheism,* the worship of one principal God (Elohim) among many. Mormonism is also tritheistic—stressing three primary earth gods, the Father, Son, and Holy Ghost—and polytheistic—accepting endless additional gods of other worlds.

*Holy Ghost:* A man with a spiritual body of matter.

*Salvation:* True salvation in Mormonism is achieved by personal merit and effort with the goal of attaining "exaltation" or godhood in the highest part of the celestial kingdom. There one may participate in "eternal increase"—that is, as a god one may beget (or fashion) innumerable spirit children just as Elohim has. All other salvation is considered "damnation," although participation in various "degrees of glory" nonetheless. Mormonism is almost universalistic, teaching that all will be saved except a very few "sons of perdition." Some Mormons teach that even these will be saved.

*Death:* Mormonism teaches that salvation is possible after physical death. Most people apparently go to a "waiting" area and are eventually assigned one of three principal kingdoms where opportunities exist for advancement—possibly to a higher kingdom, at least according to some authorities.

*Heaven/Hell:* Mormonism teaches there are three principal kingdoms of heaven—the celestial heaven is the highest, and below it are the terrestrial and telestial heavens. These constitute various "degrees of glory" and privilege.

Personal entrance is based upon individual merit in this life, which is itself based upon individual merit in preexistence.

In its most important sense, heaven consists only of three departments in the highest or celestial kingdom. Further, true salvation (exaltation or godhood) is found only by those worthy to be granted access to the highest part of the celestial kingdom.

Hell is not eternal, but a temporal purgatory. The vast majority who go there will, in their punishment, pay the penalty for their sins, be raised after the millennium and inherit a "degree of glory." The only category of persons who inherit literal, eternal hell are "the sons of perdition," principally composed of a few apostate Mormons (Mormons who deny their faith) and possibly some adulterers or murderers.

*Man:* An eternal refashioned spirit intelligence having the innate capacity to evolve into godhood. Men on earth were first created as spirit offspring of Elohim and his wife through physical sexual intercourse. Thus, men are created or fashioned as preexistent spirits and subsequently inhabit the products of human sexual intercourse (a physical body) in order to attempt to gain exaltation or godhood.

*Sin:* Mormonism holds a less than biblically orthodox view of sin in that its scriptural content is downplayed. First, the Mormon concept of works salvation teaches that good works cancel the penalty of sin. Second, its teachings give the Fall of man a positive role in fostering spiritual growth and maturity.

*Satan and Demons:* Satan is one of the innumerable preexistent spirits created by Elohim and his wife; hence the spirit brother of all men and women, including Christ Himself. Because of his primeval rebellion, he was not permitted to inherit a body as the rest of his brothers and sisters. In essence, Satan and demons once represented potential men and women, but are now consigned to live as spirits forever.

*The Second Coming of Christ:* Mormons speak of the Second Coming of the earth god Jesus, but they have also referred to the Second Coming of the god Joseph Smith (*Journal of Discourses,* 7:289; 5:19).

*The Fall of Man:* Ultimately beneficial; predestined by Elohim for the spiritual progress and ultimate welfare of all mankind.

*The Bible:* The Word of God as long as it is translated correctly. Wherever it disagrees with Mormon theology, it is considered incorrect due to textual corruption or false translation.

# Everything You
## Ever Wanted to Know About
# Mormonism

# Mormon Power and Origins

*Is the Legacy of
Joseph Smith Vindicated?*

———————————— ◆ ————————————

Mormonism, as it is called, must stand or fall on the story of Joseph Smith. He was either a prophet of God, divinely called, properly appointed and commissioned, or he was one of the biggest frauds this world has ever seen. There is no middle ground.

If Joseph Smith was a deceiver, who willfully attempted to mislead the people, then he should be exposed; his claims should be refuted, and his doctrines shown to be false, for the doctrines of an impostor cannot be made to harmonize in all particulars with divine truth. If his claims and declarations were built upon fraud and deceit, there would appear many errors and contradictions, which would be easy to detect. The doctrines of false teachers will not stand the test when tried by the accepted standards of measurement, the scriptures.

We are to be judged by our authorized doctrines and deeds

> —Tenth president and prophet of the Mormon church, Joseph Fielding Smith.[1]

N o one can deny that Joseph Smith has left a powerful legacy. In this section we will briefly examine that legacy and also begin to determine whether or not this aftermath can be justified. We will begin by discussing the power of the Mormon church in America today. We will also review the crucial question of how Mormonism first began and whether or not the unique origin of the church is credible.

Since Mormonism claims to be based on a divine revelation, we will introduce that subject and seek to determine the basis upon which anyone can know whether such a claim is valid. Two appendices are also included which discuss: 1) Joseph Smith's alleged seeking of wisdom from God (chap. 2) and 2) the Mormon claim to unjust religious persecution historically (chap. 3).

◆

# CHAPTER 1

# How Powerful Is the Mormon Church Today?

I n the minds of most people Mormonism has a good, clean reputation and is often thought to be a respectable Christian religion.
This is partly because in recent years the Church of Jesus Christ of
Latter-day Saints (Mormon) has initiated a powerful campaign to influence millions of people with its message. Sophisticated magazine,
newspaper and television ads have reached literally tens of millions of
people with the claims of Mormonism. Multiple full-page newspaper
inserts proclaim, "We believe the New Testament Scriptures are true and
that they testify that Jesus is indeed the Promised Messiah and Savior of
the world." Headlines blare, "Mormons believe Jesus Christ is Lord and
Savior" and "Mormons testify Jesus is the Christ."

These advertisements have also been placed in *Reader's Digest* (e.g.,
March 1990) and *TV Guide* (e.g., December 9, 1990) and have even provided an 800 number that respondents could call and receive a free copy
of the *Book of Mormon*, which is boldly advertised as "another testament of
Jesus Christ."

The success of these ads is evident in that in 1989 almost 260,000
requests for a free *Book of Mormon* were received, and 86,000 of those
responding wanted missionaries to make a personal visit. In addition,
forty percent of the respondents said they "believed the book was the
Word of God" and indicated that "they had a special feeling about it."[1]

Direct advertising is only one way by which the Mormon church seeks
converts. Its methods of proselytizing are as varied as its corporate
holdings. For example, the church takes advantage of the fact that every
year millions of people visit Hawaii:

Mormons own a substantial portion of Hawaii [including] the major financial institutions of this area. When you go to the [Mormon sponsored] Polynesian Culture Center they offer you a tour to [visit] their Temple . . . Soon after you return from your visit . . . you will receive a knock from a Mormon missionary asking how you enjoyed your visit and whether you would like to know more about the Church. The Mormons have many other ways of recruiting members: through door-to-door missionaries, visitor centers, the thousands of church sponsored Boy Scout troops and educational institutions, and . . . the Marriott Hotel chain which places Mormon literature in every room.[2]

The power of Mormonism also stems from the fact that it is perhaps the largest, most influential and missionary minded of the various unconventional religions of the United States. The church maintains some forty-five thousand missionaries who engage in proselytizing activities around the world, and its current membership of eight to nine million is expected to double in the next fifteen years. Moreover, the church maintains financial assets valued at billions of dollars, a testimony to the power of mandatory tithing by members. In 1991, *Time* magazine reported, "In business terms, the Church is an $8 billion-a-year conglomerate that employs about 10,000 people."[3] This makes it one of the wealthiest churches per capita in the entire world. Not unexpectedly, many of the lay leaders within the Mormon church are businessmen who help the church oversee a vast and growing worldwide financial empire.

For example, the church owns real estate management and trust holding firms which alone have assets of two billion dollars. In addition, it owns or has owned five insurance companies, a newspaper, two television stations, a chain of bookstores, a shopping mall, eleven radio stations, hundreds of thousands of acres of farmland, one of the nation's largest private television networks and most of Salt Lake City's tallest skyscrapers.[4] (Cf., the extensive report in *The Arizona Republic*, June 30, 1991.)

The church is also a large stockholder in Utah Power and Light Company, with assets of over one billion dollars. The Mormon empire also runs several colleges, such as Brigham Young University (with an enrollment of almost thirty thousand), plus other schools, factories, etc. According to Walter Martin, the church further owns Bonneville International Corporation, Zion's Securities Corporation, and Deseret Ranches of Florida, some 315,000 acres near Disney World, which alone are worth at least a billion dollars.[5] According to *The God Makers*, a critical film on Mormonism:

The Mormon Church is the second largest financial institution west of the Mississippi River. The Mormon Church wields economic power more effectively than any other organized religion in the world. They own the $2.6 million Beneficial Life Insurance Company, The Deseret Management and Trust Corp., hospitals, schools, apartment buildings, farms. They are a major stockholder in the *LA Times*. They own TV and radio stations (and) the ZCMI Department Store chain. They have vast land holdings with ownerships in all 50 American states, throughout Canada and Europe and on every continent. Two thirds of their properties are tax exempt.[6]

Mormons tend to view financial prosperity as a sign of God's blessing. Their corporate wealth confirms their belief that Mormonism is wealthy because it is pleasing to God. As noted, mandatory tithing is a principle means of church income. According to Mormon doctrine, tithing is a law of God commanded upon the people; *Doctrine and Covenants*, (hereafter cited in the text as *D&C*) 119:3,4 calls it a "standing law . . . forever." A devoted former church member estimates that many Mormons "will be paying 20%-25% of their gross income to the Church."[7] Wealthy Mormon celebrities and business executives also tend to tithe generously. For example, the Osmond and Marriott families are two large contributors to the Mormon empire.*[8]

In state and national politics, Mormons have retained more than their share of influence. Richard Peal, one of the most powerful men in the Reagan administration, was a Mormon,[11] and Mormons have headed the following posts and departments: Assistant Attorney General, head of the National Security Council, Secretary of Agriculture, Treasurer of the United States, the United States Chamber of Commerce, the Department of Interior, the Federal Communications Commission, the Department of Urban Housing and Development, the Federal Research Board, the Securities and Exchange Commission, and various state government posts.[12] Mormons also head or have headed Walt Disney Productions, Save-on Drugs, Max Factor, Standard Oil and many other conglomerates.[13]

The Mormon church is also the single largest sponsor of Boy Scout units in the United States (seventeen thousand), and Mormon officials have admitted this is an effective manner in which to share the faith.[14] For example, former Secretary of Agriculture in the Eisenhower administration and the current Mormon prophet and president, Ezra Taft Benson, comments, "Scouting is Church work. It is part of the (Mormon) Church program."[15] And,

---

*Such tithing is part of the "package" of good works that will eventually earn a Mormon his supposed exaltation or godhood (see chap. 16).[9] In fact, in Mormonism, the logical motive undergirding both tithing and missions work is the personal hope of exaltation to divinity. Any Mormon who desires godhood must tithe generously and also become a Mormon missionary.[10] In essence, two of the most effective means for expanding the Mormon empire are sustained by one of the most compelling and enticing motivators known to man—the anticipation of absolute power.

> I have been deeply impressed with the record that has been
> made by the Church. . . . In no other field do we have a better
> reputation than in the field of Scouting. . . . We have . . . a
> higher proportion of Scout troops sponsored by the Church
> than any other church or civic organization in the world. . . .
> [And] we have the highest enrollment of boys in Scouting of
> any church on the earth.[16]

In fact President Benson confesses, "Religious emphasis is a part of
Scouting" and, "Scouting helps prepare boys for [Mormon] Church responsibility. . . . We want these boys to become better men and boys and
honor their [Mormon] priesthood and to be faithful members of the
[Mormon] Church and kingdom of God."[17]

Thus, the positive image of Mormonism is undergirded by many
factors: their scouting leadership, their financial reputation, their moral
emphasis, and their Christian appearance. All this is why even many
Christians think that the Mormon church is a Christian organization and
that individual Mormons are Christians.

In fact, the Mormon church's successful portrayal of itself as Christian
explains why there may be (according to Mormons) more converts to
Mormonism from Christian churches than there are official defections
from Mormonism. According to research published in a Mormon magazine, "Far more persons convert to the Mormon Church from other
churches or from a status of no religious affiliation than leave."[18] The
report cited a 1990 study published by Mormons Howard M. Bahr and
David Hunt relying on NORC General Social Survey data from 1972-1988
and the University of Wisconsin National Survey of Families and House-
holds, 1987-1988.

This study also indicated that the conversion rates from various Christian denominations to Mormonism were proportionately similar. Jewish,
Catholic, Baptist and Christian Reformed churches had somewhat lower
conversion rates, though, than several Evangelical and Fundamentalist
denominations and some mainline denominations (Presbyterian, Episco-
pal, Christian and United Churches of Christ, among others). Studies
also indicated that among leading world religions, Mormonism has the
fourth highest retention rate: Islam (92 percent), Jewish (88 percent),
Catholic (83.5 percent), Mormon (82 percent).[19] But such studies do not
give us the whole picture.

Even though global membership of the Mormon church has climbed
sevenfold since 1947, making it the sixth largest religious denomination
in America, not all is well with Mormonism. For example, according to
the *Los Angeles Times*, several analysts familiar with the Mormon church
have stated that at least forty percent of Mormons are inactive and that
many of these are disillusioned.[20] But if even thirty percent of Mormons
are inactive or disillusioned, the Mormon empire could face some serious
future problems.

One purpose of this book is to reveal some of the reasons for this disillusionment.

We will seek to answer the following questions. What exactly is Mormonism and what does it teach? How did the Mormon religion begin? What kind of men founded the Mormon church and are they to be considered prophets according to biblical definition and standards? Can Mormonism truly be considered a Christian religion? Are the early teachings of the inspired Mormon prophets the doctrines of the church today? Has the official history of the church been suppressed or altered? Is the average Mormon aware of the early history and teachings of the church? Was the early church the victim of unjust religious persecution as it claims? Has the church engaged in deliberate suppression or alteration of its own divine revelations? Has the Temple ceremony been altered? Did the early church go so far as to kill some of its own members in order to "save" their souls? Why did the church first teach polygamy and does it still support such a practice? Should Mormonism be considered an occult religion? Why does the church baptize the living for the dead? Do modern Mormons view contacts with the dead as "faith building experiences?" Is there a Divine Mother in heaven? Was Adam of the Garden of Eden the God of early Mormonism? Does Mormonism really believe that Jesus was the product of the *physical* sexual union between God the Father and the "virgin" Mary? Are those the Mormon church labels its "enemies" really guilty of misrepresenting and distorting what Mormonism teaches? Is one branded an enemy of the church merely for raising these questions? These are only some of the issues we will seek to answer in this volume.

# CHAPTER 2

# How Did Mormonism Begin?

The official version of Mormonism's beginnings is recorded in the Mormon scripture known as *The Pearl of Great Price* (1851). By this account, the seeds of Mormonism were sown in Joseph Smith, Mormonism's founder, during a powerful divine visitation. This encounter is known as the "first vision." Allegedly, God the Father and Jesus Christ appeared to Smith as part of their plan to begin the Mormon religion and reestablish "true Christianity."

This "first vision" episode is crucial to the claims of the Mormon religion. Because of the importance of this alleged event, we will cite *The Pearl of Great Price* verbatim, after giving a brief introduction.

Joseph Smith (1805-1844) claimed that in his fifteenth year (1820), while living in Manchester, New York, a religious revival of significant proportions took place and "great multitudes united themselves to the different religious parties."[21] However, Smith alleges that the doctrinal strife among these religious parties was so great as to confuse a person entirely: with such conflicting claims, how could anyone determine which religion was correct—Presbyterians, Methodists, Baptists, or any other denomination?

Furthermore, according to Smith, the teachers of the various denominations allegedly "understood the same passage of Scripture so differently as to destroy all confidence in settling the question [of which group to join] by an appeal to the Bible."

Because of his confusion, Smith determined to seek God's counsel as to which of the various denominations was true, so that he might know which church he should join. As he explains it, James 1:5, which refers to asking God for wisdom, had a crucial impact at this juncture. In Smith's own words,

> Never did any passage of Scripture come with more power
> to the heart of man than this did at this time to mine. It seemed

to enter with great force into every feeling of my heart. I reflected on it again and again, knowing that if any person needed wisdom from God, I did; for how to act I did not know and unless I could get more wisdom than I then had, I would never know.[22]

He concluded at this point that either he must "remain in darkness and confusion" or else he must "do as James directs, that is, ask of God."[23]

In his attempt to seek God, the teenage Joseph Smith retired to a secluded place in the woods in order to pray. He notes that it was on the morning of a "beautiful, clear day, early in the spring of 1820."[24]

After finding an appropriate spot, Smith reports that he "kneeled down and began to offer up the desires of my heart to God." But what Smith encountered terrified him:

> I had scarcely done so, when immediately I was seized upon by some power which entirely overcame me, and had such an astonishing influence over me as to bind my tongue so that I could not speak. Thick darkness gathered around me, and it seemed to me for a time as if I were doomed to sudden destruction.[25]

Smith then describes how, fearing immediate death, he called upon God for deliverance:

> But, exerting all my powers to call upon God to deliver me out of the power of this enemy which had seized upon me, and at the very moment which I was ready to sink into despair and abandon myself to destruction—not to an imaginary ruin, but to the power of some actual being from the unseen world, who had such marvelous power as I had never before felt in any being—just at this moment of great alarm, I saw a pillar of light exactly over my head, above the brightness of the sun, which descended gradually until it fell upon me.[26]

Having felt the panic of imminent destruction, Smith was amazed to find himself delivered:

> It no sooner appeared when I found myself delivered from the enemy which held me bound. When the light rested upon me I saw two personages, whose brightness and glory defy all description, standing above me in the air. One of them spake unto me, calling me by name, and said—pointing to the other—"THIS IS MY BELOVED SON, HEAR HIM."[27]

At this point, the claims of Joseph Smith are clear. Having called on God for help, he has been immediately delivered by nothing less than the astonishing appearance of God the Father and His Son Jesus Christ. At this juncture, Smith collected his senses and recalled his mission:

> My object in going to inquire of the Lord was to know which of all the sects was right, that I might know which to join. No sooner, therefore, did I get possession of myself, so as to be able to speak, than I asked the personages who stood above me in the light, which of all the sects was right—and which I should join.[28]

Smith was answered immediately. In fact, to answer the question of "How did Mormonism begin?," we only need read the reply that the two supernatural personages supplied to Joseph Smith's question. According to Joseph Smith, God the Father and God the Son told him that

> I must join none of them, for they were all wrong, and the Personage who addressed me [God the Father] said that all their creeds were an abomination in his sight: that those professors [of Christian religion] were all corrupt; that "they draw near to me with their lips, but their hearts are far from me, they teach for doctrines the commandments of men, having a form of godliness, but they deny the power thereof."
> He [God the Father] again forbade me to join with any of them; and many other things did he say unto me, which I cannot write at this time. When I came to myself again [fully regained his senses], I found myself lying on my back, looking up into heaven. When the light had departed, I had no strength; but soon recovering it in some degree, I went home.[29]

Joseph Smith had found his answer. He was convinced that God had appeared to him to inform him that Christianity was a false religion. Thus, he recalls, "My mind [was] satisfied so far as the sectarian [Christian] world was concerned . . . it was not my duty to join with any of them, but to continue as I was until further directed."[30]

Smith became persuaded that, out of all the men in the world, he had been uniquely called of God. Although he admits that he "frequently fell into many foolish errors" (cf. James 1:20-22,26), he waited patiently until the next revelation.[31]

Three years later, on September 21, 1823, Smith experienced the first of several major necromantic encounters, or contacts with the dead. At this time a spirit appeared to Smith to tell him the location of certain "gold plates." These gold plates contained the purported historical records of the Jewish "Nephite" peoples concerning their early migration to the Americas (see chap. 22).

In his *History of the Church*, Smith records the visit by this spirit who identified itself as "Moroni" (the son of a "Nephite" historian named Mormon, the alleged author of the "gold plates" from which the *Book of Mormon* was "translated"):

> While I was thus in the act of calling upon God, I discovered a light appearing in my room, which continued to increase until the room was lighter than at noonday, when immediately a [spirit] personage appeared at my bed side, standing in the air. . . . He called me by name, and said unto me that he was a messenger sent from the presence of God to me and that his name was Moroni; that God had a work for me to do. . . . He said there was a book deposited, written upon gold plates, giving an account of the former inhabitants of this [American] continent, and the sources from whence they sprang. He also said that the fullness of the everlasting Gospel was contained in it, as delivered by the Savior [Jesus] to the ancient inhabitants [of America]; also that there were two stones in silver bows—and these stones, fastened to a breastplate, constituted what is called the Urim and Thummim—deposited with the plates; and the possession and use of these stones were what constituted [the category of] "seers" in ancient or former times; and that God had prepared them for the purpose of translating the book.[32]

In addition, the spirit quoted numerous passages of prophetic scripture, either implying or stating that some of them were about to be fulfilled. The spirit then departed, although it soon reappeared twice to state the same message.[33] As we will note in chapter 18, these and other necromantic contacts were probably the result of Joseph Smith's use of magic ritual to invoke the spirit world. The specific nature of the encounters frequently fit the pattern for magical contacts.

Further supernatural encounters continued to profoundly influence the young Joseph Smith. The very next day, the seventeen-year-old lad was crossing a field when suddenly "my strength entirely failed me, and I fell helpless on the ground, and for a time was unconscious of anything."[34] The first thing Smith remembered was hearing the same spirit calling his name. Regaining his senses, he was commanded to go and locate the "gold plates" buried in a certain hill named Cumorah. After that, according to the spirit, he was to return yearly to that same spot for further instructions and teaching, and in the fourth year (in 1827) the translation of the "gold plates" would be permitted. Thus, by 1829 the translation was completed, and in 1830 the *Book of Mormon* was published. Named after its author, the Nephite historian Mormon, it became one of the three scriptures unique to the Mormon faith.

In conclusion, just as the Mormon church originated in supernatural revelations, it was sustained by this means, especially by contact with various spirits, including alleged spirits of the dead such as Moroni.

In fact, from 1825 until his untimely death in 1844, Joseph Smith received several *hundred* direct revelations from the spirit world, which helped the new religious movement to grow and solidify itself.[35] Smith claimed he received revelations not only from "God," "Jesus" and "angels," but also from many of the dead. Some 135 of these revelations were printed in *Doctrine and Covenants*, the second and doctrinally most important volume of Mormon scripture.[36] For example, in this book are recorded alleged revelations from Moroni (2); the Apostles John, Peter and James (7; 27:12; 128:20); John the Baptist (13) and others (e.g., 128).[37]

Although most of the revelations claim to be from God the Father and Jesus Christ, this is not possible for reasons that will become evident Because Smith was an accomplished occultist (see chap. 18), the revelations he received were occultic, not divine. In fact, those familiar with spiritistic revelation can observe many similarities. We have read scores of such revelations and conclude that *Doctrine and Covenants* is of the same genre. In doctrinal content, practical instruction and general mannerism, its spiritistic nature seems obvious. *Doctrine and Covenants*, then, can properly be classified as a form of spiritistic and necromantic literature. It explicitly teaches, for example, that the living must be linked to the dead and that if Mormons do not help the dead to be saved, they themselves cannot be saved: "For their salvation is necessary and essential to our salvation" (*D&C*, 128:15) (see chaps. 18-20).

## ♦ ♦ *Appendix* ♦ ♦

*In Allegedly Seeking Wisdom from God, Was Joseph Smith Really Acting in Obedience to the Instructions of James?*

As a pillar undergirding the authority of the Mormon church, the importance of the first vision account cannot be overestimated. But this account raises serious questions. As we shall discuss in chapter 21, at least four and perhaps six or more different versions of the first vision account are known to exist.[38] Which account is to be trusted? Further, if we do assume the legitimacy of the official version, was the teenage Smith really obeying the injunction of the Apostle James, or was he, in fact, misapplying it?

A careful study of the incident leads us to believe that rather than obeying James, as the official account implies, Joseph Smith misinterpreted the Bible and, therefore, acted unwisely and presumptuously.

In the first place, it was unnecessary for Smith to inquire of God in the way he did. Had he consulted with Christian men or read the New Testament carefully, he could have determined that the differences among the various Christian denominations were largely on minor points, not major doctrine.

Orthodox Christian denominations have always agreed on the major historic doctrines of the faith. For example, all Christian churches of Joseph Smith's day accepted the divine authority of the Bible, the doctrine of the Trinity, the vicarious atonement of Jesus Christ, salvation by grace through faith alone, the bodily return of Christ, and many other biblical teachings. Thus, if he had wanted to, Smith could have determined that the various churches were *not* "all corrupt" as the beings in the vision maintained. And he could have determined that the spirits that appeared to him had to be lying.

In the second place, a detailed study of Smith's character and actions (e.g., see chap. 4, appendix) reveal that he was more accurately described by James 1:6,7 and 20-26, as double-minded, unstable and self-deceiving.

The official account of the first vision portrays Smith as a sincere and godly inquirer after divine wisdom. But if the hundreds of revelations that Smith received from various spirits denied what God had already revealed in the Bible, then they certainly could not have been divine revelations—nor could they contain *divine* wisdom.

Thus, if we carefully examine the teachings of James, chapter 1, we have reason to question Smith's understanding of this passage and the final result of his prayer. The "wisdom" God offers in James 1 is not an offer of extra-biblical revelation or of additional information. God did not say, "If any of you lacks information." He specifically offered to give *wisdom*. Wisdom is the godly application of knowledge one already possesses. Smith's problem was that he possessed insufficient biblical knowledge and therefore could not receive wisdom from God. Further, true prayer involves trust in God. Smith did not ultimately trust God, for as we will see he openly rejected His teachings. If one is double-minded— asking God for wisdom while rejecting His Word—one cannot logically expect to receive divine wisdom. In other words, because the young Smith rejected the teachings of those many Christians he talked with, his attitude was marked by an unwillingness to accept the plain teachings of Scripture. He was not "quick to hear" (for example, from other Christians) and "slow to speak" (for example, about their alleged "errors") (James 1:19). He did not "in humility receive the word implanted, which is able to save your souls" (v. 21).

As James 1:6,7 implies, the one who doubts what God has said sets up a barrier in his heart which prevents him from leaning upon God: "That man should not think he will receive anything from the Lord" (v. 7 NIV). According to James, we are saved by "the word of truth," but this is precisely the word that Smith rejected (v. 18). The one who *abides* in the Word and *acts upon it*, says James, "shall be blessed in what he does" (v. 25).

In spite of a zeal for his own particular religious beliefs and preferences, Smith did not prove himself a "doer of the word" as James says, but rather a hearer who deludes himself (v. 22). (See chapter 4, appendix.) James further warns of the one who "deceives his own heart," that "this man's religion is worthless" (v. 26).

In the end, Smith preferred to trust in visions that opposed the teaching of Scripture, not in Scripture itself. This was a feature of his personality that has, unfortunately, remained a characteristic of his church to this day. The Bible warns us that a man is not to take "his stand on visions he has seen, inflated without cause by his fleshly mind" but rather is to rely wholly upon the true Jesus Christ (Colossians 2:18,19).

Because the revelations in the *Book of Mormon* and *Doctrine and Covenants* oppose the most basic teachings of the Bible, we know that these revelations could not have come from God. The fact that these revelations were often delivered by spirits (later interpreted as "angels") makes the warning of Paul to the Galatians apropos to any study of Mormonism:

> I am amazed that you are so quickly deserting Him who called you by the grace of Christ, for a different gospel... there are some who are disturbing you, and want to distort the gospel of Christ. But even though we, or an angel from heaven, should preach to you a gospel contrary to that which we have preached to you, let him be accursed (Galatians 1:6-8).

The first vision narrative is interesting on one more account: its display of spiritual intimidation. Confronted by destruction from one source, Smith naturally interprets his deliverance from another as divine. But how does he know that the entire event was not staged by evil forces for just this effect? Such accounts are legion in the ranks of mediumism and other forms of spiritism. Lying spirits, which the Bible identifies as demons, often claim to be God, Jesus, angels or the human dead.[39] A similar account of evil spirits imitating divine spirits or angels is found, for example, in former medium Raphael Gasson's *The Challenging Counterfeit*: "Demons have to use some method of deception in their attempt to prove the counterfeit is of God and so they play a game of make-believe. Although they are literally evil spirits, one pretends to be the 'good' spirit while the other proclaims his 'evil'-ness."[40]

As noted, Smith was a proficient occultist (see chap. 18), and the area in which Smith encountered his visions had been a center of occult manifestations. It is hardly unexpected then that Smith could fall prey to occult powers. His account reveals numerous parallels to other occult encounters. These include speechlessness, the pillar of light, entities in the air in the midst of the light,[41] unconsciousness, lying on one's back staring into heaven at the close of the encounter, a sapping of strength, and messages given with the promise of future contact.

Nevertheless, the early Mormons followed the leading of Joseph Smith, and they continued to rely upon dramatic supernatural revelations and visions which only claimed to be divine.

## CHAPTER 3

━━━━━━━━━━━━━━━ ◆ ━━━━━━━━━━━━━━━

# Are Mormon Revelations from God?

## *How Can We Know? If They Are Not from God, Where Did They Come From?*

We can determine whether or not these revelations were from God by comparing them with what God has already said in His Word, the Bible. If these revelations deny His Word, then they cannot logically originate in God. As Abraham Lincoln noted during the Civil War, when both sides were claiming God's support, "God cannot be for and against the same thing at the same time."

If Joseph Smith or anyone else claims to have divine visions, this does not automatically prove the visions are from God; people may invent stories of divine visions for various reasons or they may even be suffering from mental delusions. Even if Joseph Smith was the recipient of supernatural manifestations, how do we know they were not clever counterfeits by deceiving spirits who were lying when they claimed to be God, Jesus, angels or saints? Counterfeit revelations are notoriously deceptive.[42]

Literally thousands of people claim to have seen divine visions or to have received revelations from angels, the spirits of the dead, etc., and yet subsequent events have typically proved them wrong. Thus, no one should automatically assume Joseph Smith's revelations were truly divine. Before such a conclusion may be accepted, the teachings and consequences of the visions must be carefully tested as the Bible itself commands (1 Thessalonians 5:21). The Bible further teaches, "Dear friends, do not believe every spirit, but test the spirits to see whether they are from God, because many false prophets have gone out into the world" (1 John 4:1 NIV).

The issue of whether or not Mormon revelations are divine is finally decided by one simple test. If Joseph Smith's revelations deny, contradict, and oppose the Bible, then, whatever their source, they cannot possibly have originated in God. And if they did not originate in God, they have no divine authority and should not be heeded.

Most of this book will be devoted to supplying thorough documentation that Mormon revelations and the doctrines derived from them cannot be considered biblical, and hence are not divine. If you are a Mormon, we ask you to carefully weigh the arguments presented. Every person has a responsibility to himself and his family to be certain that what he claims to be from God really is.

Spiritistic revelations are deeply consequential. In relying wholeheartedly upon supernatural visions and manifestations, the young church was led into great pain and suffering. The appendix to this chapter and chapters 28 and 29 illustrate this suffering.

## ◆ ◆ *Conclusion* ◆ ◆

No one can deny that the Mormon church is a powerful social and religious institution in modern America. But we cannot conclude that the legacy of Joseph Smith has been vindicated. Power, money and social prestige alone do not answer questions about the ultimate origin or fruit of a religious movement. Only the actual beliefs and practices of a religion can determine whether or not its legacy is vindicated. The remainder of this book will be devoted to answering that question.

## ◆ ◆ *Appendix* ◆ ◆

*Was the Early Mormon Church Unjustly Persecuted As It Claims—Or Did It Bring Suffering Upon Itself?* (See also chaps. 28,29.)

Mormons interpret their early history as one of unjust religious persecution, and certainly not the fault of the early Mormons who were attempting to do God's will. But the church's tragedies were largely of its own making. Mormons were attempting to live consistently with supernatural revelations that were anti-biblical and often anti-social. In some cases, there may have been persecution. But it is more accurate to say that Mormons were rejected by other people largely because of their highly unorthodox, sinful or illegal activities—practices that had resulted from these new revelations. Biographies and histories of the period make this clear. Polygamist practices, for example, caused the church no end of grief (see chap. 29), and the practices of many church leaders were positively evil (e.g., see chap. 28).

Thus, the early Mormons experienced great hardship as the fledgling church was driven from one place to another either by angry residents or because they were seeking to obey the cruel commandments of spiritistic revelations.

As documented by Jerald and Sandra Tanner in "Works of Darkness" in *The Mormon Kingdom–Volume II* and elsewhere, the Mormons' own beliefs plus the lifestyles of some or many of their members were the real cause of their persecution.[43] Many Mormons disobeyed the laws of the land, including committing serious crimes against non-Mormons. Some Mormons verbally attacked the United States government, prophesying its overthrow. Obviously attacking the country and its President was unlikely to generate neighborly compassion.[44] Indeed, "one of the most important factors leading to Joseph Smith's death was his interference in politics."[45]

Perhaps more relevant was the excessive violence committed by some Mormons. John Whitmer, one of the original Eight Witnesses to the *Book of Mormon*, observes that Smith and others had formed a secret society ("The Brotherhood of Gideon") wherein they took Masonic-like oaths to support fellow Mormons "right or wrong, even to the shedding of blood."[46] Whitmer alleges, "The formation of these things together with adultery, wickedness and abominations which grew and multiplied in the heads and members of the Church of Christ of Latter-day Saints brought Joseph Smith and his brother Hyrum to an untimely end as also the scattering of the Church."[47] As history records, Joseph Smith and his brother were killed by angry residents while in jail in 1844.

To cite an example of the violence, many leaders in the early church advocated and some practiced a doctrine of blood atonement (see chap. 28)—the putting to death of members who committed various sins, as well as whipping and castrating disobedient members.[48] Non-Mormons ("Gentiles") were also dealt with brutally. Brigham Young, the second president and prophet of the church, "was very prone to use violent methods in dealing with apostates and enemies of the Church."[49] Even some Mormons were appalled at his evil practices (see chap. 28). At one point he was actually indicted for murder, although characteristically the case never came to trial because of Mormon power in Utah.[50]

From Mormon and other credible sources, primary documentation can be supplied for numerous examples of whippings, castrations and executions of both Mormons and non-Mormons—but crimes were committed particularly against non-Mormons. When one reads account after account of these criminal activities, one finds it impossible to accept current Mormon teaching that such things never happened.[51] For example, a formerly devout Mormon wrote in 1875 that in Missouri,

"Murders, thefts, and the most shameful atrocities were of daily occurrence, and the history of those terrible doings would fill a good-sized
volume."[52]

Obviously, such activities are not practiced today; the fact that Mormon critics are alive in Salt Lake City is evidence enough. But Mormons
must certainly be concerned about the moral character of those who
helped found the Mormon church upon the basis of such practices.
Indeed, if Mormons would take the time to do the necessary reading,
including checking the original documents, they might find themselves
horrified at the excesses committed. Some of these church leaders were
capable of the most brutal of crimes and coverups—for example, the
Warren Snow case.[53]

In light of actual Mormon history, including statements by Mormon
authorities themselves, it is difficult not to classify many early Mormon
leaders as immoral men who engaged in lying, corruption and criminal
activity, all the while justifying their actions in the name of God. This,
and little else, was the cause of the persecution of the church. One
Mormon wrote of Brigham Young as follows:

> In him the Saints, from the smallest to the greatest, placed
> implicit trust, and it was in his power to mould them at his
> will. . . . But he has basely betrayed that sacred trust, . . . he has
> been guilty of the most grievous wrong-doing. He has set at
> nought all morality with his horrible and debasing teachings
> respecting a "blood-atonement"—in other words, the duty of
> assassination. He has outraged decency and riven asunder the
> most sacred social and domestic ties by his shameless intro-
> duction of Polygamy . . . both by his preaching and his practice
> he has set an example so bad as to be utterly without parallel in
> this civilized age.[54]

Surely a Mormon who knows this true history should question the
likelihood of a divine religion emerging from such roots. Do we find the
New Testament apostles engaging in anything even remotely resembling
the actions of these men? In an analogy concerning false prophets, Jesus
taught that it was impossible for diseased trees to bear good fruit (Matthew 7:15-27). Jesus also noted that even apparently sincere men could
mistakenly commit terrible crimes, even murder, thinking they were
working on God's behalf (John 16:23 NIV). Yet, the Lord noted, "They will
do such things because they have not known the Father or me" (v. 3).

It is probably true that it was often the leaders of the Mormon church
and not the laity who were responsible for the crimes committed. But
even so, the laity shared in the responsibility as followers: they empowered
the leaders. Without the many Mormon people who submitted to and
endorsed such leaders, there would have been no church platform upon
which these crimes could have been committed.

Further, it is one thing for a few dissident or evil members of a church to deny the truly moral and good teachings they profess, and thereby commit evils which are justly and logically condemned by the larger membership. But it is another thing entirely for the leaders of a church to do evil in accordance with the teachings they profess—that is, to find that crimes follow logically from their religious teachings—and to also have the church's support.

Certainly then, the "persecution" experienced by early Mormons had a different cause than that claimed by Mormon officials. In his 1904 "Introductory History" to the confession of Mormon murderer Bill Hickman, J.H. Beadle, a man well acquainted with early Mormon history, wrote:

> A religion in which it is the chief hope of its devotee to crush his opponents, not to convert or soften and unite with them, can produce but one class of fruits: hatred, malice, and all uncharitableness, strife and animosity against all who dissent. Hence the Mormons' bitter hatred of "apostates." Other churches pray for the backslider; the Mormon curses them with hideous blasphemy. Said Heber Kimball: "I *do* pray for my enemies; I pray God Almighty to damn them."
>
> Can a bitter fountain send forth sweet water? Can a people's whole inner life be bad, and their outer life good? If the Mormons are truly that peaceful, quiet, and industrious people we sometimes hear of, fitted for good citizens, *why* have they come into violent conflict with the people in all their seven places of settlement? For they have tried every different kind of people, from New York through Ohio, Illinois, and Missouri, to Salt Lake. Are *all* the people of *all* those places incurable vicious, mobbers and trespassers on religious right? This is your only possible conclusion, if you start with the hypothesis that the Mormon religion makes its devotees good citizens.[55]

But aren't these past events largely irrelevant to the modern church? Why do we mention them? We mention them because 1) they are part of the "truth about Mormonism," and 2) because such knowledge *is* relevant to the modern Mormon church. For example, Utah *today* contains more polygamists than in the nineteenth century—a direct result of early Mormon teaching. Some leaders of these polygamous sects are also murderers. Further, if it can be independently established, as we will later show, that the supernatural revelations received by the early Mormon presidents, prophets and other leaders in the church were anti-biblical, then they could not possibly have originated in God. And if these revelations rejected God, Christ and the Bible, it is not surprising they could also reject biblical morality.

Thus, to the extent that these revelations directly and indirectly supported criminal activity, this commentary is certainly relevant in establishing the source for Mormon religion as divine or non-divine. If the revelations of the early church were unbiblical and many of its practices ungodly, on what basis can Mormonism logically claim to be a revelation from God?

# Mormon Belief and Practice

*Are They Defensible?*

═══════════════════════ ◆ ═══════════════════════

I n this section, we will examine four key claims of the Mormon church. Each claim relates to a central characteristic and/or practice of Mormon faith. Understanding these subjects will enable us to better understand Mormonism and prepare the way for discussion of other Mormon teachings. These four claims are 1) that Joseph Smith was a true prophet of God; 2) that the canon of Scripture remains perpetually open and that individual members receive divine inspiration for daily guidance in life; 3) that Mormonism is the only true Christian church on earth; and 4) that only those who hold the Mormon priesthood have spiritual authority, power and privilege before God.

These four themes form an indivisible unit. If any single point is demonstrated to be false, the other three are seriously or fatally undermined. But if Mormonism is to be considered a genuine revelation from God, as it claims, all four points must be established. If none can be established, Mormonism cannot logically be considered a divine religion.

In this section we have also included a brief appendix on Joseph Smith (chap. 4).

◆

# CHAPTER 4

# Was Joseph Smith a True Prophet of God?

## Is Joseph Smith's Centrality in the Mormon Church Justified?

The Mormon church claims that Joseph Smith was a true prophet of God in the biblical sense of that term.[1] Brigham Young claimed:

> Every intelligent person under the heavens that does not, when informed, acknowledge that Joseph Smith, JUN., is a Prophet of God, is in darkness, and is opposed to us and to Jesus and his kingdom on the earth.[2]

And, in even stronger terms,

> Every spirit that confesses that Joseph Smith is a Prophet, that he lived and died a Prophet and that the *Book of Mormon* is true, is of God, and every spirit that does not is of anti-Christ.[3]

The current president of the Mormon church, Ezra Taft Benson, concurs:

> Joseph Smith was a prophet of the Living God, one of the greatest prophets that has ever lived upon the earth. . . . we have standing at the head of the Church today a prophet . . . who holds all the keys and authority necessary to carry forward our Father's program for the blessing of His children.

And, in fact,

> The greatest activity in this world or in the world to come is directly related to the work and mission of Joseph Smith—man of destiny, prophet of God.[4]

Furthermore, President Benson claims that Joseph Smith continues to guide the Mormon church even from the spirit world:

> The Prophet Joseph Smith was not only "one of the noble and great ones" [i.e., one of the spirits personally designated by God as a ruler for Him in the preexistent state before the world was created] but he *continues to give* attention to important matters here on the earth even today from the [spirit] realms above. . . .[5]

Mormons agree that upon the prophethood of Joseph Smith rests the legitimacy or illegitimacy of all Mormonism. Smith himself claimed the church began with his divine call to be a prophet for God, and Mormonism continues to depend entirely upon Smith's purported divine revelations as recorded in the *Book of Mormon, Doctrine and Covenants,* and *The Pearl of Great Price.*

But was Joseph Smith really a true prophet of God? How can we test such a claim? Since Mormonism freely confesses that Joseph Smith met all the biblical requirements for prophethood, anyone who wishes can examine those requirements and see whether or not he fulfilled them.

Did Smith meet the biblical requirements of a true prophet? No. Can this be proven? Yes. In fact, Smith didn't fulfill even a single requirement for being a prophet—and we challenge the Mormon church to prove otherwise.

First, the true prophet must speak in the name of the Lord and be commissioned by the one true God. But we shall prove in chapters 10-12 that Smith prophesied in the name of a different god and, therefore, could never have been commissioned by the God of the Bible. Under Old Testament law, such a person was to be put to death: "But a prophet who presumes to speak in my name anything I have not commanded him to say, or a prophet who speaks in the name of other gods, must be put to death" (Deuteronomy 18:20 NIV).

Second, the true prophet must have a perfect record concerning his predictions. Demonstrated error by an alleged prophet proves him a false prophet who must not be heeded or feared. But as we shall prove in chapter 25, Joseph Smith was guilty of many false prophecies, and therefore his claims to prophethood must be rejected. God Himself warned His people: "You may say to yourselves, 'How can we know when a message has not been spoken by the Lord?' If what a prophet proclaims in the name of the Lord does not take place or come true, that is a message the Lord has not spoken. That prophet has spoken presumptuously. Do not be afraid of him" (Deuteronomy 18:21,22 NIV).

But even if a so-called prophet performs a genuine miracle or prophesies accurately, he is still to be rejected *if* he counsels people to follow other gods. The Bible teaches that false prophets are often empowered by lying spirits who can perform genuine miracles through them (Acts 16:16-19); 1 Timothy 4:1; 1 John 4:1, etc.). But the fact that these "prophets" counsel rebellion against the one true God is proof of their fraud:

> If a prophet, or one who foretells by dreams, appears among you and announces to you a miraculous sign or wonder, and if the sign or wonder of which he has spoken takes place, and he says, "Let us follow other gods" (gods you have not known) and "let us worship them," *you must not listen* to the words of that prophet or dreamer. The Lord your God is testing you to find out whether you love Him with all your heart and all your soul. It is the Lord your God you must follow, and Him you must revere. Keep His commands and obey Him; serve and hold fast to Him. *That prophet or dreamer must be put to death,* because he preached *rebellion against the Lord your God,* ... he has tried to turn you from the way the Lord your God commanded you to follow (Deuteronomy 13:1-5, emphasis added).

Thus, no one who has fairly examined the evidence can accept the claim of the Mormon church that Joseph Smith was a prophet of the biblical God. But Joseph Smith should also be rejected as a prophet on other grounds. He never fulfilled the moral requirements for a prophet such as humility, honesty and integrity, all of which are characteristic of the biblical prophets (see appendix).

For example, as well as wrongly assuming his own prophethood, Smith had a rather high view of his person. He believed that all of Christendom was in ignorance, but because he had the Holy Ghost he could say, "I am learned, and know more than all the world put together."[6]

He even had his secret "Council of Fifty" ordain him "as King on earth"[7] and run him for the office of President of the United States in the 1844 election.*[8]

Smith also boasted that he comprehended "heaven, earth and hell," and that God was his "right-hand man." He further claimed, "I have more to boast of than ever any man had. I am the only man that has ever been able to keep a whole church together since the days of Adam. ...

---

* Some scholars have theorized that Smith had in mind to rule the United States as its King, and to place the government under the rule of the Mormon priesthood.[9] Early Mormons apparently believed they would rule the earth. For example, " 'Mormonism' will rule every nation. ... God has decreed it"; "the Nations will bow to this (Mormon) kingdom."[10] According to Thomas Marsh, president of the Council of Twelve Apostles, Smith said the plan was to take the nation first, and then "the whole world."[11]

Neither Paul, John, Peter nor Jesus ever did it. I boast that no man ever did such a work as I."[12]

Unfortunately, Smith's supernatural revelations didn't exactly encourage humility. Rather, as is common to spiritistic inspiration, they deliberately nourished a pridefulness and egotism within him. For example, *Doctrine and Covenants*, 135:3 declared that "Joseph Smith the Prophet and Seer of the Lord, has done more, save Jesus only, for the salvation of man in this world than any other man that ever lived in it." Likewise, in section 124:58, Smith is promised by "God," "In thee and in thy seed shall the kindred of the earth be blessed," a promise in Scripture given exclusively to Abraham to be fulfilled by the coming Messiah, Jesus Christ Himself (Genesis 12:3; Galatians 3:19).

In keeping with the above assertions, perhaps not surprisingly, Mormons have praised Joseph Smith almost as if he were another Christ. Brigham Young, the second president and prophet of the Mormon church declared:

> He who confesseth not that Jesus has come in the flesh and sent Joseph Smith with the fullness of the gospel to this generation, is not of God, but is Antichrist. All who confess that Joseph Smith is sent of God in the latter days . . . are born of God. All those who believe in their hearts and confess with their mouths that Joseph Smith is a true Prophet, at the same time trying with their might to live the holy principals the Prophet has revealed, are in possession of the Holy Spirit of God.[13]

Joseph F. Smith, the sixth president and prophet of the Mormon church, predicted:

> The day will come, and it is not far distant either, when the name of the Prophet Joseph Smith will be coupled with the name of Jesus Christ of Nazareth, the Son of God. . . . JOSEPH SMITH'S NAME WILL NEVER PERISH. . . . The name of Joseph Smith . . . will by and by be increased that his name shall be held in reverence and honor among the children of men as universally as the name of the Son of God is held today.[14]

Likewise, the tenth president and prophet of the Mormon church, Joseph Fielding Smith, said bluntly that there was "no salvation without accepting Joseph Smith," and that a man "cannot enter the kingdom of God" if he rejects the truth of Joseph Smith's prophethood.[15]

Along similar lines, Brigham Young even stated that Joseph Smith's *permission* was required to enter the "celestial kingdom" (Mormonism's highest heaven), and that even today he reigns in the spirit world as supremely as God Himself does in heaven:

No man or woman in this dispensation will ever enter the celestial kingdom of God without the *consent of Joseph Smith* ... Every man and woman must have the certificate of Joseph Smith, Junior, as a passport to their entrance into the mansion where God and Christ are ... I cannot go there without his consent. He holds the keys of that kingdom for the last dispensation—the keys to rule in the spirit world; and he rules there triumphantly, for he gained full power and a glorious victory over the power of Satan while he was yet in the flesh ... He reigns there as supreme a being in his sphere, capacity, and calling, as God does in heaven.[16]

In fact, when Brigham Young died, his last words to be heard were, "Joseph, Joseph,"—a rather telling contrast to the dying Stephen's calling upon the name of Jesus at his martyrdom (Acts 7:59).[17]

Although the Mormon church believes in the second coming of Christ, the early church also believed in the second coming of Joseph Smith:

I will now tell you something that ought to comfort every man and woman on the face of the earth. Joseph Smith, Junior, will again be on this earth dictating plans and calling forth his brethren to be baptized.[18]

And,

When Joseph comes again, will brother Brigham be removed? No, never.[19]

And Smith is compared in terms of his moral character to the biblical prophets and even to Christ Himself:

Well, now, examine the character of the Savior, and examine the characters of those who have written the Old and New Testaments; and then compare them with the character of Joseph Smith ... and you will find that his character stands as fair as that of any man mentioned in the Bible. We can find no person who presents a better character to the world.[20]

Mormonism, then, holds Joseph Smith in very high regard. But is such unswerving trust justified by the life and deeds of the real Joseph Smith? No. Unfortunately, an entirely fictionalized image of Smith has been invented and maintained by the Mormon leadership. This is characteristic of many historically recent religions, which have whitewashed their founders' lives and characters. For example, this was true of Mary Baker Eddy, founder of Christian Science, and it is also true of Joseph Smith.

Literally and figuratively the real Joseph Smith was buried long ago. Regrettably, Mormons today have little, if any, comprehension of the true character of their prophet (see appendix). In his place, the church has carefully crafted and resurrected a sterling version—principally to support its evangelistic efforts and its claims to divine authority.

Because of this sterilized image, Mormons genuinely believe that Smith's nature and character were on a par with the biblical prophets and even Christ Himself. But again, this is not the portrait painted by Joseph Smith's own words and actions. Even he said of himself, "I am not so much of a 'Christian' as many suppose I am"[21]—and such an assessment was generous.[22] Jerald and Sandra Tanner, who are among the most knowledgeable people on Joseph Smith and Mormonism in the world today, conclude:

> Today the Joseph Smith of Mormon adoration is a highly romanticized version of the real Joseph Smith. While possessing natural abilities and talents, his personal character was far from the saintly image his followers mold him into. His strong egotism and drive for power, together with his deceptive practices led ultimately to his destruction.[23]

Was Joseph Smith a true prophet of God? Is his saintly image justified? The facts of history and Smith's own life prove the answer to be no.

However, Mormons should not take our word for it. They should vigorously and impartially research the issue in a manner commensurate with its importance. (See appendix.)

## ◆ ◆ *Appendix* ◆ ◆

*Who Was the Real Joseph Smith?*

Mormons have claimed that the character of Joseph Smith was like that of Jesus Christ. However, the chart below shows the contrast between them:

| Joseph Smith | Jesus Christ |
| --- | --- |
| Occult necromancer (chap. 18) | God incarnate |
| Polytheistic (chap. 10) | Monotheistic |
| Polygamous (chap. 19) | Monogamous (celibate) |
| False prophet (chap. 25) | True prophet |
| Opposed government and laws (passim) | Obeyed government and laws |
| Egotistical, immoral, evil (passim) | Humble, moral, righteous |

Even a *partial* listing of subheadings under "Joseph Smith" in the index to the Tanners' *Changing World of Mormonism* gives one an indication of his character. For full details the reader should see the Tanners' documentation and other sources:

> Adds to Genesis over 800 words containing his own name, 391-92 adds to Genesis words discrediting blacks, 392 advises Robert Thompson to get drunk, 474 alters revelations, 39, 55, 65-66 approves concubinage, 281 argues with wife over polygamy, 218, 230 asks for other men's wives, 236... beats up a number of men, 451-52 becomes a Mason and incorporates Masonic ritual into temple ceremony, 534-47... breaks laws of land by living in polygamy, 219-20 changes his concept of Godhead, 162-63... claims to be a god to his people, 432... departs from *Book of Mormon's* teachings, 147... disobeys *Word of Wisdom* by drinking wine and beer and using tobacco, 470-72... encourages breaking *Word of Wisdom*, 33 encourages cursing of enemies, 484-85... engages in money-digging and "glass looking," 67-70... fails to fulfill commandment to publish "Inspired Revision,"... found guilty by Justice Neely in 1826, 67-73... gives revelation endorsing divining rod, 86... indicted for polygamy, 220 ignores own "inspired" renderings, 388 jailed at Carthage and attacked by mob, 464-65... marries five pairs of sisters as well as a mother and daughter, 245 married to at least twelve women when 1843 revelation received, 219... mistakenly claims revival in Palmyra in 1820, 167-71... orders *Nauvoo Expositor* destroyed because it exposes polygamy and political schemes, 460-63... possesses magic talisman, 89-90... publicly denies plural marriage, 258-60... racist tendencies of, 303 revised and rerevised his own "inspired" renderings, 396-97... teaches Blood Atonement, 490 ... tells Heber C. Kimball he would lose apostleship and be damned unless he entered polygamy, 258... violates rules of revelation by taking wives without Emma's consent, 222-23....[24]

To conclude, is it credible to believe that Joseph Smith was God's prophet? Was his life Christ-like? Despite the attempt of devout Mormons to believe in both Jesus Christ and Joseph Smith, this is logically impossible. Belief in one cancels belief in the other. Even Jesus said no man can serve two masters (Matthew 6:24).

◆

# CHAPTER 5

# Does the Mormon Church Accept New, Supernatural Revelations?

## How Do These Revelations Relate to Scripture and Personal Guidance? What Logical Problem Does the Acceptance of New Revelation Present for Mormon Belief?

Another key theme of Mormon teaching is the necessity for new supernatural revelation from God. The thirteen *Articles of Faith* represent a condensed version of Mormonism's current doctrinal beliefs, and Article nine declares: "We believe all that God has revealed, all that He does now reveal, and we believe that He will yet reveal many great and important things pertaining to the kingdom of God."[25]

As a result of its acceptance of new revelation, the Mormon church has added to the biblical canon three additional volumes of scripture: the *Book of Mormon*, *Doctrine and Covenants* and *The Pearl of Great Price*. Moreover, Mormonism believes that divine revelation is necessary on two levels:

1. For the church canon (as a source of new scripture); and

2. For individual Mormon leaders and laity (as personal inspiration for daily guidance).

We discuss these in turn:

### 1. *New scripture*

As far as the canon is concerned, it remains perpetually open: "The canon of Scripture is still open; many lines, many precepts are yet to be added; revelation, surpassing in importance and glorious fullness any that has been recorded, is yet to be given to the Church and declared to the world."[26]

Thus, the *Book of Mormon* teaches that the Bible does not contain the entire Word of God (2 Nephi 29:7-10) and that the person who denies additional revelation is ignorant of Christ's true gospel and lacks a proper understanding of the Scriptures (Mormon, 9:7-9; see chap. 27). But this is not what the Bible teaches. For example, when the New Testament emphasizes that the faith, or doctrine, of the church was "*once for all* delivered unto all the saints," it forcefully rejects the concept of new or post-apostolic revelation (Jude 3).

Nevertheless, the first president and prophet of the church, Joseph Smith himself, taught that any who reject the new Mormon revelations "cannot escape the damnation of hell."[27] Ezra Benson, the current president and prophet, agrees when he says, "Joseph Smith received many revelations from Jesus Christ, as have the [Mormon presidents and] prophets who have succeeded him, which means that new scripture has been given."[28]

Thus, Mormonism teaches that to reject the concept of continuous revelation, as Protestantism does, is a "heresy and blasphemous denial" of God Himself.[29]

### 2. *Individual revelation*

On the individual level, the Mormon church teaches the necessity of personal revelation from God. That is, in addition to revealed scripture, one must also accept direct supernatural guidance from God on a daily basis. These revelations may involve such things as an audible voice from God (*D&C*, 93:1; 67:10-14), supernatural dreams, the use of "angelic" messengers, communications from the dead, or other means.[30] Without this supernatural guidance, one cannot discern truth from error or what is from God from what is from Satan. As a result, the church actively promotes the concept.[31]

Thus, the late Mormon theologian Bruce McConkie teaches in his authoritative *Mormon Doctrine* that every good Mormon receives supernatural revelation and that it is the duty of Mormons to "gain personal revelation and guidance" for their personal affairs.[32]

Further, church leaders also claim that direct revelation from God is daily guiding the church: "The Spirit is giving direct and daily revelation to the presiding Brethren in the administration of the affairs of the Church (*D&C*, 102:2,9,23; 107:39; 128:11)."[33]

Unfortunately, the concept of continuous revelation places the church on the horns of a dilemma. Its doctrine requires the acceptance of new revelation, yet it has no authoritative basis to guard against false information. Why? Because there is no objective, unchanging standard by which to test its truth or falsehood. As we will prove later, Mormon scripture contradicts itself, as do the church's "divinely inspired" presidents and prophets (chap. 24). Church doctrine has thus placed both laity and leadership in a precarious position: How does one determine truth? In Mormonism there is no trustworthy objective standard to prove any revelation has divine authority.

What logical problem does this concept of new revelation present for Mormons? First, how can any Mormon objectively determine the real source of the inspiration, whether it is 1) divine, 2) demonic, or 3) personal delusion? Second, whether a person is merely deluded or actually supernaturally inspired, the "revelation" has been pre-defined as truth before it is even received. Third, once an openness to supernatural revelation is required, it cannot be expected that the faithful will deny any supernatural information they receive, especially if the test of its truthfulness is entirely subjective.[34]

All this is crucial for understanding how easily Mormonism was (and is) led into unbiblical teachings.

Let us illustrate the seriousness of the problem by discussing the claims of both an early and modern Mormon prophet—Brigham Young and Ezra Taft Benson. We begin with Brigham Young, who was the second president and prophet of the church. Even though his sermons emphatically contradicted biblical teaching, he claimed that all his sermons were divinely inspired scripture. Young himself illustrates the crux of the problem:

> In my doctrinal teachings I have taught many things not written in any book. . . . I have never looked into the Bible, the *Book of Mormon*, or the *Doctrine and Covenants*, or any of our Church works to see whether they agreed with them or not. When I have spoken by the power of God and the Holy Ghost, it is the truth, *it is scripture*, and I have no fears but that it will agree with all that has been revealed in every particular.[35]

Unfortunately, it did not always agree. Young had merely accepted supernatural inspiration, assuming it to be divine, and concluding that it would therefore agree with other scripture. But on what logical basis can anyone think that the mere *claim* of "divine revelation" proves that it originates in God? Could it not also originate from the deceptions of a prideful heart, or even from Satan himself—particularly if it profanes God and denies and opposes what God has already said is true in His Word?

No wonder Young received revelation that was unbiblical. He naively assumed that whatever he received was "of God," never bothering to check Scripture as the standard. But time and again the Bible warns against this approach. It should not be surprising, then, that those who violated the principle outlined in Acts 17:11,12 ("examining the Scriptures daily, to see whether these things were so") might become easy targets for spiritual deception, particularly in a church where spiritistic inspiration had already been accepted for two decades (see chap. 18).

Nevertheless, Young believed he spoke under divine inspiration and that, therefore, his transcribed lectures were literally scripture: "I say now, when they are copied and approved by me they are as good Scripture as is couched in this Bible"[36] and, "I have never yet preached a sermon and sent it out to the children of men, that they may not call it Scripture. Let me have the privilege of correcting a sermon, and it is as good Scripture as they deserve. The people have the oracles of God continually."[37]

In spite of some Mormons' claims to the contrary, Young's sermons were recorded accurately, so, according to him, they are to be regarded as God's Word.[38] Additional evidence that his sermons *were* regarded as scripture is provided by Mormon apostle Orson Pratt.[39]

Consider the extent of Young's own assertions for his divine inspiration and guidance. He claimed that whatever was accomplished by him was neither by his wisdom nor ability, "But it was all by the power of God, and by intelligence received from Him."[40] In the same vein he says, "I have had many revelations; I have seen and heard for myself, and know these things are true. . . . What I know concerning God, concerning the earth, concerning government, I have received from the heavens, not through my natural ability."[41]

At this point, Mormonism has a problem in determining what constitutes a spiritual authority. Since Young claimed to have divine inspiration, the modern church cannot logically *reject* his teachings and simultaneously *maintain* his prophethood. But they *do* reject his teachings, for example the "Adam-God" doctrine and the reprehensible teaching of blood atonement, as we will later show (see chaps. 11 and 28).

The church's doctrine of supernatural guidance has thus proven to be its Achilles' heel. It has always maintained that its presidents and prophets were spiritual authorities because they were divinely inspired— then turned around and denied their teachings whenever convenient. But if the church leadership does not respect its own prophets, why should any other Mormon? How do Mormon leaders respond?

Mormon authorities claim that Mormon doctrines are official only if they are found in the standard works of the church—the Bible, the *Book of Mormon, Doctrine and Covenants* and *The Pearl of Great Price*—or if they are sustained by the Mormon church in general conference. They can thus claim that the writings of the Mormon presidents and prophets are *not* scripture or not *necessarily* scripture. A prophet is only a prophet when acting as such they say.

But this approach does not solve the problem. Mormons cannot claim that their prophets' words are and are not scripture at the same time merely for convenience. They cannot deny a prophet a prophet's authority when *as a prophet* he teaches that his words are scripture.

So, was Brigham Young correct or incorrect when he claimed that his sermons were scripture? If correct, the modern church has rejected the Word of God. If incorrect, then how can anything Young taught be trusted? But doesn't the same reasoning hold true for *all* Mormon presidents and prophets?

Let's bring our discussion into the present. Consider the seven-hundred-dred-page volume *The Teachings of Ezra Taft Benson*. Remember, Benson is the current president and prophet of the Mormon church. The following statement claims that *the words in this book are scripture*:

> President Ezra Taft Benson is the 13th President of The Church of Jesus Christ of Latter-day Saints. As the Prophet, Seer, and Revelator, his inspired words are considered by members of the Church *to be the word of God*. President Benson has been uniquely prepared by the Lord to serve *as His mouthpiece* to the whole world. . . . The excerpts that make up this teaching volume have come from his speeches or public writings after he was called to the apostleship and sustained as a Prophet, Seer, and Revelator.
>
> President Benson personally reviewed the entire manuscript, as did his counselors in the First Presidency.[42]

Mormon leaders further emphasize that each of their presidents and prophets have given "living Scripture." Each one speaks with "the authority of God. . . . God is speaking directly through him. . . . The prophet [is] the man on the earth who is the mouthpiece for God."[43]

Obviously, if the revelations of Benson and other recent presidents and prophets *are* scripture, then logically they cannot possibly contradict the scriptural revelations of the early Mormon presidents and prophets—Joseph Smith, Brigham Young, etc. But because they do contradict them, the Mormon church continues to be faced with a serious predicament.

It can accept these damaging contradictions and their implications. This would either prove that a) Smith and Young, etc., were false prophets or b) that the presidents and prophets of the modern church are false prophets.

Or, it can simply ignore its earlier prophets and concentrate on modern "revelation." It is by this second approach that modern Mormon leaders think they have resolved the problem of contradictory theology.

But have they? If the modern Mormon church claims that it can identify which portions of its presidents' and prophets' lectures and writings are scripture, then it should do so. If it cannot, then it should not hold out this material as the Word of God to Mormon believers. If we examine Mormon revelation historically, we discover that God has changed His mind so frequently that a uniform theology cannot be built.

For in so many places one revelation here denies another there, it becomes impossible to believe that God had anything to do with the process.

This is why in 1980, the current president and prophet, Ezra Taft Benson, went so far as to declare that the president of the church is the only man who can speak for God on everything and that God's new revelation actually *replaces* the old. Consider the comments of former thirty-five year Mormon Arthur Budvarson, who quotes Benson verbatim and reports on the current president's view of his own importance:

> Ezra Taft Benson . . . has "outlined the way to follow the (Mormon President and) Prophet." He offered fourteen fundamentals, making it perfectly clear that the President of the Mormon Church is God's prophet, and that his word is law on all issues, including politics. Mr. Benson stated in no uncertain terms that the Mormon prophet is the only man who speaks for the Lord in everything! "We are to give heed unto *all his words* as if from the Lord's own mouth." He also stated that as a prophet, the Mormon President can receive revelations on all issues. However, the President does *not* have to preface his revelations with "thus sayeth the Lord" to give scripture.[44]

Note that the current prophet of the Mormon church has stated that the Mormon prophet and president does *not* have to say "thus sayeth the Lord" in order to give scripture. So, should we believe Mormon apologists when they claim that past prophets and presidents are giving scripture only when they begin with "thus sayeth the Lord?"

Budvarson then discusses Benson's approach to dealing with the thorny issue of conflicting teachings among past and present Mormon revelation. Note that the words of the president are held to have authority over the Bible as well since it too is past revelation:

> Then too, Benson made it clear that "the living prophet is more important to the Mormon system than any dead prophet." He warned of "those who would pit the dead prophets against the living prophets, for the living prophets always take precedence." He also stated that the words of the prophet are more "vital than the Standard works" (the Bible, the *Book of Mormon, Doctrine and Covenants* and the *Pearl of Great Price*), "for those books do not convey the word of God direct to us now, as do the words of a prophet or a man bearing the holy priesthood in our day and generation."
>
> This means that what the Mormon President says is to be regarded as "law" to the Mormon people, and even if he contradicts the Bible, the Mormon Standard works, or any past

prophet of Mormonism, he is to be obeyed, since "nothing a Mormon President says can be incorrect."[45]

This is true at least until a Mormon president becomes "out of date." Then his words—words that were once God's words and binding "law"—are no longer relevant because a current Mormon president and prophet has rejected them. Anyone who wishes can read this lecture of President Benson and decide for themselves its implications. (See Resource List.)

In conclusion, the very basis for determining false revelation—inconsistency with an immutable standard of revealed doctrine—is rejected in Mormonism. Even the late doctrinal authority Bruce McConkie taught that what is literally God's Word and important in one generation may be wholly insignificant in another. "For the future, there are to be new revelations that will dwarf into comparative insignificance all the knowledge now revealed from heaven."[46]

The problem such teaching raises is this. How does a Mormon *know* that the latest revelation wasn't just invented by the president and prophet for the sake of expediency? (See chaps. 24, 29 and 30.) Or how does a Mormon know that it isn't a product of self-deception, or even a result of demonic inspiration? By what authoritative standard can *any* Mormon doctrine or teaching be objectively evaluated? If there is no standard, on what logical basis can anything a Mormon president and prophet says be trusted?

Any religion that permits its leaders the authority of God with no checks or balances is asking for problems. The nature of Mormon revelation since 1830 proves the point. Remember, we are not speaking here of progressive revelation—where God reveals new information that does not contradict old revelation. The New Testament is new revelation, but it never contradicts the Old Testament. Rather, it fulfills it. Jesus Himself said He came not to abolish the law and prophets, but to fulfill them (Matthew 5:17). What the Mormon church is claiming is not revelation that is *progressive*, but revelation that is *open* and ultimately *relative*. Because it is relative, it has no authority.

━━━━━━━━━━━━━ ◆ ┝━━━━━━━━━━━━━

# CHAPTER 6

# Does the Mormon Church Claim to Be the One True Church on Earth?

*Was There a Great Apostasy of Orthodox Christianity? Are Mormons the Best People on Earth?*

God directed Joseph Smith to reestablish the true Church of Jesus Christ.... The Lord has proclaimed that it is "the only true and living Church upon the face of the whole earth" (*D&C*, 1:30).

—*The Restoration, Study Guide 3*, 3-4

A third central tenet of Mormon belief is the claim that only they constitute the one true church of God on earth. *Doctrine and Covenants* declares that Mormonism is "the only true and living Church upon the face of the whole earth."[47]

Mormon apostle Orson Pratt, one of the early church authorities, taught in 1854 that "all other churches are entirely destitute of all authority from God."[48] And this is the teaching of modern Mormonism as well. Theologian Bruce McConkie claimed that "Mormons...have the only pure and perfect Christianity now on earth."[49] Elsewhere he declared,

"All other systems of religion are false."[50] And in a discussion of John 1:4-6 he avows: "We Latter-day Saints are of God; we alone have the truth; we alone have the gospel; we alone can save men in the celestial kingdom. Unless men hear us and receive our message they shall be damned. What we have is true; what the world has is error; all things are judged by the gospel standard which we have."[51]

Even the Mormon Sunday School text, *The Master's Church Course A*, informs children, "We cannot accept that any other Church can lead its members to salvation in the kingdom of heaven."[52]

Mormons claim they alone are the true church because they trust in the "first vision" account of Joseph Smith, where God allegedly told Smith that all of Christianity was false and apostate.

Mormons believe that soon after the time of Christ there was a total apostasy or abandonment of the original Gospel. *Gospel Principles*, a book published by the Mormon church, gives this account: "More and more error crept into Church doctrine, and soon the destruction of the Church was complete. The period of time when the true church [of Jesus Christ] no longer existed on earth is called the *Great Apostasy*."[53]

Thus Mormons are taught that orthodox Christian teaching was not restored until 1830 when God and Jesus appeared to Joseph Smith promising to reinstate the true church. The fact that Mormons claim they are the "restored church" tells us that they believe they are the only church. On this belief rests every assertion of Mormon religion.

If there has been a universal apostasy, then the Mormon church *might* be correct in asserting that God has restored true Christianity through it, rather than through some other denomination. But if the Christian church has never apostatized, there would be no need for God to restore orthodox teaching, and so the claims of Mormonism would be proven false.

Let us further document Mormon claims about this "great apostasy" and then show why they are wrong. Calling it "a complete apostasy from the truth," current Mormon president and prophet Ezra Taft Benson explains that "by the second and third centuries, widespread changes had been made in the pure doctrines and ordinances given by the Savior. The Church that Jesus had established and sanctioned was no longer on this earth."[54] Joseph Smith himself taught that "there was a complete and universal apostasy . . . the Church of Christ then established was destroyed."[55] And furthermore,

> When the Apostles were all fallen asleep, then corruptions ran riot in the Church, doctrines of men were taught for the commandments of God! . . . [The] Church which while it clung to forms of godliness, ran riot in excesses and abominations . . . and thus they lay for ages. . . . The Gospel was taken from the earth, divine authority lost, the Church of Christ destroyed.[56]

Apostle Orson Pratt paints the same picture in the January 1854 issue of a Mormon publication, *The Seer*:

Q. After the Church of Christ fled from earth to heaven, what was left?

A. A set of wicked Apostates, murderers, and idolaters, who, after having made war with the saints [apostles], and overcame them, and destroyed them out of the earth, were left to follow the wicked imaginations of their own corrupt hearts, and to build up [false] churches.[57]

Joseph Fielding Smith, the tenth president and prophet of the church, and one who is acclaimed as being "universally esteemed as the chief doctrinal authority of the [Mormon] Church,"[58] also describes the extent of the alleged apostasy:

For hundreds of years the world was wrapped in a veil of spiritual darkness, until there was not one fundamental truth belonging to the plan of salvation that was not, in the year 1820 [the year of Joseph's vision], so obscured by false tradition and ceremonies, borrowed from paganism, as to make it unrecognizable, or else it was entirely denied.[59]

Likewise, Bruce McConkie, another leading doctrinal theologian, concludes that "every basic doctrine of the gospel... has been changed and perverted by an apostate Christendom."[60]

Thus, no one can deny that the Mormon church teaches that for approximately seventeen-hundred years, from A.D. 100 to A.D. 1830, there was literally *no church on the earth*. The apostasy was absolute and universal. Not until Joseph Smith received his new revelations did true apostolic Christianity appear once again. This is why Mormonism teaches, "The Church of Christ was restored to the earth in 1830,"[61] the publication date of the *Book of Mormon*.

According to the tenth president and prophet, Joseph Fielding Smith,

By heavenly direction and command of our Lord Jesus Christ, Joseph Smith restored all these [gospel] principles in their primitive beauty and power.... True Christianity, so far as the Latter-days are concerned, is very young, for it has only been since 1830 that the Church of Jesus Christ has been organized in the earth, and the gospel restored.[62]

These claims are astounding, and it is difficult to believe that Mormonism makes these claims in the face of what the Lord Jesus Christ has told us Himself: that even "the gates of Hades shall not overpower" His church (Matthew 16:18). However, Mormon apostle Orson Pratt and modern Mormons do teach that "the gates of hell have prevailed and will continue to prevail [over the church]."[63] Thus, in making these assertions, Mormonism not only disregards what the Bible itself teaches, but also disregards the facts of Christian history in order to sustain its claims that Joseph Smith was a true prophet who "restored" the church to the earth.

Both biblically and historically it can be proven to anyone's satisfaction that a universal apostasy never occurred. Apostolic doctrine is easily determined, because historical facts prove that the teachings of the New Testament are the teachings of Jesus and the apostles. Any good systematic theology will give us the basic teachings of the New Testament.

Further, church history and historical theology prove that from the first century onward these same doctrines have continued to be upheld in the church. One may go through century after century from the first to the twentieth and prove that the apostasy claimed by Mormonism is a myth. No one denies there were periods of darkness but the true apostolic faith was never lost in any generation.

We are told in the Bible that God has received glory "throughout all ages" (Ephesians 3:21 NIV), that God's "kingdom cannot be shaken" (Hebrews 12:28 NIV), and that God always retains a remnant of believers for Himself (Romans 9:29; 11:4,5). Obviously, if the Mormon teaching is right—that Christianity was completely destroyed soon after the apostolic period—then God has not received glory in all ages, His kingdom has been shaken, and He has not retained a remnant for Himself in every generation. In other words, the gates of hell have prevailed against His church.

Why does the Mormon church continue to proclaim a universal apostasy in spite of massive evidence, biblically and historically, to the contrary? Simply because it has no choice. If there was no universal apostasy, then Joseph Smith's claim that God *restored* true Christianity through him must have been false, and if false, Joseph Smith could not have been a true prophet of God.*

Although Mormonism typically assigns Christianity to the status of apostate "sectarianism," the shoe is actually on the other foot. We must conclude with Dr. Anthony Hoekema, an authority on Mormonism, that "by relegating all of present-day and most of past Christendom to the status of apostasy, Mormonism reveals its utterly anti-Scriptural sectarianism."[64]

Given the Mormon church's belief that it is the "restored" and only true church, are Mormons the best people on earth? Unfortunately, Mormon exclusivism has tended toward a prideful self-glorification. For

---

*Further, even if the Christian Church did apostatize, if its teachings *today* are established to be biblical (those of Jesus and the apostles), Mormon claims would still be false—because its official teachings deny those of Jesus and the apostles.

example, Heber Kimball, a member of the First Presidency, said in 1857 that in spite of the church's sins, "It is true that we are the best people there are on the earth."[65] And even though Brigham Young admitted, "We have the meanest devils on the earth in our midst, and we intend to keep them" he also said, "We are the smartest people in the world."[66] John Taylor, the third president and prophet of Mormonism, boasted, "We in fact are the saviours of the world"—because only Mormons know how to both save themselves, and others as well.[67] The tenth president and prophet of the Mormon church, Joseph Fielding Smith, while observing that Mormons are "not arrogant, pretentious or self-righteous," declares, "We are, not withstanding our weaknesses, the best people in the world.... We are morally clean, in every way equal, in many ways superior to any other people."[68]

Indeed, most Americans consider Mormons to be clean, decent, morally pure citizens—and many are. But is the squeaky clean image the church likes to portray really valid?

Unfortunately, social statistics in Utah do not seem to bear out these opinions. Even with the recent large influx of non-Mormons, at least seventy percent of Utah's population of 1.7 million are still Mormon.[69] But Professor Nancy Amidei of the School of Social Work at the University of Utah commented in 1991 that "Utah is not that different from the rest of the country in terms of the social and economic problems it faces."[70] An educational film on Mormonism noted that "Utah, which is seventy-five percent Mormon, leads the nation in bankruptcy and stock fraud" and it also ranks above the national average in divorce, suicide, child abuse, teenage pregnancy, venereal disease and bigamy.[71]

*The Salt Lake Tribune* of April 24, 1989 revealed that Salt Lake City is "one of the nation's crime capitals" according to FBI figures. For example, Salt Lake City leads the entire country in larcenies. According to *The Salt Lake Tribune* of August 13, 1982, "Utah's murder rate for children under fifteen is about five times as high as the national figures." *The Salt Lake Tribune* of February 14, 1989 noted that between 1987 and 1988 homicides in Salt Lake City were up almost thirty-one percent.

On the home front, *The Salt Lake Tribune* for January 9, 1989, disclosed that domestic violence is frequently ignored in Utah, with only one in ten cases being reported. And according to the Division of Family Services, "forty percent of all married couples have some sort of abusive situation" in the home. Furthermore, *The Salt Lake Tribune* of April 3, 1988, revealed that child abuse cases had set a record in Utah County and that the severity of the cases was increasing. In fact, *The Salt Lake Tribune* of January 24, 1990, announced that child abuse and neglect was spiraling upwards with substantiated cases climbing forty-four percent since 1987. Unfortunately, according to *The Salt Lake Tribune* of November 30, 1984, prosecution of child sex offenders "has been made more difficult because of intervention by local leaders of The Church of Jesus Christ of Latter-day Saints, ..."

*The Salt Lake Tribune* of April 10, 1988 indicated that polygamy was also on the rise in Utah and that seventy percent of all American polygamists are found in Utah. The June 28, 1991 Geraldo Show, "The Secret World of Polygamy," underscored the terrible personal and social cost of this frequently cruel lifestyle (see chap. 29). Moreover, because of Utah's past history condoning polygamy, virtually nothing is done by state or federal officials to stop the practice.

Furthermore, *The Salt Lake Tribune*, February 2, 1975, revealed that the "frequency of adultery . . . and the number of illegitimate births . . . have reached an appalling figure" within Utah Mormonism. *The Salt Lake Tribune* of January 26, 1987 announced that Utah's statistics in the areas of divorce rates, prescription drug abuse, teenage drug use and teen suicide are above the national average. According to Mormon expert Sandra Tanner (citing Mormon church figures), the divorce rate within Mormonism is about thirty-five percent.[72] *The Salt Lake Tribune* of October 22, 1985 divulged that the suicide rate for males aged fifteen to nineteen increased thirty-three percent from 1960 to 1970 in Utah. Then from 1970 to 1980 the increase was sixteen percent. *The Salt Lake Tribune* of July 8, 1985 revealed that Utah ranked fourteenth in the nation for teenage suicide.

*The Salt Lake Tribune* of December 25, 1987 revealed that sexually active teenagers in Utah "are as likely to have their first sexual encounter at the same age as teens across the country." Even worse, seventy percent of "teenage first births in Utah are pre-marital conceptions."[73]

Even the previous president and prophet of the Mormon church, Spencer W. Kimball, admitted in his *The Miracle of Forgiveness* that numerous years of ministry as Stake President and Apostle gave him "many experiences in dealing with transgressors, especially those involved in sexual sins, both inside and outside of marriage." He confessed that he encountered "almost daily" people with broken homes and delinquent children and noted the "prevalence and gravity of sexual and other major sins, . . ."[74]

When the *Los Angeles Times* of February 2, 1988 announced that "Utah today is the only state that still lives by the teachings of a Church" and that seventy percent of the state's population is Mormon, it would appear to cast doubt upon the claim of the Mormon church to being morally and ethically unique.

It would seem the picture the Mormon church paints of itself is less accurate than many Mormons suppose. Despite a strong emphasis on family and its sterling image, Mormonism doesn't seem to work that well at home. Why is this? Although the reasons are probably complex, one answer appears to lie in the Mormon emphasis on complete self-perfection—and the guilt, frustration and even self-hatred that can be produced by constant failure to live up to an unrealistic standard.[75] Former members indicate that there is an eighty to ninety percent failure rate among Mormons in achieving their own standards for full salvation.[76] In other words, the vast majority of church members fail to live up to the standards the church sets for them—standards which have become their own personal standards and apart from which they cannot attain true eternal life or godhood. (See chaps. 13, 14 and 16.) As a formerly devoted Mormon writes:

> In Mormonism there is a great burden because you've got to strive all the time. If you work at it hard enough, you can become a God. So there is a burden of guilt that lays there on you all the time. You're not working hard enough. You didn't do all you could.[77]

And,

> Utah has a higher than the national average rate of divorce, it has higher than the national average rate of suicides. Especially teen suicide is much higher in Utah than it is nationally. This is partly due to the fact that Mormons emphasize perfection. And so many of these young people feel defeated in their striving for Godhood, they can't measure up to everything the Church is asking of them and it...so demolishes their self-esteem that they can't go on...they take their life.[78]

In other words, belonging to a religion which teaches one can become a god on the basis of intense self-striving cannot be an untroubled road to walk.

CHAPTER 7

# What Are the Mormon Priesthoods?

## Why Are These Priesthoods Vital to Mormon Claims? Do They Have Biblical Justification?

A fourth major declaration of Mormonism is its assertion regard-ing the priesthood. The Mormon church claims that the priest-hood confers divine ability and authority to act in God's name.

The power conferred by holding the Mormon priesthood is allegedly a tremendous, supernatural power. The current Mormon president and prophet, Ezra Taft Benson, teaches, "The greatest power in this world is power presented in this priesthood. That is the power that brought this earth into existence."[79] The Mormon publication *Gospel Principles* ex-plains priesthood power in the following manner:

> Our Heavenly Father has great power. This power is called the priesthood. By his priesthood power, the heavens and the earth were created. By this power, the universe is kept in perfect order. Our Heavenly Father shares his priesthood power with his children on the earth. . . . We must have priest-hood authority to act in the name of God.[80]

The Mormon priesthood is divided into two parts: the Melchizedek and Aaronic. Mormonism claims that the Aaronic priesthood was di-rectly restored to Joseph Smith through the spirit of the dead John the Baptist; similarly the Melchizedek priesthood was restored to Smith through the spirits of the dead apostles Peter, James and John (cf. *D&C*, 27:8,12).[81] But in essence, there is only one priesthood, the Melchizedek, with the Aaronic priesthood being a lesser office within the Melchizedekian department. McConkie explains the distinction:

> As pertaining to man's existence on this earth, priesthood is the power and authority of God delegated to man on earth to act in all things for the salvation of men. It is the power by which the gospel is preached. . . . As there is only one God and one power of God, it follows that there is only one priesthood, the eternal priesthood is Melchizedek, but there are different portions or degrees of it.[82]

The offices of the Aaronic priesthood include those of deacon, teacher, priest and bishop. For example, a Mormon boy may be ordained as a teacher when he is fourteen years old. A Mormon boy may be ordained a priest, with the privileges of baptizing, administering the sacrament and ordaining other priests, teachers and deacons, when he is sixteen years old.[83]

The offices of the Melchizedek priesthood include those of elder, high priest, patriarch, member of the "Seventy" (special missionaries) and apostle. The Mormon president and prophet is the presiding high priest over the Melchizedek priesthood.

The almost papal nature of the Mormon priesthood is revealed in the following statement: "God reveals His will to His authorized priesthood representative on the earth, the prophet. The prophet, who is president of the Church, serves as the spokesman for God to all the members of the Church and all people on the earth."[84]

Why else does Mormonism think the priesthood is vital? Mormonism claims that through revelations given to Joseph Smith in *Doctrine and Covenants* and elsewhere that God has restored these two priesthoods to their church alone. The concept is crucial to established Mormon authority, because without the priesthood it is allegedly impossible for one to have either God's enablement or approval.

The Melchizedek priesthood was supposedly transferred directly from Jesus Christ to Joseph Smith and then to all presidents/prophets of the church. Smith and all other presidents/prophets thus hold the leadership of the Melchizedek priesthood.

Thus, without the priesthood, one is without spiritual authority and power—and essentially without God. And because it is available only within the Mormon church, all non-Mormons are without it. For example, because Christianity is allegedly without the priesthood, it is also without God: "This people [Mormons] have the true knowledge; they [Christians] have it not. We have the Priesthood; they have it not. We have the way of life and salvation; they have it not. We know how to be Saints—how to save ourselves and all who will harken to our counsel; they do not."[85]

But is the Mormon concept of priesthood biblically valid? No. In fact, it is flawed both biblically and in terms of Mormon history itself. It is also flawed spiritually because, as we shall show in section 4, the true power of the priesthood is occult, not divine.

Mormonism claims that the Melchizedek priesthood was transferred to Joseph Smith from the spirits of the dead, allegedly acting under the direction of Jesus Christ. But whatever the spirits told Smith, it is also true that Mormonism derived part of its Melchizedek priesthood straight from Masonry.[86] Furthermore, the Melchizedek priesthood of Christ was modeled after Melchizedek, a King of Jerusalem (Genesis 14:18-20), who is portrayed as a prefigurement of Christ. It could never have been transferred to Joseph Smith. Why? Because it was reserved by God for Christ alone, and only Christ holds it forever. Biblically, the Melchizedekian priesthood is limited to Christ alone because it is inseparably tied to both His deity and His atonement for sin. In other words, only one who is God and the atoning Savior can hold the Melchizedek priesthood. This is the plain teaching of Scripture. "For it is witnessed of Him [Christ], *Thou art a priest forever, according to the order of Melchizedek. . . . The Lord has sworn and will not change His mind, Thou art a priest forever. . . .* Because He [Jesus] abides forever, holds His priesthood *permanently* [and] because this [death for sin] He did once for all when He offered up Himself [atonement]" (Hebrews 7:17,21,24,27). Only if Christ were somehow removed could the priesthood be transferred, but Scripture itself declares this too is impossible (Hebrews 5:6,10; 6:20; 7:11,12,17-25). Thus, despite their claims, Mormons cannot be considered Melchizedekian priests: the very idea of giving the saving office of Christ to those who reject Him is blasphemous (see chap. 12).

Nor is the Mormon concept of the Aaronic (Levitical) priesthood legitimate. For one to be an Aaronic priest, Aaronic descent had to be proven. Thus, the Aaronic priesthood was only for Jews who were descendants of Aaron of the Tribe of Levi (Hebrews 7:5; Exodus 28:1; 29:9,44; 31:10; Numbers 3:1-10). As a result, the Aaronic priesthood could never be held by Gentile Mormons, for it is impossible for them to be Aaron's literal descendants.

Further, according to the Bible, the Aaronic priesthood *ended* at the cross (Hebrews 8:13; 9:6; 10:9), so how can Mormons claim to be Aaronic priests? Why would God restore what He had already eliminated?

But even if such a priesthood existed, Mormons do not fulfill the Aaronic priesthood's ordination requirements (Leviticus 8:21-23; Exodus 29). In addition, Mormons ignore the following facts concerning this priesthood:

◆ There is no New Testament basis or authority for an Aaronic priesthood, since the very reason for it (to be a mediator between the people and God as to sins) no longer existed after the atonement of Christ, which paid for all sin (Hebrews 10:10-14).

- The Aaronic priesthood was superseded by the eternal Melchizedekian priesthood (singular) of Jesus Christ (Hebrews 7:11,12, 15,26-28). The first Aaronic priesthood of *men* is stated to be faulty (Hebrews 8:6-8), but the second Melchizedekian priesthood of Christ is held to be perfect; thus the first is classified as obsolete (Hebrews 8:13; 10:9). Again, why would God restore a faulty priesthood?

- No one who understands the true reason why the Aaronic or Levitical priesthood was abolished would ever wish it restored— for it would mean our High Priest (Jesus Christ) had failed in His atonement and role as mediator for us (Hebrews 9:15; 10:11,12).

- The biblical priesthood was strictly religious, not political.

- Under Old Testament law, false pretenders to the Aaronic priesthood were to be judged and put to death or killed by God (Numbers 3:10; 16:1-35; 2 Chronicles 26).

Further, the Aaronic priesthood had to be transferred because the priests died, but if the Aaronic priesthood has been replaced by one eternal better priest, Jesus Christ, it could never be transferred because He lives forever. Christ lives eternally to fulfill all the functions of the human priest, which were but types of Christ's greater Melchizedekian priesthood:

> So much the more also Jesus has become the guarantee of a better covenant. And the *former* priests, on the one hand, existed in greater numbers, because they were prevented by death from continuing, but He, on the other hand, because He abides forever, holds His priesthood permanently. Hence, also, He is able to save forever those who draw near to God through Him, since He always lives to make intercession for them (Hebrews 7:22-25).
>
> Therefore, ". . . there is one God, and one mediator also between God and men, the man Christ Jesus" (1 Timothy 2:5).

When Mormons claim they are mediators between God and men because they hold the office of priest, they usurp the prerogative of Jesus Christ. When they further claim they are in a sense saviors of men through baptism for the dead rites (see chap. 19) and that Christ's atonement alone does not forgive sin (see chap. 15), they reveal not only their unChristian nature, but their confusion over the biblical concept of priesthood and its relationship to forgiveness of sin.

Finally, the Mormon concept of priesthood has serious additional problems. As the late Dr. Walter Martin pointed out, "Scores of documents could be appended to illustrate the contradictions about the priesthoods which the Mormons claim to hold."[87]

# ♦ ♦ *Conclusion* ♦ ♦

We have now discussed several key claims of Mormonism: 1) the alleged prophethood and centrality of Joseph Smith, 2) Mormonism's continuing revelation, 3) Mormon exclusivism and 4) the Mormon priesthood. These beliefs represent four vital doctrines of the Mormon church. If any one is false, the authority of the Mormon church is seriously or fatally undermined. But as we have indicated, and will continue to indicate, all four are false and, therefore, Mormonism cannot be considered a true revelation from God.

For example, in the next section we will discuss Mormon theology, and we will continue to prove that these four claims cannot be substantiated. Thus, if Mormon theology itself originated from Joseph Smith—who declared he was 1) a unique prophet who 2) had received new revelations from God that 3) restored the true Church and that 4) gave priesthood authority—then the Mormon church must have *as its doctrine* the same teachings revealed by God through Jesus Christ and the apostles in first-century Christianity. In other words, because Mormonism claims to be a divinely restored Christianity, this means that the true teachings of Jesus and the apostles were originally *Mormon* teachings. Thus, for Mormon claims to stand, the church must prove that New Testament theology *is Mormon theology.*

In essence, the Mormon church must prove that Jesus Christ and His apostles were really Mormons. Mormonism claims this is so: "The [Mormon] Church of Jesus Christ today teaches the same principles and performs the same ordinances as were performed in the days of Jesus."[88]

But Mormonism will never be able to prove that the teachings of Jesus Christ and His apostles were Mormon. It is an historical fact that the New Testament accurately records what Jesus and the apostles taught and did; this is the general consensus of informed biblical scholarship. So one only need compare and contrast Mormon theology with biblical teaching to prove the two are diametrically opposed and therefore that earliest Christianity was not Mormon.

Thus, we now move into a discussion of Mormon theology to prove that Mormonism is not the Christian religion it so confidently maintains it is.

# Mormon Religion and Christianity

## *Are They Compatible?*

Convince us of our errors of doctrine, if we have any, by reason, by logical arguments, or by the Word of God, and we will be ever grateful for the information, and you will ever have the pleasing reflection that you have been the instruments in the hands of God of redeeming your fellow beings from the darkness which you may see enveloping their minds. Come, then, let us reason together, and try to discover the true light upon all subjects, connected with our temporal or eternal happiness.[1]

—Apostle Orson Pratt

◆

... A prophet will never be allowed to lead the Church astray. ... The Lord will never allow the President of the Church to teach us false doctrine.

—Official Mormon Publication,
*Gospel Principles* [2]

The Lord will never permit me or any other man who stands as President of this Church to lead you astray. It is not in the programme. It is not in the mind of God.

—President Wilford Woodruff, October 6,
1890,[3] (from *D&C* 1982, 292)

I n this section, we will examine two key issues: 1) Mormonism's claim to be Christian and 2) Mormonism's true beliefs about Christianity. First, we will show that the claim to be Christian is considered false by almost everyone but Mormons. Second, when Mormons assert they are the "friends" of Christianity, this is often merely a ruse to gain converts. In truth, Mormonism considers Christianity to be an apostate church and a subtle enemy of the truth. We have also included an appendix providing chart comparisons between Mormonism and Christianity (see chap. 8).

In subsequent sections we examine the theological beliefs of Mormonism in some detail. In order to settle the question of whether or not the Mormon religion is Christian, we will examine the following topics: the Mormon view of God and the Trinity (chaps. 10 and 11); the Mormon teaching on Jesus Christ (chap. 12); the Mormon concept of salvation (chaps. 13 and 14); the Mormon view of Christ's atonement (chap. 15); the Mormon teaching on the nature of man, sin and the Fall (chap. 16); and the Mormon beliefs about the afterlife (death, heaven and hell) (chap. 17).

By carefully examining what the Mormon church teaches concerning these doctrines, and comparing them with Christian teaching, we can prove whether or not Mormonism's claim to be Christian is valid. We will begin by evaluating Mormon claims to being Christian.

# CHAPTER 8

◆

# Is Mormonism a Christian Religion?

I t is a hapless sign of the time that tens of millions of people sincerely believe they are Christians and yet are wrong. Unfortunately, they have little idea either of the significance of the term "Christian" or what it means to be one.

The term Christ (Gk *Christos*, from the Hebrew *Mashiach* or "anointed one") originally identified Jesus of Nazareth as the prophesied Jewish Messiah. Thus, to be a follower of Jesus (the) *Christ* was to be a follower of Jesus, the promised Jewish Messiah. It was to accept the truth of Jesus' own claim to be the true Messiah—the incarnate God and Savior of humanity (Isaiah 9:6; 53:1-12; John 4:26; 5:18; 10:30).[4]

In other words, to be a Christian is to be a devout follower of the biblical Jesus Christ. It is to wholeheartedly believe in what He believed—in the Bible as God's inerrant Word and in the doctrines of historic Christianity derived from God's Word. This is why the *Oxford American Dictionary* defines "Christian" as "of the doctrines of Christianity, believing in or based on these." "Christianity" is defined as "the religion based on the belief that Christ was the incarnate Son of God and on his teachings."[5]

This explains why a true Christian is one who has personally received Jesus Christ as his or her Lord and Savior and is one who leads a comprehensive lifestyle based on that fact in concert with biblical teaching. Above all, Christianity involves a committed, loving relationship with the God of the Bible. It is not merely going to church on Sundays, believing in Jesus in an intellectual sense or attempting to live "a Christian life." And, it is certainly not merely claiming to be a Christian while simultaneously rejecting Christian doctrine. Being a true Christian incorporates adherence to accurate doctrine and a godly lifestyle centered around a personal relationship with the living Jesus Christ.

No one can deny that the Mormon church deliberately seeks to be seen as a Christian religion. Indeed, to most people, Mormons appear to be genuine Christians who live their faith. Mormons express bafflement when anyone expresses the idea that they are not Christians. One Mormon Sunday school text asserts: "To members or missionaries of the Church of Jesus Christ of Latter-day Saints, it is an astonishing circumstance to find an individual who asks, with a note of disbelief in his voice, 'Are Mormons Christians?' "[6] James Talmage, one of the church's twelve apostles, states in his authoritative *Articles of Faith*, "The Doctrines taught by Joseph Smith, and by the Church today, are true and scriptural."[7] The current president and prophet of the Mormon church, Ezra Taft Benson, answers a resounding "yes" to the question, "Are Mormons Christians?"[8]

Jack Weyland, a member of the Rapid City, South Dakota Stake Mission Presidency, mentions that several times he has faced the situation where someone has told him or another Mormon that they are not Christian. "And every time it happens I'm astonished. I usually respond by saying, 'but the name of the church is the Church of Jesus Christ of Latter-day Saints. Every prayer we utter is offered in his name. Every ordinance we perform we do in his name. We believe all the Bible says about him, . . .' "[9] Dr. Harold Goodman, a Brigham Young University professor and Latter-day Saints mission president argues, "Anyone that believes in Christ is a Christian. And we believe that we are Christians."[10]

As noted earlier, Darl Andersen is a leader in the Mormon movement to evangelize Christians. He too expresses disbelief that anyone could possibly think that Mormonism is not Christian. He often refers to Mormons as "Mormon Christians" and says that "the very purpose of the *Book of Mormon*, as well as the life of Joseph Smith, is to proclaim Jesus Christ as Lord." But in his book he never once deals with the central issue: the teachings of Mormonism vs. the teachings of the Bible. In fact, he even says, "Doctrinal arguments are [only] the evidence of ill will."[11]

Perhaps the most comprehensive defense of the idea that the Mormon religion is Christian is found in Dr. Steve Robinson's *Are Mormons Christians?* Robinson received a Ph.D. in biblical studies from Duke University and is one of the few Mormons to have been tenured in religion at a non-Mormon school.*

Robinson agrees that the charge that Mormons are not Christians "is often the most commonly heard criticism of the LDS Church and its doctrines."[12] And he allows that "the charge that Mormons are not Christians is a serious charge indeed."[13] However, he argues:

> Most of the time the charge that the Latter-day Saints are not Christians has absolutely nothing to do with LDS belief or non-belief in Jesus Christ, or with LDS acceptance or rejection

---

* While his book will undoubtedly convince many that Mormonism is really a Christian religion, it will be convincing only to those who are unfamiliar with how to spot logical fallacies and are ignorant in Mormon history/doctrine and biblical/historic/systematic theology.

of the New Testament as the word of God. If the term *Christian* is used, as it is in standard English to mean someone who accepts Jesus Christ as the Son of God and the Savior of the world, then the charge that Mormons aren't Christians is false.[14]

But even Robinson, despite his effort, freely concedes that Mormonism 1) rejects traditional Christian orthodoxy;[15] 2) rejects the historic orthodox view of the Trinity;[16] and 3) rejects the specific orthodox Christian teaching concerning God—confessing that Mormonism teaches that God was once a human being and that He has a tangible body.[17] Nevertheless, Robinson proceeds to express utter astonishment that Mormonism cannot be considered Christian!

Thus, wherever one cares to look within the Mormon church, one finds the label "Christian." Unfortunately, this has caused great confusion among non-Christians and even among many Christians. Millions of people today continue to hold the mistaken belief that Mormonism is a true Christian religion. The late Harry Ropp was Director of Missions to Mormons in Roy, Utah, an organization founded to "stem the flow of converts from Christian churches to Mormonism."[18] He observes that, "Over the past several years Mormonism has been trying to gain acceptance as a Christian denomination" and that "in recent days...the Mormons have reached their goal in the minds of many."[19] He further observes that "many Christians today accept Mormons as brothers and sisters in the faith."[20]

We also have talked with numerous Christians who see nothing at all wrong with Mormonism, believing it is simply another Christian denomination. Former Mormons Jerald and Sandra Tanner direct what is perhaps the most significant organization in the country for disseminating valuable historical materials on Mormonism. For thirty years they have diligently sought to help both Mormons and Christians alike to understand what Mormonism really teaches and why it can not be considered Christian. In a personal conversation with Sandra Tanner in 1990, she informed us that, according to her own widespread experience, the greatest problem the Christian church faces concerning Mormonism is that far too many Christians think Mormonism is a Christian religion.

Even the Navy Chief of Chaplains, Rear Admiral Alvin B. Koeneman, has officially designated Mormon Navy chaplains as "Protestant." We have in our files a copy of a letter from the Protestant Chapel Council, Naval Air Station, Alameda, California to the Navy Chief of Chaplains RADM, Alvin B. Koeneman, Office of the Chief of Naval Operations, Department of the Navy, Washington, D.C. officially protesting this designation.

The influential Mason and father of positive thinking, Norman Vincent Peale referred to the former Mormon president, Spencer W. Kimball, as "a godly man," noting it was correct to consider him "a prophet" and as one whose love approached that "of the Savior."[21] Occasionally, influential Mormons have even appeared on national Christian television shows presenting their faith in Mormonism as a true Christian religion.[22]

But no matter what Mormons may say or claim, they are wrong. Mormonism is not true Christianity, and true Mormons cannot, in any sense, be considered Christians. Mormon teachings are explicitly anti-Christian and, with no disrespect intended, the Mormon religion is almost as far from Christianity as one can go. In fact, individual Mormons, both theologically and often practically, can only be classified as "pagan."*

Because there is such widespread uncertainty concerning the religious status of the Mormon church, we will document our claims in detail. The issue is an important one for Mormons because to claim to be something you are not is a deceptive practice.

Mormonism freely invites everyone to test its claims, spiritual and otherwise. Brigham Young himself urged others to "take up the Bible, compare the religion of the Latter-day Saints with it, and see if it will stand the test."[24] A modern booklet published by the Mormon church, "Apostasy and Restoration" says, "We invite all men to test our claims to know the truth for themselves."[25] So let's test these claims.

The Apostle John stated of the gnostic believers, an early heresy in the church, "They went out from us, but they were not really of us; for if they had been of us, they would have remained with us; but they went out, in order that it might be shown that they all are not of us" (1 John 2:19, see v. 26).

Similarly, since its earliest days, the Mormon church has willfully removed itself from the Christian church. Yet, Mormons demand to be called Christian. This situation became so intolerable that in July, 1986 a group of evangelical Christians and former Mormons held a news conference in Salt Lake City, Utah and subsequently presented a petition to the Mormon church asking that it stop calling itself a Christian church. According to the Mormon publication, *Deseret News*, July 15, 1986, the petition was signed by over twenty thousand persons from forty-nine states and thirty-one foreign countries.

Religious scholars and authorities on Mormonism everywhere, both Christian and non-Christian, classify Mormonism as a non-Christian religion. (Even the liberal World Council of Churches refuses to classify Mormonism as a Christian religion.) Sterling M. McMurrin is E.E. Ericksen Distinguished Professor, Professor of History, Professor of Philosophy of Education, and Dean of the Graduate School at the University of

---

*Regrettably, their theology comprises a crude sexual polytheism, and many historical and modern Mormon beliefs and practices are pagan, immoral and/or occultic. This is documented in chapters 10-12,16,18-20,28-29. According to no less an authority than the late Dr. Walter Martin, "It is eternally polygamous and it is thoroughly pagan."[23]

Utah. In his book *The Theological Foundations of the Mormon Religion* he sets as a goal the purpose of "facilitating understanding of Mormonism."[27] Noting that Mormon theology has "a radically unorthodox concept of God," he observes that "in its conception of God as in its doctrine of man, Mormonism is a radical departure from the established theology, both Catholic and Protestant."[28]

Gordon Fraser, the author of four books on Mormonism, states in his book *Is Mormonism Christian?*, "We object to Mormon missionaries posing as Christians, and our objections are based on the differences between what they are taught by their General Authorities and what the Bible teaches."[29]

The late Dr. Walter Martin, an acknowledged authority on comparative religion and biblical theology, observes in his work *The Maze of Mormonism*, "In no uncertain terms, the Bible condemns the teachings of the Mormon Church."[30]

Former Mormons turned Christians, Jerald and Sandra Tanner, who have done perhaps more in-depth research into Mormonism than anyone else, declare unequivocally, "The Mormon Church is certainly not built upon the teachings of the Bible. . . . Mormonism . . . is not even based on the *Book of Mormon*."[31]

In his *The Four Major Cults*, theologian Dr. Anthony Hoekema emphasizes that "we must at this point assert, in the strongest possible terms, that Mormonism does not deserve to be called a Christian religion. It is basically anti-Christian and anti-biblical."[32]

The *Evangelical Dictionary of Theology* observes that the Mormon attempt to be Christian "does little justice to either Mormon theology or the Christian tradition."[33]

Even the *Encyclopedia Britannica* classifies Mormonism as a non-Christian religion: "Mormon doctrine diverges from the orthodoxy of established Christianity, particularly in its polytheism, in affirming that God has evolved from man and that men might evolve into gods, that the Persons of the Trinity are distinct beings, and that men's souls have preexisted. . . . Justification is by faith and obedience to the ordinances of the Church."[34]

*The New Schaff-Herzog Encyclopedia of Religious Knowledge* comments:

> So far as the Bible is concerned, Joseph Smith and his successors have taken such liberties with its meaning, and even with its text, that it cannot be said to have any authority for a Mormon. . . . Its doctrine of God, for example, is widely different from that of the Christian Church. The Mormon conception of deity rather resembles that of Buddhism. From it a system of anthropomorphisms has been developed, which far exceeds that of any Christian sect in any age. . . . The supreme God . . . begot other gods. All have bodies, parts, and passions, . . . A chief occupation of these gods is to produce

souls for the bodies begotten in this and other worlds. The sex idea runs through the whole Mormon conception of the universe.[35]

*The New International Dictionary of the Christian Church* concludes: "An examination of the doctrines taught by the Mormon Church will reveal that they deny most of the cardinal teachings of the Christian faith."[36]

So, are Mormons Christians? Can a person be a Christian who rejects the Trinity and accepts polytheism, who denies that God always existed and instead maintains that God was once a man who evolved into godhood, who denies the Virgin Birth by the Holy Spirit, who affirms that there is a mother God, who rejects the Bible as God's only revelation to mankind, and who teaches that salvation is by law-keeping instead of grace? Can Mormons logically call themselves Christian when they will not submit themselves to the words of Jesus Christ and the New Testament?

On the other hand, one cannot deny that a few encyclopedias and secular works on religion do classify Mormonism as a Christian religion or sect. That such incorrect classifications exist is testimony to the tremendous power of the Mormon church's public relations programs.

The Mormon church apparently does not desire that its true feelings about Christianity be widely known; rather it stresses "similarities" with Christian faith whenever possible. Nevertheless, the Mormon church teaches that Christianity is an evil religion. Because Mormonism today has such an effective program of public relations in both its relationship to the Christian church and society in general, we will document this claim in our next chapter.

## ♦ ♦ *Appendix* ♦ ♦

### Mormonism Vs. Christianity

#### *Chart A: Mormon Definitions of Biblical and Christian Terms*

In order to illustrate that Mormon teachings are not biblical, we have provided a selected list of key biblical/Christian words and the false definitions that the Mormon church gives to them. This redefinition of words underscores the problem that Christians face when discussing religious issues with Mormons. Mormons may use the same words that Christians use, but they use them with different, or even opposite, meanings. Unless Christians pursue the meaning of such words, and unless Mormons are frank in giving them their true Mormon definition, Christians and the public in general will continue to be confused over the religious status of Mormonism.

In any discussion with a Mormon, the following redefinition of biblical/ Christian terms must be kept in mind. Although Mormons themselves may be ignorant of some of the definitions cited below, they represent true Mormon teaching according to standard Mormon theological works.

*Christianity:* sectarianism; a false and damnable apostate religion.

*God:* "Elohim"; one of innumerable self-progressing bodily deities; formerly a man, a finite creature. In early Mormon theology, Adam (of the Garden of Eden) was considered by many Mormons as the true earth deity.

*Jesus Christ:* a self-progressing deity, Jehovah of the Old Testament, and the first spirit child of Elohim and his wife.

*Holy Ghost:* a man with a spiritual body of matter.

*Trinity:* tritheistic; coordinated under general Mormon polytheism; thus the Father, Son, and Holy Ghost are separate deities.

*The Gospel:* Mormon theology.

*Born-again:* water baptism into Mormonism.

*Immortality:* Mormon salvation by grace (limited to the universal resurrection of all men).

*Atonement:* the provision God has supplied for individuals to earn their true salvation by obedience to the laws and ordinances of the Gospel.

*True salvation/eternal life/redemption:* "Exaltation" to godhood in the highest part of the celestial kingdom based upon individual good works and personal merit; exaltation incorporates ruling a new world and sexual procreation in order to produce spirit children who will eventually be embodied and inhabit that world, each then having the opportunity to be exalted.

*The Fall:* a spiritual step upward; a blessing permitting the production of physical bodies for preexistent spirits to inhabit and thus have the possibility of attaining their own exaltation or godhood.

*Death:* generally a step upward; death represents the possibility of a form of salvation (if not exaltation) for those who have never heard of Mormonism.

*Heaven:* three "kingdoms of glory" comprising various spiritual gradations.

*Hell:* generally purgatorial; possibly eternal for a very few (primarily apostate Mormons).

*Virgin birth:* the birth of Christ through a *physical* sex act between God the Father (the Mormon earth god Elohim) and Mary (hence, not a virgin birth).

*Man:* a preexistent eternal spirit with the potential to earn godhood by obedience to Mormon dictates.

*Creation:* the reorganization of eternal matter.

*The Scriptures:* the Book of Mormon; Doctrine and Covenants; The Pearl of Great Price; and the Bible "as far as it is translated correctly."

*The Bible:* an erring and often unreliable inspired record, properly interpreted only by Mormons and only in light of Mormon theology.

## Chart B: Contrasting Mormon and Christian Belief

Because Mormon theology diverges so far from Christian theology, it is easy to compare the beliefs of Mormonism with the beliefs of Christianity. Below we offer the following chart contrasting basic Mormon and Christian teaching.*

| Mormonism | Christianity |
|---|---|
| *Bible* | *Bible* |
| Unreliable | Reliable |
| Incomplete as it is | Complete as it is |
| Adds new revelations to God's Word | Rejects new revelations |
| Unbiblical theological presuppositions utilized in interpretation | Accepted historical, grammatical principles utilized in interpretation |
| *God* | *God* |
| Tritheism/polytheistic | Trinity/monotheistic |
| Physical (evolved man) | Spirit |
| Finite | Infinite |
| Morally questionable | Holy |
| Organizer of eternal matter | Creator of matter from nothing |
| Sexual polygamist | Nonsexual |
| *Jesus* | *Jesus* |
| A god | God |
| Created | Eternal |
| Earned salvation (exaltation to godhood) | As eternal God neither salvation nor exaltation was required |
| Not virgin born | Virgin born |
| Polygamist** | Unmarried (celibate) |
| *Salvation* | *Salvation* |
| By works | By grace |
| Denies biblical atonement | Affirms atonement |
| Possible after death | Impossible after death |
| *Afterlife* | *Afterlife* |
| "Purgatorial"; three celestial kingdoms; almost universalistic | Eternal heaven or hell; no purgatory; not universalistic |

For anyone to maintain that Mormonism and Christianity teach the same thing is logically, historically, and doctrinally an indefensible position.

---

* Taken from *Cult Watch*, Part 1, Question 3, p. 16.
** According to some early Mormon authorities.

CHAPTER 9

‌

# What Is the
# Mormon View of
# Christianity?

God the Father and Jesus Christ . . . told Joseph [Smith] not to
join any of the churches because the churches were teaching
incorrect doctrines. . . . We must come to Christ by belonging
to his Church. . . . By being baptized and joining the true
Church of Christ [the Church of Jesus Christ of Latter-day
Saints], we show that we accept Christ.

—*The Restoration, Discussion 3, 8, 12*

In this chapter we will document the true view of Christianity
held by the Mormon church, not the neighborly image they
currently seek to uphold. Once we understand the true teachings of
Mormonism, we can see that the friendship with Christianity is only
pretended for the sake of appearance and/or evangelism. We will begin
with authoritative historical teaching and then proceed to modern views.
Once again, it must be stressed that the first vision experience of Joseph
Smith permanently set the stage for all subsequent beliefs relating to
Christianity. The following illustrations are categorized by subject for
reader convenience.

### Christians Are Unbelievers

Brigham Young dogmatically insisted that "Christians profess to
believe in Jesus Christ; but, if be told the truth, not one of them really
believes in him."[36]

Leading church historian Brigham Henry Roberts' (1857-1933) introduction to Joseph Smith's *History of the Church* declares that those who profess belief in the great creeds of Christianity (the Nicean, Athanasian, etc.) "are wandering in the darkness of the mysticisms of the old pagan philosophies."[37] He further claims that these creeds "exhibit the wide departure—the absolute apostasy—that has taken place in respect of this most fundamental of all doctrines of religion—the doctrine of God. Truly, 'Christians' have denied the Lord that bought them, and turned literally to fables."[38]

### Christians Are Satanic False Teachers

Joseph Smith, who still remains the most influential man in Mormonism, agreed that Christian pastors, "Are of their father the devil. . . . We shall see all the priests who adhere to the sectarian [i.e., Christian] religions of the day, with all their followers, without one exception, receive their portion with the devil and his angels."[39] In 1 Nephi, chapters 13,14 and elsewhere, the *Book of Mormon* itself calls the Christian church "a church which is most abominable above all other churches," "the great and abominable church" founded by the devil, "the mother of abominations" and the great "whore of Babylon."[40]

In an official compilation of Joseph Smith's writings, *Teachings of the Prophet Joseph Smith*, we find the following assessments of Christianity by the founder of Mormonism:

> What is it that inspires professors of Christianity generally with the hope of salvation? It is that smooth, sophisticated influence of the devil, by which he deceives the whole world.[41]

> Respecting the Melchizedek Priesthood, the sectarians [Christians] never professed to have it; consequently they never could save anyone, and would all be damned together.[42]

> I have the truth of God, and show that 99 out of every 100 professing religious ministers are false teachers, having no authority.[43] (Cf. note 44.)

In the *Journal of Discourses*,* an official twenty-seven-volume set of authoritative speeches by early church presidents and prophets, and other leaders, we find sentiments like the following:

---

* Mormon authorities may deny that *Journal of Discourses* is authoritative and even encourage Mormons to avoid it (e.g., *A Sure Foundation*, pp. 199-201). This is only because it contains such embarrassing material, proving the modern church is often apostate in its teachings. Nevertheless, Mormons sometimes do quote from it, as an authority, when it suits their purposes.[45] Further, the *Deseret News 1989-1990 Church Almanac* officially lists it under the title "Church Publication" (p. 188). When Mormons claim this material is not authoritative, not relevant for today, or not an official church publication they are either misinformed or lying.

## Christians Are Fools and Ignorant
## Concerning the Things of God

The second president and prophet of the Mormon church, Brigham Young, declared:

> With regard to true theology, a more ignorant people never lived than the present so-called Christian world.[46]

> The Christian world, so called, are heathens as to their knowledge of the salvation of God.[47]

> The Christian world, I discovered...was grovelling in darkness.[48]

> While brother Taylor was speaking of the sectarian [Christian] world, it occurred to my mind that the wicked do not know any more than the dumb brutes, comparatively speaking.... We may very properly say that the sectarian [Christian] world do not know anything correctly, so far as pertains to salvation.... They are more ignorant than children.[49]

The third president and prophet of the church, John Taylor, held the same view:

> We talk about Christianity, but it is a perfect pack of nonsense.... And the Devil could not invent a better engine to spread his work than the Christianity of the 19th century.[50]

And,

> I consider that if I ever lost any time in my life, it was while studying the Christian theology. Sectarian [Christian] theology is the greatest tomfoolery in the world.[51]

And,

> What does the Christian world know about God? Nothing; yet these very men assume the right and power to tell others what they shall and what they shall not believe in. Why, so far as the things of God are concerned, they are the veriest fools, they know neither God nor the things of God.[52]

He also exclaimed, "What! Are Christians ignorant? Yes, as ignorant of the things of God as the brute beast."[53] Similarly Mormon apostle Orson Pratt declared that "the whole of Christendom is as destitute of Bible Christianity as the idolatrist Pagans."[54]

Likewise B.H. Roberts, noted church historian and member of the "First Council of Seventy," referred to Christians as those, "who are blindly led by the blind."[55]

## Christians Are Wicked

Mormon apostle Orson Pratt repeatedly emphasized the evils of Christianity:

> Will Christendom have the unblushing impudence to call themselves the people of God...? How long will the heavens suffer such wickedness to go unpunished![56]
>
> Another evil of no small magnitude is the vast amount of false doctrines which are taught, and extensively believed, and practiced throughout Christendom. Doctrines which are calculated to ruin the soul.... These soul-destroying doctrines... are taught in Christendom, and... millions have had the wickedness to believe [them].... Now what will become of all these false teachers... and what will become of the people who suffer themselves to be led by such hypocrites? They will, every soul of them, unless they repent of these false doctrines, be cast down to hell.... Such heaven-daring wickedness is calculated to sink these vile impostors to the lowest hell. And unless the people repent of having received baptism and other ordinances of the Gospel at the hands of such deceivers.... And embrace the fulness of the Gospel which God has revealed anew in the *Book of Mormon*... Everyone of you will, most assuredly, be damned.[57]

Given this historical stance, what position does modern Mormonism take? Although the rhetoric is toned down, the same attitudes remain. We have noted that Joseph Fielding Smith, the tenth president and prophet of the church, and Bruce McConkie are acknowledged to be two of the leading doctrinal theologians of the modern Mormon church. Joseph Fielding Smith is the author of *Doctrines of Salvation* (three volumes), *Answers to Gospel Questions* (four volumes) and other works. Bruce McConkie is author of the three-volume *Doctrinal New Testament Commentary* and the authoritative *Mormon Doctrine*. Smith states that "gospel truth has been perverted and defiled" by Catholicism until it became a pagan abomination and that even the Reformation "perpetuated these evils and, therefore, the same corrupted doctrines and practices were perpetuated in these Protestant organizations."[58]

In his *Mormon Doctrine*, Bruce McConkie universally condemns all non-Mormon churches. He asserts that "a perverted Christianity holds sway among the so-called Christians of apostate Christendom."[59] He also observes their satanic nature:

The *Church of the Devil* and the *Great and Abominable Church* are [terms] used to identify all churches or organizations of whatever name or nature... which are designed to take men on a course that leads away from God and his laws and thus from salvation in the kingdom of God [the Mormon Church].... There is no salvation outside this one true Church, the Church of Jesus Christ.[60]

In his *Doctrinal New Testament Commentary*, McConkie alleges that Christians are the true enemies of God. Why? Because the true teachings of God "have been changed and perverted by an apostate Christendom."[61] And as a whole, modern Christians are ignorant of God's true purposes.[62] In fact, Christian doctrines are the "doctrines of devils."[63] Thus, the Christian church is part of "the great and abominable church" of the devil preparing men "to be damned."[64]

From the above statements and many others, we must conclude that Mormonism, either historically or in the present, cannot be considered neutral toward Christianity. Rather, it takes a confrontational approach, viewing Christianity as its spiritual enemy.[65]

## ♦ ♦ *Conclusion* ♦ ♦

Despite the claims of the Mormon church and the sincere conviction of Mormon people, Mormonism is not a Christian religion. From its inception, Mormonism has sought to distance itself from historic Christian faith, believing that Christianity is an apostate religion which only serves to damn the souls of men.

Although Mormons use many of the same terms that Christians use, unfortunately they supply these terms with new meanings that are not Christian. In our next section we will document Mormon doctrine in some depth and further prove that it cannot be classified as Christian.

# Mormon Theology and Its Doctrine of God

### Is Mormonism a Pagan and Polytheistic Religion?

---

I n this section we will examine the Mormon view of God and compare it with the Christian view. We will examine what Mormonism believes about God in general and about each Person of the Trinity, individually. In other words, we will examine what Mormonism teaches about God the Father, God the Son, and God the Holy Ghost/ Spirit.

We will show that the Mormon view of God is not compatible with Orthodox Christianity but instead represents a form of pagan polytheism. Besides documenting the Mormon view of God, we will also reveal that—the claims of modern Mormon church authorities notwithstanding—Brigham Young and many other leaders in the early Mormon church did teach that Adam, of the Garden of Eden, was the true Mormon God. We have also included appendices on the Mormon view of the Holy Ghost/Spirit (chap. 10) and the "eternality" of Christ (chap. 12).

# CHAPTER 10

# What Is the Mormon View of God and the Trinity?

Our doctrine of God is clear.

—Current president and prophet,
Ezra Taft Benson, *Teachings*, 4

Jesus Himself emphasized the importance of having an accurate knowledge of the one true God. He stated, "And this is eternal life, that they may know Thee, the only true God, and Jesus Christ whom Thou hast sent" (John 17:3).

The Mormon church also emphasizes the importance of a correct understanding of God. For example, *Doctrines of the Gospel*, published by the Mormon church, emphasizes that "central to our faith as Latter-day Saints is a correct understanding of God the Father."[1] And this is the student manual used at Brigham Young University for courses Religion 231 and 232. But the Mormon church also claims that only they understand God in truth; all other conceptions are wrong. Joseph Smith testifies, "There are but a few beings in the world who understand rightly the character of God."[2] Likewise the leading Mormon theologian James Talmage claims, "[The] sectarian view of the Godhead [contains]...numerous theories and dogmas of men, many of which are utterly incomprehensible in their inconsistency and mysticism."[3]

Nevertheless, Mormonism proceeds to claim that its confession of faith is in the one true God, the God *of the Bible*.

But when Mormons claim they believe in the *biblical* God, what they *mean* is that the Bible teaches the *Mormon* concept of God. Because of its alleged apostasy, Christianity lost the true teaching of God, and therefore the historic Christian doctrine of God is not truly biblical.

Thus, Mormons do freely concede that their concept of deity is contrary to traditional Christian faith. William O. Nelson, Director of the Melchizedek Priesthood Department, confesses, "Some who write anti-Mormon pamphlets insist that the Latter-day Saint concept of Deity is contrary to what is recognized as traditional Christian doctrine. In this they are quite correct."[4] So the real issue becomes one of ascertaining the true biblical teaching on the nature of God. For the rest of this chapter we will document that the Mormon teaching on God is not biblical.

Here is a brief chart noting major differences between the Mormon concept of God and the biblical or Christian view:

| Mormon Concept of Deity | Biblical (Christian) Concept of Deity |
|---|---|
| *(Pagan Polytheism)* | *(Monotheism)* |
| 1. The Gods are many (polytheistic) | God is one (monotheistic) |
| 2. The Gods are evolving (changing; mutable) | God is immutable (unchanging) |
| 3. The Gods are material (physical) | God is immaterial (spirit) |
| 4. The Gods are sexual (physically procreating divine "spirit children") | God is asexual (having no literal descendants) |
| 5. The Gods are polygamists (taking wives and husbands) | God is celibate (unmarried) |
| 6. The Gods are imperfect, requiring salvation | God is eternally holy |

In the pages below, we will discuss these topics in turn.

*Mormon Teaching No. 1—The Gods Are Many: Pagan Polytheism*

How do we know that the Mormon concept of God is pagan? Merely by examining its teachings.

The *Encyclopedia Britannica* defines paganism as "practices and beliefs that are incompatible with monotheism." According to the normal understanding of "pagan," any religion teaching that 1) there are many gods and that 2) God is finite; He evolves and changes and 3) that matter and spirit are eternal, then Mormonism is properly classified as a heathen religion offering pagan theology.

Monotheism—the belief in one Supreme God—stands in contrast to paganism which rejects that central belief. The three great monotheistic religions, Christianity, Judaism and Islam, all teach that there is one eternal, sovereign, immutable and merciful God who created the universe. By contrast—unlike many polytheistic occult religions of the East—they do not teach that God changes over the aeons (that God is finite), or that there are many gods (which is polytheism) or that matter and God are both eternal and inseparably divine.

Of course, Mormons are very uncomfortable with the charge of polytheism and rightly so. Historically, polytheism has been a teaching of great consequence in the world.

It is thus not surprising that Mormons emphatically deny they are polytheists and that they wish to consider such charges false and "damnable." No less a church authority than Bruce McConkie categorically insists that "the saints [Mormons] are not polytheists."[5] Stephen Robinson, chairman of the Department of Ancient Scripture at Brigham Young University and author of Are Mormons Christians? (which he emphatically affirms), argues that "the Latter-day Saints [doctrine does not]...constitute genuine polytheism."[6] And he takes pains to argue that "the Latter-day Saints [should] be considered worshipers of the one true God."[7] He argues that only by "distorting and misinterpreting our doctrine" can others charge Mormonism with polytheism.[8]

But if Mormons are really polytheists, why do they think they are monotheists? Principally, it is through the uncritical acceptance of the statements of church authorities, and secondarily, it is by a process of seemingly deliberate self-deception caused by the improper use of words. When Mormons deny the charge of polytheism, they illustrate a characteristic feature of Mormon apologetics—equivocation (see chap. 26). Equivocation involves the ambiguous use of words in order to conceal something.

The truth is that Mormons are polytheists by any standard definition of the term. For example, the Oxford American Dictionary defines polytheism as "belief in or worship of more than one god."[9]

Technically, Mormon theology is "henotheistic"—a form of polytheism which stresses a central deity. In Mormonism, the central deity is Elohim, whom Mormons call "God the Father." But henotheism also accepts other deities. In Mormonism the other deities accepted include Jesus, the Holy Ghost, and endless other gods who were once men and have now evolved into godhood. As noted earlier, even the Encyclopedia Britannica classifies Mormonism as polytheistic.

The fact is, when pressed, Mormons must confess that they are polytheists, not monotheists. In his discussion of polytheism in Mormon Doctrine, Bruce McConkie freely confesses that Mormons believe in "three Gods."[10] Nevertheless, he equivocates by vainly attempting to distinguish pagan polytheism from Mormon polytheism.

Further, only by stressing their primary belief in Elohim, are Mormons able to convince themselves they are really monotheists. But this is self-deception.

Mormons claim they are "monotheistic" merely because their *principal* concern is with the one central deity, the earth god Elohim. In other words, even though they freely confess, at least when pressed, to be *doctrinal* polytheists,[11] they think they are *practical* monotheists. But whatever Mormons may claim, they are equally concerned with at least two other gods, the earth God Jesus and the strange God they call the Holy Ghost.

Consider the following discussion in the student manual used at Brigham Young University, *Doctrines of the Gospel*. Note the initial claim to worship one supreme, absolute being: "By definition, God (generally meaning the Father) is the one supreme and absolute Being; . . . God is the only supreme governor . . . who is omnipotent, omnipresent, and omniscient; without beginning of days or end of life."[12]

This sounds like monotheism, but as we read further the discussion digresses from monotheism to henotheism. Thus, "Our relationship with the Father is supreme, paramount, and preeminent over all others [i.e., Mormon relationships with other gods]. He is the God we worship. . . . He is the one who was once as we are now [i.e., a man]."[13]

Further, the three members of the Godhead (the Father, Son and Holy Ghost), all of whom were once men, remain "three separate and distinct entities. Each occupies space and is and can be in but one place at one time, but each has power and influence that is everywhere present."[14]

In an attempt to quell the charge of polytheism, the manual resorts to equivocation: "There is a *oneness* in the Godhead as well as distinctness of personality. This oneness is emphasized in the sayings and writings of prophets and apostles *in order to guard against the erroneous idea that these three may be distinct and independent deities.*"[15]

In other words, the claim is clearly made that the Father, Son and Spirit are *not* "distinct and independent deities." But just a few pages later, in this very same text appears: "Both the Father and Son, being omnipotent Gods, are designated by the name-titles, *Almighty . . . Almighty God . . . Lord Almighty . . .* and *Lord God Almighty. . . .* These holy beings have all power and unlimited might."[16]

Joseph Smith himself is quoted as declaring, "In the beginning, the head of the Gods called a council of the Gods; and they came together and concocted a plan to create the world and people in it."[17] This is polytheism, not monotheism.

Consider the following excerpts from Joseph Smith's new revelation of the Creation account in the Mormon scripture known as *The Pearl of Great Price*. Does the following sound like monotheism or polytheism?

At the beginning... the Gods organized and formed the heavens and the earth.... And the Gods called the light Day. ... And the Gods also said: let there be an expanse in the midst of the waters.... And the Gods ordered the expanse, so that it divided the waters.... And the Gods called the expanse Heaven.... And the Gods pronounced the dry land Earth. ... And the Gods said: let us prepare the earth to bring forth grass.... And the Gods organized the lights in the expanse of the heaven.... And the Gods organized the two great lights, the greater light to rule the day, and the lesser light to rule the night.... And the Gods set them in the expanse of the heavens.... And the Gods organized the earth to bring forth the beasts after their kind.... And the Gods took counsel among themselves and said: let us go down and form man in our image.... So the Gods went down to organize man in their own image.... And the Gods said: we will bless them.... And the Gods said: Behold, we will give them every herb bearing seed.... And the Gods formed man from the dust of the ground.... And the Gods planted a garden, eastward in Eden.... And the Gods took the man and put him in the Garden of Eden.... And the Gods said: let us make an help meet for the man.[18]

In fact, *Abraham* chapters 4 and 5 refer to the activity of the "Gods" almost fifty separate times. Anyone who thinks this is monotheism is deceiving himself.

### Different Aspects of Mormon Polytheism

Mormon polytheism encompasses two aspects. First, there is a predominant "local" polytheism as far as the earth is concerned. The earth has three distinct gods who "rule it." Thus, Mormonism's concept of the biblical Trinity is tritheistic, not monotheistic. In *Mormon Doctrine*, McConkie declares, "There are three Gods—the Father, the Son and the Holy Ghost."[19]

The principal deity is the Father, a physical god named "Elohim," said to be the primary and most "advanced" god. Mormonism teaches, "The Father is the supreme member of the Godhead."[20] The Son is the physical God "Jehovah" of the Old Testament: "Jesus Christ is Jehovah, the God of the Old Testament."[21] The Holy Ghost is another former man who has become a god (see appendix), although unlike the Father and the Son, he does not have a concrete physical body, but is a man with a spiritual body of matter.

These three beings, again, all former men, are the three gods that Mormons are to concern themselves with. Again, because Mormonism claims that extra-solar gods are not the church's particular concern, this belief in tritheism is somehow held to be monotheistic. In any case, Mormons will assure absolutely everyone that they believe in only one true God.

The second aspect of Mormon polytheism is not geocentric, but universal. If there are an infinite number of earths, each with its god or gods, there are also an infinite number of gods, and whether or not Mormons are "concerned" with them they do believe in them, hence the denial of polytheism is once again spurious. Even McConkie confesses this when he refers to the three principal Gods of our earth:

> To us, speaking in the proper finite sense, these three are the only Gods we worship. But in addition there is an infinite number of holy personages, drawn from worlds without number, who have passed on to exaltation [Godhood] and are thus gods. . . . This doctrine of plurality of Gods is so comprehensive and glorious that it reaches out and embraces every exalted personage [God]. Those who attain exaltation are gods.[22]

Brigham Young taught the same, declaring, "How many Gods there are I do not know, but there never was a time when there were not Gods."[23] As we will document later, Joseph Smith claimed that he always taught polytheism, so it is odd to find modern Mormons claiming they are monotheists if indeed they respect Smith as God's true prophet.

To claim that one is a monotheist when it is evident from one's own official doctrines that one is a polytheist is religious deception. When Mormon missionaries look people straight in the eye and confidently claim they are monotheists—and even that they believe in the Holy Trinity—they are equivocating. The truth is they are polytheists who regret the doctrine of the Trinity.

Again, for Mormons to claim to be monotheists solely because one of their gods plays a more prominent role in their affairs than other gods is like a polygamist claiming he is really a monogamist merely because he has a favorite wife. Notice the argument of Mormon theologian Duane S. Crowther:

> Thus it becomes obvious that there are now, and will continue to be, many [omnipotent] gods who will rule and reign throughout eternity on an ever increasing number of worlds which they will create. This is not in opposition to the Biblical concept of "one God," for an earth serves as the dwelling place for the children of only one God, and he alone reigns over his children there as Father and God.[24]

In other words, Mormons are monotheists because they believe in only one god per earth! The fact that there is an endless number of earths each with its own god(s) is somehow irrelevant. Mormons are still not polytheists!

Who then denies that Mormons are polytheists? Only Mormons.

Even though Mormonism repeatedly claims to believe in what the Bible teaches, the Bible clearly rejects polytheism in the most straightforward terms. God Himself declares in Isaiah: "Before Me there was no God formed, and there will be none after Me" (43:10). He also teaches, "I am the first and I am the last, and there is no God besides Me. . . . Is there any God besides Me? . . . I know of none" (44:6,8). He further emphasizes, "I am the Lord, and there is no other; besides Me there is no God. . . . There is none except Me" (45:5,21). From Genesis to Revelation, the Bible teaches there is only one God.

### The Mormon "Trinity"

Mormonism claims that it believes in the Trinity. Dr. Stephen E. Robinson is chairman of the Department of Ancient Scripture at Brigham Young University and director of *Pearl of Great Price* research for the Religious Studies Center. First, he claims that Mormonism believes in the biblical God. He emphasizes, "The Latter-day Saints accept unequivocally *all the biblical teachings* on the nature of God."[25] He further claims that Mormons believe in the biblical doctrine of the Trinity: "Latter-day Saints believe in the *biblical* Father, Son, and Holy Ghost."[26] Even more explicitly, "If by 'the doctrine of the Trinity' one means *the New Testament teaching* that there is a Father, a Son, and Holy Ghost, all three of whom are fully divine, then Latter-day Saints *believe in the doctrine of the Trinity*. It's as simple as that. The Latter-day Saints' first *Article of Faith*, written by Joseph Smith in 1842, states, 'We believe in the God, the Eternal Father, and in His Son, Jesus Christ, and in the Holy Ghost.' "[27]

Richard L. Evans, a member of the Council of Twelve, as interviewed in Leo Rosten's *Religions of America*, answered yes to the question of "Do Mormons believe in the Holy Trinity?"[28]

To the contrary, Mormons do not believe in the Trinity; they believe in *tritheism*. Again, they believe in three gods for this particular earth and accept the existence of endless other gods on endless other earths. The very fact that they caricature the biblical teaching on the Trinity indicates that they reject the concept of one triune God. We cite three examples from early and contemporary Mormonism. Joseph Smith himself ridiculed the biblical Trinity:

> Many men say there is one God; the Father, the Son and the Holy Ghost are only one God. I say that is a strange God anyhow—three in one, and one in three! It is curious organization. . . . All are to be crammed into one God according to sectarianism [Christian faith]. It would make the biggest God in all the world. He would be a wonderfully big God—he would be a giant or a monster.[29]

This is why Joseph Smith stated that whenever he preached on the subject of God, it was always in reference to polytheistic belief. In his own words, he declared while preaching on Genesis 1:1: "I will preach on the plurality of Gods. I have selected this text for that express purpose. I wish to declare that I have always and in all congregations when I have preached on the subject of the Deity, it has been on the plurality of Gods."[30]

Also referring to the Christian Trinity, William Nelson, director of the Melchizedek Priesthood Department, comments, "It was hard to fathom a Deity of this nature, let alone love him."[31] And Bruce McConkie is even more skeptical:

> Who or what is God? Is he the incomprehensible, uncreated, immaterial nothingness described in the creeds of Christendom, . . . A three-in-one nothingness, a spirit essence filling immensity, an incorporeal, uncreated being incapable of definition or mortal comprehension. . . . An Unknown God who does not appear to men?[32]

But, these caricatures are irrelevant; the Bible clearly does teach the historic orthodox doctrine of the Trinity.

### The Biblical Teaching

Christians believe the Bible teaches that the one true God exists eternally as three Persons. The doctrine of the Trinity can be seen from five simple statements supported by the Bible.

1. There is only one true God: "For there is one God and one mediator also between God and men" (1 Timothy 2:5; cf. Deuteronomy 4:35; 6:4; Isaiah 43:10).

2. The Father is God: "There is but one God, the Father, from whom are all things . . ." (1 Corinthians 8:6; cf. John 17:1-3; 2 Corinthians 1:3; Philippians 2:11; Colossians 1:3; 1 Peter 1:2).

3. Jesus Christ, the Son, is God: ". . . but he [Jesus] was even calling God his own Father, making himself equal with God" (John 5:18). ". . . while we wait for the blessed hope—the glorious appearing of our great God and Savior, Jesus Christ" (Titus 2:13; cf. John 20:28; John 1:1; Romans 9:5; 2 Peter 1:1).

4. The Holy Spirit is a Person, is eternal, and is therefore God. The Holy Spirit is a Person: "But when he, the Spirit of truth, comes, he will guide you into all truth. He will not speak on his own; he will speak only what he hears, and he will tell you what is yet to come" (John 16:13). The Holy Spirit is eternal: "How much more,

then, will the blood of Christ, who through the eternal Spirit offered himself unblemished to God, cleanse our consciences..." (Hebrews 9:14). The Holy Spirit is therefore God: "Then Peter said, 'Ananias, how is it that Satan has so filled your heart that you have lied to the Holy Spirit.... You have not lied to men but to God'" (Acts 5:3,4).

5. The Father, Son and Holy Spirit are distinct Persons: "Therefore go and make disciples of all nations, baptizing them in the name of the Father and of the Son and of the Holy Spirit" (Matthew 28:19); "May the grace of the Lord Jesus Christ, and the love of God, and the fellowship of the Holy Spirit be with you all" (2 Corinthians 13:14).

It is clear from these verses that the Bible teaches that one true God exists eternally as Father, Son and Holy Spirit. For almost two thousand years the Christian church has found in the Bible the doctrine of the Trinity as defined above. This can be seen by anyone who reads the Church Fathers and studies the historic Creeds.*

Our incomplete comprehension of this truth is insufficient grounds to reject what Scripture teaches. For example, scientists long believed that all energy existed either as "waves" or "particles": two contradictory forms. They could not understand how light, for example, could consist of *both* waves and particles because their natures were different. Even when scientific testing proved this to be true, some scientists found it difficult to accept this conclusion because it was "unreasonable." Nevertheless, scientists were eventually forced by the *evidence* to conclude that light was both waves and particles. Scientists may not be able to explain it logically, but they are honest enough to accept that this is what light is.

In the same manner, God has told who He is. The evidence of Scripture forces us to accept that the one true God exists eternally as Father, Son and Holy Spirit. We cannot fully understand it or explain it logically, but we accept it because this is where the facts have led us.

Indeed, Father, Son and Holy Spirit are so effortlessly and consistently linked in Scripture that assuming that God is not three Persons makes it impossible to understand numerous passages (e.g., Matthew 28:19; 2 Corinthians 1:21,22; 13:14; Ephesians 2:18; 3:11-16; 5:18-20; 1 Thessalonians 1:1-5).

Try answering the following questions without concluding that the Bible teaches the doctrine of the Trinity:

---

* For an indepth study of the historical development of the doctrine of the Trinity from apostolic times through the final form of the Nicean Creed adopted at the Council of Constantinople in A.D. 381, including a line-by-line comparison of the Creed with New Testament teaching, see Calvin Beisner's *God in Three Persons*. Another excellent study is E. Bickersteth's *The Trinity*.[33]

1. Who raised Jesus from the dead? The Father (Romans 6:4; Acts 3:26; 1 Thessalonians 1:10)? The Son (John 2:19-21; 10:17,18)? The Holy Spirit (Romans 8:11)? Or God (Hebrews 13:20; Acts 13:30; 17:31)?

2. Who does the Bible say is God? The Father (Ephesians 4:6)? The Son (Titus 2:13; John 1:1; 20:28)? The Holy Spirit (Acts 5:3,4)? The one and only true God (Deuteronomy 4:35)?

3. Who created the world? The Father (John 14:2)? The Son (John 1:1-3; Colossians 1:16,17)? The Holy Spirit (Genesis 1:2; Psalm 104:30)? Or God (Genesis 1:1; Hebrews 11:3)?

4. Who saves man? Who regenerates man? The Father (1 Peter 1:3)? The Son (John 5:21; 4:14)? The Holy Spirit (John 3:6; Titus 3:5)? Or God (1 John 3:9)? Who justifies man? The Father (Jeremiah 23:6; 2 Corinthians 5:19)? The Son (Romans 5:9; 10:4; 2 Corinthians 5:19,21)? The Holy Spirit (1 Corinthians 6:11; Galatians 5:5)? Or God (Romans 4:6; 9:33)? Who sanctifies man? The Father (Jude 1)? The Son (Titus 2:14)? The Holy Spirit (1 Peter 1:2)? Or God (Exodus 31:13)? Who propitiated God's anger against man for his sins? The Father (1 John 4:14; John 3:16; 17:5; 18:11)? The Son (Matthew 26:28; John 1:19; 1 John 2:2)? The Holy Spirit (Hebrews 9:14)? Or God (2 Corinthians 5:1; Acts 20:28)?

In conclusion, it is simple to see why the Christian church has been taught the doctrine of the Trinity for two thousand years—the Bible unmistakably teaches it.*

*Mormon Teaching No. 2—The Gods Are Evolving: Each God Was Once a Finite Man*

Mormonism teaches that God was not God from all eternity, but that He was once a man who evolved into godhood. This is a doctrine that Mormonism holds is true for all who are currently gods—and there are endless numbers of them. As noted elsewhere, both historic Mormon theology and contemporary Mormonism teach that there are an infinite number of earths throughout the universe, each one presided over by its own god or gods.

How do men become gods? Mormonism believes that all current gods have attained the status of godhood through the good works they performed when they were once finite men. Joseph Smith describes the process by which men may become gods: "When you climb up a ladder, you must begin at the bottom and ascend step by step, until you arrive at

---

* This discussion on the Christian Trinity was excerpted from the authors' *Cult Watch: What You Need to Know About Spiritual Deception.*

the top; and so it is with the principles of the Gospel—you must begin with the first, and go on until you learn all the principles of exaltation [becoming a God]."[34] The official Mormon publication *Gospel Principles* cites this passage and then comments, "This is the way our Heavenly Father became a God."[35] It then quotes Joseph Smith's own evaluation of "The First Principle of the Gospel," which is to realize that God the Father was once a man: "It is the first principle of the gospel to know for a certainty the character of God, and to know that we may converse with him as one man converses with another, and that he was once a man like us; yea that God himself, the father of us all, dwelt on an earth, the same as Jesus Christ himself did; and I will show it from the Bible."[36]

This same source includes the observation, "God is a glorified and perfected man, a personage of flesh and bones. Inside his tangible body is an eternal spirit (see *D&C*, 130:22)."[37] Mormon authorities claim that this teaching "in no way degrades God, but certainly elevates the status of man. And sure He's a man. He's got a body of flesh and bones like you and I have."[38]

Even though the Bible teaches, "For I, the Lord, do not change" (Malachi 3:6), Mormonism thinks that God was once a man, who was Himself created by another god. As Joseph Smith taught, "The Father of Jesus Christ had a Father":

> If Jesus Christ was the son of God, and John discovered that God the Father of Jesus Christ had a Father, you may suppose that he had a Father also. Where was there ever a son without a father? And where was there ever a father without first being a son?[39]

Mormonism thus teaches that God the Father had a father who created Him and gave Him the opportunity to become God.

This is why Joseph Smith specifically rejected the Christian teaching:

> God Himself was once as we are now, and is an exalted man, and sits enthroned in yonder heavens! That is the great secret. . . . If you were going to see him today, you would see him like a man in form. . . . I am going to tell you how God came to be God. We have imagined and supposed that God was God from all eternity. I will refute that idea, and take away the veil, so that you may see. . . . He was once a man like us. . . . Here, then, is eternal life—to know the only wise and true God; and you have got to learn how to be gods your-selves.[40]

Hence, it is not surprising that Joseph Smith stated that the true translation of Genesis 1:1 taught polytheism. According to Smith, "It read first [in its original version] 'The head one of the Gods brought forth the Gods.' That is the true meaning of the words. . . . Thus the head God brought forth the Gods in the grand council."[41] After that, "The heads of the Gods appointed one God for us [i.e., Elohim]"—and thus Elohim became the God of this world.[42]

Modern Mormons have continued to accept these early polytheistic teachings. Bruce McConkie declares that "God is a Holy Man."[43] He further teaches that "God is . . . an exalted, perfected, and glorified Man of Holiness (Moses 6:57) and not a spirit essence that fills the immensity of space."[44] Mormons everywhere affirm that "God is a man."[45]

The Mormon student manual, *Doctrines of the Gospel*, teaches that "God Himself is an exalted man, perfected, enthroned, and supreme."[46] Even Dr. Stephen Robinson, who is convinced that Mormonism is Christian, confesses, "It is indisputable that Latter-day Saints believe that God was once a human being and that human beings can become gods." The famous couplet of Lorenzo Snow, fifth president and prophet of the LDS Church, states: "As man now is, God once was; as God now is, man may be."[47]

But Mormonism is divided on how far the process of divine evolution extends. Historically, the church has been uncertain as to whether or not the gods continue to evolve forever. Many Mormon presidents and prophets taught that the gods evolve eternally in power, knowledge, etc.—which, of course, would never quite make them truly omnipotent, omniscient, etc.[48] This is conveyed in the following early teachings:

> God himself is increasing and progressing in knowledge, power and dominion, and will do so worlds without end.[49]

> The greatest intelligence in existence can continually ascend to greater heights of perfection. We are created for the express purpose of increase. . . . It is the Deity within us that causes increase. . . . He is in every person upon the face of the earth.[50]

The writings of the second president and prophet, Brigham Young, are a rebuke to many a modern Latter-day Saint, such as Bruce McConkie, who teach that God is omniscient, omnipotent and omnipresent,[51] that is, that God does not forever increase in power and knowledge. In rebuking early Mormon apostle Orson Pratt, Young emphasized that such reasoning was a reflection of ignorance:

> Brother Orson Pratt has, in theory, bounded the capacity of God. According to his theory, God can progress no further in knowledge and power; but the God that I serve is progressing eternally, and so are his children; they will increase to all eternity, if they are faithful. But there are some of our brethren who know just so much, and they seem to be able to learn no

more. You may plead with them, scold them . . . and try in various ways to increase their knowledge; but it seems as if they would not learn.[52]

In fact, Young refused to believe in an omniscient deity: "Do not lariat the God that I serve and say that he cannot learn anymore; I do not believe in such a character."[53]

Modern Mormons deny all this and teach that the state of omnipotence, omniscience, etc. will finally be attained, which would logically stop the process of divine "increase."

What kind of god does Mormonism believe in? Whether we take early or late Mormonism, one fact is clear: They have no genuine concept of God in the Christian meaning of the term. Even if we assume the truth of the heresies of the modern Mormon church (heresies in contrast to its earlier prophets), their god *evolved* to godhood, hence he was not an eternal being of divine attributes.

Thus, Orson Pratt naturally wondered, with his mind "wearied and lost in the multiplicity of [divine] generations and successive worlds . how far back the genealogy extends, and how the first world was formed, and the first father was begotten?" Although concluding that the search was futile, he raised a relevant question, for why and how "do you seek for a *first* personal Father in an endless genealogy?"[54]

Mormonism's apparent solution is to say that matter and spirit are eternal. Matter is merely a variation of spirit, a denser form of spirit, although still eternal. Apparently, in the "beginning" divine spirit/matter somehow coalesced into a man and woman who eventually evolved into godhood and became capable of sexual intercourse and the production of spirit offspring. But how did matter and spirit exist eternally without a creator? If matter is eternal and in some sense divine, is this not similar to pantheism? Further, if one eternal god did begin the process, are not Mormons to be classed as idolaters for actually obeying and worshipping lesser deities created by him?

Regardless, the above concepts are not Christian teaching. The Bible asserts in the clearest terms that God is immutable—that is, that God never changes in terms of His being, essence or attributes.*

For all eternity God has remained God. God was never originally a man who, incredibly, somehow became God through personal effort.

The following Scriptures all testify that God never changes: "For I, the Lord, do not change; therefore you, O sons of Jacob, are not consumed" (Malachi 3:6). "Every good thing bestowed and every perfect gift is from above, coming down from the Father of lights, with whom there is no variation, or shifting shadow" (James 1:17). "God is not a man, that He

---

*The incarnation of Jesus Christ is not an exclusion to this reality, for in taking on a sinless human nature, the Second Person of the Godhead did not alter His essential divine nature.

should lie, nor a son of man, that He should repent" (Numbers 23:19). "For I am God and not man, the Holy One in your midst" (Hosea 11:9). "For He is not a man as I am that I may answer Him, that we may go to court together" (Job 9:32). "From everlasting to everlasting, Thou art God" (Psalm 90:2).

In conclusion, none can deny that the Mormon god is ultimately a finite god. As Dr. McMurrin concludes in his study: "He is therefore finite rather than absolute."[55] And, "In its rejection of the classical concept of God as eternal, Mormonism is a most radical digression from traditional theism. This is perhaps its most important departure from familiar Christian orthodoxy, for it would be difficult to overestimate the importance to [Mormon] theology of the doctrine that God is a temporal being."[56]

Unfortunately, when Mormons claim their god is infinite, omnipotent, etc., they are only engaging in further equivocation, and for obvious reasons:

> The word "finite" stirs nothing in the soul of the worshiper. But "infinite," "omnipotent," and "omniscient" are words made to order for the preacher and the popular writer. So Mormon theological writing and sermonizing are more often than not replete with the vocabulary of absolutism. But, like it or not, the Mormon theologian must sooner or later return to the finitistic conception of God upon which both his technical theology and his theological myths are founded. Here Mormonism reveals the radical nature of its heresy.[57]

*Mormon Teaching No. 3—The Gods Are Material, Not Spirit*

Mormonism teaches that its gods are physical creatures, except for the Holy Ghost. In contrast to John 4:24, where Jesus Himself emphasized that God is spirit, Mormonism teaches that God is not spirit. Joseph Smith himself declared, "There is no other God in heaven but that God who has flesh and bones."[58] The Mormon scripture, *Doctrine and Covenants*, 130:22, asserts: "The Father has a body of flesh and bones as tangible as man's; the Son also; but the Holy Ghost has not a body of flesh and bones, but is a personage of spirit. Were it not so, the Holy Ghost could not dwell in us." (One wonders how Mormons explain the many biblical references teaching that both Christ and the Father also personally dwell within the believer.)

The current Mormon president and prophet, Ezra Taft Benson, reemphasizes this "basic and important" Mormon doctrine of a material god, claiming that the Christian view is false:

> The Father and Son have tabernacles of flesh and bones, and the Holy Ghost is a personage of Spirit. . . . An understanding of these basic truths is of the utmost importance.

... Instead of accepting God as he has declared himself to be, the Christian sects have sought by human reason and wisdom to describe God. ... [But] Joseph's first vision clearly revealed that the Father and Son are separate personages, having bodies as tangible as man's.[59]

The Mormon text *A Sure Foundation: Answers to Difficult Gospel Questions* also emphasizes that the Christian teaching concerning the nature of God as spirit is wrong:

... there is meager evidence in the Bible to support belief in a God who is a spirit essence. ... Those who have received their understanding about God from errant traditional Christianity need no longer struggle with that confused and confusing doctrine. The [Mormon] Prophets' inspired declarations about the Godhead are in total agreement with the biblical evidence that Jesus and the Father have distinct, material bodies.[60]

Doctrinal theologian Bruce McConkie calls God, "A glorified resurrected Personage having a tangible body of flesh and bones."[61] The Brigham Young University student manual, *Doctrines of the Gospel*, teaches, "God is a holy, perfected personage, or being, with a body of flesh and bones (see Moses 6:57; 7:35; D&C, 130:22; Matthew 5:48)."[62]

In response to John 4:24, Mormons claim that God has a *spiritual* resurrected body of flesh and bones, hence that he is a true spirit. They believe that all spirit is matter although of a finer or purer form. But even Jesus taught that a true "spirit does *not have flesh and bones*" (emphasis added, Luke 24:39).

*Mormon Teachings No. 4 and No. 5—The Gods Are Sexual Polygamists: Divine Procreation and the Begetting of Spirit Children by the Gods*

How are the gods created in the first place? As in many primitive and pagan religions, Mormonism teaches that the gods are sexually active. Through sexual intercourse, they beget spirit children who have the opportunity to become "exalted"—to become gods themselves through complete faithfulness to Mormon teachings.

In Mormonism, the sex act plays an important divine function that is inseparably integrated with the church's doctrines of exaltation and celestial or eternal marriage[63] (see chap. 30). In other words, to be "exalted" in Mormonism is to become a god who is continually active sexually, begetting offspring throughout all eternity. But this is a privilege reserved *only* for those who are married in the Mormon temple.[64] If men and women are married in the temple, and through good works finally achieve exaltation (godhood), then they may continue the process of producing spirit children who will in turn also have the opportunity to become gods. President Benson states that "Temple marriage is a gospel ordinance for exaltation."[65] Bruce McConkie explains: "Marriages performed in the temples for time *and eternity*, by virtue of the sealing keys restored by Elijah, are called *celestial marriages*.... By definition exaltation consists in the continuation of the family unit in eternity.... Celestial marriage is a holy and an eternal ordinance.... Its importance in the plan of salvation and exaltation cannot be overestimated."[66] The Mormon emphasis upon the family originated primarily from this doctrine: the teaching that men and women married in the temple can become gods with the privilege of ruling an eternal family of spirit offspring on another world.[67]

The text *Gospel Principles*, published by the Mormon church, cites the sixth president and prophet of the Mormon church, Joseph F. Smith, as teaching the current Mormon doctrine that "all men and women are... literally the sons and daughters of Deity.... Man, as a spirit, was begotten and born of heavenly parents, and reared to maturity in the eternal mansions of the Father, prior to coming upon the earth in a temporal [physical] body."[68] Further:

> Our heavenly parents... wanted us to develop every god-like quality that they have. To do this, we needed to leave our celestial home to be tested and to gain experience... to be clothed with a physical body.... Since we could not progress further in heaven, our Heavenly Father called a Grand Council... to present us his plan for our progression. We learned that if we followed his plan, we would become like him. We would have a resurrected body; we would have all power in heaven and on earth; we would become heavenly parents and have spirit children just as he does (*D&C*, 132:19,20).[69]

Because of the belief that there are so many spirits waiting for bodies to indwell, the Mormon church has always emphasized the importance of large families. Bodies are desperately needed to supply the spirit children with fleshly houses. This was, ostensibly, the early rationale for Mormon polygamy. If one wife could produce ten bodies for the spirit children, twenty wives could produce two hundred bodies.

This emphasis on large families is still present in the church. The current president and prophet, Ezra Taft Benson, happily quotes Brigham Young in *Discourses of Brigham Young*: "There are multitudes of pure and holy spirits waiting to take tabernacles [bodies]. Now what is our duty?—to prepare tabernacles for them;... It is the duty of every righteous man and woman to prepare tabernacles for all the spirits they can."[70] And President Benson himself comments, "We know that every spirit assigned to this earth will come [to this earth], whether through us or someone else. There are couples in the Church who think they are getting along just fine with their limited families but who will some day suffer the pains of remorse when they meet the spirits that might have been part of their posterity."[71]

### The Role of the Mormon Woman

Unfortunately, as in Hinduism and Islam today, Mormon women are accorded a secondary status. The Tanners note that the early Mormon doctrine toward women probably played a crucial role in preparing them for polygamist marriage. Citing early sources, they document that Mormon leaders taught that a woman was inferior to a man and that her salvation depended on her husband. For example, Brigham Young taught that "the man is the head and God of the women." They also cite the comments of early Mormon women who accepted this teaching.[72]

In response to this acceptance, former Mormon Einar Anderson observes,

> It has been a source of amazement to me that Mormon women so vigorously defend and cling to these doctrines when we know that in reality the Mormon husband is believed to be the "savior of the Mormon woman." He alone has the authority to call her forth in the resurrection. All one has to do is to attend the funeral of a Mormon wife to know that, when most of the congregation has left, the Priest places the veil over the dead woman's face, to be there until her husband calls her forth in the resurrection.[73]

Mormonism thus teaches that the husband is "God of the wife and that he will call her into resurrection to begin this eternal marriage," where their "spirit progeny will 'continue as innumerable as the stars.' "[74] In other words, the only way a Mormon wife is going to gain exaltation is if her husband chooses to call her forth "by her secret name on the morning of the first resurrection."[75]

But consider the following excerpt from the "John Ankerberg Show," which reveals the kind of pressure placed upon Mormon women that, in part, may help explain the high divorce rate in Mormonism:

> Decker (on film): "The pressure on the Mormon women is incredible. They must be perfect. They swear an oath of total obedience to the husband in the Mormon Temple. There is a whole area of psychiatric care dealing with the depression in the Mormon woman."
>
> Woman's voice: "I have a friend who is a nurse in the psychiatric ward and she came to me and asked, 'Why is it that there are so many Mormon women in my wing? What's the trouble?' And I believe that it is simply because it is an

impossibility to live up to the standards that are put upon these Mormon women."

*Decker (on film):* "They must be perfect so that they can go to exaltation with their husbands. They don't even get out of the grave unless the husband calls them forth on the morning of the first resurrection. And if you do make it to celestial exaltation, heaven to the Mormon woman is being pregnant for all eternity. One spirit baby after the next."

*Woman's voice:* "There came a point in my life as a Mormon woman when things were not going right at all. My whole time was spent in doing what the Mormon leaders had told me to do. In fact, I came to the point where I felt like life just wasn't worth living anymore."[76]

One Mormon woman recalls how a distorted appeal to motherhood helped promote Mormon theology:

Ever since I was a little girl I was taught that my primary purpose was to become a goddess in heaven so that I could multiply an earth. I wanted that. I wanted to be eternally pregnant and look down on an earth and say, "That's mine. I populated that whole earth and all those little babies I had."[77]

In part, the apparent glory of the Mormon male is to be sexually virile forever with his wife or many wives;[78] some early Mormons boasted of the hundreds or thousands of wives they would have in the resurrection.[79] In early Mormon history and in contemporary polygamist sects, Mormons actually secured dozens and even scores of wives for eternity, including being sealed to dead women in "baptism for the dead" rites.[80]

Although the Utah church has abandoned polygamy (at least for this life), it continues to teach that polygamy will exist in the afterlife.

Nevertheless, the sexual theology of Mormonism is why the church teaches there are divine mothers in heaven:

We are the offspring of God. He is our Eternal Father; we have also an Eternal Mother. There is no such thing as a father without a mother, nor can there be children without parents. We were born as the spirit children of Celestial Parents long before the foundations of this world were laid.[81]

Implicit in the Christian verity that all men are the spirit children of an Eternal Father is the usually unspoken truth that they are also the offspring of an Eternal Mother. An exalted and glorified Man of Holiness (Moses 6:57) could not be a Father unless a Woman of like glory, perfection, and holiness was associated with him as a Mother. . . . This doctrine that there is a Mother in heaven was affirmed in plainness by the First Presidency of the Church (Joseph F. Smith, John R. Winder, and Anthony Lund) when, in speaking of preexistence and the origin of man, they said . . . "all men and women are in the similitude of the universal Father and Mother, and are literally the sons and daughters of Deity." . . . Mortal persons who overcome all things and gain an ultimate exaltation will live eternally in the family unit and have spirit children, thus becoming Eternal Fathers and Eternal Mothers (*D&C*, 132:19-32, Talmage, *Articles of Faith*, 443).[82]

Mormon president and prophet Joseph Fielding Smith realized that this doctrine of an eternal Mother was not taught in the Bible, or even in the Mormon scriptures. Nevertheless, it was required as a logical inference and, therefore, was deemed valid on the basis of "common sense." He stated, "The fact that there is no reference to a mother in heaven either in the Bible, *The Book of Mormon* or *Doctrine and Covenants*, is not sufficient to prove that no such thing as a Mother did exist there. If we had a Father, which we did, for all of these records speak of him, then does not good common sense tell us that we must have had a mother there also?"[83] In commenting on Genesis 1:26,27 he asks, "Is it not feasible to believe that female spirits were created in the image of a mother in Heaven?"[84]

The Mormon concept of female deities apparently caused many early Mormons to accept celestial polygamy. Brigham Young stated in 1870, "The scripture says that he, the Lord, came walking in the Temple with his train; I do not know who they were, unless his wives and children."[85]

This is why apostle Orson Pratt wrote in *The Seer* of November 1853, that God honors polygamy since he himself is a polygamist, along with his son Jesus and his people, the Mormons:

We have now clearly shown that God the Father had a plurality of wives, one or more being in eternity, by whom he begat our spirits as well as the spirit of Jesus his First Born, and another [wife] being upon the earth by whom he begat the tabernacle of Jesus [Jesus' mother Mary], as his Only Begotten in this world. We have also proved most clearly that the Son followed the example of his Father, and became the great Bridegroom to whom kings' daughters and many honorable Wives were to be married. We have also proved that both God the Father and our Lord Jesus Christ inherit their wives in eternity as well as in time. . . . Oh, ye delicate ladies of [apostate] Christendom . . . if you do not want your morals corrupted, and your delicate ears shocked, and your pious modesty put to the blush by the society of polygamists and their wives, do not venture near the holy Jerusalem [Mormon-ism] nor come near the New Earth; for Polygamists will be honored there, and will be among the chief rulers in that Kingdom.[86]

Pratt further stated, "If none but Gods will be permitted to multiply immortal children, it follows that each God must have one or more wives."[87] Thus, if the earth god became the divine standard for Mormon behavior, it is not surprising that polygamy was an important doctrine in the early church.

To conclude, the spirit children of male and female gods require physical bodies. After probation in a preexistent state, they require life upon an earth so that they might have the opportunity to progress to godhood just as their "parents" did. Each spirit child, produced sexually by a male and female god, inhabits a body prepared for it and grows up as a man or woman. Through diligence and good works and obedience to the Mormon church, these spirits may attain exaltation. After they die, they may become gods on new earths who then procreate with their spouses and produce more spirit children. Then these spirit children, based on their good works in the preexistent state, are in turn given an earth upon which to have the opportunity for self-perfection and evolu-tion into godhood.

Apparently the process continues forever, with the newly-exalted spirits being their own gods over a planet or planets—just as was true for the heavenly Father and the Mother of Jesus who procreated all the former spirit children who now reside in physical bodies upon this earth. Brigham Young commented: "The Lord created you and me for the purpose of becoming Gods like Himself. . . . We are created . . . to become Gods like unto our Father in heaven so that we then create 'worlds on worlds.' "[88]

Although most Mormons today deny that God and Christ are polyga-mists, no one can deny the logical basis for such a doctrine in early Mormon teaching. In fact, perhaps one reason why Mormon history is disgraced with sexually-related sins is because of the sexual emphasis and practices of the gods it worships.

*Mormon Teaching No. 6—The Gods Are Imperfect and Require Salvation* (see chap. 16 and its Appendix One).

Because Mormonism teaches that the gods have evolved into godhood from the status of mere men, who have struggled with good and evil and perfected themselves, it cannot logically deny that all the gods were once imperfect and required salvation. Milton Hunter, a member of the First Council of Seventy commented:

> God the Eternal Father was once a mortal man. . . . He be-came God—an exalted being—through obedience to the same

eternal Gospel truths that we are given opportunity today to obey.... We must accept the fact that there was a time when Deity was much less powerful than he is today. Then how did he become glorified and exalted and attain his present status of Godhead? In the first place, aeons ago God undoubtedly took advantage of every opportunity to learn the laws of truth.... From day to day he exerted his will vigorously, ... he gained more knowledge.... Thus he grew in experience and continued to grow until he attained the status of Godhood. In other words, he became God by absolute obedience to all the eternal laws of the Gospel.[89]

But because the gods were once finite men who earned their deity, they must have at one time been imperfect and, by implication, sinful. In fact, because the Mormon God intended the Fall of man on earth, and because Mormon theology teaches that experience of sin may have a beneficial influence on the process of exaltation, it is hardly surprising that Mormonism teaches that its gods were once imperfect. Orson Pratt taught:

The gods who dwell in the Heaven from which our spirits came, are beings who have been redeemed from the grave in a world which existed before the foundations of this earth were laid. They and the Heavenly body which they now inhabit *were once in fallen state*. Their terrestrial world was redeemed, and glorified, and made a Heaven: their terrestrial bodies, after suffering death, were redeemed, and glorified, and made Gods. And thus, as their world was exalted from a temporal to an eternal state, they were exalted also, *from fallen men to Celestial Gods* to inhabit their Heaven forever and forever. These Gods, being redeemed from the grave with their wives, are immortal and eternal, and will die no more.[90]

If, as Mormonism teaches, every god was once an imperfect and sinful man who was saved by good works which exalted him to godhood, then the logical conclusion is that God Himself requires salvation. Thus Marion G. Romney, a member of the First Presidency, taught that "God is a perfected, *saved soul* enjoying eternal life."[91]

But again, this is not what the Bible teaches. The Scripture is clear that God is an eternally-righteous, holy and perfect God; because He was never an imperfect and sinful man, He could never require salvation (1 Samuel 15:29; Titus 1:2).

We have now examined several key contrasts between the God of Mormonism and the God of the Bible. There are also others, as the following summary chart indicates:

| God(s) of Mormonism | God of the Bible |
| --- | --- |
| Material (a physical body of flesh and bones) | Immaterial (spirit) |
| Mortal | Immortal |
| Changeable, evolving | Immutable |
| Physically localized | Omnipresent |
| Polygamous and/or incestuous | Monogamous (celibate) |
| Polytheistic | Monotheistic |
| Tritheistic (three earth gods) | Trinitarian |
| Exalted saved man | Eternal deity |
| Eternally progressing in certain attributes (early Mormonism) | Eternally immutable in all characteristics |
| Feminine counterpart (heavenly mother) | No feminine counterpart |
| Adam, once considered God (early Mormonism) | Adam, a creation of God |
| Jesus, begotten by Elohim's physical intercourse with Mary | Jesus, begotten supernaturally by the Holy Spirit (virgin birth) |
| Polygamist Jesus (early Mormonism) | Celibate Jesus |

How can anyone maintain that the God of Mormonism is the God of the Bible? Yet, Mormons continue to insist that they believe in the biblical God. Again, in his book *Are Mormons Christians?* Dr. Stephen Robinson writes, "The Latter-day Saints accept unequivocally all the biblical teachings on the nature of God."[92] And, "Latter-day Saints believe in the biblical Father, Son, and Holy Ghost."[93]

# ◆ ◆ *Conclusion* ◆ ◆

Mormons assert that their concept of God is clear and precise while the Christian concept is confused and unintelligible. The current president and prophet of the church claims, "Our doctrine of God is clear."[94] However, as the Tanners observe, "a careful examination of Mormon teachings concerning the Godhead reveals a serious state of confusion."[95]

The Mormon church cannot consistently answer the following questions: Is God holy? Who or what is God in His essential nature and attributes?

Does God evolve forever? Are the standard attributes of deity applicable to God? What is the Holy Ghost? Was Jesus a polygamist? Conflicting answers have been given on all these issues.

This is one reason we encounter a state of confusion among Mormon laymen, missionaries and scholars as to what they believe or don't believe about God—and as we shall see, about other issues as well. This is also why the average Mormon will actually deny much of Mormon theology, claiming that those who think Mormonism teaches the above beliefs are "ignorant." When no less of a leader than McConkie says that it is the Christian and not the Mormon concept of God that is "utterly incomprehensible in its inconsistency" (quoted earlier), one can only wonder whose theology he has been reading.

Not infrequently, Mormons will also accuse Christians of "blasphemy" in their view of God. But Bruce McConkie himself defined blasphemy as follows: "Blasphemy consists in either or both of the following: 1) speaking irreverently, evilly, abusively, or scurrilously against God or sacred things; or 2) speaking profanely or *falsely* about [the] Deity."[96]

McConkie defines blasphemy correctly. Unfortunately, it is Mormonism that is guilty of it. Mormonism speaks irreverently, evilly and abusively against God when it teaches He was once a sinful man. Mormonism speaks falsely about God concerning His fundamental nature and essence when it teaches polygamy and a theology of finitism.

In addition, Mormons profane God, as when Joseph Fielding Smith, the tenth president and prophet of the church, committed blasphemy in calling the biblical God "a cruel monster."[97]

In conclusion, given the pagan, polytheistic nature of the Mormonism God, it would appear that the challenge of Joshua remains open to the Mormon church: "But if serving the LORD seems undesirable to you, then choose for yourselves this day whom you will serve, whether the gods your forefathers served beyond the River, or the gods of the Amorites, in whose land you are living. But as for me and my household, we will serve the LORD" (Joshua 24:15 NIV).

# ◆ ◆ *Appendix* ◆ ◆

*What Does the Mormon Church Teach About the Holy Spirit?*

The Mormon church claims that it believes in the Holy Spirit and what it terms the Holy Ghost. [Technically, the Holy Ghost (an exalted man) and the Holy Spirit (sometimes a synonymous term, but also the mind, power or influence of God the Father) are divided into two separate concepts and/or confused with the Person of Christ; see McConkie, *Doctrinal New Testament Commentary*, 3:337-340.] Mormon authority James Talmage asserts that only Mormons possess the Holy Ghost (Spirit):

> The Holy Ghost may be regarded as the minister of the Godhead, carrying into effect the decisions of the Supreme Council [of Gods]. . . . The power of the Holy Ghost . . . is the spirit of prophecy and revelation. . . . God grants the gift of the Holy Ghost unto the obedient. . . . The authority to so bestow the Holy Ghost belongs [only] to the higher or Melchizedek Priesthood.[98]

Thus, the officiating elder, acting in the name and by the alleged authority of Jesus Christ, says to new converts, *"Receive the Holy Ghost."* And, "I confirm you a member of the Church of Jesus Christ of Latter-day Saints."[99]

But, Mormonism presents a significantly confused portrait of the God it calls the Holy Ghost. It is unclear whether or not he has a body, is personal or impersonal, married or single, male or female, the mind of God or a distinct deity.

The modern church has clarified some of these issues, believing the Holy Ghost is without a tangible body, personal, a separate God, unmarried and presumably male. As space does not permit the citing of specific quotations for these many issues, we merely provide documentation and conclude with Mormon authorities Jerald and Sandra Tanner that "one of the most confusing areas of Mormon theology is that area dealing with the Holy Ghost."[100] Thus, throughout Mormon history, the Holy Ghost/Spirit has been variously interpreted as:

A personal being[101]

Something like electricity[102]

A personage of spirit[103]

The "influence" of deity[104]

The third deity in the Mormon "Trinity" or Godhead[105]

*Not* the third deity in the "Trinity"[106]

The mind of the Father and Son[107]

A male (a few have suggested female) spirit[108]

Without a body[109]

May yet receive a body[110]

Impersonal[111]

Personal[112]

A spirit who "has no other effect than pure intelligence"[113]

The Lord Jesus Christ Himself[114]

> A localized spirit man or the power or gift of the Holy Ghost,
> or an impersonal omnipresent substance, or the spirit body
> of Jesus Christ[115]

Biblically, however, the Holy Spirit is God, the Third Person of the Trinity. Below we present a brief outline of scriptural teaching on the Holy Spirit:

1. He is distinguished from both the Father and the Son (Isaiah 48:16; Matthew 28:19; Luke 3:21; John 14:16,17; Hebrews 9:8).

2. He is personal. He loves (Romans 15:30); wills (1 Corinthians 12:11); convicts of sin (John 16:8); commands and forbids (Acts 8:29; 13:2; 16:6); speaks messages (1 Timothy 4:1; Revelation 2:7); intercedes for believers (Romans 8:26); teaches, comforts and guides into the truth (John 14:26); can be grieved (Ephesians 4:30), blasphemed (Mark 3:29) and insulted (Hebrews 10:29).

The seemingly impersonal and even inanimate terminology used to describe the actions of the Holy Spirit such as "filling," "pouring out," etc., (Ephesians 5:18; Isaiah 32:15; Ezekiel 39:29) does not imply the impersonality of the Holy Spirit as some cults maintain. Rather, such terminology refers to the intimacy of the believer's personal relationship with Him.

3. He is God. The Holy Spirit has the attributes of deity: omnipresence (Psalm 139:7,8), omniscience (1 Corinthians 2:10,11); eternality (Hebrews 9:14) and omnipotence (Job 33:4). He is the Creator of the universe (Genesis 1:2; Job 33:4) and the giver of eternal life (John 3:3-8).

   He is also identified as God by the divine associations Scripture freely lends to Him: He indwells the believer (1 Corinthians 6:19 with 2 Corinthians 6:16); strives with man (Genesis 6:3 with 1 Peter 3:20); inspires the Word of God (2 Peter 1:21 with Luke 1:68-70 with Acts 1:16 and 28:25; Isaiah 6:1-13; Hebrews 10:15-17 with Jeremiah 31:31-34); sanctifies the believer (2 Thessalonians 2:13,14 with 1 Thessalonians 4:7); speaks to Isaiah (Acts 28:25,26 with Isaiah 6:8,9); sends forth laborers (Matthew 9:38 with Acts 13:2-4); can be tested (Psalm 95:6-9 with Hebrews 3:7-9) and inspires divine love (Romans 5:5 with 1 Thessalonians 3:12,13 and 2 Thessalonians 3:5).

According to Acts 5:3,4 when Ananias lied to the Holy Spirit, he really lied to God. According to Jesus, there is only one eternal sin. That is the sin against the Holy Spirit (Matthew 12:32). He is also called the Lord in 2 Corinthians 3:18 and Hebrews 10:15,16 (see 1 Thessalonians 3:11-13).

Note also the Holy Spirit's relationship to Jesus in John 14:16-18 (see the Greek text).

Consider too the importance of the Holy Spirit in regeneration and salvation, in sanctification, in bringing glory to Jesus Christ and in inspiring the holy Scriptures, not to mention many other areas (John 3:6-8; 16:13,14; 1 Peter 1:2). All this proves the Holy Ghost/Spirit of Mormonism is not the Holy Spirit of the Bible.

Unfortunately, Mormonism does not even know who the Holy Spirit is. How then can Mormons logically claim to be genuine children of God when it is the Holy Spirit and Him alone who gives spiritual life (John 3:3-8)? "Jesus answered, 'Truly, truly, I say to you, unless one is born of water and the Spirit, he cannot enter into the kingdom of God. That which is born of the flesh is flesh and that which is born of the Spirit is spirit' " (John 3:5-6). "The Spirit gives life; the flesh counts for nothing" (John 6:63). And, "For all who are being led by the Spirit of God, these are sons of God. . . . The Spirit Himself bears witness with our spirit that we are children of God" (Romans 8:14,16).

◆

# CHAPTER 11

# Did the Mormon Church Ever Teach that Adam Was the True God?

The Mormon church has long been embarrassed by an odd teaching of its early prophets. They believed that the God of this earth was not Elohim, as the modern church holds, but rather Adam of the Garden of Eden.

Brigham Young started the controversy April 9, 1852, by stating of Adam, "He is our father and our God, and the only God with whom we have to do."[116] (This sermon is quoted at length in chap. 12, point 2.) He further added, "There are many who know that doctrine to be true."[117] Young had no doubts on this issue; in fact, he declared that the doctrine was "the word of the Lord":

> Concerning the item of Doctrine alluded to . . . that Adam is our father and God, I have to say do not trouble yourselves, neither let the Saints be troubled about the matter. . . . If, as Elder Caffall remarked, there are those who are waiting at the door of the Church for this objection to be removed tell such, the Prophet and Apostle Brigham Young has declared it, and *that it is the word of the Lord.*[118]

Many other Mormons, including leaders, agreed: "Adam is really God! And why not?"[119] Elder James Little remarked, "I believe in the principle of obedience; and if I am told that Adam is our father and our God, I just believe it."[120] Another observed that because President Young "says that Adam is our God—the God we worship—that most of the people believe this."[121]

Naturally, if Adam were God, then Jesus must be his son—the offspring of the sexual union of Adam and one of his celestial wives. There is plenty of evidence for this belief. Hosea Stout observed, "President B. Young taught that Adam was the father of Jesus and the only God to us."[122] Heber Kimball noted, "That first man [Adam] sent his own Son to redeem the world!"[123] An early Mormon hymnal contained the following hymn titled "We Believe in Our God," which included the phrase "Our own Father Adam, earth's Lord, as is plain. . . . We believe in His Son Jesus Christ."[124] George Cannon, a member of the First Presidency, emphasized that "Jesus Christ is Jehovah" and that "Adam is his father and our God."[125]

These are only a few of the citations that could be listed. Mormon polygamist John Musser, the late Christian authority on Mormonism, Dr. Walter Martin, and former Mormons Jerald and Sandra Tanner cite literally dozens of similar statements that include evidence to corroborate that early Mormon leaders believed in Adam as their God.[126]

In conclusion, it *was* believed that Adam was Elohim, the father of Jesus Christ, and that he became Jesus' father through his sexual union with Mary (see chap. 12). However although Brigham Young taught this doctrine as scripture, as he taught all his sermons were, any Mormon who teaches it today faces excommunication.

How does the church deal with this major discrepancy? In general, the church has attempted to ignore this teaching. For example, a recommended apologetic text published by the Mormon church, *A Sure Foundation: Answers to Difficult Gospel Questions* doesn't even mention the issue. When confronted, Mormons have also denied that it was ever even taught. Bruce McConkie called it an *invention* of "cultists and other enemies of the restored truth [Mormonism]."[127]

But whether the Adam-God doctrine is vehemently denied, simply ignored, or craftily reinterpreted, no one familiar with the evidence can say that it was never a genuine teaching of Brigham Young and other early Mormon leaders—for it clearly was.

Another explanation is put forth by the tenth president and prophet of the Mormon church, Joseph Fielding Smith. He alleges that the April 9, 1852 sermon in which Brigham Young first taught this doctrine "was erroneously transcribed."[128] However, according to Dr. Walter Martin this sermon was "written down by four Mormon scholars so there was no doubt that he said it and he signed it."[129]

If the Adam-God doctrine was somehow a scribal error, how did so many Mormons come to believe it? Once the doctrine was circulating, it is incredible to think that Young would not have stepped forth, corrected the problem and pronounced true doctrine in the hearing of all. But even when this doctrine was causing many Mormons to leave the church, he never did this. There is no record of a retraction or correction, despite the fact that according to a formerly devout Mormon of the time, "This public declaration [of April 9, 1852] gave great offense and led to the apostasy of many."[130]

Why would Brigham Young ever permit heresy to be circulated under his name without so much as a protest? No evidence exists that Young complained his lectures were distorted by copiers. And certainly no devout Mormon scribe would seek to deliberately pervert the words of a revered prophet—words they confidently considered as coming from the mouth of God Himself! If there were a suspicion of error, would not these copiers seek clarification? Finally, how could it be a scribal error when so many other Mormon leaders accepted the teaching *because* Brigham Young himself had declared it was "God's word?" The scribal error theory is thus not credible.

Nevertheless, Joseph Fielding Smith says only "the enemies of the Church" teach such a doctrine. If so, this would make Brigham Young himself one of the "enemies of the Church." Smith asserts that "Adam is not Elohim, or the God whom we worship, who is the father of Jesus Christ."[131]

Mormon apologist Mark Peterson in *Adam: Who Is He?* also maintains the scribal error theory.[132] He too confesses that "Adam was not Deity" and that "to say that Adam is God is, of course, opposed utterly and completely to the Scriptures as well as to our *Articles of Faith*."[133]

But no one argues that this teaching is currently held. The question is, did early Mormon authorities hold to this doctrine? And if so, doesn't this mean they too were "opposed utterly and completely to the Scriptures . . . [and] the *Articles of Faith*?"

Mormons who are more frank with the evidence at least concede that Brigham Young made some strange statements. An example of this is Dr. Stephen Robinson, chairman of the Department of Ancient Scripture at Brigham Young University. He confesses—a bit sheepishly—that Brigham Young "made some remarks about the relationship between Adam and God that Latter-day Saints have never been able to understand."[134] Noting that Young's teachings on Adam not only conflict with Young's other teachings but also with those of the modern church as well, he asks, "So how do Latter-day Saints deal with the phenomenon? We don't; we simply set it aside. It is an anomaly."[135]

Dr. Robinson seems to imply this was *only* a teaching of Brigham Young and that, besides, it is a largely irrelevant issue. Further, he says that whatever Brigham Young taught, it was never a doctrine of the church because it was never presented to the church for a sustaining vote. Finally, he falsely charges critics with distorting what Brigham Young really taught. But read the larger portion of Young's sermon in chapter 12, Section 2; then consider Robinson's arguments below and see if they are credible:

> According to them [critics] Brigham Young taught that Adam, the husband of Eve and the father of Cain, is identical to that Elohim who is God, the father of spirits and the father of Jesus Christ. But for Latter-day Saints this interpretation has always been simply impossible. It contradicts the LDS

scripture; it contradicts the teachings of Joseph Smith; it contradicts other statements by Brigham Young... it contradicts
the teachings of all the prophets since Brigham Young.

Latter-day Saints have never believed that Brigham Young
taught the "Adam-God theory" as explained in anti-Mormon
literature, and that whether Brigham Young believed it or not,
the "Adam-God theory" as proposed and interpreted by non-
Mormons simply cannot be found in the theology of the
Latter-day Saints. I do not believe it; my parents do not believe
it; and neither did their parents before them. Yet, there are few
anti-Mormon publications that do not present this "Adam-
God theory," the doctrinal creation of our opponents, as one
of the most characteristic doctrines of the Latter-day Saints.
This is certainly misrepresentation; I believe it is also dishon-
est.[136]

In other words, he also claims that Brigham Young never really taught
the doctrine, but that even if he did, it isn't current doctrine.

But we know of no responsible Christian apologist who has ever
maintained that the Adam-God teaching is the current doctrine of the
modern church. But Young did call it "the word of the Lord," and the
Mormon church has rejected it. Further, over twenty years later, in 1873,
Brigham Young remarked concerning this teaching, "How much unbelief exists in the minds of the Latter-day Saints about one doctrine which I
revealed to them and which God revealed to me."[137] Thus, we do not
think Dr. Robinson is correct when he implies the issue is unimportant or
irrelevant. We already documented that Young himself claimed all his
sermons were scripture. If so, how can the modern church logically reject
the teaching? But if he was wrong, how can the modern church uphold
him as a true authority from God? And if Young contradicts both himself
and the modern church, so much the worse for the credibility of both.

Let us cite an illustration of why we think this issue *is* important. Billy
Graham is certainly as important to the Christian church of the twentieth
century as Brigham Young was to the Mormon church of the nineteenth
century. If Billy Graham preached a sermon in which he taught that the
biblical God was really the Hindu god Krishna—and he continued to
emphasize this was "the word of the Lord"—he would have his ordination revoked and be discredited. If Dr. Graham continued to maintain
such heresy, it would result in his spiritual discipline, and his ministry
would be ended.

Likewise, for someone as influential and important to Mormon history and doctrine as Brigham Young to teach the Adam-God theory
places not only his judgment, but also certainly his knowledge of the
Scriptures into serious doubt. But Young was never subjected to church
discipline—he continues today to be revered by all Mormons as "God's

Prophet." But given such heresy, how can he be upheld as a true prophet of God? And if he is an impostor, why did the early Mormon church accept him as God's messenger?

No one knows why this doctrine was introduced. Brigham Young could simply have received a revelation. Nevertheless, it is at least possible that it was because Adam was so highly regarded for his role in the Fall, and the alleged blessings it produced for mankind, that in gratitude Young and other early Mormons gave him the status of a god.[138] (See chap. 16, appendix.) One could also suspect that this entire episode is one more example of how spiritistic revelation leads to contradictory (and often embarrassing) theology.

The fact that Mormons now deny this doctrine might be attributed to ignorance of historical theology, but consider the words of noted Mormon apologist and historian, Brigham Henry Roberts on the subject. Roberts is praised, even in the modern Mormon church, as a devoted Mormon with a great intellect. For example, John W. Welch, Professor of Law and president of the Foundation for Ancient Research and Mormon Studies (FARMS) at Brigham Young University, describes Roberts as "fiercely loyal to the Church of Jesus Christ of Latter-day Saints," and that for "all of his life, B.H. Roberts sought after truth, spiritually and intellectually."[139] He is further described as "one of the most intellectual General Authorities of his day."[140] Roberts was president of the Eastern States Mission from 1922 to 1927 as well as one of the seven Presidents of the Seventy from 1888 until his death in 1933. Again, he is described as one "whose search for truth was an all-consuming passion."[141] Yet in his *Mormon Doctrine of Deity*, Roberts wrote as late as 1903:

> Some of the sectarian [Christian] ministers are saying that we "Mormons" are ashamed of the doctrine announced by President Brigham Young to the affect that Adam will thus be the God of this world. No, friends, it is not that we are ashamed of that doctrine. If you see any change come over our countenances when this doctrine is named, it is surprise, astonishment, that anyone at all capable of grasping the largeness and extent of the universe . . . should be so lean of intellect, should have such a positive understanding, as to call it in question at all.[142]

In conclusion, when Mormons claim that the Adam-God doctrine is irrelevant, a fabrication of the enemies of the church or a scribal error, they are refusing to acknowledge the confusion and heresy of their own second president and prophet. As we note in chapter 12, point 2, they are also attempting to avoid even more embarrassing implications.

# What Is the Mormon View of Jesus Christ?

Joseph Smith is a powerful witness of Jesus Christ.

—*The Plan of Our Heavenly Father*, 11

When the Savior shall appear we shall see him as he is. We shall see that he is a man like ourselves.

—Joseph Smith, (*D&C*, 130:1)

From the beginning, the Mormon church has confessed its devoted allegiance to Jesus Christ. Around the world, Mormon literature emphatically claims to accept and revere the biblical Christ. For example, the publicity booklet published by the Mormon church, "What the Mormons Think of Christ" asserts:

Christ is our Redeemer and our Savior. Except for him there would be no salvation and no redemption, and unless men come unto him and accept him as their Savior, they cannot have eternal life in his presence.[142]

This booklet further states that "He—Jesus Christ—is the Savior of the world and the Divine Son of God."[143]

In his book *Are Mormons Christians?*, written in an attempt to prove to the world that Mormons are Christians, Dr. Stephen Robinson emphasizes over and over that Mormons believe in the true biblical Jesus Christ.

In fact, he claims that the evidence is so persuasive that Mormons believe in Jesus Christ that critics have never even dared to raise the issue!

> ... of all the various arguments against Latter-day Saints being considered Christians, *not one—not a single one*—claims that Latter-day Saints don't acknowledge Jesus Christ as Lord. ... When the charge is made that "Mormons aren't Christians," the very first impression created in the minds of the average individual is that Latter-day Saints don't believe in Jesus Christ. ... Yet in the arguments offered to support the assertion the only issue that really matters is *never even raised*: Do the Latter-day Saints believe in Jesus Christ? Do they accept him as Lord? Do they believe that he is the way, the truth, and the life, and that no man cometh unto the father but by him? These crucial questions are never asked.[144]

Dr. Robinson has apparently not read very many Christian apologetic works. Christian treatments of Mormonism consistently maintain that Mormons do *not* acknowledge the true Jesus Christ as Lord—they cannot do this because they do not believe in the true Jesus Christ. But Dr. Robinson proceeds to make another false claim: "Nor do the LDS scriptures teach anything about Christ that the rest of the Christian world would find offensive." Finally he winds up the discussion by saying, "Though all the world may say that Latter-day Saints do not know or love or worship Jesus Christ, I know that we do, and if this is not the issue in question, or if this is not enough to be counted a Christian, then the word has lost its meaning."*[145]

But Dr. Robinson is still wrong. The real issue is which "Jesus Christ" one believes in. The simple truth is that Mormons may proclaim their belief in Jesus Christ throughout the entire world, but like countless other sects and cults they believe in a false, pagan Christ who has nothing whatever to do with the biblical Jesus. In fact, as the chart below shows, the Mormon Christ and the biblical Christ are so incompatible that not a single resemblance can be found between them.

Nevertheless, the proliferation of statements by Mormons that they reverently believe in Jesus Christ has even confused some Christians. For example, Frank Morley of Grace Presbyterian Church in Alberta, Canada permits the Mormon church to publish and promote a lecture by him supporting Mormonism. In it he explains, "It had been said to me that

---

\* In fact, far from "loving and worshipping" Him, Mormonism teaches it is an abomination to pray to Jesus—that is unless, as a resurrected personage, He is standing immediately before one. For example, "To whom did Stephen pray? Sectarian [Christian] commentators say he prayed to Jesus and not to the Father, and they accordingly claim this instance as justification for the apostate practice of addressing prayers to the Son."[146] Further, "As an indication of how far removed most of them are from the true form of prayer is the fact many of them ... are addressed directly to Christ."[147]

Mormons don't believe in Jesus Christ! [It is] such superstitions and misunderstanding we have regarding them, you see, that need clearing up."[148]

In this chapter we will prove that the Mormon Jesus Christ and the biblical Jesus Christ are as far apart as day and night. Likewise the Apostle Paul had occasion to warn some of the Corinthians that they were receiving "another Christ," a false Christ that was not the true biblical Christ. "For if someone comes to you and preaches a Jesus other than the Jesus we preached, . . . you put up with it easily enough" (1 Corinthians 11:4). This is the only issue concerning Mormonism's claims about Jesus. Does it believe in the true Jesus Christ, or not? Before we begin our discussion, we supply the following chart for contrast:

| The Mormon Jesus Christ | The Biblical Jesus Christ |
| --- | --- |
| ◆ A created being; the elder brother of Lucifer | Uncreated God |
| ◆ Common (one of many gods) and of minor importance in the *larger* Mormon cosmology | Unique (the Second Person of the one and only Godhead) and of supreme importance throughout time, eternity and all creation |
| ◆ Conceived by a physical sex act between God the Father (Adam or Elohim) and Mary, thus not through a true virgin birth | Conceived by the Holy Spirit, who supernaturally "overshadowed" Mary, thus a true virgin birth |
| ◆ Once sinful and imperfect | Eternally sinless and perfect |
| ◆ Earned his own salvation (exaltation) | As God, never required salvation |
| ◆ A married polygamist? | An unmarried monogamist |

Anyone who concludes that these two teachings offer the same Jesus Christ simply isn't thinking. We will now proceed to document the Mormon view of Christ. We will prove that they have taken the biblical Jesus Christ and because of their new, occult revelations, transformed Him into a pagan deity.

For the convenience of the reader, we divide most of this data into three basic sections:

1. The Mormon rejection of Christ's unique deity.

2. The Mormon denial of Christ's virgin birth.

3. The Mormon impugning of Christ's eternal sinlessness.

*Mormon Teaching No. 1—Mormons Deny Christ's Unique Deity*

Mormonism maintains it believes and teaches the true deity of Jesus Christ. However, although it is correct that Mormons believe that Christ is *a* god, they do not in any sense accept Christ's deity according to Christian or biblical orthodox teaching. For example, Mormons teach that a) Christ is a created being, b) Christ is a "common god" who is not unique in essence, but primarily in mission—in His function and priority, and c) Christ is Satan's brother. We discuss these in turn.

a. *Mormonism teaches that Jesus Christ is a created being.*

To understand the Mormon view of Christ, we need to remember that Mormonism teaches that every person has two births—first, birth as a spirit child in preexistence and second, much later, birth as a human being.

According to Mormon theology Christ was the first and foremost of subsequent billions of spirit children created through sexual intercourse between the male earth god and his celestial wife. Later, in order to produce the body for this special spirit child, the earth god again had sexual intercourse, this time with the "virgin" Mary, who then became Jesus' earthly mother.

As we saw in our discussion of the Adam-God doctrine, early Mormon prophets taught that Christ (spirit and body) was the offspring of both the earth god *Adam* and his celestial wife—and then later of Adam and Mary. Modern Mormons maintain that Christ was the offspring of a different exalted man (*Elohim*, not Adam) who was nevertheless still the literal, physical father of Jesus Christ. Whatever view is held, Mormonism asserts that Jesus Christ is a created being. (See appendix.) He was created in preexistence, and through "probation, progression, and schooling" exalted himself as the premier spirit child. Theologian Bruce McConkie describes the creation of Jesus Christ in these words:

> From the time of their spirit birth, the father's preexistent offspring were endowed with agency and subjected to the provisions of the laws ordained for their government. They had power to obey or disobey and to progress in one field or another. . . . The preexistent life was thus a long period—undoubtedly an infinitely long one—of probation, progression, and schooling. . . . Christ, the Firstborn, was the mightiest of all the spirit children of the father (*D&C*, 93:21-23).[149]

Mormons also claim that Jesus is the "Jehovah" of the Old Testament. Thus, whenever the Bible refers to Jehovah, for Mormons, it refers to Jesus Christ in his preexistent state. (Christians, on the other hand, teach this term refers to God.) Mormon authority James Talmage explains in his

*Articles of Faith*, "Among the spirit children of Elohim the firstborn was and is Jehovah or Jesus Christ to whom all others are juniors."*[150]

**b.** Mormonism teaches that Jesus Christ is a "common" god and of minor importance in the larger Mormon cosmology.

We have now seen that Mormonism teaches that Christ was a created being. But Mormon church teaching logically implies Christ is also a common god of only relative importance. Mormons do refer to Christ as being "greater" than all other spirit children on earth. But remember, this earth is only one of an infinite number of earths, each having their own gods who have existed and evolved for aeons longer than Christ. Further, Christ is our "senior" only by achievement and position, *not* by nature or essence.

The *essence* of Christ is no different from the essence of any spirit child of Elohim, whether of men, or Satan and his demons. Every person on earth has the same nature and essence as Jesus Christ, and He as they. Although Christ performed better than others in preexistence, He is nevertheless of one nature with all men. Thus, Mormons universally refer to Him as their "elder brother." No one can deny then that Mormonism logically teaches that Jesus Christ is not unique in essence, but only in His achievement and mission. For example, Christ is not unique in His deity, His incarnation, or His capacity as Creator.

His "divinity" is not unique, for every exalted man will attain a similar godhood.

Neither is His "incarnation" unique, for *all men* are incarnated spirit beings—in preexistence the offspring of the sexual union of the gods, who then take tabernacles of flesh. Indeed, Christ was only "unique" in His *physical* birth in that rather than having a merely human father like the rest of us, His mother had physical sex with God. (See point 2 below.)

Christ is also not unique as creator of this earth, because Mormonism teaches that Adam, Joseph Smith and others *helped* Him to create it. Christ "was aided...by 'many of the noble and great' spirit children of the Father...Adam...Noah...Joseph Smith..." etc.[151]

Thus, the Mormon Jesus Christ is, in almost all respects, rather like the rest of us—at least as far as Mormons conceive of men. He just worked harder to exalt Himself in preexistence—He had more ambition, devotion and perhaps intelligence. But in basic nature He was no different from any of us. Mormon leader Milton R. Hunter, a member of the First Council of Seventy, asserted, "Jesus is man's spiritual brother. We dwelt with Him in the spirit world as members of that large society of eternal intelligences, which included our Heavenly Parents."[152] Mormon authority James Talmage explains: "Human beings generally were similarly existent in spirit state prior to their embodiment in the flesh. . . . There is

---

*For a discussion of why Mormons refer to Christ as "eternal," see the appendix.

no impropriety, therefore, in speaking of Jesus Christ as the Elder Brother of the rest of humankind."[153]

c: Mormonism teaches that Christ is Satan's brother.

Indeed, Mormon theology holds that Jesus Christ is even the spirit brother of Satan himself. Since Satan (and his demons) were also preexistent spirit creations of Elohim and his celestial wife, Satan is therefore Christ's brother as well. In fact, the devil and all demons are the spirit brothers of everyone on earth! In other words, Christ, the devil and all of us are literally brothers! Jess L. Christensen, director of the LDS Institute of Religion at Utah State University in Logan, Utah, writes in *A Sure Foundation*, "But both the scriptures and the prophets affirm that Jesus Christ and Lucifer are indeed offspring of our Heaven Father and, therefore, spirit brothers. . . . Jesus was Lucifer's older brother."[154] Thus, one Mormon writer concludes, "As for the devil and his fellow spirits, they are brothers to man and also to Jesus and sons and daughters to God in the same sense that we are."[155] In essence then, according to Mormon theology, the difference between Christ and the devil is not really one of kind, but only one of degree.

Who can maintain that this is Christian or biblical teaching? In light of the above doctrines—and many more—we must be careful *not* to accept Mormon claims concerning their belief in Christ's uniqueness or His deity. They may claim to exalt Him, for, as McConkie says, "He shall reign to all eternity as King of Kings and Lord of Lords, and God of Gods."[156] But what is often not understood is that literally millions of other people will likewise reign, for as Brigham Young emphasized, all men are "the king of kings and lord of lords in embryo."[157]

*Mormon Teaching No. 2—Mormons Deny Christ's Virgin Birth Through the Holy Spirit: Mormonism's Spirit Adultery and Incest—The Father and Mary's Sexual Union*

In his controversial Adam-God discourse of April 9, 1852, Brigham Young taught that the body of Jesus Christ was the product of sexual intercourse between God (Adam) and Mary, who then subsequently married Joseph. But since God (Adam) was also the literal, physical Father of Mary (Mary being his literal spirit offspring through celestial intercourse), this amounts to an incestuous and adulterous relationship, for at the same time she was betrothed in marriage to Joseph.

In essence, Mormonism teaches that Mary had sex with both her literal Father in heaven (God Himself) and her literal spirit brother, Joseph! Unfortunately, one apparent effect of this teaching, at least in the minds of some, was to give divine sanction to "spiritual" adultery and even incest—and thus to render the incidents of incestuous polygamy and adultery in Mormon history more acceptable. "After all," they must have reasoned that "God Himself engaged in such practices." (See chap. 29.)

In any case, because of this teaching, Mormonism denies that Jesus Christ is the product of the Holy Ghost and maintains He is the offspring of the Father only. Why? Because according to Mormon theology the Holy Ghost does not have a physical body. As such, He could not have literally had sexual intercourse with Mary in order to produce the body of Jesus. On the other hand, Mormon theology teaches that the Father does have a physical body "of flesh and bones." He could easily have had physical sex with Mary to produce the body of Jesus. This is why Brigham Young taught that if Christ had been conceived by the Holy Ghost it would have to have been through physical, sexual intercourse. And, if this were true, it would be "very dangerous" to give women the Holy Ghost lest He impregnate them and Mormon elders be held accountable for fornication! Also, it would of necessity require that Jesus be the literal son of the Holy Ghost rather than the literal son of the Father, which was not acceptable to Brigham Young and also to modern Mormons. Thus, the role of the Holy Spirit in the virgin birth of Jesus Christ, so clearly stated in Matthew 1:18 and Luke 1:35, is rejected by Mormons. Below we produce a lengthy portion of Brigham Young's "inspired" pronouncements which, as we have documented in chapter 5, he defined as "the word of the Lord":

> I will tell you how it is. Our Father in heaven begat all the spirits that ever were, or ever will be, upon this earth; and they were born spirits in the eternal world. Then the Lord by his power and wisdom organized the mortal tabernacle of man. We were made first spiritual, and afterwards temporal.
>
> Now hear it, O inhabitants of the earth, Jew and Gentile, Saint and Sinner! When our Father Adam came into the Garden of Eden, he came into it with a *celestial body*, and brought Eve, *one of his wives*, with him. He helped to make and organize this world. He is MICHAEL, *the Archangel*, THE ANCIENT OF DAYS! about whom holy men have written and spoken—he *is our* Father *and our God, and the only God with whom we have to do.* Every man upon the earth, professing Christians or non-professing, must hear it, and will know it sooner or later. . . . When the Virgin Mary conceived the child Jesus, the Father had begotten him in his own likeness. He was not begotten by the Holy Ghost. And who is the Father? He is the first of the human family [i.e., Adam]; and when he took a tabernacle [body], it was begotten by *his Father* in heaven, after the same manner as the tabernacles of Cain, Abel, and the rest of the sons and daughters of Adam and Eve.
>
> Jesus, our elder brother, *was begotten in the flesh by the same character that was in the Garden of Eden* [i.e., Adam], and who is our Father in heaven. Now, that all who may hear these doctrines [will] pause before they make light of them, or treat

them with indifference, *for they will prove their salvation or damnation.*

Now remember from this time forth, and forever that *Jesus Christ was not begotten by the Holy Ghost.* . . . "If the son was begotten by the Holy Ghost, it would be very dangerous to baptize and confirm females and give the Holy Ghost to them, lest he should beget children to be palmed upon the Elders by the people, bringing the Elders into great difficulties."[158]

No wonder this bizarre and even blasphemous doctrine has caused the Mormon church so much trouble. And no wonder Mormons don't know what to do with this statement of Brigham Young!

Thus, Mormons today accept the "virgin" birth of Jesus Christ to have been accomplished through physical sexual intercourse between God (now Elohim) and Mary, but they deny that God was Adam. Nevertheless, because "sexuality . . . is actually an attribute of God . . . [and] God is a procreating personage of flesh and bone, Latter-day prophets have made it clear that despite what it says in Matthew 1:20, the Holy Ghost was not the father of Jesus."[159]

In his *Doctrines of Salvation*, the tenth Mormon president and prophet, Joseph Fielding Smith, taught, "Christ was begotten of God. He was not born without the aid of Man and *that Man was God!*"[160] Theologian McConkie declares, "Christ was begotten by an Immortal Father *in the same way* that mortal men are begotten by mortal fathers."[161]

The current president and prophet of the Mormon church, Ezra Taft Benson, also believes that God the Father had physical sex with Mary:

> The paternity of Jesus Christ is one of the "mysteries of godliness" comprehended only by the spiritually minded. . . . An ancient [Mormon] prophet had a vision. He saw Mary and described her as "a virgin, most beautiful and fair above all other virgins." He then saw her "carried away in the Spirit . . . for the space of a time." When she returned, she was "bearing a child in her arms . . . even the Son of the Eternal Father" (1 Nephi 11:15,19-21). . . . Jesus Christ is the Son of God in the most literal sense. The body in which he performed his mission in the flesh was sired by that same Holy Being we worship as God, our Eternal Father. Jesus was not the son of Joseph, nor was he begotten by the Holy Ghost. He is the son of the Eternal Father.[162]

The logical implication of Mormon theology seems evident. Mary was apparently a bigamist, being married to both God Himself and Joseph! (Either that or, if she was not married to God, she was a fornicator with Him.) Brigham Young stated: "The man Joseph, the husband of Mary, did not, that we know of, have more than one wife, but Mary the wife of Joseph had another husband [i.e., God]."[163]

Mormons believe that Mary had to be the "legitimate" wife of God, of course, otherwise even God would have been guilty of adultery! Apparently, while Mormons will accept God having sex with many different wives, they will not have Him engaging in illicit sex! In *The Seer* of October, 1853 apostle Orson Pratt was more than frank—freely confessing that God Himself is not bound by the moral laws He gave to men (on adultery, for instance):

> The Father and Mother of Jesus, according to the flesh, must have been associated together in the capacity of Husband and Wife; hence the Virgin Mary must have been, for the time being, the lawful wife of God the Father.... It would have been unlawful for any man to have interfered with Mary, who was already a spouse to Joseph; for such a heinous crime would have subjected both the guilty parties to death, according to the law of Moses. But God having created all men and women, had the most perfect right to do with his own creation, according to his holy will and pleasure: He had a lawful right to overshadow the virgin Mary in the capacity of a husband, and beget a Son, although she was a spouse to another; for the law which he gave to govern men and women was not intended to govern himself, or to prescribe rules for his own conduct. It was also lawful in him, after having thus dealt with Mary, to give her to Joseph as her espoused husband.... Inasmuch as God was the first husband to her, it may be that he only gave her to be the wife of Joseph while in this mortal state, and that he intended after the resurrection to again take her as one of his own wives to raise up immortal spirits in eternity.[164]

Thus, God had sex with Mary, "instead of letting any other man do it"—and therein lies the alleged "uniqueness of Jesus!" As Brigham Young wrote:

> When the time came that his first born, the Saviour, should come into the world and take a tabernacle [body], the Father came Himself and favoured that spirit with a tabernacle instead of letting any other man do it.... And that is all the organic difference between Jesus Christ and you and me.... If you see and understand these things, it will be by the Spirit of God; you will receive them by no other spirit.[165]

Not everyone would agree with that last statement. The lying spirits the Bible identifies as demons characteristically teach such doctrines to men who listen to them (1 Timothy 4:1).

Such teachings are hardly biblical; they are similar to occult and pagan teachings, not Christian ones. Dr. Anthony Hoekema appropriately concludes:

> What these men are saying is that, according to Mormon theology, the body of Jesus Christ was a product of the physical union of God the father and the virgin Mary. One shudders to think of the revolting implications of this view, which brings into what is supposed to be "Christian" theology one of the most unsavory features of ancient pagan mythology![166]

The Bible clearly denies Mormon teaching when it affirms Christ's true virgin (Gk *parthenos*) birth:

> Now the birth of Jesus Christ was as follows. When his mother Mary had been betrothed to Joseph, before they came together, she was found to be with child by the Holy Spirit (Matthew 1:18).
>
> "And behold, you will conceive in your womb, and bear a son, and you shall name him Jesus." . . . And Mary said to the angel, "How can this be, since I am a virgin? [*parthenos*]" And the angel answered and said to her, "The Holy Spirit will come upon you, and the power of the Most High will overshadow you; and for that reason the holy offspring shall be called the Son of God" (Luke 1:31,34,35).

*Mormon Teaching No. 3—Mormons Impugn the Eternal Sinlessness of Christ*

Having discussed the Mormons' rejection of Christ's unique deity, and their denial of His virgin birth, our final concern is to document their rejection of Christ's eternal sinlessness. While Mormons staunchly claim they affirm that Christ is sinless, this is unfortunately more equivocation.[167] Mormons accept the sinlessness of Christ while on this earth, but they do not logically maintain he was sinless for all eternity past.

Mormon theology holds that men can only become gods after an extended period of pre-life probation where they are free to choose between good and evil. All Mormon spirits of the past have learned to choose good by their experience of evil. Thus, if Mormon theology teaches that Christ (a good Mormon) earned His own salvation and godhood through moral trial and error, they can hardly maintain that He was forever sinless. We will now document this.

Mormonism teaches that Christ earned His own salvation and godhood.

As we have shown, Jesus was only one of innumerable spirit offspring of the earth god and his celestial wife, and therefore no different in nature from any other spirit. He, too, had to undertake schooling and progression in the spirit world for aeons upon aeons and then attain his own salvation. He had to be tested with good and evil, initially at least, falling into evil like every other spirit son. As we will see in the appendix to chapter 16, Mormonism teaches it is only by direct experience of evil that men learn to choose good. Further, just like every good Mormon, Jesus also had to *earn* the right to become God.

The following statements indicate that Mormonism views Jesus Christ as a created being who earned His own salvation, eternal life and godhood. Bruce McConkie confesses that "Christ... is a saved being."[168] The official student manual, *Doctrines of the Gospel*, teaches that "the plan of salvation which he [Elohim] designed was to save his children, Christ included; and that neither Christ nor Lucifer could of themselves save anyone."[169] (According to Mormon theology, in pre-history both Lucifer and Christ presented plans of salvation to Elohim; Elohim chose Christ's plan, which provoked Lucifer's rebellion.)

The same manual also quotes the tenth president and prophet Joseph Fielding Smith on the subject:

> The Savior did not have a fullness [of deity] at first, but after he received his body and the resurrection all power was given unto him both in heaven and in earth. Although he was a God, even the Son of God, with power and authority to create this earth and other earths, yet there were some things lacking in which he did not receive until after his resurrection. In other words, he had not received the fullness until he got a resurrected body.[170]

Thus, even though, according to current president and prophet Ezra Taft Benson, "Jesus was a God in the pre-mortal existence" He was still imperfect and lacking certain necessary things.[171]

Bruce McConkie taught, "These laws [of salvation], instituted by the father, constitute the gospel of God, which gospel is the plan by which all of his spirit children, Christ included, may gain eternal life."[172]

McConkie also stated that "Jesus Christ is the Son of God.... He came to earth to work out his own salvation."[173] And that "by obedience and devotion to the truth he attained that pinnacle of intelligence which ranked him as a God."[174] A Mormon publicity booklet, "What the Mormons Think of Christ" asserts that "Christ, the Word, the First Born, had of course, attained unto the status of Godhood while yet in preexistence."[175]

Remember, this was an indeterminate period of time that involved endless aeons. If Christ learned to choose good over evil by experience and *attained* perfection by "probation, progression and·schooling," it is difficult indeed to logically conceive of Christ as being perfectly sinless throughout the entire period of his probation and preexistence.

*Was Christ a Polygamist?*

Some early Mormons taught that both God and Christ were polyga-mists. Thus, even on earth, Christ would have violated the will of God concerning at least one sin—polygamy. In Deuteronomy 17:17 and Levit-icus 18:18 God warned against plural marriage, both for kingly rulers and others. The New Testament also upholds marriage to only one woman (1 Timothy 3:2,12; Titus 1:6). Jesus Himself upheld the standard of mar-riage to only one woman based on the pattern of Adam and Eve, which was obviously God's choice, for He brought to Adam only one wife, not several (Matthew 19:4,5; Mark 10:2-8). Nevertheless, Jedediah M. Grant, second counselor to Brigham Young, stated in 1853 that "a belief in the doctrine of a plurality of wives caused the persecution of Jesus and his followers. We might almost think they are 'Mormons.' "[176] Grant implies Jesus was persecuted and crucified because "He had so many wives," including Elizabeth (he possibly refers to the wife of Zecharias), Mary, "and a host of others."[177] If Jesus was married to another man's wife, of course, that was adultery.

Nevertheless, if some Mormons taught that Jesus was married to another man's wife, we should not be surprised. As we will later docu-ment, both Joseph Smith, Brigham Young, and many other Mormon leaders were married to other men's wives while they themselves were married to their own numerous wives (chap. 29). Apostle Orson Hyde observed:

> I discovered that some of the Eastern papers represent me as a great blasphemer, because I said, in my lecture on Mar-riage, at our last Conference, that Jesus Christ was married at Cana of Galilee, that Mary, Martha, and others were his wives, and that he begat children. All that I have to say in reply to that charge is this—they worship a Savior that is too pure and holy to fulfill the commands of his Father.... If Jesus begat chil-dren, he only "did that which he had seen his Father do."[178]

Orson Pratt stated, "The founder of the Christian religion, was a Polygamist.... The Messiah chose to... by marrying many honorable wives himself, show to all future generations that he approbated the plurality of Wives under the Christian dispensation."[179]

While Mormons today generally teach that Christ was not a polyga-mist, a significant number do, especially among the many polygamist Mormon cults.[180]

In conclusion, this then is the Mormon Jesus Christ—a vague, eternal "spirit element" organized into a spirit child by sexual intercourse of the earth god and his celestial wife; the common brother of Lucifer, one of many spirit children who earned his salvation, immortality and god-hood, and perhaps, as some Mormons say, a polygamist as well.

Yet Mormon missionaries will come to the prospective convert's door with this crude polytheism and say in full sincerity they are committed Christians who believe in the biblical Jesus Christ! True Mormons do not believe in Christ; they do not even know Christ. Indeed, they officially reject and attack as heresy the idea that a man or woman should seek a personal relationship with Christ.[181] In his lecture, "Our Relationship With the Lord" Mormon apostle Bruce McConkie does just this (see Resource List).

The Mormon church is thus *not* the church of Jesus Christ—it is the church of Joseph Smith.

Yet even Mormons will admit, "If a professing minister of salvation is not a witness for Christ, he is not a prophet." We find that assessment hard to disagree with.

But in conclusion, note once again the contrast between the biblical Christ and the Mormon Christ.

| Biblical Christ | Mormon Christ |
| --- | --- |
| Deity | Not true deity (earned godhood) |
| Sinless | Sinful |
| Virgin born | Not virgin born |
| Eternal | Created |
| Unmarried | Polygamist? |

## ◆ ◆ *Conclusion* ◆ ◆

As we have seen, the Mormon view of God is not Christian. Mormonism denies the God of the Bible in 1) accepting polytheism and 2) teaching the doctrine of the Trinity as a belief in tritheism or three separate Gods. Mormons may claim that they believe in the biblical God and Trinity, but, in fact, they have invented a new God, a new Jesus Christ, and a new Holy Ghost/Spirit that have little to do with the God of Orthodox Christian faith.

## ◆ ◆ *Appendix* ◆ ◆

### Why Do Mormons Refer to Christ As Eternal?

When Mormons refer to Christ as "eternal" many Christians assume this to be an affirmation of Christ's deity. But this is only another illustration of Mormon equivocation. Mormonism does not accept that Jesus is eternal as the Second Person of the Godhead, which is Christian teaching. The only sense in which "Jesus" is eternal is according to their vague, mercurial doctrine of spirit intelligence. Mormonism believes that *all life* existed eternally as some type of seemingly undifferentiated mass of incorporeal intelligence. Human life apparently passes through at least four stages:

1. As vague, undefined, uncreated, eternally-existing "intelligences";

2. As "spirit children" in the pre-mortal spirit world, having been mysteriously remolded by means of the physical, sexual intercourse of God and one of his wives; (We then enter a lengthy period of probation, schooling and progression which determines the nature and quality of our life on earth—being born into a Mormon family is a reward for attained excellence in preexistence).

3. As earthly beings, where we inhabit physical bodies and, if we are good Mormons, have the opportunity to earn exaltation (attain godhood); and

4. As resurrected beings in postmortem states of various degrees of glory determined by our achievement on earth (the celestial, terrestrial or telestial kingdoms).

Christ must have "existed" then in some nebulous form before His spirit birth, probation and schooling, and His subsequent fleshly life on earth. The Mormon scripture *Doctrine and Covenants* teaches that "man was also in the beginning with God. Intelligence, or the light of truth, was not created or made, neither indeed can be" (*D&C*, 93:29). Thus, just as "the [material] elements are eternal" (*D&C*, 93:33), so "Spirit element (that is, 'the intelligence of spirits') always existed.     'The intelligence of spirits had no beginning.'"[182]

The spirit children or offspring of the gods are apparently the result of fashioning or "remolding" of "spirit intelligence" (in whatever form) through sexual union. Apparently, sexual intercourse between the gods somehow has the power to refashion this mercurial spirit "intelligence" into spirit children. Doctrinal theologian McConkie explains:

> Spirit entities as such, in their organized form as the offspring of Deity, have not existed as long as God has, for he is their Father, and he begat them as spirits. Thus, there are two principles: 1) That "man was also in the beginning with God," meaning that the spirits of men were created, begotten, and organized, that they came into being as spirits at the time of their spirit birth; and 2) That "intelligence, or the light of truth, was not created or made, neither indeed can be" (*D&C*, 93:29), meaning that spirit element, "the intelligence of

spirits, 'the substance from which they were created as entities, has always existed and is as eternal as God himself.' "[183]

It would seem evident then that one reason Mormons think they can
become literal gods is that they existed as eternal "spirit element" prior to
their birth as spirit children and that this spirit element "substance"
partakes in some sense of the very nature of deity (see chap. 16). Nevertheless, this teaching denies and rejects the nature of Jesus Christ as the
eternal, Second Person of the Godhead. Biblically, Christ was never some
nebulous, unformed spirit element who came into existence as a preexistent spirit by the sexual intercourse of pagan gods. In nature and
essence, He always existed as the eternal Second Person of the Trinity:
"Jesus Christ is the same yesterday, today and forever" (Hebrews 13:28).

# Mormon Salvation and the Quest for Godhood

*How Do Mormons Become Gods?*

———————————— ◆ ——————————————

In this section we will discuss the Mormon concept of salvation. To begin, we will examine what Mormonism believes concerning salvation as a whole. Here we will examine how they divide salvation into two basic categories. First, there is general salvation—a "redemption" which comes to all men. Second, there is individual salvation, or the personal quest for godhood.

Next, we will show why the claim of the Mormon church to accept salvation by grace is false. After this, we will document the Mormon view of Christ's death on the cross. Although Mormons claim to believe in the atoning death of Christ, we will reveal that their belief is not orthodox. While they may believe that Christ paid for sin, it is only in a potential sense. Actual forgiveness of sin results only from obedience to Mormon law. Thus, what the atonement of Christ accomplished according to Mormonism was to present men and women with the opportunity to become gods themselves through obedience to Mormon precepts.

Finally, we will discuss what the Mormon church teaches about the afterlife and see whether or not its views on death, heaven and hell are biblical.

In this section we have also included five appendices concerning 1) the Mormon view of faith (chap. 13), 2) the Mormon attempt to morally distinguish Mosaic versus Gospel Law (chap. 14), 3) the biblical doctrine of justification by faith (chap. 14), 4) the Mormon view of sin and the Fall of man (chap. 16), and 5) the Mormon view of Satan and demons and the reason for their Fall (chap. 16).

CHAPTER 13

# What Does the Mormon Church Teach Concerning Salvation?

What does Mormonism believe about salvation as a whole? First, as noted earlier, Mormonism claims that it alone offers salvation to the world. No other church on the face of the earth can tell a man or woman how to be saved other than the Mormon church. This teaching flows from its claim to be the only true church on earth; therefore, "There is no salvation outside the Church of Jesus Christ of Latter-day Saints."[1]

Second, Mormon salvation is dependent upon the Fall of man.

According to the Mormon church, God planned that the Fall and sin would play an essential role in human salvation. God intended for there to be sin so that 1) mankind would be *capable* of having children who 2) could then grow in spiritual experience and discernment of right and wrong. In other words, the Fall *enabled* Adam and Eve to conceive children who would then have the opportunity to become gods by learning to choose good rather than evil.

Without the Fall there would have been no progeny of Adam and Eve, no physical bodies for the preexisting spirit children, no mankind for the earth god to rule, no increase of his kingdom from his children, and no experiential growing into godhood for any Mormon.

The Fall is thus a disguised blessing of nearly unparalleled proportions to Mormon people. Mormons are grateful to Adam for bringing about the Fall—which works to permit the true salvation (exaltation) of Mormons. Thus, Adam's role in salvation—his disobedience and Fall—is almost as important as that of Christ's. (See chap. 16, appendix.)

Third, the Mormon church distinguishes two kinds of redemption: "general" and "individual" salvation. Although the term "salvation" is used to describe the general category of redemption, it is only a partial redemption at best, not true or complete salvation. This general redemption is wrought by the atonement of Christ. It covers the effects of the Fall (physical and spiritual death) and produces resurrection from the dead.

It also determines, on the basis of personal merit, where among several options, any given individual will finally spend eternity.

In this chapter we will discuss the Mormon teaching on salvation as a whole. We will look at its basic division into the general and individual categories. In chapter 14, we will examine what Mormonism claims concerning salvation by grace. In chapter 15, we will see what the church teaches concerning the atonement of Jesus Christ. Because these three areas are interrelated, the material we discuss in this chapter overlaps to a degree with the others.

## A. General Redemption: Partial Salvation (Resurrection)

In Mormonism, general redemption is resurrection from the dead. Bruce McConkie teaches concerning the resurrection or general redemption, "In and of itself the resurrection is a form of salvation meaning that men are thereby saved from death, hell, the devil, and endless torment (2 Ne. 9:17-27). . . . In this sense, the mere fact of resurrection is called salvation by grace alone. Works are not involved."[2]

But, even in this so-called "general" redemption of grace, that is mere resurrection, men are still judged according to their works and consigned on that basis to different states in the afterlife. (In the *general* category of redemption this would be either the terrestrial or telestial kingdom; see below and chap. 17.) Thus, one can hardly argue that the "redemption" of such men is entirely by grace when their placement is dependent upon their works (Romans 11:6).

Those with less than appropriate works are consigned to lower kingdoms, and have no chance for full salvation or deification. Despite Mormon claims that they are saved from death, hell, the devil, and endless torment, they are only saved from annihilation. In general, when Mormons speak of eternal torment or punishment they refer to the punishment of forever remaining single and never becoming a god.[3]

But again, it must be stressed that while works are not required in order to *be* resurrected, they *do* determine whether one is consigned to the celestial, terrestrial or telestial kingdoms and one's placement within those kingdoms (see chap. 17).

Further, to properly understand Mormon salvation, we must learn their unique use of terms. These may sound Christian, but they are given new meanings. Thus, in Mormon theology "immortality" is not the same condition as described by the term "eternal life." "Immortality" means resurrection alone, and it can even involve "damnation." To be "damned" in Mormonism is, generally, not to be granted entrance into the celestial kingdom. Thus, Mormonism equates redemption by grace with a condition of damnation: "Immortality [general salvation] comes by grace alone, but those who gain it may find themselves damned in eternity" (Alma 11:37-45).[4] On the other hand, "eternal life" means inheriting godhood, or at least inheriting the celestial kingdom. "Eternal life, the kind of life enjoyed by eternal beings [gods] in the celestial kingdom, comes by grace plus obedience."[5]

Consider the following definitions and discussion of general salvation by Mormon theologian McConkie:

> Unconditional or general salvation, that which comes by grace alone without obedience to gospel law, consists in the mere fact of being resurrected. In this sense, salvation is synonymous with immortality; it is the inseparable connection of body and spirit so that the resurrected personage lives forever.[6]

He then proceeds to discuss the implications of general salvation:

> This kind of salvation eventually will come to all mankind, accepting only the sons of perdition [primarily apostate Mormons]. . . . But this is not the salvation of righteousness, the salvation which the saints [Mormons] seek. Those who gain only this general or unconditional salvation will still be judged according to their works and receive their places in a terrestrial or a telestial kingdom. They will, therefore, be damned; their eternal progression will be cut short; they will not feel the full measure of their creation, but in eternity will be ministering servants to more worthy persons [better Mormons].[7]

Refer to the following chart, The Mormon Concept of Salvation, in order to see the hierarchy of these kingdoms:

### The Mormon Concept of Salvation

| | |
|---|---|
| True salvation by personal merit made possible by the atonement. | **Celestial Kingdom** (three levels) <br><br> 1. Exaltation for Perfect Mormons [godhood and eternal increase (spirit children)] <br> 2. lesser servant status <br> 3. same |
| "Damnation": Immortality (resurrection) or salvation by grace (degrees of glory determined by personal merit). | **Terrestrial Kingdom** (righteous non-Mormons) |
| | **Telestial Kingdom** (the wicked; their purgatorial expungement of sins was accomplished before their resurrection in the Mormon Spirit prison) |
| Salvation denied. | **Sons of Perdition** (e.g., apostate Mormons) |

In essence, general salvation means salvation to one of two kingdoms:

1. The terrestrial kingdom, where righteous non-Mormons go;

2. The telestial kingdom, where the wicked go.

But do those in the telestial kingdom progress into the terrestrial one? No. Theologian Crowther states,

> This is not to say there will be no progress by those who inherit the lesser glories, only that there are limits set beyond which they cannot pass. The passages cited above strongly imply that there is no progression from one kingdom of glory to another kingdom of a higher degree, though the church has never taken a formal doctrinal stand on this point.[8]

Only a few have taught that those in the telestial kingdom can and will progress into the terrestrial kingdom. But Mormons do seem to agree that those in the terrestrial kingdom cannot apparently progress into the celestial kingdom. Further, only in the highest part of the celestial kingdom do marriage and procreation continue for eternity. In the other kingdoms everyone is single and so never inherit the joys of deification and eternal marriage.

There is also said to be room for "eternal" advancement within each kingdom. In the citation below we can see that the concepts of purgatory and salvation after death are part of Mormonism's general salvation. The tenth president and prophet, Joseph Fielding Smith, stated:

> Those who reject the [Mormon] gospel, but who live honorable lives, shall also be heirs of salvation, but not in the celestial kingdom. The Lord has prepared a place for them in the terrestrial kingdom. Those who live lives of wickedness may also be heirs of salvation, that is, they too shall be redeemed from death and from hell *eventually*. These, however, must suffer in hell the torments of the damned *until* they pay the price of their sinning, *for the blood of Christ will not cleanse them*. This vast host will find their place in the telestial kingdom.[9]

Finally, there is another class of people who are termed "sons of perdition." These are not the "damned" of the two lower kingdoms, and their fate, at least according to Mormon theology, is not easily determined. Some Mormons hold there is an eternal hell while most others deny it, a disagreement that reflects the contradictions in their scriptures, prophets, and historical theology.

Devout Mormons have no desire to achieve any of the lower kingdoms or even to live in the lower portions of the celestial kingdom. Their desire is to achieve the highest portion of the celestial kingdom where they will be gods and have sexual increase. George Q. Cannon, a member of the First Presidency, commented in a conference report, "I never heard a prayer offered, especially in the family circle, in which the family does not besiege God to give them [the highest] celestial glory. Telestial glory is not in their thoughts. Terrestrial glory may be all right for honorable Gentiles, . . . but celestial glory is our aim. . . . All that I am on this earth for is to get celestial glory."[10]

In conclusion, the relationship between *general* and *individual* salvation may be seen in the following summary statement by James Talmage in his work *Jesus the Christ*:

> . . . general salvation, in the sense of redemption from the effects of the Fall, comes to all without their seeking it; but . . . individual salvation or rescue from the effects of personal sins is to be required by each for himself by faith and good works.[11]

Even for the category of general salvation, works are important and determinative. But in addition to this first and inferior kind of redemption there is also a second and full redemption. This is a fully conditional salvation, entirely based upon good works, personal merit and strict obedience to what Mormons term "gospel law."

## B. Individual Redemption: True Salvation

On the one hand, we have seen that *general* redemption is merely resurrection to one of two lower kingdoms of "damnation." On the other hand, true salvation affords resurrection to the highest kingdom, the celestial kingdom. It is this salvation alone which is crucial to Mormons, which forgives all sin, and which determines whether one has the opportunity for deification. This salvation is not by grace at all. McConkie teaches, "Salvation in the celestial kingdom of God, however, is not salvation by grace alone. Rather, it is salvation by grace coupled with obedience to the laws and ordinances of the gospel."[12] There are three heavens within the celestial kingdom, but only in the highest heaven do Mormons actually attain godhood. Again, this is the salvation all Mormons seek, for it constitutes the possibility of becoming a god. Here is full salvation by which Mormons may earn the eternal sexual right to produce never-ending spirit offspring and kingdoms in which to rule them.

Mormons do not believe that they become gods immediately after death. They must continue to accumulate personal merit and attain divine attributes through aeons of effort and progression in the post-mortem state. If they are finally successful, they believe they will become gods.

But these doctrines must be *believed* in order for one to actually achieve true salvation. For example, in order to be exalted, one must believe that God is an exalted man: "God revealed himself to Adam by this name to signify that he is a Holy Man, a truth which man must know and comprehend if he is to become like God and inherit exaltation."[13] Further, the doctrine of exaltation is vitally integrated with the doctrines of celestial marriage (temple marriage) and the concept of eternal increase, or having children in eternity. These doctrines must also be accepted for one to have the possibility of exaltation.

Thus, in the most alluring way possible Mormonism cements loyalty to its doctrines. The promises of eternal marriage, eternal sexual pleasure, eternal family and eternal godhood itself are offered to those who truly believe.

Nevertheless, in the celestial kingdom as well, we find a distinction between "immortality" and "eternal life." Those who do not gain "eternal life" do not become gods, and have only another form of "immortality." Along with those in the two lower kingdoms, individuals in the two lower levels of the highest (celestial) kingdom are only "angels" who will serve those more worthy Mormons who have become gods or attained exaltation. Thus, Mormonism teaches that in this sense, even those in the celestial kingdom may be considered "damned" because they have not inherited *full* salvation—godhood and eternal increase.[14] As McConkie explains:

> Even those in the celestial kingdom, however, who do not go on to exaltation, will have immortality only and not eternal life. Along with those of the telestial and terrestrial worlds they will be "ministering servants, to minister for those who are worthy of a far more, and an exceeding, and an eternal weight of glory." They will live "separately and singly" in an unmarried state "without exaltation, in their saved condition, to all eternity" (*D&C*, 132:16,17). Salvation in its true and full meaning is synonymous with exaltation or eternal life and consists in gaining an inheritance in the highest of the three heavens within the celestial kingdom. With few exceptions this is the salvation of which the scriptures speak. It is the salvation which the saints [Mormons] seek. . . . This full salvation is obtained in and through the continuation of the family unit in eternity, and those who obtain it are gods (*D&C*, 131:1-4; 132). . . . If it had not been for Joseph Smith and the restoration, there would be no salvation.[15]

Again, to be "damned" in Mormonism is to have a *limit* placed on one's eternal progression. "Those who inherit the telestial glory, the terrestrial glory, and even lower degrees in the celestial glory *will all be damned*, for there are boundaries set beyond which they can never pass, throughout all eternity."[16] Thus, "Damnation means a limit to eternal progression."[17]

Whatever else Mormonism teaches, the only true salvation in Mormonism is attaining the highest portion of the celestial kingdom—which is the same as becoming a god. To be saved in Mormon theology is to become of like nature with God the Father. As McConkie emphasizes:

> With three or four possible exceptions all of the revelations of all the ages speak of salvation as being wholly, completely, and totally synonymous with eternal or everlasting life, with exaltation in the highest heaven of the celestial world, with attaining Godhood and being like God the Eternal Father.[18]

Thus, the student manual, *Doctrines of the Gospel*, teaches Mormons, "Each one of you has it within the realm of his possibility to develop a kingdom over which you will preside as its king and god. You will need to develop yourself and grow in ability and power and worthiness, to govern such a world with all of its people."[19]

And,

> It is the blessed privilege of resurrected beings who attain an exaltation in the celestial kingdom [the highest portion] to enjoy the glory of endless increase, to become the parents of generations of spirit offspring, and to direct their development through probationary stages analogous to those through which they themselves have passed.[20]

In conclusion, the Mormon church teaches that salvation comes only through the Mormon church and that it comprises various conditions of existence after death. Worthy Mormons will attain exaltation or deification in the highest heaven within the celestial kingdom. With their celestial wife or wives, they will have spirit children forever and rule worlds upon worlds. All others are "damned" which means they inherit a servant status in lesser kingdoms with successively worse restrictions and/or punishments, but "kingdoms" nonetheless. Mormons agree that progression is possible within each of the two lower kingdoms, but they debate whether or not progression from one kingdom to another is possible.

This is the Mormon concept of salvation. It has nothing whatever to do with the biblical doctrine of salvation which teaches four things (see pp. 182-195):

1. Christ alone wrought full and complete salvation on the cross (Ephesians 1:7; Hebrews 10:14).

2. Full salvation can be freely received by anyone merely by receiving Christ as his or her personal savior from sin (John 1:12; 3:16; 5:24; 6:47).

3. Salvation is not a lengthy process of becoming the same as God, but rather, it involves men and women who as God's redeemed children honor and enjoy Him and experience eternal life with Him forever (Revelation 21:1-7; 1 John 2:25).

4. Salvation is wholly by grace, not by works (Ephesians 2:8,9).

Nevertheless, Mormons argue that they accept and promote the biblical doctrine of salvation by grace. It is to a discussion of this vital issue that we turn to in our next chapter.

## ◆ ◆ *Appendix* ◆ ◆

*What Does the Mormon Church Teach Concerning the Object and Nature of Faith?*

All people exercise faith in something, whether in God, themselves, the State, a personal philosophy, etc. Mormon theologian Bruce McConkie cites Joseph Smith's own definition of faith as "the first principle in revealed religion and the foundation of all righteousness."[21] The issue is not whether Mormons exercise faith, but what they place their faith in and whether or not their exercise of faith is truly biblical. Mormonism is a religion claiming to believe in the biblical doctrine of faith.

First of all, Mormonism claims it exercises faith in the proper object— Jesus Christ. The current president and prophet of the church, Ezra Taft Benson emphasizes that "the fundamental principle of our religion is faith in the Lord Jesus Christ. . . . Faith in Jesus Christ consists of complete reliance on him."[22]

But biblically, faith is to be placed in the true Jesus Christ alone for forgiveness of sins (see John 3:16-18; 5:24; 6:47). We have already proved that Mormons do not believe in the true Jesus Christ and, therefore, do not place their faith in the proper object, but rather in a false Christ, an idol derived from the occult revelations given to Joseph Smith (see 2 Corinthians 11:3,4,11-13).

Not only does Mormonism place faith in the wrong object, it also distorts the true nature of faith. The Bible teaches that it is faith alone that saves a person, not good works (John 6:47; Ephesians 2:8,9). But in the Mormon religion, faith and good works are *not* separated as far as salvation is concerned. In this sense "faith" is not ultimately and solely trust in Christ to save one from sin; it is ultimately trust in oneself, one's personal righteousness and one's good works to save. Note the teaching of doctrinal theologian McConkie:

> Both Mormon [the man] and Moroni [the spirit] taught that miracles also accompany faith and that where there are no

miracles, there is no faith. . . . Faith then includes signs, miracles, and good works. Unless these are present, there is no faith. . . . Faith in the Lord Jesus Christ, faith unto life and salvation, presupposes works; it requires miracles. *Works are part of the definition of faith and without them there is no faith.*[23]

Notice that McConkie has just said that "works are part of the definition of faith"—something that is neither biblical nor Christian teaching. Scripturally, true regenerating faith will lead to good works, because a person's *heart* is changed, but works are not part of faith *per se*. This is why it is possible for a person to be saved solely by faith in Christ even if he has no works (the thief on the cross, for example, and other genuine "deathbed" confessions)—something Mormonism adamantly rejects.

In addition, the nature of faith is further distorted by James Talmage when he teaches that faith is only given to those who have already shown by their works that they are *worthy* of it:

Faith . . . is given to those only who show by their sincerity that they are worthy of it, and who give promise of abiding by its dictates.[24]

But Christians have always taught that no one is worthy of salvation and that even the most *unworthy* person can still exercise true saving faith in Jesus. The Bible teaches that all of us were unworthy prior to faith, even that we were God's enemies. It emphasizes that *no one* is worthy before God at the point of faith (Romans 3:10-12; 5:6-10; Ephesians 2:1-3; Colossians 1:21).

Finally, the Mormon church claims that true faith in God can be exercised *only* by Mormons—not by anyone else. It is therefore, according to Mormonism, impossible for Christians to exercise true faith. For example, in an allusion to the Christian doctrine of God we are told:

If a person believes . . . that Deity is a power or essence that fills the immensity of space [an allusion to the Christian God] . . . he stops himself from gaining faith. . . . Faith can be exercised only by those who conform to the principles of truth which come from the true God who actually exists [the Mormon God(s)]. . . . Faith is a gift of God bestowed as a reward for personal righteousness.[25]

This last sentence supplies the key to the Mormon concept of faith. As McConkie teaches, for true faith to be present, Mormons must 1) actively exercise spiritual gifts and perform miracles, 2) possess knowledge of Mormon theology, and 3) be morally righteous—"where these things are not, faith is not."[26]

Note again that faith is bestowed as a *reward* "for personal righteousness." But none of this is scriptural. Biblically, faith is declared to be a gift. But how can faith be bestowed as a *gift*, if it is really bestowed only as a reward for merit, personal righteousness and good works? As we will see in our next chapter, when Mormonism speaks of "faith," what it really means more than anything else is "individual works of righteousness which secure salvation only on the basis of personal merit."

◆

# CHAPTER 14

# What Does the Mormon Church Believe About Salvation by Grace?

M ormonism vigorously claims that it believes in the biblical teaching of salvation by grace. One Mormon promotional brochure declares, "Salvation by grace is one of the glorious doctrines of Christ."[27]

In his apologetic text defending the assertion that Mormons are Christians, Dr. Stephen E. Robinson goes out of his way to argue that both the Mormon scriptures and the Mormon church do in fact believe that salvation is *wholly by grace*.

Because approaches like these so easily confuse both Mormons and uninstructed Christians concerning the nature of the Mormon religion, we shall begin our analysis with Dr. Robinson's book *Are Mormons Christians?*

Significantly, Robinson assigns this discussion of grace to his section of "Lesser Arguments" as to why critics think Mormonism should not be classified as Christian. But relegating so vital an issue as salvation by grace to the status of a "lesser argument" is itself indicative of the Mormon confusion over the biblical doctrine of salvation.

Nevertheless, Robinson makes the following claims against the critics of Mormonism:

> One sometimes hears that Latter-day Saints are not Christians because all true Christians believe in salvation by grace, while the Mormon believes in salvation by works. . . . *this idea of salvation by works . . . has nothing to do with LDS doctrine. . . .* The charge that this is what Latter-day Saints believe *badly misrepresents the LDS position.*[28]

However, it is not the critics who are engaging in distortion here. It is the Mormon church and its apologists who distort matters and love to equivocate. Robinson further argues, "The charge that Latter-day Saints believe in salvation by works *is simply not true*. That human beings can save themselves by their own efforts is *contrary* to the teachings of the *Book of Mormon*, which eloquently states the doctrine of salvation by grace."[29]

But Dr. Robinson is wrong. The *Book of Mormon* does not "eloquently" state the *biblical* doctrine of salvation by grace—far from it. Thus, in defending his views, the best Dr. Robinson can do is cite a few weak, if not entirely irrelevant, scriptures from the *Book of Mormon* (Mosiah 2:21,24; 5:7,8; 2 Nephi 2:3,5-8; 25:23; Alma 5:14,15; Ether 12:27; Moroni 10:32,33). Even the strongest of these passages (2 Nephi 2:3-8) is not considered as teaching salvation by grace through faith according to Mormon prophets, presidents and doctrinal theologians—at least not in any orthodox Christian or biblical sense.

Thus, when Mormonism speaks of "salvation by grace" or maintains that salvation does not come by "keeping the law," it means something different from what Christians mean by these terms. As noted earlier, for Mormons "salvation by grace" is the means of general redemption or merely a physical resurrection from the dead—not true or complete Mormon salvation. Further, the Mormon argument that men are not saved by "keeping the law" only refers to *Mosaic* law. Mormons know full well that they demand that people keep all the requirements of the "Gospel law"—requirements far more severe than the Mosaic law. (See Appendix One.)

It is significant that Robinson cites only the *Book of Mormon*. He never cites *Doctrine and Covenants*, which is the Mormon scripture that most accurately reflects current Mormon beliefs and from which Mormon doctrines were originally derived. Robinson never once mentions that *Doctrine and Covenants* adamantly and repeatedly teaches salvation by works. One can only wonder why.

Further, Robinson at times betrays his own awareness that a problem exists with his definition of grace.

> Some critics may object that the Latter-day Saints do not insist that we are saved by grace *alone* . . . but *the fundamental LDS belief regarding grace and works is well within the spectrum of traditional Christianity*, with strong affinities to the Wesleyan position. While not every Christian will agree with *this specific LDS concept of grace*, the Latter-day Saints have never believed in salvation by any other means—*and especially not by individual works. . . . The LDS scriptures are clear—we are saved by grace.*[30]

But again, what does Mormonism mean by the word "grace?" Not the Christian or biblical meaning, as we will show in point one below.

Further, to say that Mormon teaching on grace and works "is well within the spectrum of traditional Christianity" is about as gross a misrepresentation of Mormon belief, Christian belief, and historical Christian theology as can be found. Further, if Mormonism really teaches salvation by grace, how did literally every Mormon president and prophet, theologian and layman end up so confused, all of them staunchly maintaining that salvation is by works? We document this below.

Indeed, one of the few Mormon doctrines that has never been altered, suppressed, or simultaneously affirmed and denied is the doctrine that salvation *is* by personal merit and works of righteousness. Mormonism teaches that personal salvation is *never* a free gift secured by grace through faith alone as the Bible teaches. Rather, it is secured by personal merit through zealous good works and impeccable law keeping. As in the theology of Armstrongism and many other cults, "the Gospel" is not having one's sins forgiven through exercising faith in Christ's atonement; it is earning salvation by good works and becoming a god in the process. Thus, the biblical doctrine of salvation by grace through faith alone is one teaching the Mormon church never has tolerated, and never will tolerate.[31]

From the beginning the Mormon prophets and their gods have emphasized that such an idea is an "abomination." This is why Mormon theologians reject this doctrine so passionately—they are zealously obeying their gods as quoted in their scriptures. Let us give you a few illustrations of what Mormons really believe about salvation by grace, or justification by faith (see also the appendix for the biblical teaching on justification).

In his *Articles of Faith*, James Talmage refers to "a most pernicious doctrine—that of justification by belief alone."[32] We are further told that "the sectarian [Christian] dogma of justification by faith alone has exercised an influence for evil" and leads to "vicious extremes."[33] Theologian McConkie called it a "soul-destroying doctrine."[34] The tenth president and prophet, Joseph Fielding Smith, emphasized that "Mankind [is] damned by [the] 'faith alone' doctrine" and "we must emphatically declare that men must obey these [Gospel] laws if they would be saved."[35]

Likewise, Mormon apostle LeGrand Richards declared:

> One erroneous teaching of many Christian churches is: By faith alone we are saved. This false doctrine . . . would teach man that no matter how great the sin, a confession [of faith in Christ as personal savior] would bring him complete forgiveness and salvation.[36]

And the early Mormon apostle Orson Pratt is just as definite:

> Faith alone will not save men; neither will faith and works save them, unless they are [works] of the right kind. . . . True

faith and righteous works are essential to salvation; and without both of these no man ever was or ever can be saved. . . . There are some who believe that faith alone, unaccompanied by works, is sufficient for justification, sanctification, and salvation. . . . [They] . . . are without justification—without hope—without everlasting life, and will be damned, the same as unbelievers.[37]

Before we continue our discussion, it is important to recall that Mormonism consistently redefines biblical or Christian terminology in order to make it conform to its own unbiblical standards. In order to fully understand what Mormons believe salvation to be, we have to know how they have redefined the following key terms: "grace," "justification," "the new birth," "salvation," "gift," "repentance" and "sanctification." Notice how all these terms (and many others) are redefined to incorporate works salvation.

*1. The term "Grace" incorporates works.*

As we noted in chapter 13, for Mormons "salvation by grace" merely refers to being resurrected from the dead. But one's place of residence in eternity is determined wholly by good works. Second, according to Mormonism, salvation by grace is merely an infusing of grace based on good works. This is similar to the Roman Catholic doctrine wherein grace itself becomes a "work," so that as men increase in personal righteousness more and more "grace" is granted them. In other words, "grace" is secured from God only on the basis of individual merit and personal righteousness. Thus, Bruce McConkie explains how the Mormon god grants grace:

Grace is granted to men proportionately as they conform to the standards of personal righteousness that are part of the gospel plan.[38]

Further,

Grace, which is an outpouring of the mercy, love, and condescension of God .  . [is] received—not without works, not without righteousness, not without merit—but by obedience and faith![39]

This is why McConkie, emphasizing the *false* definition of grace in classical Christian belief, argues:

Many Protestants . . . erroneously conclude that men are saved by grace alone without doing the works of righteousness.[40]

Thus, Mormonism teaches that grace *alone* cannot possibly save anyone. Mormons are to save themselves, "with the help of the Lord." This brings us to the next significant aspect of the Mormon concept of grace— that Christ's death, although it did *not* forgive sin, did grant the possibility of salvation through good works. (See chap. 15.)

Mormonism teaches that the atonement of Christ provides men the opportunity to earn their own salvation by "trusting in the Lord" to help them attain a personal righteousness that fulfills all the requirements and laws of the Gospel:

> Complete salvation, which is full and eternal life, results from man's full endeavor to conform to the laws of life, the gospel of the Lord Jesus Christ. That is why we often say that men save themselves with the aid of the Lord.[41]

Sterling M. McMurrin is E.E. Ericksen Distinguished Professor of History at the University of Utah. In his study of Mormon theology, he shows how the Mormon definition of grace incorporates a doctrine of works:

> Mormon theology is not without a doctrine of grace, but it undertakes to conform that doctrine to the belief in merit. . . . The orthodox position that there is no salvation except by the atonement through Jesus Christ is thoroughly affirmed. But . . . the meaning of the atonement is that by the grace of God through Christ it is made possible for man, who is by nature neither corrupt nor depraved, to merit his salvation by free obedience to the law.[42]

In other words, Mormonism teaches a concept of grace—but one that bears no resemblance whatever to the biblical teaching.

### 2. The term "Justification" incorporates works.

Biblically speaking, "justification" is the act of God that declares a sinner righteous entirely apart from works and predicated only upon his/her faith in the atoning death of Christ for their sins. (See appendix for documentation.) But in Mormon theology the concept of justification is inextricably bound with conditions of personal merit and righteousness. According to the Mormon church, justification does *not* declare one perfectly righteous before God; it only gives one the opportunity to earn righteousness before God. Notice McConkie's reformulation: "The very atoning sacrifice itself was wrought out by the Son of God so that men might be justified, that is, so they could *do the things* which will give them eternal life in the celestial realm (*D&C*, 20:21-30, emphasis added)."[43]

What are some of those "things" necessary for salvation in the celestial heaven? Consider the following discussion of justification as provided by

McConkie. Here we clearly see that Mormons have no understanding of the biblical definition of justification:

> What is lacking in the sectarian [Christian] world is a true knowledge of the law of justification. Simply stated, that law is this: "All covenants, contracts, bonds, obligations, oaths, vows, performances, connections, associations, or expectations" (*D&C*, 132:7), in which men must abide to be saved and exalted . . . must be entered into and performed in righteousness so that the Holy Spirit can justify the candidate for salvation in what has been done (1 Ne. 16:2; Jac. 2:13,14; Alma 41:15; *D&C*, 98; 132:1,62). . . . As with all other doctrines of salvation, justification is available because of the atoning sacrifice of Christ, but it becomes operative in the life of an individual only on conditions of personal righteousness.[44]

In other words, Mormon justification 1) only gives one the opportunity to earn salvation and 2) is completed only after the individual has met all of the severe requirements of law keeping. This is why the *Doctrines of the Gospel: Student Manual* emphasizes that "justification comes [both] through faith in Jesus Christ and through individual righteousness." And it proceeds to supply a list of specific requirements, such as overcoming evil, keeping oneself unspotted from the world, etc., that Mormons must meet in order to be "justified before God."[45]

### 3. The term "New Birth" incorporates works.

The tenth president and prophet of the Mormon church, Joseph Fielding Smith, taught that even "the new birth is also a matter of obedience to law."[46] Smith was echoing the teachings of the *Book of Mormon* (Alma 5:14-30), which declares that to be "born again" a person has to fulfill a number of prerequisites, such as being blameless before God, having an absence of pride and envy, etc. In other words, the new birth is a spiritual *process* secured by good works, not a one-time event secured by faith in Christ. Commenting on this same passage of scripture, McConkie declares that its guidelines enable Mormons "to determine whether and to what extent they have overcome the world, which is the exact extent to which they have in fact been born again."[47]

Biblically, of course, being born again is something that happens in an instant—it is not a process. Scripture repeatedly refers to the fact that every believer has already been (past tense) born again, simply by faith in Jesus (1 Peter 1:3,23; Titus 3:5, cf. John 3:16; 5:24; 6:47).

### 4. The term "Salvation" incorporates works.

In a discussion of the subject of salvation in his work *The Miracle of Forgiveness*, former president and prophet Spencer W. Kimball emphasizes that terms must not be misunderstood—a reference to supposedly false Christian teaching:

Of course we need to understand terms. If by the word "salvation" is meant the mere salvation or redemption from the grave, the "grace of God" is sufficient. But if the term "salvation" means returning to the presence of God with eternal progression, eternal increase, and eventual godhood, for this one certainly must have the "grace of God," as it is generally defined, plus personal purity, overcoming of evil, and the good "works" made so important in the exhortations of the Savior and his prophets and apostles. . . . Immortality [resurrection] has been accomplished by the savior's sacrifice. Eternal life [exaltation or godhood] hangs in the balance awaiting the works of men.[48]

### 5. The term "Gift" incorporates works.

Even the meaning of the word "gift" is redefined, at least as far as salvation is concerned. Here we see that a gift is not something freely given; rather, it is something that must be earned. The apostle LeGrand Richards asserts: "Nevertheless, to obtain these 'graces,' and the gift of 'eternal salvation,' we must remember that this gift is [given] only to 'all them that obey him.'"[49] Thus, as McConkie emphasizes, "One thing only comes as a free gift to men—the fact of the atoning sacrifice. All other gifts must be earned. That is, God's gifts are bestowed upon those who live the law entitling them to receive whatever is involved."[50] Notice how McConkie redefines the word gift to denote the idea of incorporating works:

What price must men pay for this precious gift [of salvation]? Not conformity to Mosaic standards, . . . but the price of faith, faith in the Lord Jesus Christ, faith that includes within itself enduring works of righteousness, *which faith cannot so much as exist unless and until* men conform their lives to gospel standards.[51]

Certainly Mormonism has little concept of what a gift is. Any dictionary definition of the word "gift" will indicate that it is something given, not something earned. A man does not tell his wife that he is giving her flowers on the condition that she wash his car. A gift is a gift. Mormonism has perverted the most important gift of all—salvation—by requiring that men attempt the impossible feat of earning it.

### 6. The term "Repentance" incorporates works.

In Mormonism, the term "repentance" means nothing less than strict obedience to law rather than the biblical meaning of turning from one's sins. After a discussion of all the requirements and commandments that must be fulfilled until the end of one's life in order to achieve salvation,

Spencer Kimball comments that many people do not understand repentance properly. "They are not 'doing the commandments,' hence they do not repent."[52] In other words, repentance equals obedience. In fact, "Repentance must involve an all-out, total surrender to the program of the Lord," which amounts to everything Mormonism says is necessary to salvation. Indeed, a "transgressor is not fully repentant who neglects his tithing, misses his meetings, breaks the Sabbath, fails in his family prayers, does not sustain the authorities of the Church, breaks the *Word of Wisdom* [church regulations], does not love the Lord nor his fellowman.... God cannot forgive unless a transgressor shows a true repentance which spreads to all areas of his life.... 'Doing the commandments' includes the many activities required of the [Mormon] faithful."[53]

*7. The term "Sanctification" incorporates works.*

Similarly distorting the biblical concept of sanctification (meaning to be "set apart" to God), *Doctrines of the Gospel: Student Manual* teaches:

> Members of the Church of Jesus Christ are commanded to become sanctified.... *To be sanctified is to become holy and without sin.*... Sanctification is attainable because of the atonement of Jesus Christ, but *only if we obey his commandments.*... Sanctification is the state of saintliness, a state attained *only by* conformity to the laws and ordinances of the gospel.[54]

But biblically, sanctification involves three aspects. First, we are (past tense) "set apart" to Christ at the moment of regeneration or saving faith. Second, we are progressively being sanctified as we grow in the grace, knowledge and obedience of our Lord, and third, we are fully sanctified—that is, fully set apart to God and His purposes—when we become glorified at the moment of our going to be with Him. The first and third of these aspects are entirely by grace, whereas Mormonism makes all of sanctification a matter of works.

These are only a few of the Mormon redefinitions of theological terms. They should be kept in mind in any discussion with individual Mormons. Now, we proceed to document, in some detail, the Mormon reliance upon good works.

In order to show how thoroughly Mormonism teaches salvation by works, we have divided the following material into four basic sections:

1. The teaching of Mormon scriptures;

2. The teaching of Mormon presidents and prophets;

3. The teaching of Mormon theologians and church leaders; and

4. A listing of specific requirements held to be necessary to achieving Mormon salvation.

We discuss these in turn. Since this section is deliberately lengthy for purposes of documentation, the reader may wish to read only those sections of personal interest.

### 1. Do the Mormon scriptures teach that salvation is by works?

Even though Mormon leaders such as Dr. Robinson have claimed that the Mormon scriptures teach that salvation is by grace, this is not so biblically.

The *Book of Mormon* teaches works salvation. For example:

*Alma 7:16 teaches works salvation:*

And whosoever doeth this [is water baptized], and keepeth the commandments of God from thence forth, the same... shall have eternal life.

*Mosiah 5:8,9 teaches works salvation:*

...All you that have entered into the covenant with God that ye should be obedient unto the end of your lives.... Whosoever doeth this shall be found at the right hand of God.

*2 Nephi 9:23,24 teaches works salvation:*

And he [God] commandeth all men that they must repent, and be baptized in his name, having perfect faith in the Holy One of Israel, or they cannot be saved in the kingdom of God. And if they will not repent and believe in his name, and be baptized in his name, and endure to the end, they must be damned; for the Lord God, the Holy One of Israel, has spoken it.

*3 Nephi 27:14,15,17,21,22 teaches works salvation:*

[Jesus is allegedly speaking: men will] stand before me, to be judged of their works, whether they be good or whether they be evil—... That they may be judged according to their works.... He that endureth not unto the end, the same is he that is also hewn down and cast into the fire, from whence they can no more return, because of the justice of the father.... Verily, verily, I say unto you, this is my gospel; and ye know the things that ye must do in my church; for the works which ye have seen me do that shall ye also do;... Therefore, if ye do these things blessed are ye, for ye shall be lifted up at the last day.

Mormons almost universally cite these passages as evidence that salvation must come by works and *not* by grace. For example, Jack Weyland, a member of the Rapid City, South Dakota Stake Mission presidency, refers to these last verses, noting that they present the true definition of the "gospel" of Jesus Christ. In answering the question, "When non-members say we're not Christians, what is the best way to respond?" he comments that Christians don't think Mormons are saved because "we don't subscribe to their notions of the doctrine of grace." Then, after discussing why the Mormon doctrine of grace incorporates works, he comments on the passages just cited:

> It is unfortunate that nonmembers do not have the *Book of Mormon's* definition of the gospel of Jesus Christ, a definition given by the Savior Himself in 3 Nephi 27. Here the Savior described what constitutes true Christianity.[55]

He then observes that for salvation "we have much work to do as followers of Jesus Christ, works that require more than just acceptance of him as the Savior and Redeemer."[56]

A Mormon believes he is saved "by grace" only after he first meets all the numerous requirements outlined for him according to the Mormon church. If he is successful in fulfilling all these requirements to the end of his life, *then* he believes he is saved by "grace."

Thus, the *Book of Mormon's* true teaching on salvation is given in 2 Nephi 25:23: "For we know that it is by grace that we are saved, *after all we can do*" (emphasis added). In Mormon theology, then, we see once again that grace does not *provide* salvation; it only makes earning it possible.

*Doctrine and Covenants* also teaches salvation by works and not by grace. For example:

*Doctrine and Covenants, 7:37 teaches salvation by works:* "Be faithful, keep my commands and ye shall inherit the kingdom of heaven."

*Doctrine and Covenants, 18:46 teaches salvation by works:* "If you keep not my commandments you cannot be saved in the kingdom of my father."

*Doctrine and Covenants, 130:20,21 teaches salvation by works:* "There is a law, irrevocably decreed in heaven before the foundations of this world, upon which all blessings are predicated—and when we obtain any blessing from God, it is by obedience to that law upon which it is predicated."

*Doctrine and Covenants, 132:12 teaches salvation by works:* "I am the Lord thy God; and I give unto you this commandment—that no man shall come unto the father but by me or by my word, which is my law, sayeth the Lord."

The above are only a few of the citations from Mormon scriptures teaching salvation by personal merit.

## 2. Do Mormon presidents and prophets teach that salvation is by works?

From Joseph Smith onward, literally every Mormon president and prophet—without exception—has strenuously maintained that salvation comes only by good works and personal merit. Below we supply examples:

*The first president and prophet of the Mormon church, Joseph Smith, taught works salvation.*

Joseph Smith was the author of the Mormon church's standard doctrinal confession known as the thirteen Articles of Faith. Point 3 teaches that men are saved "by obedience to the laws and ordinances of the gospel."[57] Elsewhere Smith wrote, "I . . . spoke to the people, showing them that to get salvation we must not only do some things, but *everything* which God has commanded."[58] Further, "If . . . all God's people were saved by keeping the commandments of God, we, if saved at all, shall be saved upon the same principle."[59]

*Brigham Young, the second president and prophet of the Mormon church, taught works salvation.*

The following citations are taken from the selection on "obedience" in the text *Discourses of Brigham Young*. The numbers after the quotations refer to *Journal of Discourses* (vol. 13, p. 21), where the original sermon (which Young himself classified as "scripture") is found:

> I cannot save you. I can tell you how to save yourselves, but you must do the will of God (10:317). How shall we know what to do? By obedience to every requirement of the Gospel (8:148). . . . Strict obedience to the truth will alone enable people to dwell in the presence of the Almighty (7:55). The Lord has sent forth his laws, commandments, and ordinances to the children of men, and requires them to be strictly obeyed (16:31).[60]

In this same text, citing *Journal of Discourses* 3:132 and 1:312:

> Though our interest is one as a people, yet remember, salvation is an individual work; it is every person for himself. . . . There are those in this Church who calculate to be saved by the righteousness of others. They will miss their mark. . . . I am the only person that can possibly save myself.[61]

Young also taught:

> Unless we believe the Gospel of Christ and obey its ordinances we have no promise of the life to come. . . . It is a fact that all who receive eternal life and salvation will receive it on no other conditions than believing in the Son of God and obeying the principles that he has laid down.[62]

Finally, Young taught that strict obedience even in extremely minor matters (such as making one's own clothes) was necessary in order to become a "saint."[63]

*Wilford Woodruff, the fourth president and prophet of the Mormon church, taught works salvation.*

Woodruff commented that "the labours of the saints are for their own salvation, and not to enrich the Lord."[64] Further:

> I want the brethren to understand this one thing, that our tithing, our labour, our works are not for the exaltation of the almighty, but they are for us. . . . In paying our tithing, in obeying every law that is given to exalt us and to do us good, is all for our individual benefit . . . which leads to salvation and eternal life.[65]

*Joseph Fielding Smith, the tenth president and prophet of the Mormon church, taught works salvation.*

Smith emphasized that "obedience to law is the order throughout the universe."[66] Commenting on James 2:10, he stresses the *extent* of the obedience to law required for salvation:

> Therefore each who enters the kingdom must of his own free will accept all of the laws and be obedient to them, finding himself in complete accord with all. Anything short of this would cause confusion. Therefore the words of James are true. Unless a man can abide strictly in complete accord, he cannot enter there, and in the words of James, he is guilty of all. In other words, if there is one divine law that he does not keep he is barred from participating in the kingdom. . . . So in the celestial kingdom, we must be worthy in every point, or we fail to receive the blessing. The Kingdom of God must exist in absolute unity. Every law must be obeyed, and no member of the Church can have a place there unless he is in full accord.[67]

*Spencer W. Kimball, the twelfth president and prophet of the Mormon Church, teaches works salvation.*

In his *The Miracle of Forgiveness* this theme is emphasized again and again. For example, chapter 15 is titled "Keeping God's Commandments Brings Forgiveness." He says,

> Jesus Christ, our Redeemer and Savior, has given us our [spiritual] map—a code of laws and commandments whereby we might attain perfection and, eventually, godhood. . . . The Church of Jesus Christ of Latter-day Saints is the sole repository of this priceless program in its fullness, which is made available to those who accept it.[68]

Thus, he teaches, "All transgressions must be cleansed, all weaknesses must be overcome, before a person can attain perfection and godhood."[69]

Kimball emphasizes that good works enable one "to pile up credits against the accumulated errors and transgressions" that one commits.[70] Characteristically, he attacks the biblical teaching of salvation by grace through faith alone:

> One of the most fallacious doctrines originated by Satan and propounded by man is that man is saved alone by the grace of God; that belief in Jesus Christ alone is all that is needed for salvation.... Church members are fortunate indeed to have [Mormon] scriptures brought forth in this age which clarify this and other doctrinal questions beyond all doubt.[71]

*Ezra Taft Benson, the current Mormon president and prophet, teaches works salvation.*

He follows in the footsteps of his predecessors when he says,

> We accept quite literally the savior's mandate: "Be ye therefore perfect, even as your father which is in heaven is perfect."[72]

And,

> Immortality [resurrection] is a free gift to all men because of the resurrection of Jesus Christ. Eternal life [Mormon salvation] is the quality of life enjoyed by our Heavenly Father. Those who fully comply with his commandments believe the promise that they will have this quality of life.[73]

And finally,

> God, our Heavenly Father, governs his children by law. He has instituted laws for our perfection. If we obey his laws, we receive the blessings pertaining to those laws.... A spiritual person obeys all the Lord's commandments.[74]

### 3. Do Mormon presidents and prophets teach that salvation is by works?

We are aware of no Mormon theologian or church leader who teaches that salvation is by grace in the biblical sense. Even the strongest defense of Mormonism as teaching salvation by grace—that of Dr. Robinson cited above—is equivocation at best. If Dr. Robinson were really teaching salvation by grace through faith alone according to the Bible, he would certainly be excommunicated from the Mormon church. Below we cite examples of Mormon leaders who emphasize over and over that salvation occurs only by personal righteousness.

*James Talmage* is certainly one of the most respected Mormon leaders. He refers to "the absolute requirement of individual compliance with the laws and ordinances of His [Jesus] gospel as the means by which salvation may be attained."[75]

The late *Bruce McConkie* is perhaps the leading doctrinal theologian within Mormonism. He emphasizes literally hundreds of times throughout his writings that salvation comes only by works and never by grace in a biblical sense.

For example, his three-volume *Doctrinal New Testament Commentary* contains hundreds of statements demanding works salvation, so much so that any Mormon with any real awareness of God's holiness and his own sinfulness could easily be driven to despair:

> For salvation comes by obedience to the laws upon which its receipt is predicated and in no other way.... Paul is the apostle of good works, of personal righteousness, of keeping the commandments, of pressing forward with a steadfastness in Christ, of earning the right to eternal life by obedience to the laws and ordinances of the gospel.[76]

> Salvation is available because of the atonement, but it is gained through personal righteousness, as Paul proclaims again and again.... Since salvation consists in having the character, perfections, and attributes of Deity, and since all things are governed and controlled by law, it is a self-evident truth that some people are nearer to gaining eternal life than are others.[77]

Notice his other comments on the Apostle Paul:

> Paul is the great expounder of the doctrine that through God's grace salvation is available to those who keep the commandments after baptism.... Paul deals with obedience; pure, diamond, unadulterated obedience; obedience to the whole law of God; not a presumptuous, self-serving hope that salvation comes through Christ, without more on man's part than a whispered confession of belief; but obedience, obedience, obedience, obedience.[78]

McConkie goes even further: "Salvation comes by obedience to the whole law of the whole gospel.... Thus, *a man may be damned for a single sin*.... Obedience to the whole law is required for salvation."[79]

Predictably, like all Mormon leaders, he explicitly denounces the Christian teaching concerning salvation by grace through faith:

[The Apostle John] now announces how it is possible to know God. It is by obedience to the laws and ordinances of the gospel! And in no other way! Which is to say, among other things: There is not one scintilla of spiritual sense in the sectarian [Christian] supposition that salvation is gained simply by saying: "I accept Jesus as my personal savior." Since the very fact of knowing God, in the ultimate and full sense [exaltation or becoming God], consists of thinking what he thinks, saying what he says, doing what he does, and of being like him, thus having exaltation or godhood—it follows that saved souls must advance and progress until they acquire his character, perfections, and attributes, until they gain his eternal power, until they themselves become gods.*[80]

Finally, the *Doctrines of the Gospel: Student Manual*, which contains quotations from numerous Mormon prophets and presidents, church theologians and leaders, emphasizes repeatedly in chapter 17, "Obedience, a Law of Heaven," that salvation comes only through personal merit. Obedience is defined as "complete subjection to God and his commands."[81] Thus, "God demands strict obedience to his requirements."[82] Further, "Christ, himself, set the perfect example of obedience for his brethren." And, "To get salvation we must not only do some things, but everything which God has commanded."[83]

To cite *The Teachings of Spencer W. Kimball*, we are told:

Man can transform himself and he must. Man has in himself the seeds of godhood, which can germinate and grow and develop. As the acorn becomes the oak, the mortal man becomes a god. It is within his power to lift himself by his very bootstraps from the plane on which he finds himself to the plane on which he should be. It may be a long, hard lift with many obstacles, but it is a real possibility.[84]

All of this is proof that the Mormon church teaches salvation by works. When it claims that it teaches salvation by grace, it is not only deceiving the public as to the biblical meaning of grace, but it is deceiving them concerning its own teachings as well. Having documented that the Mormon church teaches salvation wholly by works, we now proceed to discuss some of the important details of how that salvation is achieved.

Mormons believe that in order for them to achieve full salvation they must literally become perfect—absolutely sinless. However, they do not believe such a condition is attainable in this life. Rather, it must be

---

*Similar statements to those above are found in *DNTC*, 2:41-44,212,215,220,240-260,274,282,290, etc.; 3:66,86,87,138,175-248,252,254,258-260,266,284-286; and throughout his *Mormon Doctrine*.

attained at some point in the *next* life. Thus, when Mormons claim that they must eventually attain such a state of absolute perfection and one hundred percent compliance with every iota of God's laws and requirements, they mean to fulfill such a condition quite literally. It simply will take longer than this life allows.

Gerald N. Lund, zone administrator for the Church Educational System, comments:

> At some point, then, if we are to become like God, we must become perfect, without any flaw or error. But must we achieve that state in this life? Here the prophets have spoken plainly.[85]

He then proceeds to quote Joseph Smith who teaches that absolute perfection "is not all to be comprehended in this world; it will be a great work to earn [more of] our salvation and exaltation even beyond the grave."[86] He also cites the tenth president and prophet, Joseph Fielding Smith:

> Salvation does not come all at once. . . . It will take us ages to accomplish this end, for there will be greater progress beyond the grave. . . . I believe the Lord meant just what he said: That we should be perfect, as our Father in heaven is perfect. That will not come all at once, . . . But here we lay the foundation.[87]

Thus, Lund concludes that "[Absolute literal] Perfection is our eternal goal: It is what we must eventually achieve."[88]

But what are the means by which a Mormon begins to achieve his or her perfection *now*, here on earth? This takes us to our fourth point concerning the Mormon doctrine of salvation—those specific laws and requirements that are essential to begin the process of salvation.

### 4. *What specific requirements are necessary to achieve salvation?*

In addition to general works of righteousness that are required of Mormons in order to attain salvation, a host of other requirements are also necessary, many of which we mention below.

In fact, Mormonism goes so far as to teach that a person is actually not saved until he has perfected himself to the level of Jesus Christ! (Compare this with 1 John 5:11-13.)

> If we can find a saved being, we may ascertain without much difficulty what all others must be in order to be saved. . . . there will be no dispute among those who believe the Bible, that it is Christ: all will agree in this, that he is the prototype or standard of salvation; or in other words, that he is a saved

being. . . . If he were anything different from what he is, he would not be saved; for his salvation depends on his being precisely what he is and nothing else. . . . And no being can possess it [salvation] but himself or one like him.[89]

The purpose of this section is not only to show the extent of Mormonism's reliance on personal merit and effort, but also to underscore the practical impossibility of any person ever accomplishing all that the Mormon church claims is required for salvation. Mormons may think they can meet the requirements listed below, but most people would consider this a self-deception.

*Personal Revelation*

Saving knowledge of God comes only by revelation from the Holy Ghost as a consequence of obedience to the laws and ordinances of the gospel.[90]

*Physical Labor*

Temporal work is *essential to salvation*. Man cannot be saved in idleness. It is not enough simply to believe the great spiritual realities. We could do that as spirits in preexistence. . . . Work is a commandment of the Lord.[91]

*Obedience to Leaders*

Mormon people are intimidated into obeying church leaders through fear of losing their eternal salvation:

To gain salvation the saints *must be subject* to God's ministers. The doctrines and ordinances of the gospel cannot be separated from those appointed to teach Christ's gospel and perform his ordinances. . . . It is an eternal, unvarying verity that *salvation seekers must submit* to the direction of those whom God has placed over them in this kingdom; otherwise they *cannot be saved.* . . . Thus when the President of the Church, the stake president, the bishop, or any duly commissioned church officer counsels those over whom he presides to follow a certain course, the Church members involved must do so *at the peril of losing their salvation.* Paul's pronouncement, as restored to its original state by the Inspired Version [see chap. 27], so specifies.[92]

*Overcoming Temptation*

Overcoming temptation is an essential part of working out one's salvation.[93] If Mormons "fall into the practices and abominations of the sectarians; if they use tea, coffee, tobacco or liquor; if they fail to pay an honest tithing; if they find fault with the Lord's anointed; if they play cards; if they do anything contrary to the standards of personal righteousness required by the gospel [Mormonism]—then to that extent they are in personal apostasy. . . ."[94]

### Intelligence or Knowledge

Because Mormons believe that "the glory of God is intelligence" (*D&C*, 93:36), they stress this subject and seek after intelligence as they work to become gods. Specifically, Mormons seek after God's own intelligence: "In our pre-earth life, as now, some spirits were more intelligent than others. Abraham recorded: ". . . I am the Lord thy God, I am more intelligent than they all" (Abraham 3:19).[95]

Therefore, the more "intelligence" we achieve now the fuller our salvation will be later. According to *Doctrine and Covenants*:

> Whatever the principle of intelligence we attain unto in this life, it will rise with us in the resurrection. And, if a person gains more knowledge and intelligence in this life through his diligence and obedience than another, he will have so much the advantage in the world to come.[96]

Thus, contrary to what is said in 1 Corinthians 1:26-30, it is being "intelligent in this life" that helps save a person. Joseph Smith stated:

> The first principles of man are self-existent with God. God himself, finding he was in the midst of spirits and glory, *because* he was more intelligent, saw proper to institute laws whereby the rest could have a privilege to advance like himself. The relationship we have with God places us in a situation to advance in knowledge. He has power to institute laws to instruct the weaker intelligences, that they may be exalted with himself, so that they might have one glory upon another, and all that knowledge, power, glory and intelligence, *which is requisite in order to save them in the world of spirits*. . . . This is good doctrine. It tastes good. . . . [It is] given to me by the revelation of Jesus Christ.[97]

Mormonism is thus gnostic in stressing proper *knowledge* as a means of salvation:

> Knowledge saves a man; and in the world of spirits no man can be exalted but by knowledge.[98]

The principle of knowledge is the principle of salvation.[99]

It is impossible for a man to be saved in ignorance.[100]

It [salvation] cannot be obtained without some effort. It cannot be obtained without knowledge of the things of God. . . . [i.e.,] the saving principles and ordinances by which salvation comes! [Still] knowledge of them will not in itself save us! Obedience thereto will![101]

## Perseverance

He that would be saved must not only be sincere, but embrace the true gospel, be baptized into the true church, and continue a faithful member of the same unto the end. This is the *only way to be saved* with a full salvation.[102]

## Prayer

This course is essential if men are to be saved; *there is no salvation without prayer.*[103]

## Baptism

Without being immersed in water *no man can enter* into the fullness of Celestial glory. . . . Many have been taught to seek forgiveness by prayer, and have been told that baptism, being only an outward ordinance, would not avail anything. . . . These are doctrines of false teachers, and they are the wicked traditions handed down by apostate Christendom. *Baptism is a condition of forgiveness* . . . cursed be that man or angel who preaches another gospel, or perverts the true gospel of Christ.[104]

## Laying on of Hands

Baptism in water for the remission of sins, and the laying on of hands for the gift of the Holy Ghost, constitute the birth of the water and of the Spirit. *This is essential to salvation.* . . . The law governing this matter has been unalterably fixed.[105]

## Marriage/Clothing of Spirit Children

Remember that an early rationalization for Mormon teaching on polygamy was the necessity of "clothing" spirit children with physical bodies. Although most Mormons today reject polygamy (for this life), the making of bodies is still a high priority, in fact it is essential to salvation.

No man can be saved and exalted in the kingdom of God without the woman, and no woman can reach the perfection and exaltation in the kingdom of God alone.[106]

> Birth Control Is Wickedness.... *It is the duty of every righteous man and woman to prepare tabernacles for all the spirits they can.* ... Moreover, *may we not lose our own salvation if we violate this divine law?* ... *Those who willfully and maliciously design to break this important commandment shall be damned.*[107]

### Church Membership

> Salvation is in the church, and of the church, and is obtained *only through the church.*[108]

### Tithing

> The law of tithing is an eternal law ... that God has instituted for the benefit of the human family, for their *salvation and exaltation.*[109]

### Temple Work

> Temple work involves a variety of activities including 1) sacred rites of marriage both for the living and the dead (chap. 30) and 2) proxy baptism to allegedly help save the souls of the dead[110] (see chap. 19). Thus, in Mormon temples, "Sacred ordinances, [baptism] rites, and [marriage] ceremonies are performed which pertain to salvation and exaltation."[111] These temple ordinances not only claim to seal families together for eternity, but also actually involve pagan ceremonies where the living are ritually used to redeem the dead. The Mormon publication *Gospel Principles* comments, "These ordinances and covenants are *necessary for our salvation.* They must be performed in the temples of the Lord."[112]

In this section, we will briefly discuss the Mormon doctrine of proxy baptism and marriage for the dead primarily as it relates to salvation. But we will also briefly introduce the subject of temple occultism, which is discussed in more detail in chapter 19.

## Mormonism's Ritual for Saving the Dead (Second Chance Salvation)

Saving the dead is a vital work for every Mormon who wishes to attain godhood. For every committed Mormon, temple work involving rituals for the dead is an absolute requirement for salvation.

But as we show in chapter 19, most Mormons are unaware that these rituals may involve them in occultic activities that God has forbidden in the Bible (Deuteronomy 18:9-12). In attempting to save the dead, Mormons not infrequently encounter supernatural revelations from the alleged human dead or other spirits plus additional occultic phenomena. Mormons reject the idea that these spirits and their revelations are spiritual deceptions intended to lead them astray from biblical truth and to give the spirits more influence over their lives. But this is exactly what happens.

Joseph Heinerman is the author of several books discussing spiritistic manifestations and contacts within Mormon temples. Among them are *Temple Manifestations, Eternal Testimonies,* and *Spirit World Manifestations: Accounts of Divine Aid in Genealogical and Temple Work and Other Assistance To Latter-day Saints.* In the preface to the latter book he notes that the inhabitants of the spirit world are anxious to accommodate Mormons in their rites for the dead:

> The inhabitants of the spirit world have received special permission to visit their mortal descendants [Mormons] and assist them and impress upon their minds the primary importance of assimilating genealogical information and performing vicarious ordinance work in the temples.... Spirit world manifestations and angelic appearances have played and continue to play a major role in the upbuilding of God's kingdom [Mormonism] in these latter days.[113]

For this reason, the Mormon church requires such activity be undertaken for any Mormon who desires to please God and become a god himself. In other words, all those who desire salvation in Mormonism are required to engage in these pagan, occultic practices. In *Improvement Era,* Joseph Smith is recorded as declaring, "The greatest responsibility in this world that God has laid upon us is to seek after our dead."[114] In *Times and Seasons,* Smith emphasized, "Those Saints who neglect it [baptism for the dead], in behalf of their deceased relatives, do so at the peril of their own salvation."[115] Joseph Heinerman cites both of these statements and then comments, "Work for the dead is an important determining factor in the Latter-day Saints' attempt to attain their ultimate salvation and exaltation [godhood] in the Kingdom of God."[116]

Mormons hold that their proxy baptisms for the dead are proof that they are the one true church: they honestly believe they are saving those who have already died. Incredibly, some Mormons teach that "through baptism for the dead [rites] the Mormons have saved more souls than Christ did when he died on the cross"![117]

Even though the Bible explicitly denies that men can perform any action on behalf of another person's salvation, or that salvation is possible after death, Mormons take this role as the "saviors" of the dead. This conviction is what accounts for one of the world's largest genealogical archives being found within the confines of the Mormon church.

But this conviction is in direct conflict with the Bible's warning that "no man can by any means redeem his brother, or give to God a ransom for him—for the redemption of his soul is costly, and he should cease trying forever" (Psalm 49:7,8). Further, the Bible also warns that salvation is not possible after death, because "it is appointed for men to die once, and after this comes judgment" (Hebrews 9:27).

But Joseph Smith and Mormonism reject these biblical teachings. Smith said of the biblical doctrine that salvation must happen in this life, "Such an idea is worse than atheism."[118] And as we have seen, he warned Mormons that failure to save their dead meant loss of their own salvation.

So when Mormons speak of themselves as being the "saviors of men," it is specifically in regard to their saving the dead. In *The Way to Perfection*, sixth president and prophet Joseph F. Smith emphasized the importance of the individual Mormon becoming a savior to other men: "But greater than all this, so far as our individual responsibilities are concerned, the greatest is to become saviors, in our lesser degree which is assigned us, for the dead who have died without a knowledge of the [Mormon] gospel."[119] This concept is explained in greater detail by the tenth president and prophet, Joseph Fielding Smith, in his *Doctrines of Salvation*. Because water baptism is required for salvation, which is physically impossible for the dead, there must be a live stand-in:

> If a man cannot enter the kingdom of God without baptism, then the dead must be baptized. But how can they be baptized in water for the remission of their sins [when they are dead]? . . . The only way it can be done is vicariously, someone who is living acting as a substitute for the dead.
>
> When we go into the temple and act for somebody else, we are . . . doing for him just what he would have to do if he were [still] in mortal life. Thus, *we bring to pass his salvation.* . . . By this means we may help to save those who have gone before and in our limited way become saviors to many people. . . . There is no work equal to that in the temple for the dead in teaching a man to love his neighbor as himself. Jesus so loved the world that he was willing to offer himself as a sacrifice for sin that the world might be saved. We also have the privilege, in a small degree. . . . Will not we have to answer for the blood of our dead, if we neglect these ordinances in their behalf? . . . If we willfully neglect the salvation of our dead, then also *we shall stand rejected of the Lord*, because we have rejected our dead (emphasis added).[120]

Thus, Joseph Fielding Smith taught that after seeking one's own salvation, "The Lord says that our greatest *individual responsibility* is to seek after our dead."[121] Why? Because Mormonism teaches that its role in saving the dead is in many ways just as important as that of Christ's role in salvation on the cross. Mormons are saviors just as Christ is—by their sacrificial action they actually help forgive the sins of men in the afterlife and thus save them. Again, Joseph Fielding Smith emphasizes the importance of this work:

The reason for this [proxy baptism] is that all the dead must be redeemed from their sins through obedience to the gospel just as the living are. It is required for us to perform this labor in their behalf. . . . Therefore our salvation and progression depends on the salvation of our worthy dead with whom we must be joined in family ties. This can only be accomplished in our temples. The Prophet [Joseph Smith] further declared that the doctrine of salvation for the dead is the "most glorious of all subjects belonging to the everlasting gospel." The reasons for this are the great magnitude of the labor, and the fact that we have the privilege of officiating for the dead and assisting in giving to them the privileges that we also enjoy, through our obedience to the gospel. . . . Do we Latter-day Saints fully realize the importance of the mighty responsibility placed on us in relation to the salvation of the world?[122]

In other words, if, comparatively speaking, only a few people have been saved historically by the death of Christ on the cross—and a much larger number of people are able to be saved by Mormonism's rites for the dead—then none can deny that Mormonism plays a *larger* role in the salvation of the world than even Christ Himself! Mormons may or may not accept this conclusion, but it is the logical result of their doctrine.

The *Doctrines of the Gospel: Student Manual* also emphasizes the absolute necessity of engaging in close contact with the dead in order to achieve salvation. It explains that God Himself has commanded that "vicarious baptisms" be performed to enable spirits in the spirit world to receive the gospel and enter God's kingdom.[123] It further states that a spirit claiming it was the prophet Elijah appeared to Joseph Smith in the Kirtland Temple, restoring the power for men to influence the destiny of the dead.[124] Thus, "Latter-day Israel [Mormons] cannot be made perfect without doing the ordinance work for their dead, nor can the dead be made perfect without this work having been done for them."[125] These ordinances are said to "provide the dead with the opportunity to receive full salvation" or godhood. In other words, "It is through the temple that we will be able to reach our dead and not otherwise. To pray for the dead may not be of any real assistance to them. To actually help them, we must do a work for them."[126]

Mormons are further told that it is not sufficient for husband and wife to be sealed in the temple in order to guarantee that they become gods— "they must also be eternally linked with their progenitors [dead ancestors] and see that the work [proxy temple marriage] is done for those ancestors."[127] To cite Joseph Smith's *History of the Church*, "It is not only necessary that you should be baptized for your dead, but you will have to go through all the ordinances [proxy temple marriage] for them, the same as you have gone through to save yourselves."[128] Joseph Fielding Smith, in *Doctrines of Salvation*, is quoted as saying that "none is exempt from this great obligation. It is required of the apostle as well as the humblest elder. . . . [Nothing] will . . . entitle one to disregard the salvation of one's dead."[129] Finally, we are told the spirits themselves are anxiously awaiting Mormon activity on their behalf. Former president and prophet Spencer W. Kimball stated, "We know that the spirit world is filled with the spirits of men who are waiting for you and me to get busy."[130]

Mormons must particularly attend to their own family history as far back as it can be traced. However, because God is no respecter of persons, they are also required to help save non-Mormons. Thus, they teach that every spirit who has not heard the gospel in this life will hear it in the next life and have the opportunity to have his or her sins forgiven through proxy baptism.[131]

Unfortunately, as we will see in our section on Mormonism and the occult, this teaching is an open door to spiritism, especially in light of the Mormon emphasis placed upon ties to family members after death. All people are naturally close to their families, and both Mormonism and the spirit world use this fact to their advantage.

Here we have one more tie to ancient paganism within Mormonism. Although not involving literal ancestor worship, the extreme emphasis on the dead causes an acute awareness among Mormons of their importance to their own deceased. As in pagan cultures, in Mormonism dead ancestors are dependent upon the living for advancement in the next life. Therefore, the living must serve the needs of the dead. The Tanners' comments are relevant:

> Because of this emphasis on work for the dead, one Mormon has compared the church to the ancient Egyptians. The Egyptians, of course, spent a fantastic amount of time and money building pyramids and doing other work for their dead. The *Book of Mormon* says that the false churches "rob the poor because of their fine sanctuaries" (2 Nephi 28:13), yet the Mormon Church is spending millions of dollars building beautiful temples. . . . The Mormon leaders are planning to build temples in a number of other countries in the near future. Most of the "endowments" performed in Mormon temples are for the dead; therefore, when we add the millions of dollars spent for temples and their upkeep to the millions spent on genealogical research, we find that the Mormons are similar to the ancient Egyptians in their attitudes toward the dead. The obsession with the dead approaches very close to ancestral worship.[132]

But there is one final example of Mormonism's connection to paganism.

## The Mormon Doctrine of Preexistence

A final illustration of the Mormon emphasis on salvation by works is related to the Latter-day Saints' doctrine of preexistence. As with the pagan doctrine of reincarnation, Mormons teach that our position on earth is determined by good works and personal merit in a previous life. The difference between Mormon preexistence and reincarnation is that these previous actions were done in the spirit world, not here on the earth—and, of course, in the number of incarnations. Mormonism teaches that there is only one. As with reincarnation, however, Mormons agree that "God has drawn a veil of forgetfulness across our minds." In other words, Mormons do not remember their previous existence as a test of their personal faithfulness to God.[133]

Nevertheless, it was personal virtue in a past life that determined the rewards experienced in this life:

> Men are elected, called, foreordained, all on the basis of preexistent preparation. Thus Joseph Smith was called to stand as one of the mightiest prophets of the ages . . . because of the talents and capacities earned in the pre-mortal life.[134]

> Is there reason then why the type of birth we receive in this life is not a reflection of our worthiness or lack of it in the preexistent life? . . . Can we account in any other way for the birth of some of the children of God in darkest Africa, or in flood ridden China, or among the starving hoards of India, while some of the rest of us are born here in the United States? We cannot escape the conclusion that because of performance in our preexistence some of us are born as Chinese, some as Japanese, some as Latter-day Saints.[135]

Thus, personal merit and good works are the determining factor, not only for a Mormon's place in the afterlife, but also for his or her place in this life.

In conclusion, Mormonism may claim to believe in salvation by grace. But the written testimony—of its three scriptures, of all its presidents and prophets, of numerous theologians and church leaders—and their entire ecclesiastical system betray this claim to be false.

From the moment a person joins the Mormon church, he is depending upon his own works of righteousness to exalt him and make him a god; he is not depending on the finished work of Jesus Christ on the cross.

Because the Mormon church has preached "another gospel" than the one God has revealed, it stands condemned before Him as a false gospel. Rather than saving, it will ultimately damn the souls of those who accept it. This is why the Apostle Paul was so severe in his condemnation of all false gospels. He perceived that there were many who wanted "to distort the Gospel of Christ." For that reason he gave this warning: "But even though we, or an angel from heaven, should preach to you a gospel contrary to that which we have preached to you, let him be accursed. As we have said before, so I say again now, if any man is preaching to you a gospel contrary to that which you received, let him be accursed" (Galatians 1:8,9).

## The Biblical Teaching on Salvation

What the Bible teaches about salvation is completely opposed to Mormon doctrine. The Bible clearly reveals that salvation does not come through personal righteousness or personal merit and good works, but only through the grace of God and the individual's faith in Christ's finished work on the cross.[136] Consider just a few Scriptures from Jesus and the New Testament. Each one teaches that salvation comes by faith— not works (emphasis added).

> I tell you *the truth*, whoever hears my word and believes him who sent me *has eternal life* and *will not be condemned*; he *has crossed over* from the death to life (John 5:24 NIV).

> Truly, truly, I say to you, he who believes *has eternal life* (John 6:47).

> Jesus answered and said to them, "*This* is the work of God, that you *believe* in Him whom He has sent" (John 6:29).

> Of Him all the prophets bear witness that through His name every one *who believes* in Him receives forgiveness of sins (Acts 10:43).

> For we maintain that a man is justified *by faith* apart from works of the Law (Romans 3:28).

> Just as David also speaks of the blessing upon the man to whom God reckons righteousness *apart from works* (Romans 4:6).

> For Christ is the end of the law for righteousness to everyone who *believes* (Romans 10:4).

> But if it is by grace, it is *no longer on the basis of works*, otherwise grace *is no longer grace* (Romans 11:6).

> For by grace you have been saved through faith; and that not of yourselves, it is *the gift of God*; not as a result *of works*, that *no one* should boast (Ephesians 2:8,9).

> I do not nullify the grace of God; for if righteousness comes through the Law, then Christ *died needlessly* (Galatians 2:21).

> Now that *no one* is justified *by the Law* before God is evident; for, the righteous man shall live by faith. However, the Law is not of faith; on the contrary, "He who practices them shall live by them." Christ

redeemed us from *the curse of the Law*, having become a curse for us—for it is written, "Cursed is everyone who hangs on a tree" (Galatians 3:11-13).

He saved us, *not on the basis of deeds which we have done in righteousness*, but *according to His mercy*, by the washing of regeneration and renewing by the Holy Spirit (Titus 3:5).

Before his conversion, the attitude of the Apostle Paul was like that of many religious people, in particular many Mormons. He accepted the idea that God's way of salvation was through his own ability to keep the Law—in this case, the law of Moses. In fact, in Philippians 3 he says that if *anyone* had a right to "confidence in the flesh," he did (v. 3), and that "as to the righteousness which is in the law" he was "found blameless" (v. 6). In Mormon theology, this would certainly earn him his exaltation.

But what was Paul's response to his own zealousness for salvation by good works and personal merit? After his salvation, how did he view his own personal righteousness? Compared to knowing Christ personally, he declares that it was all "rubbish":

More than that, I count all things to be loss in view of the surpassing value of knowing Christ Jesus my Lord, for whom I have suffered the loss of all things, and count them but rubbish in order that I may gain Christ, and may be found in Him, *not having a righteousness of my own derived from the Law*, but that which is through faith in Christ, *the righteousness which comes from God on the basis of faith* (Philippians 3:8,9, emphasis added).

Paul puts "no confidence in the flesh" (v. 3) because he has a new understanding of God's holiness. God Himself calls even the best of our righteousness "filthy rags" (Isaiah 64:6 NIV; cf. Proverbs 16:5). Thus, Paul declares that whatever he thought was gain for him, for example, blamelessness as to the Law, was but "loss" and "rubbish" compared to knowing Christ personally. In other words, all his good works and obedience to Law were *nothing* compared to his experience of salvation by faith in Christ alone (v. 7-9).

This is what Mormons need to find: the same salvation that Paul did, "For if a law had been given that could impart life, then righteousness would certainly have come by the law" (Galatians 3:21 NIV).

## ♦ ♦ *Appendix One* ♦ ♦

*Is Mormonism Correct in Morally Distinguishing Between Mosaic and Gospel Law?*

Mormons argue that Paul only condemned the belief in keeping the *Mosaic* law as a means to salvation; he never condemned the belief in keeping the *Gospel* law as a means to salvation. In other words, when Mormons claim they do *not* teach salvation by works, what they mean is that they do not teach that salvation comes through *Mosaic* works—the ceremonial law as found in Leviticus for example.[137] But other works, what Mormonism calls "Gospel" works, *are* necessary for salvation. Obedience in keeping the more difficult Gospel law means that failure to keep the Mosiac law (as defined in Mormonism) does not condemn someone.[138] Understanding this Mormon distinction between Gospel law and Mosaic law is crucial:

> But did not Paul say that salvation came by faith alone, without works? Yes, he most assuredly did; and he also said that the works he was talking about were the performances [ceremony] of the Mosaic Law.[139]

Theologian McConkie explains that because the Mosaic law is now abrogated, God has substituted a better law in its place—the Gospel law—and that keeping this law *is* essential for salvation:

> In effect Paul is saying that the law of Moses was good in its day, that God gave it for a purpose, but that now it is dead, and in place thereof God has given a higher law *to which all men must now turn for salvation.* . . . Now, Paul philosophizes, *since he obeys* the higher gospel law, he cannot be condemned for failure to keep the lesser Mosaic standard. . . . But even after the gospel law is imprinted in his mind, carnal desires persist; *and if they are not subdued, he is not justified.*[140]

The Mormon church must maintain this distinction so that it may be claimed that when Paul rejected "law keeping" as a way of salvation, he was *only* referring to the (e.g., ceremonial) law of Moses and not the moral law itself. But Mormonism is wrong. In Galatians 2 and 3 it is the *moral* law of God, not the ceremonial law, which Paul says *cannot* be a way of salvation since "the Law" requires—even demands—man to be sinlessly perfect (Galatians 3:10-12). Because no one is, or ever can be, sinlessly perfect (Romans 3:10-17), all men who approach God by moral law keeping are condemned (Romans 3:19; 4:6,15). Further, Paul never stated—anywhere—that he successfully kept the "Gospel Law"; to the contrary, he said he could *not* keep it (Romans 7; Philippians 3).

Thus, this distinction between Mosaic and Gospel law is not only arbitrary, but also it is false. The Mosaic law and Gospel law are "one" law as far as moral requirements before God are concerned. For example, Jesus' teaching on "Gospel law" in the Sermon on the Mount simply amplifies and extends the teachings of the Mosaic Law. Jesus came to fulfill the law of Moses, both in His life and actions. And certainly if Christ came to fulfill the law of Moses, then His personal emphasis on moral law over ceremonial law indicates the moral nature of the law of Moses.

Jesus emphasized the true meaning of the Mosaic law. When God said, "Thou shalt not kill," it involved an attitude of the heart as well. Just as lusting after a woman was committing adultery in the heart, so hatred was murder in the heart, and whether in the heart or in the act, both violated the moral law of God (Matthew 5:20-28). This inner sense of the law was evident in the Mosaic law itself (Exodus 20:17).

Thus, when Mormonism attempts to make a distinction between Mosaic and Gospel law, it is not doing justice to the underlying moral unity of those laws. It cannot claim that when New Testament Scripture speaks of the "law of Moses" it refers primarily or only to the "lower teachings" of Moses—the "carnal commandments" of "ordinances and performances" in Leviticus, Exodus, etc.[141]

Since it is biblically true that the Mosaic law included the moral law of God, one cannot imply that if the ceremonial aspects of the Mosaic law are now ended, that the moral aspects of the Mosaic law have no authority over us. God's moral law does not change, nor the human inability to keep it.

And as we have abundantly documented, Mormons do hope to attain salvation by keeping the moral law. But the claim to be able to keep the "higher" moral law of God (the Gospel law) not only denies scriptural teaching, it also makes the atonement of Christ unnecessary, for "if righteousness comes through the Law, then Christ died needlessly" (Galatians 2:21), and "if a Law had been given which was able to impart life, then righteousness would indeed have been based on Law" (Galatians 3:21). Obviously, then, such a law was never given.

Righteousness does not come through moral law because Christ did *not* die needlessly; the law *cannot* impart eternal life because it has no *power* to do so. These facts undermine the central pillar of Mormonism: that salvation comes through actually keeping the moral law of God.

As we have seen, the Apostle Paul taught that he did not come to know Christ on the basis of personal righteousness. He only came to know Christ by faith. If Paul rejected Mosaic works as an impossible standard for salvation, how could he possibly accept the far more difficult Gospel standards that Mormons claim they can keep (Philippians 3:9,10)? Anyone who carefully examines the standards of the "Gospel law" can only conclude they are impossible to uphold. One only need read the Sermon on the Mount to see that what is required is absolute perfection. No Mormon will ever meet such a standard—whether in this life, or the next or a thousand others.

Thus, James 2:10 (cf. 3:2) condemns every form of self perfectionism: He who stumbles in one point of the law has become guilty of breaking the entire law. This was one point of the Sermon on the Mount. For example, the smallest sin (such as calling your brother a fool) is judged worthy of eternal punishment (Matthew 5:22). This places all men under the guilt of sin. And one who is entirely guilty needs God's grace and mercy—not the pride engendered by a system that teaches that works will save you and make you a god.

In trusting their own righteousness for salvation, Mormons will never be saved, let alone be exalted as Gods; unfortunately they will only be condemned as unforgiven and unrepentant sinners.

## ♦ ♦ *Appendix Two* ♦ ♦

*The Biblical Doctrine of Justification by Faith*

I. *"Justification" is the act of God whereby He forgives the sins of believers and declares them righteous by imputing the obedience and righteousness of Christ to them through faith.* (See Luke 18:9-14.)

Justification is arguably the single most important doctrine in the Bible. It is without question a doctrine that is rejected and opposed by all cults and indeed all religions outside of Christianity. In his book *Know Your Christian Life: A Theological Introduction*, theologian Sinclair Ferguson discusses its importance, not only for the church but also for the Christian:

> Martin Luther, whose grasp of the gospel was better than most, once said that the doctrine of Justification was the article by which the Church stands or falls. "This article," he said, "is the head and cornerstone of the Church, which alone begets, nourishes, builds, preserves and protects the Church; without it the Church of God cannot subsist one hour." Luther was right. Although for our understanding of the general shape and direction of the Christian life we have suggested the doctrine of regeneration is important, the doctrine of justification is central. Not only is it the article of the standing or falling Church, but also of the standing or falling Christian. Probably more trouble is caused in the Christian life by an inadequate or mistaken view of this doctrine than any other. When the child of God loses his sense of peace with God, finds his concern for others dried up, or generally finds his sense of the sheer goodness and grace of God diminished, it is from this fountain that he has ceased to drink. Conversely, if we can gain a solid grounding here, we have the foundation for a life of peace and joy.[142]

He then explains why this doctrine is difficult—for some to accept:

> The practical importance of this cannot be exaggerated. The glory of the gospel is that God has declared Christians

to be rightly related to him in spite of their sin. But our greatest temptation and mistake is to try to smuggle character into his work of grace. How easily we fall into the trap of assuming that we only remain justified so long as there are grounds in our character for that justification. But Paul's teaching is that nothing we do ever contributes to our justification. So powerful was his emphasis on this that men accused him of teaching that it did not matter how they lived if God justified them. If God justifies us as we are, what is the point of holiness? There is still a sense in which this is a test of whether we offer the world the grace of God in the Gospel. Does it make men say: "You are offering grace that is so free it doesn't make any difference how you live"? This was precisely the objection the Pharisees had to Jesus' teaching![143]

Here are the characteristics that distinguish justification:

II. *What justification is not:*

1. It is not a *reward* for anything good we have done.

2. It is not something in which we cooperate with God. (It is not sanctification.)

3. It is not infused righteousness which results in good works which become the basis of justification (the Mormon and Catholic concept of justification).

4. It is not accomplished apart from the satisfaction of God's justice, i.e., it is not unjust.

5. It is not subject to degrees—one cannot be more or less justified; one can only be fully justified or fully unjustified.

III. *What justification is:*

1. Justification is an undeserved free gift of God's mercy (Romans 3:24; Titus 3:7).

2. Justification is entirely accomplished by *God, once* for all. (It is not a process like personal sanctification, but knowledge of it does help produce sanctification.)

One of the leading theologians of our time, James Packer stated:

> This justification, though individually located at the point of time at which a man believes (Rom. 4:3; 5:1), is an eschatological once-for-all divine act, the final judgment brought into the present. The justifying sentence, once

passed, is irrevocable. "The Wrath" (Rom. 5:9) will not touch the justified. Those accepted now are secure forever. Inquisition before Christ's judgment seat (Rom. 14:10-12; 2 Cor. 5:10) may deprive them of certain rewards (1 Cor. 3:15) but never of their justified status. Christ will not call into question God's justifying verdict, only declare, endorse and implement it.[144]

In other words, if God the Father *justified* us at the point of belief, is it possible the Son would ever repudiate the Father's legal declaration?

3. Justification involves an *imputed* righteousness entirely apart from works: the righteousness of God Himself has been given to the believer. It has nothing to do with a person's own righteousness (Romans 4:5,6,17-25).

It is not only that God overlooks our sin and guilt, but also that full and entire holiness is credited to our account. Bruce Milne describes the transaction this way:

> Our justification is not simply a matter of God's overlooking our guilt; our need can be met only if righteousness, full and entire holiness of character, is credited to us. This is the amazing gift of grace. Christ's law-keeping and perfect righteousness are made ours by faith in Him (1 Cor. 1:30; Phil. 3:9). It is not simply that our abysmal failure in life's moral examination is overlooked; we pass with 100%, First Class Honours! Well may Athanasius speak of "the amazing exchange" whereby, as Calvin puts it, "the Son of God though spotlessly pure took upon Himself the ignominy and shame of our sin and in return clothes us with His purity."[145]

Righteousness is imputed because the believer actually is united to Christ. In other words, because the believer is "in Christ," the righteousness of Christ is imputed to him. Justification is the subsequent legal recognition of that fact. We are declared (past tense) righteous. We *now* have perfect righteousness before God (not personally, but legally).

> But by His doing you are in Christ Jesus, who became to us wisdom from God, and righteousness and sanctification, and redemption (1 Corinthians 1:30).

> He made Him who knew no sin to be sin on our behalf, that we might become the righteousness of God in Him (2 Corinthians 5:21).

In his book *God's Words: Studies of Key Bible Themes*, J.I. Packer discusses the meaning of justification and contrasts it with the Catholic and Mormon view:

> To "justify" in the Bible means to "declare righteous": to declare, that is, of a man on trial, that he is not liable to any penalty, but is entitled to all the privileges due to those who have kept the law. . . . The Church of Rome has always maintained that God's act of justifying is primarily, if not wholly, one of making righteous, by inner spiritual renewal, but there is no biblical or linguistic ground for this view, though it goes back at least as far as Augustine. Paul's synonyms for "justify" are "reckon (impute) righteousness," "forgive (more correctly, remit) sins," "not reckon sin" (see Rom. 4:5-8)—all phrases which express the idea, not of inner transformation, but of conferring a legal status and cancelling a legal liability. Justification is a judgment passed on man, not a work wrought within man; God's gift of a status and a relationship to himself, not of a new heart. Certainly, God does regenerate those whom he justifies, but the two things are not the same.[146]

Thus, as *Baker's Dictionary of Theology* points out, every believer in Christ is now treated by God as if they are righteous (on the basis of their imputed righteousness), not as if they are sinners:

> "The righteousness of God" [i.e., righteousness from God: see Philippians 3:9] is bestowed on them as a free gift (Romans 1:17, 3:21 ff.; 5:17, cf. 9:30; 10:3-10): that is to say, they receive the right to be treated and the promise that they shall be treated, no longer as sinners, but as righteous, by the divine Judge. Thus they become "the righteousness of God" in and through Him who "knew no sin" personally but was representatively "made sin" (treated as a sinner, and punished) in their stead (1 Corinthians 5:21). This is the thought expressed in classical Protestant theology by the phrase "the imputation of Christ's righteousness," namely, that believers are righteous (Romans 5:19) and have righteousness (Philippians 3:9) before God for no other reason than that Christ their Head was righteous before God, and they are one with Him, sharers of His status and acceptance. God justifies them by passing on them, for Christ's sake, the verdict which Christ's obedience merited. God declares them to be righteous, because He reckons them to be righteous; and He reckons righteousness to them, not because He accounts them to have kept His law personally

(which would be a false judgment), but because He accounts them to be united to the one who kept it representatively (and that is a true judgment). For Paul, union with Christ is not fantasy, but fact—the basic fact indeed in Christianity; and the doctrine of imputed righteousness is simply Paul's exposition of the forensic aspect of it (see Romans 5:12 ff.).[147]

4. Justification is accomplished in harmony with God's justice. It displays His holiness; it does not deny it. The only way for the sinner's justification to be truly just in God's eyes is for two requirements to be absolutely satisfied. The first is that every requirement of the law must be satisfied. The second is that the infinitely holy character of God must be satisfied. J.I. Packer comments:

> The only way in which justification can be just is for the law to be satisfied so far as the justified are concerned. But the law makes a double demand on sinners: it requires both their full obedience to its precepts, as God's creatures, and their full endurance of its penalty, as transgressors. How could they conceivably meet this double demand? The answer is that it has been met already by the Lord Jesus Christ, acting in their name. The eternal Son of God was "born under the law" (Galatians 4:4) in order that he might yield double submission to the law in his people's stead. Both aspects of his submission are indicated in Paul's words: "he . . . became *obedient—unto* death" (Philippians 2:8). His life of righteousness culminated in his dying the death of unrighteous according to the will of God: he bore the penal curse of the law in man's place (Galatians 3:13) to make propitiation for man's sins (Romans 3:25).
>
> And thus, "through one act of righteousness"—the life and death of the sinless Christ—"there resulted justification of life to all men" (Romans 5:18 NASB).[148]

He concludes:

> Paul's thesis is that God justifies sinners on a just ground, namely, that the claims of God's law upon them have been fully satisfied. The law has not been altered, or suspended, or flouted for their justification, but fulfilled—by Jesus Christ, acting in their name. By perfectly serving God, Christ perfectly kept the law (cf. Matthew 3:15). His obedience culminated in death (Philippians 2:8); He bore the penalty of the law in men's place (Galatians 3:13), to make propitiation for their sins (Romans 3:25). On the grounds of

Christ's obedience, God does not impute sin, but imputes righteousness, to sinners who believe (Romans 4:2-8; 5:19).[149]

This is exactly what Scripture teaches—that God can be both just and the justifier of those who place their faith in Jesus:

> For all have sinned and fall short of the glory of God, being justified as a gift by His grace through the redemption which is in Christ Jesus; whom God displayed publicly as a propitiation in His blood through faith. This was to demonstrate His righteousness, because in the forbearance of God He passed over the sins previously committed; for the demonstration, I say, of His righteousness at the present time, that He might be just and the justifier of the one who has faith in Jesus (Romans 3:23-26).

IV. *Scripture Proof:*

| | |
|---|---|
| Genesis 15:6 | "Then he believed in the Lord; and He reckoned it to him as righteousness." |
| Psalm 32:2 | "How blessed is the man to whom the Lord does not impute iniquity, . . ." |
| Isaiah 54:17 | " 'No weapon that is formed against you shall prosper; and every tongue that accuses you in judgment you will condemn. This is the heritage of the servants of the Lord, and their vindication is from Me,' declares the Lord." |
| Jeremiah 23:6 | "In His days Judah will be saved, and Israel will dwell securely; and this is His name by which He will be called, the Lord our righteousness." |
| Habakkuk 2:4 | "Behold, as for the proud one, his soul is not right within him; but the righteous will live by his faith." |
| Romans 3:28 | "For we maintain that a man is justified by faith apart from works of the Law." |
| Romans 4:3-6 | "For what does the Scripture say? 'And Abraham believed God, and it was reckoned to him as righteousness.' Now to the one who works, his wage is not reckoned as a favor but as what is due. But to the one who does not work, but believes in Him who justifies the ungodly, his faith is reckoned as righteousness, just as David also speaks of the blessing upon the man to whom God reckons righteousness apart from works." |

| | |
|---|---|
| Romans 5:1 | "Therefore having been justified by faith, we have peace with God through our Lord Jesus Christ." |
| Romans 5:9 | "Much more then, having now been justified by His blood, we shall be saved from the wrath of God through Him." |
| Romans 9:30-10:4 | "What shall we say then? That Gentiles, who did not pursue righteousness, attained righteousness, even the righteousness which is by faith; but Israel, pursuing a law of righteousness, did not arrive at that law. Why? Because they did not pursue it by faith, but as though it were by works. They stumbled over the stumbling stone, just as it is written, 'Behold, I lay in Zion a stone of stumbling and a rock of offense, and he who believes in Him will not be disappointed.' Brethren, my heart's desire and my prayer to God for them is for their salvation. For I bear them witness that they have a zeal for God, but not in accordance with knowledge. For not knowing about God's righteousness, and seeking to establish their own, they did not subject themselves to the righteousness of God. For Christ is the end of the law for righteousness to everyone who believes." |
| 1 Corinthians 6:11 | "And such were some of you; but you were washed, but you were sanctified, but you were justified in the name of the Lord Jesus Christ, and in the Spirit of our God." |
| Galatians 2:16 | "Nevertheless knowing that a man is not justified by the works of the Law but through faith in Christ Jesus, even we have believed in Christ Jesus, that we may be justified by faith in Christ, and not by the works of the Law; since by the works of the Law shall no flesh be justified." |
| Galatians 3:8,9 | "And the Scripture, foreseeing that God would justify the Gentiles by faith, preached the gospel beforehand to Abraham, saying, 'All the nations shall be blessed in you.' So then those who are of faith are blessed with Abraham, the believer." |
| Galatians 3:21,24 | "Is the Law then contrary to the promises of God? May it never be! For if a law had been given |

which was able to impart life, then righteousness would indeed have been based on law.... Therefore the Law has become our tutor to lead us to Christ, that we may be justified by faith."

**V.** *Important applications of justification include the following:*

1. Justification demands we trust in Christ's righteousness alone and not our own.

| | |
|---|---|
| Acts 13:39 | "And through Him everyone who believes is freed from all things, from which you could not be freed through the Law of Moses." |
| Philippians 3:8-10 | "More than that, I count all things to be loss in view of the surpassing value of knowing Christ Jesus my Lord, for whom I have suffered the loss of all things, and count them but rubbish in order that I may gain Christ, and may be found in Him, not having a righteousness of my own derived from the Law, but that which is through faith in Christ, the righteousness which comes from God on the basis of faith, that I may know Him, and the power of His resurrection and the fellowship of His sufferings, being conformed to His death." |
| Galatians 5:4,5 | "You have been severed from Christ, you who are seeking to be justified by law; you have fallen from grace. For we through the Spirit, by faith, are waiting for the hope of righteousness." |

2. Justification properly orients Christian morality.

a. The motive for Christian service and living becomes obedience out of love and gratitude to a Savior whose gift of righteousness made law keeping unnecessary, not pride and self-exaltation in self-righteousness and good works.

| | |
|---|---|
| Romans 12:1,2 | "I urge you therefore, brethren, by the mercies of God, to present your bodies a living and holy sacrifice, acceptable to God, which is your spiritual service of worship. And do not be conformed to this world, but be transformed by the renewing of your mind, that you may prove what the will of God is, that which is good and acceptable and perfect." |

b. The doctrine of justification encourages morality and discourages licentiousness when we consider the One who redeemed us and the cost of our redemption. (Cf. Romans 6:10-18.)

| | |
|---|---|
| Romans 6:1,2 | "What shall we say then? Are we to continue in sin that grace might increase? May it never be! How shall we who died to sin still live in it?" |
| Colossians 1:10 | "So that you may walk in a manner worthy of the Lord, to please Him in all respects, bearing fruit in every good work and increasing in the knowledge of God." |
| 1 Thessalonians 2:12 | "So that you may walk in a manner worthy of the God who calls you into His own kingdom and glory." |
| Romans 6:17,18 | "But thanks be to God that though you were slaves of sin, you became obedient from the heart to that form of teaching to which you were committed, and having been freed from sin, you became slaves of righteousness." |

3. Justification means Christians may be assured that they *now* possess eternal life.

a. A divine gift is perfect and cannot be taken back. The gifts and calling of God are without repentance (Romans 11:29).

Perfect righteousness is a gift (James 1:17; Romans 3:24). God can only give perfect righteousness if we are declared perfectly righteous by Him. What condition can exist in the future so that we can lose our righteous standing? If righteousness is a gift to sinners and enemies (if He did the most for us when we hated Him and were His enemies), will God do *less* for us now that we are His precious children (Romans 5:8,9)?

b. Eternal life could only be a present condition on a just basis: if from the point of belief we were "eternally righteous" i.e., declared eternally righteous. This is why Scripture teaches that the believer now has *eternal* life.

| | |
|---|---|
| John 5:24 | "Truly, truly, I say to you, he who hears My word, and believes Him who sent Me, *has eternal life*, and does not come into judgment, but has passed out of death into life." |
| John 6:47 | "Truly, truly, I say to you, he who believes *has eternal life*." |

John 6:54 "He who eats My flesh and drinks My blood *has eternal life*, and I will raise him up on the last day."

1 John 5:10-13 "The one who believes in the Son of God has the witness in himself; the one who does not believe God has made Him a liar, because he has not believed in the witness that God has borne concerning His Son. And the witness is this, that God *has given us eternal life*, and this life is in His Son. He who has the Son has the life; he who does not have the Son of God does not have the life. These things I have written to you who believe in the name of the Son of God, in order that you may *know* that you *have eternal life*" (cf. 3:14).

◆

# CHAPTER 15

# What Do Mormons Believe About the Atoning Death of Jesus Christ?

Mormonism repeatedly claims that it believes in the biblical atonement of Jesus Christ. One frequently finds statements in Mormon literature to the effect that "Christ died for our sins." When talking with Mormons, they will affirm over and over that they believe Christ has died for their sins. But Mormons mean something different by these statements from what Christians mean.

First, let us give you some examples of what Mormonism claims about the atonement. Theologian Bruce McConkie claims that "salvation comes because of the atonement."[150] James Talmage argues that Jesus "bore the weight of the sins of the whole world, not only of Adam but of his posterity."[151]

The *Doctrines of the Gospel: Student Manual* emphasizes:

> No doctrine in the gospel is more important than the atonement of Jesus Christ. . . . The Savior . . . suffer[ed] for the sins of all the children of God. . . . The infinite atonement affects worlds without number and will save all of God's children except sons of perdition.[152]

The current president and prophet of the Mormon church, Ezra Taft Benson, teaches, "In Gethsemane* and on Calvary, He worked out the

---

* Mormons believe that most or all of Christ's atonement was wrought at Gethsemane, not on the cross. See *Achieving a Celestial Marriage Student Manual*, p. 6.

infinite and eternal atonement. . . . It was in Gethsemane that Jesus took on himself the sins of the world, . . . That holy, unselfish act of voluntarily taking on himself the sins of all other men is called the Atonement."[153]

The *Book of Mormon* also claims that Christ died for our sins. It has Jesus saying, "I . . . have been slain for the sins of the world" (3 Nephi 11:14). And it teaches that "the sufferings and death of Christ atone for their [men's] sins, through faith and repentance" (Alma 22:14).

But while these statements sound Christian, Mormons mean something different by them. Mormons really do *not* believe that Christ has effectively died for their sins and paid the actual penalty of divine justice necessary for their forgiveness. As we show below, Christ's death made forgiveness of sins possible but it was conditioned upon obedience to law.

Further, Mormons believe that forgiveness of sins is *not* immediately received upon true faith, repentance, baptism, etc. True forgiveness of sins requires a lengthy probationary period. Worse yet, serious sins will cause the *loss* of salvation. In this sense, even *Mormon* salvation does not necessarily constitute forgiveness of "serious sins."[154]

In Mormonism, the death of Christ accomplished two principal things, neither of them directly equivalent to actually forgiving a person's sins.[155]

First, Mormons claim that Christ's atonement produced a release from physical death. Christ defeated physical death so that all men will one day be raised from the dead. Second, Christ's atonement defeated spiritual death in that men now have the opportunity to earn the right to come back into the presence of God through obedience to law. We may thus document at least three principal Mormon teachings concerning the atonement: 1) the atonement delivers from physical death by way of resurrection from the dead; 2) the atonement delivers from spiritual death in that it makes forgiveness of sins possible by law keeping, and 3) the Christian view of the atonement is therefore a delusion. We discuss these in turn:

### 1. The atonement delivers from physical death.

The *Book of Mormon* asserts that Christ's death paid the penalty for Adam's fall: "The Messiah cometh in fullness of time, that he may redeem the children of men from the fall" (2 Nephi 2:26). Mormonism teaches that the Fall not only brought physical death but also some degree of spiritual death, often defined as removal from God's presence, and death to the "things of righteousness."*[156]

---

* Mormonism has had a difficult time defining what it means by "spiritual death." As McMurrin, points out: "It is the state of being cast out of the presence of the Lord, i.e., banishment from the garden, but beyond this, 'spiritual death' has been difficult for the Mormon theologians to define and they have usually passed over it somewhat casually. . . . It is typical of the Mormon theologians . . . to concentrate primarily on the factor of physical death rather than spiritual death. . . . [Adam's] condition of exclusion from the divine presence does not in any way constitute sin; he is not by nature sinful, nor does a necessary compulsion to actual sin condition his freedom. . . . Nothing is more evident than the determination to avoid any suggestion that Adam's guilt can in any way be imputed to mankind.[157]

Christ's atonement conquered physical death in freely providing a resurrection for all men and it conquered "spiritual" death *insofar* as men keep the law.

Thus, the only *actual* accomplishment of the atonement was that it made possible the resurrection of all men. As Mormon theologian Duane Crowther comments, "The Lord died in order to bring about the resurrection of the dead."[158] Again, this was all it *actually* accomplished. Any other benefits derived from the atonement must be earned by good works and obeying Mormon requirements.[159]

Likewise, when Mormonism claims that Christ's death brought immortality, that does not mean that it brought true salvation. As we saw in chapter 13, one can be resurrected to immortality and still be "damned." Thus, along with Jehovah's Witnesses and other cults, Mormonism teaches that the atonement merely provides the opportunity to earn salvation through personal merit. Just as a college degree does not actually secure a salary, but only makes earning one possible, so Christ's death does not actually secure salvation, but only makes earning it possible by good works. In fact, even if all the faith in the world were placed in Christ's death on the cross, this still would not forgive a single sin—not apart from law keeping.

In Mormonism, then, the actual *saving value* of the atonement is virtually nonexistent. As Dr. McMurrin observes:

> Mormon theology has with considerable ingenuity constructed its doctrine of salvation around the fall and the atonement, but with radically unorthodox meanings. . . . The meaning of the grace of God given through the atonement of Christ is that man by his freedom can now merit salvation. . . . But that Christ has taken the sins of the world upon himself does not mean, in Mormon theology, that he has by his sinless sacrifice brought the free gift of salvation to mortals steeped in original and actual sin and therefore unworthy of the grace bestowed upon them. In the Mormon doctrine, Christ redeems men from the physical and spiritual death imposed upon them by the transgression of Adam; . . . But he does not in any way absolve them of the consequences of their own actual evil or save them with high glory in the absence of genuine merit.[160]

In fact, while denying the blood atonement of Christ, the *early* Mormon church, quite logically, accepted the blood atonement of men! Mormonism actually taught that the forgiveness of certain sins required a man's death (see chap. 28). Should certain sins be committed (for example, lying, adultery, stealing), the guilty person was to have his own blood shed in order to atone for them because the death of Christ could not forgive such sins. Brigham Young himself emphasized, "I could refer you to plenty of instances where men have been righteously slain, in order to atone for their sins."[161]

Perhaps we may question whether or not much change has taken place in the modern church's view of the atonement compared with its early prophets' teaching. The early church taught that the blood atonement of men was necessary because the atonement of Christ was *partial*—"men can commit sins which it can never remit."[162] Today, the atonement is *still* partial: it only brings resurrection from the dead, and it doesn't offer even the *possibility* of forgiving *all* sins. At least one sin cannot always be forgiven—murder (and perhaps also apostasy).[163] For example, the previous president and prophet of the church stated that "all sins [can be forgiven by good works] but those excepted by the Lord—basically, the sins against the Holy Ghost, and murder."[164]

*2. The atonement delivers from spiritual death in that it makes forgiveness of sins possible by law keeping. (The atonement per se does not forgive sins: personal righteousness does.)*

Some Mormon claims to the contrary, the death of Christ did *not* forgive anyone's sins; again, it only made possible the forgiveness of sins by law keeping. The Mormon scriptures teach this. For example, *Doctrine and Covenants* 76:50,52 declares, "This is the testimony of the gospel of Christ concerning them who shall come forth in the resurrection of the just. . . . That *by keeping the commandments they might be washed and cleansed from all their sins*" (emphasis added).[165]

Likewise, the 1961 *Mormon Missionary Handbook* instructs Mormon missionaries to carefully teach new converts that Christ's death has *not* removed their sins—that only obedience can do this. Under the section titled "Fourth Discussion: The Gift of God is Eternal Life," point 7, it supplies the proper dialogue with new converts:

> Elder: Why is it so important for you to live the commandments then, Brother Brown?
>
> Brown: If I keep the commandments the Lord removes my sins.
>
> Elder: I testify that is true. He has already paid for your sins, Brother Brown. BUT WHEN ARE THOSE SINS REMOVED FROM YOU?
>
> Brown: When I keep the commandments, including repentance and baptism.
>
> [Correct] He removes our sins if we keep his commandments.[166]

Under the "Fifth Discussion: Law of Eternal Progression," point 2 reads, "Through the atonement and by obedience my sins will be removed."[167] Under the "Sixth Discussion: Be Ye Therefore Perfect," points 6-11 teach:

> 6. I must conform to the first principles and ordinances of the gospel to receive a remission of my sins.

7. I will live under the Ten Commandments.

8. I will continue to live the Word of Wisdom.

9. God has given us the law of tithing to teach us unselfishness.

10. I will live the law of tithing.

11. By obedience and through the grace of Christ I will be saved from spiritual death.[168]

The thirteenth president and prophet of the Mormon church, Spencer W. Kimball, emphasizes, "This progress toward eternal life is a matter of achieving perfection. *Living all the commandments guarantees total forgiveness of sins* and assures one of exaltation.... Perfection therefore is an achievable goal."[169]

Current president and prophet Ezra Taft Benson teaches that the atonement of Christ's death is effective for "redeeming all of us from physical death, and redeeming those of us from spiritual death *who will obey the laws and ordinances of the gospel.*"[170]

The *Doctrines of the Gospel: Student Manual* claims that Jesus only came to save those who would obey him because mercy is extended only to those who keep God's commandments. Thus, "if we do not keep God's commandments, we must suffer for our own sins."[171]

This is why the Mormon text *A Sure Foundation* concludes, "We believe that it is Christ's atonement that saves us but that we must endure to the end in doing good works *if his atonement is to take effect on our behalf....* It is by the atonement of Christ that we are saved, but *it is necessary that we keep the commandments* and obey the ordinances God has given us."[172]

In his *Articles of Faith*, James Talmage writes of the justness of having sins be forgiven by good works:

> As ... these sins are the result of individual acts *it is just that forgiveness for them should be conditioned on individual compliance with prescribed requirements—"obedience to the laws and ordinances of the gospel."*[173]

In essence, although without Christ's atonement salvation would not be possible, salvation *itself* is the reward for individual merit. This was why point 3 of the Articles of Faith of Joseph Smith stated, "We believe that through the atonement of Christ, all mankind may be saved, by obedience to the laws and ordinances of the gospel." Dr. McMurrin correctly observes,

> Here is a clear statement that, although the atonement is necessary, salvation is earned. Though the atonement brings immortality and resurrection to all men, salvation is a matter

of degree, and the degree attained is a consequence of merit. Every man must answer for his own sins and salvation can come through obedience to law. Here is the opposite pole from Luther's justification by faith only.[174]

All of this is why Mormon discussions of the atonement are noticeable for their *lack* of affirming actual forgiveness of sins through Christ's death alone. This is why Mormons don't know the true Gospel—they have never heard it. The claim of one former twenty-year Mormon (who taught doctrine in the church) was that he never once heard that Christ actually died on the cross for *his* sin. This is not unique for Mormonism; it is characteristic.[175] Thus, forgiveness of sins comes indirectly through Christ's death, which cancels the effects of the Fall, but directly only by good works, which themselves cancel sin. Hence, "The spiritual death of the Fall is replaced by the spiritual life of the atonement, in that all who believe and obey gospel law gain spiritual or eternal life."[176] Obviously then, the atonement alone *does not* forgive sins, no matter what Mormons may claim—only law keeping does. All this is why Christ's atonement is "really just a starting point," and that true salvation and actual forgiveness of sins must be earned.[177] The Mormon publication *Gospel Principles* reiterates, "The Savior atoned for us by suffering in Gethsemane and by giving his life on the cross," and "Christ did his part to atone for our sins. Each of us must repent and obey to make Christ's atonement effective in our lives."[178]

But consider this. This same text shows how difficult it actually is for Mormons to find forgiveness. It teaches that forgiveness of sins is conditioned upon repentance.[179] But what is "repentance" in Mormonism? "The privilege of repenting is made possible through the atonement of Jesus Christ."[180] This text then tells us that repentance means we must 1) recognize our sins, 2) feel sorrow for our sins, 3) forsake our sins, 4) confess our sins, 5) make restitution, 6) forgive others, and 7) keep the commandments of God.[181]

And what does it mean to keep the commandments of God? Keeping the commandments involves 1) paying tithes, 2) keeping the Sabbath day, 3) obeying the *Word of Wisdom* (such as not drinking coffee), 4) sustaining the authorities of the church, 5) loving the Lord, 6) loving humanity, 7) consistently saying family prayers, etc.[182]

Repentance involves all this and *then* spending "the balance of your lives trying to live the commandments of the Lord so he can eventually pardon you and cleanse you."[183] In other words, a Mormon's sins are not forgiven at all until *all of this is accomplished*. Thus, "As a result of repentance, the atonement of Jesus Christ becomes effective in our lives, and our sins are forgiven."[184] If this is true, how can *any* Mormon know his sins are ever forgiven?

Because the atonement has not forgiven sins, no Mormon can know he or she is saved *until* all the requirements for salvation are met. But these requirements involve spiritual progression even beyond the grave. As in reincarnation, it may literally take aeons before one attains to the status of a god. If one's "sins may be forgiven beyond the grave,"[185] and if it allegedly took the earth god Elohim a *very* long time to gain salvation, certainly, as embryonic deities, Mormons cannot expect salvation in this brief life alone.[186] This teaching has been previously documented.

All this denies the biblical teaching that Christ's death paid the full penalty for our sins, resulting in complete forgiveness at the moment of faith (see Hebrews 9:12; 10:10-14; 1 Corinthians 15:3, etc., below).

But if the atonement of Christ has already remitted the penalty of sin, how can keeping the commandments do so? Conversely, if it is taught that keeping the law forgives sin, how can Mormonism logically teach that the atonement accomplishes this? All this is why Mormons have to regard the Christian view as erroneous.

*3. The Christian view of the atonement is classified as a great error and a pernicious delusion.*

Consider the words of early Mormon theologian C. W. Penrose, which are, in various ways, frequently echoed by modern church authorities:

> The Latter-day Saints are often accused by the people in the Christian world of being very much deluded. Our religion is counted a delusion and snare. I was thinking, however, during the meeting this afternoon about the great number of Christian preachers who today are standing up in various parts of the world informing the people who listen to them that simple belief on the Lord Jesus, who died on Calvary, is all that is necessary to save them and exalt them in the presence of God the Father. And it seems to me that if there is one delusion more pernicious than another it is that very doctrine, which seems to be a fundamental principle of all the various Christian sects. . . . [We find] . . . preached the great error that mere belief in the work which Jesus Christ wrought out is sufficient for the salvation of the people. The inhabitants of the earth are informed that it is not by any works of righteousness which they may perform that they can gain any favor whatever in the sight of God, but it is the righteousness of Christ alone which is acceptable to the Father and which they can gain the benefit of if they simply believe in him.
>
> [However], the plan of the true Gospel . . . does not consist in mere belief in the righteousness of another. . . . It is men who are *not* sent who preach the nonsense we hear in the world. It is the men who are *not* sent who deceive mankind with their strong delusions, and then turn round and call the Latter-day Saints deluded. If they were sent of God they would

not preach such nonsense, they would not deceive mankind and thus become the cause of so much sin and evil in the world.[187]

In conclusion, as many other researchers have shown, Mormonism does not believe in the biblical atonement of Jesus Christ. It teaches that, at best, Christ's death only supplies the opportunity whereby individuals may work to forgive their own sins, eventually perfect themselves and become exalted as gods. When Mormons claim that Christ died to save all men or that Christ died for their sins, one must understand that such phrases do not have biblical or Christian meanings. But when Mormonism claims that Christ's death does not forgive the believer's sins, they deny what the Bible clearly teaches:

> For I delivered to you as of first importance what I also received, that Christ died for our sins according to the Scriptures (1 Corinthians 15:3).

> The next day he saw Jesus coming to him, and said, "Behold, the Lamb of God who takes away the sin of the world!" (John 1:29).

> Who gave Himself for our sins, that He might deliver us out of this present evil age, according to the will of our God and Father (Galatians 1:4).

> In Him we have redemption through His blood, the forgiveness of our trespasses, according to the riches of His grace (Ephesians 1:7).

> In whom we have redemption, the forgiveness of sins (Colossians 1:14).

> And He Himself is the propitiation [atoning sacrifice] for our sins; and not for ours only, but also for those of the whole world.... In this is love, not that we loved God, but that He loved us and sent His Son to be the propitiation for our sins (1 John 2:2; 4:10).

> ...But He entered the Most Holy Place once for all by his own blood, having obtained eternal redemption (Hebrews 9:12 NIV).

> Because by one sacrifice He has made perfect forever those who are being made holy (Hebrews 10:14 NIV).

We agree with the Mormon church when it emphasizes that "no doctrine in the gospel is more important than the atonement of Jesus Christ."[188] What is regrettable is that in Mormonism "the atonement of Christ becomes merely a handy tool to be used by the individual in his or her own do-it-yourself salvation kit."*[189]

---

* Robinson uses these words to convey an alleged *distortion* of Mormon belief—which is why we have quoted them.

◆

# CHAPTER 16

# What Does the Mormon Church Teach About the Nature of Man?

## Are Men Eternal Gods?

Mormonism is first and foremost a *humanistic* religion. In the end, man is the measure of all things. God Himself was once a man like us, and all men have a latent divine nature such that they may become gods. The principal purpose of man is his own joy and self-glorification. For example, Brigham Young taught that "the whole object of the creation of this world is to exalt the intelligences that are placed upon it."[190] The *Book of Mormon* teaches that the very reason men exist is "that they might have joy" (2 Nephi 2:25; cf. McMurrin, 4).

The Mormon church claims that man is 1) eternal and 2) potentially a god. Both concepts deny the biblical doctrine of man which teaches that man was created at a specific point in time (Genesis 2:7; Deuteronomy 4:32), and created to glorify God, not himself (Isaiah 43:2).

Because man is a creature, Christianity maintains he could never become a god. Historically, Mormonism has rejected and ridiculed the biblical doctrine of creation precisely because it denies that man can ever be like God. Joseph Smith asserted concerning the Christian doctrine of creation, "I do not believe the doctrine; I know better."[191] Mormon leader Boyd K. Packer, writing in the Mormon publication *Ensign*, commented, "The idea that mortal birth is the beginning [of human life] is preposterous."[192] This is why Dr. McMurrin, dean of the graduate school at the University of Utah, observes: "The Mormon concept of man is distinguished from the classical Christian doctrine primarily in its denial that man is essentially and totally a creation of God."[193] In the material below, we will document two key aspects to Mormonism's teaching on man. First, that man—in another form—is an eternal being, and second, that man can become a god.

*The Mormon doctrine of preexistence: Man as an eternal being.*

Mormons claim that the essence of man is eternal—and, in fact, divine—and that it was apparently fashioned or formed into spirit bodies through sexual intercourse among male and female parental deities. How the process began—how the first god or gods were created—Mormonism cannot say. Nevertheless, Mormons go beyond the early church father Origen's unbiblical doctrine* of preexistence (that souls existed as *created* spirits prior to inhabiting a body) and declare that man is an eternal entity.

*Doctrine and Covenants*, 93:29 teaches, "Man was also in the beginning with God. Intelligence, or the light of truth, was not created or made, neither indeed can be." Joseph Smith confessed,

> We say that God Himself is a self-existent being. . . . Who told you that man did not exist in like manner upon the same principles? Man does exist upon the same principles. . . . The mind or the intelligence which man possesses is co-equal with God Himself. . . . The intelligence of spirits had no beginning, neither will it have an end. . . . The first principles of man are self-existent with God.[194]

This teaching is related to the Mormon idea that intelligence itself, in some "material" form, is eternal. Mormonism believes that God did not and cannot create from nothing (the biblical doctrine of creation *ex-nihilo*).[195] Thus, according to Mormonism, God's "creation" had to involve the *reorganizing* of already existing intelligence. This eternal intelligence was somehow refashioned to create the spirit children which are the offspring of the gods. Apparently, because the spirit children needed spirit *bodies* involving a "material" substance, preexistent matter was utilized in creating them. Mormon theologian Bruce McConkie explains:

> Matter or element is self-existent and eternal in nature, creation being merely the organization and reorganization of that substance which "was not created or made, neither indeed can be" (*D&C*, 93:29). . . . If there had been no self-existent spirit element, there would have been no substance from which those spirit bodies could have been organized.[196]

---

* 1 Corinthians 15:42-47; Zechariah 12:1; for refutation see L. Berkhof, *Systematic Theology*, Eerdman's 1974, 197; A. Strong, *Systematic Theology*, Revelle 1976, three volumes in one, 488-491.

Spencer W. Kimball, the thirteenth president and prophet of the Mormon church, comments, "Our spirit matter was eternal and co-existent with God, but it was organized into spirit bodies by our Heavenly Father. Our spirit bodies went through a long period of growth and development and training and, having passed the test successfully, were finally admitted to this earth and to mortality."[197]

The tenth president and prophet of the Mormon church, Joseph Fielding Smith, comments:

> Some of our writers have endeavored to explain what an intelligence is, but to do so is futile, for we have never been given any insight into this matter beyond what the Lord has fragmentarily revealed. We know, however, that there is something called intelligence which always existed. It is the real eternal part of man, which was not created nor made. This intelligence combined with the spirit constitutes a spiritual identity or individual.[198]

Apparently, then, through the process of sexual intercourse between the male and female gods, part of this eternal intelligence is "reorganized" to produce spirit children who then enter a period of probation and finally are permitted entrance into a human body on earth.

"Spirit" and "element" (or spirit and body), which together constitute the soul,[199] must be "connected" for man to have joy and be fulfilled. *Doctrine and Covenants*, 93:33-35 asserts:

> For man is spirit. The elements are eternal, and spirit and element, inseparably connected, receive a fullness of joy. And when separated, man cannot receive a fullness of joy. The elements are the tabernacle of God; yea, man is the tabernacle of God, even temples; . . .

Indeed, to be a spirit alone without a body is viewed as something horrible. Thus, the divine judgment upon the preexistent spirits—our brothers and sisters—who rebelled against the earth god, and finally became the devil and his demons, is to be without a body forever. Paradoxically, Mormonism teaches that although the Father and Son both have bodies, the Holy Ghost is also forever without a body.

Moreover, the Mormon doctrine of preexistence extends to other creatures besides man, even to the earth itself and minerals, vegetables and animals. Bruce McConkie claims in *The Millennial Messiah*:

> The earth was created first spiritually. It was a spirit earth. . . . Man and all forms of life existed as spirit beings and entities before the foundations of this earth were laid. There were spirit men and spirit beasts, spirit fowls and spirit fish, spirit

plants and spirit trees. Every creeping thing, every herb and scrub, every amoeba and tadpole, every elephant and dinosaur—all things—existed as spirits, as spirit beings, before they were placed naturally upon the earth.[200]

Every Mormon is taught that, because of his personal merit and good deeds in his preexistent life, he has earned the right to become a Mormon and have an opportunity to become a god himself over some other world. McConkie observes that, "We dwelt with our eternal Father in the pre-mortal life for an immeasurably long period of time. . . . We developed an infinite variety and degree of talents and capacities."[201] Thus, "During the ages in which we dwelt in the pre-mortal state we not only developed our various characteristics and showed our worthiness and ability, or the lack of it [but also] . . . our Father [was able] to discern and choose those who were most worthy [to be Mormons]."[202]

Dr. Stephen Robinson argues, "Despite what our critics claim, the Latter-day Saints do not believe that human beings will ever become the equals of God."[203] Rather, "They [human beings] remain eternally his [Elohim's] begotten sons and daughters—therefore, never equal to him nor independent of him."[204] But when Robinson claims that men will never become the equals of God, one should interpret this in the context of the larger Mormon perspective. This does *not* mean they can never become like God in the fullest sense. What it means is that they can never become the equals of God because He *continually* evolves. Elohim has existed prior to his creatures for unidentified millennia—so of course if he continues to progress, none of his spirit children will ever be his *exact* equals, even after they become gods.

Nevertheless, Mormonism does teach that men will become gods in the fullest sense of the term, and we will proceed to document this below. But before we do so we must examine how Mormons attempt to defend this concept as a Christian teaching. Consider the arguments of Dr. Robinson.

Robinson appeals to three separate points 1) the figurative expression in Psalm 82 that refers to the ancient rulers of Israel as "gods" and Jesus' citation of it (John 10:34); 2) the concept of "deification" in, for example, the Eastern Orthodox church, and 3) the modern "Positive Confession" doctrines of Christians such as Paul Crouch, Robert Tilton, Kenneth Copeland, etc., who also teach that men are "gods." Robinson argues that the Mormon concept of men becoming gods is not only biblical, it is also not distinct from the teachings of many Christians.

But he never establishes his case. First, the specialized theological concept of "deification," found primarily in the Eastern Orthodox churches, is not the Mormon view. Robinson confesses this up to a point:

> Critics of the Latter-day Saints may respond that the early
> Christian saints, the later Greek theologians, and C.S. Lewis

all understand the doctrine of deification differently than the Latter-day Saints do, but this is untrue in the case of the early Christians and C.S. Lewis. Anyway, such a response amounts to a quibble, for it retreats abjectly from the claim that deification is a pagan doctrine wholly foreign to true Christianity.[205]

But it all depends on what we mean by the term "deification," doesn't it? Christian saints, the later Greek theologians and C.S. Lewis all *do* understand the doctrine of deification differently than Mormons—quite differently. And it is hardly a quibble. If Mormonism claims that man can become a god as God is now God, this is hardly a Christian or biblical teaching. Certainly it is something that the historic church and C.S. Lewis never taught. This can be seen by revealing exactly what Mormonism means when it teaches deification.

*The Mormon doctrine of deification: Man as potential God.*

Those who claim that Mormonism does not teach that men will one day become fully like God apparently do not understand Mormon doctrine or historical theology. Either that or they have something to hide.

In Mormonism, God and man are ultimately one species. Following the tradition of the East, Mormonism teaches that man must turn inward to know God: "... to know God man has but to know himself. By introspective search in his own soul, man comes to a degree of understanding of God, including Deity's character, perfections, and attributes. As Joseph Smith said, 'If men do not comprehend the character of God, they do not comprehend themselves' (*Teachings*, 343)."[206]

Perhaps this is why Joseph Smith also taught,

> The mind or the intelligence which man possesses is co-equal with God himself.... There never was a time when there were not spirits; for they are co-equal [co-eternal] with our Father in heaven.... God never had the power to create the spirit of man at all. God himself could not create himself.[207]

Thus we are told that "there is identity of race between Gods and men."[208] Theologian Bruce McConkie also teaches, "Man and God are of the same race."[209] The Mormon apostle John Widtsoe further emphasizes, "God and man are of the same race, differing only in their degrees of advancement."[210]

Time and again Mormon prophets and presidents, theologians and lay writers have described the ultimate state of man who is exalted to godhood. Consider a few statements and ask yourself whether Mormonism teaches that men will only be gods in some finite sense—or whether it teaches they will become like God in the fullest sense. Exalted men will have the same nature as God: having "eternal power" and "enjoying and possessing all that Deity himself has"; and they will "know what he knows; possess the character, perfections and attributes embodied in him; have all power, might, and dominion as he does."[211] Finally, "Those who obtain exaltation will gain all power and thus themselves be omnipotent (*D&C*, 76:95; 88:107; 130:20)."[212]

The official Mormon publication *Achieving a Celestial Marriage: Student Manual*, (4,130) promises that all who are married in the Mormon temple and are fully obedient will become fully gods. In chapter 1, "Celestial Marriage–Key to Man's Destiny," it teaches:

> God was once a man who, . . . advanced to his present state of perfection through obedience and celestial [temple] marriage. . . . God became God by obedience to Law. . . . in his mortal condition, man is God in embryo. However. . . any individual. . . may attain to the rank and sanctity of godship. . . . [Question to prospective marriage partner:] "Do you realize the implications of this doctrine?. . ." [Answer:] "I think so. If God became God by obedience to all the gospel law with the crowning point being the celestial law of marriage, then that's the only way I can. . . become God."

The same manual explains on page 130 that the potential to become a god was transmitted to all men by their spiritual birth. "There is the nature of deity in the composition of our spiritual organization; in our spiritual birth, our Father transmitted to us the capabilities, powers and faculties which he himself possessed."

The thirteenth president and prophet of the Mormon church, Spencer W. Kimball, stated that, "Having within him the seeds of godhood and thus being a god in embryo, man has unlimited potential for progress and attainment."[213] And that it is the goal of every Mormon "to perfect himself and to become as God, omniscient and omnipotent."[214] The Mormon text *Gospel Principles* comments that exalted Mormons "will have everything that our heavenly Father and Jesus Christ have, all power, glory, dominion, and knowledge."[215] A representative of the Mormon church appearing on The John Ankerberg Show stated that anyone who progresses properly within Mormonism "can expect to become God."[216] Former twenty-year Mormon Ed Decker recalled, "I believed that God was another man just like me who earned his celestial glory [godhood] through works of righteousness." Therefore Decker believed that he could do the same.[217]

Brigham Young stated in the *Journal of Discourses* that Mormons who are exalted are "worthy to be crowned Gods, even the sons of God, and will be ordained to organize matter [or be divine creators]."[218]

Mormon theologian Duane Crowther observes that "a fundamental principle of the gospel of Jesus Christ [Mormonism] is that man may be exalted and attain the highest of all goals: godhood."[219] He quotes Mormon apostle Melvin J. Ballard, who stated, "I wish to say that few men will become what God is. And yet, all men may become *what he is* if they will pay the price."[220] Sandra Tanner, a descendent of Brigham Young and formerly a devout Mormon, recalls her own beliefs: "If we work at it hard enough, we can achieve Godhood just like the Father."[221]

In his work titled "The Powers of Godhood," Crowther proceeds to discuss the attributes of Mormons who are exalted and become gods. He notes "They will be blessed with *the full array of divine power*."[222] Among the attributes and characteristics cited are 1) power to create worlds, 2) power to make worlds pass through the exaltation process, 3) power to create mortal bodies for spirit beings, 4) power over mortal man's life and death, 5) power of judgment, 6) power to resurrect, 7) power over the elements, 8) power to see all things past, present and future, 9) power to know all things, 10) power to determine the bounds of man's habitation, 11) power to forgive and pardon, 12) power to hear and answer prayers, etc.[223] He goes on to state that "these are but examples of the powers of godhood." Thus, "As a god is omnipotent, such a list would have to expand to cover all the powers of eternity, for all of them are God's."[224]

In conclusion, Mormonism does teach that man can become just like God. The fact that there are an infinite number of other gods does not lessen the implications of this teaching. The fact that all the gods are apparently evolving in some sense does not mean that the condition of exaltation is anything less than full godhood. Again, even Robinson confesses, "It is indisputable that Latter-day Saints believe that God was once a human being and that human beings can become gods. The famous [divinely revealed] couplet of Lorenzo Snow, fifth president and prophet of the LDS Church, states: 'As man now is, God once was; as God now is, man may be.'"[225]

But if God (Elohim), whom even Robinson would accept is full, absolute deity, was once a man like us—on what basis can he say that men will never be what God now is?

Mormons should no longer equivocate on this issue. If, like the devil, they want all the power, glory and attributes of God, they should state it clearly. As George Q. Cannon, a member of the First Presidency, remarks in *Gospel Truth* 1:16, "The devil in tempting Eve told a truth when he said unto her that when she should eat of the tree of knowledge of good and evil they should become as Gods. He told the truth. . . ."[226] (See Appendix One.)

♦ ♦ *Appendix One* ♦ ♦

*What Does the Mormon Church Teach About Sin and the Fall of Man?*

The Mormon concepts of sin and the Fall of man are controversial and unusual to say the least. That they are neither Christian nor biblical is recognized by many scholars of Mormonism. For example, in his analysis of Mormon theology, *Theological Foundations of the Mormon Religion*, Dr. Sterling McMurrin comments, "It is here in its vigorous denial of original sin that Mormonism takes its stand in radical opposition to the essential character of traditional Christianity."[227] Thus, in evaluating the Mormon concepts of sin and the Fall, we may note the following six points of opposition to the Christian view:

*1. The biblical account of the Fall is false.*

The sixth Mormon president and prophet, Joseph F. Smith, asserted, "It is evident that if we were dependent solely on the account of the Fall as it is presented in the book of Genesis, we would be led astray and reach a very erroneous conclusion."[228]

This statement is not surprising given the following Mormon teachings:

*2. God actively intended sin and evil.*

Joseph F. Smith also taught that "the fall was a very essential part of the divine plan. Adam and Eve therefore did the very thing that the Lord intended them to do."[229]

The second president and prophet of the Mormon church, Brigham Young, also defended God's promotion of sin:

> Some may regret that our first parents sinned. This is nonsense. . . . I will not blame Adam and Eve, why? Because it was necessary that sin should enter into the world; no man could ever understand the principle of exaltation [achieving Godhood] without its opposite. . . . How did Adam and Eve sin? . . . They transgressed a command of the Lord, and through that transgression sin came into the world. The Lord knew they would do this, and he had designed that they should.[230]

The tenth president and prophet, Joseph Fielding Smith, also comments that even death was the intentional plan of God: "We came into this world to die. . . . When Adam was sent into this world, it was with the understanding that he would violate a law, transgress a law, in order to bring to pass this mortal condition [of sin and death]."[231]

*3. The Fall brought untold blessings to humanity.*

According to Mormon scripture, the Fall of man was something beneficial. The *Book of Mormon* teaches, "Adam fell that men might be; and men are, that they might have joy" (2 Nephi 2:25; cf. Moses 6:48).

According to Mormons, the Fall was a spiritual blessing, for there was no other way for Adam and Eve to produce children; no other way for billions of bodies to be manufactured for the spirit children anxiously awaiting to inhabit them; no other way for man to learn to distinguish good from evil (through experiencing both), and no other way for men to thereby slowly evolve and progress into self-made godhood. *Gospel Principles* comments in the following manner on the Fall of man:

> Some people believe that Adam and Eve committed a serious sin when they ate of the tree of knowledge of good and evil. However, Latter-day scriptures help us understand that their fall was a necessary step in the plan of life *and a great blessing to all mankind*.[232]

Irrespective of Mormon claims to the contrary,[233] Mormon theology implicates God with sin and glorifies evil for the alleged "good" it produces, as the citations below reveal.

Brigham Young emphasized that the Fall of man was something wonderful, for, apart from the Fall, none of the blessings that Mormons claim God gives to men would have occurred. Thus, he praises both God and our first parents for their active part in the Fall:

> We should not have been here today if she [Eve] had not [eaten the fruit]; we could never have possessed wisdom and intelligence if she had not done it. It was all in the economy of heaven. . . . We should never blame Mother Eve, not the least.
> . . . if I had the tongue of an angel, the tongues of the whole human family combined, I would praise God in the highest for his great wisdom and condescension in suffering the children of men to fall into the very sin into which they have fallen, for he did it that they, like Jesus, might descend below all things and then press forward and rise above all.[234]

Young also commented, "I am glad he [Adam] did eat. I am glad the fruit was given to Mother Eve, that she ate of it, and that her eyes were opened, and that my eyes are opened."[235] The older *Catechism for Children* (1854, p. 31) by John Jacques teaches, "Did Adam and Eve lament or rejoice because they had transgressed the commandment? . . . Answer: They rejoiced and praised God." Tenth president and prophet Joseph Fielding Smith claims:

> When Adam was driven out of the Garden of Eden, the Lord passed a sentence upon him. Some people have looked upon that sentence as being a dreadful thing. It was not; it was a blessing.[236]

Modern Mormons too are so grateful for the Fall that they also praise Adam and Eve for disobeying God! In an address to seminary and institute personnel on July 13, 1966, Marion G. Romney spoke of Adam's disobedience to God in the following manner, "For his service we owe Adam an immeasurable debt of gratitude."[237]

### 4. *The Fall brought testings for salvation.*

Mormon theology teaches that only with direct experience of sin and evil can choices be made on behalf of good. Again, it was God's plan to introduce sin into the world in order to help men choose good and to eventually become gods. Bruce McConkie explains:

> According to the foreordained plan, Adam was to fall.... Adam was to introduce mortality and all that attends it [sin, death, etc.], so that the opportunity for eternal progression and perfection might be offered to all the spirit children of the Father.... Man... became subject to corruption, disease, and all the ills of the flesh.... A knowledge of good and evil could now come to him by actual experience; and being mortal he could now have children, thus providing bodies for the preexistent [spirit] hosts.[238]

The sixth president and prophet of the Mormon church, Joseph F. Smith, agreed when he wrote:

> It was part of the divine plan that man... would be shut out of the presence of God and be subject to all the vicissitudes of mortality, the temptations and trials of the flesh, thus gaining experience and being placed in a position of trial, temptation, and be purified by passing through the trials and tribulations of the flesh.[239]

### 5. *The Fall provided children and physical homes for the awaiting spirits.*

In *The Pearl of Great Price* (Moses 5:10,11) Adam and Eve are portrayed as praising God for the Fall and rejoicing over the consequences:

> Blessed be the name of God, for because of my transgression my eyes are opened, and in this life I shall have joy.... And Eve, his wife, heard all these things and was glad, saying: Were it not for our transgression we should never have had seed [children], and never should have known good and evil, and the joy of our redemption, and the eternal life [Godhood] which God giveth unto all the obedient.

The *Book of Mormon* affirms this in 2 Nephi 2:23, "And they would have had no children; wherefore they would have remained in a state of innocence, having no joy, for they knew no misery; doing no good, for they knew no sin."

As noted, the Fall of Adam and Eve was absolutely essential because without it they never could have produced physical bodies for the billions of spirit children waiting to inhabit them, so that they might have their own opportunities to become gods—just like Elohim their Father.

In other words, in Mormon theology the Fall of man is an essential *part* of attaining exaltation or godhood. *Gospel Principles* teaches that after Adam and Eve fell they "began to have children. . . . Thus, spirit children of our Heavenly Father began leaving his presence to come to the earth" in order to inhabit the bodies of the children produced by Adam and Eve.[240]

In light of the above, the following assertion by James Talmage is not surprising. Such statements seem incredible to many, but they are only the logical outcome of Mormon teaching:

> It has become a common practice with mankind to heap reproaches upon the progenitors of the family and picture the supposedly blessed state in which we would be living but for the fall; whereas [in truth] our first parents are entitled to our deepest gratitude for their legacy to posterity—the means of winning title to glory, exaltation [godhood], and eternal lives. But for the opportunity thus given, the spirits of God's off-spring [the spirit children] would have remained forever in a state of innocent childhood, sinless through no effort of their own; negatively saved, not from sin, but from the opportunity of meeting sin; incapable of winning the honors of victory because prevented from taking part in the conflict. As it is, they are heirs to the birthright of Adam's descendents— mortality, with its immeasurable possibilities and its God-given freedom of action. From Father Adam we have inherited all the ills to which flesh is heir; but such are necessarily incident to a knowledge of good and evil, by the proper use of which knowledge man may become even as the Gods.[241]

### 6. The Fall was therefore not sin.

*The Pearl of Great Price* illustrates that even though the Mormon God had commanded Adam and Eve not to disobey him, his conviction about the matter was less than absolute, presumably because he knew the harmful consequences of divine obedience:

> And I, the Lord God, commanded the man, saying: Of every tree of the garden thou mayest freely eat, but of the tree of the knowledge of good and evil, thou shall not eat of it, nevertheless, thou mayest choose for thyself, for it is given unto thee; but remember that I forbid it, for in the day thou eatest thereof thou shalt surely die (Moses 3:16,17).

According to Mormonism, God had clearly forbidden Adam and Eve to disobey him and so to eat of the fruit—the penalty was death. Yet that very action was absolutely necessary to their spiritual welfare and progress. No wonder God seemed to take the issue of disobedience lightly.

The ethical implications of this unique approach to the Fall have perplexed more than one Mormon prophet and theologian. As the tenth president and prophet of the Mormon church, Joseph Fielding Smith, commented:

> Mortality could not come without violation of that [Edenic] law and mortality was essential, a step towards our exaltation. Therefore, Adam partook of the forbidden fruit, forbidden in a rather particular manner for it is the only place in all the history where we read that the Lord forbade something and yet said, "Nevertheless, thou mayest choose for thyself." He never said that of any sin. I do not look upon Adam's fall as a sin, although it was a transgression of the law.[242]

It is hardly surprising that Mormon presidents and theologians are a little bewildered. How do they resolve the issue of explaining that a *transgression of the law* is *not* sin, when God clearly teaches in 1 John 3:4, that a transgression of the law *is* sin? "Everyone who sins breaks the law; in fact, sin is lawlessness." Even, the Mormon publication *Doctrines of the Gospel: Student Manual* cites this statement by President Smith and then two pages later (!) defines sin in the following manner: "Sin is the willful breaking of the law."[243] So, how do Mormons justify their belief that the Fall did not involve sin, especially when Romans 5:12-19 explicitly teaches it did?

The *Doctrines of the Gospel* argues as follows:

> If we correctly understand the role of Adam and Eve, we will realize that those who long labeled them sinners responsible for the universal depravity of the human race are completely misguided. The truth is that Adam and Eve opened the door for us to come into mortality, a step essential to our eternal progress. . . . If Adam and Eve had not transgressed, they would have [been responsible for] . . . frustrating God's plan of salvation. . . . Death is a necessary part of God's plan.[244]

Joseph Fielding Smith argues,

> I am very, very grateful in that in the *Book of Mormon*, and I think elsewhere in our scriptures, the Fall of Adam has not been called a sin. It wasn't a sin. . . . What did Adam do? The very thing the Lord wanted him to do; and I hate to hear anybody call it a sin, for it wasn't a sin. Did Adam sin when he partook of the forbidden fruit? I say to you, no, he did not![245]

So really it was not in the true sense a transgression of a divine commandment. Adam made the wise decision, in fact, the only decision that he could make.[246]

And he reiterates it:

The transgression of that law, contrary to the view of many, was not a sin. . . . It was not a sin to bring to pass mortality, a condition which was essential to the eternal welfare of man.[247]

In other words, Mormons never deal with what the Bible teaches—that the Fall was sin—they merely deny that a sin was ever committed in the first place and proceed to rationalize the Fall as a spiritual blessing.

So, what are we to make of this bizarre doctrine that the Fall of man is really an unparalleled blessing to humanity? Consider its impact in just two areas: 1) the degradation of the atonement and 2) the promotion of sin. In the end, the sin of Adam and Eve plays almost as important a role in man's salvation as that played by Christ on the cross. Although, like Christ's atonement, their actions never secured man's salvation, they provided the *opportunity* for man to earn his own salvation. Thus, the sin of Adam and Eve on the one hand and the death of Jesus Christ on the other have both, in their own way, opened the doors for man to earn his own salvation. Because of the Fall, the possibility exists for godhood just as because of the atonement the possibility exists for godhood. In this sense, then, the Fall is as much a spiritual blessing for mankind as is the atonement! Adam and Eve on the one hand and Jesus Christ on the other are almost equals in providing the possibility of salvation for man. But in the Bible we find exactly the opposite—the Fall of man and the death of Christ are presented in stark contrast to one another (see Romans 5:6-21).

Second, it is possible to theorize what such a view of the Fall might do to one's sensitivity to sin. Sin becomes not only relative, but also potentially good.[248] This doctrine tells Mormons that the Fall was not really a spiritual descent or a rebellion against God. It also tells them that disobedience to God is not necessarily a sin. The Fall is then perceived as a "moral" advancement for mankind, a spiritual step upward—and indeed the means to salvation. If God actively intended evil so that by *experiencing it* we might grow spiritually, then every evil, every sin, every transgression must in some sense be "good." But if we are grateful for sin, can we abhor it? If God intended sin for our welfare, should we view it as being so harmful? James Talmage declares, "A knowledge of good and evil is essential to the advancement that God has made possible for his children to achieve; and *this knowledge can be best gained by actual experience,* with the contrast of good and its opposite plainly discernible."[249]

Thus, we are told by McConkie that God even uses Satan to tempt men to "walk in darkness, and become carnal, sensual, and devilish (Moses 6:49). This opposition is used by the Lord, as part of his plan, to test and try men . . . an essential part of progression and advancement."[250]

But if so, can we believe that the Mormon God is holy or righteous? Might such teachings explain some of the evils committed throughout Mormon history, or some of the moral problems within the church today? (See chaps. 28 and 29.) When Mormons are taught that sin is something "good," confusion over the issue of what sin is or isn't should be expected. McConkie himself, again a leading doctrinal theologian, teaches that as far as keeping God's commandments, "The issue *is not the act of sin* as such, but the feelings and desires . . . in the heart. . . ."[251]

Nevertheless, the Mormon concept of the Fall is in serious error: implicating God with sin on the one hand and redefining sin on the other.

In the Bible God clearly teaches that the Fall *did* involve sin. In Romans 5:12-21 we read of "those who had not *sinned* in the likeness of Adam's offense" (v. 14). In referring to rebellious people, God says, "But *like Adam* they have transgressed the covenant; there they have dealt *treacherously against Me*" (Hosea 6:7).

In Genesis 3:12-20 God's powerful response to Adam's sin hardly indicates that He was actually pleased that Adam had disobeyed Him—or that this was part of His plan for man's salvation. To the contrary, these verses clearly teach that God was deeply grieved and angered; He pronounced immediate judgment upon both Adam and Eve for their willful disobedience to His loving command.*

In conclusion, once again we see the fruit of Joseph Smith's acceptance of spiritistic revelation: the defacing of God's character, confusion over sin, and the distortion of Scripture. What Satan first accomplished in the original Fall is now repeated—and perpetually promoted—in Mormon theology.

## ◆ ◆ *Appendix Two* ◆ ◆

*What Does the Mormon Church Teach About Satan and Demons and the Reason for Their Fall?*

Mormonism holds that Satan and his demons were spirits in the preexistent state.[256] Mormonism teaches that every being was a member

---

*The above teachings explain why Mormonism holds that human nature is essentially good and why it refuses to accept that Adam's sin and its results were passed on to all of humanity. Because of its view of the Fall, Mormonism explicitly denies original sin. Thus, the second article of Mormon faith declares, "We believe that men will be punished for their own sins, and not for Adam's transgression."[252] *Doctrine and Covenants*, 93:38 apparently teaches that men are sinless in infancy; the Mormon church extends this sinlessness to the "age of accountability." Hugh B. Brown, Apostle and First Counselor in the First Presidency, stated at the 1964 General Conference, "Our doctrine of man is positive and life affirming. . . . We refuse to believe, with some churches of Christendom, that the biblical account of the Fall of man records the corruption of human nature or to accept the doctrine of original sin."[253] We conclude with the assessment of Dr. Anthony Hoekema as to the essentially Pelagian nature of Mormon theology:[254]

Since the preexisting spirits of men are held to have been sinless in the beginning, and since children are considered to be without sin until they reach the age of eight, one wonders where the universal tendency to sin comes from. It would seem that the only explanation left is the common Pelagian one: imitation of other sinners. It is certainly clear that Mormons deny both original guilt and original pollution; they are thus completely Pelagian with respect to the doctrine of original sin.[255]

of the same race of sexually-produced spirit children. Thus, Satan, along with all other spirits in preexistence, was a spirit-child of the earth God Elohim. Satan and his demons were not the fallen angels *of the Bible*, but rather potential men and women.[257] Those spirits who *could have been men and women* with bodies instead chose to rebel with Satan and as a result became demons.

In other words, Satan and his demons are simply the preexistent spirits of potential men and women who will never have the opportunity to have a body. In fact, their punishment is to forever remain without bodies. Hence the only real difference between humans and demons is that humans have material bodies: no other fundamental distinction exists. As noted earlier, Satan is thus the spirit brother of Jesus and all of us, although fallen and condemned.

How did Satan fall from heaven? In prehistory, the earth God Elohim explained to his spirit sons the need for a Fall and for a redeemer. Satan offered himself as man's redeemer. But since he nefariously intended to save all men regardless of their free choice, he opposed Elohim and was rejected as a candidate. On the other hand, Jesus chose the plan of his Father which was to bring evil into the world to allow men to grow spiritually.[258]

When Satan was rejected as savior, it caused him to declare war on his Father, who then cast him down to earth. And "Those thus cast out are denied bodies forever."[259] Put another way, had you or I made the wrong choice in preexistence, we would now be demons.

But, ironically, Satan and his followers were *condemned* for disobeying the Mormon God while, as we have just seen, for the very same action Adam and Eve were spiritually *blessed*.

Obviously, all this denies the biblical distinction between men and angels as two separate creations of God. Who then are angels in Mormonism? "Angels" is a term for Elohim's children either before or after earth life. His children were angels before coming to earth and will be after, unless they become a god. Angels are spirit sons of the earth god and his wife and "are themselves pressing forward along the course of progression and salvation."[260] Some are nonphysical spirits, some have flesh and bone bodies, and some are the spirits of just men who are now "ministering angels unto many planets."[261]

◆

# CHAPTER 17

# What Does the Mormon Church Believe About the Afterlife?

Mormonism rejects the biblical teaching on death, heaven and hell.

For example, Mormonism denies that death brings final judgment. Instead it maintains that billions of people will have an opportunity for salvation after they die.

Mormonism also rejects the biblical teaching on heaven, substituting in its place at least three different "heavens," each offering the opportunity for degrees of progression in the afterlife.

Mormonism also rejects the biblical doctrine of hell as a place of eternal punishment for all those who have willfully rejected God's gracious plan of forgiveness in this life. We briefly discuss these in turn:

*1. Mormonism denies the biblical teaching on death.*

According to Matthew 25:46, Hebrews 9:27, Luke 16:19-31, 2 Peter 2:9 and other Scriptures, the Bible teaches that the moment of death seals one's fate for all eternity. There is no chance for people to be saved after they have died. This is why the Bible warns that "Just as a man is destined to die once, and after that to face judgment" (Hebrews 9:29 NIV), and therefore "not to receive God's grace in vain," for "now is the time of God's favor, now is the day of salvation" (2 Corinthians 6:1,2 NIV).

Mormonism denies this teaching and tells people that there are abundant opportunities to be saved (and even to become gods!) after death. "Paradise" is an intermediate state wherein spirits are allowed the opportunity to believe the gospel, and those who do so then receive the benefits of salvation by proxy baptism and proxy temple marriage on their behalf.[262] President Wilford Woodruff (who received the 1890 revelation banning polygamy) provides an example. He believed he had "saved" John Wesley, most United States presidents, and all the signers of the Declaration of Independence![263]

Mormonism thus insulates people against the biblical message stressing the urgency of making a decision for Christ now, in this life. The current president and prophet of the Mormon church, Ezra Taft Benson, illustrates this Mormon teaching:

> All of them [the dead] must receive the gospel or have the opportunity to receive it. This means, of course, that missionary work is going on on the other side of the veil [after death]. . . . The work to be done on the other side of the veil is far more extensive than here. There, billions must hear the gospel preached. . . . In the world of spirits the gospel is preached to millions of people who never had an opportunity to hear it while on the earth.[264]

The tenth president and prophet of the Mormon church, Joseph Fielding Smith, in *Doctrines of Salvation*, also affirmed this doctrine of salvation after death: "The Lord has so arranged his plan of redemption that all who have died without this opportunity [to hear the gospel] shall be given it in the spirit world. There the elders of the Church who have died are proclaiming the gospel to the dead. All those who did not have an opportunity here to receive it, who there repent and receive the gospel, shall be heirs of the celestial kingdom of God."[265]

Unfortunately, when Mormonism promises people that they may have the opportunity for salvation after death, it undermines the solemn words of Jesus Himself when He said, "I told you that you would die in your sins; if you do not believe that I am the one I claim to be, you will indeed die in your sins" (John 8:24 NIV). For someone to "die in their sins" meant they would enter eternity with their sins unforgiven, therefore demanding the judgment of God's infinite justice upon them.

Another way in which Mormonism denies the biblical teaching concerning death is by teaching that the resurrection of the body occurs only after an extended period of postmortem probation. As the former president and prophet of the Mormon church, Spencer W. Kimball, explained, "Our spirits [then] go to the spirit world, where we . . . further train for our eternal destiny. After a period, there would be a resurrection or a reunion of the body and the spirit, which would render us immortal and make possible our further climb toward perfection and godhood."[266]

## 2. Mormonism denies the biblical teaching on heaven.

The biblical teaching on heaven tells us that everyone who has received Christ as their personal savior from sin—the small and the great—

will all have an equal position before God and Christ in heaven. Different responsibilities and rewards may be gained, but because everyone's salvation was solely and wholly by grace there are no degrees of earned glory that would give one earned privileges. However, Mormonism denies this and teaches that the greater one's personal merit, the closer one's proximity to God and Christ and the greater one's opportunity to become a god. It presents a vast and confusing picture of "heaven." According to Mormonism, conditions in heaven vary widely. First, there are three degrees of glory: "The three degrees of glory provide eternal homes for the vast majority of God's children who merited earth life."[267] Nevertheless, these degrees of glory incorporate various degrees of "eternal punishment":

a. The celestial glory is "provided for those who merit the highest honors of heaven" (for example, good Mormons—among whom are Mormons who earn residence in the highest part of this heaven and so become gods and have "eternal increase."[268]

b. The terrestrial glory is provided for those "whose works do not merit the highest reward" (for example, good non-Mormons).[269]

c. The telestial glory is prepared for the wicked who "are thrust down to hell" and have a period of punishment and probation before they are redeemed and allowed to enter the telestial glory or possibly a higher kingdom.[270]

With each higher kingdom, one is allegedly permitted a closer proximity to Christ and God, although only celestial kingdom inhabitants are allowed to be in Their direct presence:

All who inherit the celestial kingdom will live with our Heavenly Father and Jesus Christ forever and ever. . . . [Inheritors of the terrestrial kingdom] will be visited by Jesus Christ, but not our Heavenly Father. . . . [Inheritors of the telestial kingdom] will be visited by the Holy Ghost, but not the Father or the son, Jesus Christ.[271]

Each kingdom is also subdivided so that "the innumerable degrees of merit amongst mankind are provided for an infinity of graded glories."[272] A few Mormons teach that advancement between each kingdom is possible, although for most all such progress is prohibited.[273] Nevertheless, until these respective kingdoms are actually attained, all spirits—the righteous and the wicked—go to the spirit world—either "paradise" or the Mormon "spirit prison." As most spirit mediums teach, this may be another dimension upon this earth. In Section 6 we will see that this opens the door for Mormons to engage in spiritistic contacts.

Again, as described in the *Gospel Principles*, this is what Mormons can look forward to:

> At the final judgement we will be assigned to the kingdom we have earned. We will be sent to one of four places: the celestial kingdom, which is the highest degree of glory; the terrestrial kingdom, the middle degree; the telestial kingdom, which is the lowest degree of glory; outer darkness, which is the kingdom of the devil and is not a degree of glory.[274]

### 3. *Mormonism denies the biblical teaching on hell.*

The Mormon text *Doctrines of the Gospel: Student Manual* teaches Mormons, "We need not fear death,"[275] which is also a common occult teaching. Of course, if Mormons reject the one true God, His Son, and His offer of salvation, as we have seen they do, then they certainly should fear death. Furthermore, according to Mormonism, it is not just Mormons who need not fear death, it is everyone.

Not only does Mormonism offer an opportunity for salvation and godhood to those who have never heard of Mormonism, even those who have and rejected Mormonism in this life are offered a "kingdom of glory" in the next life, as we have seen. In the end, almost everyone will finally receive some degree of heavenly glory, no matter what his or her life has been like on this earth. Even those among the most wicked, after a time of purgatorial refinement, will be permitted entrance to a heavenly existence. *Doctrines of the Gospel: Student Manual* explains:

> The inhabitants of the telestial kingdom will include those who were murderers, liars, sorcerers, adulterers, and whoremongers—in general the wicked people of the earth.... These inhabitants of the telestial kingdom will have become clean through their [purgatorial] suffering so that they can abide telestial [heavenly] glory.[276]

This manual goes on to explain that the residents of the higher heaven, the terrestrial kingdom, will minister to individuals in the telestial kingdom and enable them to receive the Holy Ghost. Apparently, this will be after they have suffered God's punishment for their sins in hell—a period that will last until the end of the millennium, at which point they will be released.[277]

On the subject of "The Temporary Hell," H.D. Peterson, a Brigham Young University professor, comments:

> Among those at death who are assigned to hell are the heirs of the telestial kingdom and the sons of perdition. These spirits will remain in hell, or spirit prison, suffering... until

the millennial reign is over. . . . At that time, they will be resurrected, . . . Through the mercies of God, even these people ["the filthy of the earth"] will be given a degree of glory. They will be "heirs of salvation," capable of being instructed by the Holy Spirit and by ministering angels. Elder Bruce R. McConkie wrote that, "Even most murderers will come out of hell, or the spirit prison, in the last resurrection to live in telestial glory. . . . Hell, then, is a temporary part of the spirit world where the wicked are restrained in order for justice to be served and to give them a chance to repent."[278]

Once their purgatorial suffering has ended, they will inherit a heavenly glory. Thus, even the lowest "telestial glory surpasses all human understanding,"[279] and even the wicked "are heirs of salvation."[280] Those who remain in the telestial kingdom will still be servants of God; their only punishment is that they cannot directly live in the presence of God and Christ or become a god. But the glory of the eternal heaven they will inhabit "surpasses all mortal understanding" even though it is of a lesser glory than the two heavens above it.

### Does Mormonism believe in eternal punishment?

The only people who have the possibility of eternal judgment are the "sons of perdition," among whom Satan and the demons are also classed. However, it is uncertain whether or not their punishment is truly eternal. As to whether Mormons are, in fact, universalists, no one can deny that they lean in that direction—for even if the sons of perdition are punished eternally, their numbers are exceedingly small. Mormon uncertainty on this issue is reflected in the lack of agreement on the subject on the part of different researchers of the sect. Dr. Walter Martin asserts, "The largest cult embracing universalism in the United States today is the Mormon Church."[281] Dr. Anthony Hoekema says Mormonism believes that some few will go to an eternal hell.[282]

In his book *Will the "Saints" Go Marching In?* Floyd McElveen also observes the general truism for most Mormon theology—that of contradictory revelation. Thus, concerning the topic of hell:

> In trying to research what the Mormons teach on hell, we run the gamut from apostles, teachers, and inspired books that teach an endless hell, others that teach a limited hell, and still others that teach no hell at all. As it is on so many other Mormon beliefs, Mormon leaders, their books and their Church members are hopelessly divided and do not seem to know what they really believe.[283]

Brigham Young himself was uncertain over the duration of God's punishment:

> How long the damned remain in hell, I do not know, nor what degree of suffering they endure. . . . God's punishment is eternal, but that does not prove that a wicked person will remain eternally in a state of punishment.[284]

Moreover, since Young taught that "there is no such thing as annihilation,"[285] and also that God has "a place of salvation, in due time, for all,"[286] it seems logical to conclude he was a universalist. Apostle John Widtsoe also acknowledges that Brigham Young taught universalism, that even the "sons of perdition" would be redeemed.[287] In *Times and Seasons*, April 15, 1842 Joseph Smith himself also forcefully denies eternal punishment.

Mormons, however, perpetuate these contradictory viewpoints.[288] Citing *Doctrine and Covenants*, 76:44-46, Joseph Fielding Smith, the tenth president and prophet of the Mormon church, argues that *only* those "who sinned against the Holy Ghost" will spend eternity in a special place.[289] But the Mormon definition of the "sin against the Holy Ghost" is not uniform.

Smith refers to the "sons of perdition" as the only persons for whom eternal punishment is a real possibility. He believes the term includes several possible categories of people, including murderers (some Mormons say only certain murderers),[290] adulterers, and apostate Mormons.[291] Others include the category of those who seek to hinder the work of the Mormon church—presumably Mormon apostates and Christians would constitute a large part of this category.[292]

Part of the problem in understanding Mormon beliefs is, once again, a result of equivocation: the words "eternal punishment" often mean only "punishment."[293] Below we supply examples.

Joseph F. Smith argues, *"Eternal punishment, or endless punishment, does not mean that those who partake of it must endure it forever"* (emphasis added) and that, even for the "sons of perdition," "the extent of this punishment none will ever know."[294]

Although *Doctrine and Covenants* explicitly accepts eternal punishment (cf. *D&C*, 76:44-46), it also denies it just as explicitly, as seen in the following, albeit confusing, scripture:

> And surely every man must repent or suffer, for I, God, am endless. . . . Nevertheless, it is not written that there shall be no end to this torment, but it is written *endless torment*. Again, it is written *eternal damnation*. . . . I will explain unto you this mystery . . . behold, I am endless, and the punishment which is given from my hand is endless punishment, for Endless is my name. Wherefore—Eternal punishment is God's punishment (*D&C*, 19:4-12).[295]

Mormons use such scriptures to argue that eternal punishment really isn't eternal. Thus, whenever a Mormon scripture, for example, the *Book of Mormon*, refers to the "danger of death, hell and endless torment (2 Nephi 28:22,23; Moroni 8:21), or whenever a Mormon refers to endless punishment, the meaning is not intended in a biblical sense. As H. Donl Peterson, professor of Ancient Scripture at Brigham Young University, points out:

> These statements may seem to reflect the traditional Christian view of heaven and hell. . . . But the *Book of Mormon* takes us a step farther. It describes these conditions as being, for most of mankind, temporary . . . [citing *D&C*, 19:4-12, quoted on previous page]. These verses help clarify some statements in the *Book of Mormon* and the Bible that refer to the temporary hell as being endless. As Latter-day Saints we have four books of scripture, as well as Latter-day prophets, to help us understand doctrines that have confused apostate Christianity for centuries.[296]

James Talmage also rejects biblical teaching:

> The false doctrine that the punishment to be visited upon erring souls is endless . . . is but a dogma of unauthorized and erring sectaries [Christians], at once unscriptural, unreasonable, and revolting. . . . In no instance is there justification for the inference that the individual sinner will have to suffer the wrath of offended justice forever and ever. . . . Justice must have her due; but when "the utter most farthing" is paid, the prison door shall open and the captive be free.[297]

Even though the language of *D&C*, 76:31-48 clearly implies literal eternality, Talmage refers to the sons of perdition as being only "beyond the *present* possibility of repentance and salvation."[298] Mormons frequently see hell or the Lake of Fire as figurative, for example, of mental anguish.[299]

In summary:

1. Mormon writers repeatedly contradict one another and are ambiguous in their definitions of key terms. From Joseph Smith onward, every position—from a literal eternal hell, to temporary annihilation of the spirit, to purgatory, and universalism—has been advocated.[300]

2. The biblical teaching is rejected, and it is maintained that, "There is the false teaching of one heaven and one hell."[301]

Conflicting revelations and doctrines on this issue present no small problem to Mormons. If Joseph Smith himself changed his mind on the issue—first teaching eternal punishment, then universalism—and if God's own revelations contradict one another, how can Mormons hope to find consistency on such a vital subject?[302]

Most Christian writers are in agreement that, contradictions aside, Mormonism is a universalistic or almost universalistic religion and that the average Mormon has little if any real fear of hell.[303]

To conclude, Mormon teaching on the afterlife is unclear and frequently inconsistent, presenting five possible states of existence after death—eternal hell, purgatory, and the three kingdoms. In 1) rejecting the biblical doctrine of everlasting punishment, 2) teaching the opportunity for salvation after death, and 3) offering a basically universalistic view, Mormonism rejects what God teaches in His Word concerning the eternal division of all humanity into categories of either the saved or lost.

## ◆ ◆ *Conclusion* ◆ ◆

We have now documented in detail that the Mormon religion does not accept the Christian view of salvation. Indeed, Mormonism adamantly rejects the biblical teaching on salvation—all the while claiming that its teachings are Christian. Not only does Mormonism deny the biblical nature of salvation, (as given by grace through faith), but also it rejects the atonement of Jesus Christ for sin, and denies the biblical teaching on the afterlife. In addition, it distorts 1) the nature of faith, 2) the meaning of Law, and 3) the biblical Fall of man and its implications.

# Mormon Religion and the Occult

## Should Mormonism Be Considered an Occult Religion?

———————————— ◆ ————————————

F rom the inception of the Mormon church in 1830 to the present, Mormonism has shown great receptivity to and dependence upon supernatural revelations and manifestations. Although most Mormons would be offended by such a characterization, Mormonism is an occult religion and should be classified as such. The historic revelations of Mormonism fit the characteristic pattern of spiritistic inspiration. They not only offer extremely unbiblical practices and theology, but also they have the "flavor" of occult revelations—such as the appeal to pride, encouragement to spiritistic guidance, threats for disobedience, false and/or contradictory revelations, commands to publish the revelations, etc.[1]

As an illustration, consider the revelations received by medium Dr. Helen Schucman in the modern New Age bible, *A Course in Miracles* (1977), or those given through automatic writing by medium L.M. Arnold in *The History of the Origin of All Things* (1852). In spite of their occult origin, in many places these revelations sound just as biblical as Mormon scripture, with "God" and "Jesus" speaking in the same manner as they allegedly do in *Doctrine and Covenants* and the *Book of Mormon*. Nevertheless, both revelations contain the same animosity towards Christian faith that is characteristic of all spiritistic literature, including Mormon scripture.[2]

In this section, we will show why Mormonism should be classified as an occult religion just as the religions of Theosophy, Rosicrucianism, Scientology, or Eckankar are occult. In chapter 18 we will show that Joseph Smith and other founders and leaders of Mormonism were occultists. In chapter 19 we will prove that the Mormon church actively encourages two powerful forms of occult activity: spiritism and necromancy. In chapter 20 we will reveal that the Mormon church further promotes the occult by redefining occult powers (psychic abilities) as the biblical spiritual gifts. We have also included an important appendix showing

229

how Mormonism teaches occult philosophy and practice in other ways (chap. 18).

All this will prove that Mormonism is an occult religion which comes under the judgment of God for engaging in practices He specifically forbids. God warns all men: "Let no one be found among you who... practices divination or sorcery, interprets omens, engages in witchcraft, or casts spells, or who is a medium or spiritist or consults the dead. Anyone who does these things is detestable to the Lord" (Deuteronomy 18:10-12 NIV). The specific terms "divination," "sorcery," "interprets omens," "witchcraft," and "casts spells" all apply to early Mormonism, and the phrase "who is a medium or spiritist or consults the dead" describes and condemns the Mormon church as a whole. We will proceed to document this.

Hugh Nibley himself once said that if a connection could be established between Joseph Smith and occult practices, it would be "the most damning evidence in existence against Joseph Smith."*

That connection is now established.

---

* cited by former Mormon Charles W. Carpenter in "Latter-day Skeptics" *Christianity Today*, Nov. 11, 1991, p. 30.

◆

# CHAPTER 18

# Were Early Mormon Leaders Practitioners of the Occult?

Average Mormons are probably uninformed as to the occult nature of their religion. They do not know—or will not believe—that Joseph Smith was an occultist or that Mormonism had occult origins. But there are good reasons that explain Smith's proneness to occult activity.

When occultism is practiced in a family, it is often transmitted to children both by education and, for lack of a better term, "psychic" transference. This power of transference is documented in the clinical research of Dr. Kurt Koch and others and noted in such authoritative texts as Dr. Nandor Fodor's *Encyclopedia of Psychical Science*. Smith's predilection for occultism may thus have been both "hereditary" and taught—by direct instruction from his parents. As Dr. Fodor observes, "In most cases mediumship can be traced as a hereditary gift. If the heredity is not direct, it is to be found in ancestors of collaterals."[3] Significantly, as is true for many other occultists, both of Smith's parents were involved in the world of the psychic and the occult.[4] This explains Joseph's predisposition to such activities.[5]

For example, the Smith family and Joseph himself were very interested in the ancient occult* practice of astrology.

This is not the accusation of "enemies" of the Mormon church, but of perhaps its most academically qualified historian, Dr. D. Michael Quinn,

---

* See the authors' text *Astrology: Do the Heavens Rule Our Destiny?* (Harvest House, 1989), 157-257.

who holds a Ph.D. in History from Yale. (To counter charges of "anti-Mormon bias" we have frequently cited Dr. Quinn's extensively documented research.):

> Astrology was important to members of the Smith family.... Brigham Young stated in 1861 that "an effort was made in the days of Joseph to establish astrology."... The Hyrum Smith family preserved a magic dagger inscribed with Mars, the ruling planet of Joseph Smith Sr.'s birth year. The Hyrum Smith family also possessed magic parchments inscribed with the astrological symbols of the planets and the Zodiac... and the Emma Smith Badamon family preserved a magic artifact consecrated to Jupiter, the ruling planet of Joseph Smith Jr.'s birth. Based on interviews in 1886 with disaffected Mormons of early Church membership, one anti-Mormon wrote, "The only thing the Prophet believed in was astrology. This is a fact generally known to old 'Nauvoo Mormons.'"
>
> Historical evidence provides the exact or probable dates for 18 of Smith's marriages, and all of these wedding dates have astrological correlations.... The probability of "mere coincidence" diminishes in view of the fact that there is an overwhelming pattern of astrological correlations in the marriage dates for Joseph Sr. and Jr. (the only two members of the Smith family identified by neighbors as performing ritual magic), whereas there is a corresponding lack of astrological correlations in the marriage dates of other family members.... This marriage pattern is consistent with an awareness of magic and the occult.[6]

As an example of the influence of astrology upon Joseph Smith, consider the following:

> Consistent with the claim that his ruling planet, Jupiter, governed the hazel tree... Palmyra neighbors reported that Smith began using a divining rod (hazel was the traditional wood) in his early adolescence.... The astrological dominance of Jupiter in Smith's life is reflected in an [occult] artifact... of special significance to him.... Joseph Smith's [artifact was] a silver Jupiter medallion constructed according to the instructions for making "Magic Seals, or Talismans," in Barrett's 1801 [occult manual] *The Magis*.[7]

On this prized silver medallion of Joseph Smith are the astrological symbol of Jupiter, the magic sigil of Jupiter, the magic sigil of the spirit Intelligence of Jupiter, Jupiter's magic number, and the phrase (in Latin), "Make me O Lord all powerful."[8]

This "Jupiter talisman" was an amulet possessing alleged supernatural abilities that could bring wealth, influence and power to its possessor. Associated historically with paganism, magic and astrology, such implements enabled the owner to contact the spirit associated with the stone and to make use of its occult powers.[9] Usually this could be done through magical practice.

Thus, astrology was not the only occult interest of the Smith family—they also practiced ritual magic. Dr. Quinn observes,

> While the Smith family's belief in astrology can be demonstrated only circumstantially and inferentially, the Smiths left direct evidence of their practice of ritual magic. In addition to the magic dagger, among Hyrum Smith's possessions at his death were three parchments—lamens, in occult terms—inscribed with signs and names of ceremonial magic.... Palmyra neighbors reported that Joseph Smith, Sr., and Joseph Smith, Jr., were drawing magic circles in the mid-1820's. ...Several sources indicate that Joseph Jr. engaged in folk magic activities during the summers of the 1820s away from Palmyra, often in Pennsylvania.[10]

Anyone who has studied ritual magic knows that it can be a powerful and dangerous occult practice.[11] It frequently involves the attempt to conjure spirits and to use them for secret (and not infrequently evil) purposes. This appears to have been true for Joseph Smith and his family.

Joseph Smith, Jr. apparently had an occult mentor named Luman Walter, a fortune teller, astrologer, mesmerist and necromancer.[12] Quinn further observes that the "magical milieu of the Smith family included seer stones, astrology, talismans, a dagger for drawing magic circles of treasure digging and spirit invocation, and magic parchments for purification, protection, and conjuring a spirit."[13]

The familial predilection to occult activity and powers can be seen in the fact that Joseph Smith, Jr. had characteristic supernatural experiences at a young age. The original handwritten manuscript of Joseph Smith's *History* reads, "I received the first visitation of angels, which was when I was about 14 years old."[14]

Smith's extensive use of occult practices places the origins of Mormonism and the "first vision" account in an entirely new light. Whatever discrepancies exist between the various accounts (suggesting fabrication), the possibility can hardly be ruled out that Smith was subject to actual spiritistic manipulation and manifestations. Indeed, it was the first vision itself that was crucial not only in convincing Smith that occult activities were permissible but also in further cementing his ties to occultism:

> In light of the efforts of ordained clergy to suppress folk magic, Joseph Smith, Jr.'s 1820 theophany or first vision, is

important. For by the early 1820's the Smith family had already
participated in a wide range of magical practices, and there is
apparent magical context for Smith's first vision. In this conversation experience God told Smith that the teachings of the
[Christian] clergy were wrong. . . . Smith's vision of the divine
would [thus] have given him every reason to ignore clerical
instructions, *including denunciations of the occult.*[15]

Joseph Smith, Jr., of course, went on to experience scores and perhaps
hundreds of spiritistic contacts and encounters. And at least some of
these seem to have been achieved through magic ritual having the direct
intent of spirit invocation. Consider one of Smith's 1823 visitations. As
Dr. Quinn comments,

> Within traditional magic lore, the details of the [September
> 21] 1823 visitation would have suggested that Smith's initial
> meetings with the heavenly messenger [i.e., the spirit] were
> the dramatically successful result of ritual magic, specifically
> necromancy, communication with the dead (or, more pre-
> cisely, psychomancy, the communication with the visible
> spirit of a deceased person). . . . For those who shared a magic
> world view, the times and seasons of Smith's 1823 experience
> would have directly applied to instructions for spirit incanta-
> tion by Reginald Scot, H.C. Agrippa, Erra Pater, Ebenezer
> Silby, and other occult works in frequent circulation in early
> America.[16]

Quinn explains how the background and characteristics of this 1823
vision precisely fulfilled magical intent:

> Smith began praying late Sunday night on 21 September
> 1923. According to astrological guides, Sunday night was the
> only night of the week ruled by Jupiter. . . . Jupiter, Smith's
> ruling planet, was the most prominent astrological symbol on
> the Smith family's golden lamen for summoning a good spirit.
> Pseudo-Agrippa's *Fourth Book of Occult Philosophy* also spe-
> cified that "the Lord's day" was the occasion for man "to
> receive an Oracle from the good spirits," . . . Oliver Crowdery
> [a *Book of Mormon* witness] wrote that Smith began praying
> earnestly that Sunday night about "11:00 or 12:00" in order "to
> commune with some kind of messenger." . . . [Further] the
> hour and day in which Smith prayed "to commune with some
> kind of messenger" was pinpointed in magic books as being
> ideal for the invocation of spirits.[17]

As we will see in chapter 19, the basis for Mormonism's historic
fascination with necromancy (which continues to this day) can be traced

to these early activities. Clearly, Smith and other Mormons, in harmony with occult practices of the time, did not at first identify these spirits as angels—but only as spirits. In fact, they were identified as the spirits *of the dead* and thus all these practices are properly classified as necromantic. Nevertheless, Mormons soon began redefining these necromantic contacts as angelic visitations: "Until the Mormons adopted their own definition in 1830, it was not customary to use 'angel' to describe a personage who had been mortal, had died, and was returning to earth to give a message to an individual."[18]

In other words, Mormons were never communing with "angels" at all—as the modern church claims—but only with the spirits of the dead. And this is the practice of necromancy—an activity that is specifically forbidden in the Bible (Deuteronomy 18:9-12).

Thus, Smith's occult practices are not only the context in which to see his 1820 vision and other encounters, but they are also the context in which to assess the development and inspiration of the *Book of Mormon* and other Mormon scripture. To a significant degree the *Book of Mormon* was really a product of spirit invocation and necromantic divination. Dr. Quinn himself concedes this in part, although incorrectly couching the development of the *Book of Mormon* in terms of an alleged biblical prophecy:

> The *Book of Mormon*'s use of Isaiah 29:4 to describe its own coming forth through Smith was consistent with the Smith family's magic parchments of spirit invocation and with early testimony that the other worldly messenger Moroni introduced the book to Smith by appearing as a spirit three times. Within a magic setting, the *Book of Mormon* would have proclaimed itself the fulfillment of a biblical prophecy concerning divinely appointed [sic] necromancy, or psychomancy—divination through communication with spirits of the dead.[19]

From the perspective of occult revelation, Smith's dependence upon magic ritual makes the mystical origin of the *Book of Mormon* more credible. Apparently, Smith regularly participated in the occult practice of crystal gazing. He would use "peep stones" or seer stones in order to receive psychic information. He would place these stones in a hat, bury his face in the hat and then "see" visions of buried treasure, lost property, etc.[20] Of course, this was how the *Book of Mormon* was allegedly translated.

Mormonism falsely claims that Smith used the biblical "Urim and Thummim" to translate the characters written upon the gold plates—the translation eventually becoming the *Book of Mormon*. But this so-called "Urim and Thummim" were either two seer stones attached together or more probably a single stone placed in a hat through which Smith "saw" the *Book of Mormon* translation appear.[21]

The occult origin of the Mormon religion seems evident. Smith's dependence upon the supernatural for his new religion is clear: 1) the *Book of Mormon* was an occultly derived text; 2) *Doctrine and Covenants* was also an occultly derived text containing over one hundred spiritistic revelations; 3) *The Pearl of Great Price* was another occultly derived text, being a second translation done by occult power, and 4) Smith's own revision of the King James Bible, his "inspired translation," may also have been accomplished by occult means.

In other words it is the occult, spiritistic revelations given to Joseph Smith, Jr. in the *Book of Mormon, Doctrine and Covenants, The Pearl of Great Price,* etc., that form the basic foundation of the Mormon church. All this proves that Mormonism is a religion whose origin was dependent upon occult practice.

Without the occult activities of the Smith family, there would be no Church of Jesus Christ of Latter-day Saints today.

But Smith was not alone in his trust of occult practices, or in his use of occult implements.* Many early Mormon leaders and laity were actively involved in the use of seer stones, for instance. (As in modern New Age "crystal work," these were often employed as a means to contact the spirit world."[25]) When we consider Mormonism's highly praised "Eleven Witnesses" to the *Book of Mormon,* we find that most of them were involved in occult practices. This also is confirmed by the research of Mormon author and historian Dr. D. Michael Quinn.[26]

Consider the "Eight Witnesses." Joseph Smith's father, one of the Eight Witnesses, used a divining rod and seer stones, and was involved in occult healing, magical circles, and other occult activities.[27] Joseph Smith's brother Hyrum, also one of the Eight Witnesses and a member of the Mormon First Presidency, was the custodian of the family's implements of ritual magic. (Joseph Smith's younger brother William, one of

---

*Smith's use of psychic instruments to receive many of his revelations does not mean that these implements themselves possessed supernatural power. There are literally hundreds of such implements that have been used to develop psychically—dowsing rods, Ouiji boards, pendulums, Tarot cards, crystals, the I Ching, etc. These objects, whether they are forked sticks, alphabet planchetts, stones, dice, etc., have no supernatural powers. Rather they are merely vehicles through which spirits may choose to work. Eventually, the person can dispense with the instrument and yet his psychic powers remain. Thus, as Orson Pratt noted, "Joseph received several revelations to which I was witness by means of the Seerstone, but he could receive also without any instrument."[22] In fact, Smith was arrested for fortune telling in Bainbridge, New York, in 1826. Despite Mormon disclaimers,[23] the authenticity of the court record is unassailable:

Now that the authenticity of the court record has been established, the Mormon church leaders are faced with a dilemma. The court records plainly show that Joseph Smith was deeply involved in magic practices at the very time he was supposed to be preparing himself to receive the plates for the *Book of Mormon....* The fact that Joseph Smith used a stone, which he placed in a hat to translate the *Book of Mormon,* has caused a great deal of embarrassment because it so closely resembles crystal gazing.... According to witnesses, the plates didn't even have to be present when Joseph Smith was "translating." Mormon writer Arch S. Reynolds notes that "the plates were not always before Joseph during the translation." His wife and mother state that the plates were on the table wrapped in a cloth while Joseph translated with his eyes hid in a hat with the seerstone or the Urim and Thummim. David Whitmer, Martin Harris and others state that Joseph hid the plates in the woods and other places while he was translating (*How Did Joseph Smith Translate?*, 21).[24]

the first twelve apostles, accepted Joseph's divination practices and apparently saw nothing wrong with any of the other occult practices of the family.) Brother Samuel Smith, another of the Eight Witnesses, may also have shared in such beliefs.[28]

The "Three Witnesses" to the *Book of Mormon* had similar interests. Oliver Crowdery used the divining rod before he met Smith in 1829. He was convinced he was authorized by God to use this occult practice to receive supernatural information.[29] David Whitmer accepted and honored Smith's use of seer stones and may have possessed one of his own. Martin Harris, the third witness, also endorsed Smith's use of seer stones and participated in occult treasure digging after the alleged discovery of the gold plates. Finally, "Of the remaining Eight Witnesses, John Whitmer possessed a seer stone which his descendants preserved . . . his brothers Christian, Jacob, and Peter were included in their pastor's accusation of magic belief, and Hyrum Page, their brother-in-law, had a stone for revelations."[30]

If all this were not bad enough, the influence of occultism upon Mormonism's First Quorum of Apostles is also prominent:

> The influence of magic was equally pervasive among the twelve men who comprised the first quorum of apostles in 1835. As will be seen, almost half of the first apostles— Brigham Young, Heber C. Kimball, Orson Hyde, Luke S. Johnson, and Orson Pratt—gave specific evidence of a belief in various magical practices, while William Smith, Parley P. Pratt, and Lyman E. Johnson may have shared the views that their brothers expressed and implemented. Thus, *at least two thirds of Mormonism's first apostles may have had some affinity for magic.*[31]

With so many Mormon leaders promoting the occult, it is hardly surprising that occult activities were widely practiced among the first generation of Mormons. As even Quinn confesses, the preponderance of occult activity among the founders of Mormonism would seem to justify "the conclusion that magic and the occult exercised considerable influence among the first generation of Mormon converts from New York and New England, especially prior to 1831."[32]

In conclusion, none can deny that Joseph Smith was an occultist and that many of his family members were also practitioners of the occult—or that the true source of power behind the Mormon religion was occultism. The extensive research of D. Michael Quinn, Jerald and Sandra Tanner and others leaves little room for doubt.[33]

The reason Mormonism is an occult religion is that it was founded by occultists. However, Mormonism was not only begun by occultists—and is, therefore, properly classified as an occult religion in its early history— but also it continues as an occult religion to this day. This will be the subject of our appendix and the next chapter.

# ◆ ◆ Appendix ◆ ◆

*Does Mormonism Support Mediumistic and Other Occult Philosophy?*

At several points the doctrinal content of the scriptural and other revelations within Mormonism are closely aligned with the inspired writings of spiritistic mediums. Both sets of literature support common occult beliefs such as preexistence, man as God, various spirit levels of existence, eternal progression, interaction with the spirit world, contact with the dead, and others. This is why one authority on Mormonism, the late Dr. Walter Martin, emphasized that "Occultism in Mormon theology is undeniable."[34]

In *Doctrine and Covenants*, 128 Joseph Smith explains the doctrine of baptism for the dead; in *Doctrine and Covenants*, 137 Smith receives an occult vision of the celestial kingdom and second chance salvation for the dead; in *Doctrine and Covenants*, 138 the sixth president and prophet, Joseph F. Smith, sees 1) an occult vision of the "hosts of the dead, both small and great" and 2) that the unsaved dead had the Mormon gospel preached to them for their salvation.

One prominent Mormon confessed in 1875, "The Mormon idea of the other world, while in respects it differed from the teachings of certain modern 'spiritualists' [mediums] was not altogether dissimilar."[35] For example, *Doctrine and Covenants*, 130:12 explains, "The same sociality which exists among us here will exist among us there," and in verse 18, "Whatever principle of intelligence we attain unto in this life, it will rise with us in the resurrection."

Mediumistic philosophy is also seen in Brigham Young's conviction that many of the dead are schooled in the afterlife before being permitted an opportunity to progress spiritually:

> If a person is baptized for the remission of sins, and dies a short time thereafter, he is not prepared at once to enjoy a fullness of the glory promised to the faithful in the Gospel; for he must be schooled while in the spirit, and other departments of the house of God, passing on from truth to truth, from intelligence to intelligence, until he is prepared to again receive his body and to enter into the presence of the Father and the Son. We cannot enter into celestial glory in our present state of ignorance and mental darkness. . . . We have more friends behind the veil than on this side, and they hail us more joyfully than you were welcomed by your parents and friends in this world; and you will rejoice more when you meet them than you ever rejoiced to see a friend in this life.[36]

This mediumistic teaching is endorsed in modern Mormonism. The previous president and prophet of the Mormon church, Spencer W. Kimball, also teaches this mediumistic idea:

It is the destiny of the spirits of men to come to this earth and travel a [spiritual] journey of indeterminate length. . . . While we lack recollection of our pre-mortal life, before coming to this earth all of us understood definitely the purpose of our being here. . . . We understood also that after a period varying from seconds to decades of mortal life we would die, our bodies would go back to Mother Earth from which they had been created, and our spirits would go to the spirit world, where we would further train for our eternal destiny. After a period, there would be a resurrection or a reunion of the body and the spirit, which would render us immortal and make possible our further climb toward perfection and godhood.[37]

He also teaches, "Men came to earth consciously to obtain their schooling, their training and development, and to perfect themselves."[38]

As Bruce McConkie observes, "Life and work and activity all continue in the spirit world. Men have the same talents and intelligence there which they had in this life. . . . They continue, in effect, to walk in the same path they were following in this life."[39] This is why the current Mormon president and prophet, Ezra Taft Benson, comments that the line between our world and the spirit world is so extremely thin that, in fact, the spirits coexist in our world with us, only invisibly.[40]

Mormon theologian Duane S. Crowther refers to the "blessing" of death, again in characteristically mediumistic terms: "It is important to recognize that death is a blessing, a joyful experience, and often serves as a pleasant relief to those who are suffering in mortality."[41] He proceeds to discuss the alleged experiences of the dead immediately after dying—a description which parallels endless depictions of the initial afterlife experience as given by the spirit guides of modern channelers and mediums: "One of the greatest blessings of passing through the veil [of death] is the privilege of again enjoying the company of relatives and friends who have previously died. . . . Almost all the accounts of those who are permitted to visit the spirit world contain references to happy reunions with previously departed loved ones."[42]

In one of the most indepth treatments of occultism in Mormonism, *Early Mormonism and the Magic World View*, Mormon historian D. Michael Quinn discusses many parallels between Mormonism and the magical world view. For example, in describing the vision of Joseph Smith and Sidney Rigdon, recorded February 16, 1832, he comments that the "Vision's description of multiple heavens was compatible with widely published occult views."[43] He also compares the Mormon "temple endowment" (see chap. 30) and the ancient pagan mystery religions, noting that "Mormon revelations, in fact, proclaim that the endowment restored . . . the occult mysteries of the ancient world."[44] He then cites ten specific parallels between the Mormon endowment and the ancient pagan mysteries, concluding with the fact that "the ancient occult mysteries and the Mormon endowment manifest both philosophical and structural kinship":[45]

> In fact, LDS scholar Hugh Nibley has consistently turned to the occult rites of ancient Egyptian and gnostic mystery religions to demonstrate by parallel evidence the antiquity of Mormon endowment rituals.... By drawing only on authorized descriptions of the endowment by LDS leaders, I believe it is possible to see within a historical context how the Mormon endowment reflected the ancient and occult mysteries.[46]

Thus,

> From Joseph Smith's time to the present, these ancient mysteries have been viewed as the climax of the occult tradition and magic world view.... Beginning in the early 1830's, LDS revelations announced an imminent restoration of "hidden" or "secret" mysteries. As previously discussed, these words could mean "occult" in contemporary language. In February 1832, Smith's vision of the degrees of glory announced, "And to them I will reveal all mysteries, yea, all the [occult] mysteries of my kingdom from days of old, and for ages to come (*D&C*, 76:7).[47]

For example, in some ancient paganism, initiates to the mysteries would pray and ask the deity to make the truth known to them by a "burning in the bosom" type experience.[48] In ancient Corinth the pagans (e.g., the Marcionites) practiced baptism for the dead rituals and had other practices and beliefs similar to modern Mormonism.[49]

It is also significant that a number of names given in the *Book of Mormon* illustrate parallels to various spirits and magical practices:

> Several Book of Mormon names reinforce the "familiar spirit" motif.... ["Mormon" is one].... Alma also had reference to spirits and to ceremonial magic.... The name of the Book of Mormon's founding prophet Lehi has several parallels, the last of which is similar to a name used in the ritual magic of spirit incantation.... Nephi is also a name with several parallels to spirits and magic.[50]

In conclusion, the presence of 1) mediumistic philosophy, 2) "familiar spirit" motifs, and 3) parallels to the ancient mystery religions comprise additional evidence that Mormonism is properly classified as an occult religion.

# CHAPTER 19

◆

# Does the Mormon Church Encourage Spiritism and Necromancy?

While the Mormon church cannot logically deny its occult history, it does deny any association with occult activity today. Yet Mormonism remains an occult religion because of 1) its continual acceptance of spiritism and necromancy and 2) its reliance upon psychic/spiritistic powers. We will discuss these subjects in turn in our next two chapters.

In harmony with modern "Christian" parapsychology[51] and even mediumism itself, the Mormon church interprets its spiritistic activity as "spiritual" and "godly." Yet both spiritism and necromancy are clearly condemned in the Bible as an abomination before God. As we have seen in Deuteronomy 8:9-13, God not only warns against divination, but also against any contact with spirits or with the so-called human dead. Even noted Mormon theologian Bruce McConkie confesses that necromancy "has been a common practice among apostate people," and that "the Lord calls it an abomination."[52]

Strictly speaking, necromancy is defined as divination by means of contact with the dead. But in a broader sense it is seen as any contact with the dead. And this is what we find frequently in the modern Mormon church. As we have seen, the dead have always played a key role within the Mormon religion, and they continue to play a prominent role in the church today.[53] We noted earlier that when the alleged dead biblical or family personalities appeared to Joseph Smith, he welcomed them.[54]

> Joseph Smith received the Aaronic Priesthood under the hands of John the Baptist. He received the Melchizedek Priesthood under the hands of Peter, James and John.[55]

241

> Angels serve the Father and the Son and minister [to man] on their errand, whether such angels are spirit beings... translated beings... or resurrected beings [the dead], as Moroni who ministered to Joseph Smith.[56]

But the spirits must be tested as to whether or not they really are who they claim to be. Any spirit that claims to be from God and yet rejects and distorts God's Word must be lying. Unfortunately, Mormonism has not engaged in this process of testing the spirits.

Joseph Smith's supernatural contacts—allegedly from God the Father, Jesus, dead biblical characters and others—could not have been genuine because these spirits brought unbiblical messages which supported the founding of a church that has adamantly opposed the teachings of God and Jesus Christ for over 150 years. How could good spirits engage in lies and support false teachings?

But this phenomenon of spirits lying and impersonating others is not unusual. In fact, visitations from "Jesus" and other biblical personalities are a common theme in occult circles which claim a biblical orientation.[57] So, if Mormon supernatural visitations bring unbiblical teachings and support the occult, then how are they different from any other spiritistic circles which claim visitation by alleged biblical personages? For example, "Jesus" is one of the personalities who appears as an "ascended master" in the spiritistic sect known as The Church Universal and Triumphant. Just as with Mormonism, it condemns Christianity, distorts and subverts the Bible, and teaches spiritism, occultism, and anti-Christian theology. We could also mention medium Sun Myung Moon's Unification Church, Rudolph Steiner's Anthroposophy, numerous "Christian" spiritistic churches and many others.

Nevertheless, Joseph Smith and subsequent leaders in the Mormon church regularly contacted the spirit world, and this practice has continued to this day. The current president and prophet of the Mormon church, Ezra Taft Benson, confesses his personal belief when he observes that "the spirit world is close by" and that "the veil can be very thin— .. there are people over there who are pulling for us .. our loved ones... who have passed on."[58]

But here Mormonism equivocates again. Along with "Christian" parapsychology and religious spiritism in general, it makes an arbitrary division between what it considers to be "godly" and "ungodly" necromancy or spiritism. In other words, to seek unspecified contact with the spirits of the dead is "ungodly." But to seek it "in Jesus' name" somehow makes the practice "godly" and biblical. Perhaps Mormons do not realize that to deny the true Jesus and implore the name of a spiritistic Jesus cannot logically protect them from spiritual deception.

For example, Mormon theologian Duane S. Crowther argues that merely being a member in good standing with the Mormon church and invoking Jesus' name almost *guarantees* that spiritistic contacts and revelations will be "godly." One wonders how he can logically give such assurance:

> No person can receive manifestations from righteous *spirits* unless he believes in modern [Mormon] revelation. . . . Those who seek manifestations from the spirit world but not in his [Jesus] name are unlawful mediums. The priesthood holds the keys to revelation and the ministration of angels [spirits]. Spirit beings functioning *outside of this power* are not authorized messengers from God.[59]

In other words, being a good Mormon is the only safe and successful key to "godly" spirit contact. But Mormonism is wrong when it attempts to make a division between "godly" and "ungodly" spiritism. No biblical or other legitimate justification can be cited for such a philosophy. God never tells us there is such a practice as godly spiritism or mediumism; to the contrary, it is all labeled as an abomination to Him (Deuteronomy 18:9-13).

Nevertheless, Crowther goes on to describe a "handshake test" as a principal means of determining whether the spirit one is contacting is good or evil. (Joseph Smith actually taught that you could tell a false angel by the color of his hair![60]) However, Crowther is only repeating the advice of the spirits themselves as given in the Mormon scripture *Doctrine and Covenants*, 129:6-8:

> The next [spirit] revelation in the *Doctrine and Covenants* was given in 1843, . . . [It] concerned the discerning of other worldly messengers as coming from either God or from Satan. After defining angels as resurrected "just men" with glorified bodies of flesh and bone [i.e., the dead], the revelation specified: "If he be the spirit of a just man made perfect . . . ask him to shake hands with you, but he will not move, because it is contrary to the order of heaven for a just man to deceive; but he will still deliver his message. If it be the devil as an angel of light, when you ask him to shake hands he will offer you his hand, and you will not feel anything; you may therefore detect him" (*D&C*, 129:6-8).[61]

This is how Crowther explains it:

> A handshake test to aid in detecting evil spirits posing as authorized servants of God is set forth in the *Doctrine and Covenants*:
>
> > A) Resurrected beings [i.e., allegedly good spirits of the human dead, now having physical bodies] will

answer one's request to shake hands by doing so. They can be felt.

B) The disembodied spirits of just men made perfect will refuse to shake hands so as not to deceive, but will still give their message. They will be seen in light and glory. [i.e., Because they do not yet have bodies, but are still good spirits, they will refuse to shake hands, knowing that their refusal proves their goodness because:]

C) Evil spirits masquerading as angels of light will attempt to deceive mortals by shaking hands with them when requested to do so. Their hands will not be felt.[62]

But why should anyone trust a spirit's "handshake" rather than what God has already revealed—as a means to determine that spirit's nature? Furthermore, the test is useless. The history of ancient and contemporary occultism reveals that demons characteristically *are* able to engage in physical contact with men. Any Mormon who thinks he can discern the devil's activity merely by the Mormon "handshake test" is sorely deceived. In fact, former mediums such as Raphael Gasson have exposed similar tricks on the part of the spirit world. He explains that by a carefully designed ploy they deceive people into accepting their teachings by "proving" their own "goodness" and "trustworthiness." "Demons have to use some method of deception in their attempt to prove the counterfeit [messages] are of God and so they play a game of make believe. Although they are literally evil spirits, [they] pretend to be [good spirits]."[63]

Crowther further explains that according to Mormon belief there are at least five categories of spirits who can minister to Mormons and other men. There are "pre-mortal spirits," "translated beings," "righteous spirits," "evil spirits," and "resurrected beings."[64]

The fact that Mormonism offers so many opportunities for contact with the spirits is one reason why Mormonism can be classified as a spiritistic religion. In fact, Crowther himself defines one of these categories of spiritistic contact in characteristically mediumistic terms. Thus, allegedly "righteous spirits return to earth to:

A. give counsel,

B. give comfort,

C. obtain or give information,

D. serve as guardian angels,

E. prepare us for death,

F. summon mortals into the spirit world,

G. escort the dying through the veil of death."[65]

Mormons who believe this have adopted occult philosophy in the guise of divine revelation. One can but wonder if well-meaning Mormons may become ensnared in occult practices outside the church because they were conditioned to accept occult teachings within the church.

### Has Mormonism Accepted Necromancy Throughout Its History?

It is important to understand that *modern* Mormon necromancy is justified because it finds historical precedent with Joseph Smith and other early Mormon presidents. Although we have discussed many of Smith's occult activities, we have not yet evaluated him as a spiritistic medium.

It is significant that a sermon delivered by Mormon elder Parley Pratt in 1853 indicates early Mormon acceptance of Joseph Smith as a "divine" medium—virtually the same designation modern spiritistic mediums apply to themselves. This sermon was given only five years after the celebrated spiritist movement began in 1848, a moment which Pratt himself extols. Indeed, endless other allegedly divine mediums were making pretentious claims at the very same time Joseph Smith was. For example, just like Smith, L.M. Arnold claimed he was a divine medium and that God, Jesus Christ, the Holy Spirit and other spirits had given specific revelations through him. They were eventually published as *A History of the Origin of All Things*. The title page reads, "Given By The Lord Our God Through Levi M. Arnold, 1852." But like Mormonism's scriptures, this text actively 1) endorsed spiritism for "Christians" and 2) rejected biblical teaching.

Nevertheless, in the sermon by Pratt we see that Jesus Christ is also given the role of a spiritistic mediator and that spiritism was to be individually practiced within the Mormon temple. From the following extended discussion, it should be obvious to all that the true status of Joseph Smith was that of a spiritistic medium.

Pratt is discussing Smith's spiritistic contacts as proof of his alleged prophethood, even defining necromancy as "one of the leading fundamental truths of 'Mormonism'":

> Who communicated with our great modern Prophet, and revealed through him as a medium, the ancient history of a hemisphere, and the records of the ancient dead? Moroni, who had lived upon the earth 1400 years before....
> Who ordained our first founders to the Apostleship, to hold the keys of the Kingdom of God, in these times of restoration? Peter, James, and John, from the eternal [spirit] world. Who

instructed him [Joseph Smith] in the mysteries of the Kingdom, and in all things pertaining to Priesthood, law, philosophy, architecture, sacred ordinances, sealings, anointing,
baptisms for dead, and in the mysteries of the first, second,
and third heavens, many of which are unlawful to utter?
Angels and spirits from the eternal worlds.

Who revealed to him the plan of redemption, and of exaltation for the dead who had died without the Gospel and the
keys and preparations necessary for holy and perpetual converse with Jesus Christ, and with the spirits of just men made
perfect [i.e., the dead]? . . . Those from the dead!

Again—how do the saints expect the necessary information by which to complete the ministrations for the salvation
and exaltation of their friends who have died?

Shall *we*, then, deny the principle, the philosophy, the fact
of communication between worlds? No! verily no!

Editors, statesmen, philosophers, priests, and lawyers, as
well as the common people, began to advocate the principle of
converse with the dead, by visions, divination, clairvoyance,
[spirit] knocking, and writing mediums, etc., etc. This spiritual philosophy of converse with the dead, once established
by the labors, toils, sufferings, and martyrdom of its modern
founders, and now embraced by a large portion of the learned
world, shows a triumph more rapid and complete—a victory
more extensive, than has ever been achieved in the same
length of time in our world.

An important point is gained, a victory won, and a countless host of opposing powers vanquished, on one of the leading or fundamental truths of "Mormon" philosophy, viz.—
"that the living may hear from the dead."[66]

Pratt continues his discussion by offering advice concerning the distinguishing of good vs. evil spirits. Notice the similarity of Pratt's arguments with those of Crowther just cited:

The fact of spiritual communications being established,
. . . we drop that point, and call attention to the means of
discriminating or judging between the lawful and the unlawful mediums or channels of communication.

In the first place, no persons can successfully seek to God
for this privilege unless they believe in direct revelation in
modern times.

Jesus Christ is the only name given under heaven, as a
medium through which to approach to God. None, then, can
be lawful mediums, who are unbelievers in Jesus Christ, or in
modern revelation.

And moreover, the Lord has appointed a Holy Priesthood on the earth, and in the heavens, and also in the world of spirits . . . and has committed to this Priesthood the keys of holy and divine revelation, and of correspondence, or communication between angels, spirits, and men, and between all the holy departments, principals, and powers of His government in all worlds.

And again—The Lord has ordained that all the most holy things pertaining to the salvation of the dead, and all the most holy conversations and correspondences with God, angels and spirits, shall be had only in the sanctuaries of His holy Temple on the earth.

Ye Latter-day Saints! Ye thousands of the host of Israel! Ye are assembled here today and have laid these Corner Stones, *for the express purpose that the living might hear from the dead*, and that we may prepare a holy sanctuary, where "the people may seek under their God, for the living to hear it from the dead." And that heaven and earth, and the world of spirits may commune together.[67]

Nevertheless, this basic Mormon approach is explicitly rejected in Isaiah 8:19,20 (NIV): "When men tell you to consult mediums and spiritists, who whisper and mutter, should not a people inquire of their God? Why consult the dead on behalf of the living? To the law and to the testimony! If they do not speak according to this word, they have no light of dawn."

Temple spiritism is also noted by Dr. Walter Martin, who cites an earlier leading Mormon theologian, Charles Penrose. In his *Mormon Doctrine* (1888), Penrose actually taught early Mormons to believe that "godly" spiritism saves one from the deceptions of ungodly spiritism:

The living are thus authorized, under prescribed conditions, to act for the dead, and the fathers and spirit world look to the children in the flesh to perform for them the works which they were unable to attend to while in the body. . . . This glorious doctrine . . . regulates the communion of the living with the dead. It saves those who receive it from improper and deceptive spirit communications. . . . Knowledge that is needful concerning the spiritual sphere will come through an appointed place. The [Mormon] temple where the ordinances can be administered for the dead, is the place to hear from the dead. The Priesthood in the flesh, when it is necessary, will receive communications from the Priesthood behind the veil [the dead].[68]

Joseph F. Smith, the sixth president and prophet of the Mormon church, continued the support of spiritistic and mediumistic contacts within Mormonism:

> Our fathers and mothers, brothers, sisters and friends who have passed away from this earth, having been faithful... may have a mission given them to visit their relatives and friends upon the earth again, bringing from the divine Presence messages of love, of warning, or reproof and instruction, to those whom they had learned to love in the flesh. . . . Joseph Smith, Hyrum Smith, Brigham Young, Heber C. Kimball, Jed M. Grant, David Patten, Joseph Smith, Sen., and all those noble men who took an active part in the establishment of this work, and who died true and faithful to their trust, have the right and privilege, and possess the keys and power, to minister to the people of God in the flesh who live now. . . . These are correct principles. There is no question about that in my mind. It is according to the scripture; it is according to the revelation of God to the Prophet Joseph Smith; and it is a subject upon which we may dwell with pleasure and perhaps profit to ourselves, provided we have the Spirit of God to direct us.[69]

Notice that in this representative citation by a president and prophet of the Mormon church, Mormons are told that they may have the privilege of communicating with the now dead Joseph Smith and other deceased Mormon leaders and that these are stated as "correct principles." This doctrine is why, throughout Mormon history, Mormon leaders have claimed to receive spiritistic contacts and guidance from their dead presidents and prophets—Joseph Smith, Brigham Young, etc. As one of many examples,[70] the fourth Mormon president and prophet, Wilford Woodruff, stated in 1880:

> After the death of Joseph Smith I saw and conversed with him many times in my dreams in the night season. . . . I have had many interviews with brother Joseph until the last fifteen or twenty years of my life. . . . I had many interviews with President Young, and with Heber C. Kimball, and Geo. A. Smith, and Jedediah M. Grant, and many others who are dead. *They attended our conference, they attended our meetings.*[71]

In fact, the extent of the practice of occultism throughout Mormon history is amazing to contemplate. Everything from automatic writing to out-of-body excursions and other occult practices have been endorsed.[72] Not inconsistently with Mormon theology, Brigham Young even accepted the idea that evil spirits were a necessary part of Mormons' spiritual growth. By helping to tempt Mormons to do evil, they could allegedly enable them to choose good instead. Thus, the following statement by Mormonism's second president and prophet, Brigham Young, could just as easily come from the mouth of some modern spiritistic mediums commenting upon dealings with evil spirits:

> You cannot give any person their exaltation [Godhood], unless they know what evil is, what sin, sorrow, and misery are, for no person could comprehend, appreciate, and enjoy an exaltation upon any other principle. The devil with one third part of the spirits of our Father's Kingdom got here before us, and we tarried there with our friends, until the time came for us to come to the earth and take tabernacles [bodies]; but those spirits that revolted were forbidden ever to have tabernacles of their own. . . . They are continually trying to get into the tabernacles of the human family, and are always on hand to prompt us to depart from the strict line of our duty. You know that we sometimes need a prompter. . . . Well, these evil spirits are ready to prompt you. Do they prompt us? Yes, and I could put my hands on a dozen of them while I have been on this stand; they are here on the stand. Could we do without the devils? No, we could not get along without them. They are here, and they suggest this, that, and the other.[73]

Young even confessed that the *evil* spirit world supported Mormonism: "Is there communication from God? Yes. From holy angels? Yes; and we have been proclaiming these facts during nearly 30 years. Are there any communications from evil spirits? Yes; and the Devil is making the people believe very strongly in revelations from the spirit world. This is called spiritualism [spiritism], and it is said that thousands of spirits declare that 'Mormonism' is true."[74]

So where does one find a scorecard, when even evil spirits endorse Mormonism? Again, Mormons have not understood that the very reason evil spirits support Mormonism—then and now—is that Mormonism supports the activities of evil spirits.

*Temple Spiritism and Saving the Dead (cf. Salvation: "Saving the Dead")*

Another spiritistic practice of Mormonism, briefly noted earlier, involves the Mormon doctrine that acts of charity done for the dead, in particular that baptism and temple marriage, can save them in the afterlife. In fact, in order to justify such necromancy, this doctrine is actively promoted by the spirits that Mormons contact. The fourth president and prophet of the Mormon church, Wilford Woodruff, emphasized in 1877 that the spirits of the dead were *actively pursuing* Mormons to assist them:

> We have labored in the St. George Temple since January
> . . . and many things have been revealed to us concerning the

dead. . . . I feel to say little else to the Latter-day Saints wherever and whenever I have the opportunity of speaking to them, than to call upon them to build these Temples now underway, to hurry them up to completion. *The dead will be after you, they seek after you as they have after us in St. George. They called upon us, knowing that we held the keys and power to redeem them.*

I will here say, before closing, that two weeks before I left St. George, *the spirits of the dead gathered around me, wanting to know why we did not redeem them.* . . . These were the [sic] signers of the Declaration of Independence, and they waited on me for two days and two nights. . . . I straightway went into the baptismal font and called Brother McCallister to baptize me for the signers of the Declaration of Independence, and 50 other eminent men, making one hundred in all, including John Wesley, Columbus, and others; I then baptized him for every President of the United States, except three; and when their cause is just, somebody will do the work for them.

I have felt to rejoice exceedingly in this work of redeeming the dead. I do not wonder at President Young saying he felt moved upon to call upon the Latter-Day Saints to hurry up the building of these Temples. . . . This is the preparation necessary for the second advent of the Savior.[75]

### *Mormon Temples: Houses of Necromancy?* (See Appendix.)

It is perhaps significant that the Mormon temple rituals apparently attempt to seal a person to spiritual powers. Former twenty-year Temple Mormon Ed Decker describes his Mormon temple marriage as invoking "principalities and powers" over him and his children:

> There the president of the Los Angeles Temple laid hands upon us, we knelt across the altar in the patriarchal grip holding our hands and then he said, "I seal upon you the dominions and kingdoms, the powers and principalities from above, the exaltations upon you and upon your children, upon them from generation to generation." He laid a curse upon me and my family without me even knowing it . . . the President of the temple laid his hands upon our heads and sealed upon us exaltations, dominions, thrones, powers and principalities from above. And we walked out of that temple shocked . . we were dumbfounded. We were forbidden to speak about it to one another so I could not talk to my wife without breaking my vows. We walked out and got in our car and drove home in absolute fear of what we had just done.[76]

Even if done inadvertently, this invoking may be something Decker should be concerned about. The term "principalities and powers" usually refers to evil spirits the Bible identifies as demons (Ephesians 1:21; 3:10; 6:12; Colossians 2:10,15). Given the occult nature of Mormonism, it is at least possible that such a procedure could instigate occult influence.

In other words, what are Mormon temples? Mormon temples are houses to appease the dead, houses of necromancy. The sixth president of the church, Joseph F. Smith, emphasized that the practice of temple baptism for the dead must continually be stressed:

> We should take diligent heed concerning our dead, that none shall be overlooked.... We do not have to get along in years before we get the spirit of salvation for the dead.... The younger people must not get the idea that this is only an old person's work. It is for *all* the Latter-day Saints, and young people can attend to these matters and get the spirit of this work just as much as those who are advanced in years.[77]

In the same text Joseph F. Smith encouraged Mormons not to be concerned over certain natural difficulties in tracing their ancestry, for the time would come when the dead would help them directly: "The time will come when the dead . . . will work hand in hand with those who are still in mortality, and they will furnish the information. There will be no mistakes about it then."[78] This is why the current president and prophet of the church, Ezra Taft Benson, freely confesses to necromantic contacts that current Mormon leaders have encountered in the temple:

> Visitors, seen and unseen, from the world beyond, are often close to us.... Sometimes actions here, by the priesthood of God, the First Presidency and the Twelve, as we meet in the Temple, have been planned and influenced by leaders of the priesthood on the other side [the spirit world]. *I am sure of that. We have evidence of it.... These righteous spirits are close by us.*[79]

Thus,

> The veil between us and the world of spirits is very thin. I feel most strongly that there are others here besides those we can see—some of your loved ones are here, also some of the leaders of the Church who have passed on. Those in authority in the heavens above are pleased and willing that the spirits of our loved ones should be near us.[80]

In conclusion, all this proves that modern Mormonism continues to practice necromancy, or contact with the dead.

### "Angelic" Guidance

Mormonism also still accepts spiritism in the form of alleged "angelic" guidance. (Remember Mormonism's early contact with the spirits of the dead was defined as contact with angels only later.) Bruce McConkie comments that "from Adam to the present moment, whenever men have had sufficient faith, angels have ministered unto them. So invarying is this principle that it stands forth as the conclusive test of the divinity of any organization on earth.... As is well known, angels have and do minister to faithful members of the Church of Jesus Christ of Latter-day Saints."[81]

Unfortunately, as in many other alleged angelic contacts and manifestations, the teachings of these angels reveal them to be lying spirits the Bible identifies as demons.[82] No holy angel of God is going to support a philosophy that denies God, rejects His Son, distorts God's plan of salvation and promotes the occult.

### New Supernatural Revelations

Spiritistic contacts also occur in Mormonism through numerous supernatural revelations given to the Mormon church leadership. Joseph Smith and the Mormon church justify this practice by teaching the error that "the rock" upon which Jesus would build His church (Matthew 16:17,18; cf. 1 Corinthians 10:4) was supernatural revelation—rather than Peter's confession of Christ as the true Messiah. Thus, as we saw in chapter 5, the church today continually stresses the importance of supernatural revelation. This doctrine is not only identified as one of their basic "Articles of Faith" but is also said to be evidence of one's personal spirituality and commitment to the truth (i.e., Mormonism). The following excerpts from standard Mormon literature bear this out:

> The Lord has given revelation to each of the presidents of the church.[83]

> Knowledge is revealed to the saints by the Holy Ghost (*D&C*, 121:26-32), and when they speak as moved upon by that member of the Godhead, the resulting expressions are scripture (*D&C*, 68:1-4).[84]

> The Lord's church must be guided by continuous revelation if it is to maintain divine approval.[85]

> With reference to their own personal affairs, the saints [Mormons] are expected (because they have the gift of the Holy Ghost) to gain personal revelation and guidance rather than to run to the First Presidency or some other church leaders to be told what to do.[86]

Every member of the [Mormon] church should have apostolic insight and revelation.[87]

Joseph Smith himself emphasized, "We never can comprehend the things of God and of heaven, but by [supernatural] revelation."[88] This is why Bruce McConkie emphasizes so strongly that,

Personal revelation is the rock foundation upon which true religion rests. All faithful members of the true Church receive revelation.... Revelation is for everyone in the Church.... Until men receive personal revelation they are without God in the world.... Those who receive revelation are on the path leading to salvation; those who do not receive revelation are not on that path and cannot be saved, unless they repent and get in tune with the Spirit.[89]

Unfortunately, when both leaders and individual Mormons are encouraged to seek supernatural revelations, how can they logically expect them to be divine? Consider the facts. Such persons 1) are members of a church that was founded by occultists, 2) are members of a church that teaches occult philosophy, and 3) are members of a church that practices occult activity. Isn't it logical to conclude then that any supernatural revelations received will be occult and not divine?

## ♦ ♦ *Appendix* ♦ ♦

*Has There Been Satanic Infiltration of Mormonism?*

In a Mormon church memo dated July 19, 1990, Glenn L. Pace,* a general authority of the Mormon church, claims he has met with sixty individuals, all members of the Mormon church, who allege they have been victims of ritual Satanic abuse. "Forty-five victims allege witnessing and/or participating in human sacrifice" (p. 1). In fact, Pace suggests that the number of victims is in the hundreds and alleges that "bishops, a patriarch, a stake president, temple workers, and members of the Tabernacle Choir" may be involved (p. 5). Significantly, "many" who had allegedly taken part in Satanic rites claimed that they had their "first flashback" while "attending the [Mormon] temple for the first time." When they took the Mormon oaths and heard "the exact words" in the temple ceremony that they had previously heard in Satanic ritual, "horrible memories were triggered" (p. 4). Further, "most victims are [now] suicidal" (p. 4).

---

* A photocopy of this memorandum is published in Jerald and Sandra Tanner's *Salt Lake City Messenger* 80 (November 1991): 1–12.

Pace believes that this activity is not officially a part of the Mormon church but rather that occultists, sensing a good opportunity, are taking advantage of the occult aspects of Mormonism for their own purposes.

In their analysis of this issue Jerald and Sandra Tanner note that "Church history and doctrine . . . make the Church vulnerable to infiltration by occultists and others who wish to use the Church for their own ends" (p. 12). For example, prior to the 1990 revision of the temple ceremony, participants were required to go through what was known as the "Five Points of Fellowship." "This part of the ritual would have been very appealing to a Satanist who desired close physical contact with those who pass through the ceremony" (p. 11).

Until more information becomes available it is perhaps best to reserve judgment on this issue. Nevertheless, this is a worrisome development that requires careful attention by the Mormon leadership.

◆

# CHAPTER 20

# Does the Mormon Church Confuse Spiritual Gifts and Occult Powers?

I n this chapter we will discuss one additional manner in which the Mormon church supports occultism. The church teaches its members that in addition to supernatural revelation, they should be able to manifest various supernatural powers. These are defined as spiritual gifts, but they are indistinguishable from the occult practices and abilities of modern psychics, spiritists, mediums and channelers.

The true gifts of the Holy Spirit can be clearly distinguished from occult abilities. Once these distinctions are seen, it becomes evident that Mormonism's spiritual gifts are really occult powers.[90]

For instance, Bruce McConkie emphasizes the importance of individual Mormons performing miracles:

> Those who exercise faith, always and invaryingly work miracles, and possess the gifts and signs promised the faithful. Thus when Paul says a man is justified by faith, he means he is justified only if he is keeping the commandments and so living that he has [supernatural] power to work miracles and display the fruits of faith.[91]

McConkie further encourages Mormon occultism when he asks, "How does God reveal himself? Though the ways may be infinite, the perfect and crowning way is by direct revelation, by visions, by personal [supernatural] visitations."[92]

Thus, McConkie taught that Mormons could gain the occult power of precognition: "But when a person has received revelation from the Spirit certifying to the divinity of Christ, he is then in a position to press forward in righteousness and gain other revelations, including those which foretell future events."[93]

The student manual *Doctrines of the Gospel* tells Mormons that the Holy Ghost will also give them clairvoyant or telepathic abilities: "The Holy Ghost enables righteous individuals [Mormons] to discern the thoughts of others (see Alma 10:17; 12:3; 18:16-18; Jacob 2:5)."[94] Even prayer is to involve supernatural activity: "Perfect prayers are those which are [supernaturally] inspired, in which the Spirit reveals the words which should be used."[95]

The publication *Gospel Principles* lists nearly a dozen supernatural gifts that Mormons are told they can receive. These occult counterfeits include the gift of tongues and interpretation of tongues, the gift of translation, the gift of supernatural knowledge, the gift of prophecy, ("those who receive true revelations about the past, present, or future have the gift of prophecy"[96]), the gift of healing, the gift of working miracles, etc. This publication further encourages Mormons to develop psychically when it tells them, "We can develop our gifts."[97]

However, all these "gifts" are also found among occult mediums and channelers. And in order to tell the difference between true and false gifts, Mormons need to carefully evaluate the following statement from their own *Gospel Principles*: "If we truly have the gift of prophecy, we will not receive a revelation which does not agree with what the Lord has said in the scriptures."[98]

This book also warns that "mediums, astrologers, fortune tellers, and sorcerers are inspired by Satan even if they claim to follow God."[99] But how can Mormons know this? Because of their practices? In many cases, they are indistinguishable from Mormon practices. Because of their teachings? In fact, many "mediums, astrologers, fortune-tellers and sorcerers" teach basic Mormon doctrines. The problem the Mormon church faces is that of being able to objectively distinguish the supernatural manifestations found in the world of the occult from those found within its own church. So far, the Mormon church has been unable to do this. Nor do we think it ever will, for the simple reason that its own supernatural revelations *are* occult.

The late Mormon theologian Bruce McConkie confesses that "Satan has power to imitate the truth, to lead men astray, to perform false miracles."[100] Does the Mormon church imitate the truth, lead men astray and perform false miracles? If the Mormon church claims to be biblical and Christian, yet denies the God of the Bible, rejects the Christ of the Bible, distorts biblical teaching, denies salvation by grace and promotes the occult, to name a few considerations, how can any Mormon know that his or her personal religion does not conform to McConkie's assessment?

As an illustration, consider the book *Life Everlasting* by Mormon theologian Duane S. Crowther. (This is only one of a dozen similar works.) In his appendix, "Summary of supernatural manifestations cited," he lists almost three hundred different supernatural manifestations that Mormon believers have encountered: "The incidents are listed under the name of the dead individual who was seen in the spirit world or who returned to mortality" to minister to a Mormon or Mormons.[101]

Anyone familiar with the world of the occult will immediately perceive that these experiences are occult, not godly. Most of the spiritistic contacts are designed specifically to endorse and *encourage the beliefs and practices of Mormonism, especially their involvement with the dead.* Consider a few accounts of supernatural experiences that happened to various Mormons:

> Was taken by her deceased mother into the spirit world.

> ...saw in a vision that his parents were living in an enforced separation in the spirit world. They [the parents] asked the son to perform the [Mormon] sealing which would unite them in a family relationship beyond the veil.

> Observed the displeasure of spirits at the use of the term *death*.

> Obtained permission in the spirit world to return to earth.

> Saw that the wicked and unrepentant are confined in a certain district, [Mormon] missionaries are coming from the higher to the lower spheres.

> Met Joseph Smith, Brigham Young, and Joseph F. Smith in the spirit world.

> Saw the Savior and conversed with Joseph F. Smith in the spirit world.

> Saw that the John Adamson family were happy and were gathering genealogical data in the spirit world.

> Saw that authorized family representatives in the spirit world have access to the [Mormon] Temple records and are kept fully advised.

> Saw that ordinances are performed in the spirit world effectualizing the vicarious ordinances performed here.

> Saw women preparing wearing apparel for an anticipated arrival in the spirit world.

> Saw the children who die in infancy are adult spirits. The spirit world is not a habitation of [bodily] growth.

> Saw hundreds of small children convened in a Primary or Sunday School in the spirit world.

> Was asked if you wish to remain in the spirit world, and learned that his progenitors had requested his return to mortality to do genealogical work; and was shown what would happen if he remained in the spirit world.

[Heber C. Kimball, Counselor in First Presidency] appeared to Wilford Woodruff.

Saw spirits witness their [proxy] baptisms. He was shown that every spirit who comes to earth has a guardian angel who keeps its records.

Was seen preaching the gospel [Mormonism] in the spirit prison.[102]

As can be seen, these spiritistic revelations and manifestations seek to reinforce basic Mormon belief and occult practice.

The Mormon text *Gospel Principles* tells Mormons that "members of the [Mormon] priesthood continue their responsibilities in the spirit world."[103] If this is true, why shouldn't the spirits be expected to help Mormons on the earth? And, just as in seance mediumism and other forms of spiritism or contact with dead, doesn't this provide an excellent opportunity for deceiving spirits to imitate dead Mormons and promote their own plans of spiritual deception and ruin?

Consider the works of Joseph Heinerman, graduate of Brigham Young University, Mormon missionary to central Germany and author of several books on spiritistic manifestations to Mormons. These books include *Spirit World Manifestations*, *Temple Manifestations*, and *Eternal Testimonies*, and they are replete with hundreds of accounts of spiritistic assistance given to individual Mormons.

Heinerman claims that "the inhabitants of the spirit world have received special permission to visit their mortal descendants and assist them."[104] He also states that "spirit world manifestations . . . have played and continue to play a major role" in Mormonism.[105] Spirit contact is particularly important in genealogical and related temple work. Heinerman claims that providential aid from the dead "has been manifested many times in the Latter-day Saint acquisition of rare, normally inaccessible family records."[106] In other words, the spirits that contact Mormons provide special information concerning genealogical data so that baptisms and marriages can be performed on behalf of more of the dead than would otherwise be possible.

For example, "Bishop A.J. Graham was visited by his deceased parents from the spirit world who wanted him to perform temple work on behalf of those who were dead and brought three whole volumes of names who were ready to have ordinances done for them."[107] Another Mormon "received instructions from her dead father concerning doing temple work for those in the spirit world."[108] Further, "Bishop George Farnsworth had a wonderful experience in which his dead kindred from the spirit world came to earth and instructed him to do their temple work."[109]

Because of the literally thousands of such necromantic contacts, Heinerman boasts that, "Among a multiplicity of Christian creeds, sects, and denominations, the Church of Jesus Christ of Latter-day Saints is the sole claimant to spirit world visitations and angelic communications which are inseparably connected with genealogical research and temple work."[110]

Mormons are further told that they should be extremely grateful that the spirit world has chosen to provide them with such blessings: "It should be gratifying to Latter-day Saints that those in the spirit world have expressed an intense interest and are increasingly concerned with the activities of God's people [Mormons] upon the earth."[111]

As we saw earlier, Joseph Smith and other Mormon leaders have actually tied personal knowledge of the world of spirits to Mormon salvation—thus insuring their interaction with the spirit world.[112] Nevertheless, all of this is demonism. The spirits that have appeared to Mormons fit every characteristic of the biblical demons and, therefore, could not possibly be either the true human dead or the biblical angels.

As a final illustration of Mormonism's ties to the occult, we may note the connection between Mormonism and Masonry. This should be an embarrassment for Mormonism because both the *Book of Mormon* and Joseph Smith condemned secret societies.[113] However, in light of Masonry's numerous links to occultism, the fact that Smith and many other Mormon leaders admitted they were Masons makes sense.[114] In fact, the influence of Masonry can be seen in the Mormon Temple ceremony. Jerald and Sandra Tanner list some twenty-seven parallels between Masonic ritual and the Mormon Temple ritual, with full documentation.[115] Further, none can deny that Masonic emblems are found on the walls of Mormon temples. Dr. Reed Durham, Jr. is "convinced that in the study of Masonry lies a pivotal key to future understanding [of] Joseph Smith and the Church."[116] He comments:

> It appears that the Prophet first embraced Masonry and, then in the process, he modified, expanded, amplified, or glorified it. . . . Heber C. Kimball wrote to Parley Parker Pratt. . . . "We have organized a Lodge here of Masons. . . . Since that there have near 200 been made Masons [sic]. Brother Joseph and Sidney were the first that were received into the Lodge. All of the Twelve have become members except Orson P. [Pratt]. He hangs back. He will wake up soon. There is a similarity of Priesthood in Masonry.[117]

One Mormon scholar who has studied the correlations between Masonry and Mormonism observes, "I believe that there are few significant developments in the Church, that occurred after March 15th, 1842, which did not have some Masonic interdependence."[118] But as the authors have documented in *The Secret Teachings of the Masonic Lodge*, Masonry, like Mormonism, is an anti-Christian, occult religion.[119]

In light of our discussion, we may conclude that Mormonism 1) was begun by occultists, 2) has promoted occultism historically, and 3) remains an occult religion to this day.

# ◆ ◆ *Conclusion* ◆ ◆

The above material forces us to conclude that Mormonism is properly classified as an occult religion. Joseph Smith and many other Mormon leaders were practitioners of the occult. Further, Mormonism supports mediumistic and other occult philosophy. The church even encourages spiritism and necromancy through its work on behalf of the alleged dead. Thus, it is not surprising that the church would confuse spiritual gifts and occult powers.

Why should this be of concern to Mormons or those thinking of becoming Mormons? Because, as we have documented in our book *Cult Watch: What You Need to Know About Spiritual Deception*, occult practices are dangerous. Anyone who is concerned about his own spiritual welfare or that of his family should thoroughly avoid such practices.

# Mormon Revelation and New Scripture

*Can the Church's Claim to Divine Revelation Be Substantiated? (A Critical Appraisal of the Foundation, History, and Scriptures of Mormonism)*

———————————— ◆ ————————————

M ormon leaders, apologists, and laymen frequently argue that the evidence on behalf of the divine origin of their religion is impressive. Further, they encourage others to investigate their claims. Mormon apostle and historian George A. Smith wrote, "If a faith will not bear to be investigated; if its preachers and professors are afraid to have it examined, their foundation must be very weak."[1]

Dr. D. Michael Quinn received his Ph.D. in history from Yale and is professor of American History at Brigham Young University. He also expresses a conviction that personal inquiry into the historical basis underlying Mormonism should be acceptable to both Mormons and non-Mormons alike. First, he gives his personal Mormon "testimony."

> In Mormon terms, I have a personal "testimony" of Jesus as my savior, of Joseph Smith, Jr., as a prophet, of the Book of Mormon as the word of God, and of the LDS Church as a divinely established organization. . . . I also believe that no historical documents presently available, or locked away, or as yet unknown will alter these truths; and I believe that persons of faith have no reason to avoid historical inquiry into their religion or to discourage others from such investigations.[2]

When Mormon leaders openly invite others to examine their claims, they provide common agreement for assessing the credibility of the Mormon religion. Thus, those who take up the challenge are pursuing a task Mormons themselves find acceptable. It would be foolish, then, to label such individuals as "enemies" of the church when they are only engaging in an activity the church itself has encouraged. The authors of this book have accepted this invitation and—both independently and in collaboration—have studied Mormonism for many years.

261

Mormonism claims that a large amount of genuine evidence supports its religious beliefs. We disagree.

We have studied close to one hundred different religions. While the evidential base of almost all of them is weak or nonexistent, it remains true that few religions have such a substantial array of evidence against it as does Mormonism. No other fact seems to account for the reality of so many Mormons leaving the Mormon church, including some of its scholars and leaders, on the basis of an honest evaluation of critical Mormon data.

Let us give an illustration of this evidence. Perhaps the most concise gathering of this data is found in former Mormons Jerald and Sandra Tanner's dozens of heavily documented books (see Resource List). This material has been greatly compressed in their voluminous *Mormonism— Shadow or Reality?* a further major condensation of which is found in their six hundred page *The Changing World of Mormonism*.

We have talked with many Mormons who will not even read this material.[3] Instead they prefer an appeal to subjective experience—their "personal testimony"—to prove that Mormonism is true. Still, the Tanners' work has been available for almost three decades, and the Mormon church has yet to respond. This is so in spite of the fact that *Mormonia—A Quarterly Bibliography of Works on Mormonism* calls the Tanners' *Shadow or Reality?* "perhaps the most exhaustive expose of Mormonism between two covers."[4] Philosophy professor Dr. Jennings G. Olson, of Weber College, judges it to be "the most comprehensive and thorough analysis and evaluation of Mormonism ever produced in the history of the Church. . . . I will state this book of the Tanners' is a major contribution in the search for integrity and truth about Mormonism."[5]

Ethnologist Dr. Gordon Frazer, author of *Joseph and the Golden Plates, What Does The Book of Mormon Teach?* and *Is Mormonism Christian?* calls *Shadow or Reality?* "an encyclopedia of Mormonism's lack of credibility."[6]

But what has been the response of the Mormon church to this massive body of historical data which (in all editions) has sold over 100,000 copies? Almost without exception (to our knowledge), the response of the scholars within the Mormon Church has been to ignore it. Dr. Quinn, cited above, has not responded to it, and he has a Ph.D. in history from Yale—which certainly qualifies him to evaluate the credibility of the Tanners' historical sources and their conclusions. Nor have other Mormon apologists or historians. The only response has been a small sixty-three page booklet, written anonymously: *Jerald and Sandra Tanner's Distorted View of Mormonism: A Response to Mormonism—Shadow or Reality?* The Tanners responded to this booklet in *Answering Dr. Clandestine: A Response to the Anonymous LDS Historian.*

As Mormon authority Wesley Walters observes:

> The Mormon authorities have usually answered the Tanners by the silent treatment, apparently feeling that the less

exposure their work received the better it would be for the church. Recently, however, Mormon authorities have issued an anonymous reply that any reputable scholar and historian would be rightly ashamed to sign his name to. The Tanners' research has repeatedly held up under attack, especially during this most recent effort by the Mormon Church.[7]

Any Mormon who can carefully read through even the Tanners' small library of material, weigh the evidence fairly, and yet decide to remain a Mormon is simply not being impartial. We realize that religious decisions are often not made on the basis of evidence. Nevertheless, for a religious faith to be valid, objective data should undergird it. Indeed, without this, one can be certain of very little. One could even be living a lie.

But, in fact, Mormons do not need to read the Tanners' works in order to come to the same conclusion the Tanners have. Any Mormon who wishes can go to the University of Utah Library at Salt Lake City which contains many* of the originals of the historical materials cited by the Tanners. People can go and see for themselves whether or not what Mormon critics say is true. But if what they say is true, then the claims of Mormonism cannot stand.

All this leads us to some rather hard conclusions. Mormons do indeed teach others that their religion is true. But if they are wrong, they are only leading other sincere people astray. Ignorance is perhaps understandable, but in the end it offers no excuse for deceiving others. Every conscientious person is responsible to examine the evidence for himself/herself, whether or not this requires sacrificial time and effort. Dr. Charles Crane, a college professor and expert on Mormon archaeology, comments:

> It never ceases to amaze me the number of intelligent people that are in the Mormon Church that still accept things that cannot be substantiated. They get so locked in that they are afraid to even take another look. We run into them many times where they have admitted that rather than sit down and study with us, they will accept what their church leaders tell them.[8]

Ultimately, any Mormon authority who claims that the Mormon religion is established on the basis of solid historical evidence is either engaging in wishful thinking or willful deception. And it is especially reprehensible for knowledgeable Mormons familiar with the evidence to make such claims when they know better. If they have been confronted with more than sufficient data discrediting their religion and yet continue to promote it, for whatever reason, they are without excuse.

---

*Mormon leadership continues to suppress important historical information. Mormons who want the truth should demand that these materials be made available.

But when Mormons claim one thing and their critics another, how is the public to sort out the issues? The only manner in which competing religious claims can be resolved is to 1) fairly state the claims, 2) adequately examine the evidence and 3) discover who is right. In the remainder of this book we have attempted such an approach.

We stress again that—in the end—everyone is responsible to do his own independent research. No one should take the words of another when they affect his or her religious life. But neither should one ignore the issue of Mormon credibility, hoping it will go away. Unfortunately, most Mormons have uncritically trusted the claims of Mormon leaders. They owe it to themselves, their family and their friends to find out once and for all whether those claims are true. Indeed, to do anything else might be to court personal heartache and even tragedy.

In the following material, we will supply a portion of the major evidence against Mormon claims. Because our treatment is relatively brief, we present only the highlights of ten specific problem areas:

Chapter 21.  Mormonism's First Vision Account: Is This a Credible Pillar Undergirding the Establishment of New Scripture? (Problems with the vital "first vision account.")

Chapter 22.  Mormonism's *Book of Mormon*: Can It Be Defended As a Divine Revelation? (Evidence disproving specific *Book of Mormon* claims, with eight subsections.)

Chapter 23.  Mormonism's Word of God: Have Secret Changes Been Made in the Mormon Scriptures? (Inexcusable and damning changes made in the Mormon scriptures.)

Chapter 24.  Mormonism's Teachings Historically: Do Contradictory Teachings Require the Need for Suppression of Information, and What Difficulty Does This Present to the Average Mormon? (Documentation of contradictory theology within Mormonism and the fact of its suppression by church authorities.)

Chapter 25.  Mormonism's Prophetic Record: Are There Demonstrable False Prophecies Within Mormon Scripture and Literature?

Chapter 26.  Mormon Distortions of History and Religion: Are Mormon Evangelistic/Apologetic Works Factually Sound or Do They Constitute Misrepresentation? (A critical evaluation of Mormon apologetics.)

We discuss these subjects in turn.

# CHAPTER 21

# Mormonism's First Vision Account

## *Is This a Credible Pillar Undergirding the Establishment of New Scripture?*

In chapter 2 we discussed the story of Mormon origins, citing the church's official version of Joseph Smith's 1820 revelation that began Mormonism. The importance of this "first vision account" to the claims of the Mormon church cannot be overestimated. It is considered a crucial pillar supporting church authority. The current president and prophet, Ezra Taft Benson claims, "The first vision of the Prophet Joseph Smith is bedrock theology to the church."[9]

Dr. Walter Martin also discusses its relevance:

> We cannot underestimate the importance of the "First Vision," because it is the centerpiece in virtually all Mormon presentations of Smith's prophetic authority. The "First Vision" formed the basis for the key Mormon teaching relative to the nature of God (that the Father and the Son are two separate gods with flesh and bone bodies) as well as the doctrine that the Christian Church was not on the earth in Smith's time, and that Smith was the designated prophet of the restoration of true Christianity. Smith's "First Vision" was also responsible for the Mormons' subsequent strong emphasis upon the condemnation of existing Christian Churches, doctrines, and membership as "wrong," [an] "abomination," and "corrupt."[10]

Thus, Smith's 1) prophetic authority, 2) teaching concerning the nature of God, and 3) condemnation of Christian belief are all dependent upon the credibility of this first vision account.

For example, throughout their history Mormons have appealed to the first vision account as the logical basis for condemning Christian belief as an "abomination." Hoyt W. Brewster, Jr., Curriculum Planning and Development Manager of the Church Curriculum Department, comments that, based on Smith's first vision, "It is clear that God the Father and his Son were greatly displeased with the doctrines being taught in the churches. . . . Any creed, doctrine, [etc.] . . . that deliberately or inadvertently leads people from the *saving power* of Christ and his gospel [i.e., Mormon belief] is an abomination."[11]

Brewster also cites Elder John A. Widtsoe who emphasized,

> Jesus said to Joseph that all the churches were wrong, and that their creeds were an abomination in his sight, that those professors were all corrupt. This statement has given a great deal of offense. It should not amaze us, however, if we consider that Joseph went in search of truth. . . . *All untruth is an abomination.* . . . The [orthodox Christian] ministers . . . were corrupt teachers. . . . Truth is the only holy thing; and if it is violated or changed, those who teach it become corrupt and abominable.[12]

Mormons themselves confess that the first vision is second in importance only to Christ's "divinity": that it is the "foundation of the Church," that the church stands or falls on the authenticity of the event, and that the "truth and validity" of all Smith's subsequent work rests upon its genuineness.[13] In other words, if the "first vision account" is established as not credible—either on the basis of serious internal discrepancies or other factors—then, according to Mormonism itself, the legitimacy of the entire church collapses.

Smith's official account of this pivotal event was published in *Times and Seasons* in 1842, twenty-two years after the episode allegedly took place. However, at least three additional earlier accounts of the first vision, all by Smith, were suppressed by Mormon authorities because they contradicted the official story.[14]

For example, the earliest account we now possess, from 1832, varies in key details from the official 1842 version. There are discrepancies in Smith's age, in the message given and the number of divine personages in the vision. There are also details added, such as the presence of an evil power, Smith's reason for seeking the Lord, and the existence of a revival.[15] All this lends serious doubt to the credibility of the official account.

Consider, for instance, the divine persons in the revelation. In this version only "Jesus" appears. What happened to God the Father? Jerald and Sandra Tanner reveal that the first handwritten account of Joseph Smith does not even mention the existence of the Father—who plays so crucial a role in the official version:

> It is absolutely impossible for us to believe that Joseph Smith would not have mentioned the Father if he had actually appeared.... We feel that the only reasonable explanation for the Father not being mentioned in the account which was suppressed is that Joseph Smith did *not* see God the Father, and that he made up this part of the story after the writing of the first manuscript. This, of course, throws a shadow of doubt upon the whole story.[16]

Consider another of Smith's accounts written between 1835 and 1836. In this case there is no mention of God or Christ at all—only of many spirits who "testified" of Jesus. But here again, the authority of the account—and of Mormonism's divine origin—is called into question. No longer is it God and Jesus telling Joseph Smith to begin a new church because all others are abominations; it is now only a group of nebulous "spirits." Why should anyone accept the word of a fifteen-year-old boy who claimed he talked with some unidentified spirits? Even if he did, why should anyone trust such spirits in the first place? If my fifteen-year-old boy claimed he saw a vision of God or Jesus giving him divine authority, why should Mormons believe him? So why should anyone else believe their story of Joseph Smith—especially when Smith himself kept telling different stories about his alleged divine encounter?

The dilemma posed by these various accounts of the first vision is explained by the Tanners, who conclude:

> We have now examined three different handwritten manuscripts of the first vision. They were all written by Joseph Smith or his scribes and yet every one of them is different. The first account says there was only one personage. The second account says there were many, and the third says there were two. The church, of course, accepts the version which contains two personages. If we have to accept any of the versions, we would choose the first account. It was written six or seven years closer to the event, and therefore it should give a more accurate picture of what really took place. Also, this account, which mentions only one personage, is the only account in Joseph Smith's own handwriting.
>
> At any rate, when one becomes aware of the fact that there are conflicting versions of the story, it becomes very difficult to believe that Joseph Smith ever had a vision in the grove.
>
> On top of all this, there is irrefutable evidence that an important reference to the first vision in the *History of the*

*Church* has been falsified by Mormon historians after Joseph Smith's death.[17]

How does the Mormon church respond to these charges? They claim that the discrepancies in the accounts in fact *support* the conclusion that the accounts are truthful! Milton V. Blackman, Jr., professor of Church History at Brigham Young University, presents the standard argument:

> On at least four different occasions, Joseph Smith either wrote or dictated to scribes accounts of his sacred experience in 1820. Possibly he wrote or dictated other histories of the First Vision. . . . each of them emphasizes different aspects of the Prophet's experience. . . . the existence of these different accounts help support the integrity of the Latter-day Saint Prophet. It indicates that Joseph did not deliberately create a memorized version that he related to everyone. . . . [consider that] the Four Gospels do not correspond exactly concerning the great events at the Garden's empty tomb.[18]

But neither this nor similar responses deal with the real problem. Why? Because Smith never did what Mormon apologists say he did. It is one thing to recount an incident selectively. It is something else entirely to recount it in several contradictory versions. If selective reports of a single event are given accurately, they should "add up" when totaled, making one complete, coherent description of that single event. Despite the contentions of critics, this *is* what we find when examining the Resurrection narratives—as we have shown in *Do the Resurrection Accounts Conflict? And What Proof Is There Jesus Rose from the Dead?*[19] But this central coherence is not what we find when all the facts of the six (some claim nine)[20] different accounts of the first vision are combined. Ethnologist Dr. Gordon Fraser comments, ". . . there are at least six versions of the famed First Vision of the prophet, with his own final version, written about 1838, being the least credible."[21]

Here are some of the inconsistencies. If Jesus had really been standing before Joseph Smith, why would a multitude of spirits also have been necessary to "testify" of Him? How old was Smith? He couldn't have been two different ages in the same year. Was there a commanding evil power that Smith was delivered from—or not? In what year did the revival occur that precipitated Smith's alleged seeking of the divine wisdom? What exactly did God, Jesus or the spirits say? Contrary answers to these questions cannot all be true at the same time. Further, Joseph Smith never discarded only minor aspects of a larger experience which he then reported in general fashion to different audiences. Absolutely decisive elements were discarded. But key incidents are almost *never* left out of a reported event, no matter when or under what circumstances they are written—especially if they are public writings intended to make an essentially crucial point: that God was reestablishing true Christianity after an immense lapse of eighteen hundred years.

For example, the four Gospel accounts of the Resurrection do not leave out vital incidents. None of them leave out the fact of Christ's death, or the empty tomb itself, or the appearances of the risen Christ to the disciples. But consider the versions of the first vision. Is it conceivable that in any retelling of Smith's story he would leave out the crucial parts about 1) the Father or 2) both the Father and the Son together? For Smith to leave out critical details in recounting such a crucial event makes one suspect that whatever his initial experience may have been, it was later embellished by him or others. One is also forced to the conclusion that that initial experience could have been anything—from pure invention, to religious suggestion and self-deception, to spiritistic manipulation.[22]

In essence, the official account of the church cannot be accepted as reliable, and, therefore, the authority and legitimacy of the entire Mormon church is undermined by this one conclusion alone. If even Joseph Smith was uncertain as to what he experienced, or worse yet fabricated evidence, why should anyone trust his other claims?

We are not saying Smith never had a mystical experience. We are only saying it is impossible to establish evidence of the divine origin of the Mormon church on the basis of this event. Our own personal view is that, based on his occult background, Smith probably did have a vision of spirits—and that it was *their* intent, not God's, to establish the Mormon church.

Thus, we may observe that Smith's vision was not something wholly unique, as Mormon authorities emphasize. In fact, his experience fit a characteristic pattern of spiritistic contacts which have occurred throughout history. Indeed, many similar incidents were evident during the time Smith was making his own pronouncements as to divine visitations. Elias Smith, Alexander Campbell, Asa Wild and others were making similar claims.[23] Joseph Smith's story was thus only one of many similar episodes, and, therefore, it seems at least possible that after his initial vision of spirits, he later added the account of the Father and/or the Son appearing to him. Why? Because it would single-handedly give *his* claims more divine authority and make them stand out from the many other revelations of spirits that clamored for the attention of the public.[24]

But the final blow to the credibility of this account is Joseph Smith's own tarnished moral character.[25] Anyone who studies the real Joseph Smith, not the one fabricated by the Mormon church, would be hard pressed to believe anything he claimed. (See chap. 4, appendix.)

Regardless, the evidence is conclusive that the first vision account simply cannot be trusted. Even if the official version were legitimate— accurately recording what Joseph Smith thought he experienced—the revelation could not possibly have been true. It would have to have been a demonic deception. For example, we can know that Smith never saw the biblical Jesus, for Jesus would never appear to an occultist, reject His own faithful servants as "abominations" and then proceed to begin a new, heretical church that denied and opposed everything He ever taught.

In conclusion, Mormons who trust in the first vision account need to seriously reflect on the many unanswered questions surrounding this event. Did Smith actually see anything? Did he fabricate part or all of the vision? Did he change or combine elements of several different occult visions? Did church leaders suppress damaging evidence of the event? Until they can satisfactorily answer these and other questions, perhaps they should reserve judgment on the meaning and value of Joseph Smith's personal experiences.

What can be learned from the first vision episode is that 1) it is now unwise to place trust in the official account, and 2) that, as the Bible warns, one should not take "his stand on visions he has seen" (Colossians 2:18), but rather on scriptural authority alone.*

But this raises another issue. What is scriptural authority to the Mormon? When Mormons add new scripture to the canon, can these claims to divine revelation be trusted either?

In our next two sections, we will critically examine the Mormon scriptures—the *Book of Mormon*, *Doctrine and Covenants* and *The Pearl of Great Price*. First, we will examine whether or not the *Book of Mormon* can logically be considered a divine revelation, and second, we will examine the extensive changes that have been made by church officials in all the Mormon scriptures—something most Mormons know little about.

---

*The reader may pursue the issue of the various accounts in *Dialogue: A Journal of Mormon Thought*, Autumn 1966 and Spring 1971; *Brigham Young University Studies*, Spring 1969 and elsewhere.[26]

CHAPTER 22

◆

# Mormonism's
# *Book of Mormon*

## *Can It Be Defended As a Divine Revelation?*

M ormons have always stressed that their scriptures could withstand any and all critical scrutiny. Apostle Orson Pratt even boasted that Mormons "have *more than one thousand times* the amount of evidence to demonstrate and forever establish the Divine Authority of the *Book of Mormon* than in favor of the Bible!"[27] And, "If this book be of God, it must have sufficient evidence accompanying it to convince the minds of all reasonable persons that it is a Divine revelation."[28] Further, "We defy this whole generation to bring up any testimony to condemn the truth of this book."[29] Dr. Hugh Nibley is a prominent Brigham Young University professor; some Mormons consider him one of the greatest scholars in the church. He declares, "the *Book of Mormon* can and should be tested. It invites criticism."[30] In similar fashion, the tenth Mormon president and prophet, Joseph Fielding Smith, argued, "No one can read the book with a prayerful heart and not receive the testimony that it is true. Its evidence internally and externally is overwhelming."[31]

Unfortunately, the evidence is overwhelmingly negative. From almost any angle of study, the *Book of Mormon* fails to stand up to critical examination. Indeed, this is the principal reason that Mormon leaders are increasingly claiming that the *Book of Mormon* really *can't* be proven true and that, as for Mormonism itself, one must rely upon subjective experience in order to "confirm" its alleged divine origin. This is why John W. Welch, Professor of Law and president of the Foundation for Ancient Research on Mormon Studies at Brigham Young University, quotes Mormon historian B.H. Roberts as stating, "This [power of the Holy Ghost to allegedly confirm the divine origin of the *Book of Mormon*] must ever be the chief source of evidence for the truth of the *Book of Mormon*. All other evidence is secondary to this, the primary and infallible [evidence]. . . . [This] will ever be the chief reliance of those who accept the *Book of Mormon*, and expect to see its acceptance extended throughout the world."[32]

The current president and prophet of the church, Ezra Taft Benson, now teaches,

> It never has been the case, nor is it so now, that the studies of the learned will prove the *Book of Mormon* true or false. . . . God has built his own proof system of the *Book of Mormon* as found in Moroni, chapter 10, and in the testimonies of the Three and the Eight Witnesses and in various sections of *Doctrine and Covenants*. We each need to get our own testimony of the *Book of Mormon* through the Holy Ghost.[33]

Despite Benson's claim that the "studies of the learned" will never prove the *Book of Mormon* false, we suggest this is a *fait accompli*—something already done and not reversible. Below we discuss some of the irrevocable facts associated with the *Book of Mormon* which disqualify it for any serious consideration as a revelation from God. These problems are in addition to the already documented fact (Sections 3, 4) that the *Book of Mormon* contains anti-biblical teachings and could, therefore, not possibly have been inspired by the God of the Bible.

Because the *Book of Mormon* claims it is a *translation* of ancient historical records, we will emphasize evidence that collectively proves it is really only a nineteenth-century production. This not only reveals that the *Book of Mormon* itself is a forgery—and therefore unworthy of any thinking person's trust—it also casts critical doubt upon Joseph Smith's alleged ability to divinely "translate" the other Mormon scriptures known as the *Book of Abraham* and *Book of Moses*, both found in *The Pearl of Great Price*.

The importance of this issue cannot be overestimated. Joseph Smith's claim to be able to divinely translate ancient "scripture" is crucial to the Mormon emphasis that it is a divine revelation. If Smith was deceived on this point and it can be proven that his "translations" were either completely false or wrong on other grounds, Mormonism cannot possibly be what it claims to be.

What does the evidence reveal? As we will see in chapter 23, the *Book of Abraham* has been proven a forgery. We know for a fact that Abraham never wrote the so-called *Book of Abraham* nor Moses the so-called *Book of Moses*. Concerning the *Book of Mormon*, the available evidence reveals that neither the Nephites nor their alleged historian "Mormon" ever existed, so they could hardly have produced historical records. Thus, whether it is the alleged *Book of Mormon*, the *Book of Abraham*, or the *Book of Moses*, Joseph Smith could not translate something that never existed.

If Joseph Smith never actually translated ancient records, what exactly *was* he doing? As we will show (given his claims), all Smith truly achieved was to become an occult medium for the production of psychic revelation. Because he was a proficient occultist having regular contact with the spirit world (chaps. 18,19), his psychic "translation" must be reclassified as spiritistic teaching—what the Bible identifies as "doctrines of demons": "But the Spirit explicitly says that in later times some will fall away from the faith, paying attention to deceitful spirits and doctrines [teachings] of demons" (1 Timothy 4:1). Either that, or the entire *Book of Mormon* was the invention of Smith's fertile imagination. Thus, an impartial examination of the evidence reveals only three possibilities to explain the text:

1. Human invention

2. Spiritistic inspiration

3. A combination of both

The following material on the *Book of Mormon* (Sections A-H) will reveal why we believe the third possibility is the most appropriate choice. We have divided our eight sections (A-H) under two main headings, both of which suggest the essential *unreliability* of the *Book of Mormon*:

**Division I:** Proof that the *Book of Mormon* is a nineteenth-century production (not a translation of ancient records), and therefore unreliable because it is a *forgery*.

A. The *Book of Mormon*'s psychic method of production, indicating it is an occult text of the nineteenth century, not a divine translation of ancient records.

B. The *Book of Mormon*'s human sources and plagiarisms, further revealing it is a nineteenth-century production, not a translation of ancient writings.

C. The *Book of Mormon*'s complete absence of archaeological verification, again showing it is a product of the nineteenth century and therefore that its claim to be a translation of ancient records is false.

D. The *Book of Mormon*'s complete lack of manuscript evidence, supplying the final reason it should not be considered an ancient text.

**Division II:** Proof that the *Book of Mormon* is mutilated both physically and (from the perspective of Mormon teaching) doctrinally, and therefore unreliable because it is *corrupted*.

E. The *Book of Mormon*'s textual problems—including historical, grammatical and other changes made in the text—revealing corruption and fatal problems in the methodology and accuracy of the alleged divine translation.

F. The *Book of Mormon's* lack of distinctive Mormon doctrines—including even *anti-*Mormon teachings—indicating it is not even a legitimate *Mormon* text.

G. The *Book of Mormon's* problems of language and style, revealing additional evidence that the book was not divinely translated as claimed.

H. The *Book of Mormon's* "eleven witnesses" and their lack of credibility, indicating their testimony concerning its divine origin and purity cannot be trusted.

We discuss these subjects in turn.

## Division I

*Proof that the* Book of Mormon *is a nineteenth-century production (not a translation of ancient records), and therefore unreliable because it is a forgery.*

### A. The Book of Mormon's psychic method of production

We will begin our discussion by showing that the *Book of Mormon* was produced through psychic methods. Once this is established we can proceed to prove that the revelation had nothing to do with ancient history and is therefore merely a product of nineteenth-century occultism.

The Mormon church claims that Joseph Smith translated the alleged gold plates (containing the alleged historical records of the "Nephites") by the power of God using divine implements called the Urim and Thummim—which are described as two stones in silver bows fastened to a breastplate (*Book of Mormon*, introduction).*

It denies the "translation" was produced by occult means through the use of a common seer stone. Nevertheless, historical documents prove that when Smith translated the alleged *Book of Mormon* he was only engaging in his *usual* practice of crystal gazing. For example, the testimonies of 1) Emma Smith, one of Joseph Smith's wives as well as one of the scribes; 2) William Smith, Joseph's own brother; 3) David Whitmer, one of the three key "witnesses" to the *Book of Mormon*, and many others all prove that the claims of the Mormon church are false. But if Joseph Smith was merely a common crystal gazer subject to occult fascinations,

---

* We do not know exactly what the Old Testament Urim and Thummim were. Nevertheless, 1) they were restricted in usage to the high priest; 2) the God of the Bible "spoke" through them to reveal his will, and 3) apparently they were two separate objects, not a single stone. Thus, in each category Mormon claims are refuted. Whatever Smith used, it was not the biblical Urim and Thummim (Exodus 28:30; Numbers 27:21): 1) Joseph Smith was not an Old Testament High Priest who 2) used these implements to reveal God's will, but rather used 3) a (singular) occult seer stone to divine the "translation" of a "text" that denies God's Word.

why should anyone think he was subject to divine inspiration? Further, why should anyone accept the claim of the Mormon church that his occult seer stone was really the Old Testament Urim and Thummim, when not a shred of evidence exists to substantiate such a declaration?

In 1877, David Whitmer confessed that the alleged "Egyptian" characters on the gold plates and their English interpretation appeared to Joseph Smith while his face was buried inside a hat:

> I will now give you a description of the manner in which the *Book of Mormon* was translated. Joseph Smith would put the seer stone into a hat, and put his face in the hat, drawing it closely around his face to exclude the light; and in the darkness the spiritual light would shine. A piece of something resembling parchment would appear, and on that appeared the writing. One character at a time would appear, and under it was the interpretation in English. Brother Joseph would read off the English to Oliver Crowdery, who was his principal scribe, and when it was written down and repeated to Brother Joseph to see if it was correct, then it would disappear, and another character with the interpretation would appear. Thus the *Book of Mormon* was translated by the gift and power of God, and not by any power of man.[34]

(It is important to observe here that this is essentially a *mechanical dictation* theory of translation. As such, it leaves no room whatever for changes in the text. This fact will become important when we discuss the thousands of changes that have been made in the *Book of Mormon* [see "F" on p. 292] and other Mormon scriptures [chap. 23].)

Whitmer further noted in an interview: "With this stone all of the present *Book of Mormon* was translated."[35]

Emma Smith, one of Joseph's wives, also revealed the occult method by which the *Book of Mormon* was produced. She confessed, "In writing for your father, I frequently wrote day after day. . . . He sitting with his face buried in his hat, with the stone in it, and dictating hour after hour with nothing between us."[36]

It is undeniable, then, that the *Book of Mormon* was produced through a form of crystal gazing. Testimonies such as these (and others)[37] bring even some Mormons who reject the idea to conceding at least its possibility. The tenth president and prophet, Joseph Fielding Smith, opposes this view, but nevertheless confesses that "It may have been so." Apparently he had little choice but to acknowledge the possibility since he had also just confessed that the seer stone Smith owned "is now in the possession of the Church."[38]

If the *Book of Mormon* was written through occult means, this fact speaks against its divine origin. None of the Bible was ever written in such a manner. We will now prove that the supernatural information

Smith allegedly received was not a translation of ancient records, but, in all likelihood, a combination of Smith's own efforts and spiritistic inspiration. Indeed, to do his "translating," Smith didn't even require the presence of the gold plates:

> According to witnesses, the plates didn't even have to be present when Joseph Smith was "translating." Mormon writer Arch S. Reynolds notes that "the plates were not always before Joseph during the translation. His wife and mother state that the plates were on the table wrapped in a cloth while Joseph translated with his eyes hid in a hat with the seer stone or the Urim and Thummim. David Whitmer, Martin Harris and others state that Joseph hid the plates in the woods and other places while he was translating (*How Did Joseph Smith Translate?*, p. 21).[39]

### B. The Book of Mormon's human sources and plagiarisms

Mormons maintain that apart from divine revelation it would have been impossible for Joseph Smith to have written the *Book of Mormon*. They consider this one of the greatest proofs of its heavenly derivation. Unfortunately, they rarely consider other options which explain the origin of the *Book of Mormon* far better—that it could have been, for example, a combination of Smith's natural talent and spiritistic revelation. Concerning the former, there are several possible human sources for the *Book of Mormon* which lend doubt to Smith's claims.

Remember that the Mormon church believes that the *Book of Mormon* is simply a divinely *translated* account of ancient writings first inscribed on gold plates. These plates were supposedly written at least fifteen hundred years ago. They chronicled the history of the so-called "Nephite" peoples spanning a period from 600 B.C. through A.D. 421. In other words, they recorded an alleged history of the Nephites some fourteen to twenty-four hundred years *before* Joseph Smith's time.

Fawn Brodie was excommunicated from the Mormon church for her scholarly critical study on Joseph Smith, *No Man Knows My History: The Life of Joseph Smith*.[40] In this work, she cites persuasive evidence for the likelihood of a nineteenth-century origin of the *Book of Mormon*. Brodie explains why it is nearly impossible that the *Book of Mormon* could constitute a written record at least fifteen hundred years old and why it must therefore be considered a product of the nineteenth century.

For example, how is it possible that Jewish writers between 600 B.C. and A.D. 421 would discuss the social and religious issues unique to nineteenth-century Christian America?

> Any theory of the origin of the Book of Mormon that spotlights the prophet [alone] and blacks out the stage on which he performed is certain to be a distortion.

[For example,] In the speeches of the Nephi prophets one may find [discussions of] the religious conflicts that were splitting the churches in the 1820's. Alexander Campbell, founder of the Disciples of Christ, wrote in the first able review of the Book of Mormon: "This prophet Smith, through his stone spectacles, wrote on the plates of Nephi, in his Book of Mormon, every error and almost every truth discussed in New York for the last ten years. He decided all the great controversies: —infant baptism, ordination, the trinity, regeneration, repentance, justification, the fall of man, the atonement, transubstantiation, fasting, penance, church government, religious experience, the call to the ministry, the general resurrection, eternal punishment, who may baptize, and even the question of Freemasonry, Republican government and the rights of man. But he is better skilled in the controversies in New York than in the geography or history of Judea. He makes John baptize in the village of Bethabara and says Jesus was born in Jerusalem.

[Brodie continues] If one has the curiosity to read through the sermons in the book, one will be impressed with Joseph Smith's ability to argue with equal facility on both sides of a theological debate. Calvinism and Arminianism had equal status, depending upon which [Nephite] prophet was espousing the cause, and even universalism received a hearing. . . . The theology of the Book of Mormon, like its anthropology, was only a potpourri. . . . Always an eclectic, Joseph never exhausted any theory he had appropriated. He seized a fragment here and another there and of the odd assortment built his history. As we have seen, he left unused the one hypothesis that might have helped to save the book from being made so grotesque by 20th-Century archaeological and anthropological research. This neglect was probably a result of his reading *View of the Hebrews*, which had scorned the theory expounding the Asiatic origin of the Indian.[41]

We discuss *View of the Hebrews* below. Nevertheless, why 1400- to 2400-year-old records would deal with distinctly nineteenth-century theological, social and political disputes is certainly unknown. Unless, of course, they were not that old.

The following sources for the *Book of Mormon* indicate it is a nineteenth-century production, not the translation of ancient records Joseph Smith and Mormonism claim it to be.

Source No. 1: Ethan Smith's *View of the Hebrews*

In his study *A Parallel, The Basis of the Book of Mormon*, Hal Hougey observes a number of striking similarities between the *Book of Mormon* and Ethan Smith's 1823 text *View of the Hebrews*, a book that was available to Joseph Smith.[42]

In fact, the parallels between the *Book of Mormon* and *View of the Hebrews* were sufficient enough to prompt no less an authority than Mormon historian B.H. Roberts to make his own study of the issue. He concluded it *was* possible for Smith, alone, to have written the *Book of Mormon*. In the first fourteen chapters of his study, Roberts discussed similarities between the two books; the last six chapters considered the proposition that the *Book of Mormon* is of human rather than divine origin.[43] (See chapter appendix.)

Mormons respond by pointing out that similarity does not necessarily prove plagiarism, which of course is true. Nevertheless, it is the extent of similarity that is crucial. In addition to citing eighteen of Robert's twenty-six parallels, Hal Hougey adds an additional twenty-three. He then concludes: "While a few insignificant parallels between two books may prove nothing, a large number of parallels, many of them very striking in nature, are evidence which must honestly be considered."[*][44]

### Source No. 2: The King James Bible

The King James Bible provides concrete evidence of *Book of Mormon* plagiarism. According to Dr. Anthony Hoekema, there are some 27,000 words taken from the King James Bible.[45] A few examples of these plagiarisms include:

> 1 Nephi chapters 20,21 — Isaiah chapters 48,49
>
> 2 Nephi chapters 7,8 — Isaiah chapters 50,51
>
> 2 Nephi chapters 12,24 — Isaiah chapters 2-14
>
> Mosiah chapter 14 — Isaiah chapter 53
>
> 3 Nephi chapters 12,14 — Matthew chapters 5-7
>
> 3 Nephi chapter 22 — Isaiah chapter 54
>
> 3 Nephi chapters 24,25 — Malachi chapters 3,4
>
> Moroni chapter 10 — 1 Corinthians 12:1-11.[46]

Anyone who compares these sections will see that Smith has copied material from the King James Bible. If not, an inquiring Mormon might want to know how significant portions of the gold plates ended up containing perfect King James English a thousand years before King James English existed. If the *Book of Mormon* was actually finished

---

[*] To be fair, Smith himself may or may not have plagiarized from this book; because he was subject to spiritistic inspiration and the spirits themselves are known to plagiarize, he may simply have been the victim.

in A.D. 400, how could it contain such extensive citations from a book not to be written for another twelve hundred years?

How do Mormons respond to these facts? Some Mormons have happily claimed the translation was inspired in such a manner that Elizabethan English was provided for the convenience of those who read the King James Bible! But others, feeling the embarrassment more severely, have attempted to downplay the evidence. For example, in an inexplicable gaffe, Mormon historian B.H. Roberts claimed there were only "two or three" incidents of New Testament passages that are quoted in the *Book of Mormon*.[47] However, Jerald and Sandra Tanner, in their book, *The Case Against Mormonism*, have listed, one by one, over *four hundred* verses and portions of verses quoted from the New Testament.[48] Elsewhere they conclude that both the Old and New Testament were important sources for the writing of the *Book of Mormon*:

> There can be no doubt that the first books of the Bible furnished a great deal of source material for the writing of the *Book of Mormon*.... More than 18 chapters of Isaiah are found in the *Book of Mormon*. The Ten Commandments and many other portions of the Old Testament are also found in the *Book of Mormon*.... Mark Twain said that the *Book of Mormon* "seems to be merely a prosy detail of imaginary history, with the Old Testament for a model; followed by a tedious plagiarism of the New Testament" (*Roughing It*, 110).

> The ministry of Christ seems to have been the source of a good deal of the *Book of Mormon*.... Wesley M. Jones points out that "the ministry of St. Paul is duplicated almost exactly in the ministry of [the Mormon character] Alma, one of Joseph's characters—even in the manner of speech and travels" (*A Critical Study of Book of Mormon Sources*, 14,15).

> We find many New Testament verses and parts of verses throughout the *Book of Mormon*.... In *Mormonism—Shadow or Reality?* we listed over 200 parallels, and in another study we had a list of 400. We have found over 100 quotations from the New Testament in the first two books of Nephi alone, and these books were supposed to have been written between 600 and 545 B.C.

> Mormon writers have tried to explain why so much of the New Testament is found in the *Book of Mormon*, but we feel that their explanations are only wishful thinking. The only reasonable explanation is that the author of the *Book of Mormon* had the King James Version of the Bible. And since this version did not appear until A.D. 1611, the *Book of Mormon* could not have been written prior to that time. The *Book of Mormon*, therefore, is a modern composition and not a "record of ancient religious history."[49]

Additional Sources

The Tanners have also supplied evidence for many other sources for the *Book of Mormon*, including Josiah Priest's *The Wonders of Nature and Providence Displayed* (Albany, NY: 1825), *The Wayne Sentinel*, *The Apocrypha*, a dream of Joseph Smith's father and *The Westminster Confession and Catechism*.[50] All this is proof that the *Book of Mormon* could not have been a translation of ancient records.*

What then is the real source of the *Book of Mormon*? The most appropriate answer would seem to offer a combination of both human endeavor and spiritistic revelation. Given the many testimonies of Smith's occultism and use of a seer stone in the "translation," it would be difficult to completely discard the possibility of supernatural revelation. Likewise, given the numerous contemporary sources we find in the text, it is also difficult to deny Smith's own human authorship. While it is also possible that spiritistic inspiration itself may include plagiarisms or borrowings about which the medium or channeler is wholly ignorant, the fact that Smith had access to the various sources discussed would indicate the ease with which he could have made use of them.

Finally, though, all this reinforces a negative conclusion concerning the claim that the *Book of Mormon* is a divine translation of *ancient* records.

We now turn to a discussion of archaeology as further proof that the *Book of Mormon* is a nineteenth-century production.

## C. *Archaeology and the Book of Mormon*

If the *Book of Mormon* were truly an historical record of ancient peoples inhabiting a vast civilization in relatively recent history, it is virtually impossible that no evidence could be marshalled for the existence of such a civilization. In other words, if the *Book of Mormon* were really history, archaeological data would confirm it—as it has repeatedly confirmed biblical history and the history of other ancient cultures. But in fact, not a shred of archaeological evidence exists that the *Book of Mormon* is history.

In examining the *Book of Mormon* and the discipline of archaeology, we first need to understand the background of the alleged history taught in the *Book of Mormon*.[54]

The *Book of Mormon* claims to represent the history of three different groups of people, all of whom allegedly migrated from the Near East to Central and South America. Two of the groups supposedly traveled as far

---

* In 1977, circumstantial evidence for one more source theory appeared in Cowdrey, Davis and Scales' *Who Really Wrote the Book of Mormon?* The theory, first proposed in 1833, asserts the *Book of Mormon* is adapted from a novel by Solomon Spalding, *Manuscript Found*, with religious material added by Sidney Rigdon.[51] However, the evidence for the theory is doubtful. In a review of the book, Wesley Walters concludes that "their proof must be regarded as highly questionable,"[52] and Jerald and Sandra Tanner also conclude in their *Did Spalding Write the Book of Mormon?*: "It is our feeling that this new theory will not stand the test of time and the more it is advocated the more damage it will do."[53] (See Brodie, *No Man Knows My History*, Select Bibliography.)

north as Mexico and North America (the *Book of Mormon*, Ether, and 1 Nephi).*

These people, the Nephites and Mulekites, were Semitic, with the most important group being led by Lehi of Jerusalem. His descendants became the Nephites. The main history of the *Book of Mormon* concerns the Nephites.

How did the alleged Nephites originate? Around 600 B.C. the family of Lehi left Jerusalem. By the time of Christ, his descendants had migrated to North America. Earlier, two of Lehi's sons, Nephi and Laman, had a dispute and the people took sides. This began two quarreling camps named after Lehi's sons: the Nephites and Lamanites. Nephi was a righteous leader, but Laman was not, which had unfortunate consequences for his descendants. Native American Indians are held by Mormons to be descendants of Laman, and, along with blacks, their dark skins are considered the sign of a curse by God (1 Nephi 12:23; 2 Nephi 5:21; see chap. 29).

When Jesus resurrected, He allegedly came and preached to both these peoples and they were converted. Unfortunately, a few centuries later, the Lamanites apostatized and were at war with the Nephites.

The *Book of Mormon* teaches that in A.D. 385, during the final battles that wiped out the Nephites (around A.D. 380 to 420), some 230,000 Nephites died near the hill Cumorah in New York (Mormon 6:10-15; 8:2). By A.D. 421, all the Nephites had been killed, with only the apostate Lamanites left in the land. (These were the supposed "Jewish Indians" whom Columbus discovered in 1492.)

Before this time, one Nephite historian-prophet named *Mormon* (the commander of the Nephites) had gathered all the records of his predecessors. From them he penned an abridged history of his people—allegedly written on gold plates in "reformed Egyptian." This synopsis by Mormon was largely derived from plates written by Nephi (2 Nephi 5:28-31).

Thus, Mormon wrote the supposed history of his people from about 600 B.C., when they left Jerusalem, to A.D. 385. He entrusted the plates to his son *Moroni*, who allegedly finished the history and then hid the accounts in the hill Cumorah in New York around A.D. 421. Fourteen hundred years later, Joseph Smith was allegedly led to the same hill by the spirit of the long-deceased Moroni (the same Moroni, now a resurrected being) to discover the gold plates which Mormon had written. Thus, Mormonism claims that Smith translated the Egyptian hieroglyphics of the Jew called Mormon into English. Named after its author, it became known as the *Book of Mormon*.

---

* Although the traditional view is that the *Book of Mormon* story covers North and South America, some modern Brigham Young University academicians, apparently attempting to coordinate *Book of Mormon* claims and geography with existing data back pedal and accept a more limited geography.[55] (They believe, for example, that the Cumorah in New York was really in Southern Mexico.)

Mormonism has never explained how godly Jews of A.D. 400 allegedly knew Egyptian, nor why they would have written their sacred records entirely in the language of their pagan, idolatrous enemies. Nevertheless, the story recounted in the *Book of Mormon* certainly would have a great deal of archaeological verification if it were true. According to the *Book of Mormon*, two entire nations developed and grew from the two migratory families. The Nephites and Lamanites (the latter were "exceedingly more numerous") spread over the face of the land and became as myriad as "the sand of the sea." They had large cities (the *Book of Mormon* mentions thirty-eight), "nations developed," and they fought in "great *continent*-wide wars."[56] By A.D. 322 "the whole face of the land had become covered with buildings" (Mormon 1:7). Thus, the old civilizations of Mexico and Central America are claimed by Mormons to have been the people of the *Book of Mormon*, the Nephites and Lamanites.

Nevertheless, not a shred of evidence exists to substantiate these claims—despite many vigorous archaeological excavations financed by the Mormon church. This has forced any number of non-Mormon researchers to conclude the *Book of Mormon* is comprised primarily of myth and historical invention. For example, Dr. Walter Martin refers to "the hundreds of areas where this book defies reason or common sense."[57] Dr. Charles Crane, an expert on Mormon archaeology, confesses, "I am led to believe from my research that this is not an actual story but is a fairy tale much like Alice in Wonderland."[58] Ethnologist Dr. Gordon Fraser, observing that Mormons still accept their book as history, asserts that it in no way corresponds to the known facts of the ancient Americas:

> Both Mormon scientists and objective investigators have reconstructed the story of who lived where in ancient America, when they occupied certain territories, what their cultures were, and, to a large degree, what their writing methods were.
> Certainly these facts were not known when Joseph Smith wrote, but this gives the Mormons of today no right to suppress the information they have found or to ignore the scientific findings of others.... [in fact] the probable accuracy of *The Book of Mormon* can be evaluated by an examination of the book's records of situations, times, and places that are well-known and well documented.
> If, for instance, the statements of history, geography, natural history, ethnology, and anthropology in *The Book of Mormon* almost invariably prove to be untrue, it is safe to assume that completely illogical statements in the rest of the book will follow the same pattern.[59]

Nevertheless, Mormon apologists and lay writers claim that archaeology proves that the *Book of Mormon* is true. In fact, this is a standard argument frequently used by thousands of Mormon missionaries around the world in their attempts to convert people. And, in fact, there is little doubt that many people have converted to Mormonism—trusting the claims of church members that archaeology has proven the *Book of Mormon* to be historically reliable.[60] Misinformation has also proven to be useful propaganda for Mormon believers as well:

> Scores of books and pamphlets have been written by authorized writers for Mormon consumption and to be used for propaganda purposes. Mormons believe these writings because of their source. To tell a Mormon that the *Book of Mormon* has been proved by many archaeological evidences is very reassuring.[61]

For example, Ed Decker, a former Mormon of twenty years' standing, comments, "I had always been told that archaeology has proven the *Book of Mormon* to be true beyond any doubt. That . . . non-Mormon archaeologists had taken the *Book of Mormon* and actually used it as a guide. . . ."[62]

Thus, Hal Hougey observes in *Archaeology and the Book of Mormon* that most Mormons think that archaeology is on their side:

> The numerous books and articles by Latter-day Saints over the years have shown that Mormons believe that the fruits of archaeological research may properly be applied to verify the *Book of Mormon*. Dr. Ross T. Christensen, a Mormon anthropologist, agrees with this in the following quotations from the *Newsletter* of the University Archaeological Society which has its headquarters at Brigham Young University . . . : "The Book of Mormon is in such a key position in relation to the Latter-day Saint religion as a whole that the entire structure of the latter must stand or fall with the verification or refutation of the former; . . . the Book of Mormon is of such a nature that its validity can be submitted to a thorough and objective scientific test. . . . If the Book's history is fallacious, its doctrine cannot be genuine. . . . I am fully confident that the nature of the Book is such that a definitive archaeological test *can* be applied to it."[63]

But such a definitive archaeological test has already been applied, and both the *Book of Mormon* and Mormonism have failed. In fact, archaeology has not affirmed the *Book of Mormon*, but has, in fact, discredited it. The massive data accumulated by numerous archaeological excavations has failed to uncover a shred of evidence to support the *Book of Mormon*'s claims. This has recently been confessed even by some in the Mormon church.[64] Whether we consider the purported cities, rivers, crops, fabrics, animals, metals, coins, kings, wars and war implements, palaces, etc., no evidence at all supports their existence.[65] Where are the plains of

Nephaha? Or the valley of Nimrod? Where is the land of Zarahemla? Have we found coins such as the leah, shiblon and shiblum?

Mormon authority and ethnologist Gordon Fraser correctly observes that the *Book of Mormon* has already been proven a forgery:

> Mormon archaeologists have been trying for years to establish some evidence that will confirm the presence of the [Mormon] church in America. There is still not a scintilla of evidence, either in the religious philosophy of the ancient writings or in the presence of artifacts, that could lead to such a belief.
>
> The whole array of anachronisms [historical errors] in the book stamps it as written by someone who knew nothing about ancient America and presumed that no one ever would know. It is total fiction, done by one who assumed that cultures in ancient America would probably be about the same as those of our own north eastern states in the 19th Century. While certain Mormon apologists are pledged to the task of defending the credibility of the *Book of Mormon*, because the church demands it, some professors at Brigham Young University are demanding caution concerning claims that the ruins of old temples and other artifacts found in Mexico and Central America are positive evidence of the claims of the *Book of Mormon*.
>
> The problem has become a sticky one for Mormon scholars who would like to be investigators in depth but are forbidden by their church authorities.[66]

Although it is recognized by Christian and secular researchers alike that Mormonism's archaeological claims are invalid, this verdict has not yet been accepted by the vast majority of Mormons, whose misinformation has held them captive to distortion. In part, the problem stems from the publications of zealous, but misinformed, amateur archaeologists who are careless or biased with their use of data in their defense of Mormonism—Dewey Farnsworth's *Book of Mormon Evidences in Ancient America*,[67] and the books of Hugh Nibley and Milton Hunter are examples.[68]

Nevertheless, Mormon church authorities continue to support such unreliable "apologetic" works. Thus:

> Despite the absence of archaeological support for the *Book of Mormon*, Mormons continue to produce a spate of archaeological works. Most are nonsense written by amateurs. Not until 1938 did the first Mormon earn a doctorate in archaeology, and today only a few hold this degree.[69]

As Ropp, the Tanners, and others have proven by quoting these few professional Mormon archaeologists, it is *they* and not the secular "enemies" of the church who have taken the church and its amateur archaeologists to task for distorting facts.[70] For example, John L. Sorenson, a former assistant professor of anthropology at Brigham Young University, complains: "As long as Mormons generally are willing to be fooled by (and pay for) the uninformed, uncritical dribble about archaeology and the Scriptures which predominates, the few LDS experts are reluctant even to be identified with the topic."*[71]

Thus, the claims of Mormons regarding various artifacts (the Lehi Tree of Life Stone, Kinderhook Plates, etc.) and ancient sites, may all be refuted by anyone willing to take the time to research the claims.[73] As Cowan observes:

> But, thus far, everything [Mormons] have pointed to as "proof" has turned out to be a forgery or else an exaggerated interpretation which cannot stand up under investigation. There has never yet been one [*Book of Mormon*] name, event, place or anything else verified through archaeological discoveries! . . . Dozens of biblical sites have been located by using the Bible as a guide—but not one has ever been found by using the *Book of Mormon*.[74]

In their *Mormonism—Shadow or Reality?* the Tanners come to the same conclusion—that even though many claims have been made by Mormons regarding certain archaeological "discoveries," they are either bogus or misinterpreted.[75] One leading authority on New World archaeology, Michael Coe, states unequivocally that "the bare facts of the matter are that nothing, absolutely nothing, has ever shown up in any New World excavation" documenting the historicity of the *Book of Mormon*.[76]

This is highly relevant because, according to the information in the *Book of Mormon*, its alleged ancient civilizations in South and Central America are so geographically expansive they virtually demand archaeological verification:

> There are some thirty-eight cities catalogued in the *Book of Mormon*, [supplying] evidence that these were indeed mighty civilizations which should, by all the laws of archaeological research into the culture of antiquity, have left vast amounts of "finds" to be evaluated. But such is not the case as we shall

---

* When one is dealing with a Mormon who maintains his archaeological "proofs," it is important to have such a person read the material by those few responsible Mormon archaeologists who insist such claims are false, as well as professional secular authorities. The Tanners' *Archaeology and the Book of Mormon* is one good source of such information.[72] See Resource List.

show. The Mormons have yet to explain the fact that leading archaeological researchers not only have repudiated the claims of the *Book of Mormon* as to the existence of these civilizations, but have adduced considerable evidence to show the impossibility of the accounts given in the Mormon Bible.[77]

For example:

Not one of these city sites has ever been found in South or Central America. By contrast, a great amount of evidence has been uncovered concerning the ancient cities of the Mayas and Incas who occupy these areas. The historical or archaeological support, which should be virtually overwhelming for such a civilization as the Mormons claim, simply does not exist. In fact, the opposite is true.... There is not one knowledgeable archaeologist, Mormon or non-Mormon, who will claim that there is any archaeological proof to support the *Book of Mormon*.... On the other hand, *archaeologists frequently discover proof which utterly contradicts and demolishes the claims of the Book of Mormon*.... Not only is there no archaeological proof to support the *Book of Mormon* history of the vast civilizations that supposedly covered all of South and Central America, but anthropologists also deny the claims in the *Book of Mormon*. Those who specialize in anthropology and genetics refute Joseph Smith's claim that the American Indians are descendants of the Israelites.[78]

But Mormon missionaries and church authorities continue to ignore such evidence.* Incredibly, they inform potential converts that the Smithsonian Institute or other prestigious professional organizations have utilized the *Book of Mormon* as an accurate archaeological guide. In fact, the Smithsonian Institute has received so many inquiries concerning this that they send out a regular form letter adamantly denying it. The first of many points it makes in refuting Mormon claims is this: "The Smithsonian Institution has never used the *Book of Mormon* in any way as a scientific guide. Smithsonian archaeologists see no direct connection between the archaeology of the New World and the subject matter of the book."[79]

In addition, the Bureau of American Ethnology of the Smithsonian Institute declares, "There is no evidence whatever of any migration of Israel to America, and likewise no evidence that pre-Columbian Indians had any knowledge of Christianity or the Bible."[80]

---

* Both *Doctrine and Covenants* and commentaries on it supply geographical maps of the various movements of the Mormon church in its early history—from New York to Missouri to Illinois to Utah, etc. Why are no maps ever found in a *Book of Mormon*? Because there is nothing to chart.

The prestigious National Geographic Society has also denied Mormon claims:

> With regard to the cities mentioned in the *Book of Mormon*, neither representatives of the National Geographic Society nor archaeologists connected with any other institution of equal prestige have ever used the *Book of Mormon* in locating historic ruins in Middle America or elsewhere.[81]

Perhaps this is why Mormon anthropologist D.F. Green stated that he did not see how "the archaeological myths so common in our proselytizing program enhance the process of true conversion. . . . The first myth we need to eliminate is that a *Book of Mormon* archaeology exists."[82] In other words, no *Book of Mormon* cities have ever been located; no *Book of Mormon* person, place, nation, river, or name has ever been found; no *Book of Mormon* artifacts, no *Book of Mormon* scriptures, no *Book of Mormon* inscriptions, no *Book of Mormon* gold plates have ever been recovered. Nothing that demonstrates that the *Book of Mormon* is anything other than myth or invention has *ever* been found.

As archaeological expertise and data grow, this lack of verifying evidence becomes more and more embarrassing and difficult to explain. In fact, all the evidence of archaeology only tends to disprove the *Book of Mormon*.

We are once again faced with a critical contrast between the Christian Scriptures and the Mormon scriptures, although not in theology. The antithesis between the Bible, which is accepted as a reliable archaeological guide by reputable archaeologists, and the *Book of Mormon*, which is accepted by none, is striking.

For example, even skeptical scholars can seek to disprove the Bible through archaeological investigation and yet become converted to Christianity. This was the case with archaeologist Sir William Ramsay. On the other hand, Mormon scholars who try to prove Mormonism on the basis of archaeology may wind up leaving the church. The Tanners cite the case of Thomas Stuart Ferguson, who was recognized as a "great defender of the faith," and who wrote three books on Mormonism and archaeology. He was head of the Mormon New World Archaeological Foundation, which Brigham Young University supported with funds for several fruitless archaeological expeditions.

Sir William Ramsay and Thomas Stuart Ferguson represent stark contrasts. Ferguson truly believed archaeology would prove Mormonism. Ramsay, a classical scholar and archaeologist at Oxford, was a skeptic convinced that archaeology would disprove Christianity. He had little inkling that his own excavations would prove the detailed historicity of the New Testament.

In the end, Ramsay became a committed Christian who authored some one dozen texts on the reliability of the Scripture—based on careful, skeptical scholarship. Ferguson, on the other hand, became so disheartened that he repudiated the Mormon Church's prophet.

On December 2, 1970, the Tanners received a surprise visit from Ferguson:

> He had come to the conclusion that Joseph Smith was not a prophet and that Mormonism was not true. He told us that he had spent 25 years trying to prove Mormonism, but had finally come to the conclusion that all his work in this regard had been in vain. He said that his training in law had taught him how to weigh evidence and that the case against Joseph Smith was absolutely devastating and could not be explained away.[83]

Compare this with Sir William Ramsay, who wrote that his skepticism had died: "The reversal of our judgment, then, *was complete.*"[84] And he concluded, ". . . the New Testament is unique in the compactness, the lucidity, the pregnancy and the *vivid truthfulness* of its expression. That is not the character of one or two only of the books that compose the Testament; it belongs in different ways to *all alike.*"[85] Many of the greatest archaeologists, from William F. Albright, of Johns Hopkins, to Millar Burroughs, of Yale, have stated publicly that archaeology confirms the Bible historically. No archaeologist has ever stated this for the *Book of Mormon.*

When Mormons claim there is archaeological verification for both the *Book of Mormon* and their religion, they are either uninformed or distorting the facts. The interested reader should purchase appropriate materials and prove to his own satisfaction that Mormon archaeological claims are without foundation and that therefore the *Book of Mormon* is not logically to be classified as a translation of ancient records.[86]

But there is one final disproof of Mormon claims, and it is to this subject we now turn.

### D. *The Book of Mormon's lack of manuscript evidence*

Because of their perceived importance, the religious scriptures of most ancient peoples have been preserved, despite the sometimes incredible odds against it. Occasionally, the preservation is almost perfect. The Bible of the Jews and the New Testament of the Christians are unique in this regard.[87] But even with the Koran of the Muslims and the Hindu or Buddhist scriptures, evidence often exists to determine whether a religious document is genuine or a forgery. For example, sufficient extant manuscript evidence may exist to prove a document really is as old as it claims to be.

But this is not true for the *Book of Mormon*—even though such evidence should certainly exist given the character and influence of the Jewish people who allegedly wrote it. Thus, why the Jews would so carefully preserve the Bible and *not* the *Book of Mormon* is inexplicable.

Incredibly, Mormons often claim that the manuscript evidence for the Bible is of poor quality. But, in truth, while the manuscript evidence for the Bible is rich and abundant, that of the Mormon scriptures is non-existent.[88] Perhaps it is also relevant to note that the discovery of the Dead Sea Scrolls' Book of Isaiah has remarkably confirmed the extant scriptural account while it has repudiated the *Book of Mormon* excerpts from Isaiah.[89]

In fact, there is no textual evidence for either the *Book of Mormon* or for any of Smith's other alleged translations of alleged ancient records.

Is there a single ancient manuscript? No. Is there even a portion of one? No. Is there even one fragment of a page? No. Can the "gold plates" from which Smith allegedly translated the *Book of Mormon* be produced? No. Were these ancient records ever cited by another writer? No. Who can explain this? No one. That the early Mormon church would ever permit the disappearance of materials of such incalculable textual (and monetary) value is simply not credible. And regardless, undoubtedly the Nephites were not in the *habit* of writing on gold plates, so certainly some additional manuscript evidence should be forthcoming. This is the source of another major embarrassment to the Mormon church, for there is simply no credible reason that can explain the lack of textual materials. Thus, just as the content of the *Book of Mormon* argues for a nineteenth-century origin, not an ancient one, so does the manuscript evidence. This is true not only for the *Book of Mormon*, but also for all of Mormonism's "scripture":

> As far as historical and manuscript evidence is concerned, Joseph Smith's scriptures have absolutely no foundation. The "records of the Nephites," for instance, were never cited by any ancient writer, nor are there any known manuscripts or even fragments of manuscripts in existence older than the ones dictated by Joseph Smith in the late 1820's. Joseph Smith's "Book of Moses" is likewise without documentary support. The only handwritten manuscripts for the "Book of Moses" are those dictated by Joseph Smith in the early 1830's. The "Book of Abraham" purports to be a translation of an ancient Egyptian papyrus. However, the original papyrus is in reality the Egyptian "Book of Breathings" and has nothing to do with Abraham or his religion. Therefore, we have no evidence for the "Book of Abraham" prior to the handwritten manuscripts dictated by Joseph Smith in the 1830's. It would appear, then, that there is no documentary evidence for any of Joseph Smith's works that date back prior to the late 1820's.[90]

In conclusion, having demonstrated that the *Book of Mormon* is a nineteenth-century production—and therefore a forgery, we will now show that the text itself has been corrupted and is therefore doubly incapable of a person's trust.

## Division II

*Proof that the Book of Mormon Is Mutilated Both Textually and (from the Perspective of Mormon Teaching) Doctrinally, and Therefore Unreliable Because It Is Corrupted*

### E. Textual problems in the Book of Mormon

As noted earlier, those involved in the production of the *Book of Mormon* claimed it was divinely translated by a process equivalent to that of mechanical dictation. This has resulted in the Mormon church's belief that the entirety of the book is a divine translation. But if true, this would have prevented any need to make changes in the text, even down to the smallest detail. Thus, the original 1830 edition of the English text should have become God's word, letter for letter. Not a single alteration should have occurred, even in grammar or spelling. But, in fact, we find literally thousands of changes. Although the vast majority are grammatical, some are clearly of substance. We document these changes in chapter 23.

### F. The Book of Mormon's lack of distinctive Mormon doctrines: Is the Book of Mormon "Mormon"?

From the perspective of contemporary Mormon theology the *Book of Mormon* itself must be regarded as a corrupted text. Most people, including many Mormons, believe that Mormon teachings are derived principally from the *Book of Mormon*. But this is not true. Mormon doctrine is derived primarily from *Doctrine and Covenants*. This is why, "doctrinally the *Book of Mormon* is a dead book for most Mormons. . . . The *Book of Mormon* teachings have little bearing upon current Mormon doctrine."[91]

The dilemma this poses for the Mormon church is a serious one. Why? Because another Mormon scripture called *Doctrine and Covenants* emphasizes that the *Book of Mormon does contain* basic or fundamental Mormon teachings. For example, according to *Doctrine and Covenants*, the *Book of Mormon* contains "the truth and the Word of God" (*D&C*, 19:26); "the *fullness* of the gospel of Jesus Christ" (that is, Mormon teachings, *D&C*, 20:9) and "the *fullness* of the *everlasting* gospel" (*D&C*, 135:3). *Doctrine and Covenants* also has Jesus claiming that the *Book of Mormon* has "the principles of my gospel" (*D&C*, 42:12) and "*all things written* concerning the foundation of my church, my gospel, and my rock" (*D&C*, 18:4, cf. 17:1-6; emphasis added).

According to *Doctrine and Covenants*, then, the *Book of Mormon* must contain at the very least most of the central doctrines of Mormon faith.

But the *Book of Mormon* contains few major Mormon teachings. For example, it does not teach any of the following central Mormon principles which form the foundation of the Mormon church and its "gospel":

1. Polytheism;

2. God as the product of an eternal progression;

3. Eternal marriage;

4. Polygamy;

5. Human deification;

6. The Trinity as three separate gods;

7. Baptism for the dead;

8. Maintaining genealogical records;

9. Universalism;

10. That God has a physical body and was once a man;

11. That God organized, not created, the world;

12. Mother gods (heavenly mothers);

13. Temple marriage as a requirement for exaltation;

14. The concept of eternal intelligences;

15. Three degrees of heavenly glory (telestial, terrestrial and celestial);

16. Salvation after death in the spirit world;

17. A New Testament era of Mormon organizational offices and functions such as the Melchizedek and Aaronic Priesthoods, Stake President, First Presidency, etc.[92]

All this is why even some Mormon writers have noted the theological irrelevance of the *Book of Mormon* to Mormonism. For example, John H. Evans observed "how little the whole body of belief of the Latter-day Saints really depends on the revelation of the Nephite record [i.e., the *Book of Mormon*]."[93]

Some Mormons respond by saying that the above Mormon doctrines were not revealed until *after* publication of the *Book of Mormon*.[94] But this does not resolve the problem. If so, why would *Doctrine and Covenants* teach what was clearly false—that the *Book of Mormon* did contain the "fullness of the Gospel" and "all things" pertaining to the foundation of the church?

With so many major Mormon doctrines entirely absent from the *Book of Mormon*, how can *Doctrine and Covenants* declare that the "Nephite" record contains the totality of the gospel? And if it does not, how can *Doctrine and Covenants* itself be divinely inspired—or trusted? And if the same source that inspired *Doctrine and Covenants* also claimed to inspire the *Book of Mormon*, how can the *Book of Mormon* be trusted either? Finally, if all this is true, how can the current president and prophet, Ezra Taft Benson, logically claim, "The *Book of Mormon* and *Doctrine and Covenants* testify of each other. You cannot believe one and not the other. . . . The *Doctrine and Covenants* is by far the greatest external witness and evidence which we have from the Lord that the *Book of Mormon* is true."[95]

If, then, the authority of *Doctrine and Covenants* is fatally undermined, who can maintain that its testimony concerning the *Book of Mormon* is reliable? Further, if *Doctrine and Covenants* and subjective "personal testimonies" are the *only* evidence for the genuineness of the *Book of Mormon*, why should its claims be trusted either? *Doctrine and Covenants*, then, is in serious error on a most fundamental issue and certainly cannot be considered a revelation from God even on Mormon terms. (Indeed, if *Doctrine and Covenants* cannot be a divine revelation; if the *Book of Mormon* cannot establish Mormon doctrine, and if *The Pearl of Great Price* is a proven forgery (see chapter 23), what remains of Mormon claims to having authentic, divine revelation?)

In fact, as we will see in chapters 23 and 24, the *Book of Mormon* actually *denies* Mormon doctrines. So, can a Mormon prove the *Book of Mormon* contains Mormon doctrine? No. He may attempt to prove Mormon doctrine from *Doctrine and Covenants*, but *Doctrine and Covenants* teaches he must be able to do this from the *Book of Mormon*.

But if doctrinal irrelevance were not sufficiently discouraging, there are also serious problems in the *Book of Mormon*'s alleged Egyptian language and stylistic manner. We shall now turn to a brief discussion of these topics.

## G. *The language and style of the* Book of Mormon

The Mormon church claims that the "gold plates" containing the *Book of Mormon* were penned in "reformed Egyptian." They base this belief on the *Book of Mormon* itself which affirms, "And now, behold, we have written this record according to our knowledge, in the characters which are called among us the reformed Egyptian . . ." (*Mormon* 9:32).

But this is impossible for several reasons. First, no such language exists and Egyptologists declare this unequivocally. For example, R.A. Parker of the Department of Egyptology at Brown University remarks, "No Egyptian writing has been found in this hemisphere to my knowledge. . . . I do not know of any language such as Reformed Egyptian."[96]

Second, even if it were a true language, how likely is it that the allegedly Jewish Nephites would have used the Egyptian language to write their sacred scriptures? Their strong antipathy to the Egyptians and their culture makes this difficult to accept. When modern Jews copy their scripture, they use Hebrew. They do not use Egyptian or Arabic, the language of their historic enemies.

Furthermore, just as clear evidence should exist in the Americas for the *Book of Mormon's* claims regarding various civilizations, archaeology should also have uncovered evidence of the alleged reformed Egyptian, for Mormons claim it was a universal language in the Americas fifteen hundred years ago. It is difficult to accept that the evidence for so vast a civilization could have been completely lost in fifteen hundred years, but this is what the Mormon church asks us to believe. But if modern archaeology can uncover a relatively small civilization over four thousand years old (for example, Ebla in Syria), isn't it reasonable to believe that some remnants would exist for an incomparably vaster civilization a mere fifteen hundred years old?

Style is another problem for the *Book of Mormon*. Considering the Mormon claim that it is divinely translated, the first 1830 edition should have remained unchanged. But the 1830 edition has had thousands of changes, largely because its grammar was so poor. (See chap. 23 for examples.) If this book was translated by divine power, then God is certainly unfamiliar with elemental grammar. Unnecessary repetition is also a frequent occurrence. Fawn Brodie observes, "Joseph's sentences were loose-jointed, like an earthworm hacked into segments that crawl away live and whole. Innumerable repetitions bogging down the narrative were chiefly responsible for Mark Twain's ejaculation that the book was "chloroform in print."[97]

## H. The Eleven Witnesses

How do Mormons respond to the damaging evidence surrounding the *Book of Mormon*? For the most part, they remain silent. They are content to trust in their "personal testimony" experience and the fact that millions of others have had a similar testimony—going all the way back to the "Eleven Witnesses." Unfortunately, personal testimonies mean little when that which they attest to is already established as false. Nevertheless, the testimonies of the Eleven Witnesses is a key apologetic for promoting the *Book of Mormon*. Besides Joseph Smith, the Eleven Witnesses were the only witnesses to the "gold plates," hence their testimony is considered to be crucial.

We have already noted that most of the Eleven Witnesses were occultists who subjected themselves to occult practices and/or inspiration (chap. 18). On this count alone their testimony is suspect, because occult inspiration is notoriously unreliable and deceptive.[98] Nevertheless, according to Mormons, these witnesses were men of spotless reputation and integrity who testify to the truth of Mormonism.

The testimony of the Three Witnesses and the testimony of the Eight Witnesses are found in the front of every *Book of Mormon*. The Three Witnesses declare they have "seen the plates" from which the *Book of*

*Mormon* was translated, and that it was "divinely revealed" to them that Joseph Smith's translation was correct. The Eight Witnesses declare that Joseph Smith showed them the plates as well. From such testimony, one would assume that the witnesses had physically seen the plates. But no independent testimony for such an assertion exists.

In fact, the evidence suggests they may have only *thought* they saw the plates. Fawn Brodie and others have indicated that Smith had an almost hypnotic power over other people. There is also the possibility of spiritistic visions or deception. Indeed, given the probability that there was mental manipulation associated with their occult involvement, it would be easy to account for the phenomenon of these men thinking they saw something that wasn't there. Similar things happen routinely in stage hypnosis, in many types of psychic encounters (such as "astral travel" and UFO "abductions") and in many other occult manifestations. Clearly, either by religious suggestion, or hypnotism (whether of human or spiritistic origin)—or by raw occult power—men can be made to see, feel and otherwise experience things which, in fact, have no physical reality. In his commentary on Galatians, Martin Luther himself once noted that the devil had such power as to make a man swear he saw, heard and felt such and such when, in fact, he had done no such thing.

Fawn Brodie observes:

> A careful scrutiny of the *Book of Mormon* and the legendary paraphernalia obscuring its origin discloses not only Joseph's inventive and eclectic nature but also his magnetic influence over his friends. . . . what Crowdery in later years described as Joseph's "mysterious power, which even now I fail to fathom." . . . But Joseph had more than "second sight," which is commonplace among professional magicians. At an early age he had what only the most gifted revivalist preachers could boast of—the talent for making men see visions.[99]

Since the spirit entity calling itself "Moroni" took back the alleged gold plates—as visiting spirits of all kinds are wont to do with the objects they "give" to men as "proof" of the encounter—the Eleven Witnesses are the only source of credibility as to the existence of the plates. Unfortunately, we discover that the witnesses' testimony itself is suspect. Brodie again comments:

> According to the local press of the time, the three witnesses all told different versions of their experience, . . . All three witnesses eventually quarrelled with Joseph and left his church.[100]

Concerning the Eight Witnesses, she observes, "It will be seen that four witnesses were Whitmers and three were members of Joseph's own family. The eighth witness, Hyrum Page, had married a Whitmer daughter. Mark Twain was later to observe: 'I could not feel more satisfied and at rest if the entire Whitmer family had testified.' "[101]

Brodie supplies one explanation of how the witnesses may have "seen" the gold plates. Note that at first they saw nothing at all:

> One of the most plausible descriptions of the manner in which Joseph Smith obtained these eight signatures [testifying to having seen the plates] was written by Thomas Ford, Governor of Illinois, who knew intimately several of Joseph's key men after they became disaffected and left the church. They told Ford that the witnesses were "set to continual prayer, and other spiritual exercise." Then at last "he assembled them in a room, and produced a box, which he said contained the precious treasure. The lid was opened; the witnesses peeped into it, but making no discovery, for the box was empty, they said, 'Brother Joseph, we do not see the plates.' The prophet answered them, 'O ye of little faith! how long will God bear with this wicked and perverse generation? Down on your knees, brethren, every one of you, and pray God for forgiveness of your sins, and for a holy and living faith which cometh down from heaven.' The disciples dropped to their knees and began to pray in the fervency of their spirit, supplicating God for more than two hours, with fanatical earnestness; at the end of which time, looking again into the box, they were now persuaded that they saw the plates."[102]

Hence, there are several possible explanations for the alleged gold plates: spiritual intimidation, religious suggestion brought on by psychological manipulation and/or exhaustion, a spiritistically implanted vision, hypnosis, or some combination thereof. It is even slightly possible that the plates could have been temporarily apported objects, for some of the witnesses claimed to have held them.[103] But even here, a hypnotic vision or spiritistic power could have produced the same sensation.[104]

But the most damning indictment against the witnesses is their personal character and lack of credibility. It is relevant to note that "some of the most damaging statements" against the Eleven Witnesses came from the pen of Joseph Smith himself and other early Mormon leaders.[105] Some were gullible; others were psychologically unstable and religiously insecure. In other words, they "were not competent witnesses."[106]

Thus, some of the witnesses doubted their initial vision of the gold plates, as noted by Brigham Young himself.[107] More importantly, most of them later apostatized (!) and several exchanged various charges of serious immorality back and forth with Joseph Smith.[108] In the end, of the Eleven Witnesses, six (including the three key witnesses) were excommunicated from the Mormon church. Each of the three primary witnesses, all of whom later became enemies of Joseph Smith, had severely blemished records as far as their credibility was concerned.[109]

The first, Martin Harris, was described as "changeable, fickle, and puerile in his judgment and conduct."[110] Even "God" Himself—through Joseph Smith—called him a "wicked man" (*D&C*, 3:12,13, introductory remarks). He also appears to have been mentally unbalanced.[111] At various times, he was a Presbyterian, Quaker, Universalist, Baptist, Strangite, Mormon, Restorationer, etc.—in all, he changed his religious convictions some thirteen times.[112] At the end of his life he returned to the Mormon church.

According to Joseph Smith, Oliver Crowdery, the second of the three witnesses, was led astray by Hyrum Pages' (one of the eight witnesses) "seer stone" and as a result was excommunicated from the church.[113] It is disputed whether or not he ever returned, or whether he maintained until his death that Smith was a false prophet.[114] According to the Mormon *Times and Seasons* of 1841, it does appear that he, too, doubted his first testimony about the *Book of Mormon*.[115]

The last of the three witnesses, David Whitmer, never returned to the Mormon church. And he stated the following just before he died:

> If you believe my testimony to the Book of Mormon; if you believe that God spake to us three witnesses by his own voice, then I tell you that in June, 1838, God spake to me again by his own voice from the heavens, and told me to separate myself from among the Latter-day Saints.[116]

Whitmer maintained that the Mormon church had "gone deep into error and blindness"—for example, in accepting the new revelations found in *Doctrine and Covenants*.[117]

It is hard to understand why Mormonism continues to accept Whitmer's "testimony" as seen in the front of the *Book of Mormon* when he later testified that Mormonism had become a false religion.

It is even more difficult to believe that eleven men of dubious character are so readily accepted at all, since the quality of any individual's testimony is so dependent upon his or her character. Even the current president and prophet of Mormonism, Ezra Taft Benson, is forced to concede that the testimony of the Eleven Witnesses is tarnished and that even today such "wolves" continue to haunt the flock:

> Six of the original Twelve Apostles selected by Joseph Smith were excommunicated. The Three Witnesses to the Book of Mormon left the church. Three of Joseph Smith's counselors fell—one even helped plot his death.... The wolves among our flock are more numerous and devious today than when President [J.P. Reuben] Clark made [a similar] statement [in 1949].[118]

These Mormon witnesses present a stark contrast to the twelve apostles of the New Testament who are generally conceded to be men of integrity. But how would Christians feel if the twelve apostles were men of such uncertain character as these eleven Mormon men? How could their testimonies about Jesus ever be reliably accepted? Likewise, how can Mormons logically trust the testimony of the Eleven Witnesses?

So of what value are the eleven Mormon testimonies to the *Book of Mormon*? Of what value are dubious professions to dubious visions? Indeed, there are literally hundreds just like them—from innumerable conflicting religious sects and cults, all boasting equal conviction. Without the presence of the gold plates themselves, all that remains is the testimony of unreliable men who think they *may* have seen them. What's worse, "There are a *dozen variations* of the story of the finding and translating of the *Book of Mormon*'s golden plates, and several versions of the experiences of the Three Witnesses who claimed to have seen the plates."[119]

It is never wise to place faith in alleged revelations given under what are, at best, suspicious circumstances—especially when they deny what God has already taught in the Bible. As the Tanners comment:

> The evidence shows that they were gullible, credulous, and their word cannot always be relied upon.... Some of them even gave false revelations in the name of the Lord.... How can we put our trust in men who are constantly following after movements like the Shakers, Strangites, and the McLellin group? We feel that the *Book of Mormon* witnesses have been "weighed in the balance" and found wanting.[120]

## ♦ ♦ *Conclusion* ♦ ♦

Given our brief survey of the *Book of Mormon*, what may be concluded? Briefly, from examining the book as a whole—its occult origin, its various sources and plagiarisms, its anti-biblical teachings, the archaeological disproof, the inexplicable absence of textual data, its lack of (and even opposition to) Mormon teachings, the nonexistent Egyptian language, the embarrassing grammar, the forced changes in the text due to the primitive nature of the first edition, the untrustworthy testimony of the Eleven Witnesses, not to mention its myths and many errors (see appendix to chapters 22 and 23), etc.—all the evidence points to one unavoidable conclusion. *The Book of Mormon is really a piece of nineteenth-century fiction.* Whatever else it is, it cannot be a divine revelation. Writing in "The Centennial of Mormonism" in *American Mercury*, Bernard De Voto correctly described it as "a yeasty fermentation, formless, aimless and inconceivably absurd."[121]

All this is why Mormon leaders everywhere are forced to tell potential converts to *ignore criticism* of the *Book of Mormon* and instead rely entirely upon subjective "confirmation." Mormons often respond to criticism with something like the following. "I don't care what they say. I don't care what the problems are. I have a burning in my bosom and I know the Mormon Church is true."[122] But if the *Book of Mormon* is truly authentic, why do Mormons everywhere claim that the only real evidence for it is subjective?

The tenth president and prophet, Joseph Fielding Smith, counselled, "Pay no attention to the criticism, but ask yourself prayerfully, if the record is not true."[123] L.S.T. Rasmussen, Professor Emeritus of Religious Education at Brigham Young University, emphasizes, "The best support for the authenticity of the *Book of Mormon* is the testimony of the Holy Spirit."[124] And, "In contrast to the indecisive nature of [the] external evidence, the Lord has provided a way to obtain decisive support for the book's authenticity: 'The Spirit of Truth. . . . will guide [us] into all truth.'"[125]

As noted earlier, no less a figure than Mormon historian B.H. Roberts confessed that the testimony of the Holy Ghost "must ever be the chief source of evidence of the truth of the *Book of Mormon*."[126]

Likewise, Steve Gilliland, director of the LDS Institute of Religion at California State University/Long Beach comments, "It's not our responsibility to try to prove it [the Mormon Gospel] or convince the other person. The only real proof is the witness of the Spirit."[127]

Unfortunately, the church's appeal to subjective evidence does no more to prove the *Book of Mormon* than does reading the book itself. To believe without any evidence is troublesome enough, but to believe in spite of the evidence is folly. But to then demand that God confirm the "truth" of the *Book of Mormon* in sanctified prayer is not only an insult to God, who knows better, but it is also sheer self-deception. This unjustified appeal to "spiritual" experience ironically leads to the same spiritual quagmire that Joseph Smith instigated on that "beautiful clear day early in the spring of 1820" when he started the whole business (chap. 2).

Mormons should carefully reread the *Book of Mormon*. They should read it in light of history, logic, Scripture, and common sense and see whether or not they can really believe that it represents what the Mormon church claims. If it doesn't, they should know what to do.

We cannot end this section more appropriately than with the assessments of both Mormon and non-Mormon authorities. First, Dr. Walter Martin concludes:

> The world is now in a position to judge the *Book of Mormon* on three different levels. First, the book does not correspond to what we know God has already said in His Word. Second, its internal inconsistencies, thousands of changes, and persistent plagiarization of the King James Bible decidedly remove it from serious consideration as a revelation from God. Finally,

its external inconsistencies not only expose its misuse of archaeology, science, history, and language, but actually allow us to investigate its true origin.[128]

The current prophet and president of the Mormon church, Ezra Taft Benson, could not have spoken a truer word when he said,

> The Book of Mormon is the keystone of our religion. . . . A keystone is the central stone in an arch. It holds all the other stones in place, and if it is removed the arch crumbles.[129]

# ♦ ♦ *Appendix* ♦ ♦

### The Critical Work of B.H. Roberts

In 1980, new data came to light from Mormon historian and apologist B. H. Roberts. Roberts is acknowledged by Mormon leaders as "one of the most intellectual General Authorities of his day."[130] He was president of the Eastern States Mission from 1922 to 1927 and one of the seven Presidents of Seventy from 1888 until his death in 1933. Roberts was also a committed Mormon and apparently remained so until his death.

Nevertheless, as one of the first ever to make a scholarly study of the *Book of Mormon*, his faith was subjected to the severest testing. In 1979 and 1981 two manuscripts of Roberts were released by his family. They are currently available for inspection at the University of Utah and Concordia Seminary in St. Louis.*

Even John W. Welch, a committed Mormon and professor of law at Brigham Young University, describes Roberts' study of the *Book of Mormon* (not to be confused with his "Book of Mormon Difficulties," an earlier, shorter paper) in the following terms: "In the study, Brother Roberts was blunt. He stated a case against the Book of Mormon in tough terms." Welch further referred to it as "a bonanza" for critics of the *Book of Mormon*.[131]

Nevertheless, coming from a Mormon apologist and historian, such manuscripts are particularly noteworthy. It is significant that Roberts presents a strong case for the human origin of the *Book of Mormon*. In the words of Mormon authority Wesley Walters:

> In a discussion running more than 150 pages Roberts showed that Ethan Smith's book contained practically the "groundplan" of the *Book of Mormon*. . . . Roberts hauntingly asked concerning these and other parallels he found, "Can such

---

* A typeset edition published by the University of Illinois Press is now available. See Resource List.

numerous and startling points of resemblance and suggestive contact be merely coincidental?" As his third main point he established the fact (using Mormon sources exclusively) that Joseph Smith had imaginative powers of mind sufficient to have produced the *Book of Mormon*. He describes Smith's creativity as being, "as strong and varied as Shakespeare's and no more to be accounted for than the English Bard's." Roberts rounds out his case for the human origin of the *Book of Mormon* with a 115-page discussion of the blunders that result from Joseph Smith's untrained, though creative mind. Roberts points to the impossibility of Lehi's three-day journey from Jerusalem to the shores of the Red Sea—a 170-mile trek on foot, with women and children along. He cites their arrival in America, the land "kept from all other nations" where they unaccountably find *domesticated* animals—"the cow and the wild goat" (1 Nephi 18:25, emphasis added). Roberts finds an amateurish repetition of the same plot with only the characters changed. The book, he notes, attempts to outdo biblical miracles and presents some incredible battle scenes. In one instance, 2060 "striplings" fought over a 13-year period without one being killed (Alma 56-58). This leads Roberts to ask: "Is all this sober history . . . or is it a wonder-tale of an immature mind, unconscious of what a test he is laying on human credulity when asking men to accept his narrative as solemn history?"[132]

The Mormon response has been to ignore or downplay the serious nature of Roberts' study. For example, his research is described as hasty and less than careful.[133] In addition, it is claimed that most of the questions that Roberts raised "have since found answers."

But is this really true? Consider only two examples of problems that have not "found answers." Roberts raised an important issue when he cited the absence of any archaeological evidence for the *Book of Mormon*. Doesn't this remain a problem—even a far more serious problem to the modern church? Roberts also pointed out a number of incredible and erroneous passages in the *Book of Mormon*. These passages remain in the book and can be read by anyone who wishes. One passage, for example, has it that huge numbers of attacking snakes "herded" people and their flocks and built "hedges" around them to prevent escape.[134] Thus, the claim by the church that the problems represented by Roberts' research are now solved is simply not true. Even Professor Welch concludes his analysis of Roberts' studies with,

> The Lord apparently does not intend the *Book of Mormon* to be an open-and-shut case intellectually, either pro or con. If He had intended that, He would have left more concrete

evidences. Instead, the Lord has given us the opportunity to address the *Book of Mormon* as a matter of faith.[135]

The only question is, "what *kind* of faith"? Is this a faith justified by the evidence? Or is it a blind and even hypocritical faith? Since the day of B.H. Roberts, the moral, intellectual and ecclesiastical problems for the Mormon church have only been compounded to the point of no return. Yet they continue to promote a falsified text and religion as God's revelation to a frequently unsuspecting church and American public.

◆

# CHAPTER 23

# Mormonism's Word of God

## Have Secret Changes Been Made in the Mormon Scriptures?

S tandard religious bodies usually guard and protect their scriptures with unrepentant zeal.

It is inconceivable that any bona fide church would permit the alteration of what it truly believed were divine scriptures, let alone alter them itself and then keep such misrepresentations secret. This would represent total irreverence and desecration before God.

But this is exactly what the Mormon church has done. The Mormon church claims as its scripture the *Book of Mormon*, *Doctrines and Covenants*, and *The Pearl of Great Price*. Dr. Walter Martin observes (the term "standard work" refers to "inspired" work):

> There isn't a single LDS-produced standard work that hasn't undergone hundreds and even thousands of changes, additions, deletions, and corrections, many of which are much more than "typographical" in nature, and all of which were done without indications or acknowledgement of the actions taken. Even granting Joseph the "right" to revise what God had told him before (even though it is difficult to do so when we are talking about cases involving historical facts), why is there the deception associated with these changes? . . . Church leaders have even lied in public about these situations. Why?[136]

First, we will document that, given Mormon claims, no changes whatever should have been made in the Mormon scriptures. Second, we will document the fact of the extensive changes themselves. This will prove that even Mormon church authorities, apparently, do not consider their own scripture true, let alone sacred. Why they would then demand such allegiance from church members is apparently a mystery known only to them.

In his alleged history, Joseph Smith tells the story about the mode of translation of the gold plates. This story confirms the claim that the plates were translated "by the power of God" and therefore cannot permit even the slightest alteration.

It had been prearranged that after completion of the translation the "three witnesses" would see the gold plates so they could bear "testimony" to them. After a time of fervent prayer in the woods, two of the three witnesses (less Harris, who allegedly saw the same vision later):

> Beheld a light above us in the air, of exceeding brightness; and behold, an angel stood before us [not in the light]. In his hands, he held the plates. . . . he turned over the leaves, one by one, so that we could see them, and discern the engravings thereon distinctly. . . . [then] we heard a voice from [God] out of the bright light above us, saying, "These plates have been revealed by the power of God, *and they have [now] been translated by the power of God. The translation of them which you have seen is correct*, and I command you to bear witness of what you now see and hear."[137]

This testimony is clear enough. No less an authority than God Himself has declared that the plates were translated by His own person and power. God has also testified that the translation "is correct." And later, Jesus Christ Himself also allegedly stated of the translation, "As your Lord and your God liveth *it is true.* . . . And, I, Jesus Christ, your Lord and your God, have spoken unto you."[138]

In light of such witnesses, it is hardly surprising that Smith himself confessed that the *Book of Mormon* was "the most correct of any book on earth."[139]

It follows, then, that if the first edition of the text was 1) translated by God's own power, 2) described as "correct," "most correct," and "true," and then 3) confirmed as such by both God and Jesus, there is simply no way it should require drastic revision, *grammatical* or other. A divinely *translated* text is just that, and Mormons should accept the implications. How can there possibly be errors and thousands of changes in a *divinely* translated text?

Some Mormons have claimed that there are no changes in the *Book of Mormon*. But this is false. Others have claimed that the changes are only minor and not really an issue. But the issue is not simply the existence of relatively minor grammatical changes, but the vast number of them. There shouldn't be even one, but there are several thousand. Further, as we will show, there are significant changes of substance.

Let us first examine the explanations or proposed "solutions" to the problem offered by the Mormon church. One claim is that the printer of the *Book of Mormon* (John Gilbert) was incompetent or "unfriendly" to Mormonism, and therefore produced some errors. Unfortunately, this is not only denied by other Mormons, but it was also denied by the printer himself. Gilbert confessed he was told to typeset the material as it stood—for example, to leave in grammatical errors.[140] In any case, the errors are simply too numerous for any qualified printer to make. Considering it was a country press, the actual typographical errors in the 1830 edition were very few.

Another "solution" is to claim that the translation *was* inerrant; it therefore infallibly translated *errors* made by its author (Mormon). In other words, God accurately translated the errors on the gold plates made by the Nephite historian Mormon. But if so, how can an inspired translation of errant human writings be considered "the Word of God"? Also, this means we have no way of knowing how accurate Mormon was in his history. For example, if we know that there are *some* errors of substance, how can we guarantee that there are not many errors of substance, particularly when the text we now have cannot be independently corroborated?

But again, even the claim to divine translation is suspect. Recall the translating process—Smith's face buried in a hat dictating sentences which appeared through the power of a magical seer stone. As we saw, this was the testimony of one of Joseph's wives, Emma Smith, as well as the Three Witnesses, all of whom agreed that the actual plates were often *not even present*. Nevertheless, for each sentence, "if [it was] not written correctly it remained until corrected." Only then would it disappear and a new one appear.[141] "All was as simple as when a clerk writes from dictation."[142] If this claim is true, then there should not be a single error in the text. If the claim is false, then the *Book of Mormon* could have any number of errors, serious or otherwise.

We have already recorded David Whitmer's testimony that the *Book of Mormon* was produced by a process equivalent to mechanical dictation. Oliver Huntington further declared in his own journal that he heard Joseph F. Smith, the sixth prophet of the church, affirm that "Joseph did not render the writing on the gold plates into the English language in his own style of language, as many people believe, *but every word and every letter was given to him by the power of God*. . . . If there was a word wrongly written or even a letter incorrect, the writing on the stones would remain there. . . . and when corrected the sentence would disappear as usual."[143] In other words, a perfect inerrant translation. The Mormon theory of revelation simply will not allow for changes. As Dr. Hoekema emphasizes:

> This means, then, Joseph Smith's translation differs from all other translations that have ever been made; it was inspired

directly by God and is therefore errorless. This means, too, that the original manuscript of Smith's translation must be the authoritative one, since it embodies the translation as it is alleged to have come directly from God. No changes therefore may be tolerated in this original translation, since a single change would be sufficient to upset the theory that this was an errorless translation.[144]

The *1830 edition*, then, is God's Word. As the Mormon apologetic tract, "The Challenge" emphasizes, ". . . you must have no changes in the text. The first edition as you dictated to your secretary must stand forever."[145] If Mormons can live with this claim, that is certainly their option. But perhaps they should reconsider the ethics of attempting to persuade others that no changes have ever been made in their scripture.

Some Mormons have claimed that the three witnesses "made up" the idea of a word-for-word translation, or that such accounts are not official, which, of course, has little to do with their truthfulness. However, even Joseph Smith himself was reported to have taught the equivalent idea of mechanical dictation.[146] Finally, though, whether God *translated* errors or *inspired* errors, Mormons face a serious problem.

### Changes in the Book of Mormon

Jerald and Sandra Tanner have photo-reprinted the original 1830 edition of the *Book of Mormon*, noting in the current text over 3,900 changes, the majority being in spelling and grammar. Another researcher has noted a total of 11,849 changes, including capitalization, punctuation, etc., from the 1830 edition.[147] These facts prove the translation was far from perfect or "divine." And, if the issue is "inconsequential," as some Mormons claim, why did President David O. McKay attempt to suppress sales of the original editions of the Mormon scriptures? Further, why have committed Mormons said they left the church because of such errors—if the issue is really so inconsequential?[148]

Is all this why Mormon authorities eventually changed their minds?

> Finally, the Mormon church leaders became so embarrassed about the grammar that they decided to abandon the idea that God gave Joseph Smith the English that is found in the *Book of Mormon*; their new idea was that God just gave Joseph Smith the idea and that he expressed it in his own words.[149]

Unfortunately, church leaders here are denying the solemn testimony of both their prophet and their Three Witnesses. In effect, they are calling Joseph Smith and the Three Witnesses liars—or deceivers. Logically, the same charges must be brought against God and Jesus who, as we remember, also testified to the book's perfect translation. But little choice was left. Note just a few quoted portions from the first (1830) edition as catalogued by the Tanners in their *3,913 Changes in the Book of Mormon: A Photo Reprint of the Original 1830 Edition of the Book of Mormon With All the Changes Marked*. We have verified these changes by consulting our own copy of the 1830 edition, reproduced in 1958 from uncut sheets by Mormon Wilford C. Woodruff.[150]

- Diseases which was subsequent to man [i.e., to which men were subject][151]

- And whoredoms is an abomination before me: thus saith the Lord of Hosts[152]

- Wherefore, all things must needs be a compound in one.... wherefore it must needs have been created for a thing of naught. ...And all things that in them is[153]

- Lest he should look for that which he had not ought[154]

- There he found Muloki a preaching the word[155]

- A begging for his food[156]

- They did cast up mighty heaps of earth for to get ore[157]

- But it all were vain[158]

The above are only a few of the literally thousands of places where the first edition has now been corrected. Consider these examples also: "Arrest the scriptures" has been changed to "wrested" the scriptures, "ariven" to "arrive," "respects" to "respect," "fell" to "fallen," "wrote" to "written," "exceeding afraid" to "exceedingly afraid," "began" to "begun," etc. Hundreds upon hundreds of changes of this type as well as hundreds of cases of addition or deletion of words mean that the book could not have possibly been divinely translated as claimed.[159]

Some of the changes are not simply grammatical; they alter doctrine. For example, in 1 Nephi 20:1, an attempt is made to teach Old Testament baptismal practices by adding "out of the waters of baptism," even though this is *not* present in the original 1830 edition.[160]

In Alma 29:4 the words "[that God] yea, decreeth unto them decrees which are unalterable" is *removed*, yet it is present in the 1830 edition.[161] Hoekema concludes:

Does it seem likely God would "inspire" a translation in which both grammatical and doctrinal corrections would have to be made? Mormons have no right to regard the grammatical errors as excusable on the grounds of Smith's lack of formal education for this entire translation is alleged to have been made "through the gift and power of God," and is said to be

"In no sense the product of linguistic scholarship."...Mormons cannot even admit a single grammatical error in Smith's original translation.[162]

As we have seen, Mormons who admit to *Book of Mormon* changes may claim that they are grammatical only and that the basic *meaning* of the text has never been changed. This is also false. For example, the 1830 edition of Mosiah 21:28 refers to King Benjamin while modern editions read "King Mosiah."[163] According to Mormon chronology, Benjamin was dead and so no longer king at this point (Mosiah 6:3-7; 7:1), so the divinely inspired name was changed to King *Mosiah* to *cover the error*. The same change is made in the book of Ether.[164]

In similar fashion in 1 Nephi 11:18, the 1830 edition (p. 25) teaches, in reference to Mary, "The virgin which thou seest, is the mother of God after the manner of the flesh."[165] However, since Mary could not have been the literal *mother* of the Mormon earth deity Elohim, modern editions read "the mother of *the son of* God" rather than "the mother of God."

Again, the 1830 edition of 1 Nephi 11:21 reads, "Behold the lamb of God even the eternal Father!"[166] Since Mormons do not believe Jesus is the literal person of the Father, modern editions read, "Yea, even the *son of* the Eternal Father." Additional significant changes may be found in 1 Nephi 13:22; 19:20; 2 Nephi 4:12; Mosiah 29:15; Alma 37:21,24; 3 Nephi 3:23; 22:4, etc.

When asked about such things, many Mormons will say these changes are only lies perpetrated by "enemies" of the church. In his *Answers to Gospel Questions*, President Joseph Fielding Smith (who served as church historian from 1921 to 1970) claims the following:

> A careful check of the list of changes submitted by these critics shows there is not one change or addition that is not in full harmony with the original text. Changes have been made in punctuation and a few other minor matters that needed correction, but never has any alteration or addition changed a single original thought.[167]

But anyone who wishes can obtain a notarized copy of the 1830 edition of the *Book of Mormon* and mark these changes for themselves. All they need to do is to write to Utah Lighthouse Ministry (see Resource List). President Smith is wrong.

Furthermore, as if to add insult to injury, the "inspired" translation of the *Book of Mormon* even contains *translation* errors of the King James text (see Appendix Two) and, when it quotes the King James Version, it *includes* the italicized words, which of course are not present in the original Greek and Hebrew (e.g., see Mosiah 1-4 and Isaiah 53). In a "perfect translation" done by the power of God, matters should already be perfectly lucid. Why then would God add exactly the *same* words the

King James translators happened to choose to amplify the meaning of the text? And recall that the King James translators wouldn't even be born for another thousand years.

In light of these and other facts it is incredible that Mormons say they will only accept the Bible "insofar as it is translated correctly"—since it is clear they are the community having translation problems. Mormons are often critical of Christians claiming that they have changed or removed "truths of Scripture" in order to preserve false traditions and heretical doctrines.[168] Yet Mormons make these charges without providing a shred of evidence. But Mormonism has inadvertently condemned itself, for Mormonism is the party which has changed its scriptures in literally thousands of places.

In conclusion, modern Mormons have only two choices: either 1) Smith copied mistakes that were on the alleged gold plates, or 2) it was not translated by divine power. Either way, the *Book of Mormon* could contain any number of serious errors. Certainly, whatever else one may say about the *Book of Mormon*, we may say with confidence that it could not have been divinely inspired and translated. Unfortunately, from this point on matters deteriorate precipitously.

### Changes in Doctrine and Covenants

The Mormon scripture known as *Doctrine and Covenants* is clearly the most important doctrinal text for the Mormon church. The tenth president and prophet of the Mormon church, Joseph Fielding Smith, declared:

> In my judgment there is no book on earth yet come to man as important as the book known as the *Doctrine and Covenants*, with all due respect to the *Book of Mormon*, and the Bible and the *Pearl of Great Price* which we say are our standards in doctrine. The book of *Doctrine and Covenants* to us stands in a peculiar position *above them all*. . . . The Bible is [only] a history containing the doctrine and commandments given to the people anciently. That applies also to the *Book of Mormon*. . . . But this *Doctrine and Covenants* contains the word of God to those who dwell here now. *It is our book* . . . it is worth more to us than the riches of the earth.[169]

If *Doctrine and Covenants* "stands above" the Bible and other Mormon scriptures, then of all Mormon scripture it should be the least tampered with—at least if respect for things divine means something to Mormon authorities.

But if the alterations in the *Book of Mormon* are not serious enough, consider the revisions that have been in *Doctrine and Covenants*. At least *twenty-five thousand* words are removed and *three thousand* other changes have been made in this scripture.[170]

The original edition of *Doctrine and Covenants* was published in 1833 with the title *A Book of Commandments*. This text purportedly contained direct revelations from God to Joseph Smith. Thus there could have been no "translation problems" possible because Smith received word-for-word dictation of direct divine inspiration. Even the modern introduction to *Doctrine and Covenants* emphasizes the following: "Concerning this publication the elders of the Church gave solemn testimony that the Lord has borne record to their souls that the revelations were true." But strangely, in 1835 the first edition of what came to be called *Doctrine and Covenants* appeared—with literally *thousands* of changes made from God's earlier revelations and commandments as given in *A Book of Commandments*. We have a copy of the 1833 text and have proven to our own satisfaction that such changes have been made. So may anyone else.

The Tanners explain why this is such a problem: "Of all Mormon writing we would expect the *Doctrine and Covenants* to be the most pure and free from revision. The reason for this is that *Doctrine and Covenants* purports to be the revelations given directly from God to Joseph Smith—not just a translation. . . . Yet, upon careful examination, we found thousands of words added, deleted or changed. How can the Mormon leaders explain this?"[171]

They cannot. Unwilling to entirely reject their scripture, their only recourse has been to resort to subterfuge and deception. For example, they have attempted to suppress the evidence: "For many years the Mormon leaders tried to suppress *A Book of Commandments*. They would not allow us [the Tanners] to obtain photocopies of the book from Brigham Young University."[172]

Incredibly, many Mormons today will not even admit to such changes because Mormon leaders have lied to them and declared that the revelations "have remained unchanged," and that "there has been no tampering with God's word" because "there was no need for eliminating, changing, or adjusting any part to make it fit [earlier revelations]."[173]

Other Mormons who feel constrained to admit that there are vast alterations make the incredible assertion that God has the right to "change His mind" or that the scribes and publishers made thousands of errors.[174] But even other Mormons admit such ideas are absurd.[175]

Nevertheless, the fact is that the 1835 edition has been drastically altered:

> Besides the thousands of words which were added, deleted or changed in the revelations after they were published in the *Book of Commandments* and other early publications, one whole section on marriage has been removed. Also the *Lectures on Faith*, which comprise 70 pages of the 1835 edition of the *Doctrine and Covenants*, have been completely removed from later editions. . . . All of these alterations have been made in just a little over 140 years. Imagine what would have happened

to the Bible if the churches that preserved it had altered it at the same rate that the Mormons have altered the *Doctrine and Covenants*. We would be lucky to have anything the way it was originally written![176]

Perhaps it is easy to understand why the seventy pages comprising the *Lectures on Faith*—first published in the 1835 edition—were finally removed in 1921. This section was deleted to avoid contradictions with modern Mormon theology.[177] For example, these divine revelations declare that the Father is "a personage of spirit," which contradicts Mormonism's claim that He has a physical body.[178] They also teach that God is "omnipresent," again contradicting current Mormon doctrine.[179] *Lectures on Faith* contains many other teachings that the modern church rejects, and so it was removed. Likewise, thousands of other changes were made in *Doctrine and Covenants* whenever the need arose. Recently, the church canonized the 137th section of *Doctrine and Covenants*, omitting some two hundred words of the original divine prophecy of Joseph Smith—words containing false prophecies.[180] But are such actions credible with the church's claim to respect and honor the "Word of God"?

The interested reader may see for himself all these changes—not only in the *Book of Mormon*, but also in *Doctrine and Covenants*—by comparing photographic reprints of notarized first editions of the *Book of Mormon* and *Doctrine and Covenants*. These have been published under the title *Joseph Smith Begins His Work, Volumes 1 and 2* and are available at a minimum cost.*[181] (See Resource List.)

Significantly, the most recent edition of *Doctrine and Covenants* (1982) now confesses that *some* changes have been made:

> In successive editions of the *Doctrine and Covenants*, additional revelations or other matters of record have been added. . . . Beginning with the 1835 edition a series of seven theological lessons was also included; these were titled the "Lectures on Faith." . . . these lectures have been omitted from the Doctrine and Covenant since the 1921 edition. . . . It is evident that some errors have been perpetuated in past editions, . . . this edition contains corrections. . . . These changes have been made so as to bring the material into conformity with the historical documents.[182]

But while being forced to admit to such changes, it offers no explanation of them—nor an apology to church members for distorting God's Word.

---

*In his book *Are the Mormon Scriptures Reliable?* Ropp lists a number of these changes with a helpful tabular comparison of *A Book of Commandments* in parallel sections (in correct order), so that the reader may observe the changes for himself.

## The Pearl of Great Price

*The Pearl of Great Price* is Mormonism's third "inspired" scripture and, again, the church maintains that no changes have been made in the sacred text.

Nevertheless, *The Pearl of Great Price* has had literally thousands of words deleted and hundreds added, as has been documented in the Tanners' text, *Changes in The Pearl of Great Price: A Photo-reprint of the Original 1851 Edition of The Pearl of Great Price With All the Changes Marked*[183] (currently updated as *Flaws in the Pearl of Great Price*; see Resource List).

Even the most recent version of *The Pearl of Great Price* (1982) now confesses to "some changes": "Several revisions have been made in the contents as the needs of the church have required. . . . In the present edition some changes have been made to bring the text into conformity with earlier documents."[184]

But such a confession, even if forced by data which can no longer be ignored or suppressed, gives the average Mormon no idea of the *extent* of the changes made. Let us give just one example. Page 14 of the 1851 edition requires: adding 355 words, changing 63 others, and deleting 4 more to conform it to modern editions. In fact, some whole sections (e.g. pages 33-35) are missing—and such examples could be multiplied with monotony.[185]

## The Book of Abraham

The *Book of Abraham* is a portion of *The Pearl of Great Price* which contains Mormonism's racist anti-black doctrine (see chap. 29). It was supposedly written by Abraham four thousand years ago in "reformed Egyptian." Somehow it found its way into the hands of Joseph Smith who then "divinely" translated it. Smith claimed he purchased the papyrus manuscript from a traveling Egyptologist. Of course he then translated this alleged "reformed Egyptian" text when next to nothing was known about translating Egyptian and no one could disprove the translation.

Today it can be translated accurately since a copy of the papyrus manuscript was located in 1967—and it is in a *known* Egyptian script. In fact, the *Book of Abraham* is merely a false translation of a pagan text, the Egyptian *Book of Breathings*, which is an extension of the *Egyptian Book of the Dead*, relating to the alleged journeys of the dead in the afterlife.[186]

Any number of Egyptologists have now proven that the *Book of Abraham* is a fraud. They all agree that it has nothing to do with Abraham or the *Book of Breathings*. It is thus beyond question that Smith's "divine translation" has nothing at all to do with what the Egyptian papyrus actually states. Indeed, not a "single word" of Smith's alleged translation was correct. Archaeologist Dr. Richard Fales comments, "Joseph Smith did not get right even one word in this whole translation. In fact, he took one little letter that looks like a backwards 'e' and translated it into over 76 words with seven names."[187]

Gleason Archer holds a Ph.D. in comparative literature from Harvard. He is a linguist who reads in twenty-eight different languages. He also teaches Egyptian and has been reading it since 1933.[188] He observes:

> Earlier negative verdicts of scholars like Theodule Devaria of the Louvre, and Samuel A.B. Mercer of Western Theological Seminary, and James H. Breasted of the University of Chicago and W. M. Flinders Petrie of London University (who had all been shown Smith's facsimiles) were clearly upheld by a multitude of present-day Egyptologists. Their finding was that *not a single word* of Joseph Smith's alleged translation bore any resemblance to the contents of this document. It turned out to be a late even Ptolemaic copy in hieratic script of the Sensen Papyrus, which belongs to the same genre as the *Egyptian Book of the Dead*. . . . Needless to say, the completely mistaken concept of Joseph Smith as to his competence in ancient Egyptian is now clearly demonstrated to be beyond debate.[189]

In other words, Smith could just as easily have translated an Egyptian cookbook and claimed his translation was an English New Testament. The *Book of Abraham* is thus either pure imagination, deliberate hoax, or spiritistic deception. Significantly, the second largest organized Mormon body, the Reorganized Latter-day Saints, have rejected it.[190]

Yet, incredibly, the Mormon church has tried to suppress these findings while at the same time continuing to maintain the divine integrity of the *Book of Abraham* and Smith's ability to translate![191]

In the Tanners' opinion,

> That the Utah Mormon leaders would continue to endorse the "Book of Abraham" in the face of the evidence that has been presented is almost beyond belief. We feel that if any person will honestly examine this matter he will see that the evidence to disprove the "Book of Abraham" is conclusive.[192]

Why is the Mormon church so reluctant to acknowledge this fabrication? Simply because it casts a fatal pall of doubt upon Smith's claims as to his ability to translate—and hence upon his other religious claims as well. Smith maintained that the *Book of Abraham* was God's word and that he had translated it for us by the "power of God." It has now proven to be a pagan text with a completely false translation. But Smith also avowed he translated the *Book of Mormon* by the "power of God." So how does anyone know that the *Book of Mormon* is not a similar fabrication?

Consider that Smith claimed that both the *Book of Abraham* and the *Book of Mormon* were translated from "reformed Egyptian." But, if the *Book of Abraham* is an example of Smith's ability to translate "reformed Egyptian," then on what logical basis can anyone trust the *Book of Mormon*? The alleged gold plates could have contained Chinese agricultural records and it would have made no difference. Furthermore, if Smith is wrong in these crucial claims, how can anyone, especially Mormons, trust him when he tells of the first vision account, of subsequent divine revelations and manifestations—or, in fact, of anything else?

That the *Book of Abraham* is a forgery is substantiated by many scholarly works, including H. Michael Marquardt's, *The Book of Abraham Papyrus Found*, and *Why Egyptologists Reject the Book of Abraham*, and "The Fall of the Book of Abraham" in the Tanners' book *The Changing World of Mormonism*.[193] *Why Egyptologists Reject the Book of Abraham* includes the independent, unanimous testimony of "eight of the world's greatest [recent] Egyptologists and semitists."[194] The Tanners and Walter Martin also cite several of the world's foremost modern Egyptologists, such as Klaus Baer, R.A. Parker and J.A. Wilson, in confirming that,[195]

> The Mormon Church has yet to produce a single qualified Egyptologist who disagrees with those [critical] findings. Instead, what the Church has done unofficially is to promote Dr. Nibley's apologetic in an attempt to deny what archaeology, history and logic have proved untenable.[196]

Dee Jay Nelson, a Mormon lecturer who translated the book, but after doing so—like Thomas Stuart Ferguson, the Mormon archaeologist cited earlier—he too renounced Mormonism, convinced that the *Book of Abraham* was a forgery. In his letter of resignation to the Mormon church leadership, he stated:

> Following my translation (the first to be published) of the bulk of the hieratic and hieroglyphic Egyptian texts upon the Metropolitan-Joseph Smith Papyri Fragments, three of the most eminent Egyptologists now living published corroborating translations. These amply prove the fraudulent nature of the *Book of Abraham*. . . We do not wish to be associated with a religious organization which teaches lies.*[197]

Here then are the three standard works of Mormonism: the *Book of Mormon*, *Doctrine and Covenants* and *The Pearl of Great Price*. These are the "Word of God" to Mormons. We can only ask what must be an embarrassing question: On what logical basis can Mormons trust their scriptures to be the word of God? Every single one of the standard works

---

*The case against the *Book of Abraham* is not based on Nelson or his academic qualifications as some Mormons have argued. It is based firmly on the science of Egyptology and the conclusions of leading Egyptologists.

has been changed in hundreds or even thousands of places—corrections, additions, deletions, etc.—all initially done without any indication or acknowledgement of such action. Why? Why have even church leaders lied about this in public? What do church leaders know that other Mormons don't? What else are they hiding? In changing their own divine revelations, did Joseph Smith and modern Mormon church leaders think they would thereby inspire confidence in the divine authority of those "revelations?" Why is it that the latest editions of the standard works "contain new and important changes in all three books?"[198] Further, if all these books actually deny what God has already revealed in the Bible, why should anyone trust them in the first place?*

In conclusion, the following chart demonstrates the scriptural problems faced by the Mormon church:

| | Claim | Problem |
|---|---|---|
| *The Bible* | The Bible is the Word of God insofar as it is translated correctly. | The Bible is translated correctly; the *Book of Mormon* isn't. |
| The *Book of Mormon* | Joseph Smith translated the *Book of Mormon* into English through the power of God as "the most correct book of any on earth." | The *Book of Mormon* is replete with changes, errors, and myth; its translation was through occult, not divine means. |
| *Doctrine and Covenants* | *Doctrine and Covenants* is a collection of modern revelations from God. | These revelations have been drastically altered, deny many teachings in the *Book of Mormon*, and are spiritistic in nature. |
| *The Pearl of Great Price* | The *Pearl of Great Price* (the *Book of Moses*, the *Book of Abraham*, and certain writings of Joseph Smith) clarifies doctrine and teachings allegedly lost from the Bible and was divinely translated by Joseph Smith from an Egyptian Papyrus. | The *Book of Moses* was never written by Moses. The *Book of Abraham* has been proven a fraud by the world's leading Egyptologists. Joseph Smith's ability to "divinely translate" is thoroughly discredited. |
| *Joseph Smith and Other Presidents and Prophets of the Mormon Church* | "In addition to these four books of scripture, the inspired words of our living prophets become scripture to us."[199] | Joseph Smith and the Mormon presidents and prophets historically contradict one another to such a degree that building a uniform theology is impossible. |

---

*It might be asking too much to think that men who proclaim a love for truth and yet willingly alter "God's Word" would leave their own Church history unmolested—even that of their own prophet. And it is asking too much. Numerous, detailed changes are made as seem appropriate for a particular time or circumstance. In Appendix One we provide one prominent example from Joseph Smith's six-volume *History of the Church*.

In our next chapter we will document this last point and show why matters proceed from bad to worse.

## ♦ ♦ *Appendix One* ♦ ♦

### Joseph Smith's Alleged History of the Church

Unwarranted changes have also been made in other Mormon literature, perhaps the most notable being Joseph Smith's *History of the Church* (six volumes). Mormons, again, claim it has never been altered or falsified in any way, and that it contains accurate historical material.[200] The text itself maintains that "a history more correct in its details than this was never published."[201] The only confession as to changes made concerns "the correction of a few errors in dates and other details," but nothing more significant; and further, that "no historical or doctrinal statement has been changed."[202]

But none of this is true. The Tanners' text *Changes in Joseph Smith's History* has documented over 62,000 words which have been added or deleted from the first edition[203] (see Resource List). For example, embarrassing facts of Joseph Smith's own life have been deleted, doctrines have been changed and false prophecies have been removed, as the following extended citation reveals:

> Actually, Mormon historians have broken almost all the rules of honesty in their publication of Joseph Smith's *History of the Church*. . . . In many cases they have deleted thousands of words without indication. They have also added thousands of words without any indication. . . . There can be no doubt that the changes were deliberate. . . . Certainly, no one would argue that these changes happened by accident, for they bear unmistakable evidence of falsification.
>
> Mormon historians have also changed some of Joseph Smith's prophecies that did not come to pass. Many exaggerated and contradictory statements were either changed or deleted without indication. Crude or indecent statements were also deleted. . . . In the first printed version of Joseph Smith's history he cursed his enemies, condemned other churches and beliefs, and called the President of the United States a fool. Many of these extreme statements were omitted or changed. Mormon leaders do not dare let their people see the real Joseph Smith. They would rather falsify the *History of the Church* than allow Joseph Smith's true character to be known. Mormon leaders have not only changed the *History of the Church*, but they have further deceived their people by making the claim that no historical or doctrinal statement has been changed.
>
> Not only has the *History of the Church* been changed since it was first printed, but there is also evidence to prove that changes were

made before it was first published. In other words, there is evidence that even the first printed version of the history is inaccurate. It does not agree with the handwritten manuscript.

Since we published our book, *Changes in Joseph Smith's History*, a great deal of information has come to light that supports our conclusion concerning the falsification of Joseph Smith's history. For instance, a microfilm copy of the original handwritten manuscript of Joseph Smith's History, Book A-1 and part of B-1, was given to us. . . . Mormon leaders were very upset about this matter because this film provided devastating evidence against Joseph Smith's history. . . . We had only a few days to examine the documents, but a preliminary examination clearly reveals the duplicity of the early Mormon historians. Now that we have had a brief look at the entire manuscript of Joseph Smith's History—i.e., books A-1—F-1—we must conclude that the history is in a deplorable state. Thousands of words—sometimes entire pages—have been crossed out so that they could be deleted from the printed version. On the other hand, the films show that many pages of material were interpolated after Joseph Smith's death.

Since we now know that more than sixty percent of Joseph Smith's *History of the Church* was not compiled until after his death the question arises as to what sources Mormon historians used to create the purported history. . . . It was, of course, written in the first person to make it appear Joseph Smith was the author.

Our preliminary study of the diaries of Joseph Smith leads us to the conclusion that they were used as a source for the *History of the Church*. Unfortunately, however, there was no attempt to accurately follow the text of the diaries. Mormon leaders used only the parts that suited their purposes. Where a portion did not say what they wanted, they altered it or ignored it completely, sometimes using an entirely different source. The diaries of Joseph Smith, then, tend only to deal another heavy blow to the credibility of Joseph Smith's *History of the Church*. No wonder Mormon leaders suppressed these diaries for so long.

Since it was compiled by men who believed in falsification and deceit, it cannot be trusted as a reliable history of Joseph Smith.[204]

Perhaps it is about time that Mormons demand a frank and truthful account of actions by church leaders, even if it means their prophet and their religion would be seen more truthfully. Dr. Martin emphasizes,

For the average Mormon, one can but have sympathy and regard. He is, by and large, honest, industrious, thrifty and zealous in both the proclamation and promulgation of his beliefs. One only regrets that he has accepted at face value a

carefully edited "history" of the origin and doctrinal development of his religion instead of examining the excellent sources
which not only contradict but irrefutably prove the falsity of
what is most certainly a magnificent reconstructed history.[205]

## ♦ ♦ *Appendix Two* ♦ ♦

### Errors and Anachronisms in Mormon Scripture and Literature

The number of errors in Mormon scripture and other literature is
large; these errors do not speak well for Mormon claims to divine authority. Below we present a sampling.*

*The Garden of Eden is located in Independence, Missouri.*

The tenth president and prophet of the Mormon church, Joseph Fielding Smith, affirmed:

> In accord with the revelations given to the prophet Joseph
> Smith, we teach that the Garden of Eden was on the American
> continent located where the city Zion or the New Jerusalem
> will be built. When Adam and Eve were driven out of the
> Garden, they eventually dwelt at a place called Adam-Ondi-
> Ahman, situated in what is now Davies County, Missouri.[206]

Mormons may claim that the Garden of Eden was located in Missouri,
but the general consensus is that it was located in the fertile crescent of
Mesopotamia. In Genesis 2:10,14, the Bible itself teaches that it was
located near the Tigres and Euphrates Rivers—and these are certainly not
found in Missouri.

*The sun and moon are inhabited.*

Brigham Young declared:

> Who can tell us of the inhabitants of this little planet that
> shines of an evening, called the moon? . . . When you inquire
> about the inhabitants of that sphere you find that the most
> learned are as ignorant in regard to them as the ignorant of
> their fellows. So it is in regard to the inhabitants of the sun. Do
> you think it is inhabited? I rather think it is. Do you think there
> is any life there? No question of it; it was not made in vain.[207]

---

* Most are taken from Tanner, *Changing*, passim (see references) and Whitte, *Where Does It Say That?* 69-73,
passim.

Oliver B. Huntington stated Joseph Smith also believed in moon beings:

> Nearly all the great discoveries of men in the last half century have, in one way or another, either directly or indirectly, contributed to prove Joseph Smith to be a Prophet. As far back as 1837, I know that he said the moon was inhabited by men and women in the same way as this earth, and that they lived to a greater age than we do, that they live generally to near the age of 1,000 years. He describes them as averaging near six feet in height, and dressing quite uniformly in something near the Quaker style. In my Patriarchal blessing, given by the father of Joseph the Prophet, in Kurtland, 1837, I was told that I should preach the gospel before I was 21 years of age; that I should preach the gospel to the inhabitants upon the islands of sea, and—to the inhabitants of the moon, even the planet you can now behold with your eyes (*The Young Woman's Journal*, published by the Young Ladies Improvement Association of Zion, 1892, 3:263,264).[208]

Mormon historian D. Michael Quinn observes, "That the moon and sun were inhabited was [an] equally popular [belief] in early Mormonism."[209]

*Gold and silver grow.*

Brigham Young declared, "Gold and silver grow, and so does every other kind of metal, the same as the hair upon my head, or the wheat in the field."[210]

*The earth is alive and can reproduce.*

We earlier quoted Bruce McConkie as teaching that all forms of life first existed as spirit beings and entities before the earth was created. Thus, there were spirit birds and fish, and spirit plants, trees and shrubs. Every living thing, from the amoeba to the carrot to the dinosaur, existed as spirits before they were placed physically on the earth[211] (McConkie, *The Millennial Messiah*, pp. 642,43, from *Student Manual*, p. 16). *The Journal of Discourses* reports Heber Kimball as stating, "Does the earth conceive? It does. . . . Where did the earth come from? From its parent earths. Well, some of you may call this foolish philosophy, but . . . the earth is alive. If it was not it could not produce."[212]

These teachings can be explained in part by the acceptance of occult philosophy among early Mormons. For example, in Moses 3:5-9 we find a belief in a preexistent spiritual form of all created things; thus many Mormons believed in spirit rocks and vegetables, trees that are living souls, etc. Orson Pratt even believed that the "flesh and bone" Gods ate "spirit" vegetables which prevented death and allowed them to have spirit children.[213]

Nevertheless, Mormon literature aside, there are also numerous errors in Mormon scripture. For example, in *Doctrine and Covenants* (107:49) and *The Pearl of Great Price* (Moses 8:1) Enoch is declared to have been translated to heaven at 430 years old. Yet both Genesis 5:21-23 and Joseph Smith himself teach Enoch was not 430, but 365 years of age.[214]

The *Book of Mormon* also has many errors. As noted, the 1830 edition, as well as its modern counterparts, contain translation errors of the King James Bible. For example, in Isaiah 4:5/2 Nephi 14:5 the correct translation of the Hebrew "chuppah" is canopy, not "defense." In Isaiah 5:25/2 Nephi 15:25 the correct translation of the Hebrew "suchah" is refuse, not "torn."

In Helaman 14:20 the darkness over the face of the land is said to have lasted for three days instead of the biblical three hours (Matthew 27:45; Mark 15:33).

In Alma 46:15 it teaches that the name Christian was taken in the Americas in 73 B.C. whereas in Acts 11:26, "The disciples were first called Christians in Antioch" Syria around A.D. 50.

In another anachronism, "Jesus" quotes part of Revelation 21:6 to the Nephites (3 Nephi 9:18) who, having left Jerusalem in 600 B.C., would have had no knowledge of the Greek language, since Alexander had not yet conquered nor hellenized the known world. Yet, Jesus told the Greek-ignorant Nephites, "I am the Alpha and Omega," a statement which would have been meaningless to them.[215]

In a related matter, both Joseph Smith and Mormons have claimed that the gold plates/*Book of Mormon* have "no Greek or Latin" in them.[216] Yet, Alpha and Omega (3 Nephi 9:18) are distinctly Greek terms, as are the names "Timothy" and "Jonas" (3 Nephi 19:4). The "reformed Egyptian" *Book of Mormon* even has the French word, "Adieu" (Jacob 7:27).

Further, the *Book of Mormon* contains numerous absurdities. For example, it took all of 150,000 workers and overseers seven-and-a-half years to build Solomon's Temple, according to 2 Chronicles 2:2. But the *Book of Mormon* claims that in twenty years' time less than 20 people and their descendants had built a temple like Solomon's. We are told that the temple was not built with gold, silver and precious ores like Solomon's for "they were not found upon the land"—even though they also "were in great abundance" in the land (2 Nephi 5:15-24, cf. v. 28).

These and many other errors and problems of the *Book of Mormon* make it impossible to accept as a divine text.

CHAPTER 24

◆

# The
# Historical
# Teachings of
# Mormonism

*Do Contradictory Teachings Require the Suppression of Information? What Difficulty Does This Present to the Average Mormon?*

In the Church we receive continuing guidance from inspired leaders chosen by the Lord. Through these leaders, the Lord speaks to us and ensures that the true gospel of Jesus Christ is taught.

—*Membership in the Kingdom, Discussion 6, 8*

Mormons claim they have additional scripture as well as "Latter-day prophets" to help them correctly understand "doctrines that have confused apostate Christianity for centuries."[217] The current president and prophet of the Mormon church, Ezra Taft Benson, emphasizes that, "the [Mormon] gospel encompasses all truth; it is consistent, without conflict, eternal."[218] The response of Mormon apologist Hugh Nibley to Fawn Brodie's *No Man Knows My History* was this: "Of all churches in the world only this one has not found it neces-sary to readjust any part of doctrine in the last hundred years. . . . [Mormon doctrine] remains the most stable on earth."[219] Mormons repeatedly claim that their scriptures are not contradictory.[220] Neverthe-less, if early and modern Mormon teachings are compared, one discovers they present conflicting doctrines on many key issues. As Sandra Tanner points out, Mormon "leaders have [had] to go back and rework, rewrite, cover-up, change, delete and add [material] through[out] all of their books—their histories, their Scriptures. They [also] suppress their diaries because these things show the confusion and the man-made nature of their theology and religion."[221]

Because Mormon theology is replete with contradiction, this has led the church to attempt to suppress information it has found embarrassing. This includes the Reorganized Church.[222] Church leaders have appar-ently felt this approach was justified for at least two reasons:

1. The real Joseph Smith is not the one that the church desires to present to the world, hence suppression of true bio-graphical data is necessary. (See chap. 23, Appendix One.)

2. Modern Mormonism rejects many of its earlier prophets' teachings, and its earlier prophets would reject many of the teachings now approved by church leadership.

Mormon leaders have not only unconscionably suppressed important material from non-Mormon researchers, but also from their own church researchers as well![223] We refer the reader to the footnoted sources for further documentation, especially the Tanners' "Change, Censorship and Suppression" in their book *Mormonism–Shadow or Reality?* and their book *The Case Against Mormonism, Vol. 1.*[224] Even some Mormon writers have confessed to this deliberate, historical distortion:

> But the myths and myth-making persists. Striking evi-dence for this is found in the fact that currently one of the most successful anti-Mormon proselytizing techniques is merely to bring to light obscure or suppressed historical documents. . . The reasoning of those who distort or suppress reality or alter historical manuscripts to protect the delusions of the simple believer is similar to that of the man who murders a child to protect him from a violent world.[225]

Some improvements may have been made in recent years; however, the situation is far from corrected. For example, as the Tanners observe:

> A Mormon scholar told us that the journal of George Q. Cannon may never be made available because it contained so

much revealing materials concerning the secret Council of Fifty. Also, the church has still not seen fit to publish the diaries of Joseph Smith and other leading Mormons. We can only hope that the Mormon people will continue to exert pressure until the diaries are printed and all the records are made available to the public.[226]

Dr. D. Michael Quinn, who, as noted earlier, received his Ph.D. in History from Yale University, has spent years in diligent study of Mormon history, including an entire "decade probing thousands of manuscripts diaries and records of Church history."[227] As a result of his historical inquiry into Mormonism, he has produced materials which church authorities are apparently displeased with. He comments, "It is discouraging to be regarded as subversive by men I sustain as prophets, seers, and revelators."[228] Nevertheless, he correctly observes that, "Historians have not created the problem areas of the Mormon past; they are trying to respond to them."[229]

He also asks a legitimate question and then comments upon the consequences of church suppression:

> Why does the well-established and generally respected Mormon Church today need a protective, defensive, paranoid approach to its history? . . . The tragic reality is there have been occasions when Church leaders, teachers, and writers have not told the truth *they knew* about difficulties of the Mormon past, but have offered to the Saints [Mormons] instead a mixture of platitudes, half-truths, omissions, and plausible denials. . . . A so-called "faith-promoting" Church history which conceals controversies and difficulties of the Mormon past actually undermines the faith of Latter-day Saints who eventually learn about the problems from other sources (emphasis added).[230]

For these reasons, he argues, "The Mormon historian has both a religious and professional obligation not to conceal the ambivalence, debate, give-and-take, uncertainty, and simple pragmatism that often attend decisions of the prophet and First Presidency, and not to conceal the limitations, errors, and negative consequences of some significant statements of the prophet and First Presidency."[231]

In regard to the printing of historical materials that have been so damaging to the Mormon church, Dr. Quinn comments, "It is an odd situation when present general authorities criticize historians for reprinting what previous general authorities regarded not only as faith-promoting, but as appropriate for Mormon youth and the newest converts."[232]

Nevertheless, he also observes that there has recently been something of a lessening of church restriction on historical research. For example, in 1966 the critical journal *Dialogue: A Journal of Mormon Thought* was established. Also, the periodical *Brigham Young University Studies* is increasingly devoted to historical issues. Also the institutionally independent Mormon History Association, begun in 1965, has further contributed to the cause of increased exposure to the truth about Mormon history. All this is badly needed; once Mormons are frankly exposed to their true history, they will be more qualified to judge the merits of Mormon religion.

As noted, the principal reasons for suppressing historical data is to present a false portrait of Joseph Smith and to cover up important contradictions and doctrinal changes. For example, the following teachings of the second president and prophet, Brigham Young, and the late leading doctrinal theologian Bruce McConkie are exactly opposite:

*Brigham Young*

> "The only men who become Gods [are exalted]...are those who enter into polygamy."[233]

> "Every man who has the ability to obey and practice it [polygamy] in righteousness and [who] will not [do so] shall be damned."[234]

*Bruce McConkie*

> "Plural marriage is not essential to salvation or exaltation [becoming a god]....All who...engage in plural marriage in this day...will be damned in eternity."[235]

Indeed anyone who carefully examines 1) early and late editions of the *Book of Mormon*, *Doctrine and Covenants*, and *The Pearl of Great Price*, and 2) the teachings of Joseph Smith, Brigham Young and other early leaders compared with those of modern prophets and presidents of the church will find conflicting doctrines. Moreover, these doctrines are those concerning 1) God, 2) Jesus Christ, 3) the Holy Spirit, 4) the virgin birth, 5) original sin, 6) the Trinity, 7) polygamy, 8) death and the afterlife, 9) heaven and hell, 10) exaltation, 11) rebaptism, and 12) many others (some examples are provided in the appendixes).

What all Mormons, early or contemporary, do seem to agree upon is 1) the centrality of Joseph Smith, 2) salvation by works, and 3) opposition to Christianity. Beyond this, conflicting views abound.

Nevertheless, both early and modern doctrines lay equal claim to divine inspiration. Thus, only if modern revelations actually cancel and supersede past ones can any Mormon ascertain God's will: "true doctrine" is then current doctrine, and God's Word of earlier days is discarded. But, then, is not the Word of God itself suspect? On what logical basis can God's revelation today be acceptable while His revelation of a century ago is rejected? However, even putting aside the early versus modern conflicts, there is still a problem because there are serious contradictions even among the modern Mormon scriptures themselves. In light of the extent of this conflict, then, can any Mormon really be expected to know "true doctrine?"

The modern Mormon has no logical solution to the problems such changes in doctrine represent—just as he has no solution to the real person of Joseph Smith or the problems of changes in Mormon scriptures. This is why the response of church leadership has been an attempt to suppress knowledge from the devoted member. Thus, having false and/or insufficient information about their prophet, history and doctrine, Mormons are incapable of independently judging the merits of their own religious convictions.

Where does that leave the average Mormon? Should he or she accept the church's claim that the early prophets *were* true prophets and hence absolutely authoritative? If so, then he or she must charge modern Mormonism (and *not* Christianity) with apostasy—for the modern church absolutely denies many of its early divine revelations.

Or should the average Mormon discard the early Mormon prophets as men who received erroneous revelations and were, therefore, false prophets—since many of their teachings are rejected today by church leadership on the basis of modern revelation? If so, then the entire Mormon church collapses, for it is based squarely upon the divine *authority* of such men.

In the end, the individual Mormon who does not retreat into subjective experiences or wishful thinking is faced with two equally unpleasant options. Either 1) the modern Mormon church is in apostasy and cannot be trusted or 2) the early prophets were deceivers or deceived men and cannot be trusted. In either case, Mormonism is proven to be a false religion.

# ♦ ♦ *Appendix One* ♦ ♦

## Contradictions in Mormon Scripture and Theology

Mormonism and its gods have always emphasized that their church offers no conflict of doctrine. Speaking in *Doctrine and Covenants*, 3:2 "God" says: "For God doth not walk in crooked paths . . . neither doth he vary from that which he hath said. . . ." In the *Book of Mormon* "Jesus" warns: "Neither shall there be disputations among you concerning the points of my doctrine, as there have hitherto been" (3 Nephi 11:28).

In his *Mormon Doctrine*, Bruce McConkie, referring to the church's standard works (the Bible, *Book of Mormon*, *Doctrine and Covenants*, and *The Pearl of Great Price*), declares: "All doctrine, all philosophy, all history, and all matters of whatever nature with which they deal are truly and accurately presented. . . . The Lord's house is a house of order, and one truth never contradicts another."[236]

We need not deal with the contradictions between the Bible and Mormon scriptures, as this has been documented in Sections 4 and 5. We have here selected a fraction of some of the available contradictions to be found within Mormon scripture and historical writings. We compare early Mormonism against itself, early versus modern Mormonism, and modern Mormonism against itself. We should recall that it was the claim of President Brigham Young himself that all his sermons *were* scripture and that most, if not all, Mormon presidents have made similar claims.

The problem is that Mormon contradictions frequently *result* from scripture ("God's doctrine") and, as Mormons emphasize, "in God's Church, the only approved doctrine is God's doctrine."[237] Below we present selected contradictions taken verbatim:

### The Doctrine of Polygamy

Plural marriage is not essential to salvation or exaltation (McConkie, *Mormon Doctrine*, 578).

For behold, I reveal unto you a new and everlasting covenant; and if ye abide not [in] that covenant, then are ye damned; for no one can reject this covenant and be permitted to enter into my glory (*D&C*, 132:4).

Now Zeezrom said: Is there more than one God? And he answered, No (*Book of Mormon*, Alma 11:28,29).

Ques. Are there more Gods than one?

Ans. Yes, many (*Catechism* by Elder John Jacques, chap. 4, p. 13 cited in "Mormonism—Can It Stand Investigation?" p. 7) [tract from UCTS, Box 725, LaMesa, CA 92041].

### Adam in the Garden

The *Book of Mormon*, the Bible, *Doctrine and Covenants*, and *The Pearl of Great Price* all declare that Adam's body was created from the dust of the ground, that is, from the dust of *this ground, this earth* (Joseph Fielding Smith, *Doctrines of Salvation*, 1:90).

Adam was made from the dust of an earth, but not from the dust of *this* earth (Brigham Young, *Journal of Discourses*, 3:319).

When our father Adam came into the Garden of Eden, he came into it with a celestial body (Brigham Young, *Journal of Discourses*, 1:50).

We hear a lot of people talk about Adam passing through mortality and the resurrection on another earth and then coming here to live and die again. Well, that is a contradiction of the word of the Lord, for a resurrected being does not die.... *Adam had not passed through a resurrection when he was in the Garden of Eden* (Joseph Fielding Smith, *Doctrines of Salvation*, 1:91).

### The Evolution of God from Man

The Lord Omnipotent who reigneth, who was, and is from all eternity to all eternity (*Book of Mormon*, Mosiah 3:5).

There is a God in heaven, who is infinite and eternal, from everlasting to everlasting the same unchangeable God (*D&C*, 20:17).

For I know that God is not a partial God, neither a changeable being; but he is unchangeable from all eternity to all eternity (*Book of Mormon*, Moroni 8:18).

I am going to prove it to you by the Bible.... God himself was once as we are now, and is an exalted Man (Joseph Smith, *Journal of Discourses*, 6:3).

### The Omniscience and Omnipotence of God

Each of these personal Gods has equal knowledge with all the rest.... None of these Gods are progressing in knowledge: neither can they progress in the acquirement of any truth.... Some have gone so far as to say that all the Gods were progressing in truth, and would continue to progress to all eternity... but let us examine, for a moment, the absurdity of such a conjecture (Pratt, *The Seer*, Aug. 1853, 117).

God is not omniscient (Brigham Young, quoted in chapter 10).

We might ask, when shall we cease to learn? I will give you my opinion about it; never never... both in time and eternity (Brigham Young, *Journal of Discourses*, 3:203).

God is not progressing in knowledge (McConkie, *Mormon Doctrine*, 1966, 239).

[God has] knowledge of all things... (Joseph Smith, *Lectures on Faith*, 44, cited in McConkie, *Mormon Doctrine*, 545).

[The teaching that] God is progressing or increasing in any of these attributes, [knowledge, faith, power, justice, judgment, mercy, truth is] false heresy (McConkie, *Mormon Doctrine*, 263).

God ... is not advancing in knowledge.... He *is* increasing in power (Joseph Fielding Smith, as cited in *Michael Our Father and Our God*, 27, emphasis added).

## The Fall of Man

That old serpent that did beguile our first parents, which was the cause of their fall; which was the cause of all mankind becoming carnal, sensual, devilish, knowing evil from good, subjecting themselves to the devil. Thus all mankind were lost (*Book of Mormon*, Mosiah 16:3,4).

For the natural man is an enemy to God, and has been from the fall of Adam, and will be, forever and ever, unless he yields to the enticings of the Holy Spirit (Mosiah 3:19).

[God] showed unto all men that they were lost, because of the transgression of their parents (*Book of Mormon*, 2 Nephi 2:21).

In the true gospel of Jesus Christ there is *no original sin*. (John Widstoe, *Evidences and Reconciliation*, 195, in Cowan, 75).

## Treatment of Enemies

As I remarked, we were then very pious, and we prayed the Lord to kill the mob (Apostle George A. Smith, *Journal of Discourses*, 5:107).

But behold I say unto you, love your enemies, bless them that curse you, do good to them that hate you and pray for them who despitefully use you and persecute you; That ye may be the children of your Father who is in heaven (*Book of Mormon*, 3 Nephi 12:44,45).

And may God Almighty curse our enemies. (Voices: "Amen.") ... And the President of the United States inasmuch as he has turned against us.... He shall be

Let every person be in subjection to the governing authorities. For there is no authority except from God, and those which exist are established by God. Therefore he cursed, in the name of Israel's God, and shall not rule over this nation.... And I curse him and all his coadjustors in his cursed deeds, in the name of Jesus Christ (Heber Kimball, *Journal of Discourses*, 5:95).

God Almighty curse such men, (Voices all through the congregation: "Amen!") and women, and every damned thing there is upon the earth that may oppose this people (Heber Kimball, *Journal of Discourses*, 5:32).

The President... will die an untimely death, and God Almighty will curse him; and He will also curse his successor, if he takes the same stand.... God Almighty will curse them, and I curse them in the name of the Lord Jesus Christ, according to my calling.... I pray that God my Father and his Son Jesus Christ may bring the evil upon them... (Heber Kimball, *Journal of Discourses*, 5:133).

who resists authority has opposed the ordinance of God; and they who have opposed will receive condemnation upon themselves (Romans 13:1-2).

First of all, then, I urge that entreaties and prayers, petitions and thanksgivings, be made on behalf of all men, for kings and all who are in authority, in order that we may lead a tranquil and quiet life in all godliness and dignity (1 Timothy 2:1,2).

### The Indwelling of God

The Lord hath said... in the hearts of the righteous doth he dwell (*Book of Mormon*, Alma 34:36).

The idea that the Father and the Son dwell in a man's heart is an old sectarian notion, and is false (*D&C*, 130:3).

### Salvation by Grace

Remember, after ye are reconciled to God, that it is only in and through the grace of God that ye are saved (*Book of Mormon*, 2 Nephi 10:24).

Fulfilling the commandments bringeth remission of sins (*Book of Mormon*, Moroni 8:25). Except ye shall keep my commandments.... Ye shall in no case enter into the kingdom of heaven (*Book of Mormon*, 3 Nephi 12:20).

## God's Immutability

Mormon prophets have continuously taught the sublime truth that God the Eternal Father was once a mortal man (M.R. Hunter, *Gospel Through the Ages*, 104).

Behold I say unto you, he that denieth these things knoweth not the gospel of Christ; yea, he has not read the Scriptures; if so, he does not understand them. For do we not read that God is the same yesterday, today, and forever, and in him there is no variableness neither shadow or changing? And now if ye have imagined up unto yourselves a god who doth vary, and in whom there is shadow of changing, then have ye imagined up unto yourselves a god who is not a God of miracles (*Book of Mormon*, Mormon 9:8-10).

## The Creation of Man

God ... created man, as we create our children; for there is no other process of creation in heaven, on the earth, in the earth, or under the earth, or in all the eternities that is, that were, or that ever will be (Brigham Young, *Journal of Discourses*, 11:122).

By the power of his word man came upon the face of the earth which earth was created by the power of his word. Wherefore, if God being able to speak and the world was, and to speak and man was created, O then, why is he not able to command the earth or the workmanship of his hands upon the face of it, according to his will and pleasure? (*Book of Mormon*, Jac. 4:9).

## The Fall Producing Children

If Adam had not transgressed he would not have fallen. ... And they would have had no children (*Book of Mormon*, 2 Nephi 2:22,23).

Were it not for our transgressions we never should have had seed (*The Pearl of Great Price*, Moses 5:11).

And I, God, created man in mine own image. ... Male and female created I them. And I, God, blessed them, and said unto them: Be fruitful and multiply (*The Pearl of Great Price*, Moses 2:27,28).

## Child Baptism

And their children shall be baptized for the remission of their sins when eight years old (*D&C*, 68:27).

Listen to the words of Christ ... your Lord and God.... I know that it is solemn mockery before God, that ye should baptize little children.... Yea, teach parents that they must repent and be baptized (*Book of Mormon*, Moroni 8:8-10).

## Polygamy

I, the Lord, justified my servants Abraham, Isaac, and Jacob, as also Moses, David and Solomon, my servants, as touching the principle doctrine of their having many wives and concubines (*D&C*, 132:1).

Behold, David and Solomon truly had many wives and concubines which thing was abominable before me, saith the Lord.... For there shall not any man among you have save it be one wife; and concubines he shall have none (*Book of Mormon*, Jac. 2:24,27).

Thou shalt love thy wife with all thy heart, and shalt cleave unto her and none else.... Thou shalt not commit adultery (*D&C*, 42:22, 24).

We declare that we believe that man should have one wife (*D&C*, section 109 [CIX], 1866 edition).

## Salvation by Grace

"Salvation is *free*" (2 Nephi 2:4), but it must also be *purchased*; and the *price* is obedience to the laws and ordinances of the gospel. Eternal life is available *freely*, "without money and without price" (Isaiah 55:1; 2 Nephi 9:50), but it is gained only by those who *buy* it at the storehouse of the Great God who pleads with men to purchase his priceless possession (McConkie, *Doctrinal New Testament Commentary*, 3:461).

## New Revelation

God alone can add to *or diminish* from holy writ. What he has spoken, he has spoken, and none but he can alter (McConkie, *Doctrinal New Testament Commentary*, 3:593).

### God As Spirit?

The Father [is] a personage of *spirit* [meaning that he has a spiritual body which by revealed definition is a resurrected body *of flesh and bones...*] (brackets in original) (McConkie, *Doctrinal New Testament Commentary*, 2:160,161).

### Idolatry

Worship of any god rather than the true God is in fact service to the *creature* rather than the Creator.... God is an exalted *Man* from whose presence there proceeds a light and power which *fills the immensity of space* and which is called the Light of Christ or the Spirit of the Lord. In their worship of a spirit essence that *fills immensity*, the sectarians are in effect worshiping and serving the creature rather than the Creator (McConkie, *Doctrinal New Testament Commentary*, 2:218,219).

### Church Unity

[In light of more than one hundred Mormon sects historically, each one claiming to be the only true Church] Existence of the sects of Christendom is proof positive of the universal apostasy. Truth is one; Christ is not divided; *those who enjoy the Spirit all speak the same things; there are no divisions among them*; but they are "perfectly joined together in the same mind and in the same judgment" (1 Corinthians 1:10-13) (McConkie, *Mormon Doctrine*, 699).

## ♦ ♦ *Appendix Two* ♦ ♦

### Mormon Scripture and Biblical Theology: Contrasts and Denials

Hundreds of contrasts could be listed. We list twenty-five representative samples.

#### The Gates of Hell Prevailed

The gates of hell have prevailed and will continue to prevail over the Catholic Mother of Harlots, and over *all* her Protestant Daughters (*Pamphlets* by Orson Pratt, 112, cited by Jerald and Sandra Tanner, *Changing World*, 27).

The kingdoms of this world made war against the kingdom of God . . . and they prevailed against it. . . . [It has been] overcome and nothing is left (Orson Pratt, *Journal of Discourses*, 13:125).

. . . I will build My church; and the gates of Hades shall not overpower it (Matthew 16:18).

#### "Justification" by Polygamy

Abraham received concubines, and they bore him children; and it was accounted unto him for righteousness (*D&C*, 132:37).

For what does the Scripture say? "And Abraham believed God, and it was reckoned to him as righteousness." Now to the one who works, his wage is not reckoned as a favor but as what is due. But to the one who does not work, but believes in Him who justifies the ungodly, his faith is reckoned as righteousness, just as David also speaks of the blessing upon the man to whom God reckons righteousness apart from works (Romans 4:3-6).

## Hatred of Enemies

In Missouri we were taught to "pray for our enemies, that *God would damn them, and give us power to kill them*" (Letter, B.F. Johnson, 1903, cited in Jerald and Sandra Tanner, *Changing World*, p. 485, see *Journal of Discourses* 5:32,95,107,133; 7:122 for similar examples).

You have heard that it was said, "You shall love your neighbor, and hate your enemy." But I say to you, love your enemies, and pray for those who persecute you (Matthew 5:43,44).

Never pay back evil for evil to anyone. Respect what is right in the sight of all men (Romans 12:17).

## Man As Inherently Good

It is, however, universally received by professors of religion as a Scriptural doctrine that man is naturally opposed to God. This is not so. Paul says in his Epistle to the Corinthians, "But the natural man receiveth not the things of God." But I say it is the unnatural "man that receiveth not the things of God." ... *The natural man is of God* (Brigham Young, *Journal of Discourses*, 9:305).

But a natural man does not accept the things of the Spirit of God; for they are foolish to him, and he cannot understand them, because they are spiritually appraised (1 Corinthians 2:14).

This I say therefore, and affirm together with the Lord, that you walk no longer just as the Gentiles also walk, in the futility of their mind, being darkened in their understanding, excluded from the life of God, because of the ignorance that is in them, because of the hardness of their heart (Ephesians 4:17,18).

It is not natural for men to be evil (John Taylor, 3rd President, *Journal of Discourses*, 10:50).

As it is written, "There is none righteous, not even one; There is none who understands; There is none who seeks for God; All have turned aside, together they have become useless; there is none who does good, there is not even one" (Romans 3:10-12).

## Eternal Matter

We are told by our Father in heaven that *man is eternal*; that he

[The] only Sovereign, the King of kings and Lord of lords; who has always existed, and that *all life on this earth came from elsewhere* (Joseph Fielding Smith, *Doctrines of Salvation*, 1:74).

"The elements are eternal." (*D&C*, 93:33); "matter or element is...eternal in nature, creation being merely the organization and reorganization of that substance" (McConkie, *Doctrinal New Testament Commentary*, 3:225); "it is an utterly false and uninspired notion to believe the world or any other thing was created out of nothing" (McConkie, *Mormon Doctrine*, 169).

alone possesses immortality (1 Timothy 6:15,16)

By faith we understand that the worlds were prepared by the word of God, so that what is seen was not made out of things which are visible (Hebrews 11:3).

God "calls into being that which does not exist" (Romans 4:17).

"By the word of the Lord the heavens were made, and by the breath of His mouth all their host.... For He spoke, and it was done; He commanded, and it stood fast" (Psalm 33:6,9).

## Justification by Works

Man is justified by works (McConkie, *Doctrinal New Testament Commentary*, 3:260).

For we maintain that a man is justified by faith apart from works of the Law (Romans 3:28).

By the works of the Law no flesh will be justified in His sight (Romans 3:20).

## No Original Sin

In the true gospel of Jesus Christ there is no original sin (John Widtsoe, *Evidences and Reconciliations*, 195, in Cowan, 75).

Through one transgression there resulted condemnation to all men (Romans 5:18).

## Sin Is Not Transgression of Law

It is possible to transgress a law without committing sin, as in the case of Adam (McConkie, *Mormon Doctrine*, 804).

Sin is lawlessness [the transgression of law] (1 John 3:4).

## Eternal Marriage

Marriages performed in the temples for time and eternity, by

For when they rise from the dead, they neither marry, nor are virtue of the sealing keys restored by Elijah, are called *celestial marriages....* By definition exaltation consists in the continuation of the family unit in eternity.... Celestial marriage is a holy and an eternal ordinance.... Its importance in the plan of salvation and exaltation cannot be overestimated (McConkie, *Mormon Doctrine*, 117,118).

given in marriage, but are like angels in heaven (Mark 12:25).

## God in Evolution

Remember that God our Heavenly Father was perhaps once a child, and mortal like we are and rose step by step in the scale of progress (Orson Hyde, *Journal of Discourses*, 1:123).

Two of the names of God the Father are, *Man of Holiness,* and *Man of Counsel* (Moses 6:57; 7:35); that is, God is a holy Man, a Man who is perfect in counsel (McConkie, *Mormon Doctrine*, 465).

For I am God and not man (Hosea 11:9); from everlasting to everlasting, Thou art God (Psalm 90:2).

## Rejection of Christ's Deity

Jesus *became* a God ... through consistent effort (M.R. Hunter, *Gospel Through the Ages*, Salt Lake City: *Deseret*, 1945, 51, in McElveen, 154).

The Word was God (John 1:1). Jesus Christ is the same yesterday and today, yes and forever (Hebrews 13:8). His goings forth are from long ago, from the days of eternity (Micah 5:2).

## Genealogical Work

Hence, genealogical research is required (McConkie, *Mormon Doctrine*, 308).

Nor to pay attention to myths and endless genealogies, which give rise to mere speculation rather than furthering the administration of God which is by faith (1 Timothy 1:4).

But shun foolish controversies and genealogies and strife and disputes about the Law; for they are unprofitable and worthless (Titus 3:9).

## Creation Order

*Pre-existence* is the term commonly used to describe the *premortal existence* of the spirit-children of God the Father (Spiritual existence first, then physical) (McConkie, *Mormon Doctrine*, 589).

However, the spiritual is not first, but the natural; then the spiritual (1 Corinthians 15:46). (See context; biblically, our material existence is first, then the spiritual.)

Thus declares the Lord who stretches out the heavens, lays the foundation of the earth, and forms the spirit of man within him (Zechariah 12:1).

## The Gospel

Men either have the truths of salvation or they do not; they either possess the gospel which is the plan of salvation or they do not. If they have the gospel, it is in overall scope and in minutest detail, exactly what Paul had. If any part or portion of their system of religion differs from what the ancient Apostle taught and believed, what they have is in fact a perversion of the true gospel (McConkie, *Doctrinal New Testament Commentary*, 2:458).

For by grace you have been saved through faith; and that not of yourselves, it is the gift of God, not as a result of works, that no one should boast (Ephesians 2:8,9).

## The Indwelling of God

The idea that the Father and the Son dwell in a man's heart is an old sectarian notion, and is false (*D&C*, 130:3).

Jesus answered and said to him, "If anyone loves Me, he will keep My word; and My Father will love him, and We will come to him, and make Our abode with him" (John 14:23).

## Adam as God

Adam is our Father and Our God (Brigham Young, *Journal of Discourses*, 1:50).

Then to Adam He said, " .. you are dust, and to dust you shall return" (Genesis 3:17,19).

## Priesthood Authority

Priesthood is the power and authority of God delegated to man on earth to act in all things for the salvation of men (McConkie, *Mormon Doctrine*, 594).

For there is one God, and one mediator also between God and men, the man Christ Jesus (1 Timothy 2:5).

## Source of Salvation

There is no salvation outside the Church of Jesus Christ of Latter-day Saints (McConkie, *Mormon Doctrine*, 670).

But as many as received Him, to them He gave the right to become children of God, even to those who believe in His name (John 1:12).

Whoever believes in the Son has eternal life; but whoever rejects the Son will not see life, for God's wrath remains on him (John 3:36).

## The Holy Spirit and Baptism

Cornelius... could not receive the gift of the Holy Ghost until after he was baptized (Joseph Smith, *Teachings*, 199).

Cornelius received "the gift of the Holy Spirit" *before* he was baptized (Acts 10:43-48).

## The Creation

There really was no beginning because God and matter are eternal (Wallace, *Can Mormonism Be Proven Experimentally?* 163).

In the beginning God created the heavens and the earth (Genesis 1:1).

## Death

Physical death is part of the plan of happiness our Father prepared for us (*Eternal Progression, Discussion 4*, 8).

The last enemy to be destroyed is death (1 Corinthians 15:26).

◆

# CHAPTER 25

# Mormonism's Prophetic Record

## Are There Demonstrable False Prophecies Within Mormon Scripture and Literature?

**B** efore we begin this chapter, let us briefly review our findings. To date, we have shown that the claim of the Mormon church to divine revelation cannot be trusted.

In Sections 2, 3, 4 and 5, we proved that the Mormon church cannot be considered Christian because it denies and rejects virtually every Christian doctrine. In fact, we saw that Mormon religion shared many characteristics with pagan religion. In Section 6 we revealed that Mormonism should also properly be classified as an occult religion because of its strong ties to occult practice and philosophy.

In the last four chapters we have shown that a) Joseph Smith's "first vision" account cannot be accepted as a divine revelation, b) that the *Book of Mormon* cannot be believed as a divine revelation, c) that none of the other Mormon scriptures can be trusted as divine revelation—if for no other reason than the fact that Mormon authorities themselves treat them with great irreverence—and d) that Mormonism's historical theology is so contradictory that it cannot logically be interpreted as a divine revelation. All of this clearly amounts to a disproof of the Mormon religion.

Nevertheless, there is one final area relative to Mormon claims to divine revelation that must be discussed. In chapter 4 we explained that the legitimacy and validity of the entire Mormon church rested squarely upon its declaration that Joseph Smith was a genuine prophet of God. If he was not, then the Mormon church has been guilty of promoting a false prophet to the world for over 170 years.

Mormons themselves freely confess that upon the authority of Joseph Smith the church stands or falls. If he was a false prophet, the church cannot be genuine. This is why the issue of prophecy is so vital. Apostle James Talmage said of Smith, "If his claims to divine appointment be false, forming as they do the foundation of the church in this last dispensation, the superstructure cannot be stable."[238] Given this, Mormon authorities have no choice but to perpetuate the claim that Joseph Smith was a true prophet and that his hundreds of prophecies were "literally fulfilled," and are therefore the "marvelous proof" of his divine appointment. For example, the late leading doctrinal theologian Bruce McConkie argues:

> By their works it shall be known whether professing ministers of religion are true or false prophets. Joseph Smith was a true prophet. What fruits did he leave? There is probably more evidence of his divine call and mission than of any other prophet who ever lived, Jesus himself only excepted. Joseph Smith has . . . uttered hundreds of prophecies which have been literally fulfilled.[239]

Joseph Smith himself emphasized that one who claims to be a true prophet of God must have his prophecies evaluated by the standard of God's Word. By his statement "the ancient Word of God" he clearly referred to biblical standards in part:

> The only way of ascertaining a true prophet is to compare his prophecies with the ancient Word of God, and see if they agree, and if they do and come to pass, then certainly he is a true prophet. . . . When, therefore any man, *no matter who*, or how high his standing may be, utters, or publishes, anything that afterwards proves to be untrue, *he is a false prophet.*[240]

By Joseph Smith's own words, then, he is proven to be a false prophet. And by the very words of Mormon authorities the Mormon religion also is proven to be fraudulent. Not only do the many prophecies given by Joseph Smith in *Doctrine and Covenants* deny every biblical doctrine they comment upon, but Joseph Smith's specific predictions of future events have also characteristically proven wrong. While we have not studied every alleged prophecy Mormons claim for Smith, every one we did study proved false.

In 1844, while in jail, Smith was killed by an angry group of townspeople. By that time, he had uttered scores of prophecies "in the name of the Lord." But according to biblical standards, anyone who claims to be a prophet must prove himself so by establishing a perfect record of prediction (see chap. 4). Again, the biblical requirement is for absolute accuracy in prophetic revelation. What this means is that a single false prophecy—

just one—is sufficient to establish a person as a false prophet. God Himself warned all men:

> "But a prophet who presumes to speak in my name any-thing I have not commanded him to say, or a prophet who speaks in the name of other gods, must be put to death." You may say to yourselves, "How can we know when a message has not been spoken by the Lord?" If what a prophet proclaims in the name of the Lord does not take place or come true, that is a message the Lord has not spoken. That prophet has spoken presumptuously. Do not be afraid of him (Deuteronomy 18:20-22 NIV).

In other words, if anyone spoke in the name of the Lord (Joseph Smith), but spoke presumptuously (Joseph Smith), or in the name of other gods (Joseph Smith), and if the prophecy did not come true (Joseph Smith), that prophet was to die—as, unfortunately, Joseph Smith did in 1844. When Mormon authorities claim that Smith's prophetic record is infallible and that this proves him a true prophet, they are regrettably only continuing the well-established tradition of Mormon distortion in religious matters.

Mormons have in fact devised various ways to "explain" Smith's many false prophecies. There are so many different rationalizations that one wearies of reading them. For example, they may claim, as Smith himself did, that a prophet is only a prophet when he is acting as such—that is, presumably, when he claims to speak in the name of the Lord and is therefore under divine inspiration. Mormons claim that any errors which do exist were, therefore, given when Smith was not "acting" as a prophet.

However, since many of Smith's false prophecies *were* given "as a prophet," when he *was* speaking in the name of the Lord, the explanation is irrelevant.

For anyone who lets words mean what they say, the inescapable conclusion is that, according to biblical standards, Joseph Smith was a false prophet. Just as the single act of marital infidelity or a single premeditated killing makes a person an adulterer or a murderer, so a single false prophecy makes one a false prophet.[241] Joseph Smith himself agreed to that standard. In the following cases, we include examples where Smith clearly prophesied "in the name of the Lord," so there can be no mistake that the prophecy was being claimed as divine.

### The Canadian Prophecy

David Whitmer (one of the three principal witnesses to the *Book of Mormon*) tells a highly relevant story which not only reveals Smith to be a false prophet, but sprouts seeds of doubt about any purported prophecy or revelation Smith claimed to receive. Just as the Mormon scriptures, in particular *Doctrine and Covenants,* contain the "feel" of occult revelation, here we also sample the flavor of spiritistic "humor."

Here is the story in Whitmer's own words:

> When the Book of Mormon was in the hands of the printer, more money was needed to finish the printing of it.... Brother Hyrum said it had been suggested to him that some of the brethren might go to Toronto, Canada and sell the copyright of the Book of Mormon for considerable money: and he persuaded Joseph to inquire of the Lord about it. Joseph concluded to do so. He had not yet given up the [seer] stone. Joseph looked into the hat in which he placed the stone, and *received a revelation* that some of the brethren should go to Toronto, Canada, *and that they would sell the copyright* of the Book of Mormon. Hyrum Page and Oliver Crowdery went to Toronto on this mission, but *they failed entirely to sell the copyright,* returning without any money. Joseph was at my father's house when they returned. I was there also, and am *an eyewitness* to these facts. Jacob Whitmer and John Whitmer were also present when Hyrum Page and Oliver Crowdery returned from Canada.
>
> Well, we were all in great trouble; and we asked Joseph how it was that he had received a revelation from the Lord for some brethren to go to Toronto and sell the copy-right and the brethren had utterly failed in their undertaking. Joseph did not know how it was, so he inquired of the Lord about it, and behold the following revelation came through the stone:
>
> > *Some revelations are of God: some revelations are of man: and some revelations are of the devil.*
>
> So we see that [even though Smith claimed it was] the revelation to go to Toronto and sell the copyright was not of God, but was of the devil or of the heart of man.... This was a lesson for our benefit *and we should have profited by it in [the] future more than we did.*

Whitmer concludes his discussion with a warning to every living Mormon:

> Remember this matter brethren; it is very important.... Now is it wisdom to put your trust in Joseph Smith, and believe all his revelations in the *Doctrine and Covenants* to be of God?... I will say here, that I could tell you *other false revelations* that came through Brother Joseph as mouthpiece (not through the stone), but this will suffice. Many of Brother Joseph's revelations were never printed. The revelation to go to Canada was written down on paper, but was never printed (emphasis added).[242]

Let's consider this account carefully. Smith and the other Mormons were obviously convinced of the divine authority of the initial revelation—or else they would never have taken the difficult journey to Canada. When the prophecy inexplicably failed, they naturally sought an answer from God (by occult means)—and what happened? They received a reply that could not help but strike dread into their hearts: "Some revelations are of God; some revelations are of man; and some revelations are of the devil." Apparently, then, there was no way to distinguish a true prophecy from a false one!

Thus, if this *false* revelation was *indistinguishable* from the genuine revelations of Smith, how can Mormons today know that any of Smith's revelations were legitimate? And what does this fact do to the credibility of the revelations given by any Mormon president and prophet? What is worse, such revelations will never be objectively verified or invalidated. Why? Because the Bible itself is rejected by Mormonism as a reliable authority (chap. 27). This means that the only "Scripture" left to test such revelation by is Mormon scripture, which is itself contradictory and perpetually "open." New revelations can come at any time and be added to the canon of scripture. Whether or not they contradict earlier revelation is irrelevant. In the end, we see that no Mormon should logically place trust in any of Smith's prophecies (or any of his other revelations) because 1) they could just as easily be false as true, and 2) there is no way to tell the difference until it is too late.

Nevertheless, we will proceed to document some of the false prophecies of Joseph Smith. Let us begin with the alleged scripture, *Doctrine and Covenants*. The first false prophecy is found in chapter one, where "God" Himself promises that the prophecies in the book are all true and will come to pass:

> Search these commandments, for they are true and faithful, and the prophecies and promises which are in them *shall all be fulfilled*. What I the Lord have spoken, I have spoken, *and I excuse not myself*; and though the heavens and the earth pass away, my word shall not pass away, but *shall all be fulfilled*, whether *by mine own voice or by the voice of my servants, it is the same*. For behold, and lo, the Lord is God, and the Spirit beareth record, and *the record is true*, and the truth abides forever and ever. Amen (*D&C*, 1:37,38, emphasis added).

Note that this section of Mormon scripture claims first, that the commandments "are true" and that the prophecies and promises "shall all be fulfilled"; second, that the Mormon deity is placing his own authority on the line when he says, "I excuse not myself" (for having spoken them), and third, that the prophecies "shall all be fulfilled" whether by God's own voice "or by the voice of my servants"—which is the same thing.

These claims leave no room to maneuver: A single indisputable false prophecy anywhere in *Doctrine and Covenants* will completely invalidate the entire book. Obviously, then, the existence of dozens and scores of false prophecies in *Doctrine and Covenants* means that Mormons who trust this book are being deceived. If 1) the Mormon God has spoken falsely, and 2) "some revelations are of God, some revelations are of men, and some revelations are of the devil," and 3) there is no way of knowing which are which, then the logical conclusion is that 4) Mormons should not place their trust in any of them. We will now prove that *Doctrine and Covenants* contains false prophecies.

## The City and Temple Prophecy

In a revelation given to Joseph Smith on September 22 and 23, 1832, "the word of the Lord" declares that both a city and a temple are to be built "in the western boundaries of the state of Missouri" (that is, in Independence, Missouri):

> A revelation of Jesus Christ unto his servant Joseph Smith, Jun[ior]. . . . *Yea, the word of the Lord* concerning his church . . . for the gathering of his saints to stand upon Mount Zion, which shall be the city of New Jerusalem. Which *city shall be built*, beginning at the temple lot . . . *in the western boundaries of the state of Missouri*, and dedicated by the hand of Joseph Smith. . . . Verily *this is the word of the Lord*, that the city New Jerusalem shall be built by the gathering of saints, beginning at this place, even the place of the temple, which temple shall be reared *in this generation. For verily this generation shall not all pass away* until an house shall be built unto the Lord, and a cloud shall rest upon it, which cloud shall be even the glory of the Lord, which shall fill the house. . . . Therefore, as I said concerning the sons of Moses—for the sons of Moses and also *the sons of Aaron shall offer an acceptable offering and sacrifice in the house of the Lord*, which house shall be built under the Lord *in this generation*, upon the consecrated spot as *I have appointed* (*D&C*, 84:1-5,31, emphasis added).

This prophecy clearly teaches that a temple and a city will be built in western Missouri in the generation of the men *then living* and that it will be dedicated by the hand of Joseph Smith himself. This temple will stand (in western Missouri) "upon Mount Zion" and the city will be named "the city of New Jerusalem." It was to be the place Christ returned to at His Second Coming.[243]

In *Doctrine and Covenants*, 97:19 (August, 1833) and 101:17-21 (December, 1833), God further declares that He is absolutely certain as to His intent and the location of this temple: "Zion cannot fall, nor be moved out of her place, for God is there, and the hand of the Lord is there," and "there is none other place appointed than that which I have appointed; neither shall there be any other place."

It is interesting to note that on July 20, 1833, when Smith was giving this prophecy in Kirtland, Ohio—and unaware of the events taking place in Missouri—the Mormon community had already agreed to leave Missouri because of "persecution." In other words, even as Smith was giving the prophecy "in the name of the Lord," "Zion" was already being "moved out of her place."[244]

How do Mormons respond? They claim the prophecy failed because the Mormon community itself was unfaithful. However, how can Mormons credibly claim this when the church itself was being "persecuted"? Surely, if they had not been living as committed and zealous Mormons, they would never have encountered the social response they did. (See chap. 3, appendix.) It was thus undoubtedly the *faithful* Mormons who were driven from Missouri, leaving the prophecy unfulfilled. And even Mormon historians concede that when they moved to Quincy, Illinois, their promised Missouri "temple" comprised only four cornerstones.[245]

In the ensuing 160 years no temple has ever been built in western Missouri, let alone a Mormon city. Thus Joseph Smith never dedicated a temple, nor were sacrifices offered there. It was not built in "this generation," no cloud "rested upon" the temple, etc. This revelation alone thus contains at least *four* false prophecies. Neither can Mormons logically claim that Zion was "reestablished" in Salt Lake City, for the December 1833 prophecy clearly says there will be "none other place" than the western boundaries of Missouri.

Nevertheless, the Mormon reaction to this prediction illustrates the basic Mormon approach to their many false prophecies. Divine predictions are vigorously maintained until proven false. Then they are rationalized. Consider the following train of events.

In spite of being driven from Missouri, the early Mormons intended to return and fulfill the prophecy. In 1861, thirty years after the prophecy was first given, Apostle George Smith emphasized, "Let me remind you that it is predicted that this generation shall not pass away till a temple shall be built, and the glory of the Lord rest upon it, according to the promises."[246]

Then in 1870, almost forty years after the prophecy, Apostle Orson Pratt stated that Mormons could expect a literal fulfillment of the prophecy as much as they do the rising and setting of the sun. Why? *"Because God cannot lie. He will fulfill all his promises. He has spoken, it must come to pass. This is our faith!"*[247]

Perhaps sensing a growing problem, the 1890 edition of *Doctrine and Covenants* (almost sixty years later) carried a footnote declaring that a generation lasted more than a hundred years.[248] This note is not found in *modern* editions of *Doctrine and Covenants*.

Again, in 1900, almost seventy years later, the fifth Mormon president and prophet, Lorenzo Snow, reiterated that Mormons would still go back and build the divinely prophesied temple.[249]

Even in 1931, ninety-nine years after the prophecy (when "that generation" would surely have been dead), the tenth president and prophet of the Mormon church, Joseph Fielding Smith, was stating his "firm belief" that the temple and city would be built. Thus, he promises that when the temple is reared it will be by:

> Some of that generation who were living when this revelation was given. . . . I have full confidence in the word of the Lord that *it shall not fail. . . . We have not been released from this responsibility, nor shall we be. The word of the Lord will not fail. . . .* No matter what the correct interpretation may be, the fact remains that *the city Zion*, or New Jerusalem, *will eventually be built* in Jackson County, Missouri *and the temple of the Lord will also be constructed.*[250]

Incredibly, recent editions of Smith's book (e.g., 1975) continue to retain this embarrassing statement! Logically, one would think that he would have had to confess that his "full confidence in the word of the Lord" proved futile. Who could disagree with his words when he stated in a more recent text: "It is also reasonable to believe that no soul living in 1832, is still living in mortality on the earth."[251]

It is now more than 160 years since the prophecy, and neither the temple nor the city has been built. There is no way to escape the conclusion that this prophecy is false. But, of course, since Mormonism assumes that Joseph Smith was a true prophet of God, this cannot possibly be a false prophecy. So the process of rationalization sets in. For example, Joseph Fielding Smith dealt with the problem by finally claiming that the term "generation" meant an *indefinite* period of time and that, due to "persecution," God had "absolved the saints and postponed the day."[252]

Now everyone could relax. There never was a false prophecy.

For some reason, Mormon presidents, prophets and leaders see "no conflict whatever" between the outcome of the prophecy just cited and the teaching of the *Book of Mormon* in Nephi 3:7 which says, "The Lord giveth no commandments unto the children of men, save he shall prepare a way for them that they may accomplish the thing which he commandeth them."

What is most disconcerting is that modern Mormons do not seem to be concerned with such an unquestionably false prophecy and refuse to recognize the implications.[253] They continue to believe, and to teach others, that *Doctrine and Covenants* is the inerrant "word of the Lord."

**The Civil War Prophecy**

The Civil War prophecy represents another false prediction. It is found in *Doctrine and Covenants* 87:1-8, concerning a prophecy given on December 25, 1832. In his *Articles of Faith*, James Talmage refers to "the facts establishing a complete fulfillment of this astounding prophecy."[254]

However, there was no "complete fulfillment," neither was the prophecy "astounding." It was patently false. What is astounding is that Talmage applies the 1832 prophecy to World War I (1914-1918) when it has nothing at all to do with that war. Indeed, to apply the prophecy to World War I only increases the magnitude of its errors. For one thing, its own declaration requires it be applied to the "wars that will shortly come to pass, beginning... at South Carolina." The prophecy declares:

> Verily, *thus sayeth the Lord* concerning the wars that will shortly come to pass, beginning at the rebellion of South Carolina, which will eventually terminate in the death and misery of many souls; And the time will come when that war will be poured out upon *all nations*, beginning at this place.... And the Southern States will call on other nations, even the nation of Great Britain, as it is called, and they shall also call upon other nations, in order to defend themselves against other nations; and then war shall be poured out upon *all nations*.... And thus, with the sword and by bloodshed *the inhabitants of earth* shall mourn; and with famine, and plague, and earthquake, and the thunder of heaven, and the fierce and vivid lightening also, shall the *inhabitants of the earth* be made to feel the wrath, and indignation, and chastening hand of Almighty God until the consumption decreed hath made *a full end of all nations.*[255]

Joseph Smith made other predictions relating to this great war. Elsewhere he spoke another false prophecy when he declared "in the name of the Lord God" that these tumultuous events would precede the Second Coming of Jesus Christ:

> I prophecy [sic], *in the name of the Lord God*, that the commencement of the difficulties which will cause much bloodshed *previous to the coming of the Son of man* will be in South Carolina. It may probably arise through the slave question. This a voice declared to me while I was praying earnestly on the subject, December 25, 1832.[256]

But listening to voices can be perilous.

In looking at this prophecy, we should note several facts. First, it has been demonstrated historically that Smith could have expected a civil war, hence to write of an expected war, one that is public knowledge, is hardly "astounding." For example, "Joseph Smith was familiar with the fact that South Carolina had rebelled at the time he gave the revelation."[257] Also, "many people believed there would be a civil war before it actually took place."[258] For example, five months *previous* to Smith's "revelation," on July 14, 1832, Congress passed a tariff act, refused by South Carolina, and Andrew Jackson alerted the troops. So, even at this time, "the nation was fully expecting a Civil War to begin promptly in South Carolina."[259]

Second, even God Himself didn't seem to know whether or not this great war would arise over the issue of slavery. (He said, "It may *probably* arise through the slave question.")

Third, the revelation itself was wrong on numerous counts. First, the war did not start until 1861, thirty years later—it did not "come to pass shortly." Second, war was not "poured out upon all nations" but only on one nation. Third, there were no "earthquakes," "thunder of heaven," or lightening which struck the "inhabitants of the earth" as evidence of God's wrath. Nor did the remainder of the earth's population feel "the wrath of Almighty God." Fourth, there was hardly "a full end of all nations."

Finally, Smith's revelation on the war was not printed until 1851, almost twenty years *after* the revelation, and "Mormon leaders have suppressed part of Joseph Smith's diary which tended to discredit the revelation."[260] (This concerned a "dream interpretation" of the prophecy which stated that the United States Government would call on Joseph Smith to defend the "western territory" against England. Smith was obviously dead at the start of the Civil War, thus the interpretation was false, which cast doubt on the revelation itself.[261]) In conclusion, no one can deny that this is another false prophecy.

Brigham Young was also guilty of false prophecy relating to the Civil War. He predicted that the war would not end until it had emptied the land to allow Mormons to return to Missouri, something that was never fulfilled.[262] He also predicted that the slaves would *not* be freed: "Will the present struggle free the slaves? No; . . . they cannot do that."[263]

Joseph Smith's Civil War prophecy and his "Rocky Mountain" prophecy are considered his "most important prophecies."[264] We have seen that the first is a false prophecy; and the Tanners have documented that the latter is not worth considering in that it is a "forgery which was written after Joseph Smith's death."[265]

## The Second Coming

Along with Jehovah's Witnesses and Seventh-day Adventists, Joseph Smith predicted that the Second Coming of Christ would occur in the latter part of the nineteenth century. In his *History of the Church*, Smith taught that the Second Coming would occur between 1890 and 1891.

Thus, in 1835 he declared Christ's return would occur fifty-six years later; and in 1843 he predicted it would occur in forty-eight years. Smith claimed that the generation then living would not die "till Christ comes."[266] For example, under the date of April 6, 1843, in his *original* History (taken from Smith's diary, March 10, 1843, to July 14, 1843) one can read, "I prophecy [sic] *in the name of the Lord God*—& let it be written: that the Son of Man will not come in the heavens until I am 85 years old, 48 years hence or about 1890" (emphasis added).[267] Of course, Smith was dead within a year—and Christ still has not returned.

Some of the twelve Mormon apostles were told that they also would remain until Christ returned. For example, according to the Tanners, Lyman E. Johnson was told he would "see the Savior come and stand upon the earth with power and great glory"; and William Smith was told that he would "be preserved and remain on the earth, until Christ shall come."[268] Because of such a strong belief in the imminence of the Second Coming, Apostle Parley P. Pratt wrote in 1838:

> I will state *as a prophesy* [sic], that there will not be an unbelieving Gentile upon this continent 50 years hence; and if they are not greatly scourged, and in a great measure overthrown, within five or ten years from this date, *then the Book of Mormon will have proved itself false.*[269]

Perhaps not unexpectedly, the entire prophecy has been deleted from the modern versions of the *Writings of Parley P. Pratt.*

But there have been many other false prophecies throughout the history of the Mormon church, far too numerous to list. We cite only seven others for purposes of illustration:

1. In the *Book of Mormon*, 2 Nephi 3:14 it is prophesied that "that seer" (which Mormons interpret as Joseph Smith) will be protected by God: "They that seek to destroy him shall be confounded;... this promise... shall be fulfilled."

But it was not fulfilled, for "they that seek to destroy him" did in fact destroy him at a young age in 1844 when he was killed by townspeople in a gun battle in Carthage, Illinois. Smith himself had said in October, 1843, "I prophesy, *in the name of the Lord God of Israel*... they never will have power to kill me till my work is accomplished, and I am ready to die."[270] But again, less than a year later, Joseph Smith was dead. And according to accounts of his death, he certainly was not yet "ready to die." While in jail, facing the prospect of confronting the angry people that would kill him, he quickly wrote to his Nauvoo Legion to break into the jail and "save him at all costs."[271] Eyewitnesses noted that just before he was shot he gave the Masonic signal of distress and cried out, "Is there no help... ?"—and then after he was shot came the exclamation of unbelief,

"Oh Lord; my God!"[272] Furthermore, given the tremendous obstacles facing the church he had founded, who could reasonably say his work had been "accomplished?"

2. In *Doctrine and Covenants*, (114:1) it was prophesied in the name of the Lord that David W. Patten would go on a mission one year later:

> Verily *thus sayeth the Lord*: It is wisdom in my servant David W. Patten, that he settle up all his business . . . that he may perform a mission unto me next spring, in company with others, even twelve including himself, to testify of my name and bear glad tidings unto all the world.

This prophecy was given April 17, 1838. Six months later, on October 25, 1838, David W. Patten was shot and killed—he "instantly fell, mortally wounded, having received a large ball in his bowels."[273] No one can deny, then, that this is another false prophecy. But if the Mormon God is genuine, why would He prophesy that a man was to preach for Him whom He knew would shortly be killed and thus be unable to fulfill His mission? Patten's death cannot be rationalized with the claim that he was guilty of sin or apostasy because Smith's own remarks after his death claim he was a faithful Mormon until his demise.[274]

3. On May 18, 1843, in the "name of the Lord" and "in the name of Jesus Christ" Joseph Smith prophesied the complete overthrow of the United States Government. This never occurred, nor did the Government ever redress "its crimes" as Smith promised:

> President Smith, in concluding his remarks, said . . . "*I prophesy in the name of the Lord of Israel*, unless the United States redress the wrongs committed upon the saints in the state of Missouri and punish the crimes committed by her officers that in a few years the Government will be utterly overthrown and wasted, and there will not be so much as a potsherd left" (emphasis added).[275]

And,

> I prophesied by virtue of the holy priesthood vested in me, *and in the name of the Lord Jesus Christ*, that, if Congress will not hear our petition and grant us protection, *they shall be broken up as a government*, and God shall damn them, and there shall be *nothing* left of them—not even a grease spot.[276]

But again, Congress never granted the Mormons their petition. It correctly concluded that Mormon problems with other settlers were a result of their own religious excesses and evil practices such as polygamy, violence against non-Mormons and their terrible doctrine of blood atonement. (See chap. 3, appendix, and chaps. 28–29.) In fact, the Government so increased its pressure against the polygamist activity of the church that a new "revelation" in 1890 conveniently "reversed" the polygamist doctrines which had prevented Utah's entry into the Union.

Thus, the United States Government was not "utterly overthrown and wasted," nor was there "nothing" left of it, "not even a grease spot." The United States grew to become the most powerful nation on earth.

4. In *Doctrine and Covenants* (104:1) "Jesus" claimed that the Mormon "United Order"—the Mormon communities in Ohio and Missouri—would remain until He returned. However, the "United Order" failed and was disbanded, and over 150 years later Jesus still has not returned.

5. In the *Book of Mormon* (Alma 7:10) it is falsely prophesied that the Messiah will be born in Jerusalem when, of course, He was born in Bethlehem. Four biblical books of history attest to Jesus' birthplace as Bethlehem: one prophet who wrote a miraculous prediction in 700 B.C., and three contemporary biographers of Jesus (Micah 5:2; Matthew 2:4-6; Luke 2:4-7; John 7:42).

6. Heber Kimball falsely prophesied that "Brother Brigham Young will become President of the United States."[277]

7. Joseph Smith's father falsely prophesied that Joseph, Jr., "should continue in the Priest's office until Christ comes."[278]

Many other false prophecies could be listed.*

With so many false prophecies by Smith and other Mormons, one is tempted to assume that they were either carried away by false visions of their own mind or through spiritistic duplicity. Certainly a truthful God could not be the author of such wrong predictions.

In spite of all these false prophecies, again, Mormons do not show much concern about the issue. Apparently, this is because they have never come to grips with the biblical teaching on what God requires of a true prophet and what a false prophet really is:

---

* Ralson lists the following examples: *D&C*, 42:39; 62:6; 69:8; 84:114,115; 88:87; 97:19; 101:11,17; 103:6,7; 111:2,4-10; 112:15,19; 115:14,17; 117:12.[279] Walter Martin refers to several false prophecies in *Doctrine and Covenants* 97:22-24 (with *Doctrine and Covenants* commentary, appropriate section) and also in *Teachings of Joseph Smith* (pp. 17,18), for example.[280] Jerald and Sandra Tanner refer to false prophecies in *Journal of Discourses* 3:228,253,262; 4:40; 5:10,93,94,164,173,174,274,275, and in other sources.[281] The resource text, *Where Does It Say That?* by former Mormon Bob Witte, contains others.[282]

It is somewhat ironic that most Mormons are basically unimpressed by the evidence against their "prophets" concerning the many false prophecies that have issued forth from them. This behavior is so unusual because of the reverence Mormons give their Presidents as "prophets of God." Their attitude of indifference is primarily based upon ignorance and conditioning. The average Mormon is unaware of the biblical tests for a true prophet and is therefore ignorant of how to properly determine if a man is a true prophet or a false prophet. However, the greatest difficulty Mormons have is overcoming their "conditioning." They have been programmed to believe that the greatest test of a prophet is their own personal "testimony" that he is a prophet.[283]

But it must also be said that many Mormons aren't even aware of these false prophecies. For example, if one examines the *Doctrine and Covenants'* student manual, an extensive five-hundred-page commentary on *Doctrine and Covenants*, one finds that the false prophecies are either ignored or carefully reinterpreted. For example, concerning the rebuilding of the temple, the *Manual* equivocates on the word "generation" and defines it as an indefinite period.[284] Further,

The Lord later excused the Saints from building that temple because mobs prevented it . . . and because the Saints at that time had not kept the commandments as they should. . . . The day will come, however, when the holy city of God will be established in Jackson County, Missouri, and the temple will be filled with the glory of God as envisioned by the prophets.[285]

This completely ignores the clear statements of the prophecy itself that it must be built in "this generation."

Its explanation of the Civil War prophecy is equally distorting. The text cites various wars around the world spanning almost a century, from 1861 to 1958. This is the alleged pouring out of wars upon "all nations" as described in the prophecy. But anyone who actually reads the prophecy can see that such an interpretation is completely false. To claim that "the Civil War was the beginning of the war that will bring about the end of the world" (the "full end of all nations" prophesied in *D&C*, 87:6) is a statement that could be made for any war at any period of history—if we are ignoring the factor of time.[286] Again, anyone who reads the prophecy can see that it is the end of the world itself that is predicted, and this is to happen within a set period.

But again, what else can Mormon leaders do when faced with proof of false prophecies? Being unwilling to accept the implications, which would require them to accept that Joseph Smith *was a false prophet* and to thus have to forsake Mormonism, they have no choice but to rationalize his failures. However, in doing this, they are guilty of foisting a deliberate deception upon unsuspecting converts and the very Mormon people they claim to shepherd.

## ♦ ♦ *Conclusion* ♦ ♦

In the last five chapters, we have proven that the Mormon claim to divine authority is demonstrably false. The first vision account of Mormonism cannot be trusted. The *Book of Mormon* must be considered a myth. The *Book of Moses* and the *Book of Abraham* are simple frauds. Mormon authorities have made thousands of changes in their scriptures—and deliberately suppressed vital records of its early leaders from their own membership. In addition, Mormon teaching historically has such terrific internal contradictions that the church has been forced to annul all previous divine revelations through the current prophets' "revelations." Finally, the prophetic errors establishing Joseph Smith and other Mormon leaders as false prophets are there for all to see. If one can still believe that Mormonism is a divine revelation, then one can believe anything.

In our final five chapters, we will show some of the fruits of this false church and the distortion and tragedy it can bring to the lives of Mormon people. We will examine the "fruit" of Mormonism.

# Mormon Religion and Its Fruits

## What Are the Consequences of the Church's Claim to Divine Revelation?

◆

Jesus said, "Beware of false prophets, which come to you in sheep's clothing, but inwardly they are ravening wolves. Ye shall know them by their fruits."

—Joseph Smith, *The Evening and Morning Star*[1]

The Mormon church emphasizes that it is to be known "by its fruits" and, therefore, that the proof of its religion can be found in its many good deeds. Lawrence R. Flake is a Mormon leader who has trained over two hundred Mormon missionaries. He boasts, "... the Savior said, 'By their fruits ye shall know them.' And on that basis we feel we have a very strong case [for the truth of Mormonism]."[2] Apostle LeGrand Richards emphasizes, "Our [truth] claims ... would be of little weight and consequence if the fruits of the Church did not bear witness to the truth of these claims. Jesus said: '... by their fruits ye shall know them.' ... Every Church and people must be willing to stand upon this test."[3] Of course, few will deny that many or most Mormons are sincere people with a genuine desire to live spiritual lives.

Even some Christians, noting the church's welfare program, tithings, and sacrificial missions work, and also the personal lifestyle of many Mormons, conclude that the fruit of Mormonism really is good. From this they may reason that Joseph Smith was a true prophet and that Mormonism must have a divine origin. They appeal to the words of Jesus Himself in Matthew 7:15-20:

Beware of the false prophets, who come to you in sheep's clothing, but inwardly are ravenous wolves. You will know them by their fruits. Grapes are not gathered from thorn bushes, nor figs from thistles, are they? Even so, every good tree bears good fruit; but the rotten tree bears bad fruit. A good tree cannot produce bad fruit, nor can a rotten tree produce good fruit. Every tree that does not bear good fruit is cut down

357

and thrown into the fire. So then, you will know them by their fruits.

But notice that Jesus is speaking here of *false* prophets, not true prophets. He teaches it is the *false* prophets who are disguised. They only appear to be loyal and trustworthy. Like sheep, they look friendly and innocent, but their true nature is something savage. Jesus warns that, despite their good appearance, "you will *know them* by their fruits." In other words, what they are in their nature, they will produce in their actions—for their nature being what it is, they can do little else. Just as it is impossible to gather edible fruit from thorn bushes and thistles, so it is impossible for *false* prophets to produce truly *good* fruit (v. 18). So, how does this relate to Mormonism? Don't Mormons have good fruit?

What some people may forget to consider is the true *nature* and *entirety* of the fruits of Mormonism, not to mention the warnings of Jesus immediately following His earlier words:

> Not every one who says to Me, "Lord, Lord," will enter the kingdom of heaven; but he who does the will of My Father who is in heaven. Many will say to Me on that day, "Lord, Lord, did we not prophesy in Your name, and in Your name cast out demons, and in Your name perform many miracles?" And then I will declare to them, "I never knew you; Depart from Me, you who practice lawlessness" (Matthew 7:21-23).

Here, Jesus teaches that there will be *many* individuals who claimed to believe in Jesus and to even perform miracles in His name. Yet who, all along, were false believers and false prophets.

Mormons (and members of many other religions) do think that they say to Jesus, "Lord, Lord"—and yet this alone cannot gain them entrance into heaven if the Jesus they honor is false. If so, then they do not know or honor the real Jesus at all. So then, who is the person who finds entrance into the kingdom of heaven? It is, as Jesus says, "he who does the will of My Father who is in heaven" (v. 21). And what is the will of the Father? It is ". . . that you believe in Him whom He has sent" (John 6:29; cf. v. 37-40). In other words, in order to go to heaven, one must trust in the true Jesus Christ (see John 1:12; 3:16; 5:24; 6:47).

But Mormons also claim that they perform supernatural miracles in the name of Jesus. However, as we saw in chapters 12 and 15, these are done in the name of a false Christ; therefore, they cannot possibly be performed through the divine power of the true Jesus. Further, as we saw in Section 6, any supernatural manifestations Mormons may produce are really occult miracles—therefore, they cannot be divine in any sense and must be considered counterfeit. This would readily explain Jesus' response to those who falsely claimed they performed miracles in His name: "I never knew you. Depart from Me, you who practice lawlessness" (v. 23). In other words, they were really performing demonic miracles done through the power of the enemy of God. Since such actions reject God's law (Deuteronomy 18:9-12), they are properly designated by the term "lawlessness."

Finally, the social good works and personal lifestyle that many Mormons claim are hardly the *only* fruit of Mormonism, nor are they the proper tests of its truthfulness. It should not be forgotten that it is these very fruits which help perpetuate the Mormon religion. Thus, if Mormonism itself is false, the fruits that help support it cannot be entirely good.

Further, what cult doesn't boast good works? Truth has no necessary connection to religious zeal, as the Apostle Paul so aptly pointed out (Romans 9:30,31). What good *or* evil person isn't zealous for his personal convictions? If the Mormons have forty-five thousand missionaries, Jehovah's Witnesses have over half a million and boast hundreds of millions of man-hours of witnessing. They have started more "Bible studies" in people's homes than Mormonism and most other cults combined.[4] In other words, virtually every false religion can appeal to its zeal and "good works"—but, in the end, these "fruits" mean little if the religion itself is a counterfeit that brings spiritual destruction into people's lives.

So, what is the real fruit of Mormonism? The primary "fruit" of the Mormon church is new converts to the Mormon faith. Through the church's evangelism programs and its stress upon "good works," thousands of former secularists and members of the Christian church are baptized into the Mormon religion each year. This is the real fruit of the Mormon church.

But further, even the genuinely good fruit in Mormonism is rather tainted. Its welfare program is principally for its own people, not others.[5] Its strong family emphasis is apparently reserved for Mormons in good standing. A Mormon who leaves the flock may face complete rejection by family members, divorce or loss of job and friends.[6] Indeed, Mormon leaders have actively counseled some of their flock to divorce their non-Mormon spouses, and one can hardly consider this to be upholding the "sanctity of the family."[7]

In the film *The God Makers* former Mormons Ed Decker and others recall their experiences:

> Decker on film: "I look back on my own life seeing a bishop counsel me to divorce my wife, seeing the five children whom I raised in the Mormon church pulled from me, and spending all these years just trying to re-establish those relationships. I know literally hundreds of families whose stories like this could break your heart."
>
> Narrator: "Greg and Jolene divorced because of the Mormon church and have now remarried."

Jolene: "He was raised a Christian and I was raised Mormon. We just had a very beautiful relationship, but it always came back to Mormonism. I had to convert him in some way. And after two and a half years of really trying hard, I just couldn't do it and I was advised to divorce him."

2nd Woman: "Well it became obvious to the church leaders that my husband was not going to go along with the church . . . so they thought that it was perfectly fine and acceptable and encouraged me to divorce my husband."

3rd Woman: "[On] the second visit to the counselor, he went over the things that we had told him and said, 'Well, there are just some people that shouldn't be married.'"

Woman's Voice: "I went to my bishop and he advised me that it would be better for me to live without [my husband] and to be a servant in Mormon heaven than to stay married to him."[8]

Another recalls, "Since I have come out of the Mormon church, my sisters and I have had no relationship at all."[9]

In addition to these sad results we have already shown that for thousands of people some of the "fruits" of Mormonism are disillusionment, depression, higher rates of divorce, suicide, crime and other social evils (chap. 6).

But historically, there have been many other fruits of Mormonism as well, and these must not be neglected. Therefore, in this section we will seek to show why the claim that "the divine nature of Mormonism is proven by its fruits" is a false affirmation. We will reveal that some of the real fruits of Mormonism historically are as follows:

1. Distortion of history and religion (chap. 26; seen in Mormon apologetics);

2. Distortion of biblical authority (chap. 27; seen in its real beliefs about the Bible);

3. Distortion of the sanctity of life (chap. 28; seen in its earlier doctrine of blood atonement);

4. Distortion of relationships concerning race and family (chap. 29; seen in its historic racism and polygamy);

5. Distortion of trust within the Mormon church itself (chap. 30; seen in its recent changes in its Temple Endowment Ceremony).

These considerations will also prove that the fruits of the Mormon religion are more than what the church claims them to be.

CHAPTER 26

◆

# Mormon Distortions of History and Religion

## Are Mormon Evangelistic/Apologetic Works Factually Sound or Do They Constitute Misrepresentation?

We have seen that the Mormon church makes significant claims concerning the truthfulness of its religion. Its missionary program stresses the uniqueness of the Mormon faith as well as the quality of the alleged evidences in its behalf. Thus, no discussion of Mormonism is complete without briefly evaluating the quality of Mormon apologetics.[10]

In this chapter we will show that the Mormon church makes its converts largely on the basis of distortion—not on the basis of a presentation of the true gospel of Jesus Christ. Thus when forty-five thousand Mormon missionaries tell others that Mormonism is God's religion—and yet such a claim is wrong—they are engaging in misrepresentation—consumer fraud, if you will.

Consider the following characteristic claim to the truth of the Mormon religion by the tenth president and prophet, Joseph Fielding Smith:

> Had the work [of Mormonism] been based on fraud, it would have been exposed many years ago in some of the many publications and attacks made against it. For upwards of one

361

hundred years the revealed gospel has stood the test of criticism, attack and bitter opposition. I think we can say that *never before in recorded history do we have an account of truth passing through such a crucible and being put to such a test as has the truth known in the world as Mormonism. Every attack has failed,* whether that attack has been waged against Joseph Smith in person or against the *Book of Mormon,* which by the power of God he translated from ancient records, or against the revelations received by him personally from the Lord [e.g., *Doctrine and Covenants*]. *No error in his doctrine has been shown.*[11]

But such a statement is incredible. President Smith claims that if Mormonism were false, it would have been exposed. However, Mormonism was exposed the day Joseph Smith received his first revelation—when God allegedly condemned His own church as an abomination. President Smith maintains that the church is not based on fraud. But fraud has repeatedly been found in the writings and activities of both Mormonism and Joseph Smith—from occult practices, to plagiarism, to false prophecy, to suppression of data, to altering scripture, to immorality. (See Resource List.) President Smith claims that Mormonism has withstood the test of criticism. But this is also untrue. Critics' arguments have proven so successful that thousands of Mormons have left the church, confused and bitter over the extent of their deception. Errors in Smith's own doctrine have been exposed—errors in biblical theology, scientific and historical fact, and logical argument. In truth, Mormon doctrine is so replete with errors and contradictions that they can hardly be catalogued.

If Mormon presidents and prophets make these kinds of unfounded assertions publicly—and continue to prosper—who then can be trusted among the ranks of Mormon leadership?

Unfortunately, Mormons cannot trust their church authorities to be candid. When Hugh Nibley claims, "The whole structure of anti-Mormon scholarship rests on trumped up evidence. . . . [Anti-Mormon writers are] a pack of *storytellers* who have been getting away with too much for too long,"[12] he is blowing smoke. It is the Mormon leaders who are the storytellers.

Mormons should research the issue for themselves. Thankfully thousands of Mormons are no longer willing to let the church speak for them. They are now free to check every claim made by responsible critics, and to carefully examine the original sources. (See Resource List.) Einar Anderson, one researcher of Mormonism, correctly observes, "Any who wish to learn about Mormon history and doctrine are forced *to seek out the facts and sift through much misinformation. . . . No Mormon* learns the truth until he begins to search out the historical facts for himself."[13]

Indeed, Mormon leaders themselves have *invited* critical analysis, so they should not complain when Mormons take their advice.

Thus, in the following pages we will provide sufficient examples of Mormon evangelistic/apologetic endeavors that prove that the church garners its converts on the basis of misinformation and distortion of fact. In chapter 8 we examined Dr. Robinson's attempt to defend the claim that Mormonism is Christian (*Is Mormonism Christian?*). At best, his endeavor was a poor case of wishful thinking. In the area of Mormon apologetic works in archaeology, we have also revealed why, in the words of Ropp, "Most are nonsense written by amateurs."[14] We will now examine four additional representative works: 1) *A Sure Foundation: Answers to Difficult Gospel Questions*; 2) Joseph Fielding Smith's multi-volume *Answers* Series; 3) Arthur Wallace's *Can Mormonism Be Proved Experimentally?* and 4) a popular Mormon evangelistic tract titled, *The Challenge*.

(Despite their apparent popularity among Mormons, the works of Robert and Rosemary Brown are not considered here. These books comprise a multi-volume series titled, *They Lie in Wait to Deceive*.[15] Unfortunately, they largely stress *ad hominem* arguments. However, to attack the character of critics of Mormonism such as Walter Martin and Dee Jay Nelson is hardly a defense of Mormonism. What should be examined are their contentions, not their character. Because we reject an *ad hominem* approach and do not wish to dignify such methods with a response, we suggest interested readers secure these volumes for themselves. They will then discover these works almost never deal with relevant issues and, therefore, that a discussion of them is largely a waste of time. The texts we do cite at least deal with issues germaine to the subject of Mormon credibility.)

Nevertheless, in many ways even these volumes are not true apologetic works; they do *not* provide a defense of the truth of the Mormon religion. Mormonism has no facts to use in its defense, and hence what does not exist cannot be presented. What Mormon apologetic works do is to provide 1) false claims which lack support and 2) what can frequently only be described as carefully worded distortions—alleged "explanations" for the many logical, historical, biblical, and scientific problems raised by their scripture, theology and history. This is not to say that all Mormon apologists are necessarily engaging in distortion. But one can only wonder how many of them are committed to impartially examining all sides of an issue and then siding with the evidence. We will now examine representative texts of Mormon apologists.

*Apologetic Work No. 1:* A Sure Foundation: Answers to Difficult Gospel Questions

This book seeks to answer forty-five problems and issues posed by Mormon scripture, teaching and history. Because this book is written by committed Mormon apologists, its contents may appear convincing to the uninformed. Nevertheless, anyone who carefully examines the responses will discover it lacks persuasion. Below we provide examples.

Example 1: *Was Jesus Born at Jerusalem or Bethlehem?*

The *Book of Mormon* teaches that Jesus Christ was born at Jerusalem (Alma 7:10). Of course, the Bible teaches He was born at Bethlehem (Matthew 2:1). Mormons try to resolve this conflict by claiming that, in this case, the prepositions "in" and "at" mean different things. In other words, because the Mormon text did not assert that Jesus was born "in" Jerusalem (which, Mormons argue, would literally place his birth within the city of Jerusalem), but rather "at" Jerusalem, this should be interpreted as meaning *near* Jerusalem, or, in other words, six miles away at Bethlehem.[16]

But first, why say "at Jerusalem" if you really mean "at Bethlehem"? Why wasn't God more precise in the *Book of Mormon*, (which He supposedly inspired) when he was so precise in the Bible (Matthew 2:1; Micah 5:2)—saying clearly that the Messiah would be born at *Bethlehem*?

In addition, how do Mormons think the following *Book of Mormon* scriptures should be interpreted?: "My father, Lehi . . . dwelt *at Jerusalem* [Bethlehem?] in all his days" (1 Nephi 1:4); "He returned to his own house at Jerusalem" [Bethlehem?] (1 Nephi 1:7); "I, Nephi, . . . have dwelt at Jerusalem" [Bethlehem?] (2 Nephi 25:6). If Nephi and his father really lived in Bethlehem and not Jerusalem, why wouldn't they just say so?

Further, if "at" does not mean "in," why does the Mormon church itself rarely abide by this rule? In *Doctrine and Covenants* it always identifies the *specific* location where Joseph Smith gave his prophecies. But it always uses the word *at* to describe the specific city in which he gave them. In fact, "at" is used to identify a specific location in the preface of *every single prophecy* listed in *Doctrine and Covenants*: "At Hiram, Ohio" (*D&C*, 1); "at Manchester, Pennsylvania" (*D&C*, 2); "at Harmony, Pennsylvania" (*D&C*, 3), etc.

Mormon history classes may teach that Bethlehem is part of "the land of Jerusalem";[17] nevertheless, in the Bible Bethlehem is clearly said to be in "the land of Judah," not Jerusalem. Jerusalem has never been anything other than a distinct city, separate from the city of Bethlehem. Even 1 Nephi 1:4 describes Jerusalem as a separate city—and as such it could not incorporate Bethlehem.

This argument is equivalent to saying that prepositions can alter geographic boundaries—that a person's birth at San Diego is really a birth at Los Angeles. But even with directly adjacent cities no one mistakes the intent of the writer when the preposition "at" is used. For example, we might say "the Messiah will be born *at* Wilmette, Illinois" or "the Messiah will be born *at* Winnetka, Illinois." These Chicago suburbs are immediately adjacent to each other, but the meaning is nevertheless clear. The Messiah can only be born *at* one place or the other, unless He is born directly on top of the city line! How much clearer is the meaning when the ancient cities of Jerusalem and Bethlehem were separated by a full six miles. Alma 7:10 is clearly a false prophecy, and the nature of the Mormon response only reinforces this conclusion.

Example 2: *Does the Book of Mormon Contradict Doctrine and Covenants?*

Because the *Book of Mormon* plagiarizes from the King James Bible and because occult revelations are characteristically contradictory, there are several places where the *Book of Mormon* contradicts teachings in *Doctrine and Covenants*. For example, in Alma 11:26-29 it teaches that there is only one true God, denying the official Mormon doctrine of polytheism. In response to the question, "Is there more than one God?" the answer is clearly stated as "No."

The response of Mormon apologists to this contradiction is to equivocate. Since they are polytheists and believe in multiple gods, they have no other choice than to force the passage to accommodate official doctrine. Thus, the monotheistic teaching of Alma 11 is converted into polytheism: "Of course, Amulek knew that there are three separate personages in the godhead [i.e., three gods]. [Nevertheless] Since the Son and the Holy Spirit are one in purpose, mission, and glory with the 'true and living God,' [the Father, Elohim] the three are indeed 'one Eternal God.' "[18]

Consider another example. In Alma 18:26-28 God is defined as a "Great Spirit" who is the Creator of the universe. This denies the official Mormon doctrine that God has a *physical* body. (This teaching is reaffirmed in Alma 22:9,10.) But again, Mormonism equivocates. The term "Great Spirit" is cleverly applied to Jesus Christ in His preexistent state—when He was a "Great Spirit" before *He* took His physical body. Because Jesus had a part in creating the world, He is therefore both the Creator and the Great Spirit.[19] (Of course, the same could be said for Joseph Smith, since he was also a great spirit in preexistence and helped with the creation, according to Mormonism.) But this is not what Alma 18 and 22 teach; they teach that the Creator God (Elohim) *is a spirit*.

*A Sure Foundation* also seeks to prove that *Doctrine and Covenants* does not contradict the Bible. For example, in Matthew 22:29,30 Jesus clearly *denies* that marriage is an eternal covenant, therefore refuting the Mormon doctrine of eternal marriage. In effect, He says there is no marriage in heaven. This book responds to this conflict with more equivocation and an odd argument based on omission. It claims that Jesus did believe in eternal marriage—he simply never stated such a belief clearly. Thus, "The Saviour's answer... was not a full doctrinal explanation of the doctrine of eternal marriage."[20] And, it was not "the Lord's final word on the subject."[21] Hence, "The Lord *did not* say there would be no people in the married state in the resurrection, but that there would be *no marriages made* in the resurrection."[22]

In other words, the Mormon response is to equivocate and maintain that Jesus really did believe in eternal marriage. Apparently, He simply didn't think it was important to teach this doctrine clearly while He was on the earth. But is this really credible?

First, isn't the doctrine of eternal marriage possibly the most important of all Mormon doctrines? Why would Jesus neglect so vital a teaching in the Gospels? Further, why would He neglect it *again* after His resurrection—when He supposedly preached in the Americas, as recorded in the *Book of Mormon*? Even in the *Book of Mormon* Jesus neglects to teach this crucial doctrine.

Second, did Jesus ever say what Mormons claim He said?—that even though people are not married by ceremony in heaven, that their earthly marriages (if performed in the Mormon temple) would continue in heaven—and thus that people *would* be married for eternity? This is a classic illustration of Mormon *eisegesis*—of adding to the text information never stated, but assumed—because of Mormon doctrine. In fact, Jesus taught just the opposite. He said plainly there was *no marriage* in heaven—and this covers all bases. *No* marriage must include all conditions relating to marriage, even previous marriage. Jesus even qualified His statement by noting that those in the resurrection are like the angels in heaven. Does Mormonism wish to maintain that the angels in heaven are married?

Finally, in answer to the question, "What are the best evidences to support the authenticity of the *Book of Mormon*?" *A Sure Foundation* supplies no evidence. One wonders why, if evidence exists. Rather, once again the "best" evidence is said to be subjective experience, an alleged confirmation of the divine origin of the *Book of Mormon* through the witness of the Holy Ghost as according to Moroni 10:4,5. (See *Apologetic Work No. 2*, example 3, below).

This is only a sampling of the kinds of misrepresentational responses given in this text. But again, attempting to defend things that are indefensible requires distortion, not apologetics.

*Apologetic Work No. 2:* Joseph Fielding Smith's Answers to Gospel Questions

This four-volume set by "the foremost gospel scholar" in Mormonism attempts responses to two hundred questions, including many objections raised against the credibility of the Mormon religion.

### Example 1: *Does the Book of Mormon Contain Mormon Doctrine?*

What is Smith's response to the assertion in *Doctrine and Covenants* 20:8-10 that the *Book of Mormon* contains "the fullness of the gospel"? As noted earlier, major Mormon doctrines, including some essential for salvation, are absent from the *Book of Mormon*. Smith's suggested solution is to assert it does contain the "fullness of the gospel" and simply ignore the issue.[23] But again the reader may decide for himself the meaning of the term "fullness."

### Example 2: *Is the Book of Mormon or Doctrine and Covenants Correct in Its Teachings on Polygamy?*

In *Doctrine and Covenants* 132:1 it says that God "justified [i.e., accepted or declared as righteous] [His] servants... David and Solomon,... as touching the principle and doctrine of their having many wives and concubines." In verse 39 it teaches that "David's wives and concubines were given unto him by the hand of [the prophet] Nathan" and that "in none of these things did he sin against me. . . ." Why did God say this? Because polygamy is said to be an *eternal* covenant (i.e., binding for eternity), so much so that Mormons who reject it will be condemned to hell forever (v. 4,41).

But the *Book of Mormon* declares that God *hated* David's and Solomon's polygamy: "Behold David and Solomon truly had many wives and concubines, which thing was abominable before me, saith the Lord" (v. 24). This is exactly opposite to what God said in *Doctrine and Covenants*.

Nevertheless, Smith argues that there is no contradiction here—that God was only angry when David and Solomon took *extra* wives, wives he did not approve of. Those wives He did approve of were permissible.[24] But this is not what the *Book of Mormon* said. Smith has again read meaning into the text which is not present or implied.

Further, such a distinction regarding polygamy is not found anywhere else—in either Mormon scripture or the Bible. In fact, the argument flatly contradicts God's command in the Bible when He warns concerning all future kings of Israel, including David and Solomon: "He *must not* take many wives or his heart will be led astray" (Deuteronomy 17:17, emphasis added).

### Example 3: *Does Moroni 10:3-5 Prove Mormonism Is True?*

Smith's most potent apologetic is the one Mormons rely on most frequently. It is based upon a prayer offered in the *Book of Mormon*, Moroni 10:3-5:

> Behold, I would exhort you that when ye shall read these things, if it be wisdom in God that ye should read them, that ye would remember how merciful the Lord hath been unto the children of men, from the creation of Adam even down until the time that ye shall receive these things, and ponder it in your hearts.
>
> And when ye shall receive these things, I would exhort you that ye would ask God, the Eternal Father, in the name of Christ, if these things are not true; and if ye shall ask with a sincere heart, with real intent, having faith in Christ, he will manifest the truth of it unto you, by the power of the Holy Ghost.

Based on this passage, Smith argues:

> And by the power of the Holy Ghost ye may know the truth of all things.

> As far as the *Book of Mormon* is concerned, it requires no defense from me nor anyone else. Moroni has given a challenge to the world in Moroni 10:3-5. Many thousands have accepted [the challenge] and have proved the *Book of Mormon* true. This can be proved by anyone else if he will follow Moroni's teachings.[25]

Allegedly, all anyone must do is sincerely pray about the *Book of Mormon* and he or she will receive divine "assurance" that the *Book of Mormon* is God's Word. But Moroni's "challenge" in Moroni 10:3-5 is entirely subjective and therefore cannot prove anything. This appeal rejects any reasonable investigation of the evidence. It is an appeal based squarely upon one's experience: one "feels" assurance and therefore concludes that the *Book of Mormon* is divine.

But it does not logically follow that such an experience proves Mormonism is true. For those who have had the "burning bosom" testimony, as Mormons call it, how can they logically know that it was God—and not their own needs (or insecurities), or even the devil—who personally confirmed the "truth" of the *Book of Mormon* to them? Further, how can mystical experience prove something true when all the available evidence independently proves it false? Finally, note the self-confirming nature of the challenge. Anyone who prays *sincerely* will receive divine confirmation for the *Book of Mormon*. In other words, anyone who does not receive confirmation is, by definition, insincere. This subjective and double-tongued approach was never a part of the biblical authors' appeal (e.g. Luke 1:1-4).

Nevertheless, such experiences can certainly seem real. The authors remember a young Christian woman, infatuated with a Mormon man who prayed this prayer and did indeed receive a spiritual "confirmation" that Mormonism is true and "of God." As a result she was baptized into the Mormon church and became a committed Mormon. Only when it was clearly proven to her that Mormon teaching denied God, Christ, salvation, the Bible, etc., did she realize her mistake—and learn a difficult lesson about trusting spiritual experiences. To her, the "confirmational" sensations were clearly supernatural. If so, they illustrate the reality of spiritual warfare that may enter the lives of those who disregard biblical authority, either by ignorance or lack of study of sound doctrine (Titus 1:9; 2 Timothy 2:15).

### Example 4: *Are There No Textual Changes in the Book of Mormon?*

Concerning the *Book of Mormon*'s textual changes Smith alleges that "there is not one change or addition that is not in full harmony with the original [1830] text."[26] In other words, he does not deal with the issue; he simply denies that a problem exists. As we have already shown in chapter 23, Smith's statement is entirely false.

Example 5: *Do the Book of Mormon and the Bible Deny That Jesus Was Virgin Born by the Holy Spirit?*

In *Doctrines of Salvation* Joseph Fielding Smith declares:

> They tell us the *Book of Mormon* states that Jesus was begotten of the Holy Ghost. I challenge this statement. The *Book of Mormon* teaches no such thing! *Neither does the Bible.* It is true there is one passage that states so, but we must consider it in the light of other passages with which it is in conflict.[27]

Nevertheless, anyone who wishes may read the *Book of Mormon* (Alma 7:10) which tells us that the virgin Mary will "be overshadowed and conceive by the power of the Holy Ghost, and bring forth a son, yea, even the Son of God." If the *Book of Mormon* also *contradicts* this statement in 1 Nephi 11:18, so much the worse for the *Book of Mormon*.

Smith's statement that the Bible does not teach the virgin birth by the power of the Holy Spirit is also incredible. In Luke 1:34,35 (NIV) it is painstakingly clear on this point: "'How will this be,' Mary asked the angel, 'since I am a virgin [Gk *parthenos*]?' The angel answered, '*The Holy Spirit will come upon you*, and the power of the Most High will overshadow you. So the holy one to be born will be called the Son of God'" Matthew 1:18 (NIV) corroborates this: "This is how the birth of Jesus Christ came about: His mother Mary was pledged to be married to Joseph, but before they came together, she was found to be with child *through the Holy Spirit*." These verses clearly teach that the divine instrument of Jesus' birth was the Holy Spirit.

Naturally Smith and other Mormons cannot accept that the Holy Spirit is the conceiver of Jesus Christ. For according to Mormon theology, in order to have physical sex with Mary (as the Father allegedly did), the Holy Spirit would have to have a physical body, which Mormonism denies. Jesus would then also have to be the *Son of the Holy Ghost*, not the son of God the Father. Once again the Mormons' literal sexual polytheism has forced them into false interpretations of Scripture, with bizarre implications.

In conclusion, if Smith's apologetics are some of the best the church can offer, where are Mormons to turn *except* to subjective experiences in confirmation of their faith?

*Apologetic Work No. 3:* Can Mormonism Be Proved Experimentally?

Mormon apologist Arthur Wallace also stresses the overriding importance of subjective personal "revelation" as the final and best proof of Mormonism.[28] But he also makes specific claims which can be investigated.

Example 1: *Is the Book of Mormon Prophesied in the Bible?*

Leaving aside Wallace's many claims for the *Book of Mormon* (for example, the "staggering" evidence from ancient history), we might review a few "staggering" inaccuracies. For example, the false assertion that the *Book of Mormon* is prophesied in the Bible.[29] We will examine several Scriptures that Mormons misinterpret in reference to this allegation. First, consider Isaiah 29:4,11,12, where God, using vivid imagery, is speaking judgment to "Ariel" (meaning "Lion of God," another name for Jerusalem):

> Brought low, you will speak from the ground; your speech will mumble out of the dust.... For you this whole vision is nothing but words sealed in a scroll. And if you give the scroll to someone who can read, and say to him, "Read this, please," he will answer, "I can't; it is sealed." Or if you give the scroll to someone who cannot read, and say, "Read this, please," he will answer, "I don't know how to read" (NIV).

In other words, Jerusalem is as ignorant of God's purposes as an illiterate man is of writing on a scroll. But Mormons think that this Scripture "was literally fulfilled when Martin Harris took copies of the engravings of the [gold] plates of the *Book of Mormon* to Professor Anthon in New York," who was unable to read them.[30]

But, in order to properly interpret this passage, we should carefully observe that the context of Isaiah 29 deals with God's judgment on Jerusalem (Ariel) for her wickedness. Isaiah's use of simple analogy in describing God's judgment in 700 B.C. can hardly be transformed into Mormon prophetic history describing Anthon's alleged response to Smith's translation of the gold plates twenty-five hundred years later! Second, according to *The Pearl of Great Price*, *Book of Mormon* witness Martin Harris claimed that Anthon "stated that the translation was correct, more so than any he had before seen translated from the Egyptian."[31]

However, even Professor Anthon himself rejected Mormon claims as being "perfectly false."*

And apart from this repudiation, Anthon could not have said what the Mormon church represented him as saying. How could Anthon have verified copies of the characters on the gold plates as genuine Egyptian when he could not *read* them? According to the *Book of Mormon* (Mormon 9:34), the language was unknown, so how could Anthon, who was not an Egyptologist, have attested, to its authenticity as "reformed" Egyptian? Further, how could he have noted that the plates comprised several languages—Egyptian, Chaldaic, Assyriac and Arabic—and then claim

---

* For a discussion of the Anthon misrepresentation and his own repudiation of Mormon claims concerning him, see Tanner and Tanner, *The Changing World of Mormonism*, pp. 141-145, and *Mormonism—Shadow or Reality*, p. 105, and Hoekema pp. 85,86.

he could verify their translation when such a combination of Arabic Script and Egyptian characters "would be a linguistic monstrosity"?[32] In conclusion, not only is the Mormon interpretation of this passage wrong (Isaiah 29), it cannot possibly be correct according to Mormon scripture itself.

A second alleged example of a biblical passage that prophesies the *Book of Mormon* is Psalm 85:11 where it says: "Faithfulness springs forth from the earth, and righteousness looks down from heaven."

We are told that the "faithfulness" that "springs forth from the earth" refers to the gold plates that Smith allegedly dug up. But again, poetic imagery is confused with prophetic history. The meaning of this biblical passage is simply that the people of God can once again be faithful—that is, truth or faithfulness can emerge from the earth (the nation of Israel) if the people will seek their God. It has no reference to the *Book of Mormon*.

If this Scripture can literally refer to the gold plates of Mormonism being uncovered from the ground, it could also refer to the Dead Sea Scrolls, or to almost anything else being dug up from the earth.

The third and most frequently cited prophecy is from Ezekiel 37:15-19:

> The word of the Lord came to me: "Son of man, take a stick of wood and write on it, 'Belonging to Judah and the Israelites associated with him.' Then take another stick of wood, and write on it, 'Ephraim's stick, belonging to Joseph and all the house of Israel associated with him.' Join them together into one stick so that they will become one in your hand. When your countrymen ask you, 'Won't you tell us what you mean by this?' say to them, 'This is what the Sovereign Lord says: I am going to take the stick of Joseph—which is in Ephraim's hand—and of the Israelite tribes associated with him, and join it to Judah's stick, making them a single stick of wood, and they will become one in my hand'" (NIV).

Mormons claim that the "stick of Judah" is the Bible, and the "stick of Joseph" is the *Book of Mormon*. Allegedly, God is joining them together in a single testimony. But these verses have nothing to do with the *Book of Mormon*, either linguistically or contextually. The word that is translated as "stick" is the Hebrew word *"ets,"* and it means "stick." It does not mean a book or writing scroll (or gold plates!), which is what is required if a literal Bible and *Book of Mormon* are referred to. The word for scroll is *"sepher,"* which is not used here.

Historical context also disproves Mormon claims. Ezekiel was written during the Babylonian captivity while the nation had two separate divisions—the northern ten tribes known as "Israel," and the southern two tribes known as "Judah." For their idolatry and other evil practices, the northern ten tribes had earlier encountered divine judgment in the form of deportation to Assyria. The southern two tribes, Judah, had just been deported to Babylon for similar evils. Thus, the entire context of Ezekiel is that of prophetic imagery.*

Beginning in verse 16, God has Ezekiel write a message on a stick. The first stick symbolizes Israel. The same act is repeated for Judah. God then joins the two sticks together as a prophetic symbol of His bringing the dispersed captives back into the land and reuniting the nation.

This occurred historically and was a partial fulfillment of a greater regathering at the time of the return of the Messiah. Thus, verse 22 asserts, "and I will make them one nation in the land, on the mountains of Israel; and one king [the Messiah] will be king for all of them; and they will no longer be two nations and they will no longer be divided into two kingdoms" (Ezekiel 37:22). Understanding this passage accurately enables us to see that the *Book of Mormon* never enters the picture.

Further, if this were a true prophecy of the *Book of Mormon*, one might expect that God would confirm it by identifying one of the sticks as "the stick of Joseph," which it never does. Regardless, the prophecy cannot be interpreted literally, as Mormons claim, for the Bible and the *Book of Mormon* are not "one" message as the prophecy would declare according to the Mormon interpretation.

Example 2: *Were Jesus' Apostles and the Early Church Fathers Mormon Believers?*

Consider another example of Wallace's evidence for the truth of Mormonism. He asserts that the teachings of the apostolic fathers reflect *Mormon* beliefs and *not* Christian beliefs![33] This argument supposedly "proves" that Christianity (which he falsely claims cannot be traced to earlier than A.D. 325) apostatized.

However, this argument is irrelevant. First, it is an historical fact that doctrinal Mormonism didn't even exist until the nineteenth century, so it could never have constituted early Christian belief. Second, the early Christians were hardly perfect, nor did they have centuries of study in systematic theology behind them. Some of them did accept teachings that weren't biblical. Origen, for example, believed in preexistence—but he was hardly a Mormon. Also, the fathers may not have mentioned the imputation of Adam's sin—but the Bible does (Romans 5:12-19). Nevertheless, even if they were not perfect in doctrine, they were not Mormons.[34] The thrust of the fathers, as a whole, was biblical and not pagan.

Third, only the Bible is the Word of God—not the teachings of the church fathers. What any individual taught may or may not have been correct depending on whether it was biblical. Thus, even if the apostolic fathers *were* Mormons, they would still be rejected by the Bible as heretics on the basis of its own authority.

---

*Compare the "Dry Bones" imagery of verses 1-14, which refers to the near and distant future regathering of Israel.

*Apologetic Work No. 4:* The Challenge

Finally, we will briefly discuss the popular Mormon pamphlet *The Challenge.*[35] This contains a list of "conditions" that the *Book of Mormon* supposedly meets which "proves" it had to be divinely inspired. For purposes of brevity we will mention only some of these "conditions" in summary, not by fully quoting them.

"Condition No. 6" declares there must be "no changes in the text" other than "a few" in grammar. But as noted earlier, there are thousands of documented changes.

"Condition No. 11" states that the *Book of Mormon* must be "true and sacred history"—but does *any* evidence support this claim? In fact, the *Book of Mormon* is a myth.

"Condition No. 12" teaches concerning the *Book of Mormon's* twenty-one chapters on the ministry of Christ that "every testimony you write . . . must agree absolutely with the New Testament." Of course, if much of it were copied from the New Testament, this would not be surprising. Nevertheless, we have also seen that it gives the birthplace of Christ as Jerusalem, which certainly does not agree with the New Testament.

"Condition No. 16" challenges the ablest scholars of all disciplines to prove the *Book of Mormon* false. But if they have already done so, what is the point of the challenge?

"Condition No. 17" says that "thorough investigation" for the next 125 years—historic, scientific, and archaeological—must "verify its claims and prove detail after detail to be true." But again, archaeology has authenticated nothing in the *Book of Mormon*, nor has science or history—to the contrary.

"Condition No. 19" states that the book "must not contain any absurd, impossible or contradictory statements." This claim also fails, for there are a large number of absurd, impossible and contradictory statements found in the *Book of Mormon*. This is something any impartial reader may prove to his own satisfaction.

In conclusion, the above illustrations are representative of the nature of Mormon apologetics: key issues are introduced, but rarely dealt with impartially. Critical data are ignored or suppressed, and while numerous claims are made, they are never substantiated.

One should never uncritically accept what he or she is told by Mormons. Mormons may have their "scientific," "historical" and "logical" arguments for their beliefs, but so does the Flat Earth Society.

# CHAPTER 27

# Mormon Distortion of Biblical Authority

## *What Does the Church Really Believe About the Bible?*

"I have heard a few of you declare that you are greater than [the ancient apostles]. . . . This reflects the attitude of all of you. . . . I have heard one or more of you declare that you can change anything Jesus had said or taught. This also reflects the attitude of all of you."

> —Letter of George P. Lee to the First Presidency and the Twelve, photograph- ically printed in *Excommunication of a Mormon Church Leader*, 54 (cf. *Salt Lake Tribune*, September 2, 1989)

Mormonism insists that it believes the Bible is the inspired Word of God:

Members of the Church of Jesus Christ of Latter-day Saints (known informally by the nickname Mormons) believe the Bible. Indeed, so literally and completely do their beliefs and practices conform to the teachings of the Bible that it is not uncommon to hear informed persons say: "If all men believed the Bible, all would be Mormons." Bible doctrine is Mormon doctrine, and Mormon doctrine is Bible doctrine. They are one and the same.[36]

Joseph Smith was once asked, "Do you believe the Bible?" He replied, "We are the only people under heaven that [do]. . . . We believe the Bible, and all other [Christian] sects profess to believe their interpretations of the Bible."[37]

In his *Study of the Articles of Faith*, an authoritative Mormon church work, Mormon apostle James E. Talmage also discusses Mormon claims about the Bible as well as its acceptance of new revelations:

> The Church of Jesus Christ of Latter-day Saints accepts the Holy Bible as the foremost of her standard works, . . . In the respect and sanctity with which the Latter-day Saints regard the Bible, they are of like profession with Christian denominations in general, but differ from them in the additional knowledge of certain other scriptures as authentic and holy, which others are in harmony with the Bible, and serve to support and emphasize its facts and doctrines.[38]

In their official "Articles of Faith," the Mormon church further identifies its views on the Bible. In Article 8 it claims, "We believe the Bible to be the Word of God as far as it is translated correctly. We also believe the *Book of Mormon* to be the Word of God."

But none of these claims are ultimately true: Mormonism does not honor and respect the Bible as God's Word. Along with a hundred other religious cults, it only honors and respects its own biased interpretation of the Bible. Indeed, one reason no biblical scholar considers Mormonism to be a Christian religion is that Mormonism does not permit the Bible to speak for itself. Rather, the church reinterprets the Bible through the lens of its additional scriptures and developed theology. For example, consider the words of Mormon scripture scholar and Brigham Young University (BYU) faculty member Robert J. Matthews: "The *Book of Mormon* and the JST [Joseph Smith translation of the Bible; see appendix] are the proper standards by which to measure the accuracy of the ancient Bible."[39]

However, in applying the standards of anti-biblical literature to the interpretation of the Bible, the Mormon church has discarded the warnings of Scripture: "Be diligent to present yourself approved to God as a workman who does not need to be ashamed, handling accurately the word of truth" (2 Timothy 2:15). And, "Every word of God is tested, . . . Do not add to His words, lest . . . you be proved a liar" (Proverbs 30:5,6).

We repeat—the Mormon claim to trust the Bible is false. Even while pretending to honor it, the Mormon church has, from the beginning, denied it, demeaned it and attacked it as unreliable. Thus, in discussing the Mormon attitude toward the Bible, we will note:

1. The Mormon church's declaration of scriptural omissions—the Bible as canonically incomplete;

2. The Mormon church's claim of resulting doctrinal insufficiencies—the Bible as theologically inadequate, and;

3. The Mormon church's claim of alleged eventual corruption—the Bible as textually adulterated.

We discuss these allegations in turn.

*1. The Mormon Church teaches that the Bible is incomplete.*

If the Mormon church has added new scripture to the canon, then the Bible alone must be considered scripturally incomplete. Mormon apostle Orson Pratt vigorously rejected the concept of a completed canon; indeed, those who believed such were viewed as incapable of salvation. "For who, with the Bible in their hands, can expect to be saved, if they suffer themselves to believe or harbor such a wicked doctrine in their hearts? . . . For God *will not save those* who reject the doctrine of continued revelation."[40]

This idea is staunchly defended by Mormonism because the *Book of Mormon*, protecting its own claims, also assailed the idea that the Bible alone was God's Word. Second Nephi 28:29, and 29:6,10 declare:

> Woe be unto him that shall say: We have received the word of God and we need no more of the word of God, for we have enough! . . . Thou fool, that shall say: A Bible, we have got a Bible and we need no more Bible. . . . Wherefore, because that ye have a Bible ye need not suppose that it contains all my words; neither need ye suppose that I have not caused more to be written.

Thus, the tenth president and prophet of the Mormon church, Joseph Fielding Smith, emphasized, "The canon of scripture is not only *not* complete, but the Lord has greater things to reveal to the people than have yet been given."[41]

Obviously, if three additional books of scripture (plus numerous revelations from a dozen Mormon presidents and prophets) have been necessary to give the "Word of God" to mankind, then the Bible itself certainly must be considered incomplete.

In his work *As Translated Correctly*, Mark Peterson, of the Council of Twelve Apostles, presents a typical Mormon approach to the Bible. Without supplying evidence, and in ignorance of the history of the canon, he alleges that entire books were deleted from the Bible. He lists over a dozen of these pseudopigraphal texts which, for some reason, he thinks had to have been divinely inspired.[42] Thus, as to the Bible we now possess, "whole sections of the text were occasionally omitted," and it was supposedly perverted in many other ways.[43]

Nevertheless, while his allegations concerning the compilation, transmission and translation of the Bible cannot be accepted, we *can* accept his comments in the Foreword: "The author is not a Bible scholar by any means, and certainly lays no claim to any such distinction. He writes only as a journalist reporting what is come to his attention in his own rather casual reading."[44]

In his book *Are Mormons Christians?*, Mormon scholar Dr. Robinson argues that if the Gospel writers can add the New Testament to the canon of the Jewish scriptures, then, at least in theory, so can Joseph Smith. He maintains that the issue is not whether one adds to the canon of Scripture but whether one is authorized and commanded by God to do so.[45]

But this misses the point. God would never command the addition of new scripture that *contradicted* or *denied* His own Word; this would make God a fool. The issue is whether or not the alleged new revelation is scriptural. If not, then it could not possibly have been authorized and commissioned by God.

What does the Bible teach about the acceptance of additional revelation and its supposed compatibility with the Bible? In the Bible God teaches that He is a God of truth who does not contradict Himself or deny Himself. The Scriptures teach that God "cannot lie," that His Word is "true," and "pure," and that neither God nor His Word changes (Numbers 23:19; Deuteronomy 32:4; Psalm 117:2; Isaiah 25:1; John 17:17; 2 Timothy 2:15; Titus 1:2; Job 23:13; Psalm 33:11; 119:89; Malachi 3:6; Hebrews 6:17; James 1:17). Therefore, God would never deny in one place what He has clearly spoken and affirmed in another. In conclusion, if additional Mormon scriptures deny what God has already clearly taught, then they cannot have originated from God (cf. chap. 24, Appendix Two).

## 2. *The Mormon church teaches that the Bible is doctrinally inadequate.*

Obviously, if the Bible is canonically incomplete, there may be important doctrinal truths missing from it. Naturally, the Mormon church thinks the additional revelations of Mormonism supply these missing doctrinal "truths." Mormon apostle LeGrand Richards declares, "The 'everlasting gospel' could not be discovered through reading the Bible alone—the old bottles full of old wine could not contain the new wine. . . . [Mormonism] is the only Christian church in the world that did not have to rely on the Bible for its organization and government."[46]

The Mormon text *A Sure Foundation* claims that, "The Bible alone is inadequate."[47] Joseph Smith himself said of the *Book of Mormon*, "A [man] will get nearer to God by abiding by its precepts, than by any other book."[48]

But this is not the teaching of the Bible, which solemnly testifies that it is sufficient: "All Scripture is inspired by God and profitable for teaching, for reproof, for correction, for training in righteousness; that the man of God may be adequate, equipped for every good work" (2 Timothy 3:16,17). Further, the Bible and God's power have "granted to us everything pertaining to life and godliness, through the true knowledge of Him who called us by His own glory and excellence" (2 Peter 1:3). When Mormonism maintains that the Bible is doctrinally or otherwise inadequate it rejects what God Himself has taught concerning His Word.

*3. The Mormon church teaches that the Bible is textually corrupted.*

It is apparently not enough for Mormonism to teach that God's revelation in the Bible was unfinished and that it is therefore doctrinally inadequate. The church must also teach that it has suffered major corruption. From Joseph Smith onward, Mormons have denounced the Bible as adulterated and unreliable, saying, for example, "Any man possessing of common understanding knows, that the Old and New Testaments are filled with errors, obscurities, italics and contradictions."[49]

The Bible's supposed inadequacy and corruption is why Mormon counselors frequently tell Mormons who are reading the Bible too much (or attending Bible studies) to stop such activity and read only Mormon literature.[50]

Even the *Book of Mormon* itself condemns the Christian church for allegedly perverting the Bible:

> They have taken away from the gospel of the Lamb many parts which are plain and most precious; and also many covenants of the Lord they have taken away. And all this have they done that they might pervert the right ways of the Lord. . . . Wherefore, thou seest that after the book hath gone forth through the hands of the great and abominable church, that there are many plain and precious things taken away from the book, which is the book of the Lamb of God (1 Nephi 13:26-28).

Joseph Smith contended that "ignorant translators, careless transcribers or designing and corrupt priests have committed many errors."[51]

Brigham Young held to similar views in characteristically rejecting the Bible's anti-Mormon teachings as corruptions.[52] Likewise, Mormon apostle Orson Pratt stated confidently, "*almost every verse has been corrupted and mutilated.* . . . All we have left are mutilated copies containing an incredible number of contradictory readings."[53] And he questions, "Who, in his right mind, could, for one moment, suppose the Bible in its present form to be a perfect guide? Who knows that even one verse of the whole Bible has escaped pollution so as to convey the same sense now as it did in the original?"[54]

But Mormons have never provided one iota of evidence to substantiate such foolish claims. In fact, any number of scholarly works have proven that the Bible has not been corrupted—it has by far the best manuscript attestation and textual preservation of any ancient book. For example, after a thorough evaluation of the textual evidence, citing numerous scholars in confirmation, Drs. Geisler and Nix, noted Biblical scholars, conclude that the Bible we now possess comprises at least ninety-nine percent of the original. Thus, a good modern critical edition of the Bible says, "Exactly what the autographs contained—line for line, word for word, and even letter for letter."[55] Dr. F.F. Bruce's book *The New Testament Documents: Are They Reliable?* is one of many other texts that can be cited to confirm this.

Indeed, the evidence is so persuasive that even some Mormon authorities will grudgingly make concessions. James Talmage once wrote that "although the Bible was corrupted in many parts, the volume as a whole must be admitted as authentic and credible."[56]

Regardless, Mormons are forced to admit that when asked to identify translation errors or corruptions they cannot do so. Why? Because none exists. There are no translation errors that prove Mormon doctrine to be right, and there are no corruptions.

So why do Mormons continue to use the Bible when they believe it is so unreliable and corrupted? They do so because they think they can sift the wheat from the chaff. How do they claim they do this? In two ways. Either their new scriptures "properly" interpret the Bible, or personal divine "revelation" informs them as to whether a given scripture is correct or corrupt. Thus, whenever a Mormon encounters something in the Bible he does not like, he feels he is perfectly free to reinterpret it in accordance with his own beliefs.[57]

This is why President Joseph Fielding Smith tells us, that "guided by the *Book of Mormon, Doctrine and Covenants,* and the Spirit of the Lord, it is not difficult for one to discern the errors in the Bible."[58]

This explains why leading Church theologian Bruce McConkie, in his *Doctrinal New Testament Bible Commentary,* repeatedly ignores or discards biblical teaching in favor of *Book of Mormon* teaching. Here are some illustrations:

In his "commentary" on Romans McConkie argues that Paul's epistle is properly understood only in light of nineteenth- and twentieth-century Mormon teaching. Thus, the *Book of Mormon* "sets forth in a pure, plain and perfect way the true [Mormon] doctrines of Christ, so that those who have an understanding of its teachings are able to reconcile the difficulties and solve the problems of the epistle to the Romans."[59] For instance, "Paul's difficult and complex teachings on the fall and atonement, and on the blessings that flow therefrom, are presented simply and clearly by various *Book of Mormon* prophets."[60]

Not surprisingly, McConkie informs his readers that the teachings in Romans and other New Testament books will be *misinterpreted* without first understanding them in light of Mormon doctrine.

This tacit admission of the incompatibility between the plain teaching of the Bible and the teaching of Mormonism underscores the fact that for the average Mormon the Bible is a closed book. It is not the authority they claim it to be—it is merely an early and corrupted edition of Mormon doctrine. Thus, any time the pronouncements of the Mormon president and prophet contradict the Bible (a frequent occurrence) "the prophet is right and the Scriptures are wrong."[61]

All this explains why Mormons believe Christians are ignorant concerning biblical teaching. After all, Christians reject the Bible's true interpreters—the Mormon scriptures, evolving Mormon doctrine and Mormon church authorities. Thus, we are told that Romans, for example, is a sealed book to "the sectarian [Christian] world," and "it was written to and for and about the saints [Mormons] and can be understood *by them and by them only.*"[62]

## Is the Mormon View of the Bible Credible?

The Mormon church's teaching on the Bible is not only wrong, but also illogical. Is it really conceivable that God would have inspired the Bible in the first place—knowing He would permit its almost complete corruption—knowing He would have to patiently wait over eighteen hundred years for someone to interpret all of its corruptions properly? Certainly, if God is any authority, He never expected His Word to be incomplete, insufficient or corrupted: "The grass withers, the flower fades, but the word of our God stands forever" (Isaiah 40:8).

In teaching that the Bible is incomplete, inadequate and corrupted, one wonders how Mormons can logically claim to "believe and trust the Bible."

Further, if Mormons truly believed what Jesus taught, they could not possibly accept what either the *Book of Mormon* or their church teaches about the Bible. The *Book of Mormon* maintains that the gospel was seriously perverted, but in so doing it denies the teachings of Jesus Himself, who promised, "Heaven and earth will pass away, but My words shall not pass away" (Matthew 24:35). And likewise, "For truly I say to you, until heaven and earth pass away, not the smallest letter or stroke shall pass away from the Law until all is accomplished" (Matthew 5:18). And again He reiterated, "But it is easier for heaven and earth to pass away than for one stroke of a letter of the Law to fail" (Luke 16:17). Jesus also declared, "He who rejects Me, and does not receive My sayings, has one who judges him; the word I spoke is what will judge him at the last day" (John 12:48). Jesus also promised that the gates of hell would *not* prevail against His church (Matthew 16:18).

It is an historical fact that the earliest New Testament manuscripts comprise *Christian* teachings and not those of Mormonism. Not once did Jesus or the inspired apostles ever teach Mormon theology. Can Mormons expect Christians to believe that until 1830 "the plain and most precious parts" of God's words were deleted when it is promised by God Himself that "the word of our God stands forever" (Isaiah 40:8)?

In spite of Mormon claims, the Bible is complete as it stands—it requires no additional revelation. It has a logical beginning (Genesis 1) and ending (Revelation 22), wherein the entire scope of human history and eternity are compassed. It is doctrinally complete and its ethical injunctions cannot be improved. Again, containing "everything pertaining to life and godliness" (2 Peter 1:3), it provides everything a believer needs to live for God, please Him and do His will: "All Scripture is God-breathed and is useful for teaching, rebuking, correcting and training in righteousness, so that the man of God may be thoroughly equipped for every good work" (2 Timothy 3:16,17 NIV).

But, as if speaking directly to the Mormon church, the Bible sternly warns against adding anything to God's revelation or taking anything from it (Revelation 22:18,19).* We earlier cited Proverbs 30:5,6 which warns that God's Word is proven and therefore must not be tampered with: "Every word of God is tested. . . . do not add to his words, lest he reprove you, and you be proved a liar."

In conclusion, Mormons may believe either the Bible or Mormonism, but they cannot logically believe both. For the church to tell the world that it "believes the Bible" is sheer hypocrisy. And such hypocrisy is nowhere better demonstrated than in its treatment of Joseph Smith's "Inspired Version" (see appendix).

# ◆ ◆ *Appendix One* ◆ ◆

*Why Is Joseph Smith's "Inspired Version" So Embarrassing to Mormonism?*

Joseph Smith's "Inspired Version" of the Bible (a new translation) presents the Mormon church with yet another dilemma.

Appealing to Smith's alleged power of divine translation (*Book of Mormon, Book of Abraham*), Mormons teach that only an inspired translation of the Bible can be considered "absolutely reliable,"[63] and Joseph Smith, their own prophet, claimed he produced just such a volume.

Yet even though the Mormon church believes their prophet wrote this translation under "divine inspiration" (as he did the *Book of Mormon* and the *Book of Abraham*), they cannot officially accept it because it actually *denies* Mormon doctrine! The Tanners correctly explain the quandary this places the Mormon church in:

> The Mormon church is faced with a peculiar dilemma with regard to Joseph Smith's "inspired revision." They cannot

---

* While the direct application of this verse is only to the book of Revelation, it must also be relevant to the entire Bible, for the entire Bible is divine revelation.

reject it entirely without admitting he was a deceiver. On the other hand, if they were to print the revision and fully endorse it, they would be faced with equally insurmountable problems. The contents of the "inspired revision" actually contradict doctrines that are now taught in the Mormon church. Therefore, the Mormon church can neither fully accept nor fully reject the *Inspired Version* of the Bible. They claim that Joseph Smith was inspired to translate, and then turn right around and use the King James Version. . . . Since the Mormon leaders cannot come right out and say that Joseph Smith made mistakes in his Inspired Version, they have devised another excuse to keep from fully endorsing it. They claim that Joseph Smith never finished the translation.[64]

Thus, to avoid embarrassment, the Utah church claims that the translation was never "officially" recognized because it was (allegedly) never finished.[65] The only problem is that Joseph Smith himself said he *did* finish the translation on July 2, 1833. In his *History of the Church* Smith declared, "We this day finished the translating of the Scriptures, for which we return the gratitude to our Heavenly Father."[66] Smith claimed the same thing elsewhere, and so did Sidney Rigdon.[67] In fact, Smith did not translate the Bible at all since he was ignorant of Greek and Hebrew. Characteristically, he only claimed he received the translation by "inspiration."[68] Nevertheless, in *Doctrine and Covenants* God Himself commanded the printing of the new translation which He called the "fullness of my scriptures" (*D&C*, 104:58; 94:10; 124:89).*

The command of God to print these "Scriptures" was never obeyed by Joseph Smith—or the Mormon church. For some strange reason, Smith never took his own divine translation too seriously. Like his modern church, when it contradicted his other revelations, he *ignored* the new version and relied on the King James Bible![70]

Incredibly, he even *revised* parts of his "inspired" translation up to *three* times.[71] Thus, the Tanners are forced to conclude: "A careful examination of his work reveals unmistakable evidence that it is merely a human production and contains many serious errors."[72] If this is true—and anyone who impartially studies the text can prove this to their own satisfaction—how can *any* of Smith's "inspired" translations be trusted?

Nevertheless, the "Inspired Version" presents Mormons with other unanswered questions. Mormons refer to purported books of the Bible that were surreptitiously deleted by Christians. If so, why did not Smith return them to the canon? (In fact, he deleted one more—the Song of Solomon!)[73] Also, if Mormons claim they do not use his version because it

---

*Some argue the divine translation was not completely satisfactory; regardless, it was satisfactory enough for God to command its printing.[69]

was not yet finished, why do they not themselves finish it since every president is a "prophet, seer, and revelator" of the church?

Finally, Smith not only made deliberate *changes* in his "Inspired Version," he actually copied in King James translation errors—just as he did in the *Book of Mormon*![74]

Is it surprising then that Mormon authorities have recently provided additional evidence of their distrust of their own prophet? They printed a new King James Version with certain portions of the "Inspired Version" in footnotes. However, only those portions which are acceptable to *current* Mormon doctrine are reproduced. Even though Smith claimed it was a divine translation, his results are only footnoted and not canonized as scripture.[75]

Not surprisingly, other Mormon leaders disagree. They emphasize that Smith's translation *was* truly divine and must be accepted by the church. Robert J. Matthews is cited as "one of the foremost scholars in the Church."[76] He has a Ph.D. from Brigham Young University, where he also became a faculty member. He served as chairman of the Department of Ancient Scripture as well as the Dean of Religious Education for seven years. He claims that,

> It is my conviction that Joseph Smith's translation of the Bible is a unique production, divinely inspired, worthy of study, and important to every soul who wants to understand the gospel of Jesus Christ. The reader of [this translation] ... will be thrice blessed. First, he will gain an insight to the Prophet's [Joseph Smith's] understanding of various scriptures; second, he will learn many things about the gospel not found in other sources [e.g., the Bible]; and third, he will obtain a clue as to the content and meaning of the Old and New Testaments in their original form.[77]

Thus, "The JST has everything any other Bible has; but the JST also supplies additional information about God's nature, man's nature, the origin of Satan, the premortal existence, ... [etc.]."[78]

But again, Smith's alleged translation is seriously flawed and not credible. The Mormon who accepts this translation does so because he believes in Smith's prophethood and so believes that God Himself commanded its publication. The fact that it denies Mormon doctrine seems to fall on deaf ears—contradictions and errors are rationalized in various ways, only compounding the problems and further documenting the irrational nature of Mormon faith.

Below we document some of the changes Smith claimed as divinely orchestrated. We observe that "more than twice as many verses were changed in the New Testament as were changed in the Old."[79]

| Joseph Smith's "Inspired Version" | New American Standard Bible Version |
|---|---|
| John 1:1—"In the beginning was the gospel preached through the Son. And the gospel was the word, and the word was with the Son, and the Son was with God, and the Son was of God." (This verse denies the eternal deity of Christ.) | John 1:1—"In the beginning was the Word, and the Word was with God, and the Word was God." |
| John 4:26—"For unto such hath God promised his Spirit. And they who worship him, must worship in spirit and in truth." (This verse denies that God is a Spirit.) | John 4:26—[John 4:24] "God is spirit; and those who worship Him must worship in spirit and truth." |
| Romans 4:5—"But to him that seeketh not to be justified by the law of works, but believeth on him who justifieth not the ungodly, his faith is counted for righteousness." (This verse denies the justification of the ungodly.) | Romans 4:5—"But to the one who does not work, but believes in him who justifies the ungodly, his faith is reckoned as righteousness." |
| Romans 1:5—"By whom we have received grace and apostleship, through obedience, and faith in his name to preach the gospel among all nations." (This verse teaches works salvation.) | Romans 1:5—"Through whom we have received grace and apostleship to bring about the obedience of faith among all the Gentiles, for His name's sake." |
| Romans 4:16—"Therefore ye are justified of faith and works through grace, to the end the promise might be sure to all the seed." (This verse teaches works salvation and redefines grace.) | Romans 4:16—"For this reason it is by faith, that it might be in accordance with grace, in order that the promise may be certain to all the descendants, not only to those who are of the Law, but also to those who are of the faith of Abraham, who is the father of us all." |
| 1 John 4:12—"No man hath seen God at any time, except them who believe." (This verse supports the first vision account.) | 1 John 4:12—"No one has beheld God at any time; if we love one another, God abides in us, and His love is perfected in us." |

Acts 13:48—"And when the Gentiles heard this, they were glad, and glorified the word of the Lord; and as many as believed were ordained unto eternal life." (This verse denies God's sovereignty in salvation.)

Acts 13:48—"And when the Gentiles heard this, they began rejoicing and glorifying the Word of the Lord; and as many as had been appointed to eternal life believed."

In addition, the Mormon doctrine of preexistence is taught in the "Inspired Version" in Genesis 2:9 and 6:52 (the Bible stops at Genesis 6:22), and the doctrine of God being a man is taught in Genesis 7:42 ("Behold, I am God; Man of Holiness is my name"; the Bible stops at verse 24).[80]

In light of such "Mormonizing" of the Christian Bible, it is hardly unexpected that Mormon theologians such as Bruce McConkie appeal to the "Inspired Version" to supposedly "prove" Mormon doctrine from the Bible. McConkie has dealt with the Scriptures in the same manner in his so-called commentaries. (In fact, they are not true commentaries, but merely repetitions of Mormon doctrine.[81]) In his commentary on Romans 4 (verses 5 and 6), for example, he declares that "the high point of the Apostle's presentation, as *clarified by the Inspired Version account*, is that man is 'justified of faith and works, through grace' (Inspired Version, v. 16). . . . 'And that God will *not* justify the ungodly.'"[82]

It goes without saying that the "Inspired Version" is the exact *opposite* of the biblical verse, as any standard English or Greek text will prove. God says He *will* justify the ungodly through faith (Romans 4:5).

In conclusion, we have one question. Mormon leaders cite the authority of the "Inspired Version" to refute biblical teaching. Yet Mormon authorities also refuse to officially recognize the "Inspired Version" because it denies Mormon doctrine. Isn't this self-deception?

## ◆ ◆ *Appendix Two* ◆ ◆

*Is Mormon Biblical Scholarship Credible?*

The Mormon church claims that it offers the world the true interpretation of the Bible. But the following examples of false interpretation are not exceptions; they are characteristic of Mormon biblical scholarship. First, we supply the scriptural verse and then an illustration of Mormon scholarship. We emphasize the works of Bruce McConkie, but similar illustrations could be multiplied from other Mormon theologians (see note 87).

*John 3:16*: "For God so loved the world that He gave His only begotten son, that whoever believes in Him should not perish, but have eternal life."

How does Bruce McConkie's "commentary" interpret this verse? He says, "It summarizes the whole plan of salvation, tying together the Father, the Son, his atoning sacrifice, the belief in him which presupposes righteous works, and ultimate eternal exaltation [godhood] for the faithful."[83] Notice that good works are assumed as a prerequisite for salvation and that the biblical words "eternal life" are given their Mormon meaning of exaltation or achieving godhood.

*John 6:28,29* (NIV): "They asked him, 'What must we do to do the works God requires?' Jesus answered, 'The work of God is this: to believe in the one he has sent.'"

McConkie claims that the following is "the sense and meaning" of these two verses: "This is the message of the Father, this is what he would have all men do: believe in me. . . . And show that you believe by obeying the laws and ordinances of my gospel [Mormonism]."[84] Of course, McConkie has again added works salvation into these Scriptures when, in fact, they teach nothing of the kind.

Elsewhere he takes the very plain statements of our Lord—that the "one who believes has eternal life," (cf. John 3:16, 5:24, 6:47) and twists them to mean that the "one who does *works* has eternal life [godhood]." Note Jesus' words from the Gospel of John:

> I tell you the truth, whoever hears my word and believes him who sent me has eternal life and will not be condemned; he has crossed over from death to life (John 5:24 NIV).

> All that the Father gives Me shall come to Me, and the one who comes to Me I will certainly not cast out (John 6:37).

> For this is the will of my Father, that everyone who beholds the Son and believes in Him may have eternal life; and I Myself will raise him up on the last day (John 6:40).

> Truly, truly, I say to you, he who believes has eternal life (John 6:47).

Now observe what this leading doctrinal theologian of Mormonism has done to these verses. Note how he places words into the mouth of Christ, words that Jesus never even spoke (for the reader's convenience, ideas and words Jesus never spoke are italicized):

> [John 5:24] He who believes *and obeys my words . . . shall have exaltation* [godhood] and shall not be damned. . . .

> [John 6:37] Nevertheless, all those among you who believe in me and my words, *and who obey my law*, have been given to me by my father. . . .

> [John 6:40] And this also is the will of the Father who sent me, that everyone who received me as the son of God, and

who believeth that I am the Christ, and *who obeyeth the laws and ordinances of my gospel* [Mormonism], *enduring in righteousness to the end*, shall have everlasting life [godhood]. . . .

[John 6:47] Solemnly and soberly I say unto you, he that believeth in me as the very son of God, and who receiveth my gospel, *obeying all the laws and ordinances thereof*, and who *endureth in righteousness and truth* [Mormonism] *unto the end*, behold, he shall have everlasting life, *which is exaltation* [godhood] *in my father's kingdom*.[85]

In distorting the Scriptures, McConkie is merely following in the footsteps of his own alleged prophet, Joseph Smith—and all those presidents and prophets of the Mormon church who followed him, down to McConkie himself. For example, note how easily Joseph Smith dismisses scriptural authority for his own biased evaluation in his comment on Hebrews 6:1:

Look at Heb. vi:1 contradictions—"Therefore leaving the principals of the doctrine of Christ, let us go on to perfection." If a man leaves the principals of the doctrine of Christ, how can he be saved in the principals? This is a contradiction. I don't believe it. I will render it as it should be—"Therefore not leaving the principals of the doctrine of Christ, let us go on to perfection."[86]

If Joseph Smith had simply examined the biblical text, he would have seen that this verse is not teaching that we are to leave the doctrine of Christ, but merely the elementary or simple teachings and to progress onward to deeper faith. Nevertheless, the above are only the briefest possible examples of Mormon distortions of the Bible. One may read, for example, McConkie's *Doctrinal New Testament Commentary* and find literally hundreds of similar examples.[87]

◆

# CHAPTER 28

# Mormon
# Distortion
# of
# Salvation

*Did the Early Mormon Church Really
Teach a Doctrine of Blood Atonement—
That Men Must Be Killed to Atone for
Their Own Sins?*

The Mormon doctrine of blood atonement—or killing men to expiate their sins—is one of the most horrible of early Mormon beliefs. Yet Mormons claim that the doctrine was never practiced. When critics argue otherwise, they reply that the entire charge is simply a damnable invention of the enemies of the church. The tenth president and prophet of the Mormon church claimed:

> Did you know that not a single individual was ever "blood atoned," as you are pleased to call it, for apostasy or any other cause. . . . Do you know of anyone whose blood was ever shed by the command of the church, or members thereof, to "save his soul"?[88]

Theologian Bruce McConkie (and Hugh Nibley, elsewhere[89]) declared that the alleged quotes substantiating the charges of blood atonement were merely bits and pieces "wholly torn from context":

From the days of Joseph Smith to the present, wicked and evilly disposed persons have fabricated false and slanderous stories to the effect that the church, in the early days of this dispensation, engaged in a practice of *blood atonement* where-under the blood of apostates and others was shed by the church as atonement for their sins. These claims are false and were known by their originators to be false. There is not one historical instance of so-called blood atonement in this dispensation, nor has there been one event or occurrence what-ever, of any nature, from which the slightest inference arises that any such practice either existed or was taught.[90]

The tenth president and prophet of the Mormon church, Joseph Fielding Smith, called the idea a "damnable falsehood for which the accusers must answer."[91] He alleged it was "but the repetition of the ravings of enemies of the church, without one grain of truth. . . . Not a single individual was ever 'blood atoned' . . . for apostasy or any other cause."[92] Elsewhere he remarked (citing Mormon scripture itself!—[*D&C*, 42:79]):

Is it the prerogative of the Church to inflict the punishment? No! The Lord has given commandment that all offenses worthy of death shall be handled by the courts of the land as declared in the *Doctrine and Covenants*, "And it shall come to pass, that if any persons among you shall kill, they shall be delivered up and dealt with according to the laws of the land; for remember that he hath no forgiveness; and it shall be proved according to the laws of the land."[93]

In other words, while Smith himself taught that blood atonement was the only righteous and possible way for men to have certain sins forgiven, he also said that such judgment was to be inflicted by the legal authorities. While he denied that the *Mormon church* ever practiced it, yet he confessed that for certain sins the sinner's "only hope is to have their own blood shed to atone, as far as possible, in their behalf," and that "this is scriptural doctrine, and is taught in all the standard works of the church."[94]

But when all these Mormon prophets, presidents and leaders claim the church never practiced blood atonement, they are wrong. The church did practice blood atonement,[95] as even some Mormon researchers have admitted,[96] and emphatic denials by Mormon leadership cannot change the fact.

There are several reasons and substantial evidence to support this conclusion. First of all, it is hardly surprising that when the Mormon church *denies* the full atoning value of Christ's death—teaching that Christ's atonement itself *did not pay for sin* (chap. 15)—that it might also teach that the shed blood of the sinner himself was a practical necessity.

This concept is in complete harmony with the Mormon emphasis that a person can purge his own sin by meritorious works.

Second, in much of its early history, Mormonism was a law unto itself. Is it illogical to think that the early Mormons who believed this doctrine would never have put it into practice when it was the Mormon church itself that was frequently the law of the land? If secular authorities could not (or would not) uphold the doctrine, who else could secure the necessary expiation of sin? Who else could help get a man or woman to heaven?

Third, we must remember that Mormonism is an occult religion (chaps. 18-20). It was founded and undergirded by occult practitioners who, collectively, engaged in a dozen different occult practices. And we must also remember that the power behind the occult is Satan.[97] If Jesus called Satan a "liar" and "a murderer from the beginning" (John 8:44), it is hardly impossible that early Mormonism could have followed in the footsteps of the devil—whose respect for human life is less than commendable.

Fourth, even some Mormon writers have admitted that the doctrine of blood atonement *was* put into practice. The following citations speak for themselves—they are not "lies," "distortions produced by enemies of the church," or citations "wholly torn from context."

John Ahmanson was a Danish man who converted to Mormonism in 1850 and immigrated to the U.S. to join the settlement of Mormons at Salt Lake City. However, he became disillusioned with the church, and in 1876 he wrote a history of Mormonism in an effort to warn the Danish public of the dangers and deceptions of Mormonism. He called his book *Vor Tids Muhammed*, or *A Muhammed for Our Time*, evidently a reference to the violent-prone Muhammed and the Muslim religion (e.g., "holy war"). This Danish work was recently translated by Dr. Gleason Archer and published under the title *Secret History: An Eyewitness Account of the Rise of Mormonism*. As an eyewitness, Ahmanson wrote in 1876:

> Only the very smallest portion of the crimes of the Mormons have come to light, for who would recount them, after all? The dead do not talk, and murderers seldom are accustomed to bring up the matter of their guilt. Yet even so, we shudder at the number of murderers that have been legally attested in Utah. We shudder at them even more because they were committed in the interest of a religious fanaticism and because the laws out there were so trampled under foot that it has not been possible even until now to bring a single one of the murderers to justice.[98]

In other words, Mormon political and legal power in Utah was so strong that the murderers were never brought to trial.

Sixteen years earlier, non-Mormon Judge John Cradelbaugh, of the United States Federal Court, Utah Territory, wrote to William H. Hooper in a letter dated January 18, 1860:

> 1st. That the Mormon people are subject to a theocratic government, and recognize no law as binding which does not coincide with their pretended revelations.... 4th. That they teach the doctrine of "the shedding of human blood for the remission of sin," as defined by their ecclesiastical code, and these teachings *are carried into practice*. The murders of [Henry] Jones and his mother at Pondtown; of the Parrishes and Potters at Springville; of the Aiken party at Chicken Creek, the Mudforts at Salt Creek and at the Bone Yard, and of Forbes at Springville, are the natural results of these vile doctrines. 5th. That they teach the doctrine that it is right and godly that Mormons should rob Gentiles [non-Mormons] whenever they can do so with facility and escape public exposure. The Mountain Meadows Massacre is a melancholy proof of this fact.... I am prepared here and now with proofs to sustain these charges.[99]

Even Mormon writer Klaus J. Hansen confesses in his book *Quest For Empire* that Mormons did "attempt to enforce the doctrine":

> Yet because of its theological implications, and because the [Mormon] Council of Fifty was to administer it, the doctrine [of blood atonement] was surrounded with an aura of mystery, terror, and holy murder. The Council of Fifty heightened the atmosphere of fear and secrecy associated with this practice by conducting cases involving the possibility of blood atonement in utmost secrecy for fear of public repercussions.... Whether or not the Council of Fifty ever pronounced the death penalty according to the principals of blood atonement cannot be ascertained. If Smith practiced it in Nauvoo, there is no record of it.... However, shortly after the Mormons established the Government of God in Utah on what they believed to be a permanent basis, *they attempted to enforce the doctrine*.[100]

Fanny Stenhouse, a formerly devout Mormon, wrote in 1875:

> In many instances the outrages committed against persons who were known to be innocent were so revolting that no woman—nay, even no right-minded man—would venture to more than just allude to them. A few however, and only a few, and they by no means the worst, of the milder cases, I will just mention.

There was the murder of the Aikin party—six persons—
who were killed on their way to California. The same year a
man named Yates was killed under atrocious circumstances;
and Franklin McNeil who had sued Brigham for false impris-
onment and who was killed at his hotel door. There was
Sergeant Pike, and there was Arnold and Drown. There was
Price and William Bryan at Fairfield; there was Almon Babbitt,
and Brassfield, and Dr. [J. King] Robinson; there was also
James Cowdy and his wife and child, and Margetts and his
wife; and many another, too,—to say nothing of that frightful
murder at the Mountain Meadows.

Besides these there is good reason to think that Lieutenant
Gunnison and his party were also victims, although it was
said that they were shot by "Indians." The Potter and Parrish
murders were notorious; Forbes, and Jones and his mother,
might be added to the same list; the dumb boy, Andrew Bernard; a woman killed by her own husband; Morris the rival
[Mormon] Prophet, and Banks, and four women who belonged
to their party; Isaac Potter, and Charles Wilson, and John
Walker. These are but a few. *The death list is too long for me to
venture to give it.*[101]

She recalls a conversation with one of her best friends, Mary Burton,
about the difficulty of attempting to retain faith when hearing stories of
horrible atrocities being committed by Mormon leaders. She says, "I had
heard these very same stories, and told her so; and I tried to make her
believe that they were without foundation."[102] Burton herself had told
Stenhouse:

In the time of Joseph Smith a band of men was organized to
put to death anyone who was troublesome to the Church or
offended the Elders. Some people say that it was one or
perhaps more of this band who fired at Governor Boggs,
of Missouri, and who killed many other Gentiles. . . . Elder
Shrewsbury himself told me long ago that Thomas B. Marsh,
the then President of the Twelve, when he apostatized, took
oath that the Saints had formed a "Destruction Company," as
he called it, . . . Now they speak of those men as "Danites" and
"Avenging Angels." People say that those who are dissatisfied
and want to leave [Mormonism], almost always are killed after
they set out, *by the Indians*, and they dare not say boldly who
they believe those "Indians" are. Then, too, one lady told me
that she had heard from her sister that not only were apostates
killed in a mysterious way by Indians or someone else, but that
many people who were "missing," or else found murdered,
were only *suspected* of being very weak in the faith.[103]

In "Murders in Early Utah," chapter seven in the Tanners' *The Mormon Kingdom* (volume 2), we find corroboration of much of these accounts and many other instances of people who were murdered—some in a gruesome fashion (for example, Young taught that thieves should have their throats cut). Dr. J.M. Vaughan, Isaac Potter, William Parrish, John Gheen, Tom Colbourn, and Squire Newton Brassfield are only a few of the cases of murder listed by the Tanners, who note, "We could show many other cases where men were murdered."[104] Chapter 1 of the same text, "Works of Darkness," lists further examples.

At least eleven crimes, most *not* capital, were held to be worthy of blood atonement by early Mormon leaders. (See below.) Again, the idea is that not only must the person die for these sins, but that also his or her blood must actually be spilled. Even today the fact that the state of Utah offers a criminal the choice of execution by lethal injection or shooting ("blood spilling"), is traceable to the doctrine of blood atonement. For example, this doctrine seems to be the reason behind the famed double murderer Gary Gilmore choosing execution by the firing squad rather than hanging (the pre-1987 option)—to spill his blood in accordance with the doctrine.[105] In all of Utah's history there have been only six legal hangings, an apparent witness to Mormon influence.[106]

Some Mormon polygamous sects (noted for their devotion to early Mormon revelation) may even practice this doctrine today. For example, the *Deseret News* of September 29, 1977, reported on Mormon Ervil LeBaron who "has been linked to more than a dozen deaths and disappearances in the West." He is only one of several other polygamous Mormon sect leaders that is alleged to be implicated in murder.[107]

Incredibly, Mormon prophet Brigham Young taught that murdering others could actually be the way to *love* them, a sentiment also expressed by at least one member of Charles Manson's clan*[109]:

> All mankind love themselves, and let these principles be known by an individual, and he would be glad to have his blood shed. That would be loving themselves, even unto an eternal exaltation. . . . Will you love that man or woman well enough *to shed their blood*? That is what Jesus Christ meant. . . . I could refer you to *plenty of instances* where men have been righteously slain, in order to atone for their sins. . . . *This is loving our neighbour as ourselves*; if he needs help, help him; and if he wants salvation and it is necessary to spill his blood on the earth in order that he may be saved, *spill it. . . . That is the way to love mankind.*[110]

---

* Susan Atkins once said, "You really have to have a lot of love in your heart to do what I did to [Sharon] Tate."[108]

Fanny Stenhouse commented in 1875:

> The doctrine of the "BLOOD ATONEMENT" is that the murder of an Apostate is *a deed of love!* . . . Only by his blood being shed is there any chance of forgiveness for him; it is therefore the kindest action that he can perform toward him to shed his blood—the doing so is a deed of truest love. The nearer, the dearer, the more tenderly loved the sinner is, the greater the affection shown by the shedder of blood . . . —it is making atonement, not a crime; it is an act of mercy, therefore meritorious.[111]

Jedediah M. Grant, second counselor to Brigham Young, also clearly stated that murdering others was really only to *save* them. He says of Mormon leaders:

> It is their right to baptize a sinner to save him, and it is also their right to kill a sinner to save him, when he commits those crimes that can only be atoned for by shedding his blood. . . . We would not kill a man, of course, *unless we killed him to save him.* . . . Do you think it would be any sin to KILL ME if I were to break my covenants. . . . Do you believe you would kill me if I broke the covenants of God, and you had the Spirit of God? YES; and the more Spirit of God I had, the more I should strive to save your soul by spilling your blood, when you had committed sin that could not be remitted by baptism.[112]

The various crimes capable of blood atonement are catalogued below. (Unless otherwise indicated, all quotes are by presidents and prophets or other leaders of the early church. They are usually taken from the Tanners' and Martin's research and most have been checked in the original by the authors. They constitute only a *small* sampling of such statements. Emphases are added.[113]

### 1. Marrying a Black Person

Brigham Young (second president) stated:

> Shall I tell you the law of God in regard to the African race? If the white man who belongs to the chosen seed mixes his blood with the seed of Cain, the penalty, under the law of God is *death on the spot.* This will always be so.[114]

In his personal journal, Wilford Woodruff (fourth president) quoted Young as teaching that even the *children* of such a marriage would be judged:

And if any man mingle his seed with the seed of Cane [sic] the ownly [sic] way he could get rid of it or have salvation would be to come forward and have his *head cut off* & spill his Blood upon the ground. It would also *take the life of his children.*[115]

Likewise, Lester Bush, Jr., a Mormon writer, quoted Brigham Young as saying that this offense "required blood atonement (offspring included) for salvation."[116]

Even as late as 1897 some church leaders were teaching that the offender "would *be killed, and his offspring.*"[117] Joseph Smith himself apparently taught the same doctrine.[118]

## 2. Rejecting the Mormon Gospel

Wilford Woodruff (fourth president) warned:

The time is coming when justice will be laid to the line and righteousness to the plummet; when we shall ask, "Are you for God?" and if you are not heartily on the Lord's side, you *will be hewn down.*[119]

## 3 Apostasy

Brigham Young (second president) declared:

I say, rather than that apostates should flourish here, I will unsheathe my bowie knife and *conquer or die.*[120]

Heber Kimball, a member of the First Presidency, also avowed in reference to apostasy:

When it is necessary that blood should be shed, we should be as ready to do that *as to eat an apple.*[121]

## 4. Lying

Brigham Young said:

I . . . warned those who lied and stole and followed Israel that they would *have their heads cut off*, for that was the law of God and it should be executed.[122]

## 5. Counterfeiting

Brigham Young said:

I swore by the Eternal Gods that if men in our midst would not stop this cursed work of stealing and counterfeiting, *their throats should be cut.*[123]

(Perhaps it is worthy to note that Joseph Smith was himself a counterfeiter.)[124]

## 6. *Adultery and Immorality*

Brigham Young wrote the following instruction to Mormon bishops:

> Suppose you found your brother in bed with your wife, and *put a javelin through both of them*, you would be justified, and they would atone for their sins, and be received into the kingdom of God. I would at once do so in such a case; and under such circumstances, I have no wife whom I love so well that I would not put a javelin through her heart, and I would do it with clean hands.
>
> There is not a man or woman, who violates the covenants made with their God, that will not [at some point] be required to pay the debt. *The blood of Christ will never wipe that out, your own blood must atone for it.*[125]

Likewise, Heber Kimball avowed:

> If there is anything of that kind, we will slay both men and women. We will do it, as the Lord liveth—we will slay such characters . . . our females . . . are not unclean, *for we wipe all unclean ones from our midst*; we not only wipe them from our streets, but *we wipe them out of existence* . . . so help me God, while I live, I will lend my hand to wipe such persons out: and I know this people will.[126]

Apostle George A. Smith stated:

> The principle, the only one that beats and throbs through the heart of the entire inhabitants of this Territory, is simply this: *The man who seduces his neighbor's wife must die, and her nearest relative must kill him!*[127]

George Q. Cannon, a member of the First Presidency declared:

> We are solving the problem that is before the world today, over which they are pretending to rack their brains. I mean the "Social Problem." We close the door on one side, and say that whoredoms, seductions and adulteries must not be committed amongst us, and we say to those who are determined to carry on such things *we will kill you*; at the same time we open the door in the other direction and make plural marriage honorable.[128]

## 7. Stealing

Brigham Young said:

> If you want to know what to do with a thief that you may
> find stealing, *I say kill him on the spot*, and never suffer him
> to commit another iniquity. . . . I would consider it just as
> much my duty to do that, as to baptize a man for the
> remission of his sins.[129]

Apostle Orson Hyde declared:

> It would have a tendency to place a terror on those who
> leave these parts, that may prove their salvation when they
> see *the heads of thieves taken off*, or *shot down* before the pub-
> lic.[130]

## 8. Using God's Name in Vain

Brigham Young warned:

> I tell you the time is coming when that man uses the
> name of the Lord . . . the penalty will be affixed and imme-
> diately be *executed on the spot*. (*Journal of Hosea Stout*, 2,71;
> p. 56 of the typed copy at the Utah State Historical Soci-
> ety.)[131]

## 9. Covenant Breakers

Jedediah M. Grant declared:

> We have those amongst us that are full of all manner of
> abominations, those who *need to have their blood shed*, for
> water will not do, their sins are of too deep a dye. You may
> think that I am not teaching you Bible doctrine, but what
> says the apostle Paul? I would ask how many covenant
> breakers there are in this city and in this kingdom. I believe
> that there are a great many; and if they are covenant breakers
> we need a place designated, *where we can shed their blood*.[132]

> Then what ought this meek people, who keep the com-
> mandments of God do unto them? "Why" says one, "they
> ought to *pray to the Lord to kill them!*" I want to know if they
> would wish the Lord to come down and do all your dirty
> work! . . . When a man prays for a thing, he ought to be
> willing *to perform it himself*.[133]

Blood atonement was also prescribed for murder, and even for condemning Joseph Smith.[134] Smith himself clearly preferred spilling blood
to execution by other means. In a debate on the subject he once stated:

I replied, I was opposed to hanging, even if a man kill another, I will shoot him, or cut off his head, spill his blood on the ground, and let the smoke thereof ascend up to God; and if ever I have the privilege of making a law on that subject, I will have it so.[135]

John D. Lee was a close confidante of Brigham Young. He was also the executed "scapegoat" for the hideous Mountain Meadows Massacre— which involved the wholesale slaughter of 137 innocent men, women and children pioneers by Mormon zealots. He stated in his 1877 *Confessions of John D. Lee*:

I knew of *many men being killed* in Nauvoo by the Danites. It was then the *rule* that all the enemies of Joseph Smith should be *killed*, and I know of many a man who was quietly put out of the way by the orders of Joseph and his apostles while the church was there. *It has always been a well understood doctrine* of the Church that it was *right* and *praiseworthy* to *kill* every person who spoke *evil of the Prophet*. This doctrine has been strictly lived up to in Utah, until the Gentiles arrived in such great numbers that it became unsafe to follow the practice, but the doctrine is still believed [in 1877], and no year passes without one or more of those who have spoken evil of Brigham Young *being killed, in a secret manner*. Springfield, Utah, was one of the hot-beds of fanaticism, and I expect that more men were *killed* there, in proportion to population, than in any other part of Utah. In that settlement it was *certain death to say a word against the authorities, high or low*.[136]

In a macabre fashion, Brigham Young even seemed to relish the wickedness of some of his people. "And if the Gentiles wish to see a few tricks, we have 'Mormons' that can perform them. We have the meanest devils on the earth in our midst, and we intend to keep them, for we have use for them."[137] And,

Do you say there are people here who are wicked? So we say. Could I wish things to be otherwise? NO, *I would NOT have them different if I could*. . . . I have *many a time*, in this stand, *dared the world* to produce as mean devils as we can; we can beat them at anything. We have the greatest and smoothest *liars in the world*, the cunningest and most adroit *thieves*, and *any other* shade of character that you can mention.[138]

And,

Many of you know that you cannot get your endowment without the devils being present; indeed we cannot make rapid progress without the devils. I know that it frightens the righteous sectarian [Christ] world to think that we have so many devils with us, ... *we could not prosper without them.*[139]

Again, we stress that this teaching *was put into practice*, despite emphatic Mormon denial. Stenhouse and many other Mormons then living confirm this in their writings. For example, Stenhouse provides further testimony that the doctrine was, in fact, put into practice—including for "sins" as yet unmentioned:

> Certain sins cannot be forgiven here on earth—Shedding innocent blood, divulging the secrets of the Endowment House—marital unfaithfulness on the part of the wife— Apostasy;—these are unpardonable. All other crimes which Gentiles abhor may become even virtues, if done in the cause of the church. I do not, of course, mean to say that the mass of the Mormon people act up to such atrocious doctrines; for although, when among themselves, they would admit that the theory was correct, the better instincts of their nature keep them from even putting that theory into practice. But what I do mean to say is, that such doctrines have, over and over again, *been distinctly taught in the plainest words in the public hearing of thousands; that they have been printed and reprinted by authority; that they have been practiced, and that the very highest of the Mormon leaders have applauded; and that, even at the present moment, these doctrines form part of the dogmas of the church.* It is this day a matter of fact, and not a matter of question that if any Mormon Apostate were to commit any of the unpardonable sins which I have mentioned, and if he or she were to be assassinated by a private individual, all zealous Mormons— all the leaders—would maintain that not only was the deed justifiable but even meritorious![140]

Unfortunately, some of those Mormons who left the church in disgust over the policy of killing people "to save them" sometimes themselves were then murdered for their own crime of "apostasy."[141] In 1860, noted journalist Horace Greeley apparently refers to seventy-five known cases of murdered "apostates" in that year alone.[142] Stenhouse refers to a young Baptist preacher and his wife who initially "spoke of the joy which [they] had experienced in being baptized into the Mormon Church"—so much so that they moved to Salt Lake City to be with the Mormon community. However, "There they were soon utterly disgusted with what they witnessed, apostatized, and set out for England. When they had gone three-fourths of their way back to the Missouri River, the young man, his wife, child, and another apostate and his wife, were killed by 'Indians'—such, at least, was the report; but dissenting Mormons have charged their 'taking off' to the order of the leaders of the Mormon Church."[143]

Also, according to Fanny Stenhouse, when a friend of hers was said to be in a condition of "apostasy," the Mormon Bishop told her, "I would think about as much of *killing you* or any other miserable Apostate as I would about *killing a cat*. If Brigham Young were to tell me to *put you to death* I would do it with the greatest of pleasure; —and it would be for *your good*, too."[144] Apparently, then, the sin of murder was "unforgivable" only when committed against a Mormon in good standing—murdering non-Mormons or apostate Mormons was acceptable and, for some, all to the good.

As Stenhouse observes, "To murder a Gentile may sometimes be inexpedient, or perhaps even to a certain extent wrong, but it is seldom, if ever, a crime, and never an unpardonable sin."[145]

As we mentioned previously, Young himself was indicted for murder, although Federal versus territorial disputes and Mormon power in Utah prevented his going to trial.[146]

But again, is it really so surprising such murders were committed? With church leaders inflaming the minds of blindly zealous Mormons about killing others in the name of God to save them from their sins, one might expect it. Cultic religious history is certainly not without precedent.

One is also reminded of Jesus' statement about those who would kill His disciples and think that they were "offering service to God." But, in reality, "These things they will do, because they have not known the Father, or Me" (John 16:2,3). Nevertheless "offer service to God" the early Mormons did.

Bill Hickman alone claims he was responsible for scores of murders undertaken for Mormon leaders Brigham Young and Orson Hyde. He discusses many of them in his grisly personal confession *Brigham's Destroying Angel*.[147] He concludes his two-hundred page testimony with this statement:

> I would rather have died a dozen deaths than to pass through what I have, if I could only be alive again and see right and justice triumph! Thank God! I think the day has come, and now is, and in justice to myself, my posterity, the living, the dead, and my country, I think it right to come out and show the damnable course pursued by Brigham Young—guilty as I have made myself, and with no excuse to offer except my fanatical belief. Believe me or not, I was sincere. . . . I might go into the detail of family affairs—women in polygamy, property appropriations, thievings, and when, how, and by whom ordered, and the consequences when not ordered, and many other atrocious deeds of murder done by the order of Brigham Young, which I was not witness to—all of which would make a

> larger book than this. . . . But no matter what you think now,
> the day is coming fast—yes in Utah—that you will know the
> things set down in this book for truth.[148]

The infamous Mountain Meadows Massacre was also linked to the doctrine of blood atonement. Mormon church leaders have attempted to cover up the truth about this massacre of 137 people, but to no avail.[149] Both the Tanners' material and Juanita Brooks' *The Mountain Meadows Massacre* prove that the guilty parties were Mormons.

At the forefront of this violence there was the fearsome and brutal Danite Society (a secret order also denied by Mormons), who numbered about three hundred men. They were a band of men comprised largely of thugs and assassins who committed murder for specific religious purposes—somewhat reminiscent of pagan sects such as The Dacoits of India who roam the countryside offering victims to their death goddess *Kali*. Mormon William E. Berret, in his *The Restored Church*, comments, *"Such a band as the 'Danites' did exist*, as historians affirm. . . . The organization had been for the purpose of plundering and murdering the enemies of the Saints"—although he falsely maintains it was not formed by Mormon leaders.[150] However, in their books *The Mormon Kingdom* (vol. 1, chap. 5) and *Mormonism—Shadow or Reality?* (chap. 28), the Tanners show that the vicious Danite band *was* instigated, approved, and run by church leaders. Joseph Smith's control over the church would have made it virtually impossible for such a group to have gone unnoticed by him.[151]

Joseph Smith's own purported statement denying his involvement with the Danites[152] was proven to be false, another illustration of falsified Mormon history.[153] Smith and other Mormons are known to have denied things publicly that they either practiced or taught privately (for example, polygamy and thievery).[154] Even David Whitmer, one of the Three Witnesses of the *Book of Mormon*, confessed that "the Danites consisted only of those selected by Smith and Rigdon."[155]

Furthermore, many other firsthand sources contain abundant additional documentation of early Mormon crimes. These include Chief Justice of the Supreme Court R.N. Baskin's *Reminiscences of Early Utah* (1914); Missouri *Senate Document 189*; the *Reed Peck Manuscript* (1839); E.D. Howe's *Mormonism Unvailed* [sic, 1834]; William Swartzell's *Mormonism Exposed* (1838) and the photo reprint of *On the Mormon Frontiers: The Diary of Hosea Stout* (which the Tanners refer to as, "one of the most revealing documents that we have ever encountered."[156] All these materials are available in photo-reprint editions. (See Resource List.)

Thus, the picture of Mormon history one gets from the church is quite different from the reality one uncovers in historical documents. Doctrinal matters aside, the murders committed by the early Mormon church alone indicate its anti-Christian nature. Many of the founders and leaders of the Mormon church were responsible, directly or indirectly, for atrocities. They may have had others do their dirty work, but before God they are no less guilty of murder than David was for the death of Uriah (2 Samuel 11).

Should not we ask, in accordance with the teachings of Jesus in Matthew chapter seven, whether or not a bad tree can bear good fruit? Can the teachings and doctrines of such men possibly honor God and Christ? If words of plunder and murder were spoken by church leaders from the pulpit, and published openly by them, "what may have been done in secret?"[157]

How would Christians feel if the twelve apostles of Christ were revealed to have been such men, and to have taught and done what these men did? Jesus taught that it was right to love your enemies, and do good to those who hated or persecuted you (Matthew 6:44). Rejecting Jesus' teaching, Mormon leaders not only taught hatred of one's enemy, but also that it was pleasing to God to murder them! In his *Reminiscences of Early Utah*, R.N. Baskin (who served as Mayor of Salt Lake City and as a Chief Justice of Utah's Supreme Court) stated concerning the murder of three apostate Mormons:*

> Other similar cases have been stated to me, and were given in the testimony at the trials of John D. Lee. There is no doubt in my mind that all such cases *were inspired by the throat-cutting sermons and* [Masonic-like] *oath-bound covenants* of the Mormon church. The blood-thirsty spirit revealed by these sermons conclusively shows that their authors had vengeful and malignant hearts. To call an organization in which such sermons were tolerated, and afterwards reproduced and perpetuated in its official publications, the "Church of Jesus Christ of Latter-day Saints," is a disgraceful profanation of the sacred name of Jesus Christ. These disgusting sermons of Brigham Young not only emphasize the absurdity of his assumption of divine agency, but resemble the ravings of a vicious lunatic, and are such as no Christian would deliver.[158]

Chief Justice Baskin also remarks on the existence of human skeletons found scattered throughout Salt Lake City:

> In the excavations made within the limits of Salt Lake City during the time I have resided there, many human skeletons have been exhumed in various parts of the city. The present city cemetery was established by the first settlers. I have never heard that it was ever the custom to bury the dead promiscuously throughout the city; and as no coffins were ever found

---

* Regarding Baskin's reference to Lee, see the Tanners' reprint of the 1877 edition of *Confession of John D. Lee*.

in connection with any of these skeletons, it is evident that the death of the persons to whom they once belonged did not result from natural causes, but from the use of criminal means, and therefore the victims were not given a Christian burial. That the Danites were bound by their covenants to execute the criminal orders of the high priesthood against apostates and alleged enemies of the Church is beyond question. . . . How many murders were secretly committed by that band of assassins will never be known, but an estimate may be made from the number mentioned in the confessions of Hickman and Lee, and the number of human skeletons which have been exhumed in Salt Lake City. [159]

In conclusion, how can modern Mormons defend their church if they cannot honor and revere their own prophets as men of integrity and godliness? These crimes were not the "excesses" of a few disgruntled Mormons acting contrary to church teaching. They were "divinely" instituted murders advocated by Mormon leaders acting in full harmony with church policy and doctrine

‡ ◆ ‡

# CHAPTER 29

# Mormon Distortion of Human Relationships

## What Are the Terrible Fruits of Mormon Polygamy and Racism?

"The Lord has said, that those who reject this principle [of polygamy] reject their salvation, they shall be damned, saith the Lord. . . . I want to prophecy that men and women who oppose the revelation which God has given in relation to polygamy will find themselves in darkness . . . they will finally go down to hell and be damned."

—Apostle Orson Pratt, *Journal of Discourses*, (17:224,225)

T he Mormon church claims that it has always sought to serve the Family of Man: that it honors the dignity and inherent self-worth of all men, and that it seeks only their contentment and happiness. For example, Joseph Smith claimed that true "happiness is the object and design of our existence."[160] The *Melchizedek Priesthood Personal Study Guide 2* emphasizes, "The Church of Jesus Christ of Latter-day Saints accepts as fundamental the spiritual law of service. Our

Redeemer was its greatest exemplar."[161] The Mormon promotional brochure, *Faith In the Lord Jesus Christ*, tells us, "The fruits of faith include. . . . walking uprightly and dealing justly with our neighbors."[162] Many will grant that, from its own perspective, the Mormon church does what it can to foster positive relationships among its families and people in general.

Unfortunately, it has also undermined these very ideals by its acceptance of new "scripture." In this chapter we will examine two problem areas as further evidence that the "fruit" of Mormonism is not all that the church claims it is.

### Mormon Polygamy

> He must not take many wives, or his heart will be led astray.
>
> —God's Instruction to Israelite Kings, Deuteronomy 17:17 (NIV).

In *Doctrine and Covenants*, chapter 132, Joseph Smith informed the Mormon people that polygamy was "an everlasting covenant" which must be obeyed. Anyone who did not obey it risked the consequence of eternal damnation (132:1-66). The church everywhere taught this doctrine as a divine revelation. Brigham Young, reiterating *Doctrine and Covenants*, emphasized:

> Now if any of you will deny the plurality of wives, and continue to do so, I promise that you will be damned; and I will go further and say . . . deny it in your feelings, and I promise that you will be damned. But the Saints who live their religion will be exalted, *for they never will deny any revelation which the Lord has given.*[163]

Joseph Smith, Brigham Young, scores of early church leaders and seven of the first nine Mormon presidents have all been polygamists, with the result that there are more polygamists today than ever before—up to seventy thousand practicing polygamists remain in Utah alone!*

This social plague is directly attributable to Mormonism. But unfortunately, the church continues to refuse to take responsibility for the flood of suffering and destruction it has brought to thousands of devout Mormon people, most of them women. That the practice was evident in the early church all Mormons concede. But it was more prevalent than the church admits it was. As many as fifteen to twenty percent of the Mormon population in the inter-mountain west (not the claimed two percent)

---

* Figures begin at thirty thousand; because polygamy is a crime, participants are naturally reclusive and exact figures impossible to ascertain.[164]

were polygamists.[165] The paradox that more Mormons were *not* polygamists (given the threat of eternal damnation) is explained only by the cruelty of the practice itself and the practical difficulty of incorporating such liaisons.[166]

Nevertheless, monogamy was assailed as anti-Christ, narrow-minded, shameful, a "source of prostitution and whoredom,"[167] a curse, and as bigoted and degenerate. At times Mormon leaders even taught that men required fresh young women to renew their vitality.[168] Heber Kimball, a member of the First Presidency, commented, "I have noticed that a man who has but one wife, and is inclined to that doctrine, soon begins to wither and dry up, while a man who goes into plurality [of wives] looks fresh, young and sprightly."[169]

In *Doctrine and Covenants*, 132:54 "God" actually tells Joseph Smith's own wife Emma that she will be *killed* if she does not accept his taking other wives: "And let mine handmaid, Emma Smith, receive all those [wives] that have been given unto my servant Joseph, . . . for I am the Lord thy God, and will destroy her if she abide not in my law" (*D&C*, 132:52,54). Ironically, it was Joseph Smith who was killed in less than a year, while Emma lived another thirty-five years—to the end "a bitter enemy to polygamy."[170]

Yet the doctrine was also an apparent practical necessity, for the spirit children produced by the sexual intercourse of the male and female gods were depending upon human bodies ("tabernacles") for their habitation. Brigham Young himself confessed:

> I have told you many times that there are multitudes of pure and holy spirits waiting to take tabernacles, now what is our duty?—to prepare tabernacles for them; to take a course that will not tend to drive those spirits into the families of the wicked, where they will be trained in wickedness, debauchery, and every species of crime. It is the duty of every righteous man and woman to prepare tabernacles for all the spirits they can. . . . *This is the reason why the doctrine of plurality of wives was revealed, that the noble spirits which are waiting for tabernacles might be brought forth.*[171]

In the following pages we will document two certainties: 1) Mormon confusion over the issue of polygamy, and 2) the terrible personal cost of this practice.

### Mormon Confusion

Even modern Mormon apologists have confessed that among church members, "There is probably no other Church subject on which there is so much ignorance and misunderstanding and so many conflicting views."[172]

Nor is it surprising. Consider the historical confusion on the subject. The doctrine officially began on July 12, 1843. Joseph Smith received a revelation commanding the practice of polygamy as an *eternal* covenant. A theological rationale was added—that it was a vital institution necessary for producing bodies for the billions of preexistent spirit children who must come to the earth for their continued probation and own opportunity for exaltation. But because polygamy was not only a crime, but also contrary to common sense, even most Mormons had difficulty with it—and many left the fold. In fact, the practice became so divisive in the church and society that the state of Utah was forbidden entrance into the Union six different times!

Then in 1890, Mormon president Wilford Woodruff received a "revelation" *banning* polygamy, which caused further confusion—especially since the church continued to officially (though secretly) *authorize* hundreds of plural marriages for at least fifteen more years.

Finally, some time after the 1890 revelation banning polygamy, the Utah church did reject the practice—but only for those living on the earth. Even today it accepts polygamy in heaven and teaches it will be practiced on earth during the millennium.[173] Thus, in principle, the Mormon church continues to accept the correctness of polygamist practice.

On the other hand, believing it to be a *false* doctrine, the smaller Reorganized Church has rejected it completely, from the time of Joseph Smith onward.[174]

However, possibly up to one hundred thousand Mormon polygamists *continue* to practice it in America *today* and their numbers are growing. Is it surprising Mormons are confused?

Perhaps one reason for these large numbers is the refusal of many Mormons to accept a God who decrees *eternal covenants* and then reverses Himself for apparent political and social reasons. As noted, Utah applied for statehood six times before it was finally accepted into the Union in 1896. President Wilford Woodruff's 1890 ban on polygamy was the key. The tenth president and prophet, Joseph Fielding Smith, explains:

> In 1890, because of the enactment of laws forbidding this practice and because of the opposition on the part of all other people in the United States and throughout the so-called Christian world, the Lord instructed President Wilford Woodruff to call upon the members of the Church to discontinue the practice of plural marriage.[175]

However, it was not quite so easy. Many Mormons fought strenuously against abandoning the teaching which, after all, they had been assured was an eternal covenant. The *Millennial Star* had stated, "The order of plurality of wives is an everlasting and ceaseless order."[176] Also, much earlier, the same paper of October 28, 1865, had commanded that Mormons were *not* to give up the practice, that there would be *no new revelation* to rescind it, and that such talk was "*childish babble*" by "*half informed men.*" Further, it argued that only one of two choices was possible: " 'Mormonism' allowed in its entirety [with polygamy], or 'Mormonism' wiped out in blood."[177]

This position was in keeping with what Brigham Young had taught, "It is the word of the Lord. . . . The only men who become Gods . . . are those who enter into polygamy."[178] He testified that, "I heard the revelation on polygamy [given by Joseph Smith], and I believed it with all my heart, and I know it is from God—I know that he revealed it from heaven; I know that it is true."[179] In fact Young stated that if the only way Utah could enter the Union was to abandon polygamy, "We shall never be admitted."[180]

It should also be noted that before he became president, Wilford Woodruff himself declared that Mormons would *not give up* polygamy, and he even stated that he had had a revelation *from God* to that effect![181] In his journal entry for December 19, 1889, apostle Abraham Cannon recorded that Woodruff "laid the matter before the Lord. The answer came quick and strong. The word of the Lord was for us not to yield one particle of that which he had revealed and established."[182] Naturally, then, Mormons were somewhat confused over his 1890 Manifesto (less than a year later) containing God's "newest" revelation, which yielded to political and social pressure and abandoned the doctrine.

The Mormon revelation of 1890 temporarily discontinuing polygamy was clearly another revelation of convenience, for even Joseph Smith was reputed to have admitted that the practice was destroying the church and must be changed.

In an interview, he reportedly stated (in uncharacteristic terms) that polygamy "will prove our destruction and overthrow. I have been deceived; it is a curse to mankind, and we shall have to leave the United States soon, unless it can be put down, and its practices stopped in the church."[183] Nevertheless, the practice continued long after Smith passed from the scene.

But was the doctrine even abandoned upon the release of the 1890 revelation? No. Although the Manifesto itself prohibited future polygamous relations, and although it also condemned the continuation of polygamous relationships already formed, Mormon leaders characteristically disregarded the "Word of God." Thus, while Mormon leaders "were publicly stating that members of the church should observe the law, they were secretly teaching that it was alright to break the law concerning unlawful cohabitation."[184] The Tanners list numerous admissions to this effect by church leaders.[185] Noted Mormon historian D. Michael Quinn comments extensively on the problem:

A so-called "faith-promoting" Church history which conceals controversies and difficulties of the Mormon past actually undermines the faith of Latter-day Saints who eventually learn about the problems from other sources.

One of the most painful demonstrations of that fact has been the continued spread of unauthorized polygamy among the Latter-day Saints during the last seventy-five years, despite the concerted efforts of Church leaders to stop it. Essential to this Church campaign is the official historical argument that there were no plural marriages authorized by the Church or First Presidency after the 1890 Manifesto, and that whatever plural marriages occurred between 1890 and the so-called "Second Manifesto" of April 1904 were the sole responsibility of two renegade apostles, John W. Taylor and Matthias F. Cowley. A lifelong opponent of post-1890 polygamy, J. Reuben Clark spearheaded the administrative suppression of the polygamist Fundamentalists from the time he entered the First Presidency in 1933, but he ruefully noted in 1945, "that one of the reasons why the so-called 'Fundamentalists' had made such inroads among our young people was because we had failed to teach them the truth." The truth was that more than 250 plural marriages occurred from 1890 to 1904 in Mexico, Canada, and the United States by authorization of the First Presidency, and by action or assent of all but one or two members of the Quorum of the Twelve Apostles. The official denial of that fact in LDS Church statements and histories actually has given credibility to the Fundamentalists in their promotion of new plural marriages after 1904 in defiance of First Presidency authority.[186]

Thus, this hypocrisy of Mormon authorities is one explanation for why tens of thousands of people in Utah continue to live in polygamy to this day.[187]

It is admittedly difficult, then, for most Mormons *not* to be confused. Many are ambivalent over the issue for one simple reason: they are themselves the descendants and products of polygamy. And if they are not confused personally, they are certainly confused doctrinally:

1. In the *first* edition of *Doctrine and Covenants*, published in 1835, God *prohibited* polygamy (section 101). This prohibition was deleted in 1876.[188]

2. In subsequent editions, God (and other Mormon leaders) said polygamy was *justified*, an *eternal* covenant, and that it *must* be practiced to avoid damnation (132;1-66). Logically, Brigham Young taught that only polygamists are exalted to godhood.[189]

3. In the *Book of Mormon*, however, the same God teaches that only one wife is permissible and that polygamy is an "abomination" before Him (Jacob 2:24; cf. Ether 10:5).

4. Finally, President Woodruff (who said God would not change His mind) was forced to concede that "God" did change His mind and thus issued the 1890 prohibition.

5. But then church leaders disregarded the 1890 revelation and continued the practice.

6. In addition to all this, the polygamous revelation in *Doctrine and Covenants* 132 ultimately contradicted the revelation in *Doctrine and Covenants* 58:51 which states that one who keeps God's laws "has no need to break the laws of the land."

It is not surprising, then, that modern Mormons as a whole (all sects considered) are hopelessly divided on the issue, taking every position from 1) absolute condemnation, to 2) absolute acceptance, to 3) both—condemnation of the practice now but acceptance of the practice in the millennium or heaven.

Regardless, Mormons today cannot logically *condemn* polygamy without also condemning the teachings of Joseph Smith, Brigham Young, and most presidents of the church who practiced it and/or declared it an eternal covenant. Nor can they logically *accept* polygamy without causing additional Mormons to practice it, thus bringing even more social condemnation. Neither can they *remove* the polygamous teachings in section 132 of *Doctrine and Covenants*, for this is part of the very revelation containing the essential Mormon doctrine of *temple marriage*.[190]

So, the polygamists practice it, the Reorganized Church condemns it, and the Utah church accepts it in heaven but not on earth—at least for the present.

In accepting the original revelations on polygamy, polygamist leader Joseph Musser is forced to conclude that the church has paid a "terrible price" for abandoning the practice:

> There has been so much subterfuge, so much camouflaging and twisting of facts and principles. . . . The policy of the Church to popularize itself with the world has forced upon it the adoption of many sectarian ideas that are causing "dry rot" among the rank and file of its members. . . . in order to gain the friendship of the world, we voluntarily agreed to pay the terrible price—the surrender of a principle of salvation and exaltation, a principle, without the living of which Joseph Smith said the Church could go no further and that the keys would be turned—it is little wonder that we find ourselves in the sad dilemma of being, in large measure, cut off from direct communication with heaven and, too, guilty of teaching false doctrines and supposing them to be true.[191]

But in fact, the terrible price paid resulted from the church's *accepting* polygamy not from rejecting it. And the only reason the church accepted polygamy was because leaders actively promoted an obviously false prophet as God's own mouthpiece.

### The Terrible Price

Our concern here is not to document the hypocrisy of Mormon leaders, nor their many suppressed revelations (for example, the command for Mormon men to marry Indians to make them a "white" and "delightsome" people).[192] Our concern is to briefly document the moral aspects of polygamy, and the misery, tragedy, and heartbreak this evil brought to so many unfortunate Mormon women—and continues to bring today.[193] (Cf. V.T. Avery and L.K. Newall's *Enigma: Emma Hale Smith*.)

We shall also document the fact that Smith, Young, and many Mormon leaders were guilty of adultery, even given God's alleged acceptance of polygamy. The Tanners observe:

> Zina Huntington, a wife of Brigham Young and a defender of the doctrine of polygamy, counseled: "It is the duty of a first wife to regard her husband not with a selfish devotion. . . . She must *regard her husband with indifference*, and with no other feeling than that of reverence, for *love we regard as a false sentiment*; a feeling which should have no existence in polygamy."
>
> [Nevertheless] It is almost impossible to conceive of the sorrow that the Mormon women went through. Joseph Lee Robinson, who was himself a polygamist and a faithful member of the church, frankly admitted: "Plural marriage . . . is calculated in its nature to severely try the women even to nearly *tear their heart strings out of them*."[194]

The Tanners cite many examples of the misery such teachings brought—of first wives who paced the floor all night while the second wife lay in the arms of their husband, of a woman who, while her husband was with another woman, climbed to the roof of the house and willfully froze to death![195] Even Brigham Young admitted that many women were "tormented" and that "my wife . . . has not seen a happy day since I took my second wife."[196] But this did not stop him from taking up to seventy additional wives—much to his own vexation.[197] He later threatened to set them all free for, "I will go into heaven alone, rather than have scratching and fighting around me."[198] Joseph Smith suffered the same torment from his many wives.[199] While Mormons claim Smith had only one wife, the evidence suggests he may have had as many as eighty-four.[200]

In addition, it appears that a fairly common practice was to have other women (living or dead) "sealed" to a man so he could have even more wives in eternity. Joseph Smith will have around three hundred, for even some of Brigham Young's and Heber Kimball's wives will allegedly be given to him in the resurrection.[201] After his death, over 229 additional women were "sealed to him for eternity."[202] Brigham Young had at least twenty-seven wives, plus over fifty living women, and 150 dead women, sealed to him.[203] He boasted he would eventually have *millions* of wives as a god.[204]

Thus, hundreds of *dead* women were sealed to numerous Mormon leaders—polygamist "recanter" President Woodruff apparently holds the record with a total of some four hundred.[205]

But sealing to dead women was only part of the story. Many of the faithful also practiced a novel kind of polygamy, or a form of sanctified adultery. Such men would take for themselves other men's wives while they were yet living. Documentation for this can be found in *Journal of Discourses*,[206] and a dozen other sources cited by the Tanners.[207] The evidence is clear that Joseph Smith and many others appropriated for themselves the wives of other men.[208] In *Wife No. 19*, Ann Eliza Young, a wife of Brigham Young, revealed in 1876:

> Joseph not only paid his addresses to the young and unmarried women, but he sought "spiritual alliance" with many married ladies. . . . He taught them that all former marriages were null and void, and that they were at perfect liberty to make another choice of a husband. The marriage covenants were not binding, because they were ratified only by Gentile laws. These laws the Lord did not recognize; consequently all the women were free. One woman said to me not very long since, while giving me some of her experiences in polygamy: "The greatest trial I ever endured in my life was living with my husband and deceiving him, by receiving Joseph's attentions whenever he chose to come to me." . . . Some of these women have since said they did not know who was the father of their children; this is not to be wondered at, for after Joseph's declaration annulling all Gentile marriages, *the greatest promiscuity was practiced*; and, indeed, *all sense of morality seemed to have been lost* by a portion at least of the church.[209]

H. Michael Marquardt discovered a case where Sarah Ann Whitney was married to *three* men at the same time:

> Sarah Ann Whitney was married to Joseph Smith on July 27, 1842. Nine months later on April 29, 1843, she was married to Joseph C. Kingsbury with the Prophet Joseph Smith officiating. She was then eighteen years old. Since her first child David was born on March 8, 1846, she was about seven months pregnant with Heber C. Kimball's child at the time of her marriage to him in the Nauvoo Temple on January 12, 1846. It

seems that Joseph Smith married Sarah Ann Whitney for time and for all eternity and then relinquished her for time, in a pretended marriage ceremony to Joseph C. Kingsbury who then let her become pregnant with child by Heber C. Kimball.[210]

In other words, Joseph Smith had taken Whitney as a *secret* plural wife and then performed a "pretended" marriage of her to Kingsbury to cover his own sin.[211] Thus, from these and many other testimonies, "it is hard to escape the conclusion that Joseph Smith and Brigham Young were living in adultery."[212]

Furthermore, the Tanners and others document additional odd arrangements, including many cases of incestuous marriages to sisters, and even to daughters and mothers. Smith himself married "five pairs of sisters" as well as a "mother and daughter"—a sin for which Leviticus 20:14 prescribes the death penalty.[213]

Likewise, one former polygamist wife discussed the perversity that existed within "the Mormon Kingdom":

> It would be quite impossible, with any regard to propriety, to relate all the horrible results of this disgraceful system. . . . Marriages have been contracted between the nearest of relatives; and old men tottering on the brink of the grave have been united to little girls scarcely in their teens; while unnatural alliances of every description, which in any other community would be regarded with disgust and abhorrence, are here entered into in the name of God.[214]

In his weighty preface to Bill Hickman's confession, J.H. Beadle, Esquire, refers to some of the grave consequences and implications behind the Mormon doctrine of polygamy:

> Nor is their social system other than organized selfishness. The Saints must marry many wives. Why? Because he will thus "build up his kingdom for eternity." But the numbers of the sexes being equal, even in Utah, he must build it *at somebody else's expense*; if he marries ten wives, nine other men must do without one apiece. . . . Can men who entertain such an idea of God's providences have much consideration for God's creatures? Will those who hold such low and imperfect notions of their neighbor's rights have regard for that neighbor's life, or liberty, or property, if he "stands in the way of the kingdom of God"? Can a man be much better than his ideal? Can the devotee rise above the standard of his *god*? . . . If a man will crucify the wife of his youth, and put her to open shame, by introducing another woman into the family, and calling her

his wife, if he will make misery for two helpless persons and pervert nature's current in the breast of woman, whether for earthly lust or heavenly glory, he shows by that act that he will use another's misery for his own happiness, that he is a long way on the road towards doing any other mean thing which will give him an advantage over his fellow-man. Hence a nation of slave-holders cannot long remain a nation of freemen; a race of polygamists is sure to become a race of self-seeking sensualists. Love, forgiveness, kindly charity, must wither in such an air.[215]

And such consequences are exactly what we find—in detail. We stress that the horrors and tragedies of the polygamist lifestyle can often be seen in the early literature of the period. We discuss only one such book, the autobiography by Mrs. T.B.H. Stenhouse, *Tell It All: The Story of a Life's Experience in Mormonism*, with a foreword by Harriett Beecher Stowe. In the preface, Stowe refers to the sorrows and oppression that thousands of Mormon women have suffered. She condemns polygamy as "a slavery which debases and degrades womanhood, motherhood, and the family."[216]

The author herself, based on her own experience and her wide knowledge of the polygamist activities within the church in the nineteenth century, referred to the Mormon practice as "the worst oppression and degradation of woman ever known in a civilised country."[217]

Her own experience in polygamy was typical:

What now was to be a woman's lot among the Mormons? A life without hope! Who can express the terrible meaning of those words—*without hope*! Yet so it was. Hereafter our hearts were to be daily and hourly trampled upon; the most sacred feelings of our sex were to be outraged, our affections were to be crushed;—henceforth we were to be nothing by ourselves; without a husband, we were told, we could not even enter heaven!. . . . We were told that in the other world Polygamy should be the only order of marriage, and that without it none could be exalted in glory. We were told these things by men who we believed were true and holy men of God; and we trusted in them.[218]

But nevertheless, life became full of bitterness and horror:

The terrible reality—Polygamy, refused to be ignored, and I felt all the more bitterly afterwards. I was never happy, for life had lost its charm to me. Ere I slept at night one dreadful thought was haunting my pillow, . . One thought was ever present in my mind.[219]

Although Mrs. Stenhouse tried valiantly to protect her own daughter, Clara, her child was eventually married to the oldest son of Brigham Young, Joseph A. Young. Clara thus became the daughter-in-law of Brigham Young himself which brought great tragedy into her life.[220]

Stenhouse also observes that Joseph Smith himself lived in polygamy *before* he received the alleged "revelation" officially endorsing the practice:

> People who lived in Nauvoo, respectful people, and not one or two either, have assured me that four years before Joseph is said to have received the Revelation [on polygamy], he was practicing Polygamy, or something worse, and that the Revelation was given to justify what was already done.[221]

She further discusses the practice of annulling so-called "unholy" or previous "non-Mormon" marriages and the grief it brought to thousands of Mormons and their spouses and children:

> Marriages contracted by the Gentiles or by Mormons in accordance with Gentile institutions, are not considered binding by the Saints. That was partly the cause of my indignation and the indignation of many another wife and mother—we were told that we never had been married at all, and that our husbands and our children were not lawfully ours.[222]

Stenhouse describes various aspects of this polygamy, some things reminiscent of modern practice. There were two classes of "spiritual" wives. One class consisted of older women who were married for their money. A woman in this class would only become a man's true wife in eternity when he raised her from the dead. The second category of "spiritual" wives consisted of women who were already married. However, a woman from this class married again because she did not think that her current husband would be able to raise her to a very high position in the celestial world. As a result, the woman is secretly "sealed" to a Mormon man who can supposedly exalt her to a better estate. In the resurrection, she will become the wife of the one with whom she was secretly sealed.[223]

But, such beliefs became the spiritual justification for a great deal of sexual immorality. Mrs. Stenhouse comments, "I think it will be evident even to the dullest comprehension that under such a system, 'the world, the flesh, and the devil' are far more likely to play a prominent part than anything heavenly or spiritual. All this is so repugnant to the instincts and feelings of a true woman, that I feel quite ashamed to write about it."[224]

Concerning Brigham Young she observes:

Of the prophet's moral character, the less said the better. He has been remorseless and cruel in his enmities, and he has connived at and even suggested, if nothing more, some of the most atrocious crimes that have ever been perpetrated on the face of the earth. In business matters, . . . he has evinced an amount of dishonesty which can scarcely be credited. . . . The story of his sordid avarice and his contemptible meanness in the accumulation of money would fill a volume. Morally and physically the Prophet is a great coward.[225]

Stenhouse alleges, that Brigham Young amassed enormous riches from the poverty of his followers, did many other evils and "set the worst example which despot or false prophet ever presented to the world."[226]

Just as today the public perception of the Mormon religion and its reality are two different things, so it was in the nineteenth century:

People outside of Utah may be deceived, as indeed they frequently are, by representations made in ignorance of what Mormonism and the Prophet [Brigham Young] really are. But the Gentiles long resident in Utah, the Apostates, and even the Mormon people themselves, if only they would tell the truth, could testify to the truthfulness of the picture that I have drawn of Brother Brigham [and Mormonism].[227]

However, noting that the people were sincere, she comments "their fault was in their faith."[228]

The tragedy and even death that Mormon polygamy brought to the Mormon people (and even non-Mormons) is difficult to chronicle in a few short pages. The interested reader should avail himself of the literature and books of the period—only then will he discover how great an evil Mormonism was.

But we should remember that despite official censure, there are more polygamous marriages today than there were in early Mormonism. Let us give an example. The "Geraldo" TV show for June 28, 1991 discussed *modern* polygamy among excommunicated Mormon fundamentalists. Below we present selected statements made on the program by current and former polygamist wives and children:

*Myrna:* "It is done by the priesthood leader, whoever that is at the time. He believes that he gets a revelation which tells you who you should marry, who you belong to."[229]

*Geraldo:* "Donna, two of your girlfriends married your dad? . . . You had fifty-seven siblings?"

*Donna:* "That's correct."

*Ms. Spencer:* "My father had six wives and I was one of thirty-one children. . . . They figured that polygamy would be second nature [to us], but it wasn't. It was awfully hard too—like Donna says, when they bring home a little fifteen-year-old to marry—when my husband came home and told me that he wanted to marry Susan, I broke down and wept. I said, . . . 'Why, she's only two years older than our daughter,' but he thought it must be of God."[230]

*Geraldo:* "Myrna says that hearing her husband make love with another wife drove her to attempt suicide."

*Donna:* "The heartache and the pain that these women had to endure broke my heart and I chose to get out of it. . . . I have six first cousins that have committed suicide within the last ten years, all in their late teens, early twenties. . . . The stress put on these women, it was just impossible."[231]

*Ms. Spencer:* "Over the years, as my husband married more women, why many a times I lived on a dirt floor. . . . We actually lived so poor we couldn't afford toilet paper. . . . I mean, we suffered, but the thing of it is that we felt in our heart, that we were doing it for God. We felt like that any sacrifice wasn't too great to bring in these children [apparently for the spirits]. . . . when my husband married a 15-year-old, I had a nervous breakdown."[232]

*Donna:* "What I find really sad is that most of these girls are married off at such young ages."

*Ms. Larson:* ". . . The youngest girls that have been married out there were nine years old and eleven, married to their president's brother. He was the stepfather. This isn't hearsay. They've told me that with their own mouth."

*Ms. Spencer:* "They [Mormon fundamentalist men] marry a mother and she has four daughters. . . . When they come to the age of puberty, and lots of times before, they are married off to this man to keep them in [his] family kingdom."[233]

*Ms. Spencer:* "I did not have a driver's license until I was forty years of age. I never had a checkbook, could never write a check. Your husband simply, barely, minimally cared for you. I feel, as a woman, that my rights were denied—my right to love and freedom. . . . they are not in it for sex. They are in it for religion. . . . But it's heartbreaking when you are pregnant and your husband marries a 15-year-old or 17-year-old girl and you are not being fulfilled and she's—. . ."[234]

*Geraldo:* "Are most of these families on some kind of governmental assistance?"

*Donna:* "A lot of them are and they're all doing it—a lot of them are doing it in the name of God. It's OK to rip the government off because they're doing it for God's purpose. I have seen it and it's wrong."

*Myrna:* "At least eighty-five percent of the people that are leaving polygamy are on welfare or on a WIC program or some kind of thing. My mother had eighteen children, 24 pregnancies.... She has ninety-seven grandkids. By the end of the year, she'll have 102. How can they not live without being on welfare?"[235]

Given the above discussion, perhaps the reader can begin to glimpse what may be involved with possibly one hundred thousand families practicing polygamy in the United States today. But polygamy is not the only social problem for Mormonism.

## Mormon Racism

Mormon apostle Bruce McConkie wrote in his *Mormon Doctrine*:

Prejudice... is one of the chief tools of Satan.... Indeed, few things are more self-damning, more destructive of progress, more conducive to apostasy and spiritual darkness, than the smothering mantle of prejudice.[236]

But this sentiment is not an accurate reflection of Mormon belief—either historically, or, in many quarters, today. In part, Mormon racism is "justified" by Mormon scripture. *The Pearl of Great Price* teaches that God cursed the land of Canaan and "there was a blackness [that] came upon all the children of Canaan, that they were despised among all people" (Moses 7:8). Black skin, in other words, is a sign of God's curse.

The church's 150 years of racist policies and their accompanying treatment of blacks—the cursed descendants of Cain—and other dark skinned people is also reinforced by the *Book of Mormon*. In 2 Nephi 5:21 God cursed the formerly white Lamanites with dark skin and they became Indians: "He caused the cursing to come upon them... as they were white. The Lord God did cause a skin of blackness to come upon them." Again we see that dark skin is a sign of God's curse. But further, Mormon racism has also been built on Mormon theology, which teaches that the reason blacks were cursed with dark skin was because of their *lack of merit* in the preexistent state. In our appendix to chapter 16 we saw that Elohim called a great council and laid out his plan for humanity. Jesus and the devil had different approaches for instituting this plan. After a heavenly vote among the spirit children, Jesus' plan was chosen by the majority. The spirits who sided with Lucifer became demons, cursed never to have a body. Those spirits who remained neutral, refusing to side with either Jesus or the devil were cursed to be born in bodies with black skin.[237]

Thus, until President Spencer Kimball's new "revelation" of June 9, 1978, almost 150 years of denying blacks the Mormon priesthood was based on racism justified by Mormon scripture and theology.[238] Whatever the influence of the country's own social racism, Mormon scripture gave it unambiguous divine sanction.

Although current Mormon leadership denies it, Smith and many other early leaders *were* racists.[239] Smith personally accepted slavery. He stated, "We do not believe in setting the Negroes free," and elsewhere he called them "niggers."[240] Other Mormon leaders believed blacks were "an inferior race."[241] Brigham Young, although empathetic to the black man's plight,[242] also declared in 1855, "you must not think from what I say, that I am opposed to slavery. No! *The Negro is damned*, and is to serve his master till God chooses to remove the curse."[243]

Likewise, Joseph Fielding Smith, the tenth president and prophet of the church, stated that the curse on blacks, whom he labelled "an inferior race," would continue so long as "time endures":

> Not only was Cain called upon to suffer, but because of his wickedness he became the father of an inferior race. A curse was placed upon him and that curse has been continued through his lineage and must do so while time endures. Millions of souls have come into this world cursed with a black skin and have been denied the privilege of Priesthood and the fullness of the blessings of the Gospel. These are the descendants of Cain. Moreover, they have been made to feel their inferiority and have been separated from the rest of mankind from the beginning.[244]

This is why it is not surprising that Mormons have historically supported segregation until very recent times.[245] Because blacks were allegedly cursed of God with a dark skin, they were not even to be given the Gospel![246] And yet this idea clearly denied biblical teaching (Mark 16:15; Acts 8:26-39).

All this is why many Mormons remain racist today: changing God's commands still doesn't sit well. After all, in attempting to change their doctrine, Mormons have once again let social pressure and political expediency rule over God's will.[247] When millions of Mormons have been told that African-Americans are cursed by God—and that this will always be so[248]—it is not surprising that a new contrary revelation would meet with resistance.

Thus, a Brigham Young University random poll by students found that thirty-five percent of the total Mormon population sampled compared the new revelation of greater tolerance toward blacks to a major disaster, and almost forty percent of the total believed such a change would *never* occur.[249]

They felt it would never happen because church leaders promised them this.[250] Citing a speech by Brigham Young, dated February 5, 1852, the Tanners prove he taught that the blacks would not inherit the priesthood until after the resurrection. If it occurred before this, as it now has, "the Church must go to destruction."[251] Thus, "The Mormon people are now faced with a serious dilemma; if they really believe Brigham Young was a prophet, then it follows from his statement that the Church has lost the priesthood, been put under 'the curse' and is going to destruction!'"[252]

Further, Mormon leaders have deceived church members as to the gravity of the situation by deliberately misrepresenting Brigham Young "in order to make the change palatable to the Mormon people."[253]

Here we see a parallel to the problems and conflicts the church faced with polygamy. Thus, in spite of an increasingly progressive social climate, Mormons were claiming, as they did with polygamy, that the church would never bow to social, political, governmental, or other pressure.[254]

On the other hand, Bruce McConkie, who questioned the spirituality of Mormons who thought it was time for a "new revelation" in regard to blacks, turned around *after* the new revelation and reprimanded the "unbelievers" for not accepting it merely because it was contradictory to past teachings! He said they needed to "repent" for such an attitude, and to "forget everything that I have said, or what President Brigham Young or President George Q. Cannon or whomsoever has said in days past that is contrary to the present revelation."[255]

This is remarkable, since in his 1958 *Mormon Doctrine* the issue seemed, at least then, to be quite clear and settled. The Mormon teaching was based on 1) God's Word and 2) lack of merit in preexistence:

> Negroes in this life are denied the priesthood; *under no circumstances* can they hold this delegation of authority from the Almighty (Abra. 1:20-27). *The gospel message of salvation is not carried affirmatively to them* (Moses 7:8,12,22), although sometimes negroes search out the truth. . . . President Brigham Young and others have taught that *in the future eternity* worthy and qualified negroes will receive the priesthood and every gospel blessing available to any man (*Way to Perfection*, 97-111).

> The present status of the negro rests purely and simply on the foundation of pre-existence. Along with all races and peoples he is receiving here *what he merits* as a result of the long pre-mortal probation in the presence of the Lord.*[256]

---

*changed in 1979 ed.

How convenient, then, is this teaching of continuous revelation! Whenever church leaders wish, they may change God's words for whatever reason and God Himself will bless the action! Once again we see the Mormon deity changing his mind and the confusion it brings to perplexed subjects.

Some Mormons have actually left the church in disgust over the new "revelation." It should be pointed out, however, that there probably never was a revelation, but rather a simple committee decision.[257] The church has never produced a copy of the revelation, and even if they did, on what logical basis should anyone believe it?:

> That the Mormon church was forced into the revelation is obvious to anyone who seriously examines the evidence.... What probably happened was that the leaders of the church finally realized that they could no longer retain the anti-black doctrine without doing irreparable damage to the church. Under these circumstances they were impressed with the fact that the doctrine had to be changed and this impression was referred to as a revelation from God.[258]

It seems evident that there are both historical and contemporary moral crises that the Mormon church refuses to face. Blood atonement practices, polygamy and racism are three issues which should be of concern to conscientious church members. Will church authorities accept responsibility for the death and social destruction these teachings have caused? Will it concede that 150 years of racism was never warranted and that their scriptures were wrong? Will it publicly confess to the murder of innocent men, women and children? Or will it continue the practice of suppression and deception?

Moreover, will the church confess and forsake the other social damage caused by its false claims to divine revelation? What will it do with its pagan doctrines, practices and Scripture—its sexual polytheism, rites for the dead, the *Book of Abraham*, and the many occult associations? And last but not least, will the church finally admit to its unethical misrepresentation of itself as Christian?

Dr. Walter Martin's comments on this last point are relevant:

> After carefully perusing hundreds of volumes on Mormon theology and scores of pamphlets dealing with this subject, the author can quite candidly state that never in over a decade of research in the field of cults has he ever seen such misappropriation of terminology, disregard of context, and utter abandon of scholastic principles demonstrated on the part of non-Christian cultists than is evidenced in the attempts of Mormon theologians to appear orthodox and at the same time undermine the foundations of historic Christianity. The intricacies of their complex system of polytheism causes the careful

researcher to ponder again and again the ethical standard which these Mormon writers practice and the blatant attempts to rewrite history, Biblical theology, and the laws of scriptural interpretation that they might support the theologies of Joseph Smith and Brigham Young.[259]

But Mormonism historically is guilty of much more. What of the many other crimes committed against non-Mormons in their open defiance of the laws of the land? Brigham Young boasted, "I live above the law, and so do this people."[260] What about the temple ceremony's "oath of vengeance" taken against the American people, which was deleted sometime between 1914-1927?[261]

What about Mormon interference in American politics, a subject we have hardly touched upon? In 1863 Judge John Cradelbaugh, the Associate Justice of the Second Judicial District in Utah, powerfully testified before the United States House of Representatives about the various anti-American practices that occurred within Mormonism. His speech was a stirring testimony as to the consequences of "good men being silent." We cite him at length:

> Mr. Speaker, having resided for some time among the Mormons, become acquainted with their ecclesiastical polity, their habits, and their crimes, I feel that I would not be discharging my duty if I failed to impart such information as I have acquired in regard to this people. . . .
>
> Mormonism . . . not only permits, but orders, the commission of the vilest lusts, in the name of the Almighty God himself, and teaches that it is a sacred duty to commit the crimes of theft and murder. . . . And, as if to crown its achievements, it establishes . . . *a theocratic government* overriding all other government, putting the laws at defiance. . . . They teach that it is a duty to rob and steal from Gentiles. . . . the picture, true to life as it is, has yet darker shades. Murder is openly commanded, and incessant appeals from the self-constituted apostles of Almighty God prove beyond all doubt that its execution is considered and urged as one of the fundamental doctrines to be enforced and acted on by the faithful of the Latter-day Saints. . . .
>
> *The complicity of the church dignitaries, mayors of cities, and other territorial officials, in the crimes that have been committed, demonstrates that those crimes were church crimes, and Brigham is the head of the church.* . . . Mormon punishment for Mormon apostasy is like the old curse of former Popes; it extends from the soles of the feet to the hairs of the head. It separates husband and wife; it reaches from the confiscation of property to the severance of the windpipe. Armed with such power over the hearts and lives of the people, Brigham defiantly drives the barbaric chariot of Mormon robbery, murder,

polygamy, and incest over all law, in defiance of all Federal officials in the Territory. Brigham not only controls the legislation, but he controls the courts. . . .

This attempt of the Mormons to interfere with the administration of the law, and control the courts, has been one of the chief causes of difficulty between the judges sent by the Federal Government to Utah, and the Mormon people. From almost twenty judges sent to the Territory, with the exception of two—Judge Zerubbabel Snow, a Mormon, and J.F. Kinney, the present chief justice, the only territorial judge who has not been removed by the present Administration, and who bears the unenviable reputation of being the "creature and tool of Brigham Young"—the testimony has been uniformly to the effect that the laws could not be enforced. Not one of these judges, with the exception of the two named above, have been enabled to serve out the short term of four years. Some have left in disgust, while others were driven away by force. . . .

The courts being deprived of aid and protection in the administration of the law, no arrests can be made, and no criminals brought to punishment.

Marshal Dotson, holding warrants for the arrest of almost a hundred murderers, including the participants in the horrible butcheries at the Mountain Meadows, is compelled to return those warrants unexecuted, for the reason, as he solemnly states, that *he has not the ability to serve them*. In utter disgust he resigns his office, and in this connection his letter of resignation, addressed to the President, is worthy of perusal. . . .

"Sir: I hereby tender to your excellency my resignation as United States Marshal of the Territory of Utah, to take effect from the 20th instant. . . . The *courts* of the United States in the Territory, *powerless* to do good, in dreadful mockery of justice, are compelled to lend the power and majesty of the law to subserve the evil designs of the very criminals they seek to punish. Impotent to protect innocence, they encourage crime. . . . Though willing to serve the Administration from which I received my appointment, I cannot remain an officer of the Government without the *power* to maintain its dignity. . . . I am, sir, very respectfully, your obedient servant, P.K. Dotson. . . ." [He further stated, *"So great is the number of persons engaged in the commission of these crimes, and such the feeling of the Mormon Church, and the community in their favor, that I cannot rely on a civil posse to aid me in arresting them."*][262]

I have given to you instance after instance wherein they have committed their robberies and murders, I might continue the catalogue if it was necessary. . . .

The people of Utah have nothing but ill will towards our Government. The great masses know nothing of our institutions. They come to Zion—not to America. . . . Upon arriving in Utah they hear nothing but abuse of our people; the whole fountain of patriotism is polluted, and they are taught that they owe neither allegiance nor love to our Government. Treason and insubordination are openly taught.[263] (See also Resource List.)

Again, none of this is surprising. In Nauvoo, Illinois, Joseph Smith wielded the combined power of one hundred thousand church members, had a large personal fortune, his own militia (the Legion of Nauvoo), was Mayor of Nauvoo, and may have had political power equal to that of the state government.[264] When Mormons moved to Utah, their power was even greater. It is thus not incredible that so many crimes were committed with impunity.

Indeed, early Mormonism had the attitude that there was *"no law superior to 'the word of the Lord through the prophet,'"*[265] and many a modern cult reechoes these teachings. Members of the vicious Danite band were not to question their orders whether *"right or wrong"* but were to obey them "and trust God for the result."[266] The Danites "were apparently taught to obey the commands of their superiors *without question* or hesitation. The consequences of any act, however dangerous, were not to be considered."[267]

Apostle Orson Hyde stated that "a man may steal and be influenced by the spirit of the Lord to do it."[268] Heber Kimball exhorted, "Learn to do as you are told, both old and young. . . . If you are told by your leader to do a thing, do it. None of your business, whether it is right or wrong."[269] Note some comments by and about the infamous Mormon Danite band:

> The duty of all noble and loyal Danites was to waste away the Gentiles by stealing their goods and consecrating them to the Kingdom of God.[270]

> The blood of my best friend must flow by my own hands if I would be a faithful Danite should the prophet command it. Said A. McRae in my hearing, "If Joseph should tell me to kill [U.S. President] VanBuren in his presidential chair I would immediately start and do my best to assassinate him."[271]

Unfortunately, this kind of "right or wrong" attitude still seems to be present in some quarters of the Mormon church today. Marvin Cowan, in his *Mormon Claims Answered*, refers to a similar philosophy:

> Pres. Harold B. Lee quoted an earlier LDS Prophet, Heber J. Grant as saying, "Brethren, keep your eye on the president of this church. If he tells you anything and it is *wrong*, and you do it, the Lord will *bless* you for it. But you don't need to worry; the Lord will *never* let His mouthpiece lead this people astray."[272]

The Tanners also inform us that contemporary Mormonism is not free from defect at this point:

> The Mormon church condemns the Catholics for teaching that the Pope is infallible, yet it teaches essentially the same thing. . . . Since Brigham Young's death, Mormon leaders have continued to teach that the Lord will "never permit" the president of the church to lead anyone astray. Mormons are encouraged to put all their trust in the church authorities and not try to do their own thinking. The ward teacher's message for June 1945, contained this admonition: . . . "Lucifer . . . wins a great victory when he can get members of the Church to speak against their leaders and to 'do their own thinking.' . . . *When our leaders speak, the thinking has been done.* When they propose a plan—it is God's plan. When they point the way, there is no other which is safe. When they give direction, it should mark the end of controversy."[273]

In their *Mormon Spies, Hughes and the CIA*, the Tanners also uncover chilling evidence of the influence and actions of the church authorities today, including the possible existence of a modern "Secret Council of 50" (see Resource List).

We have already noted the moral problems of the state of Utah (sixty-five to seventy-five percent Mormon) regarding high divorce rates, illegitimacy, adultery, homosexuality and crime in general (chap. 6; note 274). Obviously, neither early nor contemporary Mormonism is as unblemished as the public image they would present to the world.

While no branch of the Christian church is perfect either, it is obvious that sin in the Christian church is a failure to abide by a *higher* standard. But what we have attempted to show is that in early Mormonism almost the reverse was true. The many moral transgressions resulted from doctrines received by "revelation." In many respects theirs was not a *failure* to abide by a *higher* moral standard but a living in *obedience* to a much *lower* standard. Unfortunately, this will always be the end result of accepting occult revelations.

We cannot bring ourselves to accept such revelations as "divine" when they yield such ungodly fruits. Indeed they are more correctly described as "doctrines of demons," which are instigated by "deceitful spirits" (1 Timothy 4:1) among leaders who "will not endure sound doctrine, but [who] . . . will accumulate for themselves teachers in accordance to their own desires; and will turn away their ears from the truth, and will turn aside to myths" (2 Timothy 4:3,4).

We have now discussed a number of criticisms relevant to the Mormon church: the first vision account; problems of the *Book of Mormon* (occult transmission; plagiarism; lack of Mormon teachings and textual attestation; inexcusable changes; problems in language and style; etc.); thousands of changes in other Mormon scriptures; church suppression of embarrassing material; false prophecies; Mormon misinformation masquerading as apologetics; misuse of the Bible; blood atonement, polygamy and racism—all of which make it virtually impossible to consider Mormonism as a divine revelation. But one last subject remains for discussion.

We now turn to a brief documentation of the many changes that have been made in the Mormon temple ceremony revealing why these changes are so important for Mormons to consider.

◆

# CHAPTER 30

# Mormon Distortion of Trust

*Why Is the Mormon Temple Ritual So Important? Have Drastic Changes Been Made in the Endowment Ceremony and Why Does This Matter?*

There are many reasons one should want to come to the temple.  . In the temples, members of the Church who make themselves eligible can participate in the most exalted of the redeeming ordinances that have been revealed to mankind.
. . In the temples sacred ordinances are performed for the living and for the dead alike. . . . We do not discuss the temple ordinances outside the temples.

—Boyd K. Packer, "The Holy Temple,"
*Temples of the Church, 6*

(*Note to reader:* This chapter should be read in conjunction with chapters 18-20 relating to the occult nature of Mormonism.)

The Mormon temple rituals have been a vital sacrament within the church from the beginning. Three key aspects of the ceremonies involve what are called 1) the "endowment," 2) the temple "sealing," and 3) baptism and marriages for the dead

The "endowment" concerns specific instruction in Mormon doctrinal lessons. Temple "sealing" constitutes the actual union (marriage) of a man and woman for all eternity. (In addition, when they supposedly become gods sometime after their resurrection, this ceremony allegedly functions to "seal" their spirit offspring to them for all eternity.) The rites of baptism and marriage for the dead are believed to save and exalt the dead through the proxy baptism and marriage of the living. We discuss this in point 4 below.

The official church publication *Temples of the Church* comments, "A person usually enters the temple the first time to receive what is called the *endowment* [doctrinal instruction]. After receiving the endowment, a person then is able to be married in the temple, which in temple terminology is called being *sealed*."[275]

Mormon authority James E. Talmage, a member of the Quorum of the Twelve, describes the endowment this way:

> *The Temple Endowment*, as administered in modern temples, comprises instruction relating to the significance and sequence of past [Mormon] dispensations, and the importance of the present [Mormon revelation] as the greatest and grandest era in human history. This course of instruction includes a recital of the most prominent events of the [divine] creative period, the condition of our first parents in the Garden of Eden, their disobedience and consequent expulsion from that blissful abode, their condition in the lone and dreary world [on earth] . . . the plan of redemption . . . the period of the great apostasy [of the Christian church], the restoration of the gospel [through Joseph Smith] [etc.].[276]

Elder John A. Widtsoe, then member of the Quorum of the Twelve Apostles and another authority within the church, describes the endowment as a progression: "First, there is a course of instruction relative to man's eternal journey from the dim beginning [of the Mormon pre-existence] towards his possible glorious destiny [i.e., godhood]. Then, conditions are set up by which that endless journey may be made upward in [that] direction. Those who receive this information covenant to obey the laws of eternal progress. . . . It is a very beautiful, logical and inspiring series of ceremonies."[277]

These Mormon temple rituals are crucial to church members for at least five reasons:

*Reason No. 1:* It is alleged that the ritual was supernaturally revealed directly from God to Joseph Smith.

According to *Doctrine and Covenants*, 124:26-44 God Himself revealed the temple ceremonies, and the church confesses that in writing them down, "Joseph Smith was guided by powers beyond those of mortal men."[278] Not unexpectedly, supernatural manifestations accompanied the founding of the first temple:

> In March 1836, the first temple of modern times was dedicated at Kirtland, Ohio (see *D&C*, 109). The dedicatory services were marked by divine manifestations comparable to those attending the offering of the first [Hebrew] temple of olden times; and on later occasions heavenly beings appeared within the sacred precincts with revelations of the divine will to man.[279]

And,

> On April 3, 1836, [the spirit of the dead] Elijah the Prophet appeared to Joseph Smith and Oliver Crowdery in the newly dedicated temple in Kirtland, Ohio, and gave them the authority to reinstate baptism for the dead as well as all other ordinances necessary for the salvation of the dead.[280]

But these temple ceremonies are not only important because of their supernatural origin, they are also said to be crucial for the spiritual power they allegedly impart to individuals.

*Reason No. 2:* Recipients of the ceremony are said to be "endowed with power from on high."

In light of the fact that Mormonism is an occult religion, the promise of spiritual power is significant. According to the church publication *Temples of the Church of Jesus Christ of Latter-day Saints* it is the association with the temple in particular that brings spiritual strength to church members. Incredibly, Mormonism teaches that even the powers of the gods and other spirits are called down upon the faithful. For example,

> Temples are the very center of the spiritual strength of the Church. . . . Temple work brings so much resistance because it is the source of so much spiritual power to the Latter-day Saints and to the entire Church. . . . President George Q. Cannon made this statement, ". . . every Temple completed. . . . invokes and calls down upon us the blessings of the Eternal Gods, and those who reside in their presence."[281]

This magazine goes on to comment, "No work is more spiritually refining. No work we do gives us more power."[282]

President and prophet Benson contends, "When you attend the temple and perform the ordinances. . . . You will receive the spirit of Elijah. . . .

Your heart will be turned to your fathers [i.e., your dead ancestors] and... You will be endowed with power from on high."[283]

In fact, a Mormon cannot become a missionary without passing through temple ceremonies. Because these are believed to transfer spiritual power to the participants, temple attendance is required to help empower them for their missions. But another reason Mormon temples are revered is because of the other supernatural (i.e., occult) manifestations that occur within them.

*Reason No. 3:* New supernatural revelations for church leadership and individuals characteristically originate from within the temple.

The temple is the house of supernatural, occult revelation. In fact, hundreds if not thousands of occult revelations have been received at or in conjunction with temple rites.[284] The current president of the Mormon church, Ezra Taft Benson, confesses, "I think the temple is the most sacred spot on earth.... Temples are places of personal revelation."[285] And, "Under the influence of the Spirit, sometimes pure knowledge flows to us there."[286] Mormon apostle Bruce McConkie taught that "the discerning of spirits is poured out upon presiding officials in God's kingdom; they have it given to them to discern all gifts and all spirits, lest any [evil spirits] come among the saints and practice deception."[287]

Likewise, John A. Widtsoe argues, "*The temple is a place of revelation.* The Lord may here give revelation, and every person may receive revelation to assist him in life."[288] Joseph Smith himself received supernatural revelations in the temple, for example, Section 137 of *Doctrine and Covenants* was received in the Kirtland, Ohio Temple January 21, 1836. In that revelation the Mormon doctrine of salvation for the dead was revealed. This brings us to the fourth reason why Mormon temples are considered vital.

*Reason No. 4:* Ritual ordinances are performed for both the living and the dead in order to save and exalt them.

Boyd K. Packer of the Quorum of the Twelve Apostles asserts in his *The Holy Temple*, "In the temples the sacred ordinances are performed for the living and for the dead alike. Here is the baptismal font, where vicarious baptisms for the dead are performed, with worthy members acting as proxy for those who have gone beyond the veil [i.e., died]."[289]

Young people are baptized for the dead, while adults perform marriages for the dead. In fact, children as young as *twelve* years old can be baptized for the spirits of the dead![290]

The publication *Temples of the Church* informs us that "the Lord has extended alleged gospel blessings to the deceased of all mankind.    Not only baptism, but also the covenants and blessings of the endowment and of eternal marriage are made available to all those who could not receive them in this life.  .. When these ordinances are performed on their behalf, they are able to keep to a greater degree the commandments of the Lord and continue their growth and progression [in the spirit world]."[291] Thus, it informs us that in such rituals, "Couples long since dead are being sealed in marriage to each other, children are being [eternally] bound to their parents, and parents are being [eternally] bound to their children."[292]

This publication also claims that "it is clear that baptism for the dead was practiced by the early Christians." However, this practice was not engaged in by early orthodox Christians—it was practiced by pagans, gnostic "Christians" and other heretics.

Nevertheless, Mormons are promised that unparalleled, eternal blessings will accrue to their dead loved ones on the basis of their actions for them.

> This vicarious work constitutes an unprecedented labor of love on the part of the living in behalf of the dead. . . . But its primary purpose is to afford members of the Church the resources needed to identify their ancestors that they might extend to them the blessings that they themselves enjoy. They in effect say to themselves, "If I love my wife and children so dearly that I want them for all eternity, then should not my deceased grandfather and great-grandfather and other forebears have opportunity to receive the same eternal blessing?"[293]

Very few things in the world are so emotionally binding upon people as love for their family. The Mormon church has taken advantage of this fact in its alleged ministry to the dead—and also in a related area, the last and most crucial reason temples are considered so important to Mormons.

*Reason No. 5:* Only those who have gone through the temple ceremony will be married ("sealed") for eternity, become Gods, rule their own worlds and have spirit children sealed to them for all eternity. Thus, Mormon godhood is inseparably bound to temple marriage.

For committed Mormons, marriage in the temple is a much more important event than even the Christian concept of receiving Christ as one's personal savior. As a leading manual on temple marriage teaches:

> There is probably no decision in all of life, and perhaps in eternity, that has a more profound effect on our eternal destiny than that concerning marriage. In the relationships of husband and wife and parent and child we begin to approach the divine calling of godhood. Our Heavenly Father and mother live in an exalted state [godhood] because they achieved a

celestial marriage. As we achieve a like marriage we shall become as they are and begin the creation of worlds for our own spirit children. . . . [Thus] marriage [citing Brigham Young] . . . lays the foundation for [these] worlds, for angels, and for the Gods.[294]

It is temple marriage that results in true Mormon salvation. In other words, without going through the temple ceremony, one cannot be saved or exalted—(i.e., become a god). Citing President Brigham Young, the Mormon publication *Temples of the Church* explains that temple rites enable one to learn secret words and signs that, in part, permit access to the powers of godhood:

Your endowment is to receive all those ordinances . . . necessary for you, after you have departed this life, to enable you to walk back to the presence of the Father, passing the angels who stand as sentinels, being enabled to give them the key words, the signs and tokens, pertaining to the holy Priesthood, and gain your eternal exaltation [godhood].[295]

The tenth president, Joseph Fielding Smith, agreed when he commented, "These ceremonies . . . save us now and exalt us hereafter, if we will honor them."[296]

President Spencer W. Kimball, in his article "Temples and Eternal Marriage," emphasizes, "In these temples, by duly constituted authority, are men who can seal [marry] husbands and wives and their children for all eternity. This is a fact, even though it is unknown to many [Mormons]."[297]

Most people are aware of the Mormon emphasis on the family. Gordon B. Hinkley, First Counselor in the First Presidency, claims that, "For the most part temple work is concerned with the family."[298] The Mormon church repeatedly stresses that its temple ceremonies uphold the sanctity of marriage—but is this really true? No! For example, their text *Temples of the Church* teaches that civil marriage is merely a "temporal" and "earthly" contract and vastly inferior to the "eternal" marriage they claim to offer.

In other words, because only those who are married in the Mormon temple will allegedly find true salvation and become gods, and thus inherit eternal marriage and eternal spirit offspring—all other marriage, by comparison, has an almost insignificant nature.

*There is no exaltation*—becoming a *god*—unless you are sealed (married) in a Mormon temple. Consider the following official statement by the Mormon church:

Marriages that are made only "so long as ye both shall live" or "until death do you part" are terminated when the mortal breath is no more. . . . [the Mormon God is speaking] "No one can reject this covenant [of eternal temple marriage] and be permitted to enter into my glory," says the Lord.

A civil marriage may be performed by any of the numerous people approved by laws of the respective countries, but eternal marriage must be solemnized by one properly authorized.

"Will I accept of an offering," saith the Lord, "that is not made in my name?"

"Or will I receive at your hands that which I have not appointed?" (*D&C*, 132:9,10).[299]

In other words, what Mormonism is teaching is that God Himself does not accept the *spiritual* legitimacy of non-Mormon marriages. This same publication quotes "God" in *Doctrine and Covenants*, 132:13 as teaching that all things in the world (even if they are ordained of men) "that are not [ordained] by me or by my word . . . shall be thrown down, and shall not remain after men are dead."[300]

Consider the words of the former president and prophet of the Mormon church, Spencer W. Kimball, who reflects upon these scriptures in a highly emotional soliloquy:

How lonely and barren will be the so-called single blessedness throughout eternity! How sad to be separate and single and apart through countless ages. . . . Are you willing to jeopardize your eternities, your great continuing happiness, your privilege to see God and dwell in his presence? . . . Are you willing to forego these great blessings and privileges? Are you willing to make yourself a widow for eternity or a widower for endless ages—a single, separate individual to live alone and serve others? Are you willing to give up your children. . . . Are you willing to go through eternity alone and solitary when all of the greatest joys you have ever experienced in life could be "added upon" and accentuated, multiplied, and eternalized?[301]

In other words, all who are married in normal civil or Christian marriages will end up "damned" in eternity. They will not be allowed in the direct presence of God the Father and Jesus Christ; they will not be allowed eternal marriage; they will not be allowed eternal children. They will lose everything. They will not be gods; in fact, for all eternity they will be merely servants to the gods. Thus, "Civil marriage makes servants in eternity," but "Celestial marriage makes Gods in eternity."[302]

Likewise, *Doctrine and Covenants*, 132:16,17 emphasizes that those who will not submit to eternal marriage in the temple will only become angels and "ministering servants" who must eternally serve "those who are worthy of a far more, and an exceeding, and an eternal weight of glory." These "angels" must remain separate and single without exaltation for all eternity, "and from henceforth are not Gods, but are angels of God forever and ever." Any Mormon who does not pass through the temple rituals is thus consigned to a lower servant status forever.

Imagine how strong an appeal this is to a person's emotional life. Imagine how easily such a doctrine could tear apart a supposedly "unholy," mixed marriage of a Mormon and a non-Mormon. Although Mormons will not publically admit it, what their temple doctrine teaches is that *all* marriages outside the temple are profane, unacceptable to God, and result in damnation. Why else would Mormon officials encourage Mormons to divorce their "unrepentant" spouses who leave Mormonism? Is this upholding the sanctity of marriage?

Regardless, from the above material one can see why the forty plus Mormon temples scattered about the world are of such crucial importance to Mormons and why the church continues to emphasize a vigorous plan for constructing future temples. According to church leaders, the temple is no less than "the center of the Mormon theology."[303]

John A. Widtsoe explains this when he emphasizes,

> Whatever the gospel offers may be done in a temple. Baptisms, ordinations to the priesthood, marriages, and sealings for time and eternity for the living and the dead, the endowment for the living and the dead, gospel instruction, counsels for the work of the ministry, and all else belonging to the gospel are here performed. Indeed, in the temple the whole gospel is epitomized.[304]

But not just any Mormon can enter the temple. One must be properly evaluated by a duly appointed Mormon official before one is entrusted with temple privilege. Thus, "Each person who is worthy may apply to his or her bishop for a recommendation to enter the temple.... All faithful members of the Church are invited and urged to make use of the temple and to enjoy its privileges. It is a sacred place in which holy ordinances are given to all who have proved themselves worthy to partake of its blessings."[305]

Again, the goal of all knowledgeable Mormons is to become a god; but this is impossible without partaking in the appropriate temple rituals. For a Mormon to enter true heaven and achieve true salvation he must partake of the proper rites. Joseph Smith, Brigham Young, and president after Mormon president have emphasized this.[306]

For example, the twelfth president and prophet of Mormonism, Spencer W. Kimball, stated, "Only through celestial marriage can one find the straight way, the narrow path. *Eternal life cannot be had in any other way.*"[307] He further reiterated that "the ordinance of sealing is an absolute, and that without it there can be no salvation in the eternal world, *no eternal life.*"[308]

All this is why the tenth president and prophet of the Mormon church, Joseph Fielding Smith, lamented the fact that many Mormons were being married in ceremonies outside of the temple: "I realize what it means, that they are cutting themselves off from exaltation in the kingdom of God. . . . These young people who seem to be so happy now, when they rise in the resurrection—and find themselves in the condition in which they will find themselves—then there will be weeping, and wailing and gnashing of teeth, and bitterness of soul."[309]

The Mormon publication *Temples of the Church* paraphrases what a young couple will hear in the temple—assuring them of their responsibility for *complete trust* in what they are told:

> Each of you has received your endowment. In that endowment you received an investment of eternal potential. But all of these things, in one sense, were preliminary and preparatory to your coming to the altar to be sealed as husband and wife for time and for all eternity.[310]

The magazine goes on to comment, "If we would understand both the history and the doctrine of temple work, we must understand what the sealing power is. . . . The sealing power represents the transcendent delegation of spiritual authority from God to man. The keeper of that sealing power is the Lord's chief representative here upon the earth, the President of the Church. That is the position of *consummate trust* and authority."[311] The importance of trusting those who encourage participation in—and who regulate—temple rites is stressed again and again because of the incredible powers that temple rituals are believed to hold throughout the world.

The same church magazine accordingly boasts, "In the Church [temple] we hold sufficient authority to perform all of the ordinances necessary to redeem and to exalt the whole human family."[312]

Likewise, in his *Mormon Doctrine* Bruce McConkie refers to the sealing power in the following terms, "So comprehensive is this power that it embraces ordinances performed for the living and the dead, seals the children on earth up to their fathers who went before, and forms the enduring patriarchal chain that will exist eternally among exalted beings."[313]

The importance of the Mormon temple ceremony can be further seen in the fact that Mormonism teaches that God Himself *became God* through *the temple ceremony*:

> Mormons who go through the temple ceremony and are sealed in marriage for eternity believe that they will not only become Gods, but will also continue to have children throughout all eternity. They will people other worlds with their spiritual children and these children will worship and pray to the husband as God. Mormons feel that the God of the Bible was not always God and that he also had to pass through the

same endowments to achieve deity. Wilford Woodruff, who became the 4th Prophet of the Mormon Church, proclaimed that "the Lord had his endowments long ago; it is thousands and millions of years since he received his blessings. . . . He is far in advance of us."[314]

The sanctity and solemnity of the temple and its endowments are why from earliest days Mormon leaders have sternly warned Mormons not to reveal the solemn oaths and secrets pertaining to their temple rituals. Indeed, in early Mormon times (in conjunction with the doctrine of blood atonement) these oaths were actually upheld upon threat of death: "During the 1850s Brigham Young and other church leaders were strongly teaching the doctrine of 'blood atonement'—i.e., that the shedding of the sinner's own blood could atone for their sins. A person can only begin to imagine how serious the oaths taken in the temple were to the Mormon people at the time blood atonement was publicly preached and actually practiced."[315]

Nor is it surprising that Mormon officials wanted the temple rituals to be kept secret. Many of them involved blood-curdling oaths borrowed from Masonry that would later serve to seriously embarrass the church.[316]

Nevertheless, until 1990, most Mormons maintained that there had been *no changes whatever* in their sacred temple rituals. This was a necessary position because they were held to have been revealed from God. Leading Mormons had repeatedly stated that God does not change His mind and that every aspect of the temple ceremonies was vital. Mormons have thus staunchly maintained that the temple ceremony is the same as was originally given—without changes. Let us supply a few examples.

In the early 1900s the Mormon apostle and senator Reed Smoot emphasized, "The endowments have never changed as I understand it; it has been so testified."[317]

Mormon authority John A. Widtsoe, of the Quorum of the Twelve, stated the following in the *Utah Genealogical and Historical Magazine* of April, 1921. He maintained that the temple ceremony was complete and efficacious as it stood:

> The temple ordinances encompass the whole plan of salvation. . . . There is no warping or twisting in fitting the temple teachings into the great scheme of salvation. The philosophical completeness of the endowment is one of the great arguments for the veracity of the temple ordinances.[318]

The sixth president and prophet of the Mormon church, Joseph F. Smith, likewise claimed that those who say "we have changed the ordinances, . . . are in error. The same gospel prevails today, and the same ordinances are administered today, both for the living and for the dead, as were administered by the prophet himself and delivered by him to the church."[319]

The tenth president and prophet of the Mormon church, Joseph Fielding Smith, also emphasized that there had been no change in the ceremonies and that they were "the same today" as they were when first given.[320]

More recently, an editorial published in the church section of the *Deseret News* of June 5, 1965 emphasized,

> God is unchangeable, the same yesterday, and forever. . . . The gospel cannot possibly be changed . . . the saving principles must ever be the same. They can never change. . . . The gospel must always be the same in all of its parts. . . . No one can change the gospel . . . if they attempt to do so, they only set up a man-made system which is not the gospel, but is merely a reflection of their own views. . . . If we substitute "any other gospel," there is no salvation in it. . . . The Lord and his gospel remain the same—always.[321]

Mormon apostle James E. Talmage, a member of the Quorum of the Twelve, commented, "No jot, iota, or tittle of the temple rites is otherwise than uplifting and sanctifying."[322] In other words, this statement made in 1968 implied that there was no reason whatever to change the temple ceremony.

Even as recently as 1982, W. Grant Bangerter, Executive Director of the Temple Department and a member of the First Quorum of Seventy, repeated that the temple ceremony could not be changed:

> As temple work progresses, some members wonder if the ordinances can be changed or adjusted. These ordinances have been provided by revelation, and are in the hands of the First Presidency. Thus, the temple is protected from tampering.[323]

But none of this is true. Extreme and inexplicable changes have been made in the temple ceremony. According to the *Arizona Republic* of April 18, 1990, "The changes are the most drastic revisions of the century."[324] Those items that were previously declared to be "divinely inspired," "extremely important" and "most sacred," are now removed solely at the discretion of church leadership. In fact, the changes are so drastic that Joseph Smith and the early Mormons, not to mention more recent Mormon leaders who are now deceased, would be shocked and outraged. Even many contemporary Mormons are confused.

Mormon leaders have responded in characteristic fashion by saying that the changes reflect "new revelation." This appears to be one more example of the Mormon God changing his mind. But in fact, the changes in the temple ceremony were made for the exact same reasons that changes in doctrine were made by the 1890 revelation concerning polygamy, the 1978 revelation concerning blacks, etc. The reason was social pressure from within and without the church.

As Jerald and Sandra Tanner comment, "Like the polygamy revelation, the revelation by President Spencer W. Kimball granting blacks the priesthood was given only after tremendous pressure was exerted by non-Mormon critics and members of the Church itself. With regard to the recent revision of the temple ceremony, it is clear that the 'revelation' came in the same way as the changes on polygamy and the black doctrine."[325]

A statement by Mormon church leaders appearing in the *Los Angeles Times* of May 5, 1990 noted, "We are a church that believes in modern and continuous revelation, and the changes that were recently made in our temple ceremony are reflective of that process."[326] But again, as the Tanners point out, the process of modern Mormon revelation can be summed up in the following formula: outside criticism plus inside acceptance equals new revelation. In other words, revelation with Mormonism is today frequently a process of social *accommodation*, not divine unveiling.

The Tanners also show that *modern* Mormon revelation is not what it used to be—which was specific new (often controversial) doctrines that Joseph Smith brought into the church by alleged divine inspiration. In fact, the truth is that modern Mormon presidents and prophets have used the word "revelation" to *destroy* the teachings that Joseph Smith claimed were divinely revealed.

Thus, when President Wilford Woodruff had a "revelation" banning polygamy within Mormonism, he was not adding new doctrine. Rather he was destroying an inspired doctrine that came from Joseph Smith in *Doctrine and Covenants*—one that was said to be *essential* for salvation and was held to be an *eternal* covenant.

Likewise, when President Kimball claimed new revelation concerning the right of blacks to hold the priesthood, he was not revealing new truth to the world; he was *destroying* an inspired, racist doctrine that came from Joseph Smith in the *Book of Abraham* and that was held to be valid "for all time."

In like manner, the most recent "revelation" altering the temple ceremony has not provided new doctrine, but has *destroyed* the previous temple ceremony and its doctrine. Thus,

> It seems that it is very difficult for most faithful Mormons to grasp the significance of what is really going on in the Church. The implications are too devastating for them to face. . . . To those who are paying close attention, it is obvious that the word "revelation" is really being used as a cover-up for what is going on. Church leaders are subtly destroying the original teachings of Joseph Smith. Each time they remove some major item that Smith considered vital, they clothe the action by saying it is a new "revelation" from God.[327]

That strong social pressure existed within the church to change the temple ceremony is evident from the following notation by Mormon authorities Jerald and Sandra Tanner: "Many people who have been through the Mormon temple endowment later admit that they were shocked by the ceremony. . . . Over the years a surprising number of people have told us that they had a very bad experience when they went through the temple ritual. Most of them said that their first serious doubts concerning the authenticity of Mormonism arose when they went through the endowment ceremony."[328] One Mormon confessed, "My wife told me that she could not help but feel that the temple endowment was strange and even evil. . . . I then knew that I was not alone with my doubts."[329]

Let us give only a few examples of recent changes in the ceremony. Some of these include the deletion of oaths prescribing the severest penalties for disobedience. In 1927 an Oath of Vengeance was removed. Most modern Mormons are unaware of this oath. Nevertheless, testimony given in the Reed Smoot case, the diaries of Heber C. Kimball and Abraham H. Canon, plus the research of David John Buerger and additional documentation "combine to prove beyond all doubt the Mormon Church had an 'Oath of Vengeance' which was so offensive that it had to be completely removed from the temple endowment ceremony."[330]

Initially some of these oaths, derived from Masonry,[331] were rather bloody and graphic, for example, "binding myself under no less penalty than to have my throat cut across, my tongue torn out by the roots."[332] Former twenty-year temple Mormon Ed Decker describes part of his own temple ceremony:

> It was taught that I must learn a series of secret signs, secret handshakes, secret combinations, secret penalties. I would have to swear oaths of obedience to the prophet, that if I was disobedient I would have my throat slit from ear to ear, my tongue ripped out, that I would have my chest ripped from breast to breast and my heart ripped out. That I would have my belly ripped open and my bowels and my intestines spewed upon the ground if I broke these covenants that I swore.[333]

Later, the violent wording was removed, although the symbolic gesture—drawing participants' thumbs across their throats to show the penalty—was retained. Mormon authorities apparently wished to be rid of the offensive wording, but desired to retain the implication that there was a death penalty involved if such secrets were revealed. But in the new 1990 version no trace of the penalties remains at all.[334]

Another removal (in 1990) concerned the portraying of Christian ministers as agents of Satan. Deleting this aspect of the ceremony was in line with Mormonism's *new* emphasis on attempting to convert Christians to the Mormon faith. Thus, all material degrading Protestants and Catholics is now removed. In fact, "over 700 words were deleted, and other words changed, to remove the attack on other churches."[335]

Consider the temple teaching that Christian ministers are agents of the devil. This idea, which originated in the first vision revelation of Joseph Smith, apparently evolved over the years. The earliest accounts only refer to the devil appearing to participants in the ritual and revealing that he played a role in various "apostate" churches. Then in 1857, several Christian ministers were added as agents of the devil. "Eventually there was only a single minister who was paid by the Devil for preaching the orthodox Christian religion."[336]

For example, in the 1906 printing of the endowment, the devil offers a Christian pastor $4,000 a year to work for him—a very large sum of money in 1906. The 1984 version has Satan telling the Christian minister, "If you will preach your orthodox religion to these people, and convert them, I will pay you well."[337] Today, all this is gone.

For another example of change, consider the holy priesthood garments as described by former twenty-year temple Mormon Ed Decker:

> Then they took me into another room and there they washed and anointed with oil each member of my body, speaking special incantative type blessings upon each part of my body. Then, after I was finished with that, they gave me a thing called the "garment of the holy priesthood" which is, in fact, longjohns, long underwear.... What I was told was that I would have to wear this 24 hours a day, seven days a week and that I was not allowed to remove it for anything. This is the "garment of the holy priesthood." It's magic. It's like an amulet or a talisman. And this gave me protection, but I was told that I could only keep this protection as long as I kept this on my body.[338]

But the mystical temple garments, replete with cabalistic [occult] markings, have also been altered. "The fact that the garments have been changed and abbreviated over the years is very interesting because the early Mormon leaders stressed that they could *not* be changed."[339]

There have been many, many other changes in the 1990 version of the temple ceremony, and these are discussed and documented in Jerald and Sandra Tanner's *Evolution of the Mormon Temple Ceremony: 1842-1990*. This text includes the following material: 1) the actual 1984 temple ceremony, with all the changes marked so the reader can see the "drastic alterations that were made to arrive at the 1990 version of the ritual." This was transcribed from audio tapes that have been verified as accurate and precise by Mormons; 2) the actual 1990 temple ceremony, also transcribed from audio tapes and verified as accurate; 3) documentation concerning the influence of Masonry upon the Mormon temple ceremony; and 4) additional important historical documents such as excerpts from the 1846, 1882, and 1931 Temple Endowment.[340]

What do all these changes mean for Mormon people? They mean that Mormons cannot trust the church's claim to divine guidance here, either. In the most solemn practice the church offers, Mormons have again been the victims of church deception. If the original endowment was from God, it should never have been altered. If it was not, it should never have been presented as God's revelation in the first place.

# Conclusion

━━━━━━━━━━━━━━━━━━ ◆ ━━━━━━━━━━━━━━━━━━

I n this book we have attempted to evaluate the Mormon faith historically and theologically. We have seen that the Mormon church constitutes a growing belief that may one day join the ranks of world religions. But in looking critically at the origin, history and teachings of Mormonism, we discovered that the church's claims could not be substantiated.

Mormonism claims it is a Christian religion, in fact, the only legitimate Christian religion on earth. It claims that Joseph Smith was a genuine prophet of God through whom true Christianity was reestablished in 1830.

Nevertheless, an objective evaluation of the evidence reveals that Mormonism is not Christian. The scriptural legacy that Joseph Smith left to the world—as found in *Doctrine and Covenants*, the *Book of Mormon* and *The Pearl of Great Price*—underscores a legacy that is anti-Christian.

In our examination of Mormon teaching we carefully compared and contrasted Mormon belief with Christian belief in ten different categories. We saw that Mormonism offers a pagan—e.g., polytheistic—belief to the world, not a Christian belief. The Mormon concept of God and the God of Christianity are distinct from and opposed to one another.

Further, despite its claims to believe in Jesus Christ, we saw that the Jesus Christ taught in the Mormon church bore no resemblance to the biblical Christ. For example, the church actively denies the atoning value of Christ's death, making it little more than a stepping stone in the quest for personal godhood.

Concerning the church's teachings on salvation, Mormonism does not teach the biblical doctrine of salvation by grace. Instead, it offers the world a system of works salvation with the final hope that qualified Mormons will themselves fully become gods.

But if Mormonism is not a Christian religion, is it a new religion with independently established truth claims? The answer is no. The evidence forced us to conclude that Mormon religion is, put bluntly, a falsehood.

Even research by liberal but loyal Mormon legal and historical scholars have cast grave doubt upon Mormon credibility—causing the church to retreat further and further into the abyss of subjectivism in order to substantiate its truth claims. Richard von Wagoner's *Mormon Polygamy: A History* (documenting early Mormon fraud regarding polygamy);

445

D. Michael Quinn's *Early Mormonism and the Magic World View* (documenting early Mormon occult practices), and John Kunich's study of the population statistics in the *Book of Mormon* (disproving its credibility) are representative. (Signature Books in Salt Lake City publishes other similar texts.)

We supplied proof that the *Book of Mormon* was a nineteenth-century occult production and not a translation of ancient, historical records. We also cited evidence to show that it was translated by psychic means, not divine ones, and we documented its human sources and plagiarisms. Its absence of archaeological credibility was devastating.

We further discussed the *Book of Mormon*'s lack of manuscript evidence and other serious textual problems—as well as the absence of credibility of the Eleven Witnesses and their "testimony" concerning its alleged divine origin

Unfortunately, we discovered that Mormon authorities had gravely distorted the truth about their own scriptures, their prophet and their history and then attempted to cover up the process. This was necessary because of the large number of embarrassments and contradictions in Mormon history, scripture and theology.

Another area of concern was the occult nature of the Mormon religion. We devoted several chapters to documenting that Mormonism should be classified as an occult religion because of its occult origins and practices, many of which remain to this day. The recent revelations of possible satanic-inspired ritualistic child abuse and human sacrifice existing unofficially within Mormonism are perhaps only symptoms of the deeper problem of LDS history and doctrine that makes the church susceptible to infiltration by occultism (*Salt Lake City Messenger*, November 1991*).

Finally, we examined the fruit of Mormon faith. Although the Mormon church is characteristically known for its good works, we presented a different view. We saw that the real "fruit" of Mormonism was the recruitment of new Mormons. We further saw that the true fruit of Mormonism was not as benign as the church had claimed. Social statistics from Utah in the areas of crime, divorce, drug use, teenage pregnancy and suicide, child abuse and other categories reveal that the fruit of Mormon religion bears further scrutiny. In addition, besides distortions of history and religion in the area of apologetics, we saw the Mormon church's distortion of biblical authority and scholarship in general. We also documented that the early Mormon church did, in fact, teach and practice a terrible doctrine of blood atonement, and that historically the Mormon religion has distorted family and social relationships in the areas of marriage (polygamy) and human fellowship (racism).

In conclusion, because the claims of Mormonism cannot be substantiated—and, in fact, are disproven—Mormon faith must be considered a

---

*P.O. Box 1884, Salt Lake City, UT 84110

false religion. Unfortunately, as is true with any false religion, the consequences of such belief are frequently discovered too late. The hope of the authors was to produce a volume which would enable any Mormon to reevaluate their religious commitment. But this should only be the beginning.

## A Personal Word to Mormons

If you have stayed with us this far, perhaps you are no longer certain of the truth of Mormonism. It is our desire that you continue the process of evaluation, even if painful. The issues are too crucial for any other course of action.

But perhaps one of the most important things for Mormons to realize is that the invalidation of their own faith is not an undermining of true biblical teaching or the real Jesus Christ. The distortion of Christianity by Mormonism cannot logically be considered its disproof. In other words, if you are a Mormon who has concluded that Mormonism is not true, you should not discard the real Jesus Christ. You should begin to think in terms of deception, not rejection. If you have been deceived as to the true nature of Christian faith, you should seek out that faith in truth, rather than reject it because you have been led astray. Jesus Himself said that "this is eternal life to know thee the only true God and Jesus Christ whom thou has sent" (John 17:3).

If you have concluded that Mormonism is false and would like to receive the true Jesus Christ into your life and make Him your Lord and Savior, we suggest the following prayer.

Dear God: You know my heart now, as always. In my heart of hearts my desire is to serve you, the only true God. I now renounce the false view of you that I have promoted and ask for your help and guidance in understanding you better. I have honestly searched my heart and it is my desire to trust in you. By searching my heart, I have recognized I cannot earn my own salvation and now realize that the hope of becoming a god is futile.

I recognize this especially because I am a sinner worthy of your judgment. I reject the pride in thinking that I could perfect myself on my own power and thereby become a god. I renounce every false view of Jesus Christ and receive the true Jesus Christ of Nazareth as presented in the Bible. I believe that this Jesus Christ is truly God, that He truly paid the penalty for my sins on the cross and that He rose from the dead three days later. I believe that by receiving Him into my life I will now inherit eternal life. Right now I turn from my sins and from the false teachings of the Mormon church, and I receive the true Jesus Christ as my personal Lord and savior. Help me to grow in the grace and knowledge of my true savior Jesus Christ (2 Peter 3:18). Amen.

If you have prayed this prayer, please feel free to write us at The John Ankerberg Show and request materials that will be helpful in your new Christian life.

# Notes
# Select Bibliography
# Resource List

# Notes

**The Importance of the Subject of Mormonism**
1. Ezra Taft Benson, *Teachings*, 115, 120.
2. *Deseret News 1991-1992 Church Almanac*, 332; A. Hall, "Mormon Inc.," *The Arizona Republic*, June 30–July 3, 1991.
3. *The Los Angeles Times*, January 6, 1990, F8.
4. John Ankerberg, *Mormonism Revisited*, 2.
5. Irving Hexam, in Daniel G. Reid et al., eds., *Dictionary of Christianity in America* (Downers Grove, IL: InterVarsity Press, 1990), 777.
6. Darl Andersen, *Soft Answers to Hard Questions* (Mesa, AZ: Darl Andersen, 1989), 15-16.
7. Church of Jesus Christ of Latter-day Saints, *Achieving a Celestial Marriage*, 129.
8. Jerald and Sandra Tanner, *Evolution of the Mormon Temple Ceremony*, 58.
9. Joseph Fielding Smith, *Doctrines of Salvation I*, 188, 322.
10. J. Gordon Melton, *The Encyclopedia of American Religions* (Wilmington, NC: McGraff Publishing, 1978), vol. 1, 2:8-21.

**Section 1: Mormon Power and Origins**
1. *The Salt Lake Tribune*, January 23, 1990.
2. Ankerberg, *Mormonism Revisited*, 22.
3. *Time* magazine, July 29, 1991.
4. *Time* magazine, July 29, 1991; *The Denver Post*, November 21-28, 1982; *Wall Street Journal*, November 9, 1983; *The Arizona Republic*, June 30–July 3, 1991.
5. Walter Martin, *Maze of Mormonism*, 16-21.
6. In Ankerberg, *Mormonism Revisited*, 22.
7. Ankerberg, *Mormon Officials*, 21. See *Living a Christlike Life: Discussion 5*, 14-15.
8. Martin, *Maze of Mormonism*, 21.
9. Ankerberg, *Mormon Officials*, 21-22.
10. Ankerberg, *Mormonism Revisited*, 31; *Mormon Officials*, 21-22.
11. *The Utah Evangel* (Salt Lake City, UT), November 1981.
12. Martin, *Maze of Mormonism*, 20; Einar Anderson, *Inside Story*, ix; Jerald and Sandra Tanner, *Mormon Spies, Hughes and the CIA* (Salt Lake City, UT: Utah Lighthouse Ministry, 1976), 56.
13. Martin, *Maze of Mormonism*, 16-21.
14. *Christianity Today*, October 2, 1981, 70.
15. Benson, *Teachings*, 240.
16. Ibid., 238.
17. Ibid., 237.
18. "This People," (Mormon periodical), Spring 1990, 21.
19. Ibid.
20. *The Los Angeles Times*, January 6, 1990.
21. Joseph Smith, *History of the Church*, I 3.
22. Ibid., 4-6.
23. Ibid.
24. Ibid.
25. Ibid.
26. Ibid.
27. Ibid.
28. Ibid.
29. Ibid.
30. Ibid., 8.
31. Ibid., 9.
32. Ibid., 11-12.
33. Ibid., 12-14.
34. Ibid., 15.
35. Most of these are recorded in the most important doctrinal scripture of Mormonism, *Doctrine and Covenants*; see note 36.
36. Cf. *Doctrine and Covenants*, vi-viii for a chronological listing.
37. Cf. Joseph Smith, *History*, 1:39-48, 80.
38. Jerald and Sandra Tanner, *The Changing World of Mormonism*, 10.
39. John Ankerberg and John Weldon, *Cult Watch: What You Need to Know About Spiritual Deception* (Eugene, OR: Harvest House, 1991), parts 5, 7.
40. Raphael Gasson, *The Challenging Counterfeit* (Plainfield, NJ: Logos, 1969), 125.
41. Joseph Smith, *History*, 1:8.
42. Gasson, *Challenging*, passim, and Ankerberg and Weldon, *Cult Watch*, parts 5, 7.
43. Jerald and Sandra Tanner, *The Mormon Kingdom*, 2:1-32.
44. Jerald and Sandra Tanner, *Mormonism—Shadow or Reality?* 1972, 424; cf. Brigham Young et al., *Journal of Discourses* (hereafter cited as *Journal of Discourses*), 6:204, 207, 225, 153; 7:64; 8:336, 374; 9:4, 18, 321; 2:183; 5:126, 232, 117.
45. Jerald and Sandra Tanner, *Changing World*, 460.
46. John Whitmer, *John Whitmer's History*, 24, cited in Jerald and Sandra Tanner, *Mormon Kingdom*, 2:1.
47. Ibid.
48. Jerald and Sandra Tanner, *Mormon Kingdom*, 2:2-9.
49. Ibid., 1.
50. Cf. B.H. Roberts, *Comprehensive History of the Church* (Salt Lake City, UT: Deseret Book Co.), 5:404-408; R.N. Baskin, *Reminiscences of Early Utah* (Salt Lake City, UT: 1914), 36-38; 54-56; Hurbert Howe Bancroft, *History of Utah* (1889; reprint, Salt Lake City, UT: Bookcraft, 1964), 663; Stanley Hirson, *The Lion of the Lord*, 305-308. See *Dialogue, A Journal of Mormon Thought*, Autumn 1966, 86-87, from Jerald and Sandra Tanner, *Mormon Kingdom*, 2:153-154.

51. Jerald and Sandra Tanner, *Mormon Kingdom*, 2:1-11, 32, 132-169, citing e.g., Brigham Young, *Manuscript History of Brigham Young*, original typed copy September 6, 1846, September 13, 1846; *On the Mormon Frontier: The Diary of Hosea Stout*, 1844-1861, University of Utah 1964, 1:32, 103, 190-193, 268-269, 305-306; 2:653, 663, 740; Mormon historian Juanita Brooks, *John D. Lee* (California, 1962), 143-144, 153; *Confessions of John D. Lee*, photo reprint of 1880 edition, 159, 282, 286; *The Valley Tan* (a non-Mormon Salt Lake City newspaper) of April 26, 1859; February 22, 1860, 2; T.B.H. Stenhouse, *The Rocky Mountain Saints*, 1873, 301-302; *Warsaw Signal*, January 7, 1846, April 24, 1844, etc.
52. T.B.H. Stenhouse, Mrs., *Tell It All: The Tyranny of Mormonism*, 305.
53. Jerald and Sandra Tanner, *Mormon Kingdom*, 2:4.
54. Stenhouse, *Tell It All*, 273.
55. Bill Hickman, *Brigham's Destroying Angel*, 14-15.

## Section 2: Mormon Belief and Practice

1. LeGrand Richards, *A Marvelous Work and a Wonder* (Salt Lake City, UT: Deseret Book Company, 1975), 425.
2. *Journal of Discourses*, 8:223.
3. Joseph Smith, *History*, 7:287. (Vol. 7 is from e.g., Brigham Young's *History*.)
4. Benson, *Teachings*, 104.
5. Ibid., 101-102, emphasis added.
6. Joseph Smith, *Teachings*, 350.
7. Jerald and Sandra Tanner, *Changing World*, 456-468, citing William Marks, *Zion's Harbinger and Baneemy's Organ*, July 1853, 53; and Klaus J. Hansen, *The Theory and Practice of the Political Kingdom of God in Mormon History 1829-1890*, Brigham Young University Master's Thesis, 1969, 114; *Dialogue: A Journal of Mormon Thought*, Summer 1966, 104, etc.
8. Jerald and Sandra Tanner, *Changing World*, 458; see note 7.
9. Ibid.
10. *Journal of Discourses*, 7:53, 170; cf. 2:53; and Anderson, *Inside Story*, 126; Jerald and Sandra Tanner, *Mormon Kingdom*, 1:preface.
11. Affidavit of Thomas B. March in LeLand H. Gentry, *A History of the Latter-day Saints in Northern Missouri from 1836-1839*, Ph.D. dissertation, Brigham Young University, 1965, 414, from Jerald and Sandra Tanner, *Shadow*, p. 414.
12. *Journal of Discourses*, 5:289; 6:78, 408-409, cited in Jerald and Sandra Tanner, *Changing World*, 460.
13. *Journal of Discourses*, 9:312.
14. Joseph F. Smith, *Gospel Doctrine*, 471, 479.
15. Joseph Fielding Smith, *Doctrines of Salvation*, 1:189-190.
16. *Journal of Discourses*, 7:289.
17. Jerald and Sandra Tanner, *Changing World*, 450, citing Brigham Henry Roberts, *Comprehensive History of the Church*, 5:509.
18. *Journal of Discourses*, 7:289.
19. Ibid., cf. 8:321.
20. *Journal of Discourses*, 14:203.
21. Joseph Smith, *History*, 5:335.
22. Jerald and Sandra Tanner, *Changing World*, chapter 17; Walter Martin, *Maze of Mormonism*, 333-340, Appendix D; Jerald and Sandra Tanner, *Mormonism—Shadow or Reality?* chapter 19; Fawn Brodie, *No Man Knows My History*, 405.
23. Jerald and Sandra Tanner, *Changing World*, 466.
24. Ibid., index, 587-589; see full listing.
25. James Talmage, *The Study of the Articles of Faith*, 296.
26. Ibid., 311.
27. *Journal of Discourses*, 3:155-157; cf. 2:338.
28. Benson, *Teachings*, 102.
29. Talmage, *Articles of Faith*, 311.
30. Bruce McConkie, *Mormon Doctrine*, 645.
31. McConkie, *Mormon Doctrine*, 644; see *Journal of Discourses*, 1:13-15; 2:44-46.
32. Joseph Fielding Smith, *Teachings*, 272.
33. McConkie, *Mormon Doctrine*, 650.
34. E.g., *Journal of Discourses*, 16:46.
35. In Joseph W. Musser, *Michael Our Father and Our God*, 20, citing *Deseret Weekly News*, 26:274.
36. *Journal of Discourses*, 13:264.
37. Ibid., 13:95.
38. Musser, *Michael Our Father*, 13-29; see Jerald and Sandra Tanner, *Changing*, 202-203.
39. *Journal of Discourses*, 16:375. Mormons are to receive the words of Joseph Smith and Brigham Young "as from the mouth of God."
40. *Journal of Discourses*, 16:46.
41. Ibid.
42. Benson, *Teachings*, vi-vii, second emphasis added.
43. Ankerberg, *Mormon Officials*, 11, 14.
44. The *Utah Christian Tract Society Newsletter*, 12, 8, (March/April 1980): 2; see Resource List for transcript of Benson's original lecture.
45. Ibid.
46. McConkie, *Mormon Doctrine*, 649.
47. *Doctrine and Covenants*, 1:30, 3; cf. Church of Jesus Christ of Latter-day Saints, *Which Church Is Right?* (pamphlet).
48. Orson Pratt, *The Seer*, April, 1854, 255 (see Bibliography).
49. Bruce McConkie, *Doctrinal New Testament Commentary* (Salt Lake City, UT: Bookcraft, 1976), 2:113; cf. 366, 458-459, 506-507; and his *Mormon Doctrine*, 138.
50. McConkie, *Mormon Doctrine*, 626.
51. McConkie, *Doctrinal New Testament Commentary*, 3:396.
52. Deseret Sunday School Union, *Master's Church Course A*, 6.
53. Church of Jesus Christ of Latter-day Saints, *Gospel Principles*, 100.
54. Benson, *Teachings*, 86.
55. Joseph Smith, *History*, 1:xci.
56. Ibid., xciv.

57. Pratt, *Seer*, January 1854, 205.
58. Joseph Fielding Smith, *Doctrines of Salvation*, 2:v.
59. Ibid., 3:283.
60. McConkie, *Doctrinal New Testament Commentary*, 2:274.
61. Deseret Sunday School Union, *Master's Church Course A*, 225.
62. Joseph Fielding Smith, *Doctrines of Salvation*, 3:291.
63. *Pamphlets by Orson Pratt*, 112, cited by Jerald and Sandra Tanner, *Changing World*, 27.
64. Anthony Hoekema, *The Four Major Cults*, 64.
65. *Journal of Discourses*, 6:192.
66. Ibid., 176.
67. Ibid., 163.
68. Joseph Fielding Smith, *Doctrines of Salvation*, 1:235-236.
69. *Time*, July 29, 1991, 22.
70. Ibid., 23.
71. Ankerberg, *Mormonism Revisited*, 22.
72. Ankerberg, *Mormon Officials*, 25; see *Deseret News*, church news section, Nov. 6, 1983, p. 4 (32 percent men, 35 percent women).
73. Ibid.
74. Spencer W. Kimball, *The Miracle of Forgiveness*, ix-xi.
75. Ankerberg, *Mormonism Revisited*, 10, 24; *Mormon Officials*, 5.
76. Ankerberg, *Mormonism Revisited*, 21-22.
77. Ankerberg, *Mormon Officials*, 5.
78. Ankerberg, *Mormonism Revisited*, 9.
79. Benson, *Teachings*, 219.
80. Church of Jesus Christ of Latter-day Saints, *Gospel Principles*, 73.
81. Church of Jesus Christ of Latter-day Saints, *The Restoration: Discussion 3* (pamphlet), 10; cf. *Doctrine and Covenants*, 27:8, 12.
82. McConkie, *Mormon Doctrine*, 594.
83. Church of Jesus Christ of Latter-day Saints, *Gospel Principles*, 81-82.
84. McConkie, *Doctrinal New Testament Commentary*, 3:396.
85. *Journal of Discourses*, 6:198.
86. Ankerberg, *Mormon Officials*, 25; cf. Jerald and Sandra Tanner, *Changing World*, 536-547; cf. 444-446, and their *Mormonism, Magic and Masonry*.
87. Martin, *Maze of Mormonism*, 139.
88. Church of Jesus Christ of Latter-day Saints, *Gospel Principles*, 107; cf. 99.

### Section 3: Mormon Religion and Christianity

1. Pratt, *Seer*, January, 1853, 15-16.
2. Church of Jesus Christ of Latter-day Saints, *Gospel Principles*, 46.
3. *Deseret Evening News*, October 11, 1890, taken from *Doctrine and Covenants*, 1982 ed., 292.
4. John Ankerberg, John Weldon, and Walter Kaiser, *The Case for Jesus the Messiah: Incredible Prophecies That Prove That God Exists* (Chattanooga, TN: Ankerberg Theological Research Institute, 1989).
5. *The Oxford American Dictionary*, s.v. "Christian."
6. Deseret Sunday School Union, *Master's Church Course*, 229.
7. Talmage, *Articles of Faith*, 28.
8. Benson, *Teachings*, 10.
9. Church of Jesus Christ of Latter-day Saints, *A Sure Foundation*, 155.
10. Ankerberg, *Mormonism Revisited*, 13.
11. Darl Andersen, *Soft Answers*, 58, 86.
12. Stephen E. Robinson, *Are Mormons Christians?*, vii.
13. Ibid., 2.
14. Ibid., 7.
15. Ibid., 34.
16. Ibid., 72, 77.
17. Ibid., 60, 88.
18. Harry L. Ropp, *The Mormon Papers*, 119.
19. Ibid., 13.
20. Ibid., 11.
21. *The Utah Evangel*, November 1981, 3.
22. Ibid., May 1981.
23. Ankerberg, *Mormon Officials*, 32.
24. *Journal of Discourses*, 16:46.
25. The Church of Jesus Christ of Latter-day Saints, *Apostasy and Restoration* (pamphlet), 14.
26. Sterling M. McMurrin, *The Theological Foundations of the Mormon Religion*, x.
27. Ibid., ix, 26.
28. Gordon Fraser, *Is Mormonism Christian?*, 10.
29. Martin, *Maze of Mormonism*, 45.
30. Jerald and Sandra Tanner, *Changing World*, 559.
31. Hoekema, *Four Major Cults*, 30.
32. Irving Hexham, in Walter A. Elwell, ed., *Evangelical Dictionary of Theology* (Grand Rapids, MI: Baker Book House, 1984), 736.
33. *Encyclopedia Britannica*, 15th ed., Macropaedia, s.v. "Mormonism."
34. *The New Schaff-Herzog Encyclopedia of Religious Knowledge*, s.v. "Mormonism."
35. Anthony A. Hoekema, in J.D. Douglas, ed., *The New International Dictionary of the Christian Church*, rev. ed. (Grand Rapids, MI: Zondervan, 1979), 678.
36. *Journal of Discourses*, 6:198.
37. Brigham Henry Roberts, Introduction to Joseph Smith's, *History*, lxxxvi.

38. Ibid.
39. *Elders Journal*, 1, 4:59-60; this journal was edited by Joseph Smith. From Jerald and Sandra Tanner, *Mormonism—Shadow or Reality?* 3.
40. See *Book of Mormon* index references under "Babylon," "Church of the Devil," "Church, Great and Abominable," and "Churches, False."
41. Joseph Smith, *Teachings*, 270.
42. Ibid., 322.
43. Ibid., 345.
44. Ibid., 15.
45. Church of Jesus Christ of Latter-day Saints, *Sure Foundation*, 200-201.
46. *Journal of Discourses*, 8:199.
47. *Journal of Discourses*, 8:171; cf. 7:333.
48. *Journal of Discourses*, 5:73.
49. *Journal of Discourses*, 5:229.
50. *Journal of Discourses*, 6:167.
51. *Journal of Discourses*, 5:240.
52. *Journal of Discourses*, 13:225.
53. *Journal of Discourses*, 6:25.
54. *Pamphlets by Orson Pratt*, 183; cited in Jerald and Sandra Tanner, *Case Against Mormonism*, 1:6.
55. B.H. Roberts, *The Mormon Doctrine of Deity*, 233.
56. Pratt, *Seer*, May 1854, 259-260.
57. Pratt, *Seer*, March 1854, 237, 239, 240.
58. Joseph Fielding Smith, *Doctrines of Salvation*, 3:267, 287.
59. McConkie, *Mormon Doctrine*, 132.
60. Ibid., 137-138.
61. McConkie, *Doctrinal New Testament Commentary*, 2:240, 274; cf. 3:265.
62. Ibid., 2:280.
63. Ibid., 3:85.
64. Ibid., 247, 550-551.
65. This makes its pretended friendship with Christianity all the more inexcusable. See Andersen, "Love Thy Minister Neighbor Worship Outline," photocopy and his *Soft Answers*.

**Section 4: Mormon Theology and Its Doctrine**

1. Church of Jesus Christ of Latter-day Saints, *Doctrines of the Gospel*, 6.
2. Joseph Smith, *Teachings*, 343.
3. Talmage, *Articles of Faith*, 47.
4. Church of Jesus Christ of Latter-day Saints, *Sure Foundation*, 93.
5. McConkie, *Mormon Doctrine*, 579.
6. Robinson, *Are Mormons Christians?*, 65.
7. Ibid., 69.
8. Ibid.
9. *The Oxford American Dictionary*, s.v. "polytheism."
10. McConkie, *Mormon Doctrine*, 576-577.
11. Ankerberg, *Mormon Officials*, 1.
12. Church of Jesus Christ of Latter-day Saints, *Doctrines of the Gospel*, 8.
13. Ibid.
14. Ibid.
15. Ibid., emphasis added.
16. Ibid., 10.
17. Ibid., 16.
18. *Pearl of Great Price*, Book of Abraham 4:1, 5-11, 14-17, 25-29; 5:7-8, 11, 14.
19. McConkie, *Mormon Doctrine*, 317.
20. Church of Jesus Christ of Latter-day Saints, *Doctrines of the Gospel*, 6.
21. Ibid., 9.
22. McConkie, *Mormon Doctrine*, 576-577.
23. *Journal of Discourses*, 7:333.
24. Duane S. Crowther, *Life Everlasting*, 361.
25. Robinson, *Are Mormons Christians?*, 88, emphasis added.
26. Ibid., 79, emphasis added.
27. Ibid., 71, emphasis added.
28. Richard L. Evans, interviewed in Leo Rosten's, *Religions of America* (NY: Simon & Schuster, 1975), 189.
29. Joseph Smith, *Teachings*, 372; cf. Joseph Fielding Smith, *Answers to Gospel Questions*, 1:3.
30. Joseph Smith, *Teachings*, 370.
31. Church of Jesus Christ of Latter-day Saints, *Sure Foundation*, 96.
32. McConkie, *Doctrinal New Testament Commentary*, 2:77, 113, 158.
33. E. Calvin Beisner, *God in Three Persons* (Wheaton, IL: Tyndale, 1984); Edward Henry Bickersteth, *The Trinity* (Grand Rapids, MI: Kregel, 1969).
34. Joseph Smith, *Teachings*, 347-348.
35. Church of Jesus Christ of Latter-day Saints, *Gospel Principles*, 293.
36. Joseph Smith, *History*, 6:305.
37. Church of Jesus Christ of Latter-day Saints, *Gospel Principles*, 6.
38. Ankerberg, *Mormon Officials*, 9.
39. Joseph Smith, *Teachings*, 373; cf. McConkie, *Doctrinal New Testament Commentary*, 3:434-437.
40. Joseph Smith, *Teachings*, 345-346.
41. Ibid., 348-349.
42. Joseph Smith, *History*, 6:476, cited in Crowther, *Life Everlasting*, 364.
43. McConkie, *Doctrinal New Testament Commentary*, 2:78.

44. Ibid., 3:225.
45. Ankerberg, *Mormonism Revisited*, 5.
46. Church of Jesus Christ of Latter-day Saints, *Doctrines of the Gospel*, 17.
47. Robinson, *Are Mormons Christians?*, 60.
48. E.g., *Journal of Discourses*, 1:93, 123; 6:120.
49. *Journal of Discourses*, 6:120.
50. *Journal of Discourses*, 1:93.
51. McConkie, *Mormon Doctrine*, 544-545.
52. *Journal of Discourses*, 11:286.
53. Musser, *Michael Our Father*, 25, citing *Deseret Weekly News*, 22:309.
54. Pratt, *Seer*, September 1853, 132.
55. McMurrin, *Theological Foundations*, 29.
56. Ibid., 36.
57. Ibid., 35.
58. Joseph Smith, *Teachings*, 181.
59. Benson, *Teachings*, 3-4.
60. Church of Jesus Christ of Latter-day Saints, *Sure Foundation*, 97, 99.
61. McConkie, *Mormon Doctrine*, 250.
62. Church of Jesus Christ of Latter-day Saints, *Doctrines of the Gospel*, 6.
63. McConkie, *Mormon Doctrine*, 117-118; cf. Einar Anderson, *Inside Story*, 89.
64. McConkie, *Mormon Doctrine*, 239.
65. Benson, *Teachings*, 537.
66. McConkie, *Mormon Doctrine*, 117-118.
67. Ankerberg, *Mormon Officials*, 21.
68. Church of Jesus Christ of Latter-day Saints, *Gospel Principles*, 9.
69. Ibid., 11.
70. Benson, *Teachings*, 540, citing *Discourses of Brigham Young*, 197.
71. Benson, *Teachings*, 542-543.
72. Jerald and Sandra Tanner, *Changing World*, 244.
73. Einar Anderson, *Inside Story*, 89.
74. McConkie, *Mormon Doctrine*, 238.
75. Ankerberg, *Mormonism Revisited*, 27.
76. Ibid., 8.
77. Ankerberg, *Mormon Officials*, 24.
78. Ibid.
79. Jerald and Sandra Tanner, *Changing World*, 233-234.
80. Ibid., 231-236 for documentation.
81. McConkie, *Doctrinal New Testament Commentary*, 2:160.
82. McConkie, *Mormon Doctrine*, 516-517; cf. Talmage, *Articles of Faith*, 443.
83. Joseph Fielding Smith, *Answers to Gospel Questions*, 3:142; cf. 143-144.
84. Ibid., 144. See *Achieving a Celestial Marriage*, 132, where it teaches women also become gods.
85. *Journal of Discourses*, 13:309.
86. Pratt, *Seer*, November 1853, 172.
87. Pratt, *Seer*, October 1853.
88. *Journal of Discourses*, 3:93.
89. Jerald and Sandra Tanner, *Changing World*, 177, citing Milton Hunter (a member of the First Council of Seventy), *The Gospel Through the Ages* (1958), 104, 114-115.
90. Pratt, *Seer*, February 1853, 23, emphasis added.
91. Jerald and Sandra Tanner, *Changing World*, 188, citing Marion Romney, member of the First Presidency, *Salt Lake City Tribune*, October 6, 1974, 1, emphasis added. See *Achieving a Celestial Marriage*, 129.
92. Robinson, *Are Mormons Christians?*, 88.
93. Ibid., 79.
94. Benson, *Teachings*, 4.
95. Jerald and Sandra Tanner, *Changing World*, 191.
96. McConkie, *Mormon Doctrine*, 90.
97. Joseph Fielding Smith, *Doctrines of Salvation*, 3:286.
98. Talmage, *Articles of Faith*, 160, 163, 167.
99. Ibid., 166.
100. Jerald and Sandra Tanner, *Changing World*, 188.
101. *Journal of Discourses*, 2:338.
102. Joseph F. Smith, *Gospel Doctrine*, 60-61.
103. Ibid., 60.
104. Ibid.
105. Ibid., 61.
106. *Doctrine and Covenants*, 1835 ed., 52-58.
107. Ibid.
108. Joseph Fielding Smith, *Doctrines of Salvation*, 1:39; *Journal of Discourses*, 5:179.
109. Joseph Fielding Smith, *Doctrines of Salvation*, 1:39.
110. Ibid., with Jerald and Sandra Tanner, *Changing World*, 190.
111. *Journal of Discourses*, 2:338.
112. Joseph F. Smith, *Gospel Doctrine*, 60-61.
113. McConkie, *Doctrinal New Testament Commentary*, 3:338.
114. Ibid., 341.
115. McConkie, *Mormon Doctrine*, 359, 752.
116. *Journal of Discourses*, 1:50.
117. *Journal of Discourses*, 5:331; see *Deseret News*, June 18, 1873.
118. *Millennial Star*, 16:543, from Einar Anderson, *Inside Story*, 105-106.

119. *Millennial Star*, 16:530.
120. Jerald and Sandra Tanner, *Changing World*, 199, citing *Women of Mormonism*, 196.
121. *On the Mormon Frontier*, 2:435, in Jerald and Sandra Tanner, *Changing World*, 200.
122. *Journal of Discourses*, 4:1.
123. *Sacred Hymns and Spiritual Songs for the Church of Jesus Christ of Latter-day Saints* (1856), npp 375.
124. Abraham Cannon's diary of June 23, 1889, 2:39, from Jerald and Sandra Tanner, *Changing World*, 201.
125. Musser, *Michael Our Father*, 1-136; for example, 1-6, 13-19, 31-38, 133, etc.; Martin, *Maze*, 84-90; Jerald and Sandra Tanner, *Changing World*, chapter 8; Jerald and Sandra Tanner, *Mormonism—Shadow or Reality?* chapter 10.
126. McConkie, *Mormon Doctrine*, 18.
127. Joseph Fielding Smith, *Doctrines of Salvation*, 1:96; cf. his discussion through 106.
128. Ankerberg, *Mormon Officials*, 16.
129. Stenhouse, *Tell It All*, 299-300.
130. Joseph Fielding Smith, *Doctrines of Salvation*, 1:96; this is Smith's description of Brigham Young's alleged teaching, something Smith agrees with.
131. Mark E. Petersen, *Adam: Who Is He?* 16-17.
132. Ibid., 14.
133. Robinson, *Are Mormons Christians?* 19
134. Ibid.
135. Ibid., 20.
136. Ankerberg, *Mormon Officials*, 17, in the words of Walter Martin.
137. Jerald and Sandra Tanner, *Changing World*, 192-193.
138. Church of Jesus Christ of Latter-day Saints, *Sure Foundation*, 61.
139. Ibid., 62.
140. Ibid., 61.
141. Roberts, *Mormon Doctrine of Deity*, 42-43.
142. Church of Jesus Christ of Latter-day Saints, *What the Mormons Think of Christ*, 1982 (pamphlet), 16.
143. Church of Jesus Christ of Latter-day Saints, *Faith in the Lord Jesus Christ*, 4.
144. Robinson, *Are Mormons Christians?* 111, emphasis added.
145. Ibid., 112, 114.
146. McConkie, *Doctrinal New Testament Commentary*, 2:79.
147. McConkie, *Mormon Doctrine*, 587.
148. Rev. Frank Morley, *What We Can Learn From the Church of Jesus Christ of Latter-day Saints By a Protestant Minister* (Salt Lake City, UT: Church of Jesus Christ of Latter-day Saints, n.d.), 3.
149. McConkie, *Mormon Doctrine*, 590.
150. Talmage, *Articles of Faith*, 471.
151. McConkie, *Mormon Doctrine*, 169; cf. Joseph Fielding Smith, *Doctrines of Salvation*, 1:75.
152. Jerald and Sandra Tanner, *Changing World*, 519, citing Milton Hunter, *Gospel Through the Ages*, 21.
153. Talmage, *Articles of Faith*, 472.
154. Church of Jesus Christ of Latter-day Saints, *Sure Foundation*, 224.
155. J.H. Evans, *An American Prophet*, 1933, 241, cited in Hoekema, *Four Major Cults*, 54.
156. McConkie, *Mormon Doctrine*, 129.
157. *Journal of Discourses*, 10:223.
158. *Journal of Discourses*, 1:50-51, emphasis added.
159. Jerald and Sandra Tanner, *Changing World*, 180, citing *Dialogue: A Journal of Mormon Thought*, Autumn 1967; 100-101.
160. Joseph Fielding Smith, *Doctrines of Salvation*, 1:18, emphasis added.
161. McConkie, *Mormon Doctrine*, 547.
162. Benson, *Teachings*, 6-7.
163. Jerald and Sandra Tanner, *Changing World*, 180, citing *Deseret News*, October 10, 1866.
164. Pratt, *Seer*, October 1853, 158.
165. *Journal of Discourses*, 4:218.
166. Hoekema, *Four Major Cults*, 56.
167. Joseph Fielding Smith, *Way to Perfection*, 37.
168. McConkie, *Mormon Doctrine*, 257.
169. Church of Jesus Christ of Latter-day Saints, *Doctrines of the Gospel*, 15.
170. Ibid., 9-10.
171. Benson, *Teachings*, 6.
172. McConkie, *Doctrinal New Testament Commentary*, 2:215.
173. Ibid., 3:238.
174. McConkie, *Mormon Doctrine*, 129.
175. Church of Jesus Christ of Latter-day Saints, *What the Mormons Think of Christ*, 1982 (pamphlet), 22; cf. McConkie, *Doctrinal New Testament Commentary*, 3:140.
176. *Journal of Discourses*, 1:346.
177. Ibid., 345.
178. Ibid., 2:210.
179. Pratt, *Seer*, November 1853, 172.
180. See the citations in Jerald and Sandra Tanner, *Changing World*, 254; cf. their *Mormonism—Shadow or Reality?* 128.
181. Ankerberg, *Mormonism Revisited*, 28. See Resource List.
182. McConkie, *Mormon Doctrine*, 76, citing Joseph Smith for the last clause.
183. Ibid., 77.

## Section 5: Mormon Salvation and Godhood

1. McConkie, *Mormon Doctrine*, 670.
2. Ibid., 671.
3. Ibid., 234.
4. Ibid., 671.
5. Ibid.
6. Ibid., 669.

7. Ibid.
8. Crowther, *Life Everlasting*, 329.
9. Joseph Fielding Smith, *Doctrines of Salvation*, 2:133-134, emphasis added.
10. Church of Jesus Christ of Latter-day Saints, *Doctrines of the Gospel*, 91-92.
11. James Talmage, *Jesus the Christ*, 31.
12. McConkie, *Mormon Doctrine*, 671.
13. Ibid., 29.
14. Ibid., 176-177, 234.
15. Ibid., 670.
16. Crowther, *Life Everlasting*, 327, emphasis added.
17. Ibid., 332.
18. McConkie, *Doctrinal New Testament Commentary*, 3:284-285.
19. Church of Jesus Christ of Latter-day Saints, *Doctrines of the Gospel*, 29.
20. Ibid., 77.
21. McConkie, *Mormon Doctrine*, 261.
22. Benson, *Teachings*, 66.
23. McConkie, *Doctrinal New Testament Commentary*, 3:258-259, emphasis added.
24. Talmage, *Articles of Faith*, 107.
25. McConkie, *Mormon Doctrine*, 262, 264.
26. Ibid., 264-266.
27. Church of Jesus Christ of Latter-day Saints, *What the Mormons Think of Christ*, n.d. ed., 27.
28. Robinson, *Are Mormons Christians?* 104-105, emphasis added.
29. Ibid., 109, emphasis added.
30. Ibid., 108, emphasis added.
31. Cf. Anderson, *Inside Story*, 13, 19.
32. Talmage, *Articles of Faith*, 107.
33. Ibid., 479-480.
34. McConkie, *Mormon Doctrine*, 671.
35. Joseph Fielding Smith, *Doctrines of Salvation*, 2:139.
36. Richards, *Marvelous Work*, 25.
37. Pratt, *Seer*, January 1854, 199-200.
38. McConkie, *Mormon Doctrine*, 339.
39. McConkie, *Doctrinal New Testament Commentary*, 2:215.
40. Ibid., 229.
41. Marvin W. Cowan, *Mormon Claims Answered*, 88, citing John A. Widtsoe, *Evidences and Reconciliations*, 190.
42. McMurrin, *Theological Foundations*, 70.
43. McConkie, *Doctrinal New Testament Commentary*, 2:238.
44. Ibid., 230.
45. Church of Jesus Christ of Latter-day Saints, *Doctrines of the Gospel*, 49-50.
46. Joseph Fielding Smith, *The Way to Perfection*, 189.
47. McConkie, *Doctrinal New Testament Commentary*, 3:402.
48. Kimball, *Miracle*, 207-208.
49. Richards, *Marvelous Work*, 275.
50. McConkie, *Doctrinal New Testament Commentary*, 2:248.
51. Ibid., 231, emphasis added.
52. Kimball, *Miracle*, 203.
53. Ibid., 203-204.
54. Church of Jesus Christ of Latter-day Saints, *Doctrines of the Gospel*, 49-50, emphasis added.
55. Church of Jesus Christ of Latter-day Saints, *Sure Foundation*, 157.
56. Ibid., 158.
57. Talmage, *Articles of Faith*, 1.
58. Joseph Smith, *History*, 6:223; cf. Joseph Smith, *Teachings*, 253, 357.
59. Joseph Smith, *History*, 5:65.
60. Brigham Young, *Discourses of Brigham Young*, 220.
61. *Discourses of Brigham Young*, 390.
62. *Journal of Discourses*, 13:213.
63. *Journal of Discourses*, 11:138.
64. *Journal of Discourses*, 4:189.
65. Ibid., 192-193.
66. Joseph Fielding Smith, *Way to Perfection*, 186.
67. Joseph Fielding Smith, *Answers*, 3:26-27.
68. Kimball, *Miracle*, 6.
69. Ibid., 16.
70. Ibid., 206.
71. Ibid., 207.
72. Benson, *Teachings*, 20.
73. Ibid., 26.
74. Ibid., 343.
75. Talmage, *Jesus the Christ*, 5.
76. McConkie, *Doctrinal New Testament Commentary*, 2:279, 294.
77. Ibid., 298.
78. Ibid., 3:251.
79. Ibid., 265, emphasis added.
80. Ibid., 377.
81. Church of Jesus Christ of Latter-day Saints, *Doctrines of the Gospel*, 47.
82. Ibid., 48.
83. Ibid.

84. Ibid., 52, citing *The Teachings of Spencer W. Kimball*, 28.
85. Church of Jesus Christ of Latter-day Saints, *Sure Foundation*, 205.
86. Ibid., 206, citing Joseph Smith, *Teachings*, 348.
87. Ibid., citing Joseph Fielding Smith, *Doctrines of Salvation*, 2:18.
88. Ibid., 206-207.
89. McConkie, *Doctrinal New Testament Commentary*, 3:285-286.
90. McConkie, *Mormon Doctrine*, 318.
91. McConkie, *Doctrinal New Testament Commentary*, 3:67.
92. Ibid., 2:296, emphasis added.
93. Ibid., 3:248.
94. McConkie, *Mormon Doctrine*, 45.
95. Church of Jesus Christ of Latter-day Saints, *Master's Church Course*, 21-22.
96. *Doctrine and Covenants*, 130:18-19.
97. Joseph Smith, *Teachings*, 354-355.
98. Ibid., 357.
99. Ibid., 297.
100. *Doctrine and Covenants*, 131:6.
101. Joseph Fielding Smith, *Way to Perfection*, 208.
102. Pratt, *Seer*, January 1854, 206, emphasis added; cf. McConkie, *Doctrinal New Testament Commentary*, 3:191.
103. McConkie, *Mormon Doctrine*, 581.
104. Pratt, *Seer*, April 1854, 255.
105. Joseph Fielding Smith, *Way to Perfection*, 190-191.
106. Joseph F. Smith, *Gospel Doctrine*, 272.
107. Joseph Fielding Smith, *Doctrines of Salvation*, 2:87-89, emphasis added.
108. Cowan, *Mormon Claims*, 83, citing apostle Mark E. Petersen, *Deseret News*, Church Section, April 14, 1973, 14, emphasis added.
109. Ibid., 85, citing Brigham Young, *Deseret News*, Church Section, July 20, 1968, 14, emphasis added.
110. Cf. Ibid., 91-99.
111. McConkie, *Mormon Doctrine*, 779.
112. Church of Jesus Christ of Latter-day Saints, *Gospel Principles*, 247, emphasis added.
113. Joseph Heinerman, *Spirit World Manifestations*, 7.
114. *Improvement Era*, 39 (April 1936): 200.
115. *Times and Seasons*, 2:546.
116. Heinerman, *Spirit World*, 29.
117. Einar Anderson, *Inside Story*, 84, reporting on a Dr. Ironside's quoting of a Mormon elder. Mormons frequently teach that they are the "saviors" of men.
118. Joseph Smith, *Teachings*, 192.
119. *Millenial Star*, vol. 15, p. 801.
120. Joseph Fielding Smith, *Way to Perfection*, 153.
121. Joseph Fielding Smith, *Doctrines of Salvation*, 2:141-145, emphasis added.
122. Ibid., 145.
123. Ibid., 146-148.
124. Church of Jesus Christ of Latter-day Saints, *Doctrines of the Gospel*, 85.
125. Ibid.
126. Ibid.
127. Ibid.
128. Ibid., 86.
129. Ibid., citing Joseph Smith, *History of the Church*, 6:365.
130. Ibid., citing Joseph Fielding Smith, *Doctrines of Salvation*, 2:148-149.
131. Ibid., citing Spencer W. Kimball, "Things of Eternity," 5.
132. Joseph Fielding Smith, *Doctrines of Salvation*, 2:131.
133. Jerald and Sandra Tanner, *Changing World*, 516-517.
134. Joseph Fielding Smith, *Doctrines of Salvation*, 1:60; Benson, *Teachings*, 24.
135. McConkie, *Doctrinal New Testament Commentary*, 2:291; cf. 274, 277.
136. Mark Petersen, "Race Problems As They Affect the Church," Lecture at Brigham Young University, Provo, UT: August 27, 1954, cited in Jerald and Sandra Tanner, *Changing World*, 293-294.
137. For an excellent popular study, see James I. Packer, *God's Words: Studies of Key Bible Themes* (Downers Grove, IL: InterVarsity, 1981).
138. McConkie, *Mormon Doctrine*, 434-436.
139. McConkie, *Doctrinal New Testament Commentary*, 2:254, 260.
140. Ibid., 3:259.
141. Ibid., 2:257-258, emphasis added.
142. McConkie, *Mormon Doctrine*, 434-436.
143. Sinclair Ferguson, *Know Your Christian Life: A Theological Introduction* (Downers Grove, IL: InterVarsity, 1981), 71.
144. Ibid., 73.
145. James Packer, in Everett F. Harrison et al., eds., *Baker's Dictionary of Theology* (Grand Rapids, MI: Baker, 1972), 305.
146. Bruce Milne, *Know the Truth: A Handbook of Christian Belief* (Downers Grove, IL: InterVarsity, 1982), 155.
147. J.I. Packer, *God's Words*, 139-140.
148. J.I. Packer, in *Baker's Dictionary of Theology*, 306.
149. J.I. Packer, *God's Words*, 141-142.
150. J.I. Packer, in *Baker's Dictionary of Theology*, 306.
151. McConkie, *Mormon Doctrine*, 61.
152. Talmage, *Articles of Faith*, 76.
153. Church of Jesus Christ of Latter-day Saints, *Doctrines of the Gospel*, 22.
154. Benson, *Teachings*, 14.
155. Talmage, *Articles of Faith*, 481; Joseph F. Smith, *Gospel Doctrine*, 214-215.
156. Ankerberg, *Mormonism Revisited*, 7, 25, 37.

157. McConkie, *Doctrinal New Testament Commentary*, 2:242; cf. McMurrin, *Theological Foundations*, 71.
158. McMurrin, *Theological Foundations*, 71.
159. Crowther, *Life Everlasting*, 233.
160. Ankerberg, *Mormonism Revisited*, 7; Church of Jesus Christ of Latter-day Saints, "The Gospel of Jesus Christ" (pamphlet).
161. McMurrin, *Theological Foundations*, 83.
162. *Journal of Discourses*, 4:220.
163. Ibid., 4:54.
164. Ankerberg, *Mormonism Revisited*, 37.
165. Kimball, *Miracle*, 14.
166. *Doctrine and Covenants*, 76:50, 52; cf. Joseph Fielding Smith, *Way to Perfection*, 206.
167. Hal Hougey, *Mormon Missionary Handbook*, 62.
168. Ibid., 73.
169. Ibid., 83-84.
170. Kimball, *Miracle*, 208-209, emphasis added.
171. Benson, *Teachings*, 14, emphasis added.
172. Ibid., 23.
173. Church of Jesus Christ of Latter-day Saints, *Sure Foundation*, 156, emphasis added.
174. Talmage, *Articles of Faith*, 87, emphasis added.
175. McMurrin, *Theological Foundations*, 90.
176. Ankerberg, *Mormomism Revisited*, 25.
177. McConkie, *Doctrinal New Testament Commentary*, 2:242-243.
178. Ankerberg, *Mormon Officials*, 8.
179. Church of Jesus Christ of Latter-day Saints, *Gospel Principles*, 66, 68-69.
180. Ibid., 118.
181. Ibid.
182. Ibid., 120-121.
183. Ibid., 121-122.
184. Ibid., 122.
185. Ibid.
186. Joseph Fielding Smith, *Doctrines of Salvation*, 2:131.
187. Joseph Smith, *Teachings*, 347-348.
188. *Journal of Discourses*, 21:80-81, 84.
189. Church of Jesus Christ of Latter-day Saints, *Doctrines of the Gospel*, 22.
190. Robinson, *Are Mormons Christians?* 104.
191. *Discourses of Brigham Young*, 57.
192. Joseph Fielding Smith, *Teachings*, 352.
193. Church of Jesus Christ of Latter-day Saints, *Doctrines of the Gospel*, 30.
194. McMurrin, *Theological Foundations*, 49.
195. Joseph Smith, *History*, 6:310-312.
196. Ibid., 308, 310-311.
197. McConkie, *Doctrinal New Testament Commentary*, 3:225.
198. Kimball, *Miracle*, 5.
199. Joseph Fielding Smith, *Answers*, 4:127.
200. Joseph Smith, *Teachings*, 354.
201. Church of Jesus Christ of Latter-day Saints, *Doctrines of the Gospel*, 16.
202. Ibid., 51.
203. Ibid., 14.
204. Robinson, *Are Mormons Christians?* 65.
205. Ibid., 68.
206. Ibid., 64.
207. Joseph Smith, *Teachings*, 343.
208. Ibid., 353-354.
209. Roberts, *Mormon Doctrine of Deity*, 222.
210. McConkie, *Mormon Doctrine*, 465-466.
211. John Widtsoe, *Rational Theology*, 61, from Ankerberg Theological Research Institute, "News and Views," Chattanooga, TN, January 1983.
212. McConkie, *Doctrinal New Testament Commentary*, 2:252, 349, 506.
213. McConkie, *Mormon Doctrine*, 544.
214. Kimball, *Miracle*, 3.
215. Ibid., 2.
216. Church of Jesus Christ of Latter-day Saints, *Gospel Principles*, 290.
217. Ankerberg, *Mormon Officials*, 3.
218. Ibid., 4; cf. Ankerberg, *Mormonism Revisited*, 3.
219. *Journal of Discourses*, 15:137.
220. Crowther, *Life Everlasting*, 333.
221. Ibid., 334, citing N.B. Lundwall, *The Vision*, 45, emphasis added.
222. Ankerberg, *Mormon Officials*, 8.
223. Crowther, *Life Everlasting*, 360.
224. Ibid., 360-361.
225. Ibid., 361.
226. Robinson, *Are Mormons Christians?* 60.
227. Church of Jesus Christ of Latter-day Saints, *Doctrines of the Gospel*, 20; cf. Ankerberg, *Mormonism Revisited*, 12.
228. McMurrin, *Theological Foundations*, 72.
229. Joseph Fielding Smith, *Answers*, 4:79.
230. Ibid., 80.
231. *Journal of Discourses*, 10:312.

232. Joseph Fielding Smith, *Doctrines of Salvation*, 1:86.
233. Church of Jesus Christ of Latter-day Saints, *Gospel Principles*, 31, emphasis added.
234. Joseph Fielding Smith, *Answers*, 2:215.
235. *Journal of Discourses*, 13:145.
236. Ibid., 12:70.
237. Joseph Fielding Smith, *Doctrines of Salvation*, 1:113-114.
238. Church of Jesus Christ of Latter-day Saints, *Doctrines of the Gospel*, 20, citing, *The Message of Seminary and Institute Teachers*, July 13, 1966, 5.
239. McConkie, *Mormon Doctrine*, 268-269.
240. Joseph Fielding Smith, *Answers*, 4:81-82.
241. Church of Jesus Christ of Latter-day Saints, *Gospel Principles*, 33.
242. Talmage, *Articles of Faith*, 70.
243. Church of Jesus Christ of Latter-day Saints, *Doctrines of the Gospel*, 20, citing Joseph Fielding Smith, "The Atonement of Jesus Christ," (a speech) Brigham Young University Speeches of the Year, Provo, UT: delivered January 25, 1955, 2.
244. Church of Jesus Christ of Latter-day Saints, *Doctrines of the Gospel*, 22.
245. Ibid., 19.
246. Ibid., 20, citing Joseph Fielding Smith, "Fall—Atonement—Resurrection—Sacrament" in *Charge to Religious Educators*, 124.
247. Joseph Fielding Smith, *Answers*, 4:81.
248. Ibid., 2:214-215.
249. Ankerberg, *Mormonism Revisited*, 37.
250. Talmage, *Articles of Faith*, 53-54.
251. McConkie, *Mormon Doctrine*, 193.
252. McConkie, *Doctrinal New Testament Commentary*, 3:402.
253. Talmage, *Articles of Faith*, 52.
254. Owen Kendall White, Jr., "The Social-Psychological Basis of Mormon Neo-Orthodoxy," M.A. Thesis at University of Utah, 95-101, cited in Jerald and Sandra Tanner, *Changing World*, 551.
255. See Augustus H. Strong, *Systematic Theology*, 597-601 for a discussion of pelagianism; cf. F. Hoekema, *Four Major Cults*, 53.
256. Hoekema, *Four Major Cults*, 52.
257. McConkie, *Mormon Doctrine*, 192-193, 589ff.
258. Ibid.
259. Church of Jesus Christ of Latter-day Saints, *Master's Church Course*, 22.
260. McConkie, *Mormon Doctrine*, 193.
261. Ibid., 35.
262. Ibid., 36; cf. Joseph Smith, *Teachings*, 170.
263. Cf. Hoekema, *Four Major Cults*, 74.
264. *Journal of Discourses*, 19:229.
265. Benson, *Teachings*, 36-38.
266. Church of Jesus Christ of Latter-day Saints, *Doctrines of the Gospel*, 84, citing Joseph Fielding Smith, *Doctrines of Salvation*, 2:132.
267. Kimball, *Miracle*, 5.
268. Church of Jesus Christ of Latter-day Saints, *Sure Foundation*, 49.
269. Talmage, *Articles of Faith*, 405.
270. Ibid., 406-407.
271. Ibid., 407-408; Joseph Fielding Smith, *Answers*, 2:209.
272. Church of Jesus Christ of Latter-day Saints, *Gospel Principles*, 286-287.
273. Talmage, *Articles of Faith*, 409.
274. Ibid.
275. Church of Jesus Christ of Latter-day Saints, *Gospel Principles*, 285.
276. Church of Jesus Christ of Latter-day Saints, *Doctrines of the Gospel*, 83.
277. Ibid., 90.
278. Ibid.
279. Church of Jesus Christ of Latter-day Saints, *Sure Foundation*, 48-49.
280. Church of Jesus Christ of Latter-day Saints, *Doctrines of the Gospel*, 90.
281. Ibid., 93.
282. Martin, *Maze*, 248.
283. Hoekema, *Four Major Cults*, 72.
284. Floyd McElveen, *Will the "Saints" Go Marching In?* 97, retitled *The Mormon Illusion*.
285. *Discourses of Brigham Young*, 383, citing *Journal of Discourses*, 9:147.
286. Ibid., 386, citing *Journal of Discourses*, 2:302.
287. Ibid., 390, citing *Journal of Discourses*, 16:42.
288. Cowan, *Mormon Claims*.
289. E.g., McConkie, *Doctrinal New Testament Commentary*, 3:192, 532; Church of Jesus Christ of Latter-day Saints, *Gospel Principles*, 287.
290. Joseph Fielding Smith, *Answers*, 2:210.
291. McConkie, *Doctrinal New Testament Commentary*, 3:584.
292. Talmage, *Articles of Faith*, 60; Joseph Fielding Smith, *Doctrines of Salvation*, 2:218-219.
293. Church of Jesus Christ of Latter-day Saints, *Sure Foundation*, 50; Ankerberg, *Mormonism Revisited*, 37.
294. Joseph Fielding Smith, *Answers*, 2:208-210.
295. Joseph Fielding Smith, *Doctrines of Salvation*, 2:220, 228.
296. *Doctrine and Covenants*, 19:4-7, 10-12; cf. 19:1-2.
297. Church of Jesus Christ of Latter-day Saints, *Sure Foundation*, 46, 48.
298. Talmage, *Articles of Faith*, 61.
299. Ibid., 409, emphasis added.
300. McConkie, *Doctrinal New Testament Commentary*, 2:579; Joseph Fielding Smith, *Answers*, 2:208.
301. For original documentation, see Jerald and Sandra Tanner, *Changing World*, chapter 21 and Martin, *Maze*, 248-252, 259-261.

301. Richards, *A Marvelous Work*, 27.
302. See the discussion in Jerald and Sandra Tanner, *Changing World*, chapter 21; Martin, *Maze*, 248-252; and Cowan, *Mormon Claims*, 102-104.
303. Cf. Cowan, *Mormon Claims*, 103; Ankerberg, *Mormonism Revisited*, 30.

**Section 6: Mormon Religion and the Occult**
  1. *Doctrine and Covenants*, 1:11-14; 3:2; 53:42-43, 59-66; 72:21.
  2. Ankerberg and Weldon, *Cult Watch*, 179-183; 253-257; cf. parts 5, 7.
  3. Nandor Fodor, *An Encyclopedia of Psychical Science* (Secaucus, NJ:Citadel Press, 1974), 233.
  4. See chapter 18 and especially D. Michael Quinn, *Early Mormonism and the Magic World View*, index under "Astrology"; cf. Jerald and Sandra Tanner, *Changing World*, 10; Jerald and Sandra Tanner, *Mormonism—Shadow or Reality?* 87; Einar Anderson, *Inside Story*, 22.
  5. See chapter 18.
  6. Quinn, *Early Mormonism*, 58, 60.
  7. Ibid., 64-66.
  8. Ibid., 66.
  9. See the chapter on "crystal healing/crystal work" (243-250) in John Ankerberg and John Weldon, *Can You Trust Your Doctor? The Complete Guide to New Age Medicine and Its Threat to Your Family* (Brentwood, TN: Wolgemuth & Hyatt, 1991); cf. Jerald and Sandra Tanner, *Changing World*, 88-91; Jack Adamson and Reed C. Durham, Jr., *No Help for the Widow's Son: Joseph Smith and Masonry* (Nauvoo, IL: Martin Publishing, 1980), 32-33.
 10. Quinn, *Early Mormonism*, 78, 80.
 11. Cf. David Conway, *Magic and Occult Primer* (NY: Bantam, 1966).
 12. Quinn, *Early Mormonism*, 83.
 13. Ibid., 111.
 14. Joseph Smith, *Manuscript History*, Book-1, 642, cited by Jerald and Sandra Tanner, *Changing World*, 159, citing *Deseret News*, May 29, 1852.
 15. Quinn, *Early Mormonism*, 27-28, emphasis added.
 16. Ibid., 118-119.
 17. Ibid., 120-121.
 18. Ibid., 116.
 19. Ibid., 153.
 20. Jerald and Sandra Tanner, *Changing World*, 67-80.
 21. Ibid., 80-84; Jerald and Sandra Tanner, *Joseph Smith and Money Digging*, 7.
 22. *Millennial Star*, 40, 49, cited in Jerald and Sandra Tanner, *Joseph Smith and Money Digging*, 8.
 23. Jerald and Sandra Tanner, *Changing World*, chapter 4; cf. Jerald and Sandra Tanner, *Mormonism—Shadow or Reality?* corresponding chapter and their *Joseph Smith's 1826 Trial: New Discoveries Prove Court Record Authentic* (Salt Lake City, UT: Utah Lighthouse Ministry, 1971).
 24. Jerald and Sandra Tanner, *Changing World*, 74-75, 83-84.
 25. Jerald and Sandra Tanner, *Joseph Smith and Money Digging*, 11-13, for numerous examples; cf. Jerald and Sandra Tanner, *Changing World*, 77-85; also "Crystal healing/Crystal work," in Ankerberg and Weldon, *Can You Trust?*
 26. Quinn, *Early Mormonism*, 194-195, *passim*.
 27. Ibid., 194, 310.
 28. Ibid., 194.
 29. Ben G. Hester, *Dowsing: An Exposé of Hidden Occult Forces* (Arlington, CA: Ben G. Hester, 1984).
 30. Quinn, *Early Mormonism*, 194.
 31. Ibid., 194-195, emphasis added.
 32. Ibid., 195.
 33. Ibid., *passim*; Jerald and Sandra Tanner, *Changing World*, 159, chapter 4; Martin, *Maze*, chapter 8.
 34. Martin, *Maze*, 220; cf. Joseph Fielding Smith, *Way to Perfection*, 318-319; McConkie, *Doctrinal New Testament Commentary*, 3:137-141, 225, 393, 553; McConkie, *Mormon Doctrine*, 35-36, 762.
 35. Stenhouse, *Tell It All*, 297.
 36. *Discourses of Brigham Young*, 378-380, citing *Journal of Discourses*, 7:332, 6:349.
 37. Kimball, *Miracle*, 1, 5.
 38. Ibid.
 39. McConkie, *Mormon Doctrine*, 762.
 40. Benson, *Teachings*, 18.
 41. Crowther, *Life Everlasting*, 8.
 42. Ibid., 10-11.
 43. Quinn, *Early Mormonism*, 173.
 44. Ibid., 184.
 45. Ibid., 190.
 46. Ibid., 186.
 47. Ibid., 185.
 48. Cf. Ankerberg, *Mormonism Revisited*, 19.
 49. Cf. G.W. Grogan, "Baptism for the Dead" in Merrill C. Tenny (general ed.), *The Zondervan Pictorial Encyclopedia of the Bible* (Grand Rapids, MI: Zondervan, 1975), 1:469-470; Ankerberg, *Mormonism Revisited*, 29.
 50. Quinn, *Early Mormonism*, 154-156.
 51. Ankerberg and Weldon, *Cult Watch*, 277-281.
 52. McConkie, *Mormon Doctrine*, 526.
 53. McConkie, *Doctrinal New Testament Commentary*, 1:252; Joseph Fielding Smith, *Answers*, 1:47.
 54. E.g., cf. Joseph Fielding Smith, *Answers*, 1:47; Joseph Smith, *History*, 2:380; 4:231.
 55. Richards, *Marvelous Work*, 426; cf. *Doctrine and Covenants*, 93:11.
 56. McConkie, *Doctrinal New Testament Commentary*, 3:141.
 57. E.g., the Church Universal and Triumphant founded by Mark and Elizabeth Clare Prophet; cf. Helen Schuchman's three volume occult text, *A Course in Miracles* (npp: Foundation for Inner Peace 1975), which claims to be written by "Jesus."
 58. Benson, *Teachings*, 31.

59. Crowther, *Life Everlasting*, 150, emphasis added.
60. Joseph Smith, *Teachings*, 214.
61. Quinn, *Early Mormonism*, 183.
62. Crowther, *Life Everlasting*, 150.
63. Gasson, *Challenging*, 225.
64. Crowther, *Life Everlasting*, 150-151.
65. Ibid., 151.
66. *Journal of Discourses*, 2:44-46; cf. 1:12-15.
67. Ibid., 2:44-46, emphasis added.
68. Martin, *Maze*, 225.
69. Joseph F. Smith, *Gospel Doctrine*, 436-437.
70. Cf. *Journal of Discourses*, 3:369; 7:240; *Deseret Weekly News*, 53:112.
71. *Journal of Discourses*, 21:317-318, emphasis added.
72. Martin, *Maze*, 226-228, citing *Journal of Discourses*, 3:369.
73. *Journal of Discourses*, 3:369.
74. *Journal of Discourses*, 7:240.
75. *Journal of Discourses*, 19:229.
76. Ankerberg, *Mormonism Revisited*, 15; Ankerberg, *Mormon Officials*, 23.
77. Joseph Fielding Smith, *Doctrines of Salvation*, 2:150-151.
78. Ibid., 2:150.
79. Benson, *Teachings*, 35, emphasis added.
80. Ibid., 94.
81. McConkie, *Mormon Doctrine*, 503-504; cf. 35-36.
82. E.g., John Weldon, "Positive Confession Teachings and the Occult" (discussion on alleged angelic visits), "News & Views" (Chattanooga, TN: Ankerberg Theological Research Institute, 1988), July 1988.
83. Joseph Fielding Smith, *Answers*, 2:202.
84. McConkie, *Mormon Doctrine*, 650.
85. Ibid., 644.
86. Ibid., 645.
87. Ibid., 46-47.
88. Joseph Smith, *Teachings*, 292.
89. McConkie, *Doctrinal New Testament Commentary*, 2:320-321; cf. 3:553.
90. Ankerberg and Weldon, *Cult Watch*, 270-281.
91. McConkie, *Doctrinal New Testament Commentary*, 2:232.
92. Ibid., 3:137.
93. McConkie, *Doctrinal New Testament Commentary*, 1:252.
94. Church of Jesus Christ of Latter-day Saints, *Doctrines of the Gospel*, 11.
95. McConkie, *Mormon Doctrine*, 586.
96. Church of Jesus Christ of Latter-day Saints, *Gospel Principles*, 139.
97. Ibid., 141.
98. Ibid., 129.
99. Ibid., 142.
100. McConkie, *Doctrinal New Testament Commentary*, 3:63.
101. Crowther, *Life Everlasting*, appendix: "Summary of Supernatural Manifestations."
102. Ibid., 382-387.
103. Church of Jesus Christ of Latter-day Saints, *Gospel Principles*, 279.
104. Heinerman, *Spirit World Manifestations*, 7.
105. Ibid.
106. Ibid., 34.
107. Ibid., 61.
108. Ibid., 65.
109. Ibid., 67.
110. Ibid., 277.
111. Ibid., 280.
112. Ibid., 14.
113. See *Book of Mormon*, Ether 8:19; *Times and Seasons*, 1:133, from Jerald and Sandra Tanner, *Changing World*, 544-545.
114. See Joseph Smith's admission in *History of the Church*, 4:551-552; see documentary evidence in Jerald and Sandra Tanner, *Mormonism—Shadow or Reality?* 486-489.
115. Jerald and Sandra Tanner, *Mormonism—Shadow or Reality?* 486-489; see their *Mormonism, Magic and Masonry*.
116. Adamson and Durham, *No Help*, 15.
117. Ibid., 21.
118. See Durham, *Mormon Miscellaneous*, October 1975, 11-16 in Jerald and Sandra Tanner, *Changing World*, 546.
119. John Ankerberg and John Weldon, *The Secret Teachings of the Masonic Lodge: A Christian Perspective* (Chicago, IL: Moody Press, 1990).

**Section 7: Mormon Revelation and New Scripture**

1. *Journal of Discourses*, 14:216.
2. Quinn, *Early Mormonism*, xx.
3. Cf. Ankerberg, *Mormonism Revisited*, 18.
4. *Mormonia—A Quarterly Bibliography of Works on Mormonism*, Fall 1972, 89.
5. *Salt Lake Tribune*, October 7, 1972, 22-23, cited in Jerald and Sandra Tanner, *Mormonism Like Watergate?* 4.
6. Preface in Jerald and Sandra Tanner, *Changing World*, 11.
7. Introduction in Ibid., 17.
8. Ankerberg, *Mormonism Revisited*, 18.
9. Benson, *Teachings*, 101-102.
10. Martin, *Maze*, 29.
11. Church of Jesus Christ of Latter-day Saints, *Sure Foundation*, 211.

12. Ibid., 211-212.
13. *Dialogue: A Journal of Mormon Thought*, Autumn 1966, 29; David O. McKay, *Gospel Ideals*, 85; John A. Widtsoe, *Joseph Smith, Seeker After Truth*, 19; Paul Chesman, "An Analysis of the Accounts Relating Joseph Smith's Early Visions," Brigham Young University Master's thesis, May 1975, 75, cited in Jerald and Sandra Tanner, *Changing World*, 151; Jerald and Sandra Tanner, *Joseph Smith's Strange Account of the First Vision*, 1; Jerald and Sandra Tanner, *Mormonism—Shadow or Reality?* 143; Martin, *Maze*, 26-30; Jerald and Sandra Tanner, *Changing World*, chapter 6.
14. Jerald and Sandra Tanner, *Changing World*, 152.
15. Ankerberg, *Mormonism Revisited*, 13-14.
16. Jerald and Sandra Tanner, *Changing World*, 155.
17. Ibid., 156.
18. Church of Jesus Christ of Latter-day Saints, *Sure Foundation*, 169-170.
19. John Ankerberg and John Weldon, *Do the Resurrection Accounts Conflict? And What Proof Is There Jesus Rose From the Dead?* (Chattanooga, TN: Ankerberg Theological Research Institute, 1989).
20. Ankerberg, *Mormonism Revisited*, 13.
21. Gordon Fraser, in the foreword to Jerald and Sandra Tanner, *Changing World*, 10.
22. John Weldon, chapters on "New Age Intuition," "Visualization," and "Self-help Therapy: Inner Guides and Imagination as Personal Healers," in *New Age Medicine*, largely unpublished, a manuscript of 1600 pages, 600 of which are published in Ankerberg and Weldon, *Can You Trust?*
23. Elias Smith, *The Life, Conversion, Preaching, Travels and Sufferings*, 1816, 58-59; *The Christian Baptist*, March 1, 1824, 1:148-149; *The Wayne Sentinel*, October 22, 1823, cited in Jerald and Sandra Tanner, *Changing World*, 159-160.
24. Jerald and Sandra Tanner, *Changing World*, 160.
25. Martin, *Maze*, Appendix D; cf. appendix to chapter 4 herein, "Joseph Smith Vs. Jesus Christ."
26. Jerald and Sandra Tanner, *Changing World*, 156.
27. Cited in Jerald and Sandra Tanner, *Changing World*, 368; see *Journal of Discourses*, 7:23 for a similar statement.
28. *Journal of Discourses*, 7:22.
29. Ibid., 35.
30. Hugh Nibley, *An Approach to the Book of Mormon*, 13, cited in Jerald and Sandra Tanner, *The Case Against Mormonism*, 2:63.
31. Joseph Fielding Smith, *Answers*, 2:199.
32. Church of Jesus Christ of Latter-day Saints, *Sure Foundation*, 61-62.
33. Benson, *Teachings*, 48.
34. David Whitmer, *An Address to All Believers in Christ By a Witness to the Divine Authenticity of the Book of Mormon* (1887, reprint, Concord, CA: Pacific Publishing Co., 1972), 12.
35. *The Saints Herald*, November 15, 1962, 16, citing the Chicago *Inter-Ocean*, October 17, 1886, from Jerald and Sandra Tanner, *Joseph Smith and Money Digging*, 9.
36. *The Saints Herald*, May 19, 1888, 310.
37. See Jerald and Sandra Tanner, *Joseph Smith and Money Digging*, passim.
38. Joseph Fielding Smith, *Doctrines of Salvation*, 3:225-226.
39. Jerald and Sandra Tanner, *Changing World*, 84.
40. Einar Anderson, *Inside Story*, 61.
41. Fawn M. Brodie, *No Man Knows My History*.
42. Ibid., 69-70, 72-73.
43. Hal Hougey, *A Parallel*, 4; Ropp, *Mormon Papers*, 36.
44. Originally cited in *The Rocky Mountain Mason*, Billings, MT, January 1956, 17-31; also in Jerald and Sandra Tanner, *Did Spaulding Write the Book of Mormon?* 17.
45. Hougey, *A Parallel*, 21.
46. Hoekema, *Four Major Cults*, 85.
47. Cf. Martin, *Maze*, 68.
48. B.H. Roberts, *Defense of the Faith and the Saints*, Salt Lake City, UT: Desert News 1907, 1:329.
49. Jerald and Sandra Tanner, *Changing World*, 115-116, 118-119, 122-124.
50. Jerald and Sandra Tanner, *Mormonism—Shadow or Reality?* 72, 84-85; *Changing World*, 112-113; *Case Against Mormonism*, 2:63-112.
51. Taken from the *Book of Mormon* and in part from McConkie, *Mormon Doctrine*, 528-529; Martin, *Maze*, 47-49; McElveen, *Will the Saints?* 59-61; Fraser, *Is Mormonism Christian?* chapter 16; and Arthur Wallace, *Can Mormonism Be Proved Experimentally?* chapter 9.
52. Martin, *Maze*, 59-69; cf. Crowdery et al., dedication section.
53. James Bjornstad, *Contemporary Christianity*, Winter 1977-1978, 4.
54. Jerald and Sandra Tanner, *Did Spaulding Write the Book of Mormon?* 5.
55. Personal conversation with Sandra Tanner, 1990.
56. McConkie, *Mormon Doctrine*, 528-529; cf. *Book of Mormon*, Mormon 1:7, Helaman 3:1-11, Jarom 5-8; 1 Nephi 5:5-6, 13-21, 28.
57. Martin, *Maze*, 328.
58. Ankerberg, *Mormon Officials*, 13.
59. Fraser, *Is Mormonism Christian?* 135.
60. Ankerberg, *Mormon Revisited*, 17.
61. Fraser, *Is Mormonism Christian?* 143, 145.
62. Ankerberg, *Mormonism Revisited*, 18.
63. Hal Hougey, *Archaeology and the Book of Mormon*, rev. ed., 3-4.
64. Jerald and Sandra Tanner, *Archaeology and the Book of Mormon*, 4-6.
65. Fraser, *Is Mormonism Christian?* chapters 16-17.
66. Ibid., 143-145.
67. See John Sorenson, *Progress and Archaeology—An Anthology* (Provo, UT: Brigham Young University Press, 1963), 103-116 for a critical review.
68. See *Dialogue: A Journal of Mormon Thought*, 4:2 (Spring 1966): 74, 145-146.
69. Ropp, *Mormon Papers*, 50-51.
70. Jerald and Sandra Tanner, *Archaeology and the Book of Mormon*, 1-6.
71. Jerald and Sandra Tanner, *Changing World*, 136, citing *Dialogue: A Journal of Mormon Thought*, Spring 1966, 149.
72. See Resource List.

73. Cowan, *Mormon Claims Answered*, 50.
74. Jerald and Sandra Tanner, *Mormonism—Shadow or Reality?* 108-116; cf. Ropp, *Mormon Papers*, 49-50.
75. *Dialogue: A Journal of Mormon Thought*, Summer 1973, 46, from Jerald and Sandra Tanner, *Changing World*, 134.
76. See Resource List.
77. Walter Martin, *The Kingdom of the Cults*, 162.
78. McElveen, *Will the Saints?* 62-64.
79. Letter on file; also cited in Jerry and Marian Bodine, *Whom Can You Trust?* (pamphlet), 16.
80. Letter of Frank Roberts, Jr., Director to Marvin Cowan, January 24, 1963, cited in Bodine, *Whom Can You Trust?* 3.
81. Letter of May 29, 1978 to G.R. Shannon from A.T. Hermansen of the Research Correspondence Department, cited in Bodine, *Whom Can You Trust?* 13.
82. *Dialogue: A Journal of Mormon Thought*, Summer 1969, 76-78, cited in Jerald and Sandra Tanner, *Changing World*, 139.
83. Jerald and Sandra Tanner, *Changing World*, 140-141.
84. Sir William M. Ramsay, *The Bearing of Recent Discovery on the Trustworthiness of the New Testament* (1915, reprint, Grand Rapids, MI: Baker, 1979), 79, emphasis added.
85. Ibid., v, emphasis added.
86. Jerald and Sandra Tanner, *Archaeology and the Book of Mormon; Changing World*, 133-148; Ropp, *Mormon Papers*, 47-54.
87. Norman L. Geisler, William E. Nix, *An Introduction to the Bible*, revised and expanded ed. (Chicago, IL: Moody Press, 1986); F.F. Bruce, *The New Testament Documents: Are They Reliable?* (Downers Grove, IL: InterVarsity Press, 1971).
88. Ibid.
89. Cf. Jerald and Sandra Tanner, *Changing World*, 370-373.
90. Ibid., 369-370.
91. Wesley Walters, "Whatever Happened to the Book of Mormon?" *Eternity* magazine, May 1980, 32.
92. From Bob Whitte, comp., *Where Does It Say That?* 4.
93. Jerald and Sandra Tanner, *Changing World*, 560, citing *Improvement Era*, 16:344-345.
94. Church of Jesus Christ of Latter-day Saints, *Sure Foundation*, 14-15.
95. Benson, *Teachings*, 4.
96. Letter to Marvin Cowan March 23, 1966; cited in Jerald and Sandra Tanner, *Changing World*, 144.
97. Brodie, *No Man Knows My History*, 63.
98. Ankerberg and Weldon, *Cult Watch*, parts 5, 7.
99. Brodie, *No Man Knows My History*, 73-74.
100. Ibid., 77-78.
101. Ibid., 79.
102. Ibid., 79-80.
103. Cf. Nandor Fodor, s.v. "Apports" and "Mediumism" in his *Encyclopedia of Psychical Science*.
104. See note 22.
105. Jerald and Sandra Tanner, *Changing World*, 95-96.
106. Ibid., 96, 102, 105.
107. *Journal of Discourses*, 7:164.
108. Jerald and Sandra Tanner, *Changing World*, 95-105; cf. *Journal of Discourses*, 7:114-115, 164; Smith, *History of the Church*, 1:109-110; 3:228-232; *Doctrine and Covenants*, 3:12-13; 10:7; 28:11; *Elders Journal*, (edited by Joseph Smith) August 1838, 59; David A. Whitmer, *An Address to All Believers in Christ*, 27-28.
109. McConkie, *Mormon Doctrine*, 842-843.
110. Jerald and Sandra Tanner, *Changing World*, 103, citing LaMar Petersen, *The Historical Background for the Doctrine and Covenants*, unpublished manuscript, 58.
111. Jerald and Sandra Tanner, *Changing World*, 103-104.
112. Ibid., 103.
113. Joseph Smith, *History*, 1:109-110.
114. Ibid., 104; cf. David Whitmer, *An Address*, i-ii.
115. *Times and Seasons*, 2 (1841): 42.
116. Whitmer, *An Address*, 27.
117. Ibid., 38.
118. Benson, *Teachings*, 89.
119. Gordon Fraser in foreword, Jerald and Sandra Tanner, *Changing World*, 10.
120. Jerald and Sandra Tanner, *Changing World*, 102, 105, 107.
121. Bernard De Voto, "The Centennial of Mormonism," *American Mercury*, 19 (1930): 5.
122. Ankerberg, *Mormonism Revisited*, 18-19.
123. Letter from President Joseph Fielding Smith to Marvin Cowan, March 18, 1966, cited in Bodine, *Whom Can You Trust?* 5.
124. Ellis T. Rasmussen, in Church of Jesus Christ of Latter-day Saints, *Sure Foundation*, 27
125. Ibid.
126. John W. Welch, in ibid., 61.
127. Steve Gilliland, in ibid., 153.
128. Martin, *Maze*, 68-69.
129. Benson, *Teachings*, 53.
130. Church of Jesus Christ of Latter-day Saints, *Sure Foundation*, 62.
131. Ibid.
132. *Eternity* magazine, May 1980, 33.
133. Church of Jesus Christ of Latter-day Saints, *Sure Foundation*, 65.
134. *Book of Mormon*, Ether 9:31-33.
135. Church of Jesus Christ of Latter-day Saints, *Sure Foundation*, 71.
136. Martin, *Maze*, 318.
137. Smith, *History*, 1:54-55; cf. 52-56.
138. Ibid., 53.
139. Ibid., 4:461.
140. See W.C. Woodruff, *Joseph Smith Begins His Work*; John Gilbert memorandum, 1-2; Jerald and Sandra Tanner, *Mormonism—Shadow or Reality?* 1-2. They cite B.H. Roberts, *Defense of the Faith*, 280-281, 295; and the Gilbert interview in George Reynolds, *The Myth of the "Manuscript Found,"* 59.

141. George Reynolds, *Myth of the "Manuscript Found,"* Salt Lake City Juvenile Instructor, 1883, 91, cited in Jerald and Sandra Tanner, *Mormonism—Shadow or Reality?* 89.
142. Reynolds, *Myth,* 71.
143. Oliver B. Huntington, *Journal of Oliver B. Huntington,* from typed copy at Utah State Historical Society, 168, cited in Jerald and Sandra Tanner, *Changing World,* 132.
144. Hoekema, *Four Major Cults,* 84.
145. Church of Jesus Christ of Latter-day Saints, California Mission, 1591 East Temple Way, Los Angeles, CA 90024.
146. *Saints Herald,* November 15, 1962, 16, from Jerald and Sandra Tanner, *3913 Changes in the Book of Mormon,* 15.
147. Jack Free, *Mormonism an Inspiration,* 111, cited in Arthur Budvarson, "Changes in Mormonism," 5 (pamphlet).
148. Jerald and Sandra Tanner, *3913 Changes,* 16.
149. Jerald and Sandra Tanner, *Changing World,* 132.
150. Wilford C. Woodruff, *Joseph Smith Begins His Work.*
151. Ibid., 353.
152. Ibid., 127.
153. Ibid., 64.
154. Ibid., 173.
155. Ibid., 284.
156. Ibid., 309.
157. Ibid., 560.
158. Ibid., 142.
159. Jerald and Sandra Tanner, *3913 Changes,* 6-9.
160. Woodruff, *Joseph Smith Begins His Work,* 52.
161. Richards, *Marvelous Work,* 275.
162. Hoekema, *Four Major Cults,* 85.
163. Woodruff, *Joseph Smith Begins His Work,* 200.
164. Ibid., 546.
165. Ibid., 25.
166. Ibid.
167. Joseph Fielding Smith, *Answers,* 2:200.
168. Mark Petersen, *As Translated Correctly* 3-5; cf. Jerald and Sandra Tanner, *Changes in The Pearl of Great Price: A Photo Reprint,* Introduction, 7, citing Joseph Fielding Smith, Jr., *Religious Truths Defined,* 175, 337.
169. Joseph Fielding Smith, *Doctrines of Salvation,* 3:198-199.
170. *Lectures on Faith* is approximately 25,000 words. For other changes see Jerald and Sandra Tanner, *Flaws in The Pearl of Great Price: A Study of Changes and Plagiarism in Joseph Smith's Pearl of Great Price,* 89-155.
171. Jerald and Sandra Tanner, *Changing World,* 64.
172. Ibid., 43.
173. John Widtsoe, *Joseph Smith: Seeker After Truth* (Salt Lake City, UT: *Deseret News,* 1951), 119; Joseph Fielding Smith, *Doctrines of Salvation,* 1:170, cited by Jerald and Sandra Tanner, *Changing World,* 39.
174. Smith, *History,* 1:173 n.
175. Jerald and Sandra Tanner, *Changing World,* 64-65.
176. Ibid., 62.
177. Ibid., 185-186.
178. *Lectures on Faith,* (originally delivered before a class of the elders, Kirtland, OH, and printed in the 1835 edition of *Doctrine and Covenants*), 53, from Jerald and Sandra Tanner, *Changing World,* 185.
179. Ibid., 12, 26.
180. Ankerberg, *Mormon Officials,* 14.
181. See Resource List.
182. *Doctrine and Covenants,* "Explanatory Introduction," 1982 ed.
183. Jerald and Sandra Tanner, *Changes in The Pearl of Great Price: A Photo Reprint;* see Resource List.
184. *The Pearl of Great Price,* "Introductory Note," 1982 ed., 1.
185. Jerald and Sandra Tanner, *Changes in The Pearl of Great Price: A Photo Reprint,* 14-15; the entire preface is also deleted from modern editions.
186. Jerald and Sandra Tanner, *Changing World,* 344-345.
187. Ankerberg, *Mormonism Revisited,* 18.
188. Personal conversation with Dr. Gleason Archer, October 19, 1991.
189. Gleason Archer, "Anachronisms and Historical Inaccuracies in the Mormon Scriptures," appendix in *A Survey of Old Testament Introduction,* rev. ed. (Chicago, IL: Moody Press, 1974), 504.
190. Jerald and Sandra Tanner, *Changing World,* 362, citing the *New York Times,* May 3, 1970.
191. Ibid., citing *Salt Lake Tribune,* May 4, 1970.
192. Ibid., 362-363.
193. See Resource List; cf. Martin, *Maze,* chapter 6.
194. F.S. Spaulding and A.B. Samuel Mercer, *Why Egyptologists Reject the Book of Abraham* (see Resource List).
195. Martin, *Maze,* 155.
196. Ibid.
197. Ropp, *Mormon Papers,* 105.
198. *The Utah Evangel,* November 1981, 1, 5; cf. *Salt Lake Tribune,* September 30, 1981; Idaho Falls, *Post Register,* September 30, 1981.
199. Church of Jesus Christ of Latter-day Saints, *Gospel Principles,* 51.
200. For example, see Jerald and Sandra Tanner, *Changing World,* 398.
201. Smith, *History,* 1:v.
202. Ibid., vi.
203. See Resource List.
204. Jerald and Sandra Tanner, *Changing World,* 399, 401-402, 412, 414-415.
205. Martin, *Kingdom of the Cults,* 156.
206. Joseph Fielding Smith, *Doctrines of Salvation,* 3:74.
207. Jerald and Sandra Tanner, *Changing World,* 25, citing *Journal of Discourses,* 13:271.
208. In Jerald and Sandra Tanner, *Changing World,* 25; see also *Journal of Oliver B. Huntington,* Book 14 at Huntington Library, 3:166 of typed copy at the Utah State Historical Society.

209. Quinn, *Early Mormonism*, 130.
210. *Journal of Discourses* 1:219.
211. Bruce McConkie, *The Millennial Messiah*, 642-643, cited in Church of Jesus Christ of Latter-day Saints, *Doctrines of the Gospel*, 16.
212. *Journal of Discourses*, 1:219. It is difficult to determine from the context whether Heber Kimball means conceived figuratively, as in bringing forth food, or literally, as in begetting earths, although the latter interpretation fits other early and modern Mormon teaching.
213. Pratt, *Seer*, March 1853, 37ff.
214. Joseph Smith, *Teachings*, 170; in Martin, *Maze*, 321.
215. Both examples are cited in Jerald and Sandra Tanner, *Changing World*, 123-124.
216. *Times and Seasons*, 4:194; J.N. Washburn, *Contents, Structure and Authorship of the Book of Mormon* (Salt Lake City, UT: Bookcraft, 1954), 161, cited in Jerald and Sandra Tanner, *Changing World*, 124.
217. Church of Jesus Christ of Latter-day Saints, *Sure Foundation*, 48.
218. Benson, *Teachings*, 116.
219. Hugh Nibley, *No Man, That's Not History*, 46, from Jerald and Sandra Tanner, *Mormonism—Shadow or Reality?* 5.
220. Ankerberg, *Mormon Officials*, 28.
221. Ankerberg, *Mormonism Revisited*, 17.
222. Jerald and Sandra Tanner, *The Case Against Mormonism*, 1:86-87.
223. Ibid., 84-86.
224. See Resource List and Jerald and Sandra Tanner, *The Case Against Mormonism*, 1: chapter 4; Martin, *Maze*, 38 and chapter 7.
225. Jerald and Sandra Tanner, *The Case Against Mormonism*, 1:35, citing *Dialogue: A Journal of Mormon Thought*, Spring 1966, 49-52.
226. Jerald and Sandra Tanner, *Changing World*, 37.
227. D. Michael Quinn, *On Being a Mormon Historian*, 5.
228. Ibid., 23.
229. Ibid.
230. Ibid., 20-21, emphasis added.
231. Ibid., 16.
232. Ibid., 8.
233. *Journal of Discourses*, 11:269.
234. *Journal of Discourses*, 30:31.
235. McConkie, *Mormon Doctrine*, 522, 523; 1966 edition, 578-579 is somewhat softened.
236. McConkie, *Mormon Doctrine*, 765.
237. See "doctrine" in Ibid., 204-205.
238. Talmage, *Articles of Faith*, 7-8.
239. McConkie, *Doctrinal New Testament Commentary*, 1:252-253.
240. *The Evening and Morning Star*, July 1833, 1, emphasis added.
241. From an analogy by Bob Whitte, "And It Came to Pass" (tract), Safety Harbor, FL: from Ex-Mormons for Jesus, Box 946, 33572, nd.
242. Whitmer, *An Address*, 30-31.
243. Ankerberg, *Mormon Officials*, 7.
244. Smith, *History*, 1:400.
245. Ibid., 394, 400, 402; Martin, *Maze*, 353-354.
246. *Journal of Discourses*, 10:344, cited by Jerald and Sandra Tanner, *Changing World*, 421.
247. *Journal of Discourses*, 13:362, cited in ibid.
248. *Doctrine and Covenants*, 1890 edition, Section 84, 289.
249. *Dialogue: A Journal of Mormon Thought*, Autumn 1966, 74, cited in Jerald and Sandra Tanner, *Changing World*, 422.
250. Joseph Fielding Smith, *Way to Perfection*, 268-270.
251. Joseph Fielding Smith, *Answers*, 4:112.
252. Ibid., 111-115.
253. E.g., Ankerberg, *Mormonism Revisited*, 19.
254. Talmage, *Articles of Faith*, 25.
255. *Doctrine and Covenants*, 87:1-8.
256. Joseph Smith, *History*, 5:324, in Jerald and Sandra Tanner, *Changing World*, 428, emphasis added.
257. See "Rebellion in South Carolina" in *The Evening and Morning Star*, January 1833 (this magazine was available to Smith in December); Joseph Smith, *History*, 1:301; Larry S. Jonas, *Mormon Claims Examined*, 1961, 52, in Jerald and Sandra Tanner, *Changing World*, 424-425.
258. A civil war was considered a possibility even before 1832. This fact was recently discussed on *American Adventure*, a two-part program on Jacksonian America on WTCI-TV 45, Saturday, November 2, 1991, 7:00 to 8:00 A.M., produced by the Dallas Community College. See also Jerald and Sandra Tanner, *Changing World*, 425; Martin, *Maze*, 357.
259. Ropp, *Mormon Papers*, 64.
260. Jerald and Sandra Tanner, *Changing World*, 430.
261. Ibid., 428-430.
262. *Journal of Discourses*, 9:142-143, cited in Jerald and Sandra Tanner, *Changing World*, 426.
263. *Journal of Discourses*, 10:250; see *The Millennial Star*, 25:787.
264. Jerald and Sandra Tanner, *Changing World*, 430.
265. Ibid., 404-408.
266. Joseph Smith, *History*, 5:336.
267. Cited in Jerald and Sandra Tanner, *Changing World*, 419.
268. Ibid., 420.
269. This was copied from the microfilm original at the Mormon Church Historian's Library; cf. Jerald and Sandra Tanner, *Changing World*, 420.
270. Smith, *History*, 6:58, emphasis added.
271. Brodie, *No Man Knows*, 392.
272. Ibid., 393-394.
273. Smith, *History*, 3:170-171.

274. Ibid., 171.
275. Joseph Smith, *Teachings*, 302; cf. Smith, *History*, 5:394.
276. Joseph Smith, *Millenial Star*, 22:455 cited, in Bob Whitte, "And It Came to Pass," (tract).
277. *Journal of Discourses*, 5:219.
278. Smith, *History*, 1:323.
279. Colleen Ralson, *Dissecting the Doctrine and Covenants*, 4-7.
280. Martin, *Maze*, Appendix G on unfulfilled prophecies.
281. Jerald and Sandra Tanner, *Mormonism—Shadow or Reality?* 195.
282. Bob Whitte, comp., *Where Does It Say That?*
283. Bob Whitte, *Witnessing to Mormons*, 17.
284. Church of Jesus Christ of Latter-day Saints, *The Doctrine and Covenants Student Manual*, 181.
285. Ibid.
286. Ibid., 194.

## Section 8: Mormon Religion and Its Fruits

1. Joseph Smith, *The Evening and Morning Star*, July 1833, 1.
2. Ankerberg, *Mormon Officials*, 29.
3. Richards, *Marvelous Work*, 395.
4. Ankerberg, *Mormon Officials*, 30.
5. McConkie, *Mormon Doctrine*, 141-142, 625-626.
6. Ankerberg, *Mormonism Revisited*, 23.
7. Ibid., 9, 23.
8. Ibid., 8.
9. Ibid., 23.
10. For examples of how Christians do apologetics, see L. Russ Bush, ed., *Classical Readings and Christian Apologetics, A.D.100-1800* (Grand Rapids, MI: Zondervan/Academie, 1983); Ronald H. Nash, *Faith and Reason: Searching for a Rational Faith* (Grand Rapids, MI: Zondervan/Academie, 1988); John Warwick Montgomery, ed., *Christianity for the Tough Minded: Essays in Support of an Intellectually Defensible Religious Commitment* (Minneapolis, MN: Bethany, 1973); John Warwick Montgomery, *Faith Founded on Fact: Essays in Evidential Apologetics* (New York: Thomas Nelson, 1978); C.S. Lewis, *Mere Christianity* (New York: MacMillian, 1971); Henry Morris, *Many Infallible Proofs* (Santee, CA: Master Books, 1988).
11. Joseph Fielding Smith, *Doctrines of Salvation*, 1:190, emphasis added to four words.
12. Hugh Nibley, *The Myth Makers*, foreword cited in Jerald and Sandra Tanner, *The Case Against Mormonism*, 1:27.
13. Einar Anderson, *Inside Story*, 44, 58. The latter parts refer specifically to the Mountain Meadows Massacre, but is nevertheless applicable; emphasis added.
14. Ropp, *Mormon Papers*, 50-51.
15. See Robert and Rosemary Brown, *They Lie in Wait to Deceive*.
16. Church of Jesus Christ of Latter-day Saints, *Sure Foundation*, 4.
17. Joseph Fielding Smith, *Answers*, 1:171-175.
18. Church of Jesus Christ of Latter-day Saints, *Sure Foundation*, 7.
19. Ibid., 10.
20. Ibid., 114.
21. Ibid., 115.
22. Ibid.
23. Joseph Fielding Smith, *Answers*, 3: chapter 22.
24. Ibid., 4:213-214.
25. Ibid., 4:212.
26. Ibid., 2:200; cf. *The Gospel of Jesus Christ, Discussion 2*, 3 (booklet).
27. Joseph Fielding Smith, *Doctrines of Salvation*, 1:19.
28. Wallace, *Can Mormonism Be Proved?* 157-158.
29. Ibid., 86-91.
30. Joseph Fielding Smith, *Doctrines of Salvation*, 3:213.
31. Joseph Smith, "History" in *The Pearl of Great Price*, Section I, Verse 64, p. 56 (1982 edition).
32. Hoekema, *Four Major Cults*, 12, cf. 85-86; Jerald and Sandra Tanner, *Changing World*, 142-143 with Joseph Smith, "History" in *Pearl of Great Price*, 1:64.
33. Wallace, *Can Mormonism Be Proved?* 90-91; cf. Smith, *Doctrines of Salvation*, 3:212-215.
34. J.N.D. Kelly, *Early Christian Doctrines* (NY: Harper & Row, 1978); Harold O.J. Brown, *Heresies: The Image of Christ in the Mirror of Heresy and Orthodoxy from the Apostles to the Present* (Garden City, NY: Doubleday, 1984); Reinhold Seeberg, *The History of Doctrines* (trans. Charles E. Hay) (Grand Rapids, MI: Baker), Vol. 1: 1978, pp. 55-81, especially 77-81; see also in any edition, Edward R. Hardy, ed., *Christology of the Later Fathers*; Maurice Wiles, Mark Santer, eds., *Documents in Early Christian Thought* (Cambridge University Press); Burnhard Lohse, *A Short History of Christian Doctrine from the First Century to the Present*; J.B. Lightfoot, *Apostolic Fathers*; J.G. Davies, *The Early Christian Church: A History of Its First Five Centuries*; Lewis Burkoff, *The History of Christian Doctrines*; Bernard Ramm, *The Evangelical Heritage: A Study in Historical Theology*; E.H. Klotsche, *The History of Christian Doctrine*; Eberhard Arnold, *The Early Christians: A Source Book on the Witness of the Early Church*; William G. Rusch, *The Trinitarian Controversy: Sources of Early Christian Thought*; Richard A. Norris, Jr., *The Christological Controversy: Sources of Early Christian Thought*; Philip Schaff, *The Creeds of Christendom* (3 Vols.).
35. "The Challenge," Los Angeles, CA: The Church of Jesus Christ of Latter-day Saints, nd., (3 page pamphlet).
36. Church of Jesus Christ of Latter-day Saints, "What the Mormons Think of Christ," 3.
37. Joseph Smith, *Teachings*, 119.
38. Talmage, *Articles of Faith*, 236.
39. Robert J. Matthews, *A Bible! A Bible!* 131.
40. Pratt, *Seer*, March 1854, 238.
41. Joseph Fielding Smith, *Way to Perfection*, 334.
42. Mark Petersen, *As Translated Correctly*, 10-14.
43. Ibid., 4; cf. 3-26.
44. Ibid., foreword.

45. Robinson, *Are Mormons Christians?* 48-49.
46. Richards, *Marvelous Work*, 41.
47. Church of Jesus Christ of Latter-day Saints, *Sure Foundation*, 138.
48. Introduction to the *Book of Mormon*.
49. *The Evening and Morning Star*, July 1883, 2.
50. Scott C. Latayne, *Ex-Mormons: Why We Left* (Grand Rapids, MI: Baker, 1990), 102.
51. Joseph Smith, *Teachings*, 327; cf. 325.
52. For example, cf., *Journal of Discourses*, 2:6.
53. Pratt, *Seer*, February 1854, 213 (see Bibliography). Yet Pratt also stated in the same article (p. 212) concerning the *Book of Mormon* and the Bible, "Both books being of Divine origin, they will of course agree; for God never disagrees with himself; and his words spoken in ancient America are just as true as his words spoken in ancient Palestine."
54. Pratt, "The Bible Alone an Insufficient Guide," in *Orson Pratt's Works* (Liverpool, England, 1851), 46; cf. 44-47.
55. Geisler and Nix, *A General Introduction to the Bible*, 375; cf. 238, 267, 365-366.
56. Talmage, *Articles of Faith*, 248.
57. Joseph Smith, *Teachings*, 37.
58. Joseph Fielding Smith, *Doctrines of Salvation*, 3:191.
59. McConkie, *Doctrinal New Testament Commentary*, 2:212.
60. Ibid., 243.
61. Ankerberg, *Mormon Officials*, 16; cf. Ankerberg, *Mormonism Revisited*, 16.
62. McConkie, *Doctrinal New Testament Commentary*, 2:211-212, emphasis added.
63. Talmage, *Articles of Faith*, 237.
64. Jerald and Sandra Tanner, *Changing World*, 385.
65. McConkie, *Mormon Doctrine*, 423.
66. Smith, *History*, 1:368; cf. 302-303.
67. Herald Publishing House, *Times and Seasons*, 5:723, 6:803; cited in *Joseph Smith's New Translation of the Bible*, 10.
68. Cited in Jerald and Sandra Tanner, *Changing World*, 387-389.
69. Herald Publishing House, *Joseph Smith's New Translation of the Bible*, 10-11.
70. Jerald and Sandra Tanner, *Changing World*, 387-389.
71. Ibid., 395-397.
72. Ibid., 397; cf. chapter 12.
73. Ibid., 393.
74. Ibid., 389-390.
75. Ibid., 562.
76. Robert J. Matthews, *A Bible! A Bible!*, dustcover; see viii where McConkie refers to him as "the world authority on the Joseph Smith translation."
77. Ibid., 115-116.
78. Ibid., 127.
79. *Joseph Smith's New Translation of the Bible*, 16.
80. Ibid., 30, 47, 53.
81. Cf. McConkie, *Doctrinal New Testament Commentary*, 1:254-255; 2:224-250, 269.
82. McConkie, *Doctrinal New Testament Commentary*, 2:235-236.
83. Ibid., 1:144.
84. Ibid., 1:352-353.
85. Ibid., 354, 356.
86. Joseph Smith, *Teachings*, 328.
87. E.g., McConkie, *Doctrinal New Testament Commentary*, 2:211-302. See also *The Restoration, Discussion 3* (pamphlet), 6; *Temples of the Church of Jesus Christ of Latter-day Saints*, 15-18.
88. Joseph Fielding Smith, *Doctrines of Salvation*, 1:137.
89. Hugh Nibley, *Sounding Brass*, 231, cited in Jerald and Sandra Tanner, *The Mormon Kingdom*, 1:32.
90. McConkie, *Mormon Doctrine*, 92.
91. Joseph Fielding Smith, *Doctrines of Salvation*, 1:135-137.
92. Ibid., 137.
93. Joseph Fielding Smith, *Answers*, 1:191.
94. Joseph Fielding Smith, *Doctrines of Salvation*, 1:135-137.
95. Cf. Einar Anderson, *Inside Story*, 57, for a reference to seventy-five cases of murder for apostasy and the Tanners' data cited in chapter 28 of the text.
96. For example, Gustavo Larson, professor of Church History, Brigham Young University in *Utah Historical Quarterly*, January 1958, 62, 39; cf. Einar Anderson, *Inside Story*, 51-60.
97. Ankerberg and Weldon, *Cult Watch*, parts 5, 7.
98. John Ahmanson, *Secret History*, 147-148.
99. Cited in *Valley Tan Newspaper*, February 22, 1860, 2, from Jerald and Sandra Tanner, *The Mormon Kingdom*, 2:3.
100. Klaus J. Hansen, *Quest for Empire*, 69-70.
101. Stenhouse, *Tell It All*, 318-319, emphasis added.
102. Ibid., 170.
103. Ibid., 169-170.
104. Jerald and Sandra Tanner, *The Mormon Kingdom*, 2: chapter 7.
105. Cf. Zola Levitt and John Weldon, *Is There Life After Death?* (Dallas, TX: Zola Levitt Ministries, 1990), 21-27; McConkie, *Mormon Doctrine*, 314; *Salt Lake Tribune*, January 28, 1968, cited in Jerald and Sandra Tanner, *Changing World*, 493-494.
106. Cowan, *Mormon Claims*, 105 (189 ed., p. 138).
107. At least four other stories have been reported in the popular press in the last 15 years.
108. See bottom note and R.C. Zaehner, *Our Savage God: The Perverse Use of Eastern Thought* (NY: Sheed & Ward, Inc., 1974).
109. *Journal of Discourses*, 4:219-220; the "instances" referred to may also refer to biblical instances of capital punishment.
110. Vincent Bugliosi, televised interview, February 16, 1976, KABC-TV, Los Angeles, 11:30 P.M.
111. Stenhouse, *Tell It All*, 312.
112. *Deseret News*, July 27, 1854, cited in Jerald and Sandra Tanner, *The Mormon Kingdom*, 1:38.
113. Jerald and Sandra Tanner, *The Mormon Kingdom*, 1: chapter 3; *Changing World*, chapter 20; Martin, *Maze*, chapter 9.
114. *Journal of Discourses*, 10:110.

115. Wilford Woodruff's journal, January 16, 1852, typed copy; original located in LDS Church archives, cited in Jerald and Sandra Tanner, *Changing World*, 497.
116. *Dialogue: A Journal of Mormon Thought*, Spring 1973, 26.
117. "Excerpts from the weekly council meetings of the quorum of the twelve apostles dealing with the rights of negros in the church, 1849-1940," cited in Jerald and Sandra Tanner, *Changing World*, 497; cf. *Mormonism—Shadow or Reality?* 582.
118. Ibid.
119. *Journal of Discourses*, 3:226.
120. *Journal of Discourses*, 1:83.
121. *Journal of Discourses*, 6:34-35.
122. Manuscript history of Brigham Young, December 20, 1846, typed copy, original in LDS Church archives, cited in Jerald and Sandra Tanner, *Changing World*, 500.
123. Manuscript history of Brigham Young, February 24, 1847, typed copy, cited ibid., 500.
124. Jerald and Sandra Tanner, *The Mormon Kingdom*, 2:51-70.
125. *Journal of Discourses*, 3:247.
126. *Journal of Discourses*, 7:19.
127. *Journal of Discourses*, 1:97.
128. *Journal of Discourses*, 14:58.
129. *Journal of Discourses*, 1:108-109.
130. Ibid., 73.
131. Jerald and Sandra Tanner, *Changing World*, 496.
132. *Journal of Discourses*, 4:49-50.
133. *Deseret News*, July 27, 1854, cited in Jerald and Sandra Tanner, *The Mormon Kingdom*, 1:38.
134. Cf. Jerald and Sandra Tanner, *Changing World*, 493-494, 500 for documentation; Jerald and Sandra Tanner, *Mormonism—Shadow or Reality?* 403.
135. Joseph Smith, *History*, 5:296.
136. Photo reprint of 1880 edition, 284, cited in Jerald and Sandra Tanner, *The Mormon Kingdom*, 2:6.
137. *Journal of Discourses*, 6:176, cited in Jerald and Sandra Tanner, *The Mormon Kingdom*, 2:6.
138. *Journal of Discourses*, 4:77, cited ibid.
139. *Journal of Discourses*, 3:50, cited ibid., 10-11.
140. Stenhouse, *Tell It All*, 312.
141. Jerald and Sandra Tanner, *The Mormon Kingdom*, 2:140, 145.
142. In Einar Anderson, *Inside Story*, 57.
143. Stenhouse, *Tell It All*, 46-47.
144. Ibid., 311, emphasis added.
145. Ibid.
146. Jerald and Sandra Tanner, *The Mormon Kingdom*, 2:150-154.
147. Bill Hickman, *Brigham's Destroying Angel*.
148. Ibid., 195-196.
149. Jerald and Sandra Tanner, *The Mormon Kingdom*, 2: chapter 6.
150. *The Restored Church*, 197-198, cited in Jerald and Sandra Tanner, *The Mormon Kingdom*, 1:60.
151. Jerald and Sandra Tanner, *The Mormon Kingdom*, 1: chapter 5; cf. 60, 65.
152. Joseph Smith, *History*, 3:178-182.
153. Jerald and Sandra Tanner, *The Mormon Kingdom*, 1:58-60.
154. Ibid., 2:10.
155. Ibid., 1:60, citing *Kansas City Daily Journal*, June 5, 1881.
156. Jerald and Sandra Tanner, *The Mormon Kingdom*, 2:7.
157. Hickman, *Brigham's Destroying Angel*, 15.
158. Jerald and Sandra Tanner, *The Mormon Kingdom*, 2:161, quoting Baskin, *Reminiscences of Early Utah*, 110.
159. Ibid., 164, citing Baskin, ibid., 154-155.
160. Joseph Fielding Smith, comp., *Teachings*, 255-256.
161. Church of Jesus Christ of Latter-day Saints, *To Make Thee a Minister and a Witness: Melchizedek Priesthood Personal Study Guide*, 2,23.
162. Church of Jesus Christ of Latter-day Saints, *Faith in the Lord Jesus Christ* (pamphlet), 7.
163. *Journal of Discourses*, 3:266.
164. Einar Anderson, *Inside Story*, 39.
165. Jerald and Sandra Tanner, *Mormonism—Shadow or Reality?* 225.
166. E.g., *Journal of Discourses*, 11:269.
167. *Journal of Discourses*, 11:128.
168. Jerald and Sandra Tanner, *Mormonism—Shadow or Reality?* 225-226 for documentation.
169. *Deseret News*, April 22, 1857.
170. Jerald and Sandra Tanner, *Changing World*, 217, 222, citing *Confessions of John D. Lee*, 288-289.
171. *Journal of Discourses*, 4:56, emphasis added.
172. John Stewart, *Brigham Young and His Wives*, 8, cited in Jerald and Sandra Tanner, *Changing World*, 204.
173. Jerald and Sandra Tanner, *Changing World*, 287 for documentation.
174. Gordon Fraser, *Sects of the Latter-day Saints*, 22.
175. Joseph Fielding Smith, *Answers*, 3:161.
176. Jerald and Sandra Tanner, *Changing World*, 287, citing *The Millennial Star*, 15:226.
177. Jerald and Sandra Tanner, *Changing World*, 268-269.
178. *Journal of Discourses*, 11:269.
179. Ibid.
180. Ibid.
181. *Journal of Discourses*, 13:166.
182. Cited in Jerald and Sandra Tanner, *Changing World*, 269-270.
183. *Zion's Harbinger and Baneemey's Organ*, 3 (July 1853): 52-53, from Einar Anderson, *Inside Story*, 26.
184. Cited in Jerald and Sandra Tanner, *Changing World*, 271.
185. Ibid., 271-285.
186. Quinn, *On Being a Mormon Historian*, 21-22.

187. Jerald and Sandra Tanner, *Changing World*, 284-285.
188. See Resource List.
189. *Journal of Discourses*, 3:215; 2:269.
190. See Chapter 30 and McConkie, *Mormon Doctrine*, 257.
191. Joseph Musser, *Michael Our Father*, 27-28.
192. Jerald and Sandra Tanner, *Changing World*, 207-214, 324; chapter 9, 204-290; *The Mormon Kingdom*, 1:25-30; and *Mormonism—Shadow or Reality?* chapter 16, for documentation.
193. Jerald and Sandra Tanner, *Mormonism—Shadow or Reality?* 209-211.
194. *Journal and Autobiography of Joseph Lee Robinson*, 60, microfilm copy in LDS Genealogical Library, from Jerald and Sandra Tanner, *Changing World*, 226-227, citing S.P. Hirshim, *The Lion of the Lord*, 229-230.
195. Jerald and Sandra Tanner, *Changing World*, 227.
196. *Journal of Discourses*, 4:55-57; 12:312.
197. *Journal of Discourses*, 6:180-181; 8:178; Jerald and Sandra Tanner, *Changing World*, 233.
198. *Journal of Discourses*, 4:55.
199. Jerald and Sandra Tanner, *Changing World*, 230-231.
200. John J. Stewart, *Brigham Young and His Wives* (Salt Lake City, UT: Mercury, 1961), 31; Brodie, *No Man Knows*, Appendix C, 434-465; Stanley Ivins, *Western Humanities Review*, 10:232-233 for the 84 figure; cf. Jerald and Sandra Tanner, *Changing World*, 231-233 and Jerald and Sandra Tanner, *Joseph Smith and Polygamy* (Salt Lake City, UT: Utah Lighthouse Ministry, 1966), 41-47, a publication cited in Jerald and Sandra Tanner, *Changing World*, 231-233.
201. *The Temple Lot Case*, 379, cited in Jerald and Sandra Tanner, *Changing World*, 233.
202. Brodie, *No Man Knows*, preface; Jerald and Sandra Tanner, *Joseph Smith and Polygamy*, 47, in Jerald and Sandra Tanner, *Changing World*, 232.
203. Jerald and Sandra Tanner, *Changing World*, 233 for documentation.
204. *Journal of Discourses*, 8:178.
205. *Daily Journal of Abraham H. Cannon*, April 5, 1894, 18:66-67, Brigham Young University Library, in Jerald and Sandra Tanner, *Changing World*, 234.
206. E.g., *Journal of Discourses*, 2:13-14.
207. Cf. Jerald and Sandra Tanner, *Mormonism—Shadow or Reality?* 213-217.
208. Jerald and Sandra Tanner, *Changing World*, 236.
209. Ibid., 239, emphasis added.
210. Michael H. Marquardt, *The Strange Marriage of Sarah N. Whitney to Joseph Smith the Mormon Prophet, Joseph C. Kingsbury and Heber C. Kimball* (Salt Lake City, UT: Utah Lighthouse Ministry, 1973), 18-19; cf. Brodie, *No Man Knows*, 471-472.
211. Ibid.
212. Jerald and Sandra Tanner, *Changing World*, 242; cf. 236-247.
213. Brodie, *No Man Knows*, 336; Jerald and Sandra Tanner, *Changing World*, 245.
214. Stenhouse, *Tell It All*, 468-469.
215. Hickman, *Brigham's Destroying Angel*, 12-14.
216. Harriet Beecher Stowe, in the preface to Stenhouse, *Tell It All*.
217. Stenhouse, *Tell It All*, ix.
218. Ibid., 139-140.
219. Ibid., 143.
220. Ibid., *passim*.
221. Ibid., 151-152.
222. Ibid., 153.
223. Ibid., 254.
224. Ibid., 255.
225. Ibid., 271-272.
226. Ibid., 274.
227. Ibid., 273-274.
228. Ibid.
229. "Geraldo," "The Secret World of Polygamy," rebroadcast date June 28, 1991, transcript, p. 6, Transcript No. 987 (R-#834), New York Investigative News Group, 1991. Transcripts available from Journal Graphics, Inc., *1991 Transcripts/Video Index: Television News and Public Affairs Programming*, NY: Journal Graphics, 1990; in the 1990 index see Geraldo Rivera Show, No. 787 on bigamy (9/21/90); Show No. 834, "The Secret World of Polygamy" (11/17/90) and "The West" syndicated, Show No. 197 (11/3/90), "The Politics of Polygamy".
230. Ibid., 5-7.
231. Ibid., 2, 8, 15-16.
232. Ibid., 8-9.
233. Ibid., 11-12.
234. Ibid., 14.
235. Ibid., 12, 15.
236. McConkie, *Mormon Doctrine*, 590.
237. Ankerberg, *Mormonism Revisited*, 6.
238. Jerald and Sandra Tanner, *Changing World*, 300-302, citing Joseph Smith, *History*, 2:436-438.
239. Joseph Fielding Smith, *Answers*, 4:170.
240. Jerald and Sandra Tanner, *Changes in Joseph Smith's History*, 75, citing *Millennial Star* (containing Joseph Smith's original history), 22:602.
241. Ibid., 303-304; cf. entire chapter.
242. *Journal of Discourses*, 10:110-111.
243. *New York Herald*, May 4, 1855; *Dialogue: A Journal of Mormon Thought*, Spring 1973, 56, in Jerald and Sandra Tanner, *Changing World*, 304.
244. Joseph Fielding Smith, *Way to Perfection*, 101.
245. Jerald and Sandra Tanner, *Changing World*, 306-308, citing e.g., McConkie, *Mormon Doctrine*, 107-108; Mark Petersen, address at Brigham Young University, August 27, 1954; and *The Salt Lake Tribune*, November 13, 1969.
246. McConkie, *Mormon Doctrine*, 477; W. Berrett, *Mormonism and the Negro*, part 2, 5; A. Richardson, *That Ye May Not Be Deceived*, 13, cited in Jerald and Sandra Tanner, *Changing World*, 300.
247. Jerald and Sandra Tanner, *Changing World*, 322-325.

248. Ibid., 316, citing e.g., Stewart and Berrett, *Mormonism and the Negro*, part 2, 16; Joseph Fielding Smith, *Way to Perfection*, 101, and many others.
249. Jerald and Sandra Tanner, *Changing World*, 319, from *The Daily Universe*, June 22, 1978.
250. Jerald and Sandra Tanner, *Changing World*, 322-325.
251. Ibid., 313, from the LDS church historical department, ms.d1234, Box 48, folder 3; cf. *Journal of Discourses*, 7:290-91, 2:143.
252. E.g., Jerald and Sandra Tanner, *Changing World*, 312.
253. Ibid., 311.
254. Ibid., 310-311, citing e.g., John Lund, *The Church and the Negro*, 104-105.
255. Jerald and Sandra Tanner, *Changing World*, 318, citing McConkie speech, "All are alike unto God," 1-2; cf. McConkie, *Mormon Doctrine*, 527.
256. McConkie, *Mormon Doctrine*, 527, emphasis added.
257. Jerald and Sandra Tanner, *Changing World*, 319, 323-326.
258. Ibid., *Changing World*, 319, 326.
259. Martin, *Kingdom of the Cults*, 181.
260. *Journal of Discourses*, 1:361; cf. Jerald and Sandra Tanner, *Changing World*, 532.
261. Jerald and Sandra Tanner, *Changing World*, 532, for documentation.
262. "Journal History," June 3, 1859, as cited in Orrin Porter Rockwell, *Man of God, Son of Thunder*, 292-293, cited by Jerald and Sandra Tanner, *The Mormon Kingdom*, 2:167.
263. "The Honorable Judge J. Cradelbaugh, "Utah and the Mormons," an address to the House of Representatives, February 7, 1863, as printed in an appendix to the *Congregational Globe*, February 23, 1863, 119-125, cited in Jerald and Sandra Tanner, *The Mormon Kingdom*, 2:167-169.
264. Einar Anderson, *Inside Story*, 26-27.
265. Jerald and Sandra Tanner, *The Mormon Kingdom*, 1:54, citing *The Reed Peck Manuscript*, 9-12, typed copy.
266. Ibid., 53; cf. Joseph Smith, *History*, 3:167.
267. Leland Gentry, *A History of the Latter-day Saints in Northern Missouri From 1836-1839*, 339, in Jerald and Sandra Tanner, *The Mormon Kingdom*, 1:63.
268. *A Mormon Chronicle: The Diaries of John D. Lee*, 1:328, n. 67, in Jerald and Sandra Tanner, *The Mormon Kingdom*, 1:62.
269. *Journal of Discourses*, 6:32.
270. Jerald and Sandra Tanner, *The Mormon Kingdom*, 1:57, citing Leland Gentry, *A History of the Latter-day Saints*, 364.
271. Ibid., 54, citing *The Reed Peck Manuscript*, 9-12, typed copy.
272. *Ensign*, October 1972, 7, cited in Cowan, *Mormon Claims Answered*, 90.
273. Jerald and Sandra Tanner, *Changing World*, 431-432.
274. See Resource List.
275. Church of Jesus Christ of Latter-day Saints, "Endowed with Covenants and Blessings," in *Temples of the Church of Jesus Christ of Latter-day Saints*, 12.
276. Ibid., 14.
277. Ibid., 14, citing John A. Widtsoe, *A Rational Theology*, 7th ed. (Salt Lake City, UT: Deseret Book Company, 1965), 125-126.
278. John A. Widtsoe, "Looking Toward the Temple," in *Temples of the Church of Jesus Christ of Latter-day Saints*, 48.
279. James E. Talmage, "A History of Temples," in *Temples of the Church*, 41.
280. Church of Jesus Christ of Latter-day Saints, "Salvation for the Dead," in *Temples of the Church*, 24.
281. Boyd K. Packer, *The Holy Temple*, 11.
282. Ibid.
283. Ezra Taft Benson, "What I Hope You Will Teach Your Children About the Temple," in *Temples of the Church*, 45.
284. See the books by Joseph Heinerman in the Select Bibliography, *Spirit World Manifestations* and *Eternal Testimonies*.
285. Benson, *Teachings*, 250.
286. Benson, "What I Hope," 42.
287. *Temples of the Most High*, 100, from Jerald and Sandra Tanner, *Evolution of the Mormon Temple Ceremony*, 15.
288. John A. Widtsoe, "Looking Toward the Temple," 47.
289. Packer, *Holy Temple*, Salt Lake City, UT: Church of Jesus Christ of Latter-day Saints, 1982, 1.
290. Church of Jesus Christ of Latter-day Saints, "Salvation for the Dead," 20.
291. Ibid., 23.
292. Ibid., 25.
293. Gordon B. Hinkley, "Why These Temples," in *Temples of the Church*, 5.
294. Church of Jesus Christ of Latter-day Saints, *Achieving a Celestial Marriage*, 1.
295. "Endowed with Covenants and Blessings," *Temples of the Church*, 14.
296. Ibid.
297. Spencer W. Kimball, "Temples and Eternal Marriage," in *Temples of the Church*, 15.
298. Hinkley, "Why These Temples," 3.
299. Kimball, "Temples and Eternal Marriage," 18.
300. Ibid., 19.
301. Ibid.
302. Joseph Fielding Smith, *Doctrines of Salvation*, 2:60, 63.
303. Ankerberg, *Mormonism Revisited*, 7.
304. John A. Widtsoe, "Looking Toward the Temple," 47.
305. Ibid.
306. E.g., *Journal of Discourses*, 2:31.
307. *Deseret News*, Church Section, November 12, 1970.
308. Spencer W. Kimball, "The Ordinances of the Gospel," address to Seminary and Institute Faculty, Brigham Young University, June 18, 1962, 9-10, as cited in *Achieving a Celestial Marriage*, 204.
309. Joseph Fielding Smith, *Doctrines of Salvation*, 2:60.
310. Packer, "The Holy Temple," 9.
311. Ibid.
312. Ibid., 10.
313. McConkie, *Mormon Doctrine*, 683.
314. *Journal of Discourses*, 4:192, cited in Jerald and Sandra Tanner, *Evolution of the Mormon Temple Ceremony*, 8.

315. Ibid., 22.
316. Ibid., 16-26.
317. Reed Smoot Case, 3:185, from Ibid., 9.
318. *The Utah Genealogical and Historical Magazine*, April 1921, 58, cited in Packer, "The Holy Temple," 8.
319. *Deseret Evening News*, December 1, 1990, cited in Jerald and Sandra Tanner, *Evolution of the Mormon Temple Ceremony*, 9-10.
320. Joseph Fielding Smith printed the affidavit by Bathsheba W. Smith containing this statement in defense of their immutability. Cited in Jerald and Sandra Tanner, *Evolution of the Mormon Temple Ceremony*, 10, citing *Blood Atonement and the Origin of Plural Marriage*, 87.
321. Editorial published in the Church Section of *Deseret News*, June 5, 1965, cited in Jerald and Sandra Tanner, *Evolution of the Mormon Temple Ceremony*, 10.
322. James E. Talmage, *The House of the Lord* (Salt Lake City, UT: Deseret Book Company, 1968), 84, cited in Church of Jesus Christ of Latter-day Saints, "Endowed with Covenants and Blessings," 14.
323. *Deseret News*, Church Section, January 16, 1982, cited in Jerald and Sandra Tanner, *Evolution of the Mormon Temple Ceremony*, 10.
324. Jerald and Sandra Tanner, *Evolution*, 7.
325. Ibid., 51.
326. Ibid., 48.
327. Ibid., 53-54.
328. Ibid., 54.
329. Ibid., 54-55.
330. Ibid., 26; cf. 22-26.
331. Cf., John Ankerberg and John Weldon, *The Secret Teachings of the Masonic Lodge: A Christian Appraisal* (Chicago, IL: Moody Press, 1990), chapter on oaths.
332. Jerald and Sandra Tanner, *Evolution of the Mormon Temple Ceremony*, 16.
333. Ankerberg, *Mormonism Revisited*, 14.
334. Jerald and Sandra Tanner, *Evolution of the Mormon Temple Ceremony*, 18.
335. Ibid., 32.
336. Ibid., 33.
337. Ibid., 32.
338. Ankerberg, *Mormonism Revisited*, 11.
339. Jerald and Sandra Tanner, *Evolution of the Mormon Temple Ceremony*, 45.
340. Ibid., *passim*.

# Select Bibliography

**Books**

Ahmanson, John. *Secret History: An Eyewitness Account of the Rise of Mormonism*, translated by Gleason L. Archer. Chicago, IL: Moody Press, 1984.

Anderson, Einar. *Inside Story of Mormonism*. Grand Rapids, MI: Kregel, 1974.

Benson, Ezra Taft. *The Teachings of Ezra Taft Benson*. Salt Lake City, UT: Bookcraft, 1988.

Brodie, Fawn M. *No Man Knows My History: The Life of Joseph Smith*. 2nd ed., rev. New York: Alfred Knopf, 1976.

Brown, Robert L. and Rosemary. *They Lie in Wait to Deceive: A Study of Anti-Mormon Deception*. Edited by Barbara Ellsworth. 3 vols. Mesa, AZ: Brownsworth Publishing, 1986.

Butterworth, F. Edward. *Divine Origin of the Restoration*. Chico, CA: Cosmic Press, 1989.

Church of Jesus Christ of Latter-day Saints. *Achieving a Celestial Marriage: Student Manual*. Salt Lake City, UT: The Church of Jesus Christ of Latter-day Saints, 1976. [Texts for Courses CDFR 160 and 161.]

————————. *The Book of Mormon*. Salt Lake City, UT: The Church of Jesus Christ of Latter-day Saints, 1947.

————————. *The Book of Mormon: An Account Written By the Hand of Mormon upon Plates Taken from the Plates of Nephi*. Salt Lake City, UT: The Church of Jesus Christ of Latter-day Saints, 1976.

————————. *Book of Mormon Student Manual*. Salt Lake City, UT: Church of Jesus Christ of Latter-day Saints, n.d. [text for Religion 121–122].

————————. *Come Follow Me: Melchizedek Priesthood Personal Study Guide, 1983*. Salt Lake City, UT: The Church of Jesus Christ of Latter-day Saints, 1983.

————————. *Doctrine and Covenants/The Pearl of Great Price*. Salt Lake City, UT: The Church of Jesus Christ of Latter-day Saints, 1968 and 1982.

————————. *The Doctrine and Covenants Student Manual*. Salt Lake City, UT: Church Educational System, The Church of Jesus Christ of Latter-day Saints, 1981. [Texts for Religion 324–325.]

————————. *Doctrines of the Gospel: Student Manual*. Salt Lake City, UT: The Church of Jesus Christ of Latter-day Saints, 1986. [Texts for Religion 231–232.]

————————. *Duties and Blessings of the Priesthood: Basic Manual for Priesthood Holders, Part A*. Salt Lake City, UT: The Church of Jesus Christ of Latter-day Saints, 1986.

————————. *Duties and Blessings of the Priesthood: Basic Manual for Priesthood Holders, Part B*. Salt Lake City, UT: The Church of Jesus Christ of Latter-day Saints, 1986.

————————. *Flip Charts: Uniform System for Teaching the Gospel*. Salt Lake City, UT: Church of Jesus Christ of Latter-day Saints, 1986, "Mission of the Church" reads: "Perfect the Saints. Proclaim the Gospel. Redeem the Dead."

————————. *Gospel Principles*. Salt Lake City, UT: The Church of Jesus Christ of Latter-day Saints, 1988.

————————. *Learn of Me: Relief Society Personal Study Guide, 2*. Salt Lake City, UT: The Church of Jesus Christ of Latter-day Saints, 1990.

————————. *The Life and Teachings of Jesus and His Apostles: Course Material*. 2nd ed. rev. Salt Lake City, UT: The Church of Jesus Christ of Latter-day Saints, 1979. [Texts for Religion 211–212.]

————————. *1991 Catalogue: Approved Materials for Church Programs and Family Resources*. Salt Lake City, UT: The Church of Jesus Christ of Latter-day Saints, 1990.

————————. *Official Report of the One Hundred Fifty-Ninth Semiannual General Conference of the Church of Jesus Christ of Latter-day Saints Held in the Tabernacle Salt Lake City, Utah, September 30 and October 1, 1989*. Salt Lake City, UT: The Church of Jesus Christ of Latter-day Saints, 1990.

————————. *Official Report of the One Hundred Sixtieth Semiannual General Conference of the Church of Jesus Christ of Latter-day Saints Held in the Tabernacle Salt Lake City, Utah, March 31 and April 1, 1990*. Salt Lake City, UT: The Church of Jesus Christ of Latter-day Saints, 1990.

————————. *Official Report of the One Hundred Sixtieth Semiannual General Conference of the Church of Jesus Christ of Latter-day Saints Held in the Tabernacle Salt Lake City, Utah, October 6 and 7, 1990*. Salt Lake City, UT: The Church of Jesus Christ of Latter-day Saints, 1991.

————————. *Old Testament: Genesis–2 Samuel, Student Manual*. Salt Lake City, UT: The Church of Jesus Christ of Latter-day Saints, 1981. [Text for Religion 301.]

————————. *Old Testament: 1 Kings–Malachi Student Manual*. 2nd ed. Salt Lake City, UT: The Church of Jesus Christ of Latter-day Saints, 1982. [Text for Religion 302.]

————————. *A Sure Foundation: Answers to Difficult Gospel Questions*. Salt Lake City, UT: Deseret Book Company, 1988.

————————. *Temples of the Church of Jesus Christ of Latter-day Saints*. Salt Lake City, UT: The Church of Jesus Christ of Latter-day Saints, 1988.

————————. *To Make Thee a Minister and a Witness: Melchizedek Priesthood Personal Study Guide, 2*. Salt Lake City, UT: The Church of Jesus Christ of Latter-day Saints, 1990.

Cowan, Marvin W. *Mormon Claims Answered*. N.p. Marvin W. Cowan Publisher, 1975, revised in 1989.

Cowdery, Wayne L., Howard A. Davis, and Donald R. Scales. *Who Really Wrote the Book of Mormon?* Santa Ana, CA: Vision House, 1977.

Crowther, Duane S. *Life Everlasting*. Salt Lake City, UT: Bookcraft, Inc., 1988.

Decker, Ed. *The Mormon Dilemma: The Dramatic Story of a Mormon Couple's Encounter with Truth*. Eugene, OR: Harvest House Publishers, 1990.

Decker, Ed, and Dave Hunt. *The God Makers: A Shocking Expose of What the Mormon Church Really Believes*. Eugene, OR: Harvest House, 1984.

Deseret Sunday School Union. *The Master's Church Course, A*. Salt Lake City, UT: Deseret Sunday School Union, 1969.

Deseret News. *1991-1992 Church Almanac*. Salt Lake City, UT: Deseret News, 1990.

*Evening and Morning Star, June 1832–Sept, 1834*. No. 1, vol. 2, no. 24. Reprint. Muhringen, West Germany: F. Wochner K.G., 1969. Microfilm.

Fraser, Gordon H. *Is Mormonism Christian?: Mormon Doctrine Compared with Biblical Christianity*. Chicago, IL: Moody Press, 1977.

_____. *Joseph and the Golden Plates: A Close Look at the Book of Mormon*. Eugene, OR: Gordon H. Fraser, 1978.

_____. *Sects of the Latter-day Saints (Part 1: The Reorganized Church of Jesus Christ of Latter-day Saints; Part 2: The Polygamous Sects of Mormonism)*. Hubbard, OR: Gordon H. Fraser, 1978.

_____. *What Does the Book of Mormon Teach?: An Examination of the Historical and Scientific Statements of the Book of Mormon*. Chicago, IL: Moody Press, 1964.

Hansen, Klaus J. *Quest for Empire: The Political Kingdom of God and the Council of Fifty in Mormon History*. Lincoln, NE: University of Nebraska Press, 1967.

Herald Publishing House. *Joseph Smith's "New Translation" of the Bible: A Complete Parallel Column Comparison of the Inspired Version of the Holy Scriptures and the King James Authorized Version*. Independence, MO: Herald Publishing House, 1970.

Heinerman, Joseph. *Eternal Testimonies: Inspired Testimonies of Latter-day Saints*. Salt Lake City, UT: Joseph Lyon and Associates, 1982.

_____. *Spirit World Manifestations: Accounts of Divine Aid in Genealogical and Temple Work and Other Assistance to Latter-day Saints*. Salt Lake City, UT: Joseph Lyon and Associates, 1986.

Hickman, Bill. *Brigham's Destroying Angel: Being the Life, Confession and Startling Disclosures of the Notorious Bill Hickman*, 1904. Reprint. Salt Lake City, UT: Utah Lighthouse Ministry, n.d. Microfilm.

Hinckley, Gordon B. *Truth Restored: A Short History of the Church of Jesus Christ of Latter-day Saints*. Salt Lake City, UT: The Church of Jesus Christ of Latter-day Saints, 1979.

Hoekema, Anthony. *The Four Major Cults: Christian Science, Jehovah's Witnesses, Mormonism, Seventh-day Adventism*. Grand Rapids, MI: William B. Eerdmans, 1970.

Hughes, Dean. *The Mormon Church: A Basic History*. Salt Lake City, UT: Deseret Book Company, 1986.

Kimball, Spencer W. *The Miracle of Forgiveness*. Salt Lake City, UT: Bookcraft, 1989.

Marquardt, H. Michael. *The Book of Abraham Papyrus Found: An Answer to Dr. Hugh Nibley's Book "The Message of the Joseph Smith Papyry: An Egyptian Endowment" as It Relates to the Source of the Book of Abraham*. Sandy, UT: H. Michael Marquardt, 1975.

Martin, Walter. *The Kingdom of the Cults*. Minneapolis, MN: Bethany, 1970.

_____. *The Maze of Mormonism*. Rev. ed. Santa Ana, CA: Vision House Publishers, 1978.

Matthews, Robert J. *A Bible! A Bible!: How Latter-day Revelation Helps Us Understand the Scriptures and the Savior*. Salt Lake City, UT: Bookcraft, 1990.

McConkie, Bruce. *Doctrinal New Testament Commentary, Matthew–Revelation*. 3 vols. Salt Lake City, UT: Bookcraft, 1976, 1977.

McConkie, Bruce R. *Mormon Doctrine*. Salt Lake City, UT: Bookcraft, 1977.

McElveen, Floyd. *The Mormon Revelations of Convenience*. Minneapolis, MN: Bethany, 1978.

_____. *Will the "Saints" Go Marching In?: A Comparison of the Mormon Faith with Biblical Christianity*. Glendale, CA: Regal, 1977, retitled *The Mormon Illusion*

McKeever, Bill. *Answering Mormon's Questions: Simple Biblical Explanations to the Most Common Questions That Mormons Ask*. Minneapolis, MN: Bethany, 1991.

McMurrin, Sterling M. *The Theological Foundations of the Mormon Religion*. Salt Lake City, UT: University of Utah Press, 1977.

Morey, Robert A. *How to Answer a Mormon: Practical Guidelines for What to Expect and What to Reply When the Mormons Come to Your Door*. Minneapolis, MN: Bethany, 1983.

Musser, Joseph W. *Michael Our Father and Our God: The Mormon Conception of Deity As Taught by Joseph Smith, Brigham Young, John Taylor and Their Associates in the Priesthood*. Salt Lake City, UT: Truth Publishing, 1963.

Naifeh, Steven and Gregory White Smith. *The Mormon Murders: A True Story of Greed, Forgery, Deceit, and Death*. New York: Weidenfeld & Nicholson, 1988.

Petersen, LaMar. *Hearts Made Glad: The Charges of Intemperance Against Joseph Smith the Mormon Prophet*. Salt Lake City, UT: LaMar Petersen, 1975.

Petersen, Mark E. *Adam: Who Is He?*. Salt Lake City, UT: Deseret Book Company, 1976.

_____. *As Translated Correctly*. Salt Lake City, UT: Deseret Book Company, 1966.

_____. *The Great Prologue*. Salt Lake City, UT: Deseret Book Company, 1975.

Pratt, Orson. *The Seer*. January 1853–August 1854. vol. 1, no. 1–vol. 2, no. 8. Reprint. np., nd., microfilm.

Quinn, D. Michael. *Early Mormonism and the Magic World View*. Salt Lake City, UT: Signature Books, 1987.

Richards, LeGrand. *A Marvelous Work and a Wonder*. Salt Lake City, UT: Deseret Book Company, 1975.

Roberts, B.H. *The Mormon Doctrine of Deity: The Roberts–Van Donckt Discussion*. 1903. Reprint. Bountiful, UT: B.H. Roberts/Horizon Publishers, n.d.

Robinson, Stephen E. *Are Mormons Christians?*. Salt Lake City, UT: Bookcraft, 1991.

Ropp, Harry L. *The Mormon Papers: Are the Mormon Scriptures Reliable?*. Downers Grove, IL: InterVarsity Press, retitled *Are the Mormon Scriptures Reliable?* 1987.

Sackett, Chuck. *What's Going On in There?: The Verbatim Text of the Mormon Temple Rituals Annotated and Explained by a Former Temple Worker*. Thousand Oaks, CA: Sword of the Shepherd, 1982.

Scott, Latayne C. *Ex-Mormons: Why We Left*. Grand Rapids, MI: Baker, 1990.

_____. *The Mormon Mirage: A Former Mormon Tells Why She Left the Church*. Grand Rapids, MI: Zondervan, 1980.

Smith, Joseph. *History of the Church*. Vols. 1-6. Salt Lake City, UT: Deseret Book Company/The Church of Jesus Christ of Latter-day Saints, 1975.

_____. *Teachings of the Prophet of Joseph Smith*. Compiled by Joseph Fielding Smith. Salt Lake City, UT: Deseret Book Company, 1977.

Smith, Joseph F. *Gospel Doctrine: Sermons and Writings of President Joseph F. Smith*. Salt Lake City, UT: Deseret Book Company, 1975.

_____. *Answers to Gospel Questions*. Compiled by Joseph Fielding Smith, Jr. 4 vols. Salt Lake City, UT: Deseret Book Company, 1976.

_____. *Doctrines of Salvation: Sermons and Writings of Joseph Fielding Smith*. Compiled by Bruce R. McConkie. 3 vols. Salt Lake City, UT: Bookcraft, 1976.

_____. *The Way to Perfection*. Salt Lake City, UT: Deseret Book Company, 1975.

Snake River LDS Seminary District. *Is There An Answer?*. Compiled by A. Lavar Thornock. Pocatello, ID: Snake River LDS Seminary District, 1968.

Spencer, James R. *Beyond Mormonism: An Elder's Story*. Grand Rapids, MI: Chosen Books, 1984.

_____. *Have You Witnessed to a Mormon Lately?*. Old Tappan, NJ: Fleming H. Revell, 1986.

Stenhouse, Mrs. T.B.H., *Tell It All: The Tyranny of Mormonism*. Hartford, CT: A.D. Worthington & Co., 1875.

Talmage, James E. *Jesus the Christ: A Study of the Messiah and His Mission According to Holy Scriptures Both Ancient and Modern*. Salt Lake City, UT: Deseret Book Company, 1962.

_____. *The Study of the Articles of Faith: Being a Consideration of the Principle Doctrines of the Church of Jesus Christ of Latter-day Saints*. Salt Lake City, UT: The Church of Jesus Christ of Latter-day Saints, 1976.

Tanner, Jerald and Sandra. *Archaeology and the Book of Mormon*. Salt Lake City, UT: Utah Lighthouse Ministry, 1969.

_____. *Changes in Joseph Smith's History*. Salt Lake City, UT: Utah Lighthouse Ministry, n.d.

_____. *Changes in The Pearl of Great Price*. Salt Lake City, UT: Utah Lighthouse Ministry, n.d.

_____. *Changes in The Pearl of Great Price: A Photo Reprint of the Original 1851 Edition of the Pearl of Great Price with All the Changes Marked*. Salt Lake City, UT: Utah Lighthouse Ministry, n.d., retitled *Flaws in The Pearl of Great Price: A Study of Changes and Plagiarism in Joseph Smith's Pearl of Great Price*. 1991.

_____. *The Changing World of Mormonism: A Behind the Scenes Look at Changes in Mormon Doctrine and Practice*. Rev. ed. Chicago, IL: Moody Press, 1981.

_____. *The Case Against Mormonism*. 3 vols. Salt Lake City, UT: Utah Lighthouse Ministry, 1967-71.

_____. *Did Spaulding Write the Book of Mormon?*. Salt Lake City, UT: Utah Lighthouse Ministry, 1977.

_____. *The Mormon Kingdom*. 2 vols. Salt Lake City, UT: Utah Lighthouse Ministry, 1969-1971.

_____. *Joseph Smith and Money Digging*. Salt Lake City, UT: Utah Lighthouse Ministry, 1970.

_____. *Joseph Smith's Strange Account of the First Vision*. Salt Lake City, UT: Utah Lighthouse Ministry, n.d.

_____. *A Look at Christianity*. Salt Lake City, UT: Utah Lighthouse Ministry, 1971.

_____. *The Lucifer-God Doctrine: A Critical Look at Charges of Luciferian Worship in the Mormon Temple, with a Response to the Decker–Schnoebelen Rebuttal*. Revised and enlarged ed. Salt Lake City, UT: Utah Lighthouse Ministry, 1988. Revised and enlarged ed.

_____. *The Mormon Kingdom*. 2 vols. Salt Lake City, UT: Utah Lighthouse Ministry, 1969-1971.

_____. *Mormonism Like Watergate?: An Answer to Hugh Nibley*. Salt Lake City, UT: Utah Lighthouse Ministry, 1974.

_____. *Mormonism—Shadow or Reality?*. Enlarged ed. Salt Lake City, UT: Utah Lighthouse Ministry, 1972.

_____. *3913 Changes in the Book of Mormon: A Photo Reprint of the Original 1830 Edition of the Book of Mormon with All the Changes Marked*. Salt Lake City, UT: Utah Lighthouse Ministry, n.d.

_____. *Mormonism, Magic and Masonry*. Second ed. Salt Lake City, UT: Utah Lighthouse Ministry. 1988.

Tanner, Sandra, *The Bible and Mormon Doctrine*. Salt Lake City, UT: Utah Lighthouse Ministry, 1971.

Unger, Merrill, *Unger's Bible Dictionary*. Chicago, IL: Moody Press, 1975.

Walker, Williston et al. *A History of the Christian Church*. 4th ed. New York: Charles Schribner Sons, 1985.

Wallace, Arthur. *Can Mormonism Be Proved Experimentally?*. Los Angeles, CA: Arthur Wallace, 1973.

Woodruff, Wilford C. *Joseph Smith Begins His Work: Book of Mormon*. 1831. Reprint. Bountiful, UT: Wilford C. Woodruff, 1963.

Young, Brigham. *Discourses of Brigham Young*. Compiled by John A. Widtsoe. Salt Lake City, UT: Deseret Book Company, 1976.

Young, Brigham and His Counselors, the Twelve Apostles, and Others. *Journal of Discourses*. Reported by George D. Watt. 26 vols. plus index. Liverpool, England: F.D. Richards, 1855. Reprint. Salt Lake City, UT: N.p., 1967. )We stress this is an official LDS publication, a photolithographic reprint of the exact original edition. See *Deseret News 1989-1990 Church Almanac*, p. 188.)

## Mormon Pamphlets

"The Challenge." Los Angeles, CA: The Church of Jesus Christ of Latter-day Saints. n.d.

The Church of Jesus Christ of Latter-day Saints. *Apostasy and Restoration*. Salt Lake City, UT: The Church of Jesus Christ of Latter-day Saints, 1983.

――――――. *Eternal Progression, Discussion 4: Uniform System for Teaching the Gospel*. Salt Lake City, UT: Church of Jesus Christ of Latter-day Saints, 1987.

――――――. *Eternal Progression, Study Guide 4*. Salt Lake City, UT: Church of Jesus Christ of Latter-day Saints, 1987.

――――――. *Faith in the Lord Jesus Christ*. Salt Lake City, UT: Deseret News Press, n.d.

――――――. *The Gospel of Jesus Christ, Discussion 2: Uniform System for Teaching the Gospel*. Salt Lake City, UT: Church of Jesus Christ of Latter-day Saints, 1986.

――――――. *The Gospel of Jesus Christ, Study Guide 2*. Salt Lake City, UT: Church of Jesus Christ of Latter-day Saints, 1986.

――――――. *Instructions for the Discussions: Uniform System for Teaching the Gospel*. Salt Lake City, UT: Church of Jesus Christ of Latter-day Saints, 1986.

――――――. *Jesus Christ Savior and Mediator of Mankind*. N.p., n.d.

――――――. *Living a Christlike Life, Discussion 5: Uniform System for Teaching the Gospel*. Salt Lake City, UT: Church of Jesus Christ of Latter-day Saints, 1986.

――――――. *Living a Christlike Life, Study Guide 5*. Salt Lake City, UT: Church of Jesus Christ of Latter-day Saints, 1986.

――――――. *Membership in the Kingdom, Discussion 6: Uniform System for Teaching the Gospel*. Salt Lake City, UT: Church of Jesus Christ of Latter-day Saints, 1986.

――――――. *Membership in the Kingdom, Study Guide 6*. Salt Lake City, UT: Church of Jesus Christ of Latter-day Saints, 1986.

――――――. *The Plan of Our Heavenly Father, Discussion 1: Uniform System for Teaching the Gospel*. Salt Lake City, UT: Church of Jesus Christ of Latter-day Saints, 1986.

――――――. *The Plan of Our Heavenly Father, Study Guide 1*. Salt Lake City, UT: Church of Jesus Christ of Latter-day Saints, 1986.

――――――. *Plan of Salvation*. N.p., n.d.

――――――. *The Prophet Joseph Smith's Testimony*. N.p., n.d.

――――――. *The Purpose of Life*. Salt Lake City, UT: Church of Jesus Christ of Latter-day Saints, 1983.

――――――. *The Restoration, Discussion 3: Uniform System for Teaching the Gospel*. Salt Lake City, UT: Church of Jesus Christ of Latter-day Saints, 1986.

――――――. *The Restoration, Study Guide 3*. Salt Lake City, UT: Church of Jesus Christ of Latter-day Saints, 1986.

――――――. *What the Mormons Think of Christ*, n.d.

――――――. *What the Mormons Think of Christ*, 1982.

Morgan, John. *The Plan of Salvation*. Salt Lake City, UT: The Church of Jesus Christ of Latter-day Saints, n.d.

Packer, Boyd K. *The Holy Temple*. Salt Lake City, UT: Church of Jesus Christ of Latter-day Saints, 1982.

Penrose, Charles W. *What the "Mormons" Believe: Epitome of the Doctrines of the Church of Jesus Christ of Latter-day Saints*. Salt Lake City, UT: Deseret News Press, n.d.

## Pamphlets, Booklets, Transcripts, Journals, Newsletters, Photocopies, and Letters

Adamson, Jack and Reed C. Durham, Jr. *No Help For the Widow's Son: Joseph Smith and Masonry*. Nauvoo, IL: Martin Publishing Co., 1980.

Anderson, Darl. "Love Thy Minister, Neighbor: Worshop Outline." Photocopy.

Anderson, Kirby. *Who Are These Good People? An Analysis of Mormonism*. Rev. ed. Dallas, TX: Probe Ministries International, 1983.

Ankerberg, John. *Former Mormons Testify*. Chattanooga, TN, 1982. Program transcript.

Ankerberg, John. *"Mormon Officials and Christian Scholars Compare Doctrines."* (Mr. K.H. Christensen, Mr. Lawrence R. Flake, Dr. James Bjornstad, Mrs. Sandra Tanner, Mr. Ed Decker, Dr. Walter Martin), Chattanooga, TN: The John Ankerberg Show, 1983. Television transcript.

Ankerberg, John. *Mormonism Revisited* (Ed Decker with excerpts from the film *The God Makers*), Chattanooga, TN: The John Ankerberg Show, 1983. Television transcript.

Bodine, Jerry and Marian. *Whom Can You Trust?*. Santa Ana, CA: Christ for the Cults, 1979.

――――――. *Witnessing to the Mormons*. Santa Ana, CA: Christ for the Cults, 1978.

*A Book of Commandments for the Government of the Church of Christ Organized According to Law on the 6th of April, 1830*. Independence, MO: Board of Publication, Church of Christ, 1977 (reprint of 1833 edition published by W.W. Phelps & Co. in Independence, MO: "Zion").

Budvarson, Arthur. "Changes in Mormonism?" La Mesa, CA: Utah Christian Tract Society.

Budvarson, Arthur. *Mormonism: Can It Stand Investigation?*. La Mesa, CA: Utah Christian Tract Society, n.d.

Church of Jesus Christ of Latter-day Saints. *Temples of the Church*. Salt Lake City: Church Magazines/*Ensign* 1988.

Ex-Mormons for Jesus. *An Interview with LeGrand Richards*. Clearwater, FL: Ex-Mormons for Jesus, n.d.

Farkas, John R. *What the Mormons Really Think of Christ and the Father*. St. Louis, MO: Personal Freedom Outreach, 1988.

Fraser, Gordon. *A Manual for Christian Workers: A Workshop Outline for the Study of Mormonism*. Hubbard, OR: Gordon H. Fraser, 1978.

Geer, Thelma (Granny). *Mormonism's Salvation . . . By Grace or By Eternal Marriage and Sex?*. Tucson, AZ: Calvary Missionary Press, n.d.

"Geraldo" TV show, June 29, 1991. Available from *Journal Graphics*. New York. (Phone: (212) 732-8552.) Hall, Andy et al. "Mormon, Inc.: Finances and Faith." *The Arizona Republic*. June 30–July 3, 1991.

Hougey, Hal. *Archaeology and the Book of Mormon*. Concord, CA: Pacific Publishing, n.d.

——————. *Archaeology and the Book of Mormon*. Rev. ed. Concord, CA: Pacific Publishing, 1976.

——————. *Latter-day Saints—Where Did You Get Your Authority?*. Concord, CA: Pacific Publishing, 1977.

——————. *A Parallel, The Basis of the Book of Mormon: B.H. Roberts' "Parallel" of the Book of Mormon to View of the Hebrews*. Concord, CA: Pacific Publishing, 1975.

——————. *Mormon Missionary Handbook—A Reprint—Accompanied By a Refutation in Parallel Columns of the Arguments Used By Mormon Missionaries*. Tucson, AZ: Roy-Co Distributors, n.d.

Kaiser, Edgar P. *How To Respond to the Latter-day Saints*. St. Louis, MO: Concordia, 1977.

Marquardt, Michael H. *The Strange Marriages of Sarah N. Whitney to Joseph Smith the Mormon Prophet, Joseph C. Kingsbury and Heber C. Kimball*. Salt Lake City, UT: Utah Lighthouse Ministry, 1973.

Martin, Walter R. *Mormonism*. Grand Rapids, MI: Zondervan, 1967.

Matthews, Robert J. *Index and Concordance for "Teachings of the Prophet Joseph Smith."* Salt Lake City, UT: Deseret Book Co., 1976.

Morley, Rev. Frank S. *What We Can Learn from the Church of Jesus Christ of Latter-day Saints By a Protestant Minister*. Salt Lake City, UT: The Church of Jesus Christ of Latter-day Saints, n.d.

Petersen, LaMar. *Problems in Mormon Text*. Concord, CA: Pacific Publishing, 1972.

Petersen, Mark E. "Which Church Is Right?" Salt Lake City, UT: Church of Jesus Christ of Latter-day Saints, 1982.

Quinn, D. Michael. *On Being a Mormon Historian (A Lecture by D. Michael Quinn, Associate Professor of History at Brigham Young University Before the Student History Association. Fall 1981)*. Salt Lake City, UT: Utah Lighthouse Ministry, 1982.

Ralson, Colleen. *Color Me Confused: A Guide for Marking Your Book of Mormon*. Rev. ed. St. Louis, MO: Watchman Fellowship, 1988.

Smithsonian Institution, Department of Anthropology. "Statement Regarding the *Book of Mormon*." Washington, D.C.: Smithsonian Institution, 1988.

——————. *Dissecting the Doctrine and Covenants: A Guide for Marking Your Doctrine and Covenants*. St. Louis, MO: Watchman Fellowship, 1990.

Spaulding, F.S. and Samuel A.B. Mercer. *Why Egyptologists Reject the Book of Abraham*. Salt Lake City, UT: Utah Lighthouse Ministry, n.d.

Tanner, Jerald and Sandra. *Joseph Smith's 1826 Trial: New Discoveries Prove Court Record Authentic*. Salt Lake City, UT: Utah Lighthouse Ministry, n.d.

——————. *Salt Lake City Messenger* (various issues). P.O. Box 1884, Salt Lake City, UT 84110.

Taylor, Sally J. to Jerald and Sandra Tanner, September 25, 1990. Discussing the Navy Chief of Chaplain's designation of the Mormon Faith as "Protestant."

Taylor, Sally J. (Mrs. Andrew R. Taylor) et al. Letter to Rear Admiral Alvin B. Koeneman, Office of the Chief of Naval Operations, Department of the Navy, Washington D.C. from the Protestant Chapel Council Naval Air Station, Alameda, CA, protesting the designation of Mormonism as Protestant. (The U.S. Army/Air Force offer the same classification), n.d. visible on Xerox copy.

Whitmer, David. *An Address to All Believers in Christ by a Witness to the Divine Authenticity of the Book of Mormon*. 1887. Reprint. Concord, CA: Pacific Publishing Co., 1972.

Whitte, Bob. *What's Going On Here?* Clearwater, FL: Ex-Mormons for Jesus, n.d.

——————. *Where Does It Say That?: A Witnessing Resource for Christians*. Safety Harbor, FL: Ex-Mormons for Jesus, n.d.

——————. *Witnessing to Mormons: Using Where Does It Say That?*. Safety Harbor, FL: Ex-Mormons for Jesus Ministries, n.d.

## Newspaper and Periodical Articles

"Analysis of FBI Figure Shows S.L. [Salt Lake City] Leads U.S. in Larcenies." *The Salt Lake Tribune*, April 24, 1989.

Anderson, Vern. "Reorganized LDS Church in Turmoil After Split in Faith." *The Salt Lake Tribune*, July 9, 1990.

"Child-Abuse Cases Set Record in Utah County." *The Salt Lake Tribune*, April 23, 1988.

Dabling, Bobby B. "Attorney Says Church Can Stall Sex Cases." *The Salt Lake Tribune*, November 30, 1984.

Dart, John. "Mormon Church Passes Seven Million Mark." *Los Angeles Times*, January 6, 1990.

Davis, V. Beason appeal from the third Judicial District Court of the Territory of Idaho argued December 9-10, 1889—decided February 3, 1890 (re: bigamy and polygamy). This decision noted, "Bigamy and polygamy are crimes by the laws of all civilized and Christian countries. They are crimes by the laws of the United States, and they are crimes by the laws of Idaho. They tend to destroy the purity of the marriage relation, to disturb the peace of families, to degrade women and to debase man. Few crimes are more pernicious to the best interest of society and receive more general or more deserved punishment. To extend exemption from punishment for such crimes would be to shock the moral judgment of the community" (p. 341, Mr. Justice Field delivering the opinion of the court).

Dockstader, Julie. "Teen Suicides Becoming 'National Tragedy,'" *The Salt Lake Tribune*, October 22, 1985.

"Health Of Utah Children Is Deteriorating Like Rest of U.S. Youth, Officials Warn." *The Salt Lake Tribune*, March 12, 1989.

Heber, G. Wolsey, "Who Are the Mormons?" *This People*, Spring 1990.

Jorgensen, Chris. "Task Force Begins Efforts to Treat Young Sex Offenders." *The Salt Lake Tribune*, February 27, 1989.

Lamb, David, "Salt Lake: A Worship of Order." *Los Angeles Times*, February 2, 1988.

"The Mormon Financial Empire," *Denver Post*, November 21-28, 1982.

"Mormons Testify Jesus Is the Christ," Augusta, GA: Newspaper insert, April 13, 1990.

"Most Polygamy Is in Utah, Professor Says." *The Salt Lake Tribune*, April 10, 1988.

Palmer, Anne. "Three Factors Contribute to Teenage Drug Use." *The Salt Lake Tribune*, January 26, 1987.

*Readers' Digest*, March 1990, p. 63.

Renolds, Michael H. "Mormon Chaplains in the Military." *The Utah Evangel*, January–February, 1992, p. 12.

Sisco, Carol. "Murder Rate of Children Ranks High: One Out of Five Victims in Utah Is Younger Than Age 15." *The Salt Lake Tribune*, August 13, 1982.

Sisco, Carol. "2 Utah Lawmakers Sponsor Legislation to Better Protect Women from Abuse." *The Salt Lake Tribune*, January 9, 1989.

Sisco, Carol. "Utah Must Cure Plague of Child Abuse, Says Analyst." *The Salt Lake Tribune*, January 24, 1990.

"S.L. [Salt Lake City] Crime Rate Rises 3.2% in '88." *The Salt Lake Tribune*, February 14, 1989.

Sowerby, Melinda. "The Church's New Magazine Ad Campaign Focuses on Message of Restoration." *The Salt Lake Tribune*, January 23, 1990.

"Teen Suicide Continues to Escalate." *The Salt Lake Tribune*, July 8, 1985.

Tracy, Dawn. "Study Says Utah Teens' Sex Life Mirrors U.S. Profile." *The Salt Lake Tribune*, December 25, 1987.

Zonana, Victor F. "Leaders of Mormonism Double As Overseers of a Financial Empire." *Wall Street Journal*, November 9, 1983.

# Resource List

## Book List
## Utah Lighthouse Ministry
## Box 1884 Salt Lake City, Utah 84110

*Mormonism—Shadow or Reality?* (1987 edition)
by *Jerald and Sandra Tanner*

Our most comprehensive and revealing work on Mormonism. Deals with: new discoveries relating to Mormon history, changes in Joseph Smith's revelations, Joseph Smith's 1826 trial for "glass looking," proof that *The Book of Mormon* is a product of the nineteenth century, changes in the *Book of Mormon*, archaeology and the *Book of Mormon*, changes in Joseph Smith's *History*, the First Vision, the Godhead, the Adam-God doctrine, the priesthood, the missionary system, false prophecy, Joseph Smith's doctrine of polygamy, polygamy after the Manifesto and in Utah today, changes in the anti-black doctrine, the rediscovery of the Joseph Smith Papyri and the fall of the Book of Abraham, Mormon scriptures and the Bible changes in *The Pearl of Great Price*, blood atonement among the early Mormons, the Word of Wisdom, the Council of 50, the Danites, the temple ceremony, changes in the temple ceremony and garments, the Mountain Meadows Massacre, Mormonism and money, plus hundreds of other important subjects.

*An Index to Mormonism—Shadow or Reality?*
by *Michael Briggs*

*Tract Pact*
A collection of 18 different tracts on Mormonism from various publishers.

*The Changing World of Mormonism*
by *Jerald* and *Sandra Tanner*

A condensed version of *Mormonism—Shadow or Reality?* Published by Moody Press. Almost 600 pages plus an index and bibliography.

*Major Problems of Mormonism*
by *Jerald* and *Sandra Tanner*

Thirty years of research on Mormonism distilled into a 256-page book. Covers the most important areas.

*The Bible and Mormon Doctrine*
by *Sandra Tanner*

A 33-page booklet dealing with the LDS view of man's eternal progression, modern revelation, the gospel, salvation by grace or works, the true church, pre-existence, kingdoms in heaven, temple work, priesthood, and the nature of God as compared with the biblical view. A great help in understanding Mormon beliefs.

*Jerald Tanner's Testimony*
by *Jerald Tanner*

An account of why he left the Mormon church and how he found a personal relationship with Jesus Christ. Tells how he met Sandra (the great-great granddaughter of Brigham Young), how they were married, and how they set up a ministry to Mormons. Also deals with the fears and problems encountered in running such a ministry, and contains a number of personal stories.

*Evolution of the Mormon Temple Ceremony, 1842-1990*
by *Jerald* and *Sandra Tanner*

Contains the *actual text* of the 1990 revision of the highly secret endowment ritual and other accounts of the ceremony dating back to 1846. Shows that Joseph Smith borrowed from Masonry in creating the ritual and that it has evolved over the years. Also shows the serious changes made in the ceremony in 1990.

*No Man Knows My History*
by *Fawn M. Brodie*

The finest book written on the life of Joseph Smith. The Mormon writer Samuel W. Taylor remarked: "Mrs. Brodie was unchurched for the writing of it and delivered to the buffetings of Satan; . . . It was not inaccuracy that raised the Mormon ire, but her documentation of that which we didn't wish to believe."

*The Mormon Mirage: A Former Mormon Tells Why She Left the Church*
by *Latayne Colvelt Scott*

*Mormon Claims Answered*
by *Marvin Cowan*

An excellent book on the teachings of Mormonism.

*Where Does It Say That?*
by *Bob Witte*

Over 100 photos of oft-quoted pages from early LDS sources.

*Mormon Scriptures and the Bible*
by *Jerald* and *Sandra Tanner*

A 53-page book dealing with such subjects as the decline of the use of the Bible in Mormon theology, the influence of Bible critics on Mormonism, the charge that the Catholics conspired to alter the Bible, a comparison of the manuscript evidence for the Bible and Mormon scriptures, Young's attempt to suppress Joseph Smith's Inspired Revision of the Bible, the way Smith ignored his own renderings, the lack of support in ancient manuscripts for Smith's "inspired" renderings, and changes in *The Pearl of Great Price*.

### *A Look at Christianity*
by *Jerald* and *Sandra Tanner*

Deals with the Flood, Noah's Ark, Egypt and the Bible, evidence from Palestine, the Moabite Stone, Assyrian records, the Dead Sea Scrolls, the importance of love, the destructive effects of hate, reconciliation with God, our testimony, the historicity of Jesus, manuscripts of the New Testament, early writings concerning Christianity, and more.

### *Mormonism, Magic and Masonry*
by *Jerald* and *Sandra Tanner*

A study of the influence of magic and Masonry on Joseph Smith and his family.

### *Joseph Smith's Bainbridge, NY, Court Trials*
by *Wesley P. Walters*

Important discoveries concerning Joseph Smith's 1826 and 1830 trials. Proves beyond all doubt that Joseph Smith was a money-digger who used a "peep stone" to find buried treasures at the very time he was supposed to be preparing himself to receive the gold plates from which *The Book of Mormon* was translated.

### *Joseph Smith and Money-Digging*
by *Jerald* and *Sandra Tanner.*

Deals with such subjects as Joseph Smith's connection with money-digging; Joseph Smith's "seer stone," the use of the "seer stone" to find *The Book of Mormon* plates and its use to translate the book itself; the relationship of money-digging to the story of the gold plates of *The Book of Mormon* and to the text of the book; the use of the divining rod by the Mormons, and the revelation regarding treasure hunting. This book also contains a photographic reprint of the affidavits regarding Joseph Smith's money-digging activities, which were published by E.D. Howe in 1834.

### *New Light on Mormon Origins from the Palmyra (NY) Revival*
by *Wesley P. Walters*

A devastating blow to the First Vision story. Mormons claim that Joseph Smith was motivated to pray in the woods in 1820 due to a revival in Palmyra. Walters, however, presents evidence that there was no revival in Palmyra in 1820.

### *Covering Up the Black Hole in the Book of Mormon*
by *Jerald* and *Sandra Tanner*

A penetrating look at *The Book of Mormon* that conclusively demonstrates it was written by Joseph Smith and did not come from gold plates written by ancient Jews. Contains *74 pages of proof* that Smith plagiarized extensively from the King James Version of the New Testament.

### *3913 Changes in the Book of Mormon*

A photomechanical reprint of the original 1830 edition of *The Book of Mormon* with all the changes marked. Contains a 16-page introduction by Jerald and Sandra Tanner that proves that the changes are not in harmony with the original text.

### *Joseph Smith Begins His Work*, Vol. 1

A photo-reprint of the original 1830 edition of *The Book of Mormon*. Bound.

### *Joseph Smith Begins His Work*, Vol. 2

Photo-reprint of both the 1833 *Book of Commandments* and the 1835 edition of the *Doctrine and Covenants*. Bound.

### *The Pearl of Great Price*

Photo-reprint of the original 1851 edition.

### *An Address to All Believers in Christ*
by *David Whitmer*

One of the three witnesses to *The Book of Mormon* tells why he left the LDS church and how Joseph changed the revelations and fell into error. Photo-reprint of the 1887 edition.

### *The Use of the Bible in the Book of Mormon and Early Nineteenth-Century Events Reflected in The Book of Mormon*
by *H. Michael Marquardt*

A good summary of the evidence showing that *The Book of Mormon* is a product of the nineteenth century.

### *An Examination of B.H. Roberts' Secret Manuscript*
by *Wesley P. Walters*

An article analyzing Roberts' compilation of evidence showing that Joseph Smith could have written *The Book of Mormon*. Includes some photographs of Roberts' original manuscript.

### *Roberts' Manuscripts Revealed*

Photo reproductions of some secret manuscripts written by Mormon historian B.H. Roberts. Roberts expressed some serious doubts about *The Book of Mormon* and frankly admitted that Joseph Smith had a vivid enough imagination and the source material to have produced the book.

### *Archeology and The Book of Mormon*
by *Hal Hougey*

By using quotations from well-known Mormon authors, Mr. Hougey shows that there is no real archeological evidence to support the claims of *The Book of Mormon*.

### *Ferguson's Manuscript Unveiled*

A significant paper on the subject of *The Book of Mormon's* archaeology and geography. Thomas Stuart Ferguson, one of the most noted defenders of *The Book of Mormon*, was finally forced to conclude that it was "fictional."

### Did Spalding Write The Book of Mormon?
by Jerald and Sandra Tanner

Explains why the Tanners oppose the theory that Spalding penned 12 pages of The Book of Mormon. Contains a photographic comparison of Spalding's handwriting with The Book of Mormon manuscript and a photo-reprint of Spalding's Manuscript Found.

### Archaeology and The Book of Mormon, 1969
by Jerald and Sandra Tanner

A 92-page book dealing with such subjects as The Book of Mormon in light of archaeological findings in the New World, the disagreement between Dr. Nibley and Dr. Jakeman over archaeology and The Book of Mormon, Nephite coins, the Anthon transcript, Mayan glyphs, the Paraiba text, the Kinderhook plates, the Newark stone, the Lehi Tree-of-Life stone, the problem of The Book of Mormon's geography, the Bat Creek inscription, Dr. Gordon's work, Adam's altar, Jewish coins in America, and many other subjects.

### View of the Hebrews
by Ethan Smith

A photo-reprint of the 1825 edition; also contains parallels between View of the Hebrews and The Book of Mormon identified by the Mormon historian B.H. Roberts. Many scholars believe that Joseph Smith used this book in writing The Book of Mormon.

### The Golden Bible; or, The Book of Mormon. Is It From God?
by M.T. Lamb

A photo-reprint of the 1887 edition. A good analysis of internal problems in The Book of Mormon.

### The Use of the Old Testament in The Book of Mormon
by Wesley P. Walters

Demonstrates many errors Joseph Smith made in The Book of Mormon. Makes it clear that Smith was plagiarizing the King James Version of the Bible rather than translating from ancient gold plates.

### 2,000 Changes in The Book of Mormon
by Lamoni Call

A photo-reprint of Call's 1898 work. A critical study of The Book of Mormon.

### Latter-day Saints—Where Did You Get Your Authority?
by Hal Hougey

A valuable study of Mormon priesthood.

### Joseph Smith Among the Egyptians
by Wesley P. Walters

Walters, one of the top scholars on Mormon history, gives a good summary of the evidence against the Book of Abraham. Deals with Dr. Nibley's attempt to defend it and shows that he is in a "state of confusion" on almost every important issue.

### Joseph Smith's Egyptian Alphabet and Grammar

A photographic reproduction of a handwritten document that was suppressed by the Mormon leaders for 130 years because it proves that Joseph Smith did not understand Egyptian and that his Book of Abraham is spurious. Also contains part of two handwritten manuscripts of the Book of Abraham. A vital document for students of the Book of Abraham.

### The Book of Abraham Papyrus Found: An Answer to Dr. Hugh Nibley's Book "The Message of the Joseph Smith Papyri..."
by H. Michael Marquardt

In this book Mr. Marquardt shows that Dr. Nibley has failed in his recent attempt to prove the authenticity of the Book of Abraham.

### Can the Browns Save Joseph Smith?
by Jerald and Sandra Tanner

A rebuttal to They Lie in Wait to Deceive.

### The Book of Abraham Revisited
by H. Michael Marquardt

A critical look at the Book of Abraham.

### Why Egyptologists Reject the Book of Abraham

A photo-reprint of Joseph Smith, Jr. As A Translator, by F.S. Spalding, D.D., 1912, and Joseph Smith As an Interpreter and Translator, by Samuel A.B. Mercer, Ph.D. Spalding sent the Book of Abraham (containing the facsimiles purported to have been copied from the writing of Abraham) to eight prominent Egyptologists and Semitists and asked them to pass judgment on the 'translation made by Joseph Smith. All of these scholars denounced the Book of Abraham as a fraud.

### Mormon Spies, Hughes and the CIA
by Jerald and Sandra Tanner

Deals with the Mullen Company (the firm that handled public relations for the Mormon church) and the Watergate break-in, the BYU spying operations, the prostitution conspiracy and the church, wiretapping and bugging, Mormons and the CIA, Robert Bennett's involvement with Hunt, Hunt's BYU spy, Bennett's cover-up, Mormons and Hughes, the possible existence of the secret Council of 50 in the church today, and many other important subjects.

### Unmasking a Mormon Spy
by Jerald and Sandra Tanner

Story of a recent LDS spy, the "enemies list," infiltration into Ex-Mormons for Jesus, intelligence gathering, Mormon church security, new material on the Council of 50.

### Mormonism Like Watergate?
by *Jerald* and *Sandra Tanner*
Contains an answer to Dr. Nibley's 1973 article in the *Salt Lake Tribune*, the 1831 revelation on polygamy (which commands Mormons to marry Indians to make them a "white" and "delightsome" people), and suppressed material on the anti-black doctrine. Filled with important information.

### The Strange Marriages of Sarah Ann Whitney to Joseph Smith the Mormon Prophet, Joseph C. Kingsbury and Heber C. Kimball
by *H. Michael Marquardt*
This pamphlet proves that Joseph Smith took Sarah Ann Whitney as a secret plural wife, but performed a "pretended" marriage ceremony between her and Joseph Kingsbury to cover up his own iniquity.

### Joseph Smith and Polygamy
by *Jerald* and *Sandra Tanner*
Contains a detailed study of the Mormon doctrine of plural marriage, the spiritual wife doctrine, the John C. Bennett book, the Nancy Rigdon affair, the Sarah Pratt affair, and also the Martha H. Brotherton affair. Also included is a list of 84 women who may have been married to Joseph Smith.

### Mormons and Negroes
by *Jerald* and *Sandra Tanner*
Covers such subjects as the protests against BYU and the Mormon church, dissatisfaction in the church, the question of a new revelation, Blacks who held the priesthood before 'the doctrine was changed, slavery and civil rights among the Mormons, and many other important subjects. Also included is the complete text of Apostle Mark E. Petersen's speech "Race Problems—As They Affect the Church."

### Excommunication of a Mormon Church Leader
Contains the letter of George P. Lee.

### LDS Apostle Confesses Brigham Young Taught Adam-God Doctrine
Contains a photographic reproduction of a 10-page letter written by Bruce R. McConkie.

### Adam Is God?
by *Chris A. Vlachos*
A well-researched pamphlet on the Adam-God doctrine.

### Tracking the White Salamander—The Story of Mark Hofmann, Murder and Forged Mormon Documents
by *Jerald* and *Sandra Tanner*
Shows how Jerald's belief that the documents were forged was confirmed by investigators. Also contains *Confessions of a White Salamander* at no extra charge.

### A Gathering of Saints: A True Story of Money, Murder and Deceit
by *Robert Lindsey*
An excellent account of the forgeries and murders of Mark Hofmann.

### Salamander: The Story of the Mormon Forgery Murders
by *Linda Sillitoe* and *Allen Roberts*
A scholarly look at Mark Hofmann and his dealings with the Mormon church.

### The Tanners on Trial
by *Jerald* and *Sandra Tanner*
A detailed study of Andrew Ehat's unsuccessful attempt to stop publication of *Clayton's Secret Writings Uncovered*. A Mormon judge awarded Ehat damages, but his decision was overturned by the 10th Circuit Court of Appeals. This book has well over 100 large pages with many photographs of the original court documents. Contains fascinating testimony by some of the Mormon church's top historians. Highly recommended.

### Mormonism Exposed, Being a Journal of a Residence in Missouri from the 28th of May to the 20th of August, 1838
by *William Swartzell*
A photo-reprint of the 1840 edition.

### An American Prophet's Record: The Diaries and Journals of Joseph Smith
Scott H. Faulring, ed.
All the diaries of Joseph Smith printed in a beautiful paper-back edition.

### Joseph Smith's Kirtland Revelation Book
Introduction by Jerald and Sandra Tanner. Photographs of Joseph Smith's early revelations in handwritten form. Does not contain a typescript.

### Heber C. Kimball's Journal, November 21, 1845 to January 7, 1846
A photographic reproduction containing some important information on the Nauvoo temple ceremony. Most of the space, however, is devoted to listing names of those who passed through temple rituals. Does not contain a typescript.

### The Lucifer-God Doctrine
by *Jerald* and *Sandra Tanner*
Demonstrates that some Mormon critics have gone too far in attempting to link Mormons to Satanism and witchcraft. Contains an answer to the Decker-Schnoebelen rebuttal.

#### The Mormon Kingdom, Vol. 1, 1969
by *Jerald* and *Sandra Tanner*

Contains an account of the temple ceremony. Also discusses the changes in the ceremony and garments, the relationship to Masonry, the "oath of vengeance," the doctrine of blood atonement, baptism for the dead, the Danites, the Council of 50, the failure of the Kirtland Bank, the war in Missouri, Joseph Smith's secret ordination as King and his candidacy for President of the United States.

#### The Mormon Kingdom, Vol. 2, 1971
by *Jerald* and *Sandra Tanner*

Deals with such subjects as the Council of 50 and how it controlled early Utah, the ordination of Mormon kings, Mormonism and money, politics in Utah, the Mountain Meadows Massacre, the Utah War, the practice of blood atonement in Utah, and Brigham Young's indictment for murder and counterfeiting.

#### The Case Against Mormonism, Vol. 1, 1968
by *Jerald* and *Sandra Tanner*

Deals with Joseph's First Vision, changes in Mormon revelations and documents, the Law of Adoption, the Mormon Battalion, suppression of the records, book-burning, the BYU spy ring, and many other subjects.

#### The Case Against Mormonism, Vol. 2, 1968
by *Jerald* and *Sandra Tanner*

Deals with *The Book of Mormon* witnesses, the gold plates, parallels between *The Book of Mormon* and other documents, the influence of the Bible and the Apocrypha upon *The Book of Mormon*, and proof that the Book of Abraham is a spurious work. Almost 70 pages are devoted to the papyri and the Book of Abraham.

#### The Case Against Mormonism, Vol. 3, 1971
by *Jerald* and *Sandra Tanner*

Deals with the meaning and changes in the facsimiles in the Book of Abraham, books Joseph Smith may have had in writing *The Book of Mormon* and the Book of Abraham, the plurality of gods doctrine, the Adam-God doctrine, the Virgin Birth, false prophecies of Joseph Smith and Brigham Young, the Word of Wisdom, the priesthood, cursing enemies, animal sacrifice after Christ, the Mormon missionary system, and many other important subjects.

#### Hearts Made Glad: The Charges of Intemperance Against Joseph Smith the Mormon Prophet
by *LaMar Petersen*

This book throws a great deal of light on Joseph Smith's Word of Wisdom and his attitude toward it.

#### Mormonism Unveiled
by E.D. Howe

A photo-reprint of the 1834 edition.

#### History of the Saints
by *John C. Bennett*

A photo-reprint of the 1842 edition.

#### Reed Peck Manuscript

This manuscript was written in 1839 by Reed Peck, who had been a Mormon. Contains important firsthand information concerning the Mormon war in Missouri and the Danite band.

#### Senate Document 189

A photo-reprint of the "testimony given before the judge of the fifth judicial circuit of the State of Missouri, on the trial of Joseph Smith, Jr., and others, for high treason, and other crimes against that State." Gives very interesting testimony on the Danite band.

#### Brigham's Destroying Angel

A photo-reprint of the 1904 edition. The confessions of Bill Hickman, who claimed that he committed murder by the orders of Brigham Young and Apostle Orson Hyde.

#### Confessions of John D. Lee

A photo-reprint of 1877 edition. Contains important information on the Mountain Meadows Massacre.

#### Under the Prophet in Utah
by *Frank J. Cannon*

A photo-reprint of 1911 edition. Cannon was United States Senator from Utah and the son of George Q. Cannon, a member of the First Presidency. Shows how the Mormon leaders broke their covenants to the nation and continued to live in polygamy after the manifesto. Also shows how the leaders interfered in politics.

#### Reminiscences of Early Utah
by *R.N. Baskin*

Photo-reprint of the original 1914 edition. Baskin was a Chief Justice of the Supreme Court of Utah who also served as mayor of Salt Lake City. He explains how the Mormon leaders tried to evade the laws of the United States, discusses marked ballots and the absurd election laws, the Mountain Meadows Massacre, the Endowment House rites, blood atonement, the Danites, and the revelation on polygamy.

#### Changes in Joseph Smith's History
by *Jerald* and *Sandra Tanner*

A study of the changes that have been made in the six volumes of the *History of the Church* since its first printing.

*Falsification of Joseph Smith's History*
by *Jerald* and *Sandra Tanner*

Proves that many serious changes were made in Joseph Smith's *History* after his death. Although the Mormon leaders claim that Joseph Smith wrote this History, research reveals that less than 40% of it was compiled before his death.

*A Critical Look: A Study of the Overstreet "Confession" and the Cowdery "Defence"*
by *Jerald* and *Sandra Tanner*

This pamphlet shows that these two documents are forgeries.

*Answering Dr. Clandestine: A Response to the Anonymous LDS Historian,* enlarged edition
by *Jerald* and *Sandra Tanner*

This is an answer to the booklet, *Jerald and Sandra Tanner's Distorted View of Mormonism.* Also deals with Joseph Smith's magic talisman and the Nag Hammadi documents.

**On Being a Mormon Historian**
by *D. Michael Quinn*

One of the best speeches ever given by a Mormon historian. *Newsweek* called it a "stirring defense of intellectual integrity." In this 1981 speech Dr. Quinn, Associate Professor of History at BYU, attacks the suppressive policies advocated by Apostles Benson and Packer.

*Following the Brethren*
Introduction by *Jerald* and *Sandra Tanner*

Contains Apostle Ezra Taft Benson's speech, "Fourteen Fundamentals in Following the Prophets." Also contains Apostle Bruce R. McConkie's speech, "All Are Alike Unto God."

**John Whitmer's History**

Joseph Smith gave a revelation in 1831 commanding John Whitmer to keep this history of the church. Very revealing.

*Elders' Journal*

A photo-reprint of a LDS paper (1837-38).

*Messenger and Advocate*

A 3-volume set. Photo-reprint of an early LDS church paper (1834-37).

*Clayton's Secret Writings Uncovered: Extracts from the diaries of Joseph Smith's Secretary William Clayton*

*Joseph Smith's History, by His Mother*

A photo-reprint of the original 1853 edition. Contains a 15-page introduction by Jerald and Sandra Tanner

*Changes in the Key to Theology*
by *Jerald* and *Sandra Tanner*

A photo-reprint of the 1855 edition, with changes marked between the first edition and the 1965 edition. Changes were made in the teachings on polygamy and the Holy Spirit.

**Our Relationship with the Lord**
by *Mormon Apostle Bruce R. McConkie*

An attack on the concept of a personal relationship with Christ.

# Cassette Tapes

*Sandra Tanner Tape No. 1*

Two lectures given at Trinity Evangelical Divinity School. A helpful overview for those who want to understand Mormonism.

*Sandra Tanner Tape No. 2*

A one-hour interview on Mormonism with a Milwaukee television station. Includes personal comments about why the Tanners left Mormonism and their faith in Christ. Helpful for both LDS and non-LDS audience.

*Problems in Winning Mormons*
by *Jerald Tanner*

Shows how to use a loving approach to win Mormons to the Lord.

*Jerald Tanner's Testimony*

Three cassette tapes concerning Jerald's life and the Utah Lighthouse Ministry.

# Other Good
# Harvest House Reading

**CULT WATCH**
by *John Ankerberg* and *John Weldon*

*Cult Watch* provides historical background and the vital facts on the major beliefs of modern religious movements and looks closely at the reasons people become entrapped in them. Drawing from years of research and interaction with representatives of each movement, the authors offer penetrating analysis of how each religious system clearly contrasts with the essential doctrines of biblical Christianity.

**WHAT YOU NEED TO KNOW ABOUT MORMONS**
by *Ed Decker*

In this informative book, the differences between Mormonism and Christianity are clearly presented through a series of conversations between neighbors, which sheds light on the basic tenets of Mormonism and the countering truths of the Bible.

**WHAT YOU NEED TO KNOW ABOUT MASONS**
by *Ed Decker*

When Jeff Moore, a young Baptist minister, resigns from the Lodge, his family and his church relationships are thrown into chaos.

The hidden dangers of Freemasonry to the family and the church are fully communicated and the secret initiation ceremonies into the Lodge exposed in this creative approach to understanding one of the least-recognized cults in America.

**THE GOD MAKERS**
by *Ed Decker* and *Dave Hunt*

This unique exposé on Mormonism is factual, carefully researched, and fully documented. *The God Makers* provides staggering new insights that go beyond the explosive film of the same title. An excellent tool in reaching Mormons.

**THE "FACTS ON" SERIES**
by *John Ankerberg* and *John Weldon*

John Ankerberg, host of the award-winning "The John Ankerberg Show," and author John Weldon deal with many controversial issues facing Christians and non-Christians alike. In concise 48-page booklets, Ankerberg and Weldon focus on the most relevant aspects of each subject in a readable, straightforward style. Topics range from astrology to the Masonic Lodge to rock music.

Dear Reader:

We would appreciate hearing from you regarding this Harvest House nonfiction book. It will enable us to continue to give you the best in Christian publishing.

1. What most influenced you to purchase *Everything You Ever Wanted to Know about Mormonism*?
   - ☐ Author
   - ☐ Subject matter
   - ☐ Backcover copy
   - ☐ Recommendations
   - ☐ Cover/Title
   - ☐ _____

2. Where did you purchase this book?
   - ☐ Christian bookstore
   - ☐ General bookstore
   - ☐ Department store
   - ☐ Grocery store
   - ☐ Other

3. Your overall rating of this book:
   - ☐ Excellent  ☐ Very good  ☐ Good  ☐ Fair  ☐ Poor

4. How likely would you be to purchase other books by this author?
   - ☐ Very likely
   - ☐ Somewhat likely
   - ☐ Not very likely
   - ☐ Not at all

5. What types of books most interest you?
   (check all that apply)
   - ☐ Women's Books
   - ☐ Marriage Books
   - ☐ Current Issues
   - ☐ Self Help/Psychology
   - ☐ Bible Studies
   - ☐ Fiction
   - ☐ Biographies
   - ☐ Children's Books
   - ☐ Youth Books
   - ☐ Other _____

6. Please check the box next to your age group.
   - ☐ Under 18
   - ☐ 18-24
   - ☐ 25-34
   - ☐ 35-44
   - ☐ 45-54
   - ☐ 55 and over

**Mail to:** Editorial Director
Harvest House Publishers
1075 Arrowsmith
Eugene, OR 97402

Name _____

Address _____

City _____ State _____ Zip _____

**Thank you for helping us to help you
in future publications!**